TONY BLAIR

Also by John Rentoul

The Rich Get Richer

Me and Mine: The Triumph of the New Individualism?

Tony Blair

Prime Minister

JOHN RENTOUL

Little, Brown and Company

A *Little, Brown* Book

First published in Great Britain in 2001
by Little, Brown and Company

Parts of this book appeared in slightly different form in *Tony Blair* by
John Rentoul, published in 1995 by Little, Brown and Company.

PICTURE CREDITS
1, 3, 15: Syndication International; 2, 4, 6, 7, 8, 9, 10, 11, 12, 13,
16, 19: Private collections; 5: Alpha; 14: South West News Service; 17:
News International Syndication; 18: North News & Pictures; 20, 23,
25, 41: Rex Features; 21, 24: Steve Eason/Hulton Getty; 22:
Financial Times; 26–29: Tom Stoddart/IPG/Katz; 30, 31, 35, 39, 40,
42: Press Association; 32, 38: Popperfoto; 33: Atlantic Syndication;
34: Martin Rowson/*Guardian*/Centre for the Study of Cartoons and
Caricature; 36: Steve Bell/*Guardian*/Centre for the Study of Cartoons
and Caricature; 37: Don McPhee/*Guardian*

A CIP catalogue record for this book
is available from the British Library.

ISBN: 0 316 85496 4

Typeset in Sabon by M Rules
Printed and bound in Great Britain by
Clays Ltd, St Ives plc

Little, Brown and Company (UK)
Brettenham House
Lancaster Place
London WC2E 7EN

www.littlebrown.co.uk

Contents

Preface ix

PART ONE: EARLY YEARS

1 Cheerful Rebel
Childhood and School Days, 1953–71 3
2 Gap Year
London, 1971–72 28
3 Purple Loons
Oxford, 1972–75 35
4 Meeting a Woman at the Bar
London, 1975–80 51
5 The Race for a Seat
Hackney, Beaconsfield, the North-East, 1980–83 65
6 After Extra Time
Sedgefield, 1983 95

PART TWO: MP

7 Up Your Ladder
Backbencher and Treasury Spokesman, 1983–87 113
8 Doubtful Capitalist
Trade and Industry, and Energy, 1987–89 136
9 Open Shop
Shadow Employment Secretary, 1989–92 153
10 Gordon's Missed Opportunity
The Modernisers Thwarted, 1992 175
11 Social Moralist
Shadow Home Secretary, 1992–94 192
12 The Battle Against the Block Vote
One Member, One Vote, 1992–94 207

PART THREE: LEADER OF THE OPPOSITION

13 BLAIR'S NUMBER COMES UP
The Leadership Campaign, 12 May–21 July 1994 221
14 SOCIAL-ISM
The Rewriting of Clause IV, July 1994–April 1995 249
15 SHADOW PRIME MINISTER
Preparation for Power, April 1995–December 1996 267
16 NOT A LANDSLIDE COUNTRY
Election Campaign, January–April 1997 296

PART FOUR: GOVERNMENT

17 WE ARE THE SERVANTS NOW
First Hundred Days, 2 May–9 August 1997 323
18 BLAIR AND THE CROWN
Death of Diana, 31 August 1997 343
19 VICAR OF ST ALBION
The Church's Nominations Rejected, September 1997 350
20 NEW LABOUR AND MONEY
The Ecclestone Affair, November 1997 358
21 WELFARE REFORM
Lone-Parent Benefit Cut, December 1997 373
22 NEIGHBOURS
'Psychological Flaws', 18 January 1998 382
23 GOVERNMENT BY HEADLINE
'The Twenty-Third Member of the Cabinet', April 1998 391
24 HAND OF HISTORY
Northern Ireland, Good Friday, 10 April 1998 400
25 AN UNCERTAIN SOUND
Hoo-Ha Over a Far-Away Country, May 1998 420
26 THIRD WAY
Egalitarianism by Stealth, September 1998 431
27 UNFINISHED BUSINESS
Scotland, Wales and the House of Lords, November 1998–November 1999 447
28 PURER THAN PURE
Mandelson's Home Loan, December 1998 461
29 REGRETS
Launch Party for the Euro, 31 December 1998 472
30 WHY LIB–LAB COALITION DIDN'T HAPPEN
Paddy Bows Out, 20 January 1999 488

31 EDUCATION, EDUCATION, EDUCATION
Only Excellence Will Do, 22 March 1999 501

32 BETTER ANGELS
Kosovo War, 24 March–3 June 1999 509

33 GETTING STUFF DONE
'Scars in My Back', 6 July 1999 533

34 BIG TENT POLITICS
Millennium Celebration at the Dome, 31 December 1999 555

35 FORWARD MARCH OF NEW LABOUR HALTED
Mayor Ken, 4 May 2000 561

36 RUNNING ON EMPTY
Fuel Protest, September 2000, and
Peter Mandelson's Final Fall, January 2001 570

37 DEFINITION DEFERRED
The Future 580

Appendix I: Chronology 587
Appendix II: Family Tree 595
Bibliography 598
Index 605

Preface

This is a different book from the one I wrote in the year after Tony Blair became leader of the Labour Party in 1994, in two ways. First, he has now been Prime Minister for a parliamentary term, fulfilling some of the promise that persuaded me in 1992 that he would be an interesting subject for a biography, but inevitably closing off some of the possibilities that were open before he came to Downing Street. Then, he was a young man who had achieved little of substance, poised on the threshold of high office, armed only with words. Now, he can be measured against his record.

Second, a great deal more information about his early life and political development has become available since then. My task this time round has been much more that of selecting and offering judgments on a large amount of material rather than simply presenting what I could find out.

In one respect, however, this book is similar. It is not an authorised biography. I wrote it and then rewrote it in order to satisfy my own curiosity rather than to promote its subject. Obviously, I began as a sympathetic observer, and that is what I remain – although perhaps inevitably a rather less sympathetic one – but I am an observer from the outside.

During my research for the first book, I interviewed Blair twice and checked facts with him and his family. He was as friendly, embarrassed and wary as might be expected, given that I knew him only in my capacity as a journalist for the BBC. I was not allowed to interview members of his family, although they have been helpful with corrections and some additions since. I interviewed him again after publication: he gently disagreed with some of my assessments and offered a few comments, some of which I took into account. Beyond that, he has had no influence over either the first book or this one.

Part I of this book, on Blair's life before becoming an MP, has been completely rewritten to take in the new material available since 1996. Some of it was provided by Blair himself during the long campaign for the 1997 election, in particular in a series of long personal interviews designed to present the human side of one of the most effortlessly professional politicians of the modern era. The story of his year off between school and university was not volunteered by him for these purposes, however, and is told here on the basis of interviews with the people who knew him then. Some of my early judgments on his political development have been revised. His contemplative Christianity ran deeper and was established earlier than I realised: his adoption of Christian socialism at Oxford was therefore less of a Damascene conversion and more of a natural progression. Later on, when he joined the Labour Party, I thought he started out on the 'soft left'; now it seems he was really on the right, albeit what might be called the 'soft right'. I may have fallen for the same mistake everyone makes of assuming he is like them.

Part II, covering his rise from Labour backbencher in 1983 to leadership contender in 1994, has been revised and shortened. Some of the positions which I took seriously in the earlier version of this book turned out to be expedient. In particular, the rhetoric of Labour Party democracy and the battle for 'one member, one vote', which seemed one of the more significant episodes in his career, turned out to be a means to an end. The conservative language on social issues, which I dressed up as 'social moralism', may have been genuine so far as it went, but that turned out to be not very far in practice.

Part III, which covers the period from the Labour leadership contest in 1994 to the General Election in 1997, has been extended and updated to take in, among other things, accounts of that period from Donald Macintyre, in his outstanding biography of Peter Mandelson, and from Philip Gould, in his memoir from within the leader's compound itself.

Part IV, on the period since the 1997 election, is different in structure from the rest. Much as Blair himself must have found when he became Prime Minister, it is possible to keep track of the big picture for a while, but then the complexity, variousness and continuousness of government becomes overwhelming, and issues can only be dealt with one at a time. After an introductory chapter on the first hundred days in office, therefore, I have adopted a thematic approach in a number of shorter chapters.

I have tried to keep the story broadly chronological by using a sequence of episodes as pegs on which to hang an account of how Blair handled each issue.

I should like to thank Andrew Gordon at Little, Brown; Sam Coates; Michael Crick; Stephen McEntee; Mick Rawsthorne; Sallyanne Godson; Georgie Grindlay; Adrian Long; Stuart Robertson; Patricia Wynn Davies; James 'Sound Judgment' Stephenson; my colleagues at the *Independent*, including Simon Kelner, Ian Birrell, David McKittrick, Adrian Hamilton, Matt Hoffman and Colin Brown, but especially Donald Macintyre, whose advice has always been invaluable; and Sean O'Grady, who helped with research, commented on drafts and suggested many historical perspectives.

PART ONE

EARLY YEARS

1

Cheerful Rebel

Childhood and School Days, 1953–71

> 'He has always been conscious of how he appears to other people, the façade is always there. He is very intelligent and calculating. Don't forget that he was a superb actor.'
>
> —*David Kennedy, one of Blair's teachers at Fettes College*

Tony Blair's political ambition began at the age of eleven, when his father Leo's ended, on 4 July 1964. At the age of forty, at the height of his powers and looking for a Conservative parliamentary seat, Leo Blair had a stroke. Tony was woken by his mother in the morning.

> A child gets an immediate sense of when something terrible has happened. My mother hadn't even spoken and I was in tears. Then she said, 'Daddy's not very well, something happened in the night,' and I knew it was dreadful and serious. Some friends had come round who then took me to school.[1]

Tony spent the day not knowing whether his father would survive. He remembers playing rugby in the late afternoon and seeing his mother on the touchline. She had spent the day at the hospital and had come to take him home. She said she thought his father was probably going to live. Leo lost the power of speech for three years. It was, said his son, 'one of the formative events of my life',[2] 'the day my childhood ended'.[3] From the rostrum at the 1996 Labour conference, he sought to explain why:

> My father was a very ambitious man. He was successful. He was a go-getter. One morning I woke to be told he had had a stroke in the middle of the night and might not live through the day and my whole world then fell apart. It taught me something. It taught me the value of the family, because my mother worked for three years to help him talk and walk again. But it taught me something else too. When that happened, the fairweather friends – they went. That's not unusual. But the real friends, the true friends, they stayed with us. They helped us, and they stuck with us for no other

> reason than that it was the right thing to do. I don't pretend to you that I had a deprived childhood. I didn't. But I learned a sense of values in my childhood.[4]

The episode offers a better clue to the origins of Blair's determination than of his left-wing beliefs. Although the crisis might have prompted a sense of sympathy for those whose misfortune is no fault of their own, the reference to fairweather friends is oddly irrelevant and non-political. Blair explained why he had subjected himself to autobiographical examination in public: 'Because I just wanted people to understand that, you know, I did learn through that, early on, that not everything in life was just a smooth run. It obviously brought with it tremendous insecurity.'[5] But it is the picture of his energetic, all-conquering father brought down in his prime which is most telling. The stroke was caused by overwork. Leo was a lecturer in law at Durham University and a practising barrister as well as chairman of the Durham Conservative Association. He had gone to university late, because of the war, and felt he had a lot of catching up to do.

> You can only guess now the appalling frustration for him. He was a highly articulate and tremendously able man, a barrister, lecturer in law and a fledgling politician. And there was a time when he could say only one word. That was: 'Good.' Otherwise he'd have to motion for a cup of tea.[6]

Leo had been a good pianist, and could no longer play, but it was the loss of the ability to speak which was hardest to bear.

> I don't think Dad was in bed for that long. A few months perhaps, maybe slightly less than that. Quite quickly he was able to get up and walk, but learning to speak was the problem. It did make me very aware of the changes that can happen overnight and the fact that you can go down as well as up in the world. We were very conscious of that.[7]

Blair is open about the spur that drove him. 'After his illness my father transferred his ambitions on to his kids. It imposed a certain discipline. I felt I couldn't let him down.'[8] The weight of that responsibility fell mostly on Tony. His brother William, three years older, had already been sent away to Fettes College boarding school in Edinburgh.

Leo had pushed himself fiercely. 'I had always had the ambition to be a British MP,' he said. 'Furthermore, my ambition was boundless – I wanted to be Prime Minister.'[9] Such drive caused tensions. Tony said his mother, Hazel, 'used to talk to us a lot about Dad's ambition. She used to say that in many ways he was a far easier person to live with after he was ill than before.'[10]

Gradually, Hazel taught her husband to speak again, and he relearnt the piano a little, enough to play some Beatles songs. Then, just as Leo was getting better, Tony's younger sister Sarah developed Still's disease, a juvenile form of rheumatoid arthritis, at the age of eight.

> My sister was in hospital for two years, as they treated the illness quite differently then. It was a terrible thing because she had to have all sorts of drugs. My mum was coping with that and my dad at the same time and she was an absolute rock. I didn't see her break down, never once, nor indeed when she was ill herself. When you think about what she must have gone through with Dad she must have been under awful strain. But she never exhibited any signs of it, so I owe her a very great debt. It's very difficult when you're actually teaching someone to speak again.[11]

The story of a leader's origins has always been important, particularly in the Labour Party, from Ramsay MacDonald's croft to Harold Wilson's unemployed industrial chemist father. Blair's story is no less distinctive. He might have been called Tony Parsons. His father had been brought up by foster parents, Glasgow shipyard rigger James Blair and his wife Mary. Tony Blair knew his father had been fostered, but had no idea who his natural grandparents were – until the *Daily Mail* researched his family tree when he emerged as the likely leader of the Labour Party after John Smith's death.

The story of his real grandparents is a colourful one, although of limited relevance to all but genetic determinists. They were actors: Charles Parsons, whose stage name was Jimmy Lynton, and Celia Ridgway. They played in comedy, music hall and straight drama around the time of the First World War.

Celia led a complicated life. Born Augusta Bridson, her mother left her retired army officer father to live with a landowner called Arthur Burton. Gussie, as she was known as a child, left home to go on stage against her parents' wishes and changed her name. 'She enjoyed the company of men and was married by the time she was seventeen,' said Pauline Harding, the elder of two daughters from her first marriage. 'Mother was always away and she didn't often answer our letters. Our father was wicked to her. He used to knock her about, though I suppose he was fed up with her carrying on. Eventually they were divorced.'[12]

Celia then married again, to a commercial photographer called Hugh Wilson, and most of the time was away from her daughters. She had a son in 1923, in Filey, Yorkshire, while she was on tour in a show with Charles Parsons. The baby was named Leo after the sign of the zodiac under which he was born. Wilson knew the baby was not his and divorced Celia. At a time when the shame of illegitimacy was severe, the baby was fostered out to the Blairs, whom Celia and Charles had met while on tour in Glasgow.

Charles and Celia were married three years after Leo was born but had no more children. In 1936, when Leo was thirteen, they tried to get him back. Celia sent a man in a car to collect him and bring him to the Central Hotel, by the railway station in Glasgow. She tried to persuade him to come to live with them in London, but 'Mrs Blair was the only mother he knew, and he obviously loved his foster parents. Mrs Blair also didn't want to let him go,' said Harding.[13] The last part was an understatement: Mary Blair, who had had two miscarriages and had given up hope of a child of her own, barricaded herself in her home and threatened to kill herself if her foster son was taken away.

Leo told his own children of his materially deprived childhood. 'I remember my father telling me about being brought up in Glasgow in the 1930s, living in a crowded tenement, five or six families sharing a toilet, foster mother finding it hard to make ends meet, his foster father, a shipyard worker subject to the casual labour of those times,' said Tony.[14] James Blair was also often unable to work through illness, and died relatively young during the Second World War. Mary, on the other hand, lived into old age, still smoking Woodbine cigarettes.

James and Mary Blair made no secret of his parentage, according to Leo, 'even with all the neighbours'. But Tony recalls

> a terrible scene. Once we were round there and I asked Dad where he was born. Dad said, 'Well, I was born in Yorkshire,' which was true. But Granny Blair absolutely flew at him. 'You were born in Glasgow,' she said. 'You were born in Glasgow.' Dad said, 'Oh, come on Ma, don't let's be silly about it,' but she wasn't having any of it.[15]

She cut all links with his past. When he was a child, his mother and two half-sisters, Pauline and Jenefee, sent Easter and Christmas cards every year, which he kept in a biscuit tin under his bed. While he was away during the war, Mary Blair burnt the contents of the tin. 'My stepmother wanted me for herself without the constant reminder that I was in fact someone else's son,' Leo explained later.[16] What he did not know was that she had also written to his natural parents to say that he was missing, presumed killed in action. The cards stopped coming, and Leo thought they had lost interest in him. It was only when a family reunion was arranged in 1994, after the newspapers traced his lost relations, that he discovered the real reason.

When his own children asked him about his parentage, Leo seems to have been unforthcoming. 'Let sleeping dogs lie,' he used to say, according to Tony. 'I think there was a bit of him that was hurt. He thought his real parents hadn't wanted him.' Although his father 'was a tremendously driven man', his son did not think he had been damaged. 'You'd think he would have been completely psychologically disturbed. What's amazing about my dad is that he had such an abnormal childhood but he turned out to be incredibly well-balanced.'[17]

Leo's son has also resisted over-explaining the origins of his own character traits. 'One of the odd things about being a politician is that people ask all about your previous life; you start to analyse things in a way that you would never . . . I mean most people don't really look back at all.'[18]

Blair's unusually confident and self-controlled personality was evident from an early age, but beyond the obvious effects both of the intensity of his father's ambition, and its frustration by his stroke, any attempt to try to explain his exceptional qualities by reference to his family dynamics is only speculative.* However, the theme of childhood loss recurs often enough in twentieth-century prime ministers to be suggestive. The so-called Phaeton theory of the loss of a father as a source of intense ambition has been applied by some historians to Asquith, whose father died when he was seven, and to Lloyd George, whose father died when he was ten.[19] James Callaghan's father died when he was nine; and when John Major was twelve the failure of his father's business forced the family to sell the house and move into a rented flat in Brixton.

Leo Blair grew up a socialist in 'Red Clydeside'. Although his foster father disliked politics and was not even a member of a trade union, Mary was a lifelong Communist, and Leo became secretary of the Govan branch of the Scottish Young Communist League at the age of fifteen in 1938, a post he held until 1941. Originally, he wanted to be a Communist MP. When he left school he worked for the Communist newspaper the *Daily Worker* until it was suppressed as a wartime measure in 1941 – not least because the Communist Party supported the Russian pact with Nazi Germany. (It resumed publication after the war and was renamed the *Morning Star* in 1966.) He worked briefly as a clerk for Glasgow Corporation before joining the army in 1942.

After serving in the Royal Signals and rising to the rank of lieutenant, however, he underwent a rapid political conversion. 'Like a number of servicemen, I voted Labour in 1945,' he said. But when he was demobilised

---

*A laughable example of such speculation is *The Man Behind the Smile*, by Leo Abse, the former Labour MP, which diagnoses Blair's personality as incomplete, androgynous and cold because his parenting left him without a clear sexual identity. It also links the themes in Blair's politics of renewal, rebirth and youth and the attack on Old Labour with the desire to kill off his father. Abse's book was given more credibility than it deserved because he famously drew attention to the fact that Margaret Thatcher did not mention her mother in her *Who's Who* entry, in his *Margaret, Daughter of Beatrice*.

in May 1947 he had been an officer for a few years, and even an acting major. He attributed his conversion to the Conservative Party simply to 'the great change from living in a tenement in Govan to life in the Officers' Mess'.

Before he was demobilised, Lt Blair was assigned to clerical work at the Ministry of National Insurance in Glasgow. While there, he said he used 'any excuse' to pop in to the typing pool on the floor above to talk to the pretty red-haired woman he kept seeing on the stairs. 'It took me quite some while to persuade Hazel to let me date her,' he said.[20] Her strongly Protestant family came from Ballyshannon, County Donegal, where she was born above her grandparents' shop in 1923. Her father, George Corscaden, who moved to Glasgow where he owned several butcher's shops, died of appendicitis just six months after she was born. When she married Leo in Glasgow in 1948 she gave her surname as Corscaden, but she was in fact known as Hazel McLay. Her mother, Sally, had married William McLay, another Ballyshannon man who moved to Glasgow to become a butcher. According to Tony Blair, Grandpa McLay

> was a real character. I used to go down to the Glasgow meat markets with him. He'd done something terrible to his leg once so he had this stick. He was a very tough guy and he'd lash the meat with it[21] . . . giving the carcasses a good whack to see what shape they were in. If we were naughty, he'd come after us with that stick and say: 'If ye dinnae stop that laddie Ah'll gie ye a richt skelping.'[22]

On the marriage certificate, Leo gave his own name as 'Blair, formerly Parsons'. He had changed his name by deed poll four months earlier, and taken Charles and Lynton as his middle names, a combination of his natural father's original and stage names. His first son William, born in 1950, was given Leo's adopted father's name James and Lynton as middle names, and his own middle names he gave to his second son, although he never told him where they came from.

Blair Two

Anthony Charles Lynton Blair was born at 6.10am on 6 May 1953, in the Queen Mary Maternity Home, Edinburgh. By then, the family had moved to a small bungalow, 5 Paisley Terrace. His birth certificate records that his father was then an Assistant Examiner for the Inland Revenue – a junior tax inspector. More importantly, he was studying by night for a law degree at Edinburgh University, and hoping to begin an academic career. He started as a law tutor at the university, but the next step up the ladder meant moving halfway around the world. Leo was offered a job as a lecturer in administrative law at the University of Adelaide. The family's only connection with Australia was that, as a Wren, Hazel had been stationed in Sydney during the war. On Christmas Eve 1954, Leo, Hazel, Bill and Tony sailed for Adelaide on the maiden voyage of the ocean liner *Iberia*, a four-week journey via Gibraltar, Suez, Bombay and Colombo. The Australian university generously paid for them to travel first-class.

Tony, only eighteen months old, was already a show-off. According to his father, he entertained passengers to a display of ballroom dancing accompanied by the band and dressed in just a nappy. 'The dance ended only when his nappy dropped to his ankles.'

The family lived in Adelaide for three years, and Tony's sister Sarah was born there. Tony continued to show an appetite for public applause. His father remembers a concert at his school in Adelaide in which, aged four, he danced and sang – as 'Mr Nobody' – and brought the house down. 'It was somewhat difficult for his mother to get him off the stage,' Leo said. But Leo never intended to stay in Australia permanently and successfully applied for a job as a law lecturer at Durham University. Hazel and the children returned by air in January 1958, and stayed with her parents in Stepps, Glasgow, for six months while Leo completed a 'slim volume' on the law of the Australian Public Service before joining them. There is a family tale of Tony, aged five, standing up for his brother Bill, eight, when he was teased by local children because of his strong Australian accent.

When the Blairs arrived in Durham they moved into an empty flat above the Chorister School, where William was to go. It had been offered to them by Canon John Grove, the headmaster, who described conditions in the top flat in No. 5, The College, in the precincts of the cathedral, as 'very primitive'. They stayed there for some months before moving into a house in the centre of Durham, which Leo bought derelict and had restored by an architect.

As well as lecturing, Leo read for the English Bar, began to practise as a barrister in Newcastle upon Tyne and became active in local Conservative politics.

Tony remembers seeing little of his father: 'Dad had a flourishing legal business and was always lecturing around the country. He was also an astute self-publicist, appearing regularly on regional television. I'm sure I saw less of him than my children see of me now.'[23]

Leo's desire to be an MP was the main reason he returned from Adelaide. By the time of his stroke, after six years in Durham, he had become chairman of the local Conservative Association and, he said, 'I was ready to try for any Conservative seat that became vacant'.[24]

His predecessor as Tory chairman, Colin Beswick, recalled him as a 'ball of fire', fiercely ambitious, 'the essence of charm' and a 'really good front man'. In that respect, said Beswick of Tony Blair, 'you are your father's son, in all the best ways'. Cherie Booth once said of her husband's charm: 'If you met his father, you'd see where he gets it.'[25]

There were similarities between father and son, but also differences. Beswick said of Leo: 'I have never come across such a ladies' man.' It was a quality which ensured Leo was a hit with the grass-roots Tory party membership, most of whom were women.

A law lecturer in those days earned a good and secure salary, and both boys went to private schools. William, aged eight, started at the Chorister School; Tony went to Western Hill pre-prep, and followed his brother to the Chorister School in 1961, where they were day boys rather than members of the cathedral choir to which the school owed its origins. The Blairs were well-off, although Canon Grove said 'our fees have always been low compared with many prep schools – a deliberate policy in the past by the Dean and chapter, so that it shouldn't be beyond the range of the clergy. And so if a clergyman can send one son, a lawyer can probably send two.' Tony Blair said: 'We had a perfectly good, average, middle-class standard of living.'[26] This is rather euphemistic code for: 'I may have enjoyed the privilege of private education, afforded to a tiny minority, but we did not live in a country house and go hunting and shooting at the weekend.'

Blair Two, as he was known, was considered academically bright enough to skip the lowest form, and came third in the exams at the end of his first year. Brian Crosby took him for maths, and remembers him partly because the word 'rhinoceros' once appeared on his test answer sheet. Blair explained cheerfully that he knew the longest side of a right-angled triangle was called something like 'hippopotamus', but that that was not right.

Blair Two was a conventional boy. He was good at athletics. One of his memories, 'and it's one of these things that stays with you all your life', was of running a race at the school:

> I tracked the boy in front all the way round and I was just coming to the last bend, and I thought, right, I'm going to put on my spurt then and overtake him, and I just found my legs wouldn't carry me at all. And ever afterwards occasionally in your dreams you rerun this and of course win, but I didn't, and so my little silver cup's rather smaller than his.[27]

Later, he played in the school team at both cricket and rugby. In his final year, he won the school's Scott Cup as 'the best rugger player in 1965–66'. He continued to appear on stage, although – with the actor Rowan Atkinson, who was at the school from 1964 to 1968 – only as a spear carrier. There was little indication of the rebelliousness of his teenage school years. He cheered the Queen, as he later told her: 'As a young boy in short trousers, I stood and waved my flag as I saw you first in Durham city back in the early Sixties.'[28] He read the same books as everyone else. 'As a boy I read avidly C. S. Lewis's *Narnia* adventures, *Biggles*, Denis Wheatley's war books and Robert Louis Stevenson's *Kidnapped*. But I enjoyed most the world created by Tolkien in *The Lord of the Rings*.'[29] And he was interested in football: 'From the age of seven my father used to take me to watch Newcastle at St James's Park.'[30] His memory of it, however, was unreliable: he recalled sitting in seats behind the goal which were not put in until the 1990s, and named Jackie Milburn as his favourite player, although Milburn had last played for Newcastle when Tony was four and living in Australia.[31]

'We spent virtually every childhood summer holiday up to when the Troubles really took hold in Ireland,' Blair told Irish MPs when he explained that their country 'is in my blood'. The family usually stayed at the Sand House Hotel in Rossnowlagh, next door to Hazel's home town of Ballyshannon. 'It was there in the seas off the Irish coast that I learnt to swim, there that my father took me to my first pub, a remote little house in the country, for a Guinness, a taste I've never forgotten and which it is always a pleasure to repeat.'[32] Given that British troops were deployed in Northern Ireland in 1969, the young Blair was obviously introduced to alcohol before he was sixteen. They also spent holidays in Scotland, and in the summer of 1966, aged thirteen, Blair remembers being on the continent. 'I watched the 1966 World Cup Final in a bar while on a family holiday in France.'[33]

Grove remembered him for his 'perpetual, almost impish' smile, and said he was 'a really good sort of small boy to have in prep school – the sort of boy that was the backbone of a school like this'. He was polite: his parents were strict about manners.

> They always said, 'Misbehave inside the family if you will, but outside make us proud of you.' Respect for others, courtesy, giving up your seat for the elderly, saying please and thank you . . . If I was told off at school, I was told off again at home. When my mother saw the teacher, she apologised for me.[34]

He was good at Latin and Scripture, coming top of his form once in each. In locating the origins of Blair's Christian beliefs, it is significant that, on the day of his father's stroke, Grove prayed with Blair in his study. 'I will always remember kneeling and praying with the headmaster,' he said later.[35] The object of their prayers, however, was a lifelong atheist. 'Dad wasn't religious at all and after my mum died he was firmly anti-religion. Mum took us to church but not as regularly as I go with my kids now,' said Blair, who grew up nominally in the Church of England. 'Mum taught us all our prayers and said them with us.'[36]

In 1963 the family bought 28 Hill Meadows in High Shincliffe, a new four-bedroomed house on an estate in a suburb a mile or two outside Durham. They had a Vauxhall estate, a big, expensive car at a time when not all middle-class families owned cars. Leo's stroke soon afterwards limited the family's means. 'We were still well-off,' said Blair, 'but not nearly as well-off as we might have been.'[37] Leo's Bar earnings stopped, but the university supported him as he made his recovery, and he insisted that his wife should not work. 'He had very fixed ideas about that sort of thing, and even though she wanted to get a job to tide the family over this difficult period, he wouldn't hear of it.'[38] Not only did Hazel nurse Leo back to health and look after Tony's sister Sarah through her illness, but she also cared for her mother Sally, who lived with the Blairs after she developed Alzheimer's disease and declined distressingly into dementia. Hazel was obviously central to Tony's early life: he described her as 'almost painfully shy' but 'an absolute rock'.[39] Her sister, Tony's Aunt Iris, said: 'When Hazel was younger she had quite a temper, but of course family life settles you down, doesn't it?'[40]

His father's zealous Conservatism was one of the dominant political influences of Tony Blair's youth. It was no surprise, then, that when he was twelve, Blair should be the school's Conservative candidate for a mock election to be held on 26 March, five days before the 1966 General Election. 'During that week speeches were held in the yard by Christopher Scott (Liberal), Tony Blair (Conservative) and Stephen Dowrick (Labour), the candidates,' records the school magazine, the *Chorister*, July 1966. Canon John Grove remembers:

> For about a fortnight beforehand the boys went around canvassing and then there came the election day. And possibly the Fates wanted to say to him, 'Conservative so far, but no further,' because on the day he was ill. Somebody else had to stand in and got elected.[41]

According to the school magazine, Richard Stewart took over as Conservative candidate for the final speeches on the night before the mock election. 'The following morning, the polling station (The Hobbies' Hut) was opened and the ballot papers were printed. On Monday, 28th of March, the Results came through.' Although there was a dramatic swing from the Liberals to Labour since the previous mock election in 1964, which reflected the national trend in Harold Wilson's favour, Stewart won handsomely with 62 votes to 26 for the Labour candidate and 24 for the Liberal.

Twenty-eight years later, during the leadership campaign of 1994, the event was inevitably recalled by contemporary witnesses. Blair himself said he could not remember it, nor could he recall whether he had stood as the Conservative under the influence of his father, or because 'we'd all got parts to play and that was the one ascribed'.[42] He gave the impression that he was embarrassed by a party label he had worn long before most people's political ideas are fixed. After all, Clement Attlee had been a Conservative and Harold Wilson a Liberal, not at school but at university.[43]

Blair did not develop settled political views of his own until he was at least seventeen or eighteen. When he did, he confounded the expectations of both heredity and environment. He rejected his father's meritocratic proto-Thatcherism, the typical outlook of the self-made man.

> Dad used to say that he had made it, so there was no reason why anyone else shouldn't. But I would say: 'Yes, but you only made it because you had a good Scottish education. You survived because there was a National Health Service to care for you and support your family as it tried to support you. Your children have done well because all those things have been there for us too.'[44]

Despite his inescapably middle-class upbringing, Tony refused to be pigeon-holed with his privately-educated peers. 'We moved around a lot when I was young, before we finally settled in Durham,' he said. 'I never felt myself very anchored in a particular setting or class.'[45] In fact he was only five when the family moved to Durham but, like many products of post-war upward mobility, he felt he lacked roots in comparison to his parents' strong sense of coming 'from' somewhere: Leo from the sandstone tenements of Govan, Hazel from the small shop in Ballyshannon. Leo had no reason for choosing Durham other than that he had seen a good job there advertised in Australia. Its location in the class system was ambiguous, an ancient cathedral city surrounded by the moderate socialist tradition of the County Durham coalfield. Blair claimed he was influenced by the miners' galas, which were in the 1960s always addressed by Labour Party leaders, including Harold Wilson: 'There was great pride in the industry and an overwhelming sense of local community. That feeling has stayed with me ever since: you don't just create your own space and inhabit it, you share it with others.'[46] But by the time he came to live in Durham, of course, most of the pits in the county had closed, and he went to school with the sons of professionals.

Blair's class background is often misunderstood because of the common assumption that the British middle classes live only in southern England. As the writer and poet James Fenton, who overlapped with

Blair at Durham Chorister School (1957–62), observed, his accent and his background are *northern* middle-class. According to him, Blair's accent has not changed since he was eight.[47] Blair left Durham at the age of thirteen, however. Sent away to a boarding school in Scotland, he became a member of the British national élite which looked to London as its hub.

Fettes College

'To be utterly frank,' Leo wrote when asked why he chose Fettes College for his sons, 'I did it for three reasons: I had read in *Scottish Field* that it was the "Eton of Scotland"; the local county judge went there, as did his son; [and] I have always found that the Scots valued a good education and its benefits more than the ordinary Englishman.' It is one of the best-known public schools in Scotland. Founded in 1870 by Sir William Fettes, its elaborate fairy-tale Gothic tower is a landmark on the outskirts of Edinburgh. Before Blair its most famous old boys were Conservative Chancellors of the Exchequer Iain Macleod and Selwyn Lloyd, and, fictionally, James Bond.[48] It is essentially an English private school in Scotland, where Blair studied A-levels instead of Scottish Highers, and where as many boys were Anglicans as Church of Scotland. Blair regards himself as English, although when he described himself thus in the Commons he corrected himself, first to say, 'well, born in Scotland but brought up in England', then to declare, 'I'm British and proud to be British.'[49]

He won an 'exhibition', a second-rank scholarship worth £50, in the school's entrance examination, and started as a boarder in 1966. Following in his brother William's footsteps, he went to Kimmerghame House, where the cubicles in the dormitory were known as the horse boxes, each with a bed, two drawers underneath and a wardrobe at the foot. Blair did not like being away from his family. He hated the harsh discipline and the practice of fagging, where junior boys were allocated as 'fags' – effectively servants – to seniors. Blair was fag to a prefect called Michael Gascoigne, now an Edinburgh solicitor, who recalled him as cheerful and efficient:

> Blair would clean my shoes, Blanco my army belt and polish the brass on it. If I couldn't see my face in it, he would have it thrown back at him. He would also, if it was a games afternoon, lay out my rugger kit on the bed for me, or my whites if it was cricket . . . There was always a requirement for toast, but we insisted that it had to be one inch thick, no thinner, no thicker, with lashings of butter and marmalade. And Blair would steam into the adjoining kitchen where he made particularly good toast.[50]

Although Gascoigne detected no 'truculence or unwillingness', Blair said: 'The house they put me in was very old-fashioned – we new boys had to "fag" for prefects and I always resented that.'[51] The boys at Fettes were called 'men', especially the 'new men', and they were required to call prefects 'Sir'. Prefects were allowed to cane junior boys, and Blair was beaten for a number of petty infractions. This was still a cruel practice, with the tradition of being allowed a day in the sanatorium in order to recover from a thrashing having only recently lapsed. Depending on the gravity of the offence, prefects would line up to take their turn with the cane and the more sadistic would take a run-up.

The headmaster, Dr Ian McIntosh, was a conservative who resisted the liberalisation of the 1960s. His response to the increasingly fashionable rebelliousness of youth, he once joked, was to listen carefully to demands for change – and only then to say 'No'. But he had one strength, which was to appoint excellent teachers who were often free-thinking progressives.

One of the bright spots of Blair's miserable first year were English lessons with a young master who had just returned to the school from a spell at Gordonstoun, where he taught the teenage Prince Charles. More than anyone else, Eric Anderson shaped Blair's Fettes career. Indeed, he had written the very article in *Scottish Field* which had so impressed Blair's father (although the 'Eton of Scotland' tag was a headline-writer's invention). He said of Blair that there was 'some sort of chemistry between us', and was responsible for Blair's unfashionable taste for Walter Scott, on whom he was an expert. Anderson featured in Blair's contribution to the government advertising campaign, 'No one forgets a good teacher', and, after his successful school career culminated in his becoming headmaster of Eton College, Blair appointed him chairman of the Heritage Lottery and National Heritage Memorial funds.

Anderson had returned to Fettes in 1966 to set up a new house, called Arniston, which he intended to run on more enlightened lines, with no beating or fagging. Towards the end of Blair's first year, the headmaster asked for volunteers from each year to join Arniston in a new building which had just been completed. Anderson said there were two kinds of boy who wrote confidential letters to Dr McIntosh asking to be chosen: 'The first kind were the idealists who wanted to build a new society; the second were those who didn't like their own house.' Blair came into both categories and was 'desperate' to be selected. Anderson recalled him asking him repeatedly, 'Sir, when shall we know? When shall we know?'

Anderson ensured that Blair was chosen, but it was just at this point, as Blair was returning to Fettes at the start of his second year, that he tried to run away from school. His desire to join the new house did little to overcome his dislike of the school as a whole. Perhaps there was also an element of simple exuberance in Blair's adventure, as he tried to see how far he could get. When his parents put him on the train at Newcastle station to go to school, he walked through the carriages and got off again at the other end of the platform. The fourteen-year-old Blair then made his way to Newcastle airport and said he managed to get on a plane to 'somewhere like' the Bahamas before being asked for his boarding pass. The airport authorities then telephoned the headmaster of Fettes, who telephoned his parents.

When he first told this story publicly in a television interview with Des O'Connor on 18 December 1996, journalists were delighted to discover that there had never been flights to the Bahamas from Newcastle – although anyone flying to the Bahamas would get a plane to London first. They also telephoned Leo, who scoffed at the idea that his son had actually boarded a plane.[52] Tony then contradicted him in the press: 'I did actually get on the plane. I was taken off by the stewardess. I think Dad was trying to help because he thought I had done something terrible.'[53] Certainly, the younger Blair's account was accepted by the school at the time.

It was the start of a running battle not just with the school authorities but with his father, by now recovered from his stroke, although his speech was a little impaired. 'I was a pretty dreadful teenager. I have this constant feeling of guilt for my poor dad,' he said.[54] (But not for his mother, to whom he remained close.)

When Blair joined the new house, his schooldays became easier. Instead of fagging, junior boys were required to do some cleaning and menial tasks for the house collectively. Some boys thought Blair looked up to Arniston's first 'head of house', Nicholas Burnett, a boy of forward-looking views who 'cared as little about being dressed properly as Blair', according to Anderson. If Burnett, now with the World Bank in Washington, DC, was an influence, he was not aware of it. He said of Blair: 'He was certainly keen on being noticed, whether it was for his views or his pranks. He liked the attention very much.'

While Blair was obviously rebellious from the start, other boys had no inkling that he had serious political views of his own. They merely thought of him as someone who was permanently 'railing against authority', infuriating masters – and many of the other boys. 'His tie was always slightly undone, he had dirty shoes, he was questioning things the whole time. He was an extremely annoying character for a lot of people,' said one more conformist contemporary. 'On the other hand, he had some endearing features. He always had an eye for a ball, and could always play any sport.' Indeed, Blair won a place in the school Junior Colts rugby team in his second term, and was captain of the Junior Colts cricket team in the summer term of 1967. His team won seven matches, lost one and drew one.

As he grew older, however, playing rugby and cricket for the school was too Establishment for him. For many boys at that time, playing for the school's First XV was all that mattered, and, although teachers said Blair could easily have played fly-half for the school and was a skilful place kicker, he would only play rugby at house level in his later years. He was also good at football – one of his persistent questions was why it was not an official sport – and he took up the more unusual sport of basketball, in which he had the advantage of being tall, and was captain of the school team.

Anderson clashed repeatedly with Blair over the enforcement of rules:

> I got used to a knock at my study door, followed by the grinning Blair face and a fifteen-minute argument about some way of doing things which the school ought, he thought, to change at once. Tony was full of life, maddening at times, pretty full of himself and very argumentative. He was an expert at testing rules to the limit, and I wouldn't swear that he stuck rigidly to the school rules on not drinking, smoking or breaking bounds. I was always telling him to get his hair cut and to pull up his tie. But he was a live wire and fun to have around.

Some of the rules were petty in the extreme, even in a liberal house like Arniston. In 1968 the requirement that the 'middle button of jacket to be buttoned up at all times' was dropped, mainly because prefects were fed up with enforcing it. It was in that year that Anderson took the entire house of sixty boys to the Cameo cinema in Edinburgh to see the film *If . . .*, in which boys blow up and machine-gun their teachers in a reactionary boarding school. The headmaster was furious with him for infecting the boys with such subversive propaganda. The analogy with a prison camp was a dominant one with the boys, and much of their energy was devoted to trying to leave the grounds to go to pubs, shops or to chat to girls. Much of the masters' energy was devoted to trying to stop them: the bell would ring at unannounced times and the register would be taken. Nick Ryden, one of Blair's fellow rebels, recalled comparing notes with boys at a reform school, or borstal, against whom Fettes played hockey, who concluded that their regime was more liberal. One of the additional perks of being in the basketball team, said Ryden, who also played, was that John Sutcliffe, the sports master, 'had been quite a sportsman himself and realised that after a tiring basketball match "up town" the exhausted players deserved to be dropped off at a pub rather than be taken straight back to the fenced compound at Fettes'.

Anderson further encouraged Blair's independence of mind by inviting his friend Sir Knox Cunningham, the Unionist MP for South Antrim and President of the Old Fettesian Association, to stay at Arniston. 'He had no children of his own, to his sadness, and made a point of coming four or five times a year,' said Anderson (one of Blair's contemporaries commented wryly on Anderson's innocence: Cunningham was 'the sort of man who liked boys – he never did anything about it as far as I know, but that was what he was about').

Cunningham liked to go through to the boys' quarters to provoke them with his outrageously reactionary views and encourage them to challenge school rules. Robert Philp, house tutor at Arniston, said, 'He used to come back rubbing his hands with glee, saying, "That's stirred things up a bit." Blair loved arguing with him.' Blair was not interested in politics at that time but, as a former parliamentary private secretary to Prime Minister Harold Macmillan, Cunningham offered him an early glimpse of the glamour of Downing Street.[55]

Anderson managed to channel some of Blair's energies into his own passion, which was drama. In the public life of Fettes, it is as an actor that Blair is mainly remembered. Whether or not it had anything to do with the showbusiness heritage of his secret grandparents, Blair knew he could hold an audience from the time he danced in his nappy on the liner to Australia: at Fettes his performances were more formally thespian.

In his second year, still only fourteen, Blair was chosen to play the role of Mark Antony in the house play, *Julius Caesar*, an early experience of being promoted at a younger age than would be expected. The reviewer for the school magazine, the *Fettesian*, saw potential: 'As the instrument of Caesar's revenge, Blair emerged as a somewhat youthful Antony, but nevertheless a very promising actor who should prove indispensable for school productions in the next few years.'

At the age of sixteen, under Anderson's influence, he formed a group with five other boys called The Pseuds, to act in and produce 'contemporary dramatic works'. Their first 'presentation' was 'an evening of contemporary drama' open to any member of the Upper School, featuring Harold Pinter's *The Dumb Waiter* and *Trouble at the Works* and N. F. Simpson's *Gladly Otherwise*.

In the autumn of 1969 Blair played Drinkwater in the school play, George Bernard Shaw's *Captain Brassbound's Conversion*. The *Fettesian* review was mixed:

> His accent was, on the first night, a little garbled, and often presented the same difficulties of comprehension experienced with the original article. This, however, was soon remedied and the slower, if slightly less convincing accent of the ensuing nights came over very well. His clearer diction, combined with his superb command of the gestures and mannerisms of the insolent, unscrupulous Cockney, provided us with an accomplished and amusing study.

Nearly thirty years later, Blair would again receive poor notices for his 'Estuary' accent, as the critics took exception to his demotic glottal stops in some of his more downmarket performances.

Blair's greatest dramatic triumph at school was as Captain Stanhope in R. C. Sherriff's *Journey's End*, the Arniston house play at the beginning of 1971. Everyone who saw it seems to remember his performance in this claustrophobic First World War drama, set in the trenches. When the play was first produced in 1928, Laurence Olivier played the part of Stanhope, the company commander who can only fight an absurd war if he dulls his moral senses with whisky. This time the *Fettesian* review was unstinting:

> Arniston were fortunate in having so experienced an actor as Blair for this central figure. From his first entrance . . . Blair brought out the febrile intensity of Stanhope, wiring himself into his ever more circumscribed troglodyte world, speculating moodily on the worm that went down when it thought it was coming up.

Robert Philp thought Blair's performance was 'brilliant'. It was a part to be seized with some relish by a seventeen-year-old rebel, for whom military uniform was anathema: Blair was among the minority at the school who opted out of the Combined Cadet Force. For the first two years, in which it was compulsory, he wore the uniform and used a rifle at the school's firing range. Until he assumed responsibility for Britain's armed forces twenty-nine years later, that was the full extent of his military experience. In his third year he chose to join the school's 'outside service', a programme of voluntary work known as 'granny-bashing', involving digging old people's gardens and running errands for hospital patients.

It was on outside service that the young Blair met another early mentor, Ronald Selby Wright, the minister at Canongate church in a slum area of Edinburgh. He had been the BBC's Radio Padre during the war, broadcasting to the Forces, working in words and phrases containing codes for the intelligence services, and would later be Moderator of the Church of Scotland, its annually-elected head. He had been the Church of Scotland chaplain to the school, and continued to work at Fettes during Blair's time. Significantly in the light of Blair's later development, he observed: 'Tony did not really have an interest in religion.'[56]

Blair was also a member of a discussion society called Paramaecium, run by another liberal master, Michael Lester-Cribb, the director of music. The society took its name from a single-cell organism which reacts to an obstacle by backing off at an angle and going forward in a new direction.

In the sixth form, Blair was a leading figure in the school's counter-culture. He was flamboyant and aloof, with a big, lippy mouth like Mick Jagger, and younger boys were in awe of him. He was capable of being quite unpleasant to boys he did not get on with, reserving a cutting scorn for conformists and being 'quite sharp' to senior boys who upheld 'the system', according to David Kennedy, who succeeded Philp as house tutor at Arniston in 1968. Although Kennedy did not teach Blair, he got to know him well, because as house tutor he had the only television in the house. Several boys enjoyed watching *Scotsport*, the Scottish equivalent of *Match of the Day*, on Saturday evenings on his black-and-white set.

Blair was always just stepping over the limit of the rules, and using his charm to get away with it. 'Hair was a big issue,' said Hugh Kellett, two years below him in Arniston. 'It had to be above the collar and behind the ears. He would put butter and crap on his hair, to grease it down inside the back of the collar. Many of the boys did.' Anderson had a simple rule. He kept a bust of Sir Walter Scott in his hall, and any boy with hair longer than Sir Walter's had to get it cut, which was a relatively relaxed measure. But Ian McIntosh, the headmaster, was less tolerant, and once frog-marched Blair into the school barber's and stood over him while his hair was cut.[57]

Most teachers nevertheless found him stimulating. David Kennedy said:

> Some boys are rebellious because they are stupid. Tony was rebellious because he wanted to question all the values we held to. In a boarding school there are obviously lots of rules as to how the day runs and what one does at various times. You had to have simplified sets of rules. And Tony would always question them.

Philp saw Blair's later career as rooted in this schoolboy attitude:

> He was always interested in pointing out the defects of the institution of which he was a part, and that kind of analytical stance is probably fundamentally some kind of political stance, even when it isn't attached to any party-political feeling.

He was an intellectual rebel rather than a simple trouble-maker. He worked hard and read a lot. Philp said Blair was 'not the very cleverest, but he had a good mind'. He studied English, French and History at A-level, and applied to read law at Balliol College, Oxford, once again following his brother. Balliol, a popular college with a progressive reputation, rejected him but passed him on to St John's, a rather duller place which eagerly offered him a place, on the notional condition that he obtained 'something like' two Ds and an E in his A-levels, according to a contemporary. Blair managed to keep the fact of this setback out of the public domain until after he became Prime Minister.[58] He has even more successfully kept his A-level grades secret (he asked Fettes within days of John Smith's death in 1994 not to release any documents). The most plausible explanation is that they were not as good as he thought they should be, but presumably that only means they were not straight As. Cherie Booth has been happy for the world to know that she gained four As. He got 'perfectly respectable high grades' said one of his teachers.

David Kennedy believes that Blair's persona as a rebel was a front, related to his skill at acting, and offered a pointed assessment:

> He was so affable that you couldn't call him reserved, but you never saw his real self. He didn't like to expose himself in case someone spotted a weakness. He could end up being a prime minister like Wilson, clever but shallow. He was always charming, but, to be cruel, he only likes to be in groups where he is the leading light. He has always been conscious of how he appears to other people, the façade is always there. He is very intelligent and calculating. Don't forget that he was a superb actor.

Behaving badly was more about exercising his ego than losing control. A contemporary said: 'He really, really got under people's skin. He was a very superior wind-up artist.' He was careful in his disrespect and most of the time he avoided disciplinary action. But when Eric Anderson left in 1970 to be headmaster of Abingdon School, his successor as house master, Bob Roberts, found Blair – then in his final year – infuriating: 'He was the most difficult boy I ever had to deal with.'[59] Blair expected to be made a prefect, and might have reached some accommodation with Anderson, but Roberts would have none of it. His brother had been a prefect, listed in the *Fettesian* under the bald heading 'THOSE IN AUTHORITY', but Tony stayed on the back benches, with all the insolence of his role model, Mick Jagger. 'Bob was a very old-fashioned, strict teacher who did not get on with him at all,' according to David Kennedy.

Blair now risked expulsion, and needed allies. Luckily Selby Wright, the former chaplain, was a 'great supporter' of his, according to Anderson. In his final year Blair volunteered to help run a summer camp for Selby Wright's boys' club. 'Some might say that if it hadn't been for going on one of those camps, Tony might have found himself leaving the school a little earlier than expected,' commented Nick Ryden, who also did outside service and testified to Blair's genuine altruism. 'But it was also an astute move on his part. If he had been shown the red card, Selby Wright would have put in a good word for him.'

Instead, Roberts beat Blair, the only master to do so, giving him 'six of the best' at the age of seventeen for persistently flouting school rules. Even in such a conservative school, beating a seventeen-year-old youth was an unusual event. 'It probably did me no harm,' Blair said twenty-four years later, when he rather awkwardly explained that he had always been opposed to physical punishment in schools.[60] But it meant his school days both started and ended as a negative experience. And it was his government which, in September 1999, finally extended the 1986 ban on beating in state schools to the private sector.

'Masters were very worried about sex, drugs and rock 'n' roll, and Blair looked like all three,' explained Kellett. 'He was a big guy, six feet tall at sixteen.' The rock 'n' roll at Fettes was mostly heavy metal – especially Led Zeppelin – which was played in the boys' studies. In October 1970 Atomic Rooster and Anno Domini played at the school. There were 'hardly any' drugs in Fettes, according to contemporaries. From Eric Anderson's testimony it would seem that alcohol and cigarettes were the narcotics of choice. As for sex, 'boys were allowed to go "up town" three times a week, and Blair probably didn't bother getting the slip signed', according to Kellett. The opposite sex was one of the main attractions of 'up town'. Blair's father was again summoned to talk to the headmaster and house master. Leo said: 'He was always nipping over the wall to chat up the girls at the fish and chip shop.'[61]

On his last summer holiday in 1970, at a party at his friend Chris Catto's house in Forfar, Blair met a girl even more rebellious than he. Anji Hunter, who had just turned fifteen, was the daughter of a Scottish rubber plantation manager. She had been born and brought up in Malaysia until the age of ten; her mother had been killed in a car crash within months of the family returning to Scotland. She was then at St Leonard's, a girls' private school in St Andrews, forty miles away. 'I met Anji when I was about seventeen, at a party where we both stayed overnight,' Blair said, when he paid a private tribute to her after winning the Labour leadership, adding mischievously: 'It was my first defeat.'[62]

She and Blair never went out with each other, but have been like brother and sister ever since. She was expelled from St Leonard's for insubordination in 1971, around the time Blair left Fettes. Like Blair, she was bright – she took nine O-levels at the age of fourteen. She also persistently questioned the rules and was 'agin the system'. She went to take her A-levels at St Clare's sixth-form college in Oxford, so she was there during Blair's first year at university. Fourteen years later, she came to work for him as an MP. She is still one of his closest and most trusted advisers, having assumed the title of Special Assistant to the Prime Minister.

Meanwhile, Fettes's own defences against girls had just been breached. Two years earlier, as French students hurled cobbles on the streets of Paris, David Ogilvy, the founder of advertising agency Ogilvy & Mather and an old boy of the school, delivered an inflammatory speech at Founder's Day. Quoting Sir William Fettes, who endowed the school for the education of 'young people', he declared:

> What right had the first governors to decide that our Founder meant only *boy* children? He clearly intended that this great school should educate girls as well as boys. If the governors continue to ignore his wishes, I urge you boys to follow the example of your contemporaries at foreign universities – riot!

This was, he said, greeted with 'loud and prolonged applause' from the boys.[63] In Ian McIntosh, the headmaster, already fearful of the example set by *If . . .*, it induced a state of terror. Typically, however, liberalisation came from the top rather than by revolt from below. Over the second brandy at lunch on the next year's Founder's Day, one of the school's governors, Jack Mackenzie-Stuart, an Old Fettesian, judge and crossbench peer, raised 'the problem of his daughter Amanda' with McIntosh. She was tired of her Wiltshire boarding school and wanted to be a day girl at home in Edinburgh for the sixth form. Could McIntosh take her? 'I don't see why not,' was the reply.[64]

Thus, in the autumn of 1970, at the beginning of Blair's last year, Amanda Mackenzie Stuart became the first girl at Fettes. She was in Blair's class, the History Sixth. As the only girl in a school of 440 boys – until she was joined around half-term by a second member of the alien sex – she was inevitably the object of (mostly suppressed) romantic attention. In the competition for her affections, there could be only one winner, who turned out to be Blair. 'He was so bright, so engaging – and very funny,' she said later. 'He could get away with teasing the masters and, looking back, I suppose it was because he was cleverer than most of them.' Despite the competitive all-male environment, however, their relationship was not widely advertised and most boys were not aware of it. Indeed, for all his noisy, argumentative showing-off, they knew little of Blair's family life or his private thoughts. All the boys and masters who knew him express surprise at his future course, but Mackenzie-Stuart may have known him better. She said he was 'not really into politics at the time – it was more Led Zeppelin and Cream – but I was never surprised that he joined Labour. That was always there.'[65]

Amanda Mackenzie Stuart is an important witness because this is the earliest sighting of left-wing leanings. Others speak of his anti-Establishmentarianism, or his compassion, but this was the first inkling that they might take political expression. That, however, would wait until he arrived at Oxford. Before that, he would spend a year off between school and university, mostly in London. But before *that*, he had to complete his last few weeks at school after his A-levels. McIntosh had had enough and wanted to expel him straight away, but another protector stepped in: this time it was his girlfriend's father. Lord Mackenzie-Stuart went to see McIntosh and proposed a compromise, that Blair should live at his house in Edinburgh for the last few weeks of the summer term. Thus he ended his schooldays in privileged exile.

Much has been made by Tony Blair's detractors of his privileged, middle-class upbringing, as if this should automatically disqualify him from leadership of a left-of-centre party. In fact Clement Attlee, Hugh Gaitskell and Michael Foot also came from relatively privileged families, while the background of John Smith, son of a provincial Scottish headmaster, was hardly downtrodden. Like Attlee, Gaitskell and Foot, Blair was sent to a private boarding school. Like Gaitskell, but unlike Attlee and Foot, he was of a strongly anti-Establishment cast of mind, rebelling against petty school rules and regulations and striking quite a pose as a nonconformist. Although he had carved out the space to enjoy himself, he did not leave with fond memories of the school. Three years later, he visited Edinburgh with some university friends. 'We were driving past Fettes and Tony hit the floorboards,' said one of them, Peter Thomson. 'There must be something about that place.'

Much later, when he was a shadow Cabinet minister in about 1990, he was the guest speaker at a lawyers' dining club in Edinburgh, at the invitation of his old friend from Fettes, Nick Ryden. When he and Ryden entered the library for drinks beforehand, he stopped suddenly and said: 'Christ! No one told me *he* was going to be here.' He had seen Michael Gascoigne, for whom he had fagged a quarter-century before. Ryden was alarmed, and asked if he could not let bygones be bygones. 'No, I can't,' replied Blair sharply. 'That bastard beat me. I never thought I would see him again.'

Fortified with two glasses of champagne, he began his speech by saying that his evening had been 'ruined' by the presence in the room of someone whom he had last seen wielding the cane when he, Blair, was bent over being flogged for something stupid like having his shoelaces undone. Without naming Gascoigne, he went on to say that this prefect at his school had flogged a lot of people for smoking, 'so I was pleased to see that when I arrived here he was the only person in the room who was smoking'.[66]

Blair became reconciled to some aspects of Fettes at least, and later acknowledged his debt to the school. Defending his education reforms in government, he said: 'I had a privileged education. I know what it did for me. I know I would not be Prime Minister without a decent education.'[67] He emerged not only with a set of good qualifications, however, but with the confidence, style and self-discipline that are recognisably the products of the British public school system.

Notes

1. Interview with Lynda Lee-Potter, *Daily Mail*, 26 October 1996.
2. London *Evening Standard*, 16 November 1993.
3. *Woman's Weekly*, 1 January 2000.
4. Ad-lib section of speech to Labour conference, Blackpool, 1 October 1996.
5. BBC Radio 4, *Desert Island Discs*, 23 November 1996.
6. London *Evening Standard*, 16 November 1993.
7. Lynda Lee-Potter, *Daily Mail*, 26 October 1996.
8. Martin Jacques, *Sunday Times Magazine*, 17 July 1994.
9. Letter to the author, 22 January 1996. Throughout the rest of the book, quotations from the author's interviews or correspondence are not footnoted unless the date is relevant.
10. Lynda Lee-Potter, *Daily Mail*, 26 October 1996.
11. From the same Lynda Lee-Potter interview, which was Blair's most expansive about his childhood. Alastair Campbell, his press secretary, said afterwards: 'I wish it had been filmed.'
12. *Daily Mail*, 27 May 1994.
13. *Ibid.*
14. Speech in Cape Town, 8 January 1999.
15. Lynda Lee-Potter, *Daily Mail*, 26 October 1996.
16. Jon Sopel, *Tony Blair: The Moderniser*, p. 7.
17. Lynda Lee-Potter, *Daily Mail*, 26 October 1996,
18. BBC Radio 4, *Desert Island Discs*, 23 November 1996.
19. See Michael and Eleanor Brock, editors of H. H. Asquith, *Letters to Venetia Stanley*, Oxford University Press, 1985, footnote on p. 7.
20. *Daily Mail*, 6 June 1998.
21. Lynda Lee-Potter, *Daily Mail*, 26 October 1996.
22. Tom Brown, *Daily Record*, 7 March 1996.
23. Sopel, *Tony Blair: The Moderniser*, p. 7.
24. *The Times* Diary, 17 May 1994.
25. Lynda Lee-Potter, *Daily Mail*, 22 April 1997.
26. *Channel Four News*, 11 July 1994.
27. Speech at the opening of the Chorister School pre-prep, October 1993, filmed by Peter Borthwick, one of the boys.
28. Speech at Queen's golden wedding anniversary dinner, 20 November 1997.

29. *The Times*, 23 April 1998, to mark World Book Day; *The Lord of the Rings* had coincidentally topped a poll of customers of Waterstone's bookshop as the 'book of the century' the previous year.
30. *Mail on Sunday*, 31 May 1998.
31. Report of an interview on local radio in 1997, *Sunday Telegraph*, 6 February 1999.
32. Speech to the Irish Parliament, 26 November 1998.
33. *Mirror*, 11 March 1998.
34. Speech to the Women's Institute, Wembley Arena, 7 June 2000: this is a recurrent theme, although Blair's teachers remember him as well-behaved at Durham; it was only at Fettes later that he was 'told off'.
35. See Note 27.
36. Lynda Lee-Potter, *Daily Mail*, 26 October 1996.
37. Martin Jacques, *Sunday Times Magazine*, 17 July 1994.
38. Sopel, *Tony Blair: The Moderniser*, p. 10.
39. Lynda Lee-Potter, *Daily Mail*, 26 October 1996.
40. Iris Cubie, *Daily Record*, 9 July 1998.
41. BBC2, *Newsnight*, 10 June 1994.
42. *Observer*, 2 October 1994.
43. On going to Oxford University in 1901, Clement Attlee said, 'I was at this time a Conservative', *As It Happened*, p. 15; Ben Pimlott, *Harold Wilson*, pp. 47–50.
44. *Daily Record*, 5 December 1996.
45. *Observer*, 2 October 1994.
46. *Scotland on Sunday*, 24 July 1994.
47. James Fenton, *Independent*, 16 January 1995.
48. Ian Fleming's fictional *Who's Who* entry for Bond, Commander James, 'Educ.: Eton College and Fettes', is reproduced in Robert Philp, *A Keen Wind Blows*, p. 78.
49. *Hansard*, 12 January 2000.
50. Sopel, *Tony Blair: The Moderniser*, p. 14.
51. Tom Brown, *Daily Record*, 7 March 1996.
52. *The Times*, 19 December 1996.
53. *Sun*, 20 December 1996.
54. Lynda Lee-Potter, *Daily Mail*, 17 April 1998.
55. Not that Cunningham had been much use to his boss: during the Profumo affair he 'had a bad habit of getting things wrong', according to Michael Fraser, head of the Conservative Research Department, quoted in Alistair Horne, *Macmillan, 1957–1986*, p. 493.
56. *Daily Express*, 20 May 1994. He died in 1995.
57. Philp, *A Keen Wind Blows*, p. 87.
58. Richard Jenkyns, *Spectator*, 15 July 2000.
59. *Mail on Sunday*, 22 May 1994.
60. BBC1, *Panorama*, 3 October 1994.
61. Martin Jacques, *Sunday Times Magazine*, 17 July 1994.
62. Speech to supporters and campaign workers, Church House, London, 21 July 1994.

63. David Ogilvy, *Blood, Brains and Beer*, 1978, quoted in Philp, *A Keen Wind Blows*, p. 92.
64. Philp, *A Keen Wind Blows*, p. 93.
65. Keith Dovkants, London *Evening Standard*, 18 July 1994.
66. Interview, Nick Ryden, 27 October 1999.
67. BBC2, *Newsnight*, 19 July 1999.

2

Gap Year

London, 1971–72

> 'His belongings consisted of a home-made blue guitar which he called Clarence, from which the entire neck would separate during rapid riffs, and a tatty brown suitcase containing a maximum of one change of clothes.'
>
> —*Alan Collenette, friend and former business partner*

A friend of a friend had told Tony Blair that Alan Collenette was a rock promoter, so Blair arrived on his doorstep in Inverness Gardens, just off Kensington Church Street, claiming to be a gifted guitarist and suggested they should talk about going into the music business together. In fact, he had not yet learnt to play, but Collenette was not much of a rock promoter either. 'So we deserved each other,' said Collenette, who had just left St Paul's School. Thus began a happy twelve months in which Blair lived in London, which he had previously visited only once, and became the 'manager' of some bands made up mostly of public schoolboys with ambitions to be rock stars.

'It was a very good period of time for me, because I was very anxious not to have to depend on my dad for money. I just wanted to demonstrate a bit of independence,' he said.[1] He fell in with a crowd of 'weekend hippies', as one of them described themselves, but has always been reticent about what he did. 'I dabbled in the music business, helping to organise gigs.'[2]

'He should be embarrassed about that year,' said one of his friends. 'That was before he became respectable.'

He was already highly persuasive, however. He was staying at the house of a school friend of Collenette's, Chris Blishen, who knew someone at Fettes. Blishen said: 'He was a very charming guy, had that grin and was very ambitious to get things done. He was only supposed to be staying a night while my parents were on holiday and he ended up staying two weeks.'

Blair then asked if he could stay at Collenette's parents' house, and moved in with the meagre possessions listed above. Now managing director of a commercial real-estate company in San Francisco, Collenette said he and Blair 'struck up a fast friendship, based on Tony's sense of humour and self-effacing charm'. They set themselves up in business over his kitchen table. They were going to discover, promote and manage the next Led Zeppelin or Free. Had they succeeded, Blair might have ended up like Michael Levy, the pop music promoter who later raised money for him and whom Blair made a peer. Collenette said: 'Tony was an excellent partner, because he had no reservations about making a fool of himself, which gave us a sense that anything was possible.'

First they needed a band. Collenette recruited Mike Sheppard, a friend, still in the sixth form at St Paul's, who had taught himself to play guitar and whose father would let them rehearse in their Kensington basement. And he found a friend of his brother, who was at Westminster School, who could not only play guitar but was already in a band. He was Adam Sieff, son of Edward Sieff, then chairman of Marks & Spencer. His band was called Jaded, but the other members – who had included James Lascelles, son of Lord Harewood and stepson of Jeremy Thorpe – had moved on. But the name, formed from James, Adam and Ed, another boy at Westminster, appealed, and so the band was re-formed with two other friends of Sieff's.

One of the handbills advertising the band survives. It is headed: 'Blair–Collenette Promotions introduce: JADED. Exciting Rock'n'Roll band available for all Dances, Concerts and Parties.' The band's energetic promoters also offered a 'Spacematic DISCO with LIGHTS!!' The band consisted of Sieff on lead guitar, Paddy Quirke on bass, Sheppard on 'Rythm' guitar and Theo Sloot on drums.

The handbill had been printed by Sheppard using Letraset in the school art room. 'Spacematic' was not some high-tech music system, 'it was Letraset's way of making sure you've got the letters separated correctly,' said Sheppard. Sieff and Sheppard had already played together in another band. 'Jaded were heavy rock. We were hopeless. It was crap, but it was just great fun,' said Sheppard.

They were not totally hopeless, however. Indeed, compared with other schoolboy bands with dreams of stardom, some of them had real musical talent. Sheppard went on to tour the world with the Electric Light Orchestra, and Sieff, after a list of session music credits including 'The Chicken Song' on *Spitting Image*, is now head of Jazz and World Music at Sony UK.

Next, Blair–Collenette Promotions needed a venue. They searched through the *Yellow Pages*, and Blair tried to persuade several vicars to let them use their church halls. The only one who was prepared to let them stage their concerts was Norman Burt, a 'lonely and rather mysterious' figure, according to Collenette. He was a teacher and the part-time deacon at the Vineyard Congregationalist church in Richmond, where he ran the youth club in the crypt, rather unsuccessfully.

Although the youth club was not 'explicitly religious', according to Gill Hall, who helped Burt with another club later, 'he wanted the church to go out to young people, to reach out to them'. Blair and Collenette were quite happy to go along with any ulterior evangelical motive as long as they had a place to 'showcase' their bands.

However, Blair was not entirely cynical in befriending the unconventional churchman. Collenette remembers that Blair was a believer. 'He was God-fearing and that was unusual at that time in that circle of people. I respected him greatly for it.' After Amanda Mackenzie Stuart's, this is the next significant testimony to Blair's sense of mission. He had seemed rather godless at Fettes, and the former school chaplain, Ronald Selby Wright, confirmed that Blair was not religious then (see p. 19). Blair's father Leo was and is not at all religious, while his mother Hazel's faith was undemonstrative. On the other hand, his prep school headmaster Canon John Grove said Blair was a believer at the age of eleven, and it is worth noting that he did not play up in chapel at Fettes, or argue about religious observance at school, as he did over everything else.

When Blair's stay at Collenette's parents' house stretched the limits of politeness, he lodged with Burt in his house in Twickenham, across the River Thames from the Vineyard. Blair used his upstairs bedroom at 18 Cassilis Road as the base for his operations. At the bottom of the Jaded handbill is the legend, 'Booking and Management . . . Tony Blair', and the old 01 London phone number of Burt's house.

Burt also owned a cottage on the Norfolk Broads, and he and Blair organised a trip there. Sheppard said: 'I remember a magical hot summer week with various members of the clique and Mr Burt, whose primary concern seemed to be maintaining a safe separation between the boys and girls after dark.'

Burt kept in touch. When Blair was first elected as an MP, Burt wrote to him and Blair invited him to the House of Commons. But Burt did not see his long-haired, eighteen-year-old lodger become Prime Minister: he died in 1996.

Blair bought a 'decrepit' blue Ford Thames van for £50, in which they used to ferry bands and equipment around London. At one point, said Collenette, 'rounding a key intersection between Little Venice and St

John's Wood, a wheel fell off with a clunk'. On another occasion, Blair's driving skills were put to the test:

> We were driving through Richmond late one night with members of a band in the van, when Tony drove too near a parked Jaguar, and replaced much of the British Racing Green paint with a Thames Blue. The body of opinion in the van, the overwhelming consensus, was: 'He can afford it; he'll never know who did it; step on it Tony, let's get out of here.' Tony insisted on stopping, writing a note to the driver with his phone number, together with an apology and a promise to make good.

The van came in useful for earning a little extra money, and Blair used it for making deliveries. 'I got to know the streets of London very well,' he once told the London *Evening Standard*. 'So there you are. I could become a black-cab driver if things go badly.'[3]

They certainly did not make enough to live on from their bands, and hit on another scheme to supplement their income. 'My mother makes an excellent lemonade,' said Collenette,

> with a recipe involving the following three unusual ingredients: lemons, sugar and water. We hatched a plan to phone Beecham in Brentford and see if we could sell them the recipe. Tony made this possible by his absolute lack of shyness and so he and I set forth along the M4 by bus.
>
> I cannot remember the name of the head chemist, but he was very pleasant. He told us that the recipe was known to him and that the issue was that the lemonade turned an ugly brown if left on supermarket shelves for more than a few days. He drove us all the way back to London along the M4 and dropped us off on the Cromwell Road, still smarting from our rejection.

Blair and Collenette were forced to find more conventional means of earning money, stacking shelves in the food hall of Barkers of Kensington – the one time in his life when Blair had to clock in and out of work. The main excitement of working there was when a local resident, the actress Charlotte Rampling, came in, once leaning over the future prime minister to select a can of mulligatawny soup. Mr Hodge, their supervisor, took them aside at one point and told them: 'You know, young men, if you keep going the way you are going there might just be a good career for you here. Let's just say you have been noticed.'

The shop was close to Kensington Market, where Blair was marched by two friends who insisted his jeans were too far gone and told him to buy some new trousers. Egged on by his friends, he chose a pair of white flares so tight that they would only fit if he held his breath. 'The lace-up fly was unusual even for 1971,' said Collenette. Most distinctive was Blair's purple and black striped jacket, a Radley School blazer belonging to Collenette's father.

'Let's go honies'

'Tony and I promoted the Vineyard by cycling around London, or driving the van, and standing outside schools as the students came out,' said Collenette.

> Many of the schools were girls' schools, and I remember that one of the most frequently asked questions of Tony as he was handing out the posters for the next Vineyard was: 'Will *you* be there?' Tony was quite a draw and was responsible for a big part of the quite large crowds we had at the Vineyard.

Blair also used to wear a large brown fur coat and Collenette remembered him with his below-shoulder-length blond hair and chipped front tooth, hands on hips, saying: 'Let's go honies.' He loved the Rolling Stones, and 'imitated Mick Jagger constantly'.

On a few occasions at the Vineyard Blair got in some singing practice on the Stones numbers 'Brown Sugar' and 'Honky Tonk Woman' and Elvis Presley's 'Blue Suede Shoes'. But mostly he did the lights, some disc-jockeying and kept the door. On one occasion some Hell's Angels bikers turned up, and one tried to gain entry without the required 30p. 'Tony smiled his huge grin and asked him if he really expected to get in without paying. He said he did. Tony said, "I see", and let him in,' said Collenette.

Blair also looked after the accounts, carefully recorded in a diary kept jointly with Collenette. It had a ledger page for each month. For January 1972, Blair wrote in the 'Paid' column: 'Jan. 14th £22.00'; under 'Received' he wrote '£33.00'. The profit figure, '£11.00', was added in a third column. Result: happiness. The following Friday's gig, on 21 January, was even happier: paid £29, received £54, profit £25.

The financial arrangements became more sophisticated by Wednesday 16 February: 'Fee for Band – £30.00. Fee for Management – 80% of anything over £30.00. Transport – Van.' Mr Eighty Per Cent quickly became an even more ruthless capitalist. For the gig on Saturday 26 February, Blair wrote: 'Fee for Band – £15. Fee for Management – Anything left over.' Despite letting it all hang out, the inner freak was already firmly in control.

After six months of putting on discos and live bands at the Vineyard, capacity 150, Blair and Collenette felt they were ready to break into the big time and booked the Queen Alexandra Hall in Kensington, which could take 2,000. On Blair's nineteenth birthday, 6 May 1972, they put on a concert under the slogan 'Bands with a Future', with a group called Listen topping the bill. 'The band came. The people didn't,' said Collenette. Attendance was better at their second and last date, but

'Oxford was beckoning for Tony and I had to get a real job'.

The story of Blair's gap year confirms his drive. One of his new circle, Adrian Friend, in his final year as a boarder at St Paul's, said Blair 'tried quite hard to get a recording contract – his tremendous enthusiasm even then was overwhelming. He was extremely determined and able to work much harder than anyone else I knew.'

After a while at Oxford, Blair moved from the back room to centre stage, as the lead singer for a student band called Ugly Rumours. Knowing the words to 'Honky Tonk Woman' stood him in good stead when he was auditioned for the job. And he still had the white flared trousers.

Sheppard recalled a party at Collenette's in London two years later, in early 1974, when Blair was in his second year at Oxford (it is possible to date it from the fact that Alvin Stardust, produced by the future Lord Levy, was in the charts with 'My Coo-Ca-Choo' at the time). 'I remember Tony was sitting all by himself in the front room. I went and chatted to him and it was obvious that he was thinking very hard about something quite different. There was a definite change of personality, he wasn't so carefree.'

Collenette visited Blair at university, and offered a striking vignette of the two sides of Blair's character:

> I knew he took religion seriously and my impression was that this made him somewhat reserved about relations with the opposite sex. Visiting his rooms in Oxford, I remember a crowded ante-room full of friends and interested young ladies, but by contrast, off stage, his bedroom with its Bible by the bedside.

Two other features of this period are worth comment. One is that Blair continued to show no interest in politics. His formation is therefore unlike most prime ministers, and unlike the teenage William Hague, who took copies of *Hansard* out of the library, or Charles Kennedy, an MP at the age of twenty-three. Blair has, however, said that his favourite book at eighteen was Isaac Deutscher's 'superb' biography of Leon Trotsky.[4]

The other is the sheer harmlessness of the japes he got up to in his gap year. In particular, to have avoided illegal drugs in that rock music milieu would have been quite unusual. The band that Sieff and Sheppard were in before Jaded was called Acid, but Sheppard insisted: 'The name was not significant. Alkaline would have been equally valid.'

During the campaign for the Labour leadership Jeremy Paxman asked Blair if he had been 'exposed to things like drugs' in his rock 'n' roll days.

Blair's answer was unspecific: 'No, I didn't get into drugs.'[5]

The 'No' there is weightless: he was certainly 'exposed' to drugs during his gap year and at Oxford. People he knew smoked dope and did so at parties he attended. And it is obviously true that he 'didn't get into drugs'. The question is whether he tried pot once or twice, or did not try it at all.

The second is not impossible. There were people like that, even in white flared trousers in rock bands in the early 1970s. Blair was different from the other 'weekend hippies' in his gap year, not least because he had a Bible by his bedside. Collenette is emphatic. 'Tony did not smoke pot. He was fun to be around partly because he had few inhibitions and knew how to have fun instinctively without the need for artificial stimulation.' James Moon, the drummer in his Oxford band, Ugly Rumours, said: 'I have to say, because it's true, I never saw him with any drugs whatsoever, which I must say is more journalistically interesting than if I had. Particularly with that lot in the band.'

In which case it was curious that Blair did not 'just say no' to Paxman. However, he did give a definite answer to a straight question three months later. Interviewed in the *Spectator*, on 1 October 1994, he was asked by Noreen Taylor if he had ever smoked dope: 'No, I haven't. But if I had, you can be sure I would have inhaled.' The macho dig at his friend Bill Clinton slightly diluted the effect, but this denial laid the issue to rest.

Indeed, no one who knew him at school, during his year off or at Oxford, has said that they saw him smoke cannabis. He smoked cigarettes, and he drank, but rarely to excess. One or two friends suggest that he was sometimes intoxicated, but none has said they ever saw him incapacitated. In part, this may reflect the loyalty of his friends – which in itself reflects well on him – in not relating the racier episodes of Blair's growing up. But it seems he was, even at the ages of eighteen and nineteen, a self-controlled and worryingly wholesome character.

Notes

1. Charles Reiss and Anne Applebaum, London *Evening Standard*, 23 May 1996.
2. Martin Jacques, *Sunday Times Magazine*, 17 July 1994.
3. Charles Reiss and Anne Applebaum, London *Evening Standard*, 23 May 1996.
4. *The Times*, 23 April 1998; Deutscher's book was published in three parts: *The Prophet Armed*, 1954; *The Prophet Unarmed*, 1959; *The Prophet Outcast*, 1963.
5. BBC2, *Newsnight*, 23 June 1994.

3

Purple Loons

Oxford, 1972–75

> 'My Christianity and my politics came together at the same time.'
>
> —*Tony Blair, 1995*

But for God, would Tony Blair be a Conservative? 'With my class background, if all I had wanted to do was to exercise power I could and would – let's be blunt about this – have joined another party,' as Blair said after he was elected Labour leader.[1] Not that he actually joined the Labour Party – 'that would have been regarded as terribly right-wing' – until after he left university.[2]

It was not until his first year at St John's College, Oxford, in 1972, when he met Peter Thomson, who described himself as a 'renegade priest', that Blair suddenly developed a Christian socialist philosophy. Although most contemporaries had no idea he was interested in politics, those who knew him well were aware of an intense commitment. 'He used to go on and on and on about his belief in the Labour Party, about socialism and inequality; he was quite a zealot about it,' according to fellow-student Sally Brampton.

Blair met Thomson through another Australian, Geoff Gallop, a Rhodes scholar studying Philosophy, Politics and Economics. Gallop was a revolutionary Marxist and therefore pretty normal for a student interested in politics at the time. But Thomson was different. He was a 36-year-old mature student, a minister of the Australian Anglican church, reading theology at St John's. Blair described him as 'spellbinding', and 'the person who most influenced me'.[3]

David Gardner, later Brussels correspondent for the *Financial Times*, was another member of this 'group of friends which was very close' and whose centre of gravity was Thomson's 'tremendous enthusiasm'. For a year and a half, 'long meaning-of-life sessions were very much on the agenda', said Gardner. Another member, Marc Palley, who became Blair's best friend, said: 'It's what students do, putting the world to rights, pontificating about their theories.' Two or three times a week, various people in Thomson's circle would end up, usually in his room, putting the world to rights late into the night.

There is a sense about Thomson, although he does not say so directly, that he felt he had wasted a lot of his life, and was trying to make up for lost time. He wanted to discuss – endlessly – how moral philosophy should be put into practice. It was a 'project', to use a later word, which deeply interested Blair. Thomson said:

> I was an old retard who had arrived here from Australia, trying to become respectable. He was young, full of life, a person who had this *joie de vivre*. He was into life. He'd a keen intellect and a sense of compassion for other people. And we used to have these marvellous discussions that would go on for hours – you know, cigarettes and coffee and, because I was a bit older I had a bit more money than they did, they'd smoke all my cigarettes and drink all my coffee and we'd get into religion and politics.[4]

It would be a mistake to see Thomson's discussions as the late-night equivalent of Christian coffee mornings. They were informal and often irreverent, although there was an underlying seriousness of purpose. Relaxed, informal, garrulous, Thomson was also a good tennis player and taught Blair to play.

> He used to get me up at seven in the morning. He'd say, 'We've got to go and play,' and I was trying to open one eye. He got quite good. But competitive! Oh, he wanted to win every point. But he was great. It just showed the kind of dogged determination that the bloke's got. He sets his focus in a particular way and goes for it.

Blair's outward persona at Oxford was a noisy and exuberant extension of that of the public-school rebel, and even the more serious, private Blair at university combined earnestness with detachment. Marc Palley said: 'He's got a great ability to stand back from things, and I would say when one talks about being a serious person the inference is that they take themselves seriously as well, which he didn't.' He may have taken himself seriously since then, 'but it's always with things in perspective – there's always a little bit of twinkle in the eye'.

Those who took part in Thomson's discussions were a shifting set of people, united more by left-wing politics than by religious commitment. Other members of the circle included Olara Otunna, a Ugandan refugee who was later, briefly, Uganda's foreign minister in 1984–85 and a candidate for Secretary-General of the United Nations, and Anwal Velani, an Indian postgraduate student. 'It was no accident that most were from abroad and not products of the British class system,' said Blair. 'I could never stand the Oxford intellectual Establishment. They seemed to have a poker up their backsides.'[5] However, as well as his circle of Commonwealth outsiders, Blair also hung out with products of the British public-school system, however rebelliously tongue-in-cheek they were, in a rock band and in dining clubs.

Geoff Gallop said he and Thomson were 'both very political. I was very much an activist on the far left, pushing a Marxist line. Tariq Ali was my guru. Peter was a Christian socialist.' Gallop was in the International Marxist Group; David Gardner 'considered myself well to the left of the Labour Party'; Marc Palley was cynical about politics (and religion) but was 'liberal-leftish anti-Establishment' – his father was the only white MP in Rhodesia to oppose Ian Smith. Thomson's theology was broad, non-institutional and politically radical. Only Otunna was an evangelical Christian. Beyond an anti-Establishment pose and a sense of compassion, Blair's politics were unformed when he arrived at Oxford. The discussions he engaged in over Thomson's coffee and cigarettes were to change all that.

Junior love-god

Blair chose to study law, following his father and brother, although he has since said that he wished he had studied history. Law was and is a tedious subject to study, involving large amounts of rote learning and offering little opportunity for flights of intellectual exploration. And at St John's, an all-male college, and a rather dull and conservative place, he certainly stood out. 'He looked very different. He didn't go for smashing things up, but he was lively,' said David Chater, a contemporary who was later a television reporter and foreign correspondent for Sky News. Blair's father said he went to Oxford to pick him up in his first year, and met a long-haired undergraduate, shirt open to the navel, a large ceramic cross round his neck and a long, black synthetic skin coat with a red lining. 'I wondered who the hell it was. Then he said, "Hi, Dad".'[6]

In his third year, Tony Blair's appearance, as the lead singer in the rock band Ugly Rumours, was just as dramatic, the features graphically listed by bass guitarist Mark Ellen:

> Reading from top to bottom, the long hair with the rather severe fringe – a slightly medieval look about him, a sort of Three Musketeers thing – a

> T-shirt that can only be described as 'hoop-necked' and possibly even 'trumpet-sleeved', which revealed a large acreage of rippling bare torso, and beyond that the obligatory purple loons, topped off with the Cuban-heeled cowboy boots.[7]

Adam Sharples, lead guitarist, now a Treasury civil servant, said drily: 'That certainly chimes with my memory.'

When he was auditioned for the Ugly Rumours, he prepared for it as if he were going for a job interview, according to Mark Ellen. 'Tony turned up bang on time – incredibly punctual – brandishing sheaves of paper, of lyrics that he had transcribed, and we were fantastically impressed by this, because obviously we'd told him what songs we played [although] we didn't really know what the words were.'

The Ugly Rumours were public-school rebels. The band was started by Adam Sharples and Ellen, who knew each other from Winchester School, with drummer James Moon. 'We felt, looking at ourselves, that we were on the visual front a little bit tragic – yards of unconditioned hair and collective sex appeal of slightly less than zero,' said Ellen. 'What we felt we wanted was a charismatic, good-looking lead singer, and Adam suggested this guy Tony Blair. "I met this guy Tony Blair in St John's. He looks terrific. He can sing – I've seen him sing."'

So Blair was auditioned, sitting in the armchair in Sharples's room in Corpus Christi, where Sharples read Philosophy, Politics and Economics. Sharples and Ellen played acoustic guitar while Moon hit 'anything within reach in a rhythmical manner', said Ellen. And Blair sang. 'He was fantastic. He had a really good voice. It was a very high, powerful voice and he knew all the words. So we said: "Well, you're in. We're called Ugly Rumours and you can start tomorrow."'

The band's name came from a Grateful Dead album of the time called *Live at the Mars Hotel.* Blair was not a Grateful Dead fan, but Sharples and Ellen were heavily into deep and meaningful gloom rock. 'If you held this album cover upside down in a mirror, the stars in the sky spelt the words "ugly rumors", which seemed to have great significance at the time – possibly less so now,' said Ellen.

Blair's earnestness continued. Ellen said: 'I was amazed by how keen he was on the idea of rehearsal. I think we were just a little bit looser – "Hey, we'll just turn up and we'll be brilliant." And he was like, "No, I think we should actually practise this and get it right."' Ellen stayed in the music business, as a presenter of *The Old Grey Whistle Test*, editor of the music magazine *Q* and publisher of *Mojo* magazine. His account of the band's first gig, in Corpus Christi's oak-panelled, sixteenth-century hall, is something of a comedy performance in itself. They rehearsed – 'not very rigorously' – in the underground car park across the road, came on stage at 8.30 and 'shuffled into some lumpen riff'. Enter Tony Blair, in purple loons and cut-off T-shirt.

> He comes on stage giving it a bit of serious Mick Jagger, a bit of finger-wagging and punching the air. And we go into our third song and – complete catastrophe – the drums begin to fall off the drum riser. I can see it now in slow motion. One by one they just fell apart and rolled off the stage and on to the floor. And we were all absolutely frozen with horror and embarrassment. The audience are looking at us, and we're looking at them. And Tony just got straight in there and dealt with it brilliantly. He grabbed the microphone and said: 'We're the Ugly Rumours. Hope you're enjoying yourself. We're playing on Saturday at the Alternative Corpus Christi College Ball, supported by a jazz-fusion band and a string quartet. Hope you're going to come. Are you having a good time? I can't hear you at the back. Corpus Christi how are you?' All that sort of stuff – really ludicrous. He held the entire thing together, and we were just amazed. We were running around behind him trying to nail these drums back again. Got the kit back. Plugged in. Got back into this appalling riff that we were playing, and the whole thing resumed. It was brilliant, the way he dealt with it. He dealt with the hecklers at the back. He dealt with the rather worthy students in the berets who've paid their 30p admission and they're not going until they've heard a Captain Beefheart song. And he dealt with the sea of girls down at the front with the floral print dresses. You know, 95 per cent of them were probably called Amanda. And he was really funny, charming, really charismatic. I can remember standing there in the back line with my bass guitar, standing behind a sea of crash cymbals, looking at him and thinking: 'This is no ordinary junior love-god lead singer we have here. Where is this guy going to go?'

Moon, now an investment banker, concurred: 'He was quite a good front man, you know, hip-wriggler in chief.' But Blair was not a good singer. Comments on his voice ranged from 'rough' to 'he looked great'.

The band's next performance, at the Alternative Ball, was recorded by another eyewitness. Blair wore 'white skin-tight trousers and strummed his bass guitar with far less dexterity than he now applies to politics'.[8]

The Ugly Rumours were not signed up by a talent-spotting record company and required to sacrifice their artistic integrity to the commercial pressures of the music industry. The band played only about half a dozen gigs in its brief career, and restricted itself to literal cover versions of 'Honky Tonk Woman' and 'Live With Me' by the Rolling Stones, 'Black Magic Woman' by Fleetwood Mac, 'Take It Easy' by Jackson Browne, and songs by Free and the Doobie Brothers – the last being what the band most sounded like, according to one ear-witness.

Blair also appeared on stage in comic revues and straight drama, carrying on from where he left off at school. He played Matt in the St John's Drama Society production of Bertolt Brecht's *Threepenny Opera* at the Oxford Playhouse in 1974.

Blair's Oxford days also had a 'strawberries and cream' side, which took the form of aping the *Brideshead* caricature of upper-class Oxford. He rowed on the river, with Chater, in a 'joke Eight'. And he was a member of the St John's Archery Club, which had little to do with bows and arrows. Its main function was to hold parties, according to Nicholas Lowton, a contemporary member, especially in the summer, although sometimes they would 'twang around in St John's Gardens – not after we'd drunk too much, for obvious reasons. There had been trouble with it in the past.' It was arch, not to say archaic. The members wore straw boaters and blazers; women were allowed only as guests on 'Ladies' Days'.

For much of his first year, Blair went out with Suzanne (Suzie) Parsons, generally described as one of the most beautiful women in Oxford. She was at St Clare's sixth-form college with Blair's friend Anji Hunter, who, as well as being protective and even possessive of Blair, later went out with Mark Ellen. In his second and third years Blair had a (short) series of other girlfriends, and was usually being 'chased by several more', according to one friend. Blair and Marc Palley were once summoned by the deans to answer the charge that women had visited their rooms outside permitted hours. A lipstick had been found in Blair's room. 'Oh, that's mine,' he replied, casually, when confronted with the evidence.[9]

In his personal relationships, as in his later political ones, he showed a remarkable ability to leave behind a good impression. Mary Harron, a Canadian student who went out with him briefly, recalled:

> Even before he became an MP and famous I always thought of Tony as the only 'nice' person that I ever went out with at Oxford. He was very good-looking, in a kind of sweet way, and wasn't at all predatory. He was very different from most of the guys I knew, but I guess I fell for him because he was cute.[10]

Harron went on to be film critic for the *New Statesman* and later a film producer in New York (she was also director of the 1999 film *American Psycho*).

For all his front as a noisy show-off, Blair was discreet about sex, abstemious about drugs and earnest about rock 'n' roll. 'He had a more varied bunch of interests or social life than most. Most people tended to be one group or another. Tony had a slightly more catholic circle of friends,' said James Moon. 'He wasn't a particularly political animal. He had good emotional motives, decency. There was a sense of decency, and a slight sense of apartness from the mainstream.'

A philosophy

According to Thomson and Gallop, there were three broad topics to which their discussions constantly returned: the relationship between theology and politics; reform or revolution (what Gallop called 'the perpetual question'); and the concept of community. The last theme arose out of Thomson's enthusiasm for a Scottish philosopher called John Macmurray, whose work Thomson had been introduced to at theological college in Melbourne in 1955 by a priest who had lost his parish because of his former membership of the Communist Party.[11] 'If you really want to understand what I'm all about,' said Blair, just as he was elected Labour leader in 1994, 'you have to take a look at a guy called John Macmurray. It's all there.'[12]

Macmurray was considered one of Britain's leading thinkers in the 1930s, when he was Grote Professor of Philosophy at London University, and described then as 'one of the most original minds of our time'.[13] Because he used plain language, he was also popular, giving regular talks on BBC Radio. But his reputation did not survive the war, when he moved to Edinburgh University. By the time Thomson came across his work, he had been relegated to a minor figure in academic theology. But Thomson was hugely excited by the central idea of Macmurray's forgotten and rather dated books, an infectious interest he took with him to Oxford:

> I think he was one of the most important British philosophers this century. And he was on to a concept of community. He used to say that the noblest form of human existence is friendship and that instead of being on a debit and credit ledger idea of 'If you do this for me, then I'll do that for you', we ought to develop a sense of community where people were committed to the welfare of one another.

Macmurray saw his purpose as being to challenge the starting-point of modern philosophy, the idea that people are individuals first, who then choose how to relate to others. He insisted that people exist only in relation to others. The central idea of liberalism, that individuals should be free to do whatever they like provided they do not harm others, started from an unreal assumption, according to Macmurray, because it assumed that people exist in a vacuum and only impinge on others when they choose to.

He argued that individuals are created by their relationships in their families and communities. Or, as Blair put it in 1993, 'We do not lose our identity in our relations with others; in part at least, we achieve our identity by those relations.'[14]

The effect of Macmurray's rethinking was to invert Adam Smith's dictum, 'Social and self-love are the same'. Smith said that if we follow our self-interest, we benefit the whole community. Macmurray said that by pursuing the community's interests we benefit the individuals within it, including ourselves.

Macmurray made grand claims for his philosophy, although it was not the radical inversion of the assumptions of Western philosophy he thought. The British ethical and Christian socialist thinkers of the turn of the century, such as T. H. Green and L. T. Hobhouse, also believed that altruism was the highest form of self-interest.

What was distinctive about Macmurray was that he combined this Christian socialism with an attack on liberalism which resembled that of Conservative followers of Edmund Burke, who emphasise the family and tradition as the bonds that hold together organic communities, and who oppose individualism and rationalism.[15] In this, Macmurray anticipated the 'communitarian' philosophy of contemporary North American thinkers such as Charles Taylor and Michael Sandel. According to Sandel, the politics of the common good enable us to 'know a good in common that we cannot know alone'. Real societies are not 'voluntary associations', he said. The shared pursuit of a common goal is not a relationship people choose, 'but an attachment they discover, not merely an attribute but a constituent of their identity'.[16]

It was precisely the combination in Macmurray of Christian socialism and a 'conservative' critique of liberalism which underpinned the apparent novelty of Blair's political philosophy when he became leader of the Labour Party. Macmurray's other-centred philosophy crystallised Blair's thinking:

> It seemed to me a sensible explanation of the human condition. There seemed a coincidence between the philosophical theory of Christianity and left-of-centre politics. I didn't work these things out very clearly at the time, but they were influences that stayed with me. They were formative influences.[17]

Macmurray's starting-point was his personal experience of the First World War. Blair later recalled an essay on the subject of Christian duty which arose out of his observation that 'his comrades had divided into two categories in response to the horror of the conflict'. The first group reacted as Epicureans, rejecting altruism for the pursuit of sensual pleasures.

> The second group, in contrast, was gripped by a profound belief that their lives had to have a purpose – a moral purpose that encompassed the notion of duty. One could liken this to Kant's moral imperative. What Macmurray meant is that there is a human impulse within, which can be fulfilled only through duty.[18]

Macmurray was always profoundly religious, although he was not a member of a church until late in life, when he joined the Society of Friends (Quakers). The practical application of Macmurray's thought remained ambiguous, however, despite his emphasis on doing rather than thinking (curious for a full-time, life-time academic). His vision of universal community was ultimately a religious one, although not of any particular religion. 'It sounds wishy-washy, but it isn't,' said Peter Thomson.

Christian socialist

According to Thomson, Blair 'wasn't really a Christian' when he met him.[19] Blair himself said:

> I had always believed in God but I had become slightly detached from it. I couldn't make sense of it. Peter made it relevant, practical rather than theological. Religion became less of a personal relationship with God. I began to see it in a much more social context.[20]

There was no difference for him between religion and socialism. 'My Christianity and my politics came together at the same time.'[21] He started to go to the college Chapel, and asked to be confirmed in the Church of England towards the end of his second year. The importance of this event in understanding his personal development can hardly be overstated. He was prepared for confirmation by the assistant chaplain to St John's, Graham Dow, later Bishop of Carlisle, who said:

> Thomson came to me and said, 'Tony Blair would like to be confirmed.' I was pleased because he was from a group that was interested in social action, rather than the more usual groups of evangelicals – of the narrowly pietistic kind – or quiet intellectuals. He was looking for something that was active, to change society. He gave the impression of someone who had just discovered something exciting and new – he didn't know it all, that's why he was such fun to talk to.

Dow said there were usually two or three candidates for confirmation a year, and remembered the discussions he had with Blair in his study: 'Because of who I am, I would have been quite straight about the commitment faith demands.' Blair 'didn't disagree' with Dow's language of a commitment to a personal Christ and to building the Kingdom of God, but was more interested in practical change in society. Blair was hardly a deep or original thinker about religion or philosophy, but his seriousness cannot be doubted. Blair the Contemplative spent a lot of time in college, working quite hard, reading a lot and – for a law student – quite widely. As well as Macmurray and Immanuel Kant, he also read Søren Kierkegaard and Carl Jung and 'the classics: Austen, Trollope, Thackeray, as well, of course, as the big legal tomes necessary for a law degree'.[22]

Blair's religious belief was private. Oxford contemporaries who did not know him well had no idea that he was a practising Christian. Even his best friend, the atheist Marc Palley, who knew Blair was a Christian, did not know he had been confirmed:

> I've never been able to understand the logic of religion. It's not for me. We used to have long discussions, and I used to say it's a complete load of rubbish, baloney and gibberish. He wasn't a godsquadder – he was the antithesis of a stereotypical godsquadder – but he happened to believe.

For years afterwards, his beliefs were not well known. In December 1991, on a visit to New York, Gordon Brown's adviser Geoff Mulgan was surprised when, after a heavy Saturday night, Blair was up at the crack of dawn to look for a church. The journalist Peter Kellner expressed astonishment when Blair asked where the nearest church was during a weekend visit at about the same time. Blair was unruffled. 'It's not a sin, is it?' he asked. It was only with the election of Christian socialist John Smith as Labour leader in 1992 that his religion became visible, and it came as news to at least one close friend of over a decade's standing.

Blair considered going into the church. Olara Otunna remembered him discussing the possibility: 'It was at one point very much on his mind. It was certainly one of the options that he talked about seriously.'* But the ministry would not have satisfied his desire to be famous, which had prompted his ambition to be a pop star.

Instead, politics became the vehicle for his moral commitment. 'It seemed a normal consequence of what we were thinking about and doing for him to go into politics and not to be restricted by becoming a priest in the church,' said Thomson. Otunna said, 'it became clearer to him that the way to make a difference, the way to be useful and to help shape the destiny of those for whom he cared, was to work through the established political process'. Twenty-five years later, he came full circle, satirised as a trendy evangelical vicar by *Private Eye*.

It seems that Blair's early, unspecific desire to 'be something' had become more altruistic. Maybe he still wanted to attract attention, but now by 'doing something' as well.

---

*Blair has been inconsistent since, denying to Robert Harris that he had contemplated a career in the church (*Talk* magazine, May 2000), but telling others it had been 'not impossible at all'.

Into politics

It was not immediately obvious how to 'make a difference' through the established political parties, however. Blair's friends in St John's were mostly left-wing, but had no interest either in the Labour Party or in student politics. Mainstream politics was as deeply unfashionable as dark suits in the early 1970s.

Against a background of economic crisis, Edward Heath and Harold Wilson seemed interchangeably uninspiring, at least after Heath's retreat from the prototype Thatcherism of 'Selsdon Man' in 1972. In the winter of 1973, war in the Middle East almost quadrupled the oil price, and Heath announced a 'three-day week' to conserve energy supplies during the coal strike. The February 1974 election confirmed the electorate's lack of enthusiasm for the two main parties, which both saw their share of the vote fall to the benefit of the Liberals and Nationalists.

Equally, after the romance of the 1968 student rebellions, the doctrinaire and intricate Marxism into which the student left had retreated seemed much less fun. 'I was very interested in political ideas. I was reading everything from Tawney and William Morris through to Gramsci and Isaac Deutscher,' said Blair.[23] New thinking on the left was still dominated by Marxism. Some strands, such as that associated with Antonio Gramsci, were increasingly liberal and pluralistic, but all started from the same texts and were bounded by the same assumptions. And the old thinking was still working its way through the Labour Party – after Europe, the main internal struggle of the time was over how many 'major monopolies' the party wanted to nationalise.

Blair said: 'I went through all the bit about reading Trotsky and attempting a Marxist analysis. But it never went very deep, and there was the self-evident wrongness of what was happening in Eastern Europe.'[24] Thomson was excited by Marxist-influenced radical Christian thought, such as Roman Catholic 'liberation theology', but for Blair

> Christianity helped to inspire my rejection of Marxism. Whatever subtleties can be placed upon it, Marxism was essentially determinist. It was an attempt to make politics scientific. And it isn't. It is about people. And they are, of course, influenced by the conditions around them. But human nature is complex. There is free will, individual responsibility. We can choose and decide.

He was writing in 1997, and by then sounded uncannily like Margaret Thatcher in her fundamentalist anti-Marxism: 'The problem with Marxist ideology was that, in the end, it suppressed the individual by starting with society,' he wrote, to some extent contradicting Macmurray who followed Marx in starting with social relations.[25]

Blair may have become politically committed at Oxford, but he did not become active. He was not involved in the two closely fought election campaigns of 1974 – he was, therefore, not even a member of the Labour Party when it won its last General Election before he himself led it to victory in 1997. Nor did he have anything to do with the university Labour Club. He did take part in a sit-in along with 2,000 other students in the winter of 1973, when the university was convulsed by the campaign to secure a central student union rather than college-based unions. Later on he went on two demos against the National Front, which organised meetings at Oxford Town Hall. Another issue which engaged him was the campaign against apartheid in South Africa. 'I suppose the first issue which got me politically active was the anti-apartheid movement. I think the same sense of moral outrage and moral purpose which lay behind that movement fires most Labour Party members, and I am no different,' he said.[26] He only went to the Oxford Union debating society once, dragged by a girlfriend to see Michael Heseltine give a speech. Heseltine, who was just about to discover the Conservative Party conference and who had yet to swing the mace, was in his prime. Blair was impressed, but not moved.

Farewells

In the summer of 1974, at the end of Blair's second year, Gallop and Thomson left Oxford to return to Australia. Thomson returned to his post as chaplain at Timbertop School in Australia, little knowing that he had helped shape the politics of a national leader. He and Blair kept in touch. Blair visited Australia with Cherie in 1982, and then with Gordon Brown in 1990. Thomson retired from teaching in 1993, at the age of fifty-seven, to a farm 3,000 feet up in the foothills of Mount Buller, north-east Victoria, but the boredom of watching his cattle grow was soon broken by his protégé's election to the Labour leadership a year later. Journalists who tracked down the man who had been 'Blair's guru' at Oxford were told: 'Tone's come a long way since then, but he's still got the basic thrust of it all. He's developed a political realisation of the ideas, but they're still there. If he can take the people with him he can do great work, I'm telling you.'[27] He came to London the next year, to work with the church in projects among the disadvantaged, and to be part of the excitement of 'Tone's' election as Prime Minister.

Geoff Gallop, meanwhile, abandoned Marxism and became a state MP in Western Australia in 1986 and eventually leader of the state Labor Party.

Back in Oxford in his final year, Blair lived with Marc Palley and three women undergraduates in what Palley described as a 'pretty damp, extremely grotty and very cold' house, 63 Argyle Street. Blair's academic career at Oxford was summed up, rather inconsequentially, in the 'President's Collections', a kind of end-of-term report written by the President of St John's, Sir Richard Southern, a distinguished medieval historian.

> Early 1973: 'Well organised. Apt to leave things till the last minute. But a strong interest in many things.'
> June 1973: 'Pleasing structure to work, but some weakness in content.'
> February 1974: 'Seems extraordinarily happy.'
> December 1974: 'Signs of really understanding the principles of the subject.'
> March 1975: 'Needs to be tougher in thinking through his ideas.'

Blair graduated in June 1975. According to Derry Irvine, head of his barristers' chambers, he just failed to get a First, because 'he simply didn't exert himself'.[28] Marc Palley was sceptical: 'To be fair to you, Tony, I think that's overstating it. I think he got a good Second.'

When Blair left Oxford, then, he was definitely left-wing, and saw the unfashionable Labour Party as the only possible vehicle for his political interest. His beliefs were still forming, but could already be described as ethical socialist. John Macmurray was the dominant influence, but he had also read several other more familiar works of the ethical socialist canon and rejected any form of Marxism.

While many people's politics are formed primarily by their parents, this was clearly not the case with Blair. His prep school headmaster, Canon John Grove, said: 'Father was rather wry about it and said, "Oh, he'll soon grow out of it."' But he never did. Blair's basic beliefs have not changed since he was twenty. He is the Christian socialist son of an atheist Tory.

Two weeks after he graduated, Blair's mother Hazel died at the age of fifty-two. She had been diagnosed with throat cancer when he was in his final year at Fettes.

> I don't know why on earth I didn't realise how serious it was. But I suppose you think your mother is indestructible. It never occurs to you that she can die. She had an operation and then she actually survived for about four years after that, which was apparently quite lucky. She very much downplayed it. She just said that she had a lump on her throat and she had to get it removed, so she was going to go into hospital. Even when she went in for the second time and it was obvious there was something wrong, you somehow felt it would be all right.[29]

His parents kept the seriousness of Hazel's condition from Tony because they did not want to distract him during his exams. When Tony went home afterwards, Leo met him off the train and said, 'I'm afraid Mum is a lot more ill than we thought.'

'She's not going to die, is she?' Tony asked, expecting the answer that it wasn't that serious, but Leo replied: 'Yes, I'm afraid she is.'[30] They went straight to the hospital, where Hazel had only a week to live.

> It was terrible how she had suddenly aged at the end. She knew she was dying but she was very, very lucid. She saw each one of us in turn and went through things with us . . . She was very keen as to what type of future life we should lead . . . I was always the wildest of the three [and] Mum was worried I might go off the rails. Also she was very anxious that we were a credit to Dad. She was insistent on us promising that we'd get ourselves sorted out and not do stupid things.[31]

It is possible that, if Tony Blair reacted against his father's politics, his mother's gentleness and social concern provided an alternative base. 'My mother always supported Dad in his politics, but I never thought she was really a Tory. We never got around to discussing it, and she died when I was just coming out of university.'[32] Peter Thomson, who had stayed with the family in Durham, said: 'It was absolutely clear that she doted on Tony and that Tony adored her. She also had a really deep social conscience and I think Tony has turned out to be the type of human being that she would have wanted him to be.'[33]

Olara Otunna remembers him going home at the time:

> He took such trouble to care for his father who had been, I think, even more affected by this, and his younger sister Sarah, who was terribly affected by it. This was something that one could see meant a good deal. He took a great deal of trouble to make sure that the family pulled through this.

His father Leo said: 'He was very solicitous towards me, very kind. He was a very loving son. His mother adored him.'[34]

Hazel's death also heightened her son's ambition:

> As well as your grief for the person your own mortality comes home to you. And you suddenly realise – which often you don't as a young person – that life is finite, so if you want to get things done you had better get a move on[35] . . . For the first time I felt not so much a sense of ambition as a consciousness that time is short. My life took on an urgency which has probably never left it.'[36]

Many – perhaps most – people leave university not really knowing what they want to do. When Blair started his training as a barrister in London, he had gone into law for want of any strong pull in any other direction. Becoming a barrister (again following his brother) rather than a solicitor had more appeal to the show-off in him. His days as a junior love-god of the rock 'n' roll stage were over. But he saw the law as a base rather than a career. 'I would never have been satisfied as a lawyer,' he admitted in 1997, rather contradicting his presentation of himself as a rounded human being who could always give up politics and earn a living at the Bar.[37] The skills of persuasive public speaking are a good grounding for politics: there are more lawyers in the House of Commons than any other occupational group.

Blair has said of his time at Oxford, 'I had no thought of going into Parliament.'[38] However, Geoff Gallop said – of Blair's second year – that he 'was starting to see politics as a future, he was starting to be geared up to go into politics'. And Marc Palley said that when he moved to London with Blair, politics was 'definitely in his mind' as his vocation.

Notes

1. Interview, *Vanity Fair*, March 1995.
2. Martyn Harris, *Sunday Telegraph*, 18 March 1990.
3. Keith Dovkants, London *Evening Standard*, 18 July 1994; *Marxism Today*, July 1990.
4. BBC2, *Newsnight*, 10 June 1994.
5. Martin Jacques, *Sunday Times Magazine*, 17 July 1994.
6. *Ibid.*
7. BBC2, *Newsnight*, 10 June 1994.
8. Mel Johnson, in a book of Corpus Christi College reminiscences, *Corpuscles*, 1993.
9. Martin Jacques, *Sunday Times Magazine*, 17 July 1994.
10. Jon Sopel, *Tony Blair: The Moderniser*, p. 26.
11. Peter Thomson, 'Putting Spine into the Community', R. H. Tawney Memorial Lecture, 1 March 1997.
12. *Scotland on Sunday*, 24 July 1994.
13. C. E. M. Joad, *Spectator*, undated, review of John Macmurray, *Interpreting the Universe*, 1933, supplied by Peter Thomson.
14. Speech, Wellingborough, 19 February 1993.
15. For example, Alexis de Tocqueville, *Democracy in America*, and Michael Oakeshott, *Rationalism in Politics*.
16. Michael Sandel, *Liberalism and the Limits of Justice*, pp. 150, 183.
17. Keith Dovkants, London *Evening Standard*, 18 July 1994.
18. *Sunday Telegraph*, 7 April 1996.
19. Martin Jacques, *Sunday Times Magazine*, 17 July 1994.
20. *Ibid.*
21. Lesley Ann Down, *News of the World*, 29 October 1995.
22. *Sunday Telegraph*, 7 April 1996; *The Times*, 23 April 1998.
23. Martin Jacques, *Sunday Times Magazine*, 17 July 1994.
24. Martyn Harris, *Sunday Telegraph*, 18 March 1990.

25. *Sunday Telegraph*, 7 April 1996.
26. Fiona Millar, *House* magazine, 2 October 1996.
27. *Scotland on Sunday*, 24 July 1994.
28. *Ibid.*
29. Lynda Lee-Potter, *Daily Mail*, 26 October 1996.
30. Mary Riddell, *Daily Mirror*, 26 September 1996; Lynda Lee-Potter, *Daily Mail*, 26 October 1996.
31. Lynda Lee-Potter, *Daily Mail*, 26 October 1996, 22 April 1997.
32. *News of the World*, 29 October 1995.
33. Sopel, *Tony Blair: The Moderniser*, p. 36.
34. Martin Jacques, *Sunday Times Magazine*, 17 July 1994.
35. Sopel, *Tony Blair: The Moderniser*, p. 36.
36. Mary Riddell, *Daily Mirror*, 26 September 1996.
37. Lesley White, *Sunday Times Magazine*, 20 April 1997.
38. *Observer*, 2 October 1994.

4

Meeting a Woman at the Bar

London, 1975–80

'Once you succumb to Tony's charm, you never really get over it.'
—*Cherie Booth, 1997*

When Tony Blair joined the Labour Party in the autumn of 1975, the most important issue dividing the party was Europe. He was still at Oxford when he voted in the referendum, on 5 June, in favour of Britain's continued membership of the EEC, along with the 67 per cent majority in the country, and most of Harold Wilson's Cabinet, but probably against the majority of the Labour Party membership. On this central issue of British politics, Blair's private beliefs have been consistent – although, when the party's policy swung against Europe once Labour was out of power, he toed the line in public.

Blair moved into a basement flat in Earl's Court, west London, with his university friend and fellow lawyer Marc Palley. The flat, at 92 Ifield Road, SW10, was in the Redcliffe ward of the constituency of Chelsea, safe seat of Conservative Nicholas Scott. A fellow constituent was the new leader of the Conservative Party, Margaret Thatcher, elected that February in a coup of the Tory modernisers against the traditionalists. Harold Wilson, already preparing to resign the following year in favour of James Callaghan, was absorbed in a time-consuming struggle to quarantine Tony Benn in the Industry Department. Meanwhile the Labour Party was still dreaming of achieving the 'irreversible shift of wealth and power in favour of working people and their families' promised in its manifesto, through ever-more unlikely programmes of state ownership and planning agreements. Both government and party were oblivious to the threat from Thatcher, who gave the Conservative Party that autumn her vision: 'A man's right to work as he will, to spend what he earns, to own property, to have the state as servant and not as master.'[1]

The Redcliffe branch of the Chelsea Labour Party had become inactive, and Blair arrived at the same time as two long-standing members decided to try to revive it. Sandy Pringle and Tim Bolton, then chairman of the Chelsea Labour Party and now a local councillor, wrote to all the members in the ward and asked them to come to a meeting in Pringle's flat.

Blair was one of the twenty people who turned up. Pringle said he was 'very encouraged to think there were all these young people around'. Pringle became branch chairman and, at his first meeting, Blair became secretary. Branch secretaries are automatically members of the General Committee, the body which runs the constituency-wide party, and which in those days chose parliamentary candidates. Thus Blair received an early initiation into the ancient rites of Labour's internal machinery. Branch and General Committee meetings were sometimes held at the Gunter Arms pub on the Fulham Road. Although they did meet in people's homes, said Pringle, they did not meet in Blair's basement flat – 'the sort of place where students would live'.

Pringle found Blair 'exceedingly bright and engaging', a 'fairly competent' secretary, and they became quite good friends. He recognised him as a 'chap of ability', and thought his politics were like the old or *Tribune* left – as distinct from the new, more Marxist-influenced Labour left. He had 'definitely radical views in his attitude towards the Establishment', and had a 'healthy disrespect' for it, said Pringle.

Labour lawyer

Tony Blair started his one-year course at Bar school in September 1975 and early the next year turned his mind to the question of obtaining a pupillage. In order to practise as barristers, students who pass the Bar exams have to gain work experience as a pupil in a set of chambers – a group of barristers who share offices. As is still often the case, pupils were not paid, but the Inns of Court awarded scholarships to support some of them. Before Blair's interview for a scholarship in the spring of 1976, he waited in the Old Hall of Lincoln's Inn with other candidates seated in alphabetical order. He found himself next to Cherie Booth, one of the most academically outstanding of that year's students. Brought up in Liverpool, she shone at Seafield Convent Grammar School in Crosby, where every lesson began with a prayer and 'we were taught you worked hard for the glory of God and whatever you achieved was not enough', according to a classmate of Cherie's, Patricia Murphy.[2]

Cherie was 'one of the most intelligent pupils I ever taught', said her history teacher Margaret Oliver. She took four As at A-level, in History, Geography, Economics and General Studies, topped by the highest First in law at the London School of Economics. Like Blair, she was interested in politics, although she had joined the Labour Party earlier than him, at the age of sixteen in 1970. Her application for a scholarship was successful. His was not.

Blair noticed her over the next year. 'I always remember Cherie being in the Lincoln's Inn library when everyone else would go down to the pub for lunch, she would be eating her sandwiches in there, poring over her books.'[3] It soon became clear the two of them would have more to do with each other when he applied to be a pupil at the chambers of Derry Irvine.[4] At the time, individual barristers took on their own pupils, although decisions to award a tenancy – a permanent place in chambers – would be made by members of chambers as a whole (nowadays most pupils are taken on by chambers and then allocated to work with individual barristers).

Blair arrived at Irvine's office through his public school connections. He had met Colin Fawcett, the head of another chambers, at a friend's twenty-first birthday party at Beaconsfield Golf Club. His legal career thus began in the same deeply Conservative Home Counties town as his parliamentary career, launched by the Beaconsfield by-election six years later. Blair asked Fawcett for advice: he recommended Irvine, and agreed to 'effect an introduction'. Irvine had already taken on a pupil, and Blair applied late, but 'he bowled me over with his enthusiasm', said Irvine, so he took him on as well as the highly impressive student he had already recruited – Cherie Booth. As a former lecturer at the LSE's law department, Irvine would have known the lecturers who could testify to her outstanding academic ability. She said Blair's arrival 'didn't please me at all, because I'd been assured that I was going to be the only one'.[5] Indeed Irvine has always claimed that he did not intend to have two pupils, but he certainly needed them both, and he took two pupils again the following year. One of these, Julian Fulbrook, said Irvine was 'colossally overworked'. At thirty-six, he was only two years away from becoming the youngest of his contemporaries to 'take silk', that is, to become a Queen's Counsel, one of the barrister élite.

A driven and rigorous intellectual meritocrat, Irvine can be abrasive. According to Blair, on one of his first meetings with his mentor he was confronted with the question: 'So, your parents were rich enough to send you to a public school then?'

Blair tried to reply tactfully: 'Well, of course you can criticise my public school education—'

'I bloody well will!' was the terse reply.[6]

Irvine, who himself was a scholarship boy at the fee-paying Hutchesons' Boys' Grammar School in Glasgow (and whose own sons were later educated privately), joined the Labour Party at the age of seventeen at Glasgow University, where he was a friend of fellow law student John Smith. In the same year that Smith was first elected for the safe Labour seat of North Lanarkshire, 1970, Irvine stood unsuccessfully for parliament in Hendon North. More significantly, he just missed being the Labour candidate for the safe South Wales seat of Aberdare for the 1974 elections. When Blair started work in Irvine's chambers, Smith was a rising minister in the Labour government. Irvine's political contacts were to prove important in Blair's future career, although Irvine said that politics played no part in his decision to take Blair on – indeed, he thought that of the two Cherie was the fledgling politician.

In the summer of 1976 Booth confirmed Irvine's judgment by coming top in that year's Bar exams. Blair achieved an undistinguished Third class. He explained that he did not treat the exam 'with the seriousness that – well, actually I think I did treat it with the seriousness it deserved, but anyway I didn't work particularly hard at it'.[7] Booth began her pupillage straight away, while Blair spent the summer in France. He worked in the bar of the Frantour hotel in Paris, where he 'got quite good tips' from American tourists because he spoke English. This led to 'my first lesson in applied socialism', he said twenty-two years later in his address (in French) to the French National Assembly. 'The others told me to put all my tips into a communal pot. But at the end of the night I discovered it was only me who had been putting my money in.'[8] (Centre-right deputies broke into delighted laughter and applause, while their socialist opponents were unamused.) He also taught English to managers at an insurance company, which gave him a large enough bonus to pay for a cycling holiday in the Dordogne.

When he returned, he and Booth were locked in competition for a permanent place – a tenancy – at Irvine's chambers. They knew that the chambers would only take on one of them at the end of their year's pupillage. They both had to work hard in any case, because Irvine often handled four or five Employment Appeal Tribunal cases a week, as well as two conferences with clients which needed detailed preparation. Every Friday, however, Irvine would unwind, taking pupils, former pupils and – as often as not – John Smith to El Vino's in Fleet Street for a drink (Cherie taking a dim view of the fact that at that time women were not served at the bar there).

Instead of driving them apart, the competition between Booth and

Blair had the opposite effect. Initially, she appeared to have the advantage over him. 'She's a brilliant lawyer,' said Blair. 'In the first bit of the pupillage I was struggling a bit . . . She helped me enormously.'[9]

The professional and personal balance changed gradually. She said: 'I was with someone else at the time, but by the end of the pupillage I'd finished with him and started going out with Tony.'[10]

He confessed: 'She did have a boyfriend at the time, but when you've met the person you believe you want to spend the rest of your life with, you've got to go for it, haven't you?'[11]

To begin with, 'she wasn't quite sure whether I was what she was looking for. She felt I'd had it easy which in a way I hadn't. But I'd been to Oxford, which she could have done and decided not to,' he said. 'When I first met Cherie she was quite difficult. She had that slight Liverpool chippiness. She was a woman who'd had to struggle.'[12]

At a party given by a friend of Cherie's at Christmas 1976, they played a team game which involved physical contact, passing a balloon held between their knees. A few days later they went out to lunch with Irvine in Covent Garden. Irvine thought they were there to celebrate the end of a case, but eventually realised that other business was being transacted and made his excuses. 'Derry took us out for lunch, and he disappeared after a time,' said Blair. 'And I remember we were still there at dinner time, so something must have happened along the way.'[13]

In 1977, the chambers awarded Blair the tenancy on Irvine's recommendation. 'We always did what he suggested in relation to his pupils and he did not recommend taking them both, he only recommended Tony,' said Michael Burton, now a High Court judge. 'So we voted accordingly at the chambers meeting.'[14] This contradicted Irvine's account. He avoided saying he made a choice, saying she found somewhere else – but she would only have done so if it had been indicated to her that Blair would be preferred.

Blair not only won the tenancy, he got the girl. 'Once you succumb to Tony's charm, you never really get over it,' she said.[15] She had to look for a tenancy elsewhere, but at least had the consolation of going out with the intensely persuasive young man who had snatched her crown. She joined the chambers of George Carman, one of the most famous libel lawyers. It was a small set of chambers, which did not particularly fit her interests, because most of her work was in family and employment law.

Irvine said Blair was a very good lawyer: 'He was absolutely excellent. I have no doubt that he would have become a QC. He had a very keen sense of what was relevant. He was very good at getting to the point. He was a fast gun on paper, possessing an excellent facility with the English language.'[16]

Most of Blair's work was on commercial cases. One friend said: 'He is in fact basically an extremely able commercial lawyer.' But Irvine's chambers also acted for the Labour Party, and Blair also developed a practice in employment law, acting for both employers and trade unions. This prepared the ground for his future career: not only would trade union law become a political battlefield, but he could present himself as a fighter for the legal rights of trade unionists facing redundancy or victimisation, and the contacts he made, in the party and in the unions, would help his political advancement.

His ambition had become more certain. When his university friend, Geoff Gallop, returned to Oxford to study for a doctorate in 1977, 'we would talk about what we were going to do when we got elected', the Australian said.

Why did Blair want to be a politician? He was asked this question in one of the earliest profiles of him, by Martyn Harris in the *Sunday Telegraph*, 18 March 1990. His answer was curiously evasive and prosaic, as if he were slightly embarrassed by his early idealism: 'I was interested in politics, and in trade union law. I decided this was what I wanted to do.'

'But what did you want to do exactly?' asked Harris.

'Well, get into government. Actually run something.'

'Why?'

'Well, I suppose you could go into all the slightly twee motives. I suppose you just look at the world around you. Think things are wrong. Want to change them.'

That advancement was on hold, however, while James Callaghan attempted to nurse the Labour government towards a break in the electoral clouds. After little more than a year in the Chelsea Labour Party, Blair and Marc Palley had moved. Palley said they discussed 'moving into an area of London which had a stronger Labour Party'. Instead, they moved to another 'extremely grotty flat' in St Edmund's Terrace in St John's Wood, near Primrose Hill, in another Conservative constituency, Marylebone. When Palley moved out to live with his girlfriend, in September 1977, two other friends from St John's College, Oxford, David Fursdon and Martin Stanley, moved in. Blair was not active in the Marylebone Labour Party, although his new girlfriend was. Cherie Booth lived in the neighbouring Lord's–Hamilton Terrace ward and was a member of the constituency General Committee. She and Blair used to listen to Bruce Springsteen records in the flat – Blair chose one of them, 'Fourth of July, Asbury Park', for his *Desert Island Discs*.[17]

At the start of 1979, he moved again, south of the Thames, to 41 Bramford Road, SW18, by Wandsworth Bridge, the house of a lawyer friend, Charles Falconer. He transferred his party membership to the Fairfield branch of the Battersea Labour Party, of which Falconer was already a member.

The two had met in inauspicious circumstances when they were both at private schools in Scotland. Blair was going out with Amanda Mackenzie Stuart at Fettes, and was furious when she turned up at a party on Falconer's arm. 'We got on very, very badly,' admitted Falconer, who was at Trinity College, Glenalmond. After Blair left school, Mackenzie Stuart ditched him to go out with Falconer. The two rivals met again towards the end of 1976, as barristers working in different chambers in the same building, quickly put the past behind them, and became good friends. They both attended Amanda's wedding, to a business school lecturer, joking that they had moved in together in order to get over her.

Falconer said 'it never occurred to me' that Blair might one day be leader of the Labour Party. 'It is quite surprising. But he has got a sort of determined, self-disciplined, slightly obsessive quality, which makes him the sort of person who will become leader of the Labour Party – or leader of a political party. He's quite skilful.'

Blair worked hard. 'When I was a barrister I was a lark, sometimes in chambers to work on cases at 6.30 in the morning,' he said.[18] Falconer once misleadingly compared their lifestyle in Wandsworth to the student anarchy of *The Young Ones* (the other choices he was given were *Withnail and I* and *This Life*). 'I was the Rik Mayall character who was a fan of Cliff Richard,' he said.[19] His style may have been more relaxed than Blair's, but he too was certainly capable of hard work, becoming a QC at the age of thirty-nine before joining his old friend's government.

For young members of the Labour Party at the time like Blair, Booth and Falconer, their starting-point was disappointment with the governments of Harold Wilson and James Callaghan in the 1970s, and what Blair described in 1982 as the 'tired excuses of pragmatism from the Labour right'.[20] Callaghan inherited a weakening and directionless government which had, and still has, few friends. It collided first with the demands of global capital in the form of the International Monetary Fund, and then with organised labour, in the wintry guise of the public sector unions. Party members were further antagonised by a series of illiberal acts, most symbolically the virginity testing at Heathrow airport of Asian women claiming immigration rights on marriage, quickly reversed when it became public.

On 3 May 1979, James Callaghan dolefully observed 'a sea change' in

Britain as he was turned out of Downing Street by the Conservative leader he had so often patronised. It was a comforting view for a prime minister who had misjudged the timing of an election he could conceivably have won the previous autumn. However, there was no fundamental change in public attitudes, rather an impatience with trade union obstinacy and Labour's inability to deal with it, or with the mounting economic chaos. Margaret Thatcher seized her chance and the Labour Party imploded, ensuring that it would be out of power for eighteen years.

Falconer went with Blair to a meeting at which Alf Dubs, the new Labour MP for Battersea, reported back on the mood of the party at Westminster. 'Mr Callaghan was broadly quite unpopular, he was seen as a sell-out merchant by the grass roots of the party. Having lost, all that had gone before looked a miserable failure, which in some respects it was, but not in every respect,' said Falconer.

In those days, to be a Labour Party member disappointed with the Labour government was to be left-wing. And most party members were – especially the activists who dominated General Committees. But, through Derry Irvine, Blair knew personally one member of that discredited government – John Smith – even though Smith had not been in the Cabinet long enough to share fully in the collective responsibility for its failure. As a chasm opened up between the parliamentary leadership and party, Blair found himself suspended in the middle.

It was at this moment that he first took part in public politics, writing his second published article (the first was a dutifully dull review of a hundred years of drama at Fettes College for his school magazine in 1970) in the *Spectator* of 18 August 1979 – a hard-hitting and clear analysis, liberal rather than left-wing, of the arbitrary powers of the Immigration Service.

Over the next two years, 'Anthony Blair' wrote eight articles for the left-wing *New Statesman* and another for the *Spectator*. (He was called Tony at Durham Chorister School, and occasionally Anthony at Fettes. As a Labour candidate in the Beaconsfield by-election in 1982 he was Tony, and thus he has remained ever since.)

His first article in the *New Statesman*, on 16 November 1979, like most of those that followed, was on employment law. He was paid £45 for it. These early articles were significant in that they consistently advocated a broad definition of legally permissible secondary strike action. In one case, he supported the steel union ISTC calling private sector steel workers out on strike in support of their public sector colleagues. Blair had acted for the ISTC in court against the British Steel Corporation (BSC); in 1994 the union's executive was the first to nominate him for the

Labour leadership. The Court of Appeal ruled that the private sector strike was not 'in furtherance of a trade dispute', because it was 'political'. Blair accused the court, led by Lord Denning, of having 'massively over-reached itself' in a 'staggering' decision. He argued:

> Spreading the strike to the private steel sector will put pressure on the government to end the strike. No one seems to have dissented from that. If that is so, then of course the action in spreading the strike furthered the dispute with the BSC.[21]

This was a definition of legitimate strike action so wide that it would allow almost any group of workers to strike in support of any public sector employees. It would clearly have fallen foul of the definition that he was to propose ten years later, as shadow Employment Secretary. His 1990 policy was that a second group of workers must have a 'direct interest' in the outcome of a dispute to be allowed to strike.

Lord Denning was Blair's bugbear at the time. In December 1981, he attacked another Denning ruling, against Harriet Harman, solicitor to the National Council for Civil Liberties. Harman was a friend of Cherie's: Tony and Cherie were both members of the NCCL. Harman had agreed to contribute a chapter about the case to a booklet published by the National Union of Journalists called *Taking Liberties*, but she asked Blair to write it instead. The booklet was a blast against the 'sustained, deliberate and dangerous attack upon civil liberties' by the judiciary, with a retrospective salvo aimed at Labour former Home Secretaries Roy Jenkins and Merlyn Rees, and Attorney General Sam Silkin, whose photographs, framed like traitors, adorned the cover. Blair's article, however, was measured and restricted to the narrow point at issue: Harman had been prosecuted for contempt of court for showing *Guardian* journalist David Leigh documents which had been read out in open court. Leigh could have obtained the information had he been in court, or had the *Guardian* paid for an expensive transcript. The documents revealed internal Home Office doubts about the legality of its prisons policy, other aspects of which had already been criticised by the European Court of Human Rights. 'It is difficult to resist the conclusion that it was precisely to forestall such criticism of the Home Office that the judges decided the matter against Ms Harman,' wrote Blair, describing Denning and his colleagues in the Court of Appeal as 'an elderly triumvirate of black-letter lawyers'.*

---

*'Black letter' is an unusual way of saying old-fashioned, referring to the Old English or Gothic typeface. I am grateful to Tim Gopsill at the National Union of Journalists for unearthing a rare copy of this booklet.

The following year he accused Denning of effectively condoning racism and undermining the Race Relations Act in his 'momentous' ruling – later overturned – that it did not apply to Sikhs, because they were a religious rather than a racial group.[22]

The proposal

In the summer after the 1979 election, after they had been going out with each other for a little more than two years, Blair and Booth became engaged. Blair had decided beforehand that he would propose during a two-week holiday in a rented flat in Tuscany. In personal interviews in tabloid newspapers in the run-up to the 1997 election, he described the big moment:

> I was twenty-six, Cherie was twenty-four, and I'd come to the complete conviction in my own mind that this was the person I wanted to marry. I kept thinking about it, I was very nervous and then quite near the end of the fortnight I suddenly thought, 'Right, it's now or never'[23] . . . I kind of went up to her and gave her a hug and said, 'Will you marry me?'[24]

She said Yes, and they were married on 29 March 1980 in the chapel of St John's College. They chose Oxford not so much because of Blair's devotion to his old college, but because Cherie's mother Gale lived in the city. For the wedding, Cherie bought a dress in the Liberty sale – 'she's always been careful with money', said her friend Maggie Rae, who made the dresses for the bridesmaids, Cherie's sister Lyndsey and Tony's sister Sarah. Tony's brother Bill was his best man. They were married by the college chaplain, Dr Anthony Phillips. 'I had no idea I was marrying a future prime minister. They were perfectly ordinary people, both devout.' Significantly, the ceremony was Anglican: though Cherie was a devout Roman Catholic, she was theologically liberal.

She had been brought up a Roman Catholic in her father's strongly Catholic household, although her mother never became one. Cherie's father, the actor Tony Booth, was famous for his part as the 'Scouse git' in the television serial *Till Death Us Do Part*. He was also famous for drinking, womanising and supporting the Labour Party.

He married Gale, an actress who had just turned twenty-one, in London in 1954. She was the first of six wives or partners who took his name. They met in a repertory company playing *The Princess and the Swineherd* on tour the previous year: she was the snobbish, self-centred princess, he was the swineherd who taught her humility and who turns out to be a king. 'Our courtship wasn't very long, about nine or ten months, but it was pure Romeo and Juliet,' said Gale, in the only interview she has given.[25] While performing in Rhayader, mid-Wales, they stayed for a week in a café and guest house where they were charmed by Cherie Hoyle, the eight-year-old daughter of the owner. 'She climbed out of her bedroom window each night and sneaked to the theatre to meet my parents at the stage door. They were enchanted by her and promised to name any daughter of theirs after her,' said that daughter. 'It could have been worse. If I had been a boy, they would have named me Tarquin' (after Laurence Olivier's son).[26]

Cherie was born in Bury, Lancashire, on 23 September 1954, an event which was announced to 'bemused theatregoers' at the end of a performance in that Lancashire town of *No Time for Sergeants*, a madcap comedy of military life in which Tony Booth was playing, and which later transferred to the West End, running for a year.[27] Tony and Gale moved to London, and had a second daughter, Lyndsey, two years later. In 1958 they moved in with Tony's parents in Waterloo, the poorest part of Crosby that is closest to Liverpool, but Tony was often on the stage in London. In 1960, when Cherie was five and Lyndsey three, he told Gale he had met someone else in London. Cherie and Lyndsey grew up in the home of their paternal grandparents, while their father himself was rarely there. His account of this period of his life in his autobiography, *Stroll On*, is one long bacchanalia of hell-raising and 'crumpeteering', in which – at Gale's request – his wife and children are not mentioned. According to Gale, there was no clean break:

> We didn't split up exactly. It was never as clear-cut as that. He met Julia and went to live with her. I was terribly upset of course – devastated, heartbroken. But that was that. I didn't sit on the doorstep or bang the door. I thought, if that was what he wanted, then let him get on with it. And in the acting profession you don't look at things in quite the same way as ordinary people. We aren't normal people, you know. I had to get on with life.
>
> Lyndsey and Cherie knew their dad wasn't there. There was no need for me to say anything about it. They saw him now and then, but when they were older, around nine and eleven, he landed his role in *Till Death Us Do Part*. At that time he was drinking really heavily and I wasn't bothered particularly whether the children saw him. But he wasn't like that when I was with him and he isn't like that now.[28]

Gale refused to give him a divorce, but when Cherie was nine he and Julie (Julia) Allen, his new partner, had a baby and it was clear that his first marriage was over. According to Tony Blair, 'Cherie was hurt very badly as a child when he left.'[29] Her own public account is matter-of-fact:

> I had a fairly uneventful childhood until, at the age of nine, my parents split up. This was fairly unusual in those days, particularly in my school, which

> was a Catholic one. I started not paying attention to my schoolwork. But I was lucky. I had a farsighted schoolteacher who suggested to my mother that I needed a challenge and that I should be moved up a year in school. This proved to be a great success and I often think that I owed my later success to that teacher.[30]

The teacher was Denis Smerdon, a former Spitfire pilot known as Biggles.[31] Cherie was, then, an 'accelerated pupil', and the original model for a scheme proposed by her husband in January 1996 in an attempt to associate Labour with promoting the most academically able.

Gale and the children continued to live in Tony Booth's parents' house in Ferndale Road. Cherie recalled: 'There was myself, my sister Lyndsey, my mum, grandma, grandad and my great grandma, all in this little terraced house in Waterloo. God knows how we fitted in.'[32] For some of the time, Tony Booth's sister Audrey lived there too and helped look after the girls. They were, said Gale, 'a very close family'. So much so that she lived there until Lyndsey left home, when she and Tony Booth finally divorced and she moved to Oxford.

Tony Blair was obviously not allowed to forget that, while his socialism was an intellectual choice, Cherie's was a class identity into which she was born. Her mother came from a solid Labour family in Ilkeston in Derbyshire; her mother's father was a shot-firer at the pit there, a shop steward, Labour activist and cornet player in the Salvation Army. Tony Booth's family went to a different church, but were just as working-class. The matriarch of Cherie's childhood house, Tony Booth's mother Vera, 'wasn't particularly politically active'.[33] But Tony himself was a rebellious left-winger just like his famous character, Alf Garnett's bolshie son-in-law, and he was one of the leading celebrity Labour supporters of his day. His grandmother, Cherie's great-grandmother, who also lived in the house, had come to Liverpool as a poor Irish Catholic immigrant, while the male line can be traced back through four generations of factory labourers in Lancashire. Booth also claims to be related to the actor John Wilkes Booth, who assassinated Abraham Lincoln. In his memoirs he recalls his father's response when told he was going to be an actor: 'We don't want anything to do with the theatre. The last time a Booth was in the theatre was a disaster as far as our family was concerned!'[34]

Gale gave up being an actress when Lyndsey was born and took as many jobs as she could, including one in a fish and chip shop. 'It's difficult being a single mother now, but I think it was even more difficult then, and Gale was a tower of strength,' said Maggie Rae, a lawyer friend with whom Cherie shared a house before she got married. Despite the adversity of their childhood, Cherie and her sister 'certainly weren't deprived', said

Gale. She got a job at Lewis's Travel Bureau. 'We got concessions so we went on holidays that most people couldn't afford then. We went to Ibiza, the Costa Brava, Bulgaria and Rimini for £27 on a sleeper coach.'[35] The girls were brought up with middle-class, academic values. 'As a young girl I read Noel Streatfeild's *Ballet Shoes*,' Cherie said. 'My dreams of becoming a prima ballerina collapsed, though, when I realised I had two left feet and lacked any sense of balance.' Like Tony Blair, though, she continued to show an early appetite for the stage, encouraged by her mother. 'Although my career in ballet was short-lived, I continued to perform throughout my childhood as an actress and a musician.'[36]

At the age of sixteen, she was recruited to the Labour Party youth wing, the Young Socialists, by Mrs Speight, a teacher at her school who was a Quaker: 'I joined with a number of my friends and I suspect that our motives were more social than political at first, as it was a good way to meet boys!' On the other hand, the issues which engaged her were hardly trivial: 'It was the era of *Cathy Come Home* and the start of Shelter, so homelessness was a big issue, as were the docks in Liverpool.'[37] School friends had already taken seriously her declaration at the age of fifteen: 'I want to be Britain's first female prime minister.'[38] Nine years later, Margaret Thatcher beat her to it. But when she and Blair married, friends thought one of them would be prime minister while the other would be a famous lawyer, although they got them the wrong way round.

While Tony Blair's upbringing was materially privileged, he and Cherie shared a sense of insecurity. 'It has been a long journey from Crosby and I am always conscious of that,' she said.[39] 'Her childhood means Cherie doesn't take money for granted. Like lots of people who come from virtually nothing, I think that there's always a lurking anxiety it might all disappear one day,' said Blair.[40]

They were married soon after Cherie's father, bankrupted a second time and nearly burnt to death in a fire in 1979, gave up alcohol and, although he had never lost contact with them, sought forgiveness from his older daughters. Blair underwent a more minor reformation on his wedding day: 'I had my last cigarette at 1.45pm and we married at two. It was my wife's idea, one of the terms of the contract, and I'm glad to say I still think I made the right bargain.'[41]

Notes

1. Speech to Conservative Party conference, 10 October 1975; Margaret Thatcher, *The Revival of Britain*, p. 23.
2. *Sunday Mirror*, 30 April 2000.
3. BBC Radio 4, *Desert Island Discs*, 23 November 1996.

4. The chambers, at 2 Crown Office Row, were headed by Michael Sherrard QC. In 1981 Irvine set up his own chambers with nine other members of these chambers, including Blair, at 1 Harcourt Buildings, now 11 King's Bench Walk.
5. CBS, *Sixty Minutes*, 2 February 1997.
6. Interview with Imogen Gassert, a sixth-former at Fettes, by then fully co-educational, for the school magazine, the *Fettesian*, in December 1991.
7. BBC Radio 4, *Desert Island Discs*, 23 November 1996.
8. Speech, 24 March 1998.
9. BBC Radio 4, *Desert Island Discs*, 23 November 1996.
10. *New Woman*, May 1994.
11. Sue Evison, *Sun*, 19 November 1999.
12. Lynda Lee-Potter, *Daily Mail*, 22 April 1997.
13. BBC Radio 4, *Desert Island Discs*, 23 November 1996.
14. Dominic Egan, *Irvine*, p. 58.
15. Lynda Lee-Potter, *Daily Mail*, 22 April 1997.
16. *Ibid.*
17. BBC Radio 4, *Desert Island Discs*, 23 November 1996.
18. London *Evening Standard*, 16 November 1993.
19. BBC Online, 15 November 1999.
20. Australian lecture, 1982. See p. 69.
21. *New Statesman*, 1 February 1980.
22. *Ibid.*, 6 August 1982.
23. 'Tony Blair opens his heart to the *Sun*', 27 February 1997.
24. Lynda Lee-Potter, *Daily Mail*, 22 April 1997.
25. *Daily Mail*, 16 March 1996.
26. Speech at a theatrical charity function, London, 9 September 1999.
27. Cherie Booth, London *Evening Standard*, 27 July 1995.
28. *Daily Mail*, 16 March 1996.
29. Lynda Lee-Potter, *Daily Mail*, 22 April 1997.
30. Contribution to a book for the Dyslexia Institute, *A Personal Reflection*, sold at charity auction and reported in the press on 31 October 1997.
31. *The Times*, 1 November 1997.
32. Lynda Lee-Potter, *Daily Mail*, 22 April 1997.
33. Cherie Booth, article in Labour Party magazine, *Inside Labour*, April 1999.
34. Tony Booth, *Stroll On*, p. 52; the *Daily Mail*'s genealogical researches found no evidence for this link, however (8 February 1997).
35. *Daily Mail*, 16 March 1996.
36. London *Evening Standard*, 27 July 1995.
37. *Inside Labour*, April 1999.
38. *Sunday Mirror*, 30 April 2000.
39. *Inside Labour*, April 1999.
40. *Woman* magazine, 10 March 1997.
41. London *Evening Standard*, 16 November 1993.

5

The Race for a Seat

Hackney, Beaconsfield, the North-East, 1980–83

'You've got to wear all the right badges.'
—*Sandy Pringle, Blair's first Labour Party branch chairman*

After a honeymoon in Tuscany, Tony moved in with Cherie in her friend Maggie Rae's house, 14 Wilton Way, in Hackney. They shared a 'battered and temperamental Volkswagen Beetle'.[1] Later in 1980, they moved round the corner into their first home, 59 Mapledene Road. They transferred their party membership to the Queensbridge branch of the Hackney South Labour Party. Now Blair was to devote his energy to Labour politics. It was from Hackney that he launched his parliamentary ambitions, and it was here that he was to forge a set of political friendships which have stayed with him since, and through which he oriented himself in the charged and swirling politics of the Labour Party. His arrival coincided with Labour's national crisis. At the Blackpool conference in October 1980, the left had won its demand for a change in the way the party elected its leaders – which was then decided by a vote of Labour MPs alone – but delegates had been unable to agree on a new system. The conference therefore adjourned until a special session at Wembley the following January.

Thus it was that, when Tony Blair and Cherie Booth attended their first meeting of the Queensbridge branch on 6 November 1980, the minutes record that it was dominated by a debate about the principle of one member, one vote in the party – the very issue which, thirteen years later, would help propel Blair to the party leadership. Three days earlier, in order to pre-empt the election of Tony Benn as leader by a new electoral system, James Callaghan had resigned as Leader of the Opposition and

Labour MPs had chosen Michael Foot to replace him. Foot was also a left-winger, but more acceptable to the middle ground in the party.

At the Queensbridge branch meeting, two rival motions were proposed for a new system for electing the party leader in future. Both were 'model' resolutions, drafted by factions organising for the Wembley conference. One motion, which Blair and Booth supported, proposed that the leader should be elected not just by MPs but by all the individual members of the party: 'one member, one vote'.[2] The other was a standard wording circulated by activists of the Bennite left, which proposed that the leader should be elected by an 'electoral college' made up of block votes divided 30/30/40 between MPs, constituency parties and trade unions.

Both sides wanted to broaden the franchise beyond MPs, but the Bennites wanted to give power not directly to party members but to their representatives on constituency General Committees and to trade-union delegates. Some of the right-wingers who were belatedly organising against the left thought one member, one vote was the best way to outflank them, by passing power directly to the 'moderate' mass membership. But it was a dangerous idea, associated with the Gang of Four – Shirley Williams, Roy Jenkins, William Rodgers and David Owen – who were poised to leave the Labour Party. There were only ten members in the Labour Club on Dalston Lane, but the meeting followed all the fatuous procedure of Citrine's antique *ABC of Chairmanship*. One member, one vote was rejected by 5 votes to 3. The democratic choice of the Queensbridge Branch Labour Party, carried on the casting vote of the chair after a 4–4 tie, was the Bennite electoral college. This was the formula which prevailed at the special conference at Wembley on 24 January 1981, and which lasted until John Smith's reform of 1993.

Many on the left saw their victory at Wembley as a staging-post on the road to electing the one leader who could be trusted to deliver their demands: Tony Benn; many on the right thought it was the end – the day after the Wembley conference, the Gang of Four issued the Limehouse Declaration, setting up a 'Council for Social Democracy'. It had become obvious not only that they would leave to set up a new party but that it would attract wide support from the public. The mood in the Labour Party started to tilt against Benn: those right-wingers who decided to stay were galvanised, while some on the left began to doubt the wisdom of presenting Labour to the electorate as a fratricidal rabble. Most of the left, however, thought Labour's unpopularity was a temporary and necessary price to be paid, and that if the traitorous old guard departed it would be good riddance. They were determined to press on: the next battle would be for Benn to use the new system to challenge Denis Healey for the deputy leadership.

That was how things stood when Tony Blair started looking for a parliamentary seat. His first experience was daunting. In December 1980, he was one of seventeen who applied to be the Labour candidate in Middlesbrough, near his boyhood home of Durham. To be considered, he had to be nominated by a branch of the party or by a local affiliated union or society. He got one nomination, from a branch of the electricians' union, but failed to make the shortlist. Stuart Bell, a fellow barrister, was the successful candidate, and is now a backbench MP, having been overlooked for ministerial office when Blair became Prime Minister. He said: 'I met Tony Blair for the first time in the office of Tom Burlison, who said, "I've got this young lad here looking for a seat."' Blair was certainly in the right place. Burlison was a significant power-broker in Labour politics in the north, as the Regional Secretary of the General and Municipal Workers' Union (later the GMB). But Bell had already secured that union's backing. Burlison said of Blair: 'My thinking was that he had to serve his apprenticeship in the Movement. He was quite a charismatic character, but he was young, pretty fresh-looking. I didn't think he was going to get a northern seat.' In fact, Bell had the seat sewn up. Blair may have been nominated by the electricians' union, the EETPU, but Bell said: 'The EETPU did a deal with me that they would nominate him but vote for me.' It was a fitting initiation in the parliamentary selection game.

'Too fat and affluent'

Back in Hackney, Blair threw himself into the fight against the Bennites. He first organised to win a position at the lowest level of Labour's scorched grass roots. A member of the branch for just four months, he ousted the then hard-left Branch Secretary, Mike Davis, at the annual general meeting on 5 February 1981. The coup involved persuading the old-style local councillor, Miles Leggett, to ask some of the 'old ladies' from the council estate to come to the meeting. Friends of Blair's also called on members beforehand, urging them to come to vote for him, because he was 'such a nice man'. It is most unusual to have house-to-house canvassing for such a humble position in the Labour Party. But it was necessary: at the meeting, Blair was elected secretary by just 17 votes to 15 for Mike Davis. Someone who was there saw a 'glint in his eye; I realised that here was a very ambitious man'. He also made no secret of his desire to become an MP, at a time when it was often considered improper to be so open about your intentions. Another member remembers: 'You were supposed to want to be a good comrade – if others urged you to put yourself forward, you would do it reluctantly, for the good of The Cause.'

At that moment, however, the Labour Party did not seem to be a good bet for an ambitious would-be politician. On the day Blair was elected Branch Secretary, Labour's former deputy leader, George Brown, was one of many to sign a *Guardian* advertisement in support of the Limehouse Declaration. This was particularly significant to Blair because the MP for Hackney South was George Brown's younger brother Ron. Blair's father-in-law Tony Booth once shared the platform with George Brown at a Labour Party rally at Wembley during the 1964 election campaign, when Brown proudly declared that he had found his brother Ron a seat, at which Booth shouted: 'This party is against nepotism!' The cry was taken up by many in the audience: 'Nepotism, nepotism!'[3]

Blair presumably considered the possibility of succeeding Ron Brown, then fifty-nine, although it would have quickly become obvious that he was out of tune with the Bennite vanguard then sweeping to power in the constituency party. Brown himself said of Blair: 'He followed me quite closely. He supported my views on Europe – he was very supportive of Europe. He was a sensible man, very able.'

Some members of the Queensbridge branch were not prepared to wait for Brown to retire. They thought he was unacceptably right-wing and wanted to deselect him. Their first move was to demand that he repudiate the Social Democratic Party when it was launched in March. The minutes of the meeting of the Queensbridge branch on 2 April 1981 are in Tony Blair's handwriting: Item 4, correspondence, notes the receipt of a letter from the MP, Ron Brown. Skating over the intense controversy, Blair recorded drily: 'It was felt by some members that the letter did not reject in sufficiently personal terms the Social Democratic Party.'

Blair was an active member of the group of Brown supporters who organised to defend him. In the atmosphere of the time, it was an awkward task. As Chairman of the London Group of Labour MPs in 1981, Ron Brown was in the front line of the battle against the left-wing insurgency in the capital. Ken Livingstone, elected leader of the Greater London Council in a left-wing coup in May, described him as a 'particular problem' who 'did everything possible to sour relations between Labour MPs and the GLC'.[4]

With Blair's help, Brown was successfully reselected. He then almost immediately defected to the SDP, in October 1981. John Lloyd, the *Financial Times* writer and later editor of the *New Statesman*, was also a member of the Hackney South Labour Party. He thinks Brown's defection hurt Blair:

> For people like Tony and me and the others who were Ron loyalists it was an absolute smack in the face. It would have been wonderful if he had fought on for what he believed in. But actually to say then, 'I've got a magic carpet called the SDP,' was awful. So the left clearly said, 'We always told you, this guy is a traitor,' and what could we say?

Brown lost the seat at the following election, and the bitterness lasted. 'It's ruined my life, but at least we've proved the point. I'm not saying I'm happy about it, but now they're all like I am.'

Blair himself was never tempted to join the SDP. 'I wasn't born into this party, I chose it,' he later said of his loyalty to the Labour Party.[5] But his allegiance to his chosen party was just as tribal as that of someone raised in the Labour tradition.

His political views during this period are preserved in detail in the text of a lecture he delivered on the other side of the world the following year, in August 1982. He flew to Australia with Cherie to visit his friends from Oxford University, Peter Thomson and Geoff Gallop. He was also returning to the country in which he had spent three years as a small child. Gallop now taught politics at Murdoch University in Perth, and invited Blair to give a seminar to the staff and postgraduates at his faculty. Blair wrote up the lecture at the end of 1982 for publication in an Australian political journal, and Gallop kept the invaluable twenty-three-page document.[6] It provides Blair's detailed assessment of the state of the Labour Party at an extraordinary juncture in its history.

There was an edge to his hostility to the SDP breakaway at the time which was later airbrushed out of his personal history:

> To read the press, you would think that a major change in British political thought had occurred. 'We are breaking the mould,' say the SDP leaders. They are strange mould-breakers: Roy Jenkins, Shirley Williams, David Owen, Bill Rodgers. If anything, they are the failed representatives of the old mould. They all held office in the last Labour government; and not merely did they hold office in it, they were, in a very real sense, its ideological lieutenants. The SDP rank-and-file are made up largely of middle-aged and middle-class erstwhile Labour members, who have grown too fat and affluent to feel comfortable with Labour and whose lingering social consciences prevent them from voting Tory; the Tammany Hall working-class Labour politicians; and that ephemeral group of supporters that always clusters round anything new . . .

He was, of course, quite wrong to say the SDP represented continuity with the failure of Wilson and Callaghan. The main lesson it drew from the previous Labour government was the need to separate the party from the vested interests of the trade unions, an argument which would later form the basis of Blair's own claim to be a 'moderniser'. It is instructive to study the hostilities which most animate a politician: as a Labour loyalist in the early 1980s he felt the Conservatives were uncaring, the traditional Labour right complacent and the Bennite left 'misguided'. But the real acid was reserved for those closest to what he himself was to become.

He wrote that the SDP and Liberals, who had entered into an alliance, 'show a humane, bland, unobjectionable face that says very little that is not "moderate", and nothing that is efficacious. They lack any distinctive image save for one of niceness.'

One of the reasons he gave for not joining the SDP defectors was because, 'by their disastrous embracing of the Tebbit Bill, which curbed trade union rights, they have isolated themselves from organised labour, a fatal mistake for any radical party'. For an early supporter of one member, one vote, who did not think Labour should be the political arm of the trade unions, this was a curiously fundamentalist view of the role of 'organised labour' in politics. But it fits with his unreconstructed views on employment law in his *New Statesman* articles, and in his lecture he even described 'traditional trade union militancy' as one of 'the necessary strands of radical thought' within the Labour Party.

Typically, he also gave an entirely pragmatic reason for staying with Labour: 'The Social Democrats haven't a hope of winning a general election,' he wrote, because the unemployed and low-paid made up '40–45 per cent of the entire country's workforce', concentrated in the inner cities, the north, Scotland and Wales. 'Certainly under the present electoral system, they will provide Labour with a solid 200-seat base.' How astute that observation turned out to be: despite winning almost as many votes as Labour, the Liberal–SDP Alliance won only twenty-three seats.

Soft right: Solidarity and CND

Blair's hostility to the SDP, a combination of kicking against the (Old Labour) Establishment and hard political calculation, offers little help in solving the puzzle of his position in the internal politics of the early 1980s Labour Party. The right-wingers who stayed with Labour were just as contemptuous of defectors as the left. In the first edition of this book, I identified Blair as essentially of the Labour left, and one of the first to show the ideological flexibility which characterised the 'soft left' which would break up the Bennite coalition and align itself behind Neil Kinnock's leadership. Closer examination, however, suggests that it makes more sense to see Blair as essentially a Labour right-winger who showed a flexibility which could have him described as 'soft right', and which enabled him to pass himself off as one of the crowd of revisionist lefties.

Over the summer of 1981 the Benn–Healey deputy leadership contest tore the Labour Party apart in a poisonous atmosphere. As it reached its climax in September, Denis Healey was shouted down at two Labour Party meetings in Cardiff and Birmingham, and Tony Benn made the fatal mistake of refusing to condemn the intimidatory tactics of some of his supporters. It was an important moment for many MPs and party members who held no brief for the old right – and it was the moment Blair chose to join the anti-Bennite Labour Solidarity Campaign. Solidarity took its name from the Polish anti-Communist trade union movement, Solidarność, whose world-famous logo it copied. It had been set up by Roy Hattersley and Peter Shore after the Wembley conference in an attempt to rally the grass roots members who thought the left were pushing their demands too far and at too great a cost to the party's electoral prospects. Blair wrote to Solidarity's pre-conference newsletter in September 1981:

> Like many within the party, I have not joined or been associated with any particular group before. So I felt some hesitation in doing so now. But, as I understand it, Solidarity represents both traditional left and right opinion in the party, united by a growing concern at the unrest that sectarian elements from the ultra-left are causing. The effect of this unrest has been to undermine our effectiveness as an opposition to the government and to aid the defectors to the Social Democrats . . . It is only by exposing in argument the fallacies of these sectarian elements and the dangers they pose for parliamentary democracy that the wounds in our party can be healed. We all want socialism but not totalitarianism.[7]

Indeed, when Solidarity was founded it was not exclusively right-wing in Labour policy terms: it was neither pro-European (Shore was a committed anti-Marketeer) nor did it have a view on the equally divisive issue of nuclear weapons. Although most of its leading lights and certainly its organisers were identified with the old right, it tried to present itself as a broad-based opposition to the ultras. This strategy had largely failed by the time of Blair's letter, because it had been drawn into the deputy leadership contest as a front for the Healey campaign.

In any case, Blair's letter was hardly the 'Innocent of London E8 writes' which it seemed. The secretary of Solidarity was Mary Goudie, who worked as an adviser to Hattersley and was the wife of the barrister James Goudie, with whom Blair shared an office in chambers. James Goudie had stood unsuccessfully for Parliament in the 1974 elections in

Brent North, and was Labour leader of Brent council in north London in 1977–78. The Goudies were active members of Solidarity's predecessor organisation, the Campaign for Labour Victory,[8] which included David Owen as one of its leading lights and Roger Liddle as one of its organisers. The CLV broke up when many of its members left to form the SDP, and those remaining in the Labour Party formed Solidarity. (Liddle joined the SDP with Owen, but eventually returned to the Labour fold, through his friendship with Peter Mandelson, to work for Blair in Downing Street.)

Although Blair did not meet Hattersley until later, he knew John Smith, who was also a member of Solidarity although he played a less visible role. In 1981 Blair wrote a paper for Smith, who was then shadow Trade Secretary, on legal aspects of privatisation. At the time, Smith was busying himself with his legal practice in Scotland, waiting to see if the Bennite flood would ebb. But he did spend some time at Westminster, and sometimes dined at the Commons with Irvine and Blair.

Blair's early forays into seat-hunting would have taught him how important factional networks were in making contacts and mobilising support in constituencies where he would otherwise arrive as a stranger. Another Solidarity organiser, John Spellar, now a government minister, was then the political officer of the EETPU which saw itself as the Praetorian Guard of the Labour right. The union, which had nominated Blair in Middlesbrough the previous year, worked as hard as the left to secure delegates to General Committees in seats where the Labour nomination was being contested. The right won unexpected victories against the left at Labour's annual conferences in 1981 and 1982, despite the depletion of its ranks by defections to the SDP, but public association with Solidarity would have been death to the hopes of any aspiring candidate in the vast majority of constituencies.

It was around this time that Blair also joined the Campaign for Nuclear Disarmament. It was unusual to be a member of both CND and Solidarity, but not impossible. The simplest explanation for joining CND is opportunism – it was later said on Blair's behalf to be the 'minimum requirement to get anywhere' in the Labour Party of the time. This was the period of checklist socialism, when left-wing purity and commitment could be measured by ticking off the policies supported and membership cards held.

Sandy Pringle, Blair's first Labour Party mentor, from Earl's Court, recalled meeting him and Cherie Booth at a Greater London Labour Party conference in early 1982. Pringle knew that he was looking for a seat and asked, 'Any luck, Tony?'

'Not so far,' said Blair.

'You've got to wear all the right badges.'

With which, said Pringle, 'Blair ruefully agreed'.

There may have been more to Blair's membership of CND than a badge, if not much more. It later came to be seen as axiomatic that the policy of one-sided nuclear disarmament was a vote-loser, but that was not so clear in 1981, when the new Reagan administration in the United States frightened many people with plans to fight a 'limited' nuclear war in continental Europe with cruise missiles. The old Atlanticist Labour right had no patience with what it saw as pacifists or Communist fellow travellers, but someone less bound by its traditions, like Blair, might have felt the public mood was changing. While he was far from being a convinced unilateralist, he sought in his 1982 Australian lecture to harness the impulses behind the peace movement. In addition to 'traditional trade union militancy', he thought the other 'necessary strands' of Labour's revival included

> a new and vital commitment to democracy and accountability within the institutions that govern us; an appreciation of the ever-growing danger posed by the nuclear arms race; a recognition of the multicultural society in which we now live; and a traditional belief in social equality and justice through public ownership and the welfare state.

There was no doubt, he thought, that the issues of 'nuclear disarmament, ecology, race relations, feminism . . . represent a genuine, if limited, social movement'. And in a significant passage, he urged Labour right-wingers to accommodate it:

> There is a tendency on Labour's traditional right to dismiss these issues as trendy . . . irrelevant to what are the bread-and-butter issues of jobs, housing, health and education. That is an error of enormous proportions. The support of radical campaigns such as CND and environmental protection can be seen across Europe – look at the rise of the Green parties in West Germany . . . There is no point in pretending [these issues] don't exist or in attempting to mobilise the union vote to neutralise their effect. Instead, the right should be trying . . . to assist their development by lending them that pragmatism, that hard-headedness of purpose that is the quality of the right, which the left consistently underestimates.

As a by-election candidate in May 1982, the *Guardian* described him as

> highly pragmatic on the Common Market – 'come out if we must, but not as an article of socialist faith' – but firm on unilateralism. He said the older generation, accustomed to conventional warfare, has not yet awoken to the real nature of the threat, the 'warfare of the end game'.[9]

In fact, his position was contrived for two audiences. For internal party consumption, as a seeker of a safe seat, a small amount of flexibility on Europe was more possible than on the Bomb; while for public consumption, as a mere candidate he was unable to deviate far from the party line. In his lecture, he also described policies of 'unilateral disarmament, withdrawal from the EEC and incomes policy' as 'really much less fundamental to a concept of socialism than is often supposed' – an early intimation of his skill in downplaying fundamental differences of opinion.

When the moment came for the deputy leadership election, at Labour's Brighton conference at the end of September 1981, Blair as a rank-and-file party member did not have a direct vote. When asked as a by-election candidate how he would have voted had he been an MP, he plumped for the compromise candidate John Silkin. Pressed on how he would have voted in the second round after Silkin was knocked out, he backed Denis Healey, but so reluctantly that he was unwilling even to speak his name: 'Definitely not Benn.'[10]

This reluctance was presentational, however. Healey had been demonised by the left as the paymaster of Callaghan's betrayal, and his image was far from that of the avuncular polymath it later became. Open support for Healey, like membership of Solidarity, would have put the brand of Cain on Blair's forehead. His left-wing Oxford friend, David Gardner, by then a journalist on the *Financial Times*, recalled: 'Tony Blair was impressed by Healey. I certainly wasn't.'

On the other hand John Lloyd, who was firmly on the right of the Labour Party and an open admirer of Denis Healey, regarded Blair – despite his closeness to Ron Brown – as something of a 'trendy leftie'. They often disagreed over the tactics of fighting the hard left on the General Committee in Hackney. Blair was a coalition-builder, always appealing to party unity, while Lloyd's instinct was to confront what he saw as leftist nonsense: 'Blair would always say, "This is all right, we can soften it," while I would say, "No, it's rubbish, we've got to throw it out."'

If a Labour right-winger like Lloyd regarded Blair as a trendy leftie, the Bennites thought he was suspiciously right-wing. A friend of Blair's who supported Benn in 1981 remembers:

> When I first met Tony he was definitely not identified as a trendy leftie at all. I remember those of us who were trendy-leftie thinking he was quite right-wing. Nor was Cherie a trendy leftie, although she was definitely more of a feminist than him. The image that I had of him was of a very earnest, very serious person.

Blair had good contacts on the right of the party, but he also dined with MPs on the 'soft left' of the party. He introduced himself to Tom Pendry, Labour spokesman on overseas development and a friend and drinking partner of his Bennite father-in-law, Tony Booth. They had lunch at the Gay Hussar in Soho several times to discuss Blair's search for a seat.

The Labour left splits

Denis Healey won the deputy leadership in September 1981 by a margin of 0.852 per cent. Tony Benn was denied victory by the abstention of a group of MPs including Pendry and Neil Kinnock: they could not vote for Healey, but equally they were 'Definitely not Benn'. Blair recognised that Benn's defeat was a turning-point because it split the left. 'The Benn campaign in 1981 may, in retrospect, be seen not only as the high water mark of his own personal fortunes, but of that of the "far" left in the party,' he said in his Australian lecture. 'The question of the next year is going to be whether the soft left/hard left split within the PLP [Parliamentary Labour Party] and the unions becomes mirrored in the constituency parties.' The constituency parties, represented in the electoral college by delegates who were by definition activists, were overwhelmingly on the hard left. Eight out of ten voted for Benn.

However, even before the deputy leadership election, the peeling-off of the soft left was beginning to be reflected at the grass roots. Central to that process was a group of people who were friends of Blair's through the Hackney Labour Party.

The first, and perhaps most important, was Alan Haworth. Haworth lived with and later married Maggie Rae. Then a member of the Communist Party, Rae was passionately hostile to the Trotskyist groups which increasingly dominated the Labour left in London. Haworth, meanwhile, had been one of the 'Newham Seven', as Secretary of the Newham North-East Labour Party when it voted to deselect Cabinet minister Reg Prentice in 1975. The affair was central to the mythology of betrayal, to which Prentice, an increasingly unpredictable right-winger, lent credence by defecting to the Conservative Party two years later. You did not have to be a Trotskyist, although three of the Newham Seven (not including Haworth) were, to think Prentice was a traitor. But by the time he met Blair, Haworth was strongly opposed to the hard left.

Haworth has long been an important party bureaucrat as well as a personal friend, and became secretary to the Parliamentary Labour Party. When Blair was Leader of the Opposition, therefore, he was minute-taker at meetings of the shadow Cabinet. He is one of those, like Anji

Hunter, Peter Thomson and Derry Irvine, with whom Blair forged long-standing bonds of mutual loyalty.

Barry Cox, Head of Current Affairs at London Weekend Television, moved in next door to Blair and Booth in Mapledene Road at the same time as they did. He became a millionaire in 1993 when LWT gave a group of managers a 'golden handcuff' share scheme to keep them during a successful bid to retain its franchise, and he worked as fundraiser for Blair's leadership campaign.

Glenys Thornton and John Carr moved into the Queensbridge ward in 1981. Thornton was later chair of the London Labour Party and General Secretary of the Fabian Society. Carr was elected to the Greater London Council in May 1981, as a left-wing supporter of Ken Livingstone – but he too became disillusioned with the hard left. And Charles Clarke moved into the house that backed on to Blair's. He was a former president of the National Union of Students who had just started working for Neil Kinnock, the shadow Education Secretary, and had been elected to Hackney council in a by-election.

All except Cox were members of what could be described as the organisation which saved the Labour Party – although it nearly destroyed it first. The Labour Co-ordinating Committee was set up in 1978 to mobilise the left in the party and – less explicitly – to secure the leadership of the party for Benn. But during 1981 it started to metamorphose into Benn's enemy within.

When the LCC was founded, under 'acting chairman' Michael Meacher, then a junior trade minister, it put itself at the head of demands for 'real' socialism in anticipation of defeat at the imminent General Election. In order to put an end to the cycle of betrayal of 'the Labour movement' by its parliamentary leadership, the LCC advocated the automatic reselection of MPs, an electoral college to choose the leader and control of the manifesto by the National Executive. But the LCC always kept its distance from the cult of Benn's personality. Benn's deputy leadership campaign was run by the even more ornately-named Rank and File Mobilising Committee, a super co-ordinating committee to bring together even more factions and cliques of the Labour left, including the LCC and the Trotskyist Militant tendency. And when Benn's closest supporters hailed his narrow defeat as a tremendous advance for the left, and started to plan for another contest the following year, the LCC pulled out.

Haworth became Membership Secretary of the LCC and in 1982 persuaded Blair and Cherie Booth to join. With Solidarity – which Booth never joined – now identified exclusively with the old right, the LCC had become the right vehicle for the backlash against Bennism. He said: 'Tony and I had a chat about how to modernise the party, how to break up the hegemony of the Stalinist left. He mused over the possibility of starting a new organisation. I credit myself with saying that there is an organisation already.'

The Hackney clique formed the core of a group within the LCC that started to organise against the hard left in London. Charles Clarke said: 'We had a planning group and Tony and Cherie came to it. They were very keen to do whatever they could, although they felt relatively ignorant of the ways of London politics.'

Once again, Blair's pleasant smile and glazed blue eyes presented a convincing front of naïvety. If his new allies had known he was a member of Solidarity, they would have regarded him as a stealthy envoy from the enemy camp.

Blair's interest in the Australian lecture, however, was less in organisational matters than political. The central question he asked was: 'How can left and right in the party be reconciled?' His tentative answer foreshadowed the strategy which Kinnock was to follow after 1983: to weld the 'soft left' with the forward-looking right. The right, Blair declared, had to come to terms with the need for economic radicalism required by the new scale of unemployment:

> The mild tinkering with the economy proposed by the Social Democrats nowhere near measures up to the problem. A massive reconstruction of industry is needed. However, a reflation of the economy that is unplanned would lead, almost for a certainty, to inflation; and the resources required to reconstruct manufacturing industry call for enormous state guidance and intervention.

This was an unthinking regurgitation of conventional Labour assumptions: he knew there were problems with greater state control, but had not tried to work out what they were. Labour's 'difficulty will not be one of increasing central control but of containing that control and marrying it to ideas of industrial democracy', he wrote.*

> That in turn will bring any Labour government into sharp conflict with the power of capital, particularly multinational capital. The trouble with the right of the party is that it has basked so long in the praise of the leader

---

*Such were the statist assumptions of Labour policy at the time that, in one of his leaflets for the Beaconsfield by-election under the heading 'Tony Blair on the Economy', he advocated 'Price control to help fight inflation'. Industrial democracy was even in 1982 a dated idea: the idea of changing company law to require 'worker representatives' on boards of directors had been shelved by the 1974–79 Labour government.

> writers of the *Financial Times*, *Times* and *Guardian*, that it is no longer accustomed to giving them offence. It will find the experience painful but it is vital.

(Only two years later, Blair himself was to bask in the *Financial Times*'s description of him as 'one of the most promising newcomers'.[11])

The economic radicalism of his Australian lecture was confused. When he said, 'The Labour Party sits uneasily, squashed between traditional Clause IV Part Four socialism and an acceptance of the mixed economy,' he might have been describing himself. The phrase 'mixed economy' would soon come to seem dated. But the fact that Blair appeared to 'accept' it – despite his call for 'enormous state intervention' – contained a sort of logic which would lead in time to the expunging of the Labour Party's constitutional commitment to 'common ownership of the means of production'.

Blair reserved his more considered criticisms in his lecture for the left in the party. He admitted that 'the left has generated an enormous amount of quite necessary rethinking in the party'. But it was the left that now needed to rethink:

> The left is keen on democracy, and rightly so. But democracy should not be seen as something abstract, something the party has within itself. The party must have a democratic relationship with the electorate. The key word is relationship. It would be absurd if the party descended into populism, merely parroting the views of 'the electorate', however those views could be gauged. Equally absurd, though, is the view that there is anything to be gained from capturing control of the Labour Party machine and leaving the voters behind.

This had been aptly demonstrated to him in the London Labour Party. By a process of caucuses within caucuses, the left-wing faction which dominated the London-wide party found itself increasingly organised through the newspaper *London Labour Briefing*, which in turn was increasingly controlled by a Trotskyist group called the Socialist Organiser Alliance. Thus the London party found itself associated with support for the Irish Republican Army, opposition to the 'Falklands/Malvinas' War and, ultimately, violent revolution. Blair suggested in his Australian lecture that *Briefing* would be regarded by most Labour voters as 'incomprehensible at best and at worst as scary' which led him to what would become a dominant theme:

> The left's position is often inconsistent on democracy. It will advocate party democracy, yet refuse one member, one vote . . . It will talk of decentralisation yet find itself at a bizarre and remote distance from most of the opinions of those to whom 'power' is supposed to be given.

Before he had a constituency in which he could put it into practice, Blair had the idea of what the Labour Party should be like: 'A local party should grow out of a local community – the party members having roots in that community.' Blair was already formulating his view that the party needed to turn outwards and recruit far more members. Austin Mitchell MP best described the Labour Party of the time: 'A mass party without members, an ideological crusade without an agreed ideology, a people's party cut off from the people.'[12]

As an example of the party's distance from most voters, Blair cited Labour's opposition to council house sales: 'That is for perfectly sound reasons of political principle. Yet there is something mildly distasteful about owner-occupier party members preaching the virtues of public housing to council tenants.'

He cited 'my own experience, canvassing roughly 8,000 people during the Beaconsfield campaign . . . in local council estates or the cheaper end of private housing' which told him

> there are growing numbers of young, often socially upward-moving people who are simply not prepared to accept our basic ideology just because their forefathers did. There are very few of the younger age group converted to our ideology and we rely to a dangerous degree on the loyalty vote amongst older citizens.

Beyond saying that Labour's ideology should not be Marxist, however, he did not say what it should be. And he insisted that Labour did not need to change its policies – except its refusal to allow the sale of council houses. All he did in the lecture was set out some of the principles of his later ideological development.

An important clue lay in his argument against the idea of re-nationalising state assets without compensation for their shareholders, which was being seriously proposed in the party at the time: 'Quite apart from questions of parliamentary democracy, such a policy would cause much more trouble for Labour – in terms of Labour being portrayed as an extremist authoritarian party both at home and abroad – than it could possibly be worth.' He plainly did not agree with the idea for reasons of fundamental principle, but preferred to argue against it for how it would be perceived: a test which had important implications for almost all of Labour's existing programme. Despite his rudeness towards the SDP, he insisted that 'Labour needs those middle-ground voters to be sure of defeating the Tories'.

The lecture concluded with a defence of pragmatism, or what he called the 'exercise of political judgment', which he explained 'means knowing when to fight and when to accept defeat. It acknowledges that not every compromise is a sell-out. Above all, it means an appreciation that there must be some system of priorities.' He even quoted Lenin: 'To reject compromises "on principle", to reject the possibility of compromises in general, no matter of what kind, is childishness, which it is difficult ever to consider seriously.'[13]

He was already developing the intellectual apparatus which would enable him to justify almost any policy changes in order to win elections as the means of putting his principles into practice. It was this flexibility which distinguished him from Gaitskell, for example, a revisionist of fixed ideas. Over the next decade and a half, his argument that compromise did not mean sell-out was the one flame-resistant fixed point in the bonfire of Labour's commitments.

No openings

In the autumn of 1981 Cherie Booth tried unsuccessfully to become the Labour candidate for the Crosby by-election. As with Blair's decision to go for Beaconsfield the next year, this showed a willingness to take the fight not just to the Conservatives but to the Liberal–SDP Alliance, which was riding high in the opinion polls and would win the Croydon North-West by-election in October. She had joined the Labour Party while at school in Crosby eleven years earlier, inspired by 'figures such as Barbara Castle, Tony Crosland and Shirley Williams', she wrote in a Labour Party magazine in 1999.

> I was particularly keen on Shirley Williams as she was a Catholic and a woman who had made her name politically. I felt very let down when she defected to the SDP and in fact decided to throw my hat into the ring to be the candidate in Crosby in 1981 when she stood there. I was really looking in the south-east at the time because Tony was looking in the north, but I felt outraged that she was then going to stand in Crosby – my home town! I actually went up there and addressed a meeting, but didn't get the nomination.[14]

Shirley Williams's win in November was a sensation in the formerly safe Tory seat, with Labour humiliated in third place, although had Cherie been selected she might have used a brave showing in a by-election as a stepping-stone to greater things.

Meanwhile, Blair was again nominated but not shortlisted for a northern seat, Teesside Thornaby, most of which became Stockton South in the boundary changes two years later. The vacancy was created by the defection to the SDP of a sitting MP, in this case Ian Wrigglesworth. To the local party, Blair was just a 'southern smoothie'. The successful candidate,

Frank Griffiths, confirmed Blair's centre-left position. He recalled Blair protesting, 'in a friendly but firm way', to a group of members in Teesside Thornaby that he was on the left of the party because he was a supporter of *Tribune*. This was just before the newspaper – edited by Michael Foot in the 1950s – was captured by the Bennites. In fact, Blair was lucky to be unsuccessful here, because Wrigglesworth held on to the seat in 1983. Blair also spoke to various Labour Party branches and affiliates in the next-door seat – Stockton North – but failed even to be nominated.

His next attempt to become a Labour candidate was more modest. The man who was to lead the Labour Party in just twelve years' time now aspired to be a Hackney borough councillor in the 1982 local elections in London. It was a time of conflict between Labour councils and central government, and within Labour councils between right and left. When Ken Livingstone seized control of the GLC he roused the left with the rhetoric of confrontation with the Conservative government, although the left's 'Target 82' campaign was aimed with typical introspection at winning Labour councils like Hackney for the left, rather than winning Tory councils for the Labour Party. Blair wanted to be a councillor for his own safe Labour Queensbridge ward. In a vote to choose three candidates, he came fourth, and was thus saved the character-forming experience of serving on the new hard-left Hackney council.

No voting figures are recorded in the minutes, only the fact that there were twenty-eight members present. What the minutes also fail to record is that Blair himself was not there. Instead, Cherie Booth argued for him. A court case kept him away, but there was a strong feeling at the meeting that he should have been there if he wanted to be considered seriously. 'I don't know that he would have been selected anyway,' said Mike Davis, the ousted Branch Secretary. Blair had been a member there for little more than a year, and 'we weren't sure where he was coming from'. However, it soon became clearer where he was going. Two months later, he was the surprise choice as the Labour candidate for the by-election in the safe Conservative constituency of Beaconsfield.

Beaconsfield

The death of the Powellite Conservative MP Ronald Bell on 27 February 1982 was reported in the press as a chance for the Liberal–SDP Alliance to continue its spectacular by-electoral progress. A swing as great as that which delivered Crosby to Shirley Williams would have yielded up Beaconsfield, the eighteenth safest Conservative seat.

The question of who would be the Labour candidate was therefore of little public interest. As the local party began its selection, Roy Jenkins, the SDP's first leader, won a third sensational by-election for the Alliance at Glasgow Hillhead on 25 March. Blair put his name forward after taking advice from John Smith and Tom Pendry. Pendry enthusiastically encouraged him: 'It's only twenty-five minutes down the road, you'll have a high-profile campaign – and what is more, an old girlfriend of mine is the local party secretary.'

One of Blair's rivals, John Hurley, who was then the leader of Slough Borough Council, believed that Blair was the choice of the party 'organisation'. He remembers that there were two questions asked at the selection conference which seemed to him to be aimed at putting Blair in a good light. One was about a research paper on housing which he, as the leader of an urban council, 'might have been expected' to know about – and did not, but Blair did. As a disappointed candidate, he may have overestimated the forces arrayed against him. The state of Labour's national organisation at that time was such that 'fixing' a by-election candidate may have been beyond it, although Blair did use planted questions in Sedgefield the following year.

In any case, there can be no doubt that Blair was selected on merit. Doug Vangen, who later became Chair of the Beaconsfield Labour Party, recalled Blair as 'like a breath of fresh air' and 'outstanding'. He came across as sincere and honest, in contrast to people who 'just trot out the party handout'.

Blair was chosen as the Labour candidate on 1 April 1982. The next day, Argentina invaded the Falkland Islands. On 3 April, an emergency sitting of the House of Commons approved the sending of a task force, after the Labour leader Michael Foot demanded action. Three weeks later, British forces recaptured South Georgia. On 1 May, the task force bombarded the Falklands. The by-election campaign was dominated by news of the war, which helped reconnect Margaret Thatcher with popular opinion.

Blair was caught in Labour's national dilemma. 'I supported sending the task force,' he told the *Sunday Telegraph*. 'At the same time I want a negotiated settlement and I believe that given the starkness of the military options we need to compromise on certain things. I don't think that ultimately the wishes of the Falkland islanders must determine our position.'[15] That directly contradicted Thatcher's assertion that 'the wishes of the islanders must be paramount'. The *Daily Telegraph*, whose reporter Godfrey Barker hounded Blair during the campaign, alleged that his position on the Falklands was 'victory to the Argentines'. What Blair actually said was: 'There are limitations to our military ability,' and 'there must be proportionality between lives lost and the cause at issue'.[16] The weakness in his position – which was that of the Labour front bench – was that 'the cause at issue' was territorial gain by aggression. He appeared to be willing to allow a dictator to keep what he had wrongly seized. Even the *Guardian*'s friendly paraphrase of Blair's views impaled him on this hook: 'A promise of self-determination for the Falklanders could lead to a full-scale war, he said. Nor was he convinced about such an abstract purpose as preventing the aggressor from retaining his spoils.' His balanced position looked anaemic both against Thatcher's 'we fought to show that aggression does not pay', and against the moral absolutism he himself later asserted as Prime Minister in Kosovo.

Despite the hopelessness of the Beaconsfield contest, Blair was better prepared than was usual for a by-election candidate at the time. On his own initiative, he had gone to party headquarters in Walworth Road and asked to be briefed on party policy. The national party's researcher on defence policy was Mike Gapes, now the MP for Ilford South.

> In those days there was no real proper organisation of any by-election. I don't remember any other by-election candidates in the early 1980s asking for briefing. He was serious and thorough. He wanted to know what the line was. He was keen, quite diffident, but very sharp. He asked all the right questions – 'What do I do if somebody asks this?'

When Blair then turned to the economic policy researcher at Walworth Road for a briefing, he found himself in the office of the former lead guitarist from the Ugly Rumours at Oxford, Adam Sharples. He and Sharples had not discussed politics at university – they were more concerned about whether they needed backing vocals for 'Black Magic Woman'. Now they found themselves going through the finer points of the party's Alternative Economic Strategy. 'He tackled the job of being a parliamentary candidate with the same sort of enthusiasm that he'd shown in the band,' Sharples said.

According to another Oxford friend, David Gardner, Blair was horrified to come face-to-face with the small print of the huge amount of policy recently laid down by Tony Benn's subcommittees of the National Executive: 'Before the Beaconsfield by-election he said he'd been round to visit every office of the party, trying to find out what they thought of Europe and defence, and he was appalled.'

On the question of Europe, Gardner said Blair's position at the time

> was absolutely nothing to do with suggesting withdrawal. I recall in some detail conversations we had before Beaconsfield in which the view was . . . if it becomes the case that we are obstructed from carrying out the

democratically agreed socialist policy, then we confront that at the time – but that was always rather hypothetical.

However, in his campaign literature he did not play down the party's policy of withdrawal. One of his by-election leaflets said: 'Above all, the EEC takes away Britain's freedom to follow the sort of economic policies we need.' That and the cost of the 'indefensible' farm policy 'are just two of the reasons for coming out. Only a Labour government will do it.'

Inevitably, the press demanded to know where the young candidate stood in the battle raging in the Labour Party. He did take one clear stand, by making sure that Tony Benn did not come to the campaign, which was bold for a by-election candidate at that time. The *Guardian* reported: 'At the mention of Mr Benn, he merely bows his head, says that he does not agree with him, and suggests there is now a steady move away from regarding him as the focal point for radical reform.'[17] He told the *South Bucks Observer* on 8 April 1982:

> I'm basically a centrist in the party, and want to see it united. I do agree with some of Tony Benn's views but didn't support him for the deputy leadership. I want the internal differences in the party to be forgotten, so that we can expose the record of the government and put forward the socialist alternative.

This did not stop the paper putting the headline 'Benn-backing barrister is Labour's choice' on its report, and Blair wrote a letter, published on 16 April, protesting that 'alliteration is a poor substitute for accuracy', and saying 'I am emphatically not a Benn-backer'. His letter ended:

> Just so as there is no further misunderstanding: I support the Labour Party's present leadership; Labour's plan for jobs; withdrawal from the EEC (certainly unless the most fundamental changes are effected); and nuclear disarmament, unilaterally if necessary; in particular I intend to campaign against Trident and American-controlled cruise missiles on our soil. I do so as a Labour Party man, not as a 'Bennite' or any other 'ite'.

What is interesting is not that he supported withdrawal from the EEC – as a by-election candidate he could hardly oppose party policy – but that he qualified it. His public position on Europe, while still at odds with his private view, was as far from the official party line policy as it could be. The idea of changing the EEC to make it acceptable was explicitly ruled out in *Labour's Programme 1982*: 'We do not believe a further attempt to change the nature of the Community would be worthwhile . . . Britain must therefore withdraw.' However, Blair did not attempt to focus his campaign on other issues. Instead, he chose to make Europe one of his main themes. One explanation may be simple populism. It is worth remembering that public opinion between 1980 and 1983 was strongly opposed to EEC membership. Another is that he was a party loyalist who stayed close to the leader. Michael Foot had been a passionate anti-Marketeer on Benn's side in the 1975 referendum, but made it quite clear as leader that he bitterly opposed Benn's campaign to push the party ever further to the left. When Foot was asked why Benn had not been invited to Beaconsfield, he said it was a matter for the local organisers and smiled: 'I think they've exercised their discretion very well.'

Cutting teeth

The Beaconsfield campaign gave Blair the chance to be noticed by almost the entire leadership of the Labour Party. Michael Foot delivered an endorsement to BBC2's *Newsnight*, dog-eared from use ever since, as he stepped out of a fish-and-chip supper at the Stag & Hounds pub: 'We're very proud of everything he's been saying here and, whatever the result, we believe he's going to have a very big future in British politics.' It was not the kind of thing he said about every Labour by-election candidate: he famously refused to endorse Peter Tatchell in Bermondsey the following year.

The by-election campaign saw a surprisingly large number of senior Labour politicians – excluding Tony Benn – pass through this quintessentially Conservative exurb. Shadow Chancellor Peter Shore came to denounce the new monetarists in the Cabinet – Margaret Thatcher, Geoffrey Howe, Leon Brittan, Patrick Jenkin. 'What is the one thing these people have in common? – they're all lawyers,' he thundered. Beside him on the platform, barrister Blair sat expressionless.

Denis Healey, Stan Orme, Merlyn Rees and Gwyneth Dunwoody were also scheduled for the final fortnight, prompting the headline in the *Slough Observer* on 14 May 1982: 'LABOUR MODERATES ARE BACKING BLAIR'. Michael Foot and Roy Hattersley, on the left and 'moderate' wings of the party respectively, teased each other about Blair's intra-party loyalties. Foot said that when Hattersley claimed Blair as a supporter of his, he replied: 'Oh? He seemed all right to me.'

Neil Kinnock and John Smith also came to the campaign: two future Labour leaders who blessed a third. Like others, Kinnock was impressed:

> There he was in the sylvan lanes of Beaconsfield, nicely received by people because he was a pleasant, articulate but not over-smart man from London. He fought a great rearguard action because he was active, because he was accessible, because he was charming, and when he did hustings with other candidates he attracted people. He wasn't in any sense precocious or flashy,

> and he was fighting it out of duty – and curiosity, I think, to see what it was like. He couldn't have picked a better place to cut his teeth – right down to the gums as the result turned out – but it was a creditable performance in very difficult circumstances.

The Conservative press, however, showed none of its later enthusiasm. The *Daily Telegraph*'s Godfrey Barker described Blair as 'too nice and too unguarded to be a politician'. Blair told a news conference that he supported the strike by health service workers, and Barker pointed out that it could put lives at risk:

> Mr Blair began a *mauvais quart d'heure* such as no Labour candidate has known in any by-election one can recall. 'Of course it is the case that people may suffer as a result,' he responded blandly. 'It is not the fault of those taking industrial action that they are doing so.'[18]

Barker's account is no doubt an exaggeration, but Blair was also described as 'rattled' by the *Daily Express*.

Cherie Blair – as she called herself for the purposes of the by-election – joined energetically in the campaign. In one of Blair's election leaflets, she wrote 'A message from Cherie Blair', a socialist feminist pitch sold in a Tory-MP's-supportive-wife style:

> As a member for ten years I believe only the Labour Party shows real concern for the welfare of women today. At a time of economic recession, women are often the first casualties, not only in terms of employment – and unemployment – but also because the burden of public spending cuts falls most heavily on them.

In addition to this early experience of reconciling the role of politician's wife with her own political identity, Cherie asked her father, Tony Booth, to add some showbusiness autograph-chasing to the campaign with Pat Phoenix. Phoenix, whom Booth later married on her deathbed, played Elsie Tanner in *Coronation Street*, and was a megastar who drew larger crowds than the candidate himself. Like her consort, she was a committed left-winger and unilateral disarmer. She shared Booth's suspicions of politicians, writing in her 1983 autobiography: 'Strong socialist though I may be, politics in general today sickens me. I'm sick to death of the race for power, the contradictions, the changing of tunes. Let's have someone who is going to save the earth, not destroy it.'[19]

Whether or not Phoenix thought Blair would save the earth, his campaign made little impact on the local electorate. Towards the end of the campaign, on 23 May, the *Sunday Express* commented: 'Mr Blair, with his unexceptionally fashionable views (in Labour terms) on everything from the Common Market to disarmament, is cutting little ice.' On one issue, though, Blair's views were not fashionably left-wing, and that was law and order. In one election leaflet, he described the rise in crime rates as a 'tragedy' and, in an early rehearsal of one of his signature tunes, welcomed a government measure: 'The decision to put police "back on the beat" is a welcome move back to closer contact with the public and in the right direction to help reduce crime.'

However, the last week of the by-election campaign was dominated by daily reports from General Galtieri's crime wave in the South Atlantic (the theft of a small British colony). On the Friday before polling day, British troops landed at San Carlos Bay on the Falkland Islands. The following Tuesday, HMS *Coventry* was lost and SS *Atlantic Conveyor* was hit by an Exocet missile, with thirty-one killed. The Conservative candidate Tim Smith was filmed listening anxiously to the news on the radio. He drove around the constituency clutching a letter from the Prime Minister: 'I hope that the electorate will demonstrate their support for the government's resolute response to the crisis in the South Atlantic, and for our policies at home.'

Two days later the voters of Beaconsfield responded to Thatcher's call. The Liberal–SDP Alliance candidate, Paul Tyler (later Liberal Democrat MP for Cornwall North), came an ordinary second. (In a bitter footnote to Blair's Hackney years, his MP Ron Brown, now in the SDP, came to Beaconsfield to campaign for Tyler.)

At the count Blair had already prepared his press release, which started by congratulating Tim Smith. He stood on the balcony with the other candidates as the result was announced, smiling broadly but stiff and embarrassed, with a huge red rosette which looked like a comedy prop. His final leaflet of the campaign had been headed, prophetically, 'Why Conservatives are voting for Tony Blair.' It was not true this time. Blair's result was a poor one, the Labour share of the vote halving from 20 to 10 per cent, dropping from second to third place behind the Liberal. With just 3,886 votes, he lost his deposit.[20] It seemed an unpromising first test of his appeal to his fellow citizens.

What was more important was the favourable impression he had made on a pantheon of leading Labour politicians. In the BBC's studio that night Peter Shore, flanked by Norman Tebbit and Cyril Smith, echoed Michael Foot's endorsement: 'He really is a most entertaining, attractive and obviously first-rate candidate, and we'd very much like to have him in the Parliamentary Labour Party.' But he still had no prospect of getting into parliament. The *Daily Telegraph* had earlier, on 18 May, reported the following exchange on the campaign trail: '"I suppose you're hoping for a nice safe seat like Dagenham after losing your deposit here," a colleague solicitously inquired. "I haven't thought about it," replied Mr Blair disarmingly.' Bryan Gould had been selected as the candidate for Dagenham in January 1982, and there were now few safe seats left which had not chosen their candidates.

Blair has pointed to the timing and positioning of his start on the road of political advancement as evidence that he was not a career politician, although sometimes he protested too much:

> Believe me, fighting the '82 Beaconsfield by-election for Labour was hardly seen as a smart career move. Michael Foot was struggling with the problems of leadership, Tony Benn was in charge of policy, Arthur Scargill was leading the trade unions, and we were in the middle of the Falklands War.[21]

This last is a dash of added colour, as the war had not started when he decided to put himself forward, although his general point seems obvious. Nevertheless, it was not obvious to most Labour members and supporters even in 1982 that the party was facing extinction. For them, the electorate simply had to be given the chance to deliver a verdict on Margaret Thatcher and mass unemployment. It is unlikely that anyone applying for Labour seats at that time would have done so on the basis that the party would still be in opposition fifteen years later. Blair himself was certain that Labour would survive and recover, as he said in his Australian lecture later that year.[22]

The year of living restlessly

As Blair returned to Hackney politics from the spacious lawns of the Home Counties, it seemed that the Beaconsfield by-election had come too late to be a stepping-stone to a safe Labour seat. Cherie, meanwhile, had been selected as the Labour candidate for solidly Conservative Thanet West. He, meanwhile, was invited by the Beaconsfield Labour Party to fight the seat again at the General Election. He was inclined to accept, but consulted Derry Irvine: 'I advised him that sometimes amazing things can happen in politics, and persuaded him to ride his luck.'[23]

So Blair said no to Beaconsfield, although his only hope was that the review of constituency boundaries would come into effect before the election and shake the political kaleidoscope. The review, which reduced the number of safe Labour seats in order to reflect the move of population out of urban areas, had been delayed by a cynical legal action brought by the party.

Meanwhile, Blair pursued two campaigns in speaking engagements and journalism: against the 'Tebbit Bill', which proposed to weaken the closed shop and to allow the selective dismissal of strikers; and against a series of court decisions which constrained spending by Labour local councils. He had already attacked his own profession for doing the Conservatives' work for them in *Labour Weekly*. In an article on 5 February 1982 headed 'When the judges step into politics', he condemned the law lords' ruling against the GLC's 'Fare's Fair' policy of subsidising public transport – which sits oddly with his later sweeping condemnation of Ken Livingstone and all his works. The case developed the concept of the 'fiduciary duty' owed by councillors to their ratepayers not to put up local taxes 'unreasonably'. This mattered because of the archaic local government law which held councillors personally liable for unlawful council spending. The Queensbridge Labour Party minutes for 10 June 1982 contain a gem of historical irony. Tony Blair moved, and Cherie Booth seconded, a motion for that year's party conference condemning the courts' interference in politics. It was carried by 11 votes to 0.

> Conference reaffirms its belief that democratically elected local authorities should be answerable to their electorate and that political decisions should not be subject to the interference of the courts.
>
> Conference calls upon the next Labour government to introduce legislation which will:
>
> (a) abolish the judge-invented doctrine of fiduciary duty (which means that the duty to ratepayers takes precedence over manifesto pledges), and
>
> (b) restrict councillors' liability to surcharge or disqualification to cases of serious crime.

Of the eleven people present, who could have imagined that, when they called upon 'the next Labour government', it would be led by the proposer of the motion? Several other constituency parties backed a similar motion – it had been circulated by the Society of Labour Lawyers – and it was carried, as Composite 66, by the 1982 Labour conference. Although technically still Labour policy, it has since been overtaken by events. The idea of fiduciary duty became irrelevant when the Conservative government introduced rate capping, which put a statutory limit on local taxes; while the most spectacular victim of personal liability since then was the Tory former leader of Westminster council, Shirley Porter.

The battle against Militant

As well as passing Blair's Composite 66, the Labour Party conference in Blackpool in 1982 marked the moment when Michael Foot began to assert control over the party. His most significant victory was to win the conference's backing for action against the Militant tendency. Blair summed up the position succinctly in his Australian lecture:

> Militant is an avowedly Trotskyist group, whose links go back to the Revolutionary Socialist League in the 1960s. It has sixty-four full-time workers, including thirty-four at a regional level. Militant say that they only 'sell the *Militant* paper'. The centre and right say it is much more than just a group selling a paper; it is, in effect, a secret conspiracy, a party within the party. Following a report by the general secretary and national agent into Militant, the NEC [National Executive Committee] voted narrowly to establish a Register of all groups in the party. To qualify, the group has to show it abides by Labour's constitution. The constitution in effect outlaws parties within the party. Thus it is plain, since the report expressly said that Militant was a party within a party, that Militant will not be permitted to register.

The reason Blair knew so much about it was because the National Executive had taken legal advice from Derry Irvine. Michael Foot explained that Blair 'was the liaison between the Executive and our official lawyers, but he knew everything that was going on, and why it was so important that we get it right . . . What we wanted to make sure was we didn't offend against natural justice.' Foot had been surprised to be advised that Militant might have a good case for court action against the party if it simply tried to expel its adherents. Instead, Irvine and Blair devised the idea of a Register. Foot gave most of the credit to Irvine's junior: 'All that was based on his advice, you know. I don't want to say that he determined it, but we took full account of what he said.'

Now the 'soft' left faction to which Blair belonged was in a quandary. The Labour Co-ordinating Committee was one of the groups which was required to register. The idea of expelling people for their politics was difficult for the left of the party to accept, with its folk-memory of right-wing purges in the 1930s and 1950s. But it had also long insisted that conference decisions were sovereign – the point of the betrayal thesis was to try to force the parliamentary leadership to abide by them. In October, the LCC Executive voted to co-operate with the Register. However, as a democratic group, the LCC's position would ultimately be decided by its members at its annual meeting in Newcastle, on 21 November 1982.

It was a crunch moment for the soft left, and Haworth knew the vote might be close. Any member of the LCC could attend and vote at its annual meetings, so it was important to mobilise. He asked Tony Blair and Cherie Booth to go with him and Maggie Rae to Newcastle to 'vote against the Trots' – although their leading opponent in the LCC, Tony Benn's organiser Jon Lansman, was not actually a Trotskyist.

The meeting was on a Sunday, so the two couples stayed in a hotel on the moors above Alston for the weekend. When they arrived at Newcastle Polytechnic, there were 150 people in the Rutherford Hall. The Register was the first issue to be discussed, and the debate did not appear to be going the LCC Executive's way. Haworth sat next to Blair, and was surprised when he suddenly got up:

> That was the first time I heard him make a speech impromptu, unrehearsed, without notes. I wanted to make an intervention, because the debate was going ultra-leftie. He said, 'Oh, this is shit.' When he went forward to speak, I was worried that he might be embarrassing or counter-productive. I tended to think he was a bit naïve, inexperienced. But it was brilliant, just perfect. He was confident and courageous.

Blair knew what he thought about Militant, and was used to getting a hostile reception for his views from Labour audiences. He thought it was one reason why he had made so little headway in his search for a parliamentary seat. But this was the first time he realised he could hold and sway people in political argument. The LCC agreed to co-operate with the Register – by just 72 votes to 61.

The decision left Militant isolated, and the tendency's only defence was now to go to the capitalist courts. The next month, the members of the 'Editorial Board' of *Militant* tried to get an injunction against the Labour Party. Blair appeared in court as Derry Irvine's junior counsel for the party, and Militant's application was thrown out. The five members of Militant were in due course expelled.

However, the battle had only just started and Labour was still heading for disaster in the General Election. It was likely that Thatcher, riding high in the opinion polls, would call an election in the summer of 1983. Early in the year the legal action by the Labour Party against the new constituency boundaries collapsed in the House of Lords, and there was a scramble for a reduced number of safe seats. As a growing caravan of displaced Labour MPs chased the last few vacancies, Blair was depressed: 'I'd been getting fairly desperate to fight the election, and I could see everything disappearing.'[24] He was resigned to fighting the election campaign as the supportive husband of the candidate in Thanet North, as Thanet West had become under the new boundaries.

In March 1983, his hopes were raised. Right next door to his childhood home in Durham, the boundary commissioners had re-created the constituency of Sedgefield. The number of seats in County Durham had not changed, so all the existing Labour MPs had expected to end up with a safe seat when the music stopped. But Ernie Armstrong, MP for North-East Durham, upset the game of musical chairs when he opted for

North-West Durham instead of shuffling south to Sedgefield.[25] This left David Watkins, MP for Consett in north Durham, without a seat and a vacancy in Sedgefield, a south Durham seat to which he had no special claim. It was suspected that Armstrong was trying to create a vacancy for his daughter, Hilary (she eventually succeeded him in North-West Durham in 1987). The effect was to throw wide open the contest for a seat for life.

Blair had no contacts in Sedgefield. He went up to County Durham to help in the campaign for the by-election on 28 March in Darlington, next-door to the new seat. (He later cited the experience on the doorstep there as one of the reasons why he disliked Ken Livingstone. 'I remember canvassing in the Darlington by-election,' he said, 'and getting the antics of the London Labour Party thrown back in my face.' The London party was 'a byword for extremism and gesture rainbow politics'.[26]) He telephoned the secretary of the Sedgefield party, George Ferguson, who refused to give any information until the formal selection procedure began. Other inquiries suggested the party there had already been stitched up by the hard left. It was one of the seats eyed by Les Huckfield, whose own Nuneaton seat looked as though it would fall to the Conservatives as a result of boundary changes (it did). Once a junior industry minister (from 1976 to 1979), on the right of the Labour Party, Huckfield had transformed himself into a more-Bennite-than-Benn member of the National Executive.* After he lost to a fellow MP, Roger Stott, for the candidacy in Wigan on 24 April, he concentrated his efforts on Sedgefield.

On 28 April, Blair was the political gooseberry at a Labour Party rally in Margate Town Hall, at which Cherie, her father Tony Booth and Tony Benn all spoke. Reg Ward, the Chairman of Thanet North Labour Party, remembered Blair as 'hyperactive' and said he had to remind him that he was 'the candidate's husband, not the candidate'. The hall was packed and, in a vibrant echo of a Labour era which was about to pass, Benn spoke brilliantly. According to the next day's *Isle of Thanet Gazette*, 'Miss Booth said she was delighted to be sharing a platform with the two Tonys who have inspired her in her quest for socialism'. What the third

*Most Labour politicians do not know – or care to remember – that it was once official party policy to ban all car imports. That policy was proposed on Labour's National Executive by Huckfield in April 1980: it was too much even for Tony Benn, who doubted its feasibility and tried to amend it. When he failed, however, Benn ended up voting for it, and it was carried by 10 votes to 6 (*Labour Weekly*, 2 May 1980).

Tony thought of this was not recorded. Blair argued with Benn about Militant in the car on the way back to London.[27]

Cherie's views are another important pointer to Blair's early position in Labour politics. She was noticeably more left-wing than he was: if Blair was soft right, she was soft left. The invitation to Benn to speak in her constituency contrasted with Blair's refusal to let him come to Beaconsfield, and her tribute to Benn's 'inspiration' balances her later claim to have been inspired by the less contentious trio of Castle, Crosland and Williams. While she was not as enthusiastic in her support for Benn as her father, she was clearly more comfortable with him than her husband was. But she disagreed with Benn, too, and after the 1983 election played an active role in the LCC when it became publicly an anti-Bennite faction. Her campaign literature in Thanet also disappointed the Conservative tabloids when they later tried to dig up evidence of her extreme left-wing past – her election address was notably Blairite before its time, promising: 'Less tax: we will reduce the tax burden on the lower-paid and cut VAT.'

A week after the Margate rally, Cherie threw a surprise party for Tony's birthday. He was just thirty, but gloomy about his future. That weekend Margaret Thatcher retreated to the Prime Minister's country house at Chequers to consider the implications of the week's local elections. On Monday, 9 May, she announced that the General Election would be on 9 June. Blair decided to go to Sedgefield to 'ride his luck', in Derry Irvine's words. Cherie said: 'He went up north one day, and he never came back.'

Notes

1. *Sun*, 28 February 1997.
2. This may have been the model resolution drafted by the right-wing Campaign for Labour Victory; see David and Maurice Kogan, *The Battle for the Labour Party*, p. 87.
3. Tony Booth, *Stroll On*, p. 105.
4. Ken Livingstone, *If Voting Changed Anything, They'd Abolish It*, p. 177.
5. Speech to special Labour conference on Clause IV at Westminster Central Hall, 29 April 1995.
6. It is undated but refers to events at the Labour Party conference in October 1982 and also to 'the scale of the problems we face as a people in 1982'.
7. *Labour Solidarity*, No. 6, Vol. 1, September 1981. The papers of the Labour Solidarity Campaign are held in the Brynmor Jones Library at the University of Hull, and I am grateful to Brian Dyson, the archivist, for a copy of this letter.
8. They were signatories of a Campaign for Labour Victory advertisement in *Labour Weekly*, 26 September 1980.

9. *Guardian*, 10 May 1982.
10. *Ibid.*, 17 May 1982.
11. Peter Riddell, *Financial Times*, November 1984, quoted by Andrew Roth, *Parliamentary Profiles*.
12. Austin Mitchell, *Beyond the Blue Horizon*, p. 85.
13. Vladimir Ilyich Lenin, *'Left-Wing' Communism, An Infantile Disorder*, 1920.
14. *Inside Labour*, April 1999.
15. *Sunday Telegraph*, 9 May 1982.
16. *Daily Telegraph*, 14 May 1982.
17. *Guardian*, 10 May 1982.
18. *Daily Telegraph*, 19 May 1982.
19. Pat Phoenix, *Love, Curiosity, Freckles and Doubt*, pp. 106, 107.
20. The threshold for retaining a deposit was then 12.5 per cent of the vote; it was reduced to 5 per cent in 1985.
21. *Spectator*, 1 October 1994.
22. See p. 70.
23. Jon Sopel, *Tony Blair: The Moderniser*, p. 58.
24. BBC2, *Newsnight*, 21 November 1988.
25. *The Times*, 14 March 1983.
26. Interview, *Observer*, 21 November 1999; Labour's holding the Darlington seat was credited with saving Foot's leadership in the run-up to the 1983 election.
27. Tony Benn was not so impressed by his discussion with Blair that he recorded it in his diaries. I am grateful to Ruth Winstone for confirming this.

6

After Extra Time

Sedgefield, 1983

> 'If there was a moment when history should have noticed him, it was then.'
>
> —*Roy Hattersley*

On the day the Labour Party nearly destroyed itself, its future leader knocked on the door of a small terraced house in the former pit village of Trimdon, in County Durham. It was Wednesday, 11 May 1983. In London, Michael Foot chaired the meeting to draw up Labour's manifesto. Rather than re-open deep divisions over policy, it was decided to reprint in full a 'campaign document' published two months earlier, with a new foreword by Foot. Only the shadow Chancellor Peter Shore spoke up in the meeting for a shorter manifesto, from which things could be left out. Neil Kinnock, the shadow Education Secretary, had made his unhappiness clear in a letter to Foot the day before. But in the manifesto meeting itself he and the rest of the doubters sat on their hands. Chief doubter Gerald Kaufman called it 'the longest suicide note in history'.

Up in Durham, staying with friends, Tony Blair made the telephone call that would change his life. To be chosen as a candidate, he first needed to be nominated. 'He phoned me up and asked if he could come and see me because I was the secretary of the Trimdon Village branch,' said John Burton. 'He got a list of secretaries from the secretary of the constituency party and noticed that Trimdon hadn't nominated anybody. I said, "Well, the best time will be tonight because there are five of us having our post-election meeting."' Burton and his fellow councillor Terry Ward had just been re-elected to Sedgefield District Council in the local elections the week before, 'and we were going to send a thank-you letter out, so we were having a meeting and a few drinks in the house'.[1]

At 9pm, Blair's brown Mini Metro pulled up outside 9 Front Street South, Trimdon. He later said he nearly did not get out of the car; he nearly just drove back. One of the five Labour Party members in Burton's house that night, Paul Trippett, recalled:

> We were less than a month away from an election, he didn't have a nomination, he was going to a branch that didn't have an inclination to nominate anybody particularly, going to a stranger's house to meet some people, and he said he just thought, 'What am I doing here?' He sat for a minute or two, and then he thought, 'I've come all this way, I might as well go in.'

He knocked on the door and Burton asked him to come in and sit down. The most important item of business for that night's meeting was the football match on television, the European Cup Winners' Cup Final between Aberdeen and Real Madrid. 'So he said he quite liked football,' said Burton. 'Whether he was being polite or not I don't know. We had some beer and some wine and he came in and sat down.' Trippett said: 'He sat there, watched the match, took part in the conversation guys have when the match is on, you know, "Good shot", "Bad cross", so he was one of the guys.' The game, tied at 1–1, went into extra time, so Blair had to wait another half an hour. Aberdeen scored another goal to win. Then they asked him why they should nominate him.

Peter Brookes, another of the five, said they gave him a bit of a grilling: 'Why on earth should we give a nomination to this bloke who's just arrived and spoiled the football? We don't know him from Adam. He talks posh and he comes from London. Why on earth should we consider him at all?'

Terry Ward, a left-wing health service union activist, was the most aggressive. 'Terry gave him a bit of a hassling about the health service, and Tony acquitted himself very well,' said Trippett. Ward was impressed, but not persuaded. He wanted a 'proper socialist' of the hard left.

Burton, a local councillor who was on the right wing of the party, recalled Blair's 'ideas for change, for broadening the base of the party, which he was talking about then – and things like Europe, where he wasn't in line with party policy because he said we should play a more important part in Europe. He believed the future lay in Europe.' Blair did not bowl them over, but they liked him. Brookes, a social worker, said:

> He was very open and honest. We actually felt when we were talking, 'This guy is sincere. He means what he is saying.' You thought, 'He really wants this.' He was saying things like how much he did want to get into politics, to get a parliamentary seat, because he thought he could make a contribution to the future of society. He didn't really need to do that in terms of his personal situation because he was a very successful barrister doing

industrial law. And he was sharing this with us, 'I don't need this for the money', sort of thing.

The fifth member there was Simon Hoban, the branch's youth officer. He was favourably impressed, but said little. Trippett, a joiner for Sedgefield District Council with a dry sense of humour, was lukewarm:

> He gave us this spiel about standing in Beaconsfield and he had this letter off Foot saying that people of the calibre of Tony should be in the House. That letter swung a lot of us straight away, because we had a great affection for Michael Foot, because he was a left-winger – we didn't know what Tony's views were at that time, but we thought he must have some radical views, or Foot wouldn't have written this letter. He wasn't too bad with the questions. Nothing out of the ordinary. He came across, he was a young lad, good-looking, well-spoken, personable. I wasn't bothered one way or the other. So I thought, 'Yeah, if you want to, we'll go for it.'

It was John Burton more than the others who thought there was something special about their visitor. Inevitably, there were other calculations. Burton himself was interested in being the candidate, but as a councillor did not want to stand against the leader of the council, Warren McCourt, who had already joined the contest, in case he did not win. 'It's whether you're a prophet in your own land,' said Burton. 'As soon as I met Tony, anyway, I knew that he was the chap and not myself. That he was better able to take the party forward and change the party than I would be.'

Nine days later, Blair would be the Labour candidate for one of the safest seats in the country. Four of the five people in Burton's house that night – Terry Ward dropped out – became, with Phil Wilson who had been away that week, the 'Famous Five' who threw themselves into the campaign to get Blair selected. Burton, Brookes, Trippett and Wilson continued to be the core of the 'Sedgefield posse' which provided Blair with such a strong base as he climbed the Labour ladder over the next eleven years. They had just run a local election campaign, to re-elect Burton and Ward to Sedgefield council against presumptuous SDP opposition, and were looking for something else to do.

They knew the hard left was organising for Les Huckfield, the displaced MP, but Sedgefield was a new constituency, and the local Labour Party was assembled from bits of old parties with very different outlooks and loyalties, so its politics were fluid.

Despite not being bothered 'one way or the other', Paul Trippett took the next day off from his job to drive Blair round to visit some of the delegates to the selection conference:

> I stayed in the car, I just pointed out where they lived and what they were called, and Tony went in, because I thought, 'If this guy wants it, he's going

> to have to do a bit of work himself, I'm not going to spoon-feed him.' And what he was actually doing, he was very clever. He was going in to see them, and he wasn't saying, 'Vote for me.' What he was saying was, 'I would like to be on the shortlist first. If I get on the shortlist and you've already decided to support somebody, and if your person goes out, would you then transfer your vote to me?' That was his line, because by this time a lot of people had made their minds up. I think people took notice of that. Here was a sensible, quiet young man who wanted a chance – that was part of his appeal then, and it's part of his appeal now.

Blair moved into John Burton's house, Peter Brookes lent him his car, and Paul Trippett took more time off work. Meanwhile, Burton, as secretary, hurriedly convened a meeting of the Trimdon Village Branch of Sedgefield Labour Party for that Saturday. Unless Blair received a nomination from a branch or affiliated body, his name could not be on the shortlist, and the selection conference could not vote for him.

Nowadays, Trimdon branch has 200 members. That Saturday morning in the village's Community College there were just fifteen – as well as eight or nine would-be candidates. John Burton said:

> Tony said that of all the times, ever – then, before and since – he has never been as nervous as he was that day. He thinks he made the worst speech of his life, and was really worried. His speech was five minutes, I think, and question and answer. He was quite convinced he wouldn't get the nomination.

Burton's memory of Blair's speech is that it was 'perfectly all right – he was just nervous'. As well he might be. Sedgefield was the last constituency Labour Party in the country to choose a candidate. At each stage in the process, Blair was lucky.

The chairman of the branch, George 'Mick' Terrans, just happened to be the chairman of the new constituency party as well. 'He was the big politician in the area,' said Burton. Despite being formally pledged, as a retired miner, to his union's candidate, he liked Blair instantly, and gave him an unobtrusive boost. Terrans commented that all the applicants except Blair had already been nominated by other branches or affiliates. Burton said: 'I moved as Tony Blair didn't have a nomination that we give our nomination to him, and there was a 12–3 vote for that, which was a little bit naughty. He allowed that.' As chairman, Terrans should have asked the meeting to vote on each applicant in turn.

The next day, Sunday 15 May, Burton visited George Ferguson, secretary of the Sedgefield Constituency Labour Party, who wrote a carbon-copied letter. 'I hereby acknowledge receipt of your nomination in respect of: Anthony Charles Lynton Blair.' The selection conference was to be held on Friday, 20 May. The Blair campaign, having taxied around the obstacles of party procedure, was airborne.

The Trimdon posse

Sudden as Tony Blair's arrival at John Burton's house was, it was not just a stroke of luck. Blair had been scouring the north-east for a seat for two and a half years. And he had known about the vacancy in Sedgefield for several weeks before he contacted Burton. Giles Radice, the MP for Chester-le-Street (most of which was absorbed into his new seat of Durham North), took an interest in the battle for Sedgefield, and had already met Blair:

> I first met him at a Fabian meeting in Hackney, and I remember him as bright, nice. He'd just been the candidate in Beaconsfield. Then John Lloyd, who is a mutual friend of ours, said that he was trying to get this seat, very much at the last moment, in the north-east, and could I be of any assistance? I met him at supper with the Lloyds, in London, and I was very impressed by him, I must say.

Radice spoke to Joe Mills, the regional baron of the Transport and General Workers' Union in the north. He was also that year's Chairman of the Northern Region Labour Party. Before he went to John Burton's house, Blair went to visit him, said Mills:

> We talked at length, Tony and I, about what his philosophy was, and what I was impressed about was the fact that he was very keen on the one member, one vote issue which I was promoting in the early 1980s, much against a lot of the other people in the party. And I thought, 'Well, this is a fella we could support.'

The Northern Region of the TGWU was always right-wing in Labour Party terms, and Mills had no intention of helping Huckfield. 'I was passionately opposed to Les Huckfield and did everything I could to stop him,' he said. Huckfield 'turned up at my office with a Northern Region TGWU tie on – I don't know where he got that from. He was in my office, with the chap who was bringing him round, Alan Meale' (Meale was later MP for Mansfield and briefly a minister in Blair's government).

Huckfield asked Mills to write a letter to the Sedgefield Labour Party endorsing him, said Mills: 'I remember bringing my secretary into my office and saying to her to take down, "Les Huckfield is a sponsored member of the TGWU." He said, "Is that it?" And I told him, "I'm not recommending you, that's all I'm bound to do as an official of the union."'

Blair was (and is) a member of the TGWU. He was a TGWU delegate on the General Committee of the Hackney South Labour Party, and had spoken at a TGWU weekend school in Durham in June 1982.[2] Weekend schools were a useful network for right-wingers in a union dominated at national level by the left. The TGWU did not have many branches affiliated to the Sedgefield Labour Party, but with Mills's help Blair managed to get one of them to nominate him. The Trimdon nomination turned out not to be the single thread by which his hopes hung, but it was the more important. He went into the selection process with just two nominations, while Huckfield had a fistful. But, as John Burton said, one nomination can be as good as a hundred, because it means you can be considered for the shortlist.

Tom Burlison, Mills's equivalent in the other big general union, the General and Municipal, was also keen to help Blair, whom he had met when he went for Middlesbrough in 1980. Burlison asked his political officer, Nick Brown, to look at Sedgefield. Brown, who had himself just been chosen as the candidate for Newcastle East, checked, but all 'his' union delegates in Sedgefield were 'left-wing people who couldn't be influenced', he said. For many years afterwards, it was assumed that, because Blair's selection was unexpected, it must have been fixed by 'the unions'. The truth is that their main contribution was to fail to help his opponent.

Even before Blair arrived in the constituency, Les Huckfield was being treated by some in the Sedgefield party as the candidate. At a meeting organised by the National Union of Mineworkers on 7 May as part of its campaign against the closure of Fishburn coke works, the Labour Party was embarrassed by the fact that the Conservative and Alliance candidates for Sedgefield accepted invitations to speak. Tongue in cheek, *Newsnight* filmed the meeting for a report on 'the constituency with no Labour candidate'. In the meeting the chairman proposed a stand-in from the audience – Les Huckfield. As he took his seat on the platform, followed by the BBC's camera, there was a ripple of dissension in the hall. George Ferguson, scrupulous as ever, pointedly did not attend the meeting and told *Newsnight*: 'It could be construed that we're pre-empting who is to be the prospective parliamentary candidate. Personally I don't think it would be right to put anyone in that chair.'

As Blair and his 'Famous Five' supporters canvassed delegates to the selection conference, it became clear that many of them shared Ferguson's dislike of Huckfield's presumption. But opposition to Huckfield was split between several others – hence Blair's tactic of asking people for their second-preference votes.

The 'Five' were mostly inexperienced. Only John Burton was a delegate to the selection conference. But he was well-known and widely liked – a centre-forward for Bishop Auckland amateur football team, a PE teacher, banjo player in a folk band and, of course, a Labour district councillor. 'Lo and behold!' said Burton. 'Some of the delegates I'd been to school with. Some of the delegates I'd played football with, and some of the delegates I was related to.'

Phil Wilson, returning to Sedgefield the week after Blair's arrival, was quickly swept up in the venture. He had only joined the Labour Party – because of his support for the Campaign for Nuclear Disarmament – in March 1983, and was already active in his civil service union, the CPSA. He had been away at the union's conference in Brighton, proposing a constitutional amendment which he later discovered had been drafted by Cherie Booth, who had done some legal work for the union. As soon as he met Blair, with Burton, he knew 'there was something about him', he said. According to Wilson, Burton took him aside and said: 'We've got to support him, you know, he's Cabinet material.'

The campaign was exhilarating. 'It was a happy time, it was all new to all of us. And to Tony himself. We were treading new ground, we were having to work things out,' said Paul Trippett. Trippett had been a member of the Militant tendency, become disillusioned, and left the Labour Party. He had only rejoined the party the month before, to work for the re-election of Councillor John Burton, his former teacher. His initial motive for throwing himself into the campaign to get Blair chosen as the candidate was simply that it was a challenge. Although he had not been particularly impressed by Blair on that first night, he quickly came to admire him. He was motivated by the urgency of the campaign: 'This guy knocks on the door and asks for a nomination, we decide to give him it, and then it has to be done. Unlike council politics, where you debate things for weeks on end, and there's resolutions and everything, this was politics, moving, and it was exciting.'

The story of his life

Tony Blair's curriculum vitae for the selection is a badly-typed two-page document (see overleaf). John Burton said he got a friend to type it who was not a typist – 'you can see she wasn't a typist!' – after Blair got the branch's nomination. It was copied from Blair's handwritten version, and is full of errors and misreadings.

Like all good CVs, however, it is selective. It starts with Michael Foot's endorsement of 'Tony Glair', obviously quoted from memory, as the

NAME : TONY BLAIR

AGE : 30 years .

TRADE UNION : Transport & General Workers Union

PREVIOUS PARLIAMENTARY EXPERIENCE

I stood, during the Falklands war, in the Beaconsfield by-election, a Tory seat with a mojority of 23,000. I lost, (unsurprisingly) but gained valuable experience. Michael Foot speaking on BBC Newsnight on 26th May i982 said,
"In my view Tony Glair will make a major contribution to British Politics in the months and years ahead".

BACKGROUND
I lived in County Durham from i958 to i975, first in Durham City and then from i963 to i975 on a new housing estate at High Shincliffe.
From i972 -75 I attended Oxford University (St.John's College) where Iread Law. I graduated in i975 with a B.A. (Hons) in Law.
i975/6 I was a student at the Inns of Court School in London, passing my professional exams in the summer of i976.
i976/7 I was pupip to Alexander Irvine Q.C. At the end of my pupillage, at the age of 24 years, I was awarded a full place in Chanbers as a practising barrister. Since i977 I have worked as a practising barrister in those chambers.

NATURE OF WORK
I specialise in trade union and industrial law, which, in effect, has meant living and working in London. I also work for several major County Councils and in the area of civil liberties. In addition I have represented the Labour Party. The unions I have worked for include: T.G.W.U.; I.S.T.C.; N.U.R.; G.M.B.A.T.U.; T.S.S.A.; A.U.E.W.; N.A.L.G.O.
Amongst the major cases in which I have been involved over the past few years are;

- Defending the Labour Party in court action against the Reg Prentice and his supporters
- Defending the Labour Party in the action against it by Militant
- Defending ILEA in its decision to peg school meal prices at 35p
- Several cases arising aout of redundancies by the British Steel Corporation, inclusing winning the unfair dismissal claim of the 30 Birmingham steelworkers
- I have, in particular, worked in cases where trade unionists have been selected for redundancy, especially in the TGWU and ISTC
- Most recently, I acted for the Port Talbot steelworkers, in their case against the BSC.

PUBLICATIONS AND LECTURES
Amongst the papers I have written for are - The Guardian, New Statesman, Spectator, Labour Weekly. These articles habe concerned trade union law, civil liberties, and race relations. I have lectured regularly in Trade Union law over the years, giving the i982 Society of Labour Congress lecture on the Tebbit Act.
In addition I as a discussion leader at the TGWU weekend in Durham City in June i982, speaking on the Labour Party, and I was invited and gave a lecture on the Labout Party and its future in Perth, Western Australia to Murdoch and W.A. Universities, later published in Australia.

wording is quite wrong (Foot was actually more effusive, see p. 85). It omits any reference to his private education.* Nor would you get the impression from his description of his work as a barrister that he ever

*He was asked by *Marxism Today* in July 1990, 'What do you blame your parents for?', and answered, 'Thinking that sending me to public school was a good career move!'

PARTY OFFICES
I have held offices in three London constituencies, and been a member of each G.C. I am at present a TGWU delegate on Hackney South G.C. (a labour seat with a sitting SDP defector).
I am a member of the Executive of the Society of Labout Lawyers concentrating partioularly on trade union and logal government law.
MEMBERSHIP OF OTHER ORGANISATIONS
C.N.D.; N.C.C.L. ; L.C.C.

FAMILY
I am married to Cherie Booth, who was born and bred in Liverpool. Cherie is now a barrister (having come top in the professional exams in i976 for the whole country). She specialises in child care and adoption work. Cherie's father is the actor, Anthony Booth of 'Till Death Do Us Part' fame. Anthony and Pat Phoenix, from 'Coronation Stree', both came and canvassed for me when I previously stood for Parliament and would be happy to do so again.
Cherie and I , as yet, have no children.

SHORT STATEMENT OF VIEWS AND INTENT
I have always wanted to come back to the North East to represent the community here. I would, of course, live in the constituency if selected, and I would be a full-time M.P. Cherie's work, unlike mine, could transfer to the North.
I believe an M.P. has two tasks: to know and work with the Community he or she represents;and to put the best possible case for that community in Westminster.
I believe in a united Labout Party offering radical solutions within a framework that people understand and that touches their everyday lives.
I support Party policy as determined by Party conference. When arguments do take place, they should take place within the Party, not on the media; and in a spirit of democracy. That means not only the right to express your views, but the right to have them listened to.

engaged in corporate litigation, or represented employers. And it would take a lawyer to appreciate the careful wording of the claim to have 'written for' the *Guardian* (no published article can be found) or of the suggestion that Cherie's work 'could transfer to the North'. The CV confirms that Blair was a member of the Campaign for Nuclear Disarmament, despite his denial in September 1994.*

It may have been scrappy, but its 'Short Statement of Views and Intent' prefigures one aspect of the later, glossier Blair – it is notably bland and abstract: 'I believe in a united Labour Party offering radical solutions within a framework that people understand and that touches their everyday lives.'

This was the document that the Executive Committee of the Sedgefield Labour Party had before it when it met in Spennymoor Town Hall on Wednesday 18 May – just a week after Blair's arrival – to draw up a shortlist of candidates. Spennymoor was the largest town in the Sedgefield constituency, and the Trades Council there was the power base of the hard

*See pp. 144 and 252.

left. There were sixteen applicants who filled in the yellow nomination forms. They included David Watkins, the displaced MP for Consett, Joel Barnett, another displaced MP and former Cabinet minister, Hilary Armstrong, Sid Weighell, the recently retired railway union leader, and Ben Pimlott, later a professor and biographer of Harold Wilson – as well as Blair and Huckfield.

The Executive Committee, a small body dominated by the left, decided on a shortlist of six, which was designed to favour Huckfield.

Blair's name was not on the list.

As the General Election campaign was already under way, the selection procedure had been compressed. So the next day, the larger and more politically mixed General Committee of the constituency party met, again in Spennymoor Town Hall, to approve the shortlist. John Burton went to the meeting with one objective – to add Blair's name. This was the decisive meeting, because it was the General Committee that would meet again the following day to choose the candidate. Burton recalled:

> They went through the whole list, everybody who had a nomination, to see if they should be added to the shortlist. Barnett – No. Then they came to Blair. I got up and said, 'I've got this letter from Michael Foot saying he wants him in the House as soon as possible.' Nobody understood that it's a fairly standard letter, and it went down well.

Blair was waiting with Burton's wife Lily, Peter and Christine Brookes, Phil Wilson and Paul Trippett in the Red Lion in Trimdon. When John Burton returned from the General Committee meeting he paused on the threshold, looking downcast. 'What happened?' asked Peter Brookes, his heart sinking. 'You're not going to believe this,' said Burton. 'They only added one name to the shortlist. And that was Tony Blair.' Burton recalled: 'Wheee! The place went up with joy.' Blair's name had been added to the list by one vote. (The official constituency party records have been lost: Burton recalls that the tellers disagreed, one saying the vote was 42–41, the other 41–40; but both agreed Blair had won, so demands for a recount were ignored.)

The next day, Blair went back to Durham Cathedral, in whose precincts he had lived and gone to school, to pray. He once spoke of the 'sense of solidity and stability that it gave to my life'.[3] He did not know that John Burton, a church warden of St Mary Magdalene on the Green in Trimdon, had let himself into the church late the previous night to do the same.

On Friday night, 119 delegates attended the selection meeting at Spennymoor Town Hall. All seven of the expanded shortlist spoke for ten minutes and took five minutes of questions. Les Huckfield might have realised things were going horribly wrong when he found himself pushed on the defensive in answer to questions from the floor. Blair and Burton may have been inexperienced, but they were not innocent.

Burton has kept the scribbled notes of the questions which he planted among friendly delegates. One, on the back of an envelope, has 'Roger Stott' written at the top – it was presumably suggested by Stott, Huckfield's adversary in Wigan: 'Don't you think Mr Huckfield it counts strongly against you that you deserted Nuneaton when it became a marginal seat, allowing the opp. parties to say Labour couldn't win because the sitting MP had defected?' Three other questions, headed 'Joe Mills', the TGWU Northern Region boss, are on two scraps of paper. The sharpest was: 'The TGWU supported the Register of groups. How can Huckfield continue to oppose it. You advocated strict adherence to party conf[erence decisions].' Huckfield's defence of Militant (at whom the Register was aimed) did him no good. Even left-wing delegates had no time for Militant if Michael Foot and the party conference were against them. Mills explained:

> We had ensured that people going to the selection conference would expose Huckfield's credentials. The ordinary people in the Durham area were opposed to Tony Benn's policies. We had to get Huckfield to come over quite clearly as supporting the same policies as Benn – to ensure Huckfield could be seen for what he was.

Huckfield's assiduous organising among the local hyper-activists of the hard left had given a misleading impression of his strength. The roots of County Durham's ethical socialism went deeper.

Blair spoke last. 'He was brilliant, excellent – energetic and alive with ideas,' said Burton. He remembers that Blair mentioned Europe in his speech, because one of the delegates teased him about it:

> Ron Mahon, who was one of the officers from NUPE regional office, walked up when Tony said about playing a part in Europe and said, 'Your lad's just lost it.' And I said, 'I don't think so. The party's changing on Europe.' And of course it was changing.

When it came to the voting, Blair won fewer than a third of the votes on the first round. But he was in the lead. 'It's going to happen,' thought Burton. 'It's really going to happen.' Huckfield came a poor second, and a grass roots activist from Durham, Pat McIntyre, beat Sedgefield council leader Warren McCourt. Bill Giffin of the Fire Brigades Union, Frank Robson, a farmer and Darlington councillor, and Reg Race, another hard-left displaced MP, trailed behind. Blair led in each round of voting, but there were five rounds before he finally emerged the winner. The records may be lost, but John Burton wrote down the votes in his green book, in which as a councillor he noted the details of cases he dealt with.

	Round				
	1st	2nd	3rd	4th	5th
Pat McIntyre	17	18	20	29	
Bill Giffin	8	5			
Tony Blair	39	53	51	58	73
Warren McCourt	15	14	16		
Les Huckfield	27	27	32	32	46
Frank Robson	5				
Reg Race	8	2			

'I do believe it was the women who gave Tony the vote,' said George Ferguson. He said that after the final round the Chairman, Mick Terrans, forgot to announce the figures: 'We brought them all out on the stage to hear the result. And Mick Terrans said, "We've got a new MP, let's give him our congratulations." I had to nudge him to say, "Who is it?" He said, "Oh, Tony Blair."'

John Burton agreed that the result wasn't immediately clear, but remembers it slightly differently. 'Terrans started to say, "We've got to organise for the General Election now, less than three weeks away," and then something about having a "bright young chap" as the candidate, and the penny dropped.'

The news spread fast and far. Blair telephoned Cherie at the home of her Thanet North party chairman, Reg Ward. At about midnight that night, in a hotel in Scotland, shadow Home Secretary Roy Hattersley was woken by a hammering on his door. He was due to make an election campaign speech the next day. When he opened the door he found Mary Goudie in a dressing gown. 'Not at all what I'm used to,' he said. She was working for the Labour Party as his 'minder' at the time.

'What's the matter?' said Hattersley.

'Have you heard about Blair?' she said.

Hattersley could not remember who Blair was at that moment, so he said, 'Come in, come in.'

'Young Blair's done this extraordinary thing,' she said. 'He hadn't been shortlisted, and he's gone round and knocked on all the doors. And he's got it.'

'From then on,' said Hattersley, 'whenever anybody said to me that Blair wasn't strong and tough, I always thought of Mary Goudie beating on my door at midnight that Friday night. If there was a moment when history should have noticed him, it was then.'

However, it was the middle of a General Election campaign, and history had other things on its mind. That day shadow Foreign Secretary Denis Healey appeared to disagree with Labour's defence policy, and opened up a gap between him and Michael Foot. It was not clear that the Labour Party would survive.

Once he was selected, Tony Blair and the Trimdon posse threw themselves into the General Election campaign locally. Cherie Booth came with her father Tony Booth and Pat Phoenix who campaigned again for Blair, as promised.

Blair's election address, which later became controversial, was produced in haste, with only twenty days to polling day when he was chosen as the candidate. Written by George Ferguson but in Blair's name, it contradicted his pro-European declaration at the selection conference: 'We'll negotiate withdrawal from the EEC which has drained our natural resources and destroyed jobs.'

As a mere parliamentary candidate, Blair presumably felt that – having made his point inside the party – he should maintain party unity in public. He said in his Sedgefield CV: 'I support party policy as determined by party conference. When arguments do take place, they should take place within the party, not on the media.' Of course it would have been possible simply to have left the EEC withdrawal sentence out, and Blair's acceptance of the party line does not sit easily with his later attempts to present himself as a 'conviction politician'. But the EEC sentence appears in a long list summarising party policies, headed, ironically, 'Labour's Sensible Answers'. More difficult for Blair to explain is 'A Personal Message', on the back of the address, in which he did not mention Europe, but did attack the Trident nuclear missile programme:

> The Tories say there is no money to create new jobs. But they spend billions of pounds on dangerous nuclear weapons. They spend billions on keeping people on the dole. They encourage the rich to invest billions abroad each year. This isn't sense – it's insanity!

The 1983 General Election

The Labour manifesto, agreed on the day Blair knocked on John Burton's door, promised a non-nuclear defence policy; withdrawal from Europe; a rise in public spending, including a 50 per cent rise in local council spending, paid for by borrowing; the return of privatised industries to public ownership and 'public investment' in others; a Price Commission which could freeze or cut prices; and the reversal of council house sales.

It would have been a difficult programme to sell at the best of times. But the Labour campaign in 1983 was publicly described by Roy Hattersley as a 'shambles'. A shambles was originally a board on which meat scraps and offal would be displayed for sale, and the grisly metaphor was appropriate. Professor David Butler wrote, 'It is difficult to think of any campaign fought by a major party since the war that was more inept,' and thought that, after the turmoil since 1979, it was the beginning of the end: 'Future historians may well see the period as a crucial stage in the decline and fall of the Labour Party.'[4]

Historians may now see the period differently. But there is no denying that, on 9 June 1983, the party nearly carried out its suicide threat. Margaret Thatcher inspired adulation and loathing in roughly equal measure, but she benefited from a divided opposition. Labour gained only 28 per cent of the national vote, and just avoided getting fewer votes than the Liberal–SDP Alliance, on 26 per cent. In Sedgefield, the future leader of the Labour Party was elected with a majority of 8,281 votes. He had squeezed into Parliament not at the last minute but during extra time. His father, Leo, came to the count – intensely proud of him, despite their political differences. Nearly 300 miles away, in Thanet North, his wife was pushed into third place by the Alliance and only just saved her deposit.

Afterwards, Blair wrote to thank all the people in Trimdon who had helped him. Peter Brookes is the only one who still has his letter, dated 20 June 1983: 'There was one thing that I really wanted to do, and I have been given the chance by you to do it. I only hope your faith in me will be repaid.'

Tony Blair was asked by his school magazine in December 1991: 'What makes a Fettesian become a Labour MP?' His reply: 'A catalogue of errors and mistakes.' Actually it was luck, and a lot of hard work. John Burton was the most important person in securing the seat for Blair. After the election, when they were in a car together, Blair turned to him and said: 'I'll say this once, and I won't say it again. I can never, ever repay you for what you've done for me.' Burton is quite open about living his political ambitions through Blair. Although he considered standing for Parliament again in 1992, he worked as Blair's assistant in the constituency after retiring as a teacher at the beginning of 1994.

Blair's luck was not just in scraping into Parliament at the last possible moment, but in being elected for Sedgefield. It is a place which gave him roots. In his first speech in the Commons, Blair described the 'real community' of Fishburn, under threat from the closure of its main employer: 'The constituency of Sedgefield is made up of such communities. The local Labour Party grows out of, and is part of, local life. That is its strength.' It was true enough. And it was going to become more true.

Paul Trippett remembers celebrating Blair's election with Phil Wilson in the Red Lion until 4am. 'Then I had to get up to go to work on the Friday. I was tired. I felt empty, I just felt nothing. But then that weekend we all talked about it with Tony, about how we would make it the best constituency in the country, and it started again.'

Notes

1. Most of the quotations in this chapter are from a series of interviews with John Burton, Paul Trippett, Peter Brookes and Phil Wilson in July 1994.
2. Tony Blair, Sedgefield CV, see pp. 102–3.
3. Speech at the opening of the Durham Chorister pre-prep school, October 1993.
4. David Butler and Dennis Kavanagh, *The British General Election of 1983*, pp. 64, 274.

PART TWO

MP

7

Up Your Ladder

Backbencher and Treasury Spokesman, 1983–87

> 'To begin with, I thought there was absolutely no chance of my ever leading the Labour Party.'
>
> —*Tony Blair, 2000*

At the age of thirty, Tony Blair was the youngest member of the Parliamentary Labour Party, a bloodied rump army. The Labour left was ruined, but could not see it. Its leader Tony Benn lost his Bristol seat, but in his battle-delirium he welcomed heroic defeat as moral victory – 'eight and a half million votes for socialism'.

As Blair had observed in his Australian lecture at the end of the previous year, the electoral system almost guaranteed Labour a 'solid 200-seat base', but how solid that base really was seemed in doubt. In fact the party received a terrible shock, returning just 209 MPs – he was one of only thirty-two new Labour members – who faced a Conservative majority of 144.

Over the next four years it was often unclear whether the party had either the unity or the will to continue. Blair's first business as a new Labour MP was to take a position in the leadership election, which started on the Sunday after the election, when Michael Foot announced his resignation. Four candidates immediately emerged: Neil Kinnock, Roy Hattersley, Peter Shore and Eric Heffer. Bryan Gould, returning to the House after an absence of four years, threw himself into Shore's campaign:

> The first time I really registered Tony as a person was when we held a meeting in one of those 'W' rooms, down off Westminster Hall, and it was a fairly small meeting I'm sorry to say. Peter's candidature didn't really get off

> the ground. But one of the people who did turn up – there weren't more than a dozen or so – was Tony Blair. And I immediately thought, 'Well, here's a bright young new member, this is rather encouraging.' But I spoke briefly to Tony afterwards and it became clear that he was going to all the meetings. He obviously thought the House of Commons was like going up to university – you went to Buddhists and you went to the communists and you picked up their literature and you decided which of the clubs you'd join.

Gould supported Shore principally because they were both firmly opposed to membership of the European Community, and it was plain to Gould that Blair did not share that view. In fact, the tide of opinion in the party was turning. During the leadership election campaign, Kinnock argued that Britain had been in the Community for over ten years, and that Labour would have to accept that it was no longer practical to come out. Kinnock was the front-runner for the leadership from the moment Foot resigned – in fact, Foot's resignation had been timed deliberately to assist him.[1] Blair backed the 'dream ticket' of Kinnock for leader, Hattersley for deputy.

Over the next nine years, Blair was to develop a close relationship with Kinnock, to the point where, when Kinnock resigned in 1992, Blair was a possible contender for the deputy leadership of the party. By then, Kinnock and Blair were bound together in the common 'project' of party modernisation, with Blair at its leading edge.

In his Australian lecture in 1982, Blair had said that Labour could defeat the Conservatives 'without altering its policies at all. Its policies indeed already recognise, if sometimes unconsciously, the changes that have taken place in our social and economic attitudes.' His lawyer friend Charles Falconer observed in 1994:

> I think there was a real sea-change in Tony's attitude to things after '83. Because I think the '83 defeat is seminal. Obviously he was aware of the shortcomings of the position in 1983, but it was quite a stunning defeat in '83, not because it was unexpected but because it was large. Tony Blair in the early 1980s was less radical than now. Now he realises that the Labour Party needs to re-create itself; then he was defensive of many things in the party. His position now is much more destructive of the Labour Party as we know it, which I say is a good thing. Tony in the period after the '83 election became aware that here was a party that could not begin to cope with what was happening politically. Without change, he came to believe at that period, and always said it since '83, without fundamental change in the Labour Party, we would never win.[2]

Despite this testimony, it is difficult to trace Blair's transformation from labour movement orthodoxy to arch-revisionism in his public utterances for some time. There were clues, such as his repeated insistence on the party's need to keep up with social change. 'The image of the Labour Party has got to be more dynamic, more modern . . . Over 50 per cent of the population are owner-occupiers – that means a change in attitude that we've got to catch up to,' he said in his first television interview as a 'typical new Labour MP' in a Westminster pub on *Newsnight* on 22 June 1983. But when it came to specifics, he was guarded.

In his first speech in the House of Commons on 6 July, he made one point that the divided party could still agree on – that mass unemployment was unacceptable. He said that, without work, his constituents 'not only suffer the indignity of enforced idleness – they wonder how they can afford to get married, to start a family, and to have access to all the benefits of society that they should be able to take for granted'.

It was a measure of how out of touch the Labour Party was in 1983 that this language of marriage and family sounded out of place; it was only reclaimed by Blair as shadow Home Secretary a decade later. He spoke an older language of ethical socialism too, in a passage of some power, in which he explained how the moral beliefs of his early adulthood had sought political expression:

> I am a socialist not through reading a textbook that has caught my intellectual fancy, nor through unthinking tradition, but because I believe that, at its best, socialism corresponds most closely to an existence that is both rational and moral. It stands for co-operation, not confrontation; for fellowship, not fear. It stands for equality, not because it wants people to be the same but because only through equality in our economic circumstances can our individuality develop properly. British democracy rests ultimately on the shared perception by all the people that they participate in the benefits of the common weal.

It was an eloquent and confident personal credo, which stands well as a summary of his political beliefs at the start of his steady and unshowy rise to the top of the Labour Party. Despite the rejection of textbooks, the language – 'the common weal', 'equality' (specifically 'equality in our economic circumstances') and the Christian-socialist word 'fellowship' – reeks of R. H. Tawney and other dusty tomes.

It is instructive to compare it with the new version of Clause IV of Labour's constitution adopted twelve years later, in which 'equality' only appeared as the less distinctive 'equality of opportunity'. The ideas in 1983 were also simpler. The philosophical mantra of John Macmurray – translated in the new Clause IV as 'by the strength of our common endeavour we achieve more than we achieve alone' – is missing, despite supposedly being such a persistent influence from Oxford days. The rights and duties which arise from Macmurray's work are also absent – to be rediscovered, if not re-invented, later.

As he developed his analysis of what had gone wrong, he had to judge how much of it he could safely express. An early, bruising experience is part of the Blair mythology. Soon after the election, the hard left in Spennymoor in his constituency organised a 'public meeting' – the sort of meeting no normal member of the public would ever attend – to build on the Great Leap Forward for socialism which the 1983 election represented.

Blair agreed to speak, and described the meeting – a little dramatically – as 'the greatest humiliation I have ever experienced'. He argued that the party had to change, that it had lost touch with society, and that many of the changes in society were for the better. Although his Sedgefield fan club was there, the mood was hostile. In the version told by Blair's agent John Burton, the left-wing MP Dennis Skinner spoke after Blair, and savaged him for 'betraying socialist principles'. As Skinner was speaking, Les Huckfield, Blair's rival for the Sedgefield seat and no longer an MP, walked in. '*There* is a man true to his socialist principles,' declared Skinner, pointing, to loud applause.

After the meeting, Blair told Burton: 'Maybe I was wrong, I shouldn't have said those things.'

Burton replied: 'You must never stop saying those things. You mustn't move towards the party. The party must move towards you.'[3]

This is a moral fable which has been lovingly retouched in the memory. Skinner remembers it differently, pointing out that he would never have praised Les Huckfield, a former right-winger and ministerial rival to his ally Bob Cryer. Nor does he remember attacking Blair personally, although he would certainly have disagreed with him.

Much of the reformation that took place in the Kinnock years appears in retrospect obvious and inevitable, but the task of rebuilding the party took a long time. Although the shock of near oblivion in the 1983 election convinced many that the party had to change, the party's instinctive reaction to specific changes was to suspect betrayal. Many of those who voted for Kinnock as leader were the kind of socialists, once identified by Richard Crossman, who were 'always looking around for someone to betray them'.

Although Foot had moved against Militant in 1982, for example, it was not until Kinnock's 1985 conference speech that the battle was really won, and two supporters of the tendency were still Labour MPs until they were expelled from the party in 1991. When Blair was first allocated an office as a new MP he had to share with one of them, Dave Nellist. There was hardly a meeting of minds between the Militant and the lawyer who had devised the tendency's expulsion.

After a few months Blair found more palatable company.

Two bright boys

Blair and Gordon Brown shared a windowless office in the Palace of Westminster until Brown was elected to the shadow Cabinet in 1987. They got to know each other soon after Blair noticed Brown's debut in the House on 27 July 1983. Brown's speech does not read well now – it is a wall of statistics about poverty and the meanness of the social security system – but (like Blair's) it was delivered with confidence and authority and (unlike Blair's) some wit. He recalled what the then Minister for Social Security, Rhodes Boyson, a gothic item of mill-town splendour, had written five years earlier about the ease of gaining self-employed work: 'To become a window cleaner little equipment is needed – a bucket, a leather or two and a ladder.' Brown commented: 'When the Prime Minister talked regularly during the election about ladders of opportunity, I had not realised that the next Conservative government would have something quite so specific in mind.' To 'On your bike' Brown now added 'Up your ladder' as a Conservative solution to unemployment.

Like Blair's, Brown's underlying message was different from his later teachings. The implication then was that the most urgent business of socialism was to increase social security benefits.

Only two years older than Blair, Brown was an established politician when he entered the House of Commons. He was Chairman of the Scottish Labour Party, had written and edited books about Scottish politics, first stood for Parliament in 1979 and had been an elected student politician at Edinburgh University in the early 1970s, when Blair was at Oxford. Brown was a leader of the mainstream Labour left in Scotland, where the new Bennite left was less successful.

Whereas Blair could equally have supported Kinnock or Hattersley for the leadership in 1983, Brown was a purer Kinnockite. He joined the centre-left Tribune Group of MPs, of which Kinnock was the leading member, and was appointed to Kinnock's leadership campaign committee. (While the *Tribune* newspaper had fallen to the Bennites, the Tribune name was kept by what now became the centre grouping of MPs, and the hard left contingent broke away to form the Campaign Group.)

Blair's faction, the Labour Co-ordinating Committee, operated at the party's grass roots but not in Parliament. Paul Convery, then the secretary of the LCC, recalls the only meeting of the group's MPs just before the party conference in September 1984. Blair was there, along with Harriet Harman and Robin Cook (who was also a leading Tribunite). 'Tony Blair said he had no intention of working in any formal organisation of MPs and didn't see any value in it. The core of his case was that he saw correct argument and merit as the way to move the party, rather than factional organisation,' said Convery. This lofty attitude did not last long. The next year, 1985, Gordon Brown persuaded Blair to join the Tribune Group, partly because it was an instrument of Kinnock's tactic of detaching the soft from the hard left, but partly because it was a 'ladder of opportunity' to the shadow Cabinet.

From the start of their partnership, Brown was the senior member, better versed in the ways of the Labour Party, and – as a former television reporter and editor – in the ways of the media. He also expounded with some authority a compelling and damning analysis of the state of the party at the time. Falconer is one of several witnesses who attest to Blair's awe of Brown. He said Blair was 'mammothly dazzled by Brown's power. I don't think he ever thought at that stage that he would be leader of the party. People always regarded Brown as the obvious man.'[4]

The relationship was not wholly unequal. Blair had a better sense of how middle-class English voters thought, and was more in touch with people who were not in politics. But he knew little about journalism. He watched admiringly as Brown made the headlines, often with leaked government documents. Blair, meanwhile, could not even get Labour Party bodies to publish his Great Thoughts. The Fabian Society rejected his draft for a pamphlet on the subject of 'community' soon after the 1983 election.

Blair and Brown had their first taste of political advancement through the patronage of the right of the Labour Party. John Smith had spotted their talent before they entered the House. He knew Brown as the candidate in his home constituency of South Edinburgh in 1979, and Blair through his friend Derry Irvine.

As soon as Blair came into the House, Smith was recommending him. The Labour MP Tam Dalyell, still indefatigably pursuing conspiracy theories about the sinking of the *Belgrano* in the Falklands War, sought Smith's opinion on a point of international law:

> John said, 'I can't do this, my mind is on all sorts of other things, but if you want to ask a lawyer, go and search out Tony Blair, who has worked for me and Derry Irvine, who is an absolutely brilliant lawyer, a better lawyer than I am, in these matters, and ask him for an opinion.' Now, I explained this problem to Tony Blair as an educated layman would. All I can say is, the following day, he produced a two-page handwritten synopsis of the

major legal points, and it was extremely skilfully done. I've always said that he had an extremely elegant, sharp mind.

Outside Parliament, Blair had opposed the 'Tebbit Bill', which became the 1982 Employment Act. Inside Parliament, he now had the chance to oppose the next Bill to reform trade union law, brought in by Tom King, Norman Tebbit's successor as Employment Secretary. This Bill, which became the 1984 Trade Union Act, brought in the legal requirement on unions to hold ballots before calling strikes, opposition to which now appears quixotic. Indeed, in his parliamentary debut in policy debate, Blair appeared a youthful Don Quixote, tilting enthusiastically at windmills in a well-meaning but over-excited fashion.

Unlike his 'maiden' speech, Blair's first engagement in the regular rough and tumble of the Commons contained no hint of future promise. Called to speak in the first debate on the Bill, on 8 November 1983, he denounced it as 'a scandalous and undemocratic measure'.[5] Another participant in that debate, a new Conservative MP and fellow barrister called Michael Howard, would throw those words back at him six years later, when he and Blair faced each other from the front benches over yet another Employment Bill. By then, Labour had accepted the central principles of the 1984 legislation.

Blair declared that the issue 'is not whether elections are good or bad, but whether it is right for the state to intervene and dictate to trade unions how they should conduct their affairs'.[6] That was not the issue at all. What mattered was whether union members needed to be protected, and whether there was a wider public interest in how unions conducted their internal affairs. Other provisions of the Bill may have been biased, such as that requiring unions to ballot on political donations while imposing no equivalent obligation on companies, but Blair went too far when he declared that the Bill as a whole 'has nothing to do with democracy – it has everything to do with interfering with the rights of British trade unionists to organise freely in the association of their own choice'. He came close to calling on the unions to rise up against the legislation: 'It is a disgrace that we should be debating today the taking away of fundamental freedoms for which British trade unionists have fought for a long time. Having fought long and hard for them, they will not give them up lightly.'[7]

Hobnailed boots

If Blair did not make an immediate mark in House of Commons debates, he had fallen among people, like Smith and Brown, who could teach him. As the new shadow Employment Secretary, John Smith chose the Labour backbenchers who would serve on the committee to examine the Bill line by line. From the new intake, he chose Brown and Blair. In the more informal atmosphere of committee proceedings, Blair's performance was initially even more fevered and histrionic. In November 1983 he opened with a tirade about how it was 'unacceptable in a democratic society' for a government to interfere in the internal affairs of a union – an association in which 'people come together voluntarily and decide how their constitution will be run' – by telling them 'to have elections, and when, where and how to have them'.

The wind of indignation was taken out of his sails by the Conservative MP John Townend, who asked mildly if he would describe closed shops, in which union membership was a condition of employment, as voluntary organisations. Blair was suddenly on the defensive:

> One reason why closed shops exist and are accepted by both sides is that it is much easier for collective bargaining purposes to have a trade union dealing with the employer. If people are to have the benefit of that collective bargaining process, there should be some commensurate duty placed on them also.[8]

He was back on his high horse the next month, over the clause in the Bill which required that paid officials of a union who had a vote on its ruling body be directly elected by union members – again, a reasonable measure at a time when some unions wielded considerable power, sometimes on the basis of a closed shop, but to which Blair proposed an amendment. 'We have heard a lot of self-righteous and sanctimonious pap about the rule of law from the government over the past four weeks, but here we see the government's true attitude to the rule of law,' he declared, self-righteously and sanctimoniously. The Bill would breach contracts entered into in good faith by a union general secretary, he said:

> He may alter his whole life; he may move his family and give up lucrative alternative employment to give his services to the trade union movement . . . It is the amalgamated association of contract breakers on the government benches who are the true bully boys when it comes to the rule of law. It is they who . . . impose a mass legal picket to prevent him [from entering] his place of work in accordance with his contract . . . It is a disgraceful notion that an agreement freely entered into by two contracting parties should be torn up or smashed to smithereens in this cavalier and irresponsible fashion. It is the hooligan element on the government benches whose disrespect for the rule of law is made obvious by their opposition to the amendment.

The committee chairman, the genial Conservative MP for Maidstone, John Wells, called Blair to order: '"Hooligan element" is a very strong term – it is not actually unparliamentary – to apply to a body of men who look like a vicarage tea party.'

Like a cheeky schoolboy, Blair immediately took the joke too far:

> I must stand corrected, Mr Wells, but I am sure that you appreciate the extreme provocation under which we are constantly put. Despite the ties and suits worn by Conservative Members, I am sure that if we looked under the desks we should see their hobnailed boots ready to trample over the rights of trade unionists.

Wells was not amused: 'I tried in jocular fashion to ask the Honourable Member to moderate his language. If he will not take the jocular hint, I must ask him to continue to be humorous, because that makes our proceedings pleasant, but to stick strictly to the amendments.' Realising his mistake, Blair now backpedalled, retracting as best he could the most damaging phrase: 'Of course, Mr Wells, I was referring only metaphorically to intellectual hobnailed boots.'[9]

But it was not long before he was again carried away when concluding the Opposition's argument:

> Trade union officials are taken on and given a contract on a certain basis and then these sanctimonious preachers of the rule of law intend to drive a coach and horses through the contractual rights of these officials and apply a straitjacket which is not wanted by the official, the executive of the union, or the membership . . .

John Selwyn Gummer, the Minister of State replying for the government, mocked his mixed metaphors:

> The temperature has been raised many times this morning over what is a simple matter . . . He suggested we were sanctimonious preachers and that we were driving coaches and horses and seeking to apply a straitjacket – all in one sentence! All that we are saying is that a person who has a vote on a principal executive committee should be elected.[10]

Despite the allegedly transforming effect of the 1983 election defeat on Blair's outlook, the committee minutes reveal no evidence that he recognised that the perception that the unions were above the law was damaging to Labour. 'I believe that one of the most dangerous things for the rule of law is the involvement of courts in industrial relations,' he told the committee.[11]

Gummer was a seasoned minister whom Labour MPs could not ruffle. The new junior member of the government's employment team, Alan Clark, was another matter. During his first, woefully unprepared speech to the committee, the Labour old stager Ian Mikardo asked the Secretary of State in a loud aside: 'Where did you find this geezer, Tom?'[12] It was that experience on 6 December 1983 that Clark described as 'ghastly' in his *Diaries*: 'Labour has a very tough team. Little John Smith, rotund, bespectacled, Edinburgh lawyer. Been around for ages . . . And two bright boys called Brown and Blair.'

Clark got little help from his own side while Labour MPs were 'bobbing up all over the place, asking impossible, spastic questions of detail'. He was ambushed by the chairman on 24 January 1984, who asked him what GMBATU stood for – it was John Smith's union. He got as far as 'General' before having to be prompted by Conservative MPs on the Municipal, then guessed the B was for Building and, when told it was Boilermakers, kept calling it the Boilerbuilders and Allied Trades Union. He was also reluctant to let Blair interrupt his speech because Blair had missed the previous session, he noticed. 'While we were debating on Thursday—'

'Do not go on,' interjected John Smith.

'—the Honourable Gentleman was otherwise occupied, whether gainfully I do not know. I do not know whether he has any industrial relations clients left . . .'

Blair rose gleefully: 'I was present at the birth of my first child. I can assure the Under-Secretary that that was not gainful employment. This morning I am feeling the first effects of spending nights in the same house as the baby, having just brought it home.'

To Labour hoots of 'We did warn you', Clark apologised fulsomely: 'Yes, in their friendly and communicative way Honourable Members warned me, but I went straight on into the ambush, as I fully accept. I congratulate the Honourable Member for Sedgefield on an event which I have experienced periodically.'

The chairman intervened again: 'Order. The Honourable Gentleman cannot experience the birth of his first child periodically.'

'I have never actually attended—'

'Order,' repeated Wells. 'This is far too enjoyable.'

New man

The arrival of Tony and Cherie's first son, Euan, had been coyly advertised in Blair's CV for the Sedgefield seat eight months before: 'Cherie and I, as yet, have no children.' Nicholas and Kathryn followed at approximately two-year intervals:

> I attended the births of Euan and Kathryn, and only missed the arrival of Nicholas because he was early. I was in the constituency and had to race through the night to get back to London. Euan took ages, a day more or

less, and had to be induced. Kathryn was a Caesarean and all over in forty-five minutes. You feel pretty useless. But I'm pleased I was there. It's good for your partner, I think, and you're humbled by what she goes through.[13]

That year, the family also bought 'Myrobella', a large old house tucked behind a terrace of miners' cottages in Trimdon station, in the centre of his Sedgefield constituency. The house came with an Aga, dating from the time before such a thing became a sociological marker, but which matched their lifestyle. The family began a life based in London, with a weekend home in an unusual part of the country. In 1986 they moved 'up' in London from Hackney to Islington, the modern equivalent of Hugh Gaitskell's liberal Hampstead. When Blair became leader, Charles Falconer said: 'They've got a life firmly based in London – quite sensibly. They go to Sedgefield a lot, but they live as a family together, rather than living these etiolated lives that a lot of politicians live.'[14]

Cherie continued to be active in the Labour Party. At the end of 1983 she was elected to the Executive of the Labour Co-ordinating Committee, as it developed first as a source of 'critical support' for Kinnock's leadership, and then as a 'moderniser' faction arguing the case for heretical rethinking of policy, and for one member, one vote democracy in the party. Despite sharing a platform with Tony Benn in the election campaign, and despite her father's campaigning for him in the 1984 Chesterfield by-election, she was now one of the minor leaders of the counter-revolution. Her manifesto for the Executive said, in language identical to her husband's: 'The Labour Party must be more than just a party of activists. It must be part of the community and have a democratic relationship with the community as a whole.' She was re-elected for another year in December 1984.

The LCC was also becoming a platform for centre-left activists to become better known in the party as a step up into Parliament. Eight of Cherie's fellow members of the Executive later became MPs – Peter Hain, Kate Hoey, Mike Gapes, John Denham, Mike Connarty and Barbara Roche – or Euro-MPs – Wayne David and Anita Pollack. Cherie, however, decided that one politician in the family was enough, and her priorities became 'family and work – politics comes third', said friend Islington neighbour Margaret Hodge, MP for Barking. Although she ceased to be active, she and Blair were still members when the LCC was finally wound up, its work done, in December 1998.

During her time on the LCC Executive, Cherie took sides in at least one significant debate. The testing issue for the left in 1984–85 was the miners' strike. Although she came from a mining family, some on the Executive remember her as one of those most opposed to the strike. The argument was not about the justice of the miners' cause, but the fact that they had been called out without a ballot. The clarity of her stance is to her credit, as many in the Labour Party were trapped in hand-wringing equivocation, including the leader. Neil Kinnock later felt the strike was a 'lost year' in the modernisation of Labour.

Tony's view was the same as Cherie's, but he avoided taking a public position on the strike. Before the strike began, he had expressed support for the economic case on which it was based: 'There is no inevitable or inexorable fate that dictates that mines must close. It is a matter of political choice and judgment . . . There is nothing odd about subsidising an industry. To proceed in such a way is sensible.'[15] During the strike, however, he confined himself to expressing his concern that the police were exceeding their powers when Kent miners were stopped at the Dartford Tunnel on their way to picket pits in the Midlands.

On the LCC, Cherie was better known as the daughter of Tony Booth than as the wife of Tony Blair. She later said: 'I started life as the daughter of someone, now I am the wife of someone and I'll probably end up as the mother of someone.'[16]

First rung

She started on the role of 'wife of someone' in November 1984. After only seventeen months in Parliament, Tony Blair was summoned to the Leader's Office. 'Tony was absolutely shivering,' according to Charles Clarke, Neil Kinnock's Chief of Staff. 'He had no idea what it was. What had he done? The idea that he might be on the front bench was absolutely beyond him. It was the first time he'd been called to see the leader. And he was knocked absolutely flat.'

According to Kinnock, he said to Blair: 'I'd like you to go on the front bench.' There was a long silence, and he added: 'Don't you want to go on the front bench?'

'Yes. Yes, I do,' said Blair.

'Well, listen, I want you to be in our team and that's that.'

'I want to be in the team, too.'

'What's the matter then?' Kinnock asked.

'I'm a bit surprised.'

About one-third of Labour MPs were members of the 'shadow government'. Blair now joined shadow Chancellor Roy Hattersley's team as its most junior member. His was hailed as 'the fastest promotion since David Owen's in 1968',[17] although that was in government, not in Opposition.

Hattersley had been impressed when he first met Blair during the

Beaconsfield by-election campaign the year before he was elected. Apart from Blair's intelligence and capacity for hard work, one detail had stuck in Hattersley's mind: 'Tony's one of the most polite people I've ever met. It's a very minor qualification, but I think I've probably done fifty by-elections and only two candidates sent me letters afterwards. And Tony was one of them.' (The other was Tony Benn.) However, Hattersley made no grand claims for his prescience, having told Blair's father, in the manner of an indulgent headteacher, that, if his son 'kept his nose both clean and to the grindstone, he might do quite well in politics'.[18]

Gordon Brown, meanwhile, declined the offer of a shadow Scottish Office post, because he did not want to be typecast as a Scottish politician. He joined John Smith's trade and industry team the following year.

Blair was clearly ambitious, but avoided giving the impression of self-promotion. Hattersley said he shared Kinnock's restless insistence on the need to win power: 'One of his abiding features when he was a very young Member was that he was always saying that there's no point in doing things if we didn't win.' Kinnock was contemptuous of those of his colleagues who regarded the business of Opposition as an end in itself and who talked of their front-bench positions as jobs. 'Jobs they ain't,' he snarled. Apart from 'Leader of the Opposition', Blair never listed his Opposition posts in *Who's Who*.

Blair cannot have been an MP for long before he made some calculations about the future. He never thought Labour would win the 1987 election. But he might have expected to be in the shadow Cabinet (as he was) by the election after that, which he must have thought Labour could win. High ministerial office, maybe, but probably not the premiership. 'To begin with, I thought there was absolutely no chance of my ever leading the Labour Party. For the first ten years, I would say it never crossed my mind,' he said later. 'I thought I was too moderate and too different from the archetypal Labour leader.'[19]

One consequence of his early promotion is that he hardly took part in the main event of the House of Commons, Prime Minister's Questions, until he became Leader of the Opposition. Apart from the party leaders themselves, the occasion is considered to be primarily one for back-benchers. Margaret Thatcher was at her peak: 'It was the clear sense of an identifiable project for the Tory party that I did admire. It is absolutely essential in politics. That is what keeps you going.'[20] Her admirer, Tony Blair, speaking in 1994, first clashed with her ten years earlier. Sarah Tisdall had just been jailed for leaking to the *Guardian* a memo on the concealment of the deployment of US cruise missiles to Greenham Common. He asked for a freedom of information law:

> When people can be imprisoned for six months for, in effect, telling the British public what the government should have told them, does the Right Honourable Lady not agree that there is an urgent need for legislation so that, while the interests of our national security are protected, the government cannot conceal the scale of what they are doing?

Thatcher cuffed him away. No government, she said, can carry on its business unless it can 'trust those in the civil service who have charge of secret documents to keep those documents to themselves'.[21]

His third question to her, in October 1984, produced a memorable answer. He asked how she squared Chancellor Nigel Lawson's statement that 'unemployment is not an economic problem but only a human or social one' with her recent endorsement of the 1944 Employment White Paper. Her government was considered to have abandoned 'full employment' – a cross-party goal launched by the wartime coalition which, as Blair said, 'puts the battle for jobs at the heart of economic policy'.

She claimed that the White Paper had 'a great deal in common with the policies the government are pursuing—' before being interrupted by disbelieving Labour MPs. 'I have a copy in my handbag,' she declared. She pulled it out and quoted from it: 'Without a rising standard of industrial efficiency we cannot achieve a high level of employment combined with a rising standard of living.'[22] Thus did Blair help make Thatcher's handbag famous.

Roy Hattersley was impressed with his new recruit:

> He was just as good as I expected him to be. He was hugely industrious and could always do it. If he had to do hideous things in the House of Commons, like wind up on the third day of the Finance Bill, he would always do it well. You knew there were only five people in the House, and I was one of them. One of the others was that man who was Financial Secretary and was going to be prime minister – John Moore. And John Moore would make a hideously embarrassing speech, declaiming to the House. Tony would make a complete little rounded speech that you'd be pleased to read in *Hansard*.

Having made an early impact in the House, Blair also started to become better known in the party and on the media. He remained in touch with the grass roots through the Labour Co-ordinating Committee. In the spring of 1985, LCC Secretary Paul Convery organised a series of fringe meetings at regional Labour Party conferences, and remembered Blair speaking at the Southern Region:

> We were pushing the themes of modernisation of the party apparatus, of developing it as a campaigning organisation, of building the membership. He spoke without notes to a meeting of about twelve people, most of whom

> seemed to come from Thanet North, where Cherie had been the candidate. It was a very, very interesting speech. I was struck by the themes, very much what he is saying now – the need for morality, a strong moral base. And I was struck by the style, the reflective style. I thought two things: 'I've never heard anybody speak like this,' and 'Jolly posh chap, this.'

Blair first appeared on BBC1's *Question Time* on 16 May 1985. Just to be invited into this television arena was a great step for a rising politician. Blair beat Gordon Brown to it by three years. He was articulate and confident, opening with one of his theme tunes, Bipartisan Reasonableness: 'If I could begin on a positive point and say what areas of the new public order legislation one could agree with – there are measures to tighten up the laws against racism and measures to tighten up the law against football hooliganism . . .'

It was the day the Liberal–SDP Alliance pushed the Conservatives into third place in a Gallup poll. Sir Peter Parker, aged sixty, claimed the Alliance was the force of the future and teased the 32-year-old Blair as one of the 'tired young men from the Labour Party'.

Blair returned the back-handed compliment by accepting that Labour and the Alliance desired the same ends:

> If you can accept that there is virtually a consensus against this government, the choice for the country is whether they want the politics of the Alliance, which is all words and aspirations, or whether they want the Labour Party, which has the policies to translate those aspirations into reality.

His private view, in fact, was that the Labour Party's policies were far from ready to meet anything quite so testing as reality.

Blair's main energies in this period were still directed to developing his reputation in the Commons. Although its importance is sometimes overrated, performance in the House is still an essential test for a politician aspiring to the highest office. After tackling the Prime Minister, he tussled with the Chancellor of the Exchequer, Nigel Lawson, whose intellectual clarity he admired. In January 1985, he invited Lawson to reject the 'ludicrous dogma that government intervention is always wrong and market forces are always right', which inspired a typically magisterial put-down: 'Nobody is always right, not even the Honourable Gentleman . . . Experience shows that, on the whole, it is easier for markets to correct mistakes, even though they make them, than it is for interventionist governments to do so.'[23]

The Chancellor airily patronised the most junior member of the Opposition Treasury team on another occasion, saying, 'The difference between the two sides of the House is that the Opposition discuss problems, but we solve them,' a point not lost on his opponent.[24] It was not until 1987 that Blair was getting anywhere near even in his clashes with Lawson. On 29 April, shortly before the election was called, the Chancellor tried to downplay a Treasury study which showed that tax cuts did not create jobs. When Blair commended the study as 'excellent', Lawson asked: 'Has the Honourable Gentleman read it?'

Blair replied crisply, 'I have read it,' and chided him: 'It is wrong of the Right Honourable Gentleman to commission a report and then dismiss it simply because he does not like the findings.'

Although Blair attacked free-market 'dogma', Lawson felt, like many Conservatives, that his opponent was engaged in lawyerly dispute rather than ideological disagreement:

> I was always slightly surprised that he was in the Labour Party at all. He is quite definitely the least socialist leader the Labour Party has ever had. Someone like John Smith was a moderate socialist, on the right of the party, instinctively, in his bones. I don't feel Tony Blair is – I don't want to cause trouble for him – but I don't feel he is a socialist.[25]

Blair certainly looked and sounded more like a Conservative MP. In June 1986, he took to the high life, flying by Concorde to the United States to lobby James Baker, the Treasury Secretary, against plans to impose so-called 'unitary' taxes on British companies operating in America. It was an expensive trip, paid for by a business pressure group called the Unitary Tax Campaign through a lobbying company, Ian Greer Associates. There was confusion over whether it should have been recorded in the Register of MPs' Interests. Three MPs were on the all-party trip: Ian Wrigglesworth, the Alliance economics spokesman, registered it; Sir Michael Grylls, a Conservative backbencher, listed himself as an adviser to 'the Unitary Tax Campaign (Ian Greer Associates)'; Blair, however, felt he had nothing to declare.

Nine years later, when Conservatives used the trip to attack him, Blair explained that it had been on 'quasi-official' business: Norman Lamont, Financial Secretary to the Treasury, had briefed Grylls for the trip and met the group afterwards; Lawson wrote to Baker asking him to see them.[26] Indeed, there was an element of smear in the attack, in that Ian Greer's company also acted for Mohamed Fayed, and was the conduit for his payment to Conservative MP Tim Smith for asking parliamentary questions. Blair was also clearly engaged in serious – not to say highly technical – business as an unofficial emissary of the government. However, the fact that a trip was official did not exempt MPs from registering an interest. 'A distinction seems to have arisen in the minds of some Members,' the Select Committee on Members' Interests reported later, between visits 'which were essentially connected with official duties and those which were primarily recreational. We would emphasise that no such distinction has ever been reflected in the Rules.'[27] (This was one mistake from which Blair did not learn: he was caught out on exactly the same point when he failed to register a trip with his family to Silverstone racing circuit in 1996.*) Furthermore, it would be hard to argue that the group had to fly by Concorde, and anyone scrupulous about the 'highest standards of honesty and propriety in public life', as Blair later became, would have registered it just to be on the safe side.

Premonitions

Shadowing the Treasury during Lawson's zenith gave Blair an early taste of an issue of enduring political significance – European monetary integration. It was part of the founding ambition of the creators of the European Community to achieve 'economic and monetary union'. Put simply, the authors of this vision wanted all tariffs and other barriers to trade abolished, leading in time to the establishment of one money across Europe, replacing national currencies.

This stage would be arrived at by gradually linking the currencies more closely in the Exchange Rate Mechanism. Britain's Labour government refused to join the ERM when it was set up in 1979, and for a long time monetary union seemed a distant goal. But when Jacques Delors became European Commission President in 1985, he drove the plan forward at a time when the ERM had become a stable, low-inflation club.

This forced politicians to think about the reality of greater European integration, and nowhere was the controversy more divisive than in Britain. It was the economic and political question which would destroy first Lawson, then Geoffrey Howe and then Thatcher herself.

At the beginning of 1986 Blair had to take a position on what was then the relatively obscure question of the ERM. The bulk of the Labour Party still regarded the European Community with suspicion as a capitalist club. It was one they no longer wanted to leave but still wanted to change fundamentally. They voted against the Single European Act later that year not because it was creeping federalism – the reason why Margaret Thatcher later regretted it – but because it cleared the ground for market forces without adequate social protection.

On 29 January 1986 Blair gave Labour's reasons for opposing a Liberal–SDP Alliance motion that Britain should join the ERM 'forthwith'. Some commentators had urged Britain's entry the previous autumn

---

*See p. 363.

as a defence against inflation and financial instability. Lawson later revealed that both he as Chancellor and Howe as Foreign Secretary had favoured entry in November 1985, but had been overruled by the Prime Minister.[28] In the debate, Blair started by arguing against the ERM in practice, rather than in principle. 'The balance of advantage still lies against our joining,' he said. It was

> essentially a means to an end, and for it to succeed there must be a clear and common area of agreement between members on economic policy and objectives. We are not convinced that policy objectives that are currently pursued in the European Monetary System converge sufficiently with those which we would want to be pursued domestically.

However, he then went beyond the 'balance of advantage' line to use what would later be Eurosceptical language against the principle of joining the ERM, describing it as 'essentially a Deutschmark bloc. It could be said that we would be putting Herr Pohl of the Bundesbank in 11 Downing Street.'

He went on: 'The exchange rate is important, but is a residuary [sic], not a fundamental.'[29] By this he meant that membership of the ERM would require economic policy to be directed to maintaining a certain exchange rate when the pound's value on the foreign exchanges ought to reflect the 'fundamentals' – the soundness – of the British economy. This was the orthodox economic theory espoused by Thatcher and her adviser Alan Walters, and initially by Lawson. But Lawson had come round to the view that ERM membership, by tying Britain to the conservative German central bank, would give people confidence that inflation would be lower in future.

Blair's argument appeared to be at the same time one of timing and of principle. He complained that the Alliance was suggesting immediate entry at a time when the pound was sinking, but also pointed to the difficulty of ever pursuing Britain's interests under the constraints of the ERM. He seemed to imply that, in time, the economic policies of the ERM countries might converge with 'those which we would want to be pursued domestically'. But he also seemed to say that economic policy should always be decided by national politics, and not by the Bundesbank, which dominated ERM policy-making. He stressed that Labour and the Alliance would always want to pursue a more expansionist policy than either the Conservatives or the Bundesbank.

Although his attitude to them was inconsistent, Blair had at least identified the fundamental and difficult issues. As Bryan Gould, who was to take the opposite view, remarked, 'You get the impression with Tony that there is a brain being engaged, somehow.' But Blair, for all his professed interest in economics, would never have been, like Lawson or Gordon Brown, an economists' politician. Gould also commented cruelly: 'Whatever is Labour Party orthodoxy, Tony believes that.'

Since he voted 'Yes' in the referendum in 1975, Blair's attitude to Europe reflected the tensions which pulled at the party's policy. He publicly supported withdrawal in 1982–83, while privately stating his objections. In 1986 he attacked the ERM and the Single European Act, but was now edging towards the historic switch of 1988–89 when Labour would become more pro-European than the Conservatives. In 1986, his – and his party's – position resembles an artist's impression of the missing evolutionary link. It has some of the features of its ancestors, but also a clearly discernible new outline. The evolution of Labour policy, on Europe and other issues, was incomplete when the party next presented itself to the British people in 1987.

Media savvy

The party went in to the 1987 election campaign with essentially the same policies on defence and the economy as it had had in 1983. What was really different this time, however, was the party's understanding of modern techniques of television presentation and press management.

During the 1983–87 parliament, the five people who would be responsible for the creation of 'New Labour', the most successful rebranding exercise in democratic political marketing, came together. By the 1987 election, the core partnership of Blair and Brown was well-established. Both had met Alastair Campbell, a *Daily Mirror* journalist who was friendly with Neil Kinnock. Campbell claimed to have seen leadership potential in Blair the first time they met, in the Members' Lobby at the House of Commons in 1983: 'If you had said to me then: is this the kind of guy whom you would consider could one day be leader of the Labour Party, I'd have said yes.' But it would be a while before Campbell came to admire Blair's ability to analyse complex political situations and to work closely with him – lending him his skill as a tabloid journalist in return for ideas and insights for his columns: 'For someone who was then quite young he was really quite a reassuring figure, and I saw him as the kind of rounded, full personality who has an innate understanding of what makes people tick.'[30]

Another central character entered the Blair story in October 1985, when Peter Mandelson was appointed Labour Party director of communications. A few months younger than Blair, Mandelson was at Oxford at the same time as him. Asked if they knew each other then, Mandelson is said to have replied: 'No, I was interested in politics.' The grandson of wartime Home Secretary Herbert Morrison, he had been a member of the Young Communist League at Hendon County Grammar School and worked as a volunteer in Tanzania before going to Oxford. While in Africa, he wrote to a friend that at times 'I feel that my revolutionary ardour is fading because I am a bourgeois at heart'.[31] At university he was a Labour activist, but his early idealism had resolved into a firmly social-democratic outlook, and he was considered as pragmatic and opportunistic as he was later, working for Roy Hattersley's leadership campaign in 1983.

As a producer on London Weekend Television's *Weekend World* when he applied for the Labour Party job, Mandelson gave the impression that he knew about modern communication techniques. He did not, but he knew a man who did, and drafted in Philip Gould as a volunteer. Gould got into politics during his childhood in suburban Woking, where he went to a secondary modern school, leaving at sixteen with a single O-level in geography. He had worked in advertising, but desperately wanted to work on political campaigns for Labour. He became in effect the only 'political consultant' in Britain, a profession well-known in the different American system: a hired hand who runs campaigns for candidates, carrying out opinion polling, devising strategies and creating advertising. He quickly made himself indispensable.

Mandelson, meanwhile, turned out to have a genius for presentation and the old art, about to be given a new name and a new significance, of 'spin-doctoring'.* Along with campaigns co-ordinator Bryan Gould, he was the architect of Labour's highly professional and innovative 1987 election campaign.

After the 1987 election, Mandelson, Philip Gould and Campbell became increasingly important in advising Blair and Brown, and – especially when Bryan Gould started to falter – helped present them as the faces of the future in the 'new model party' which Kinnock was trying to construct.

Twelve years later, four of the five were the subject of seven biographies and the fifth had published his memoirs. At the time, however, they were relative unknowns, although Brown was an obvious rising star. Blair attracted a little media coverage for a long-running attack during 1985 on the secrecy with which the Bank of England used public money to bale out Johnson Matthey Bankers – but outside the House of Commons he

*The phrase was popularised in the United States in the 1984 Reagan–Mondale presidential campaign and quickly imported to Britain.

was one of several intelligent but anonymous middle-ranking front-benchers.

His friend from Hackney South Labour Party, John Lloyd, became editor of the *New Statesman* in August 1986, and commented on how important it was that 'Labour has a stronger shadow Treasury team'. Damning shadow Chancellor Roy Hattersley with faint praise, he turned to the rest of the line-up:

> Oonagh MacDonald has so far battled hard without too much effect and Terry Davis shows little signs of battling at all. Tony Blair, the bright young barrister who is the junior member of the team, has taken pains to bone up on his subject, but his eagerness does not amount to weight.[32]

Blair was furious, and telephoned Lloyd to say so. 'You're saying I'm lightweight.' Lloyd was taken aback, and said he had meant that he was inexperienced. 'That is not what it says,' retorted Blair. He must have been especially hurt to be bracketed with MacDonald and Davis, of whom he shared Lloyd's low opinion. According to one colleague, Blair used to come out of Treasury team meetings saying they were 'absolutely dreadful'.

Blair was gloomy about Labour's prospects in the 1987 General Election. After losing the Greenwich by-election to the SDP in February, Labour was in third place in the opinion polls. Blair thought the party might be overtaken by the Liberal–SDP Alliance, which had nearly happened in 1983. That it was not, and instead succeeded in forcing the centre party more firmly into third place, he attributed largely to the skills of Peter Mandelson.

Blair himself had a low-profile election. Some friends remember him spending much of the time in his Sedgefield constituency – hardly a marginal seat. His name does not feature once in the log of BBC TV news programmes throughout the campaign. To make matters worse, his only significant public outing was an embarrassment to him.

At a Labour news conference on 31 May, he and Gordon Brown attacked Conservative housing and education policies. As Regional Affairs spokesperson, Brown was busy, touring the country and always in demand on regional television. Blair's lack of experience showed when he said that the Conservative plans to increase private rented housing bore Margaret Thatcher's personal 'thumb mark' and were the product of 'an unchecked and unbalanced mind'. Michael Brunson, ITN's political editor, alertly picked him up and asked if he was saying the Prime Minister was mad. Shadow Home Secretary Gerald Kaufman, chairing the news conference, quickly insisted that Blair was attacking the 'ethos of Thatcherism'. Mandelson tried to persuade Brunson afterwards that there was nothing newsworthy in Blair's words.

The timing was unfortunate because it came on a day when Labour appeared uncertain of how to tackle its dominant opponent. Bryan Gould had said that morning, 'There is one campaign issue which encompasses all others – the personality of Mrs Thatcher,' while other Labour politicians were reported to be privately anxious that concentrating their fire on her might be seen as 'over the top' by floating voters. Blair's comment was widely reported as an example of Labour's confusion and desperation. He was humbled by the experience and learned from it.

The 1987 election can be summarised simply: Labour won the campaign and the Conservatives won the votes. The soaring seagulls, the stirring Brahms and the ruthless management of television coverage contrasted sharply not just with the 1983 campaign but – less sharply – with the Conservative campaign. That contrast for a moment led Thatcher to uncharacteristically 'wobbly' behaviour, but she need not have worried.

On 11 June 1987, Blair increased his majority in Sedgefield from 8,281 to 13,058. But nationally, the result was another ghastly blow for the Labour Party. The Conservatives still had a majority of 102, and Labour's share of the vote had increased by just 3.2 points to 31.5 per cent. This time there were no excuses. The party had presented a fundamentally unpopular programme to the British people almost as well as it could plausibly be presented. Only now did the party really begin to face up to the huge amount of policy change that would be needed. Between 1983 and 1987, only the policy on Europe and some of the more baroque elements of the siege economy had changed. Between 1987 and 1992, Neil Kinnock would ensure that policies on defence, public ownership and trade unions would go – the last would be Blair's responsibility – as part of a complete policy review.

Notes

1. Robert Harris, *The Making of Neil Kinnock*, pp. 213–14.
2. Interviews, 5 and 6 September 1994.
3. Martin Jacques, *Sunday Times Magazine*, 17 July 1994.
4. Interview, 6 September 1994.
5. *Hansard*, 8 November 1983, col. 210.
6. *Ibid.*, col. 207.
7. *Ibid.*, col. 210.
8. Standing Committee F, Session 1983–84; *Hansard*, 22 November 1983, cols 32–3.
9. *Ibid.*, 15 December 1983, cols 310–12.
10. *Ibid.*, col. 313.
11. *Ibid.*, 26 January 1984, col. 768.
12. *Ibid.*, 6 December 1983, col. 149.

13. London *Evening Standard*, 16 November 1993.
14. Interview, 6 September 1994.
15. *Hansard*, 15 November 1983, cols 798–9.
16. Fiona Millar, *Today*, 22 July 1994.
17. Andrew Roth, *Parliamentary Profiles*.
18. *Guardian*, 22 November 1999.
19. Robert Harris, *Talk* magazine, May 2000.
20. *The Times*, 6 July 1994.
21. *Hansard*, 27 March 1984, col. 138.
22. *Ibid.*, 23 October 1984, col. 552.
23. *Ibid.*, 24 January 1985, col. 1114.
24. *Ibid.*, 13 February 1986, col. 1081.
25. Interview, 21 September 1994.
26. *Daily Mail*, 4 May 1995; *Observer*, 7 May 1995.
27. Select Committee on Members' Interests, Second Report, Session 1994–95.
28. Nigel Lawson, *The View from No. 11*, pp. 483–508.
29. *Hansard*, 29 January 1986, cols 983, 988–92.
30. Philip Gould, *The Unfinished Revolution*, pp. 183–4.
31. Donald Macintyre, *Mandelson*, p. 33.
32. *New Statesman*, 22 August 1986.

8

Doubtful Capitalist

Trade and Industry, and Energy, 1987–89

'Our future is surely more important than the activities of those who chase paper profits in the casino economy of the markets.'
—*Tony Blair, 1987*

After the 1987 General Election, Blair made his first assault on that plateau of political ambition, the shadow Cabinet. The annual election, in which all Labour MPs voted while the party was in Opposition, was the unlit gateway to advancement. It was an acutely timed move. There is always a clear-out of old faces just after a General Election, and it was soon but not too soon, when he might have got a derisory vote.

He asked the advice of Bryan Gould, the star of the General Election campaign, who was expected to do well in the shadow Cabinet election:

> In '87 he asked me – it's a nice quality in Tony, he wasn't interested in my view, but it was his way of canvassing support – he asked me whether I thought he was too young and too inexperienced to have a go at the shadow Cabinet. And I said, 'I think you're entirely up to having a go. I mean, don't be disappointed if you don't get in the first time, but have a go.'

Blair was aware that he needed allies and organisation. Merit was all very well, but the most important thing was to get on a 'slate', a list of approved candidates organised by one of the rival ideological factions. At that time, there were three slates, organised by the right, the centre-left Tribune Group and the hard-left Campaign Group. Although very few MPs voted blindly for a whole slate, endorsement by one of these groups was a big help. Once, in the 1950s, the Tribune Group had been a small left-wing caucus. Now it was no longer in any meaningful sense 'left-wing' on Labour's internal spectrum – after 1983, it expanded to include about half of all Labour MPs.

Blair was a prime example of the new Tribunites. When he joined in 1985, as when he joined the Labour Co-ordinating Committee in Hackney, he was a right-winger joining a left-wing faction as it moved towards him. This meant he was eligible to take part in the vote that mattered – the ballot among Tribune Group MPs to decide who should be on the slate. Despite Blair's protestation in 1984 that he was not interested in 'factional organisation', he had to use the system if he were to advance his career. Nick Brown, his ally in the Northern Labour Party, former GMB union political officer and now the MP for Newcastle East, ran a 'syndicate' for the Tribune ballot. This was effectively a caucus-within-a-caucus, and it helped get both Gordon Brown and Blair on the Tribune slate. In the election of fifteen shadow Cabinet members, Blair came seventeenth, with seventy-one votes. It was a good result for a first attempt, but not so good as to prompt envy.

Bryan Gould, who topped the shadow Cabinet poll, failed to win the post he wanted: shadow Chancellor. Roy Hattersley, vacating the Treasury portfolio for Home Affairs, ensured the succession of John Smith. The heavyweights of the pro-European right could cause more trouble for Kinnock than Gould's less committed soft-left supporters. Instead, Gould took the second ranked economic post, as shadow Trade and Industry Secretary, and Blair was appointed his deputy, after turning down the offer of legal affairs spokesman, which offered few prospects of self-advertisement. Gould and Blair had worked together for a year in Hattersley's Treasury team, Gould having been brought in as shadow Chief Secretary to the Treasury in addition to the important election job of campaigns co-ordinator.

Gordon Brown, elected to the shadow Cabinet at his first attempt, took Gould's place as shadow Chief Secretary, effectively number two to John Smith. Smith and Gould were embarking on a personal and policy feud which would culminate in the leadership contest five years later, but Blair avoided entanglement in it.

Andy McSmith, a Labour Party press officer who used to sit in on some of the trade and industry team meetings, recounted a telling vignette of the period. Gould easily dominated the meetings 'by virtue of his sharp brain and extraordinary memory', but a lot of time was wasted in 'small talk or unfunny in-jokes'. The fact that Gould did not put a stop to this silliness revealed one of the weaknesses that would be his undoing. Nor did he seem able to insist that Blair attend team meetings, which he patently regarded as a waste of his time. Once when he did attend 'he sat looking out of the window, absorbed in his own thoughts . . . My impression was that, ahead of the general opinion in Westminster, he had taken

Bryan Gould's measure and did not rate him highly.' McSmith was either unusually perceptive, or Blair later became better at concealing his low opinions of others, because one of the striking features of his rise was the self-control with which such opinions were suppressed. In any case, at the end of the meeting, as Blair was leaving, Gould asked him about a point of detail in the Copyright Bill, which Blair was handling in the Commons:

> He stopped, hands in pockets, to talk to Gould, who was still sitting, and questions and answers flashed back and forth between the pair about the impact of cheap cassette tapes and recorders on the music industry and about arcane aspects of copyright law. No one interrupted because no one else present had the slightest idea what they were talking about. During those few minutes, more real business was conducted than in the entire long-drawn-out meeting.[1]

With Brown in the shadow Cabinet as Smith's deputy, the 'seniority gap' between Blair and Brown was as wide as ever, although not quite as wide as it looked. Blair's brief included responsibility for the City of London and consumer affairs, and was 'seen as the principal job outside the shadow Cabinet at that point', according to Gould. 'The brightest people were given the job and, if they proved themselves in that, it was the obvious launching-pad.' At other times the post was held by Gould himself and Mo Mowlam. Gould said:

> One of the good things about doing the City job is that you can actually get yourself a lot of attention on the financial pages, particularly in the Sundays. There was a period when I and then Tony found ourselves on the front page of the *Observer* every second week because we would do something about Lloyd's or Barlow Clowes.

By coincidence, Blair's promotion brought him up against the next generation of Conservative leaders. As Gould's deputy, he faced Kenneth Clarke, deputy and Commons understudy to David Young, the Trade and Industry Secretary who was in the House of Lords. Blair's first parliamentary job, though, was to finish the business of opposing the Finance Bill, which had been postponed from before the election. As a result he found himself briefly facing John Major, the new Chief Secretary to the Treasury, and Norman Lamont, the Financial Secretary, who was responsible for getting the Bill through. Blair – always courteous in the House – thanked Lamont on 20 July for what was 'the most detailed explanation that I have ever heard on the Third Reading of a Finance Bill'. Lamont returned the compliment the following year:

> He's a very effective parliamentary performer. He doesn't speak for the

> sake of speaking . . . He asks very pointed questions. I did once take the Finance Bill through committee when he was my opposite number and I was very impressed (a) by how much he'd done his homework, and (b) by his ability to think quickly on his feet.[2]

Cultural revolutionary

In China, intellectuals were despatched forcibly to the countryside for re-education. Neil Kinnock attempted something much more difficult. He had to persuade the Labour Party to go voluntarily. The policy review launched at the Labour conference in Brighton in September 1987 was a unique attempt to re-educate an entire political party.

The idea for the policy review came from a memo by Adam Sharples. He had moved from Labour Party headquarters to the public sector union NUPE, where he worked for Tom Sawyer, Tony Benn's successor in the chair of the Labour National Executive's main policy committee.

Sawyer was the most Kinnockite of union leaders. He had come from the left, but had been humbled by his attachment to democracy: NUPE balloted its members in 1981 on Labour's deputy leadership, and they had backed Denis Healey over Tony Benn. Since then Sawyer became relentless in trying to reconnect Labour politics with his members, and the wider electorate. That was the gist of Adam Sharples's blueprint for the policy review, which Neil Kinnock took up, and which was approved at the September meeting of the National Executive:

> Our policy must be responsive to the concerns of the voters – particularly those we need to win over. This is not to say we should abandon our programme in favour of a collection of 'popular' policies. But policy development cannot be divorced from communication of that policy.[3]

The choice facing the Labour Party was stark. Its vote in 1987 was so low that it was fruitless to argue – although the hard left still did – that the policies should be presented with more conviction. The party either had to change its policies radically, or it had to do a deal with the third party, the Alliance. In the short term, the second course seemed perverse because the two parties of the Alliance had just begun a disastrous merger.

Many in the Labour Party, however, were persuaded that a pact between the Opposition parties was the only long-term hope for power. A pact would mean Labour would have to accept the case for reform of the electoral system, a central demand of what was temporarily called the Social and Liberal Democrats. But it was a price many were happy to pay. Fifteen motions to the Labour conference in 1987 advocated PR, proportional representation. Blair's view, set out in an article in the *New*

Statesman on 4 September 1987, remained consistent – in public at least – for the next ten years:

> Labour's new enthusiasts for PR put their case not primarily on grounds of constitutional principle, but as a strategy for power. The implications of their case are fundamental: that Labour cannot ever again win a majority of seats in Parliament; and that what cannot be achieved through the front door of majority government can be bundled in by the back door of coalitions and electoral pacts. This view rests on dangerous delusions.

One delusion, said Blair, was the notion of an 'anti-Thatcher' majority. Under proportional representation, 'there is no guarantee that the 1987 election would have produced a Labour-led coalition'. Proportional representation would at least have guaranteed a Conservative–Alliance coalition rather than an unchecked Conservative government. This was irrelevant, however, because electoral reform would have to come after a successful Labour-led pact at a General Election.

Blair's central argument was a powerful one, however, and it turned on the need for fundamental change in the Labour Party:

> The real question for the Labour Party is why it is not achieving sufficient electoral support. It must face this question irrespective of whether we retain the present electoral system or change it, whether we stand for election alone or in a pact. The campaign for PR is just the latest excuse for avoiding decisive choices about the party's future.
>
> A coalition still has to decide its economic policy, its industrial policy, what it intends to do about defence or foreign affairs or trade union law . . . There is no decision that would be justifiable for Labour to make in order to win power in a coalition that it should not be making anyway for itself.
>
> Some of the Labour Party conference resolutions betray a comforting view that electoral reform legitimises self-indulgence: we can become a true socialist movement without the need, as Colne Valley Labour Party puts it, 'to appeal to the wavering middle ground'. In practical terms, this is the most dangerous delusion of all.

Blair offered his analysis of Labour's failure to win over the 'wavering middle ground' in an earlier article in *The Times*, 1 July 1987. In a typically abstract and philosophical way, he argued that the programme just announced by Margaret Thatcher's second government reflected 'an extreme view of individual responsibility'. He explained:

> The large majority of the measures in the Queen's Speech are predicated on the basis that individual choice does not in any way depend on social opportunity; the further people are from the institutions of society, the better they will be. Thus, Mrs Thatcher's answer to education problems is to allow schools to leave the system . . . The answer to concern over pensions is to take out private insurance. The NHS is inviolate only because of

its place in the public affections. But if it did not exist, this government would never have invented it. No intellectual energy, no political impetus is given to improving what we do as a society rather than as individuals.

The strategy he would pursue as leader was here in embryo. First he set out what he saw as the fundamental philosophical divide between Labour and the Conservatives, and only then did he start to draw policy conclusions from these first principles. He thus avoided an overt challenge to Labour policies, or even any criticism of his party at all.

The policy review, however, would have to deal with the specifics. The 1987 party conference suspected betrayal, but could not put its finger on the leader's intentions. Blair was a member of the supporting chorus whose role was to help smooth the leader's path. In a television interview, he defended the review as a thorough and fundamental re-affirmation of all Labour's existing policies: 'I think once the policy review starts taking place, people will realise there's no revision, there's no scrapping, there's no bonfire of commitments. What there is, is a more practical assessment of how you translate your principles into practice.'[4] Of course, in private, destruction and rebuilding were Kinnock's twin themes, shared with his inner circle, which now included Blair. Blair had even hinted at it in his *New Statesman* article, when he wrote of Labour's need for 'profound changes in ideas and organisation', and observed: 'The key to Mrs Thatcher's political success has been in destroying and re-creating contours of electoral support.'

Bonfire of commitments

There were three important policies that Neil Kinnock wanted to destroy and re-create in the policy review: those on public ownership, trade union law, and defence. His determination to win was often underestimated. No one thought he would abandon Labour's non-nuclear defence policy, but he had already decided to do so. He drove the plan for the policy review through a sullen and uncertain conference. But the process quickly ran out of momentum as he went through a period of depression, withdrawing from many of his colleagues. In the end the strain on his personality and past beliefs was too great to carry enough conviction with the electorate.

As spokesman on the City, Blair had a small role to play in the first policy earmarked for demolition: nationalisation. Kinnock wanted to dispose of the perception that, as Bryan Gould had put it, Labour simply wanted to run the Tory privatisation video in reverse. During the annual conference, Blair urged his party to have the self-confidence to review its policies in another article in *The Times*, on 29 September 1987. Labour had spent the summer reeling before the 'bourgeois triumphalism' of Thatcherism, as commentators hailed a third election victory as proof that Margaret Thatcher had remade the nation's psyche in her own image. Blair took issue with the idea – which the Labour Party half-believed – that she was now invincible, because privatisation had turned Britain into a nation of share-owners:

> The notion that we have thereby created a generation of stock market investors is fatuous. All that has been shown is that if something is given away, it will be gratefully received. Of course, if Labour promises to take the gift back, it will not excite popularity among the beneficiaries. None of this means that privatisation is right, or means that public ownership is wrong.

This sweetly persuasive, pragmatic approach contrasted with that of his front-bench boss. The next day, Gould was unexpectedly heckled in his speech to the conference. His words the previous week had excited the suspicions of delegates: 'The idea of owning shares is catching on, and as socialists we should support it as one means of taking power from the hands of the few and spreading it more widely.'[5] The jeers and shouts of 'You are a disgrace' came at exactly the wrong time for the leadership. The conference was debating a motion to renationalise British Telecom, extend public ownership generally and reaffirm Clause IV. Kinnock did not want it passed.

Kinnock feared that with the Old Testament orthodoxy of Clause IV dragged into it, Gould's provocative revisionism was counter-productive. It was time for a loyal emissary from the leader's camp to be sent out to try to reverse the impression Gould had given. As the vote was being counted, Blair appeared on BBC TV's live coverage outside the Brighton conference hall: 'The issue is not whether we throw overboard public ownership or Clause IV. The issue is how you implement those things in practice in a modern world today.'

Vivian White, the BBC's reporter, put to him that there were some people who wanted to reinterpret Clause IV, knowing that Blair was one of them. Blair was adamant. 'It's not even a question of reinterpreting it. It's a question of giving effect to it.'

In this disingenuous deflection, Blair was making a serious point, much as he would when he eventually asked for Clause IV to be rewritten in 1994. By trying to focus the attention of a suspicious party on what it would mean to 'give effect' to Clause IV, he hoped to open up a debate which would be bound to lead to reinterpretation and rewriting. But he recognised that to start with the demand for revision, before the debate had even begun, would only end in failure.

Immediately after the election, he had hinted at an important new direction for policy, which he would try to develop – largely without success. Labour had missed a trick in responding to privatisation, he said: 'The most credible argument in favour of privatisation – competition – was discarded. A really radical policy would have addressed the interests of consumers. Instead, the only protection is a government quango.'[6] But the implication that Labour should favour competition where possible was not followed through. It was simply not possible at that time for most of the Labour Party to accept the virtues of the free market.

Nor did Blair himself appear to believe in them. He was asked by Kinnock to report on the October 1987 stock market 'crash' to the shadow Cabinet. 'I'm a one-man committee,' he told *The Times* Diary, 'with a double brief – to suggest regulation to reduce volatility and to find out if there are ways to reduce speculation.'[7] However, his views on market volatility were old-fashioned and his acceptance of free-market economics less than total. As a result of the crash, he confidently predicted: 'There will be few politicians standing for election next time on a platform advocating "free markets".' He went on: 'It is high time we reasserted the value of those who work to produce or to serve, in manufacturing and in services. Their future and ours is surely more important than the activities of those who chase paper profits in the casino economy of the markets.'[8]

In May 1988, for example, the Swiss company Nestlé launched a takeover of British confectioner Rowntree. Blair demanded that trade minister Kenneth Clarke block the bid, more out of simple populism than a socialist desire to challenge 'the power of capital, particularly multinational capital', which he had once condemned. Although he dressed up his opposition with well-known academic studies of poor performance by merged companies, and the fact that hostile takeovers were rare in Germany and Japan, Clarke accurately parodied his position thus: 'That no foreigner should be encouraged to invest in this country and that no Englishman should be encouraged to invest abroad.'[9]

If Labour's instincts on economics made the shift away from public ownership difficult, the other changes that Kinnock wanted to achieve touched equally deep emotions in the party.

As one of the leader's increasingly trusted favourites, Blair was also appointed to one of the seven groups set up to carry out the policy review, the 'People at Work' group on trade union law. In two years, Michael Meacher, the shadow Employment Secretary responsible for it, was unable to produce what Kinnock wanted from it – a decisive break from what might be called Scargillism. But, by planting Blair on the group, Kinnock ensured that it would, eventually, deliver the right result.

The third issue – which touched different but equally jangling nerves – was the party's non-nuclear defence policy. This was the change Blair was least involved in. Despite his early support for unilateral nuclear disarmament in 1982–83, he had not committed a word on the subject to the public record since entering the Commons. Sylvia Littlejohns, the part-time secretary he shared with Martin O'Neill, the MP for Clackmannan, remembered his reaction when he received a circular from the Campaign for Nuclear Disarmament in 1983, which carried a list of Labour MPs who were supporters, including him. 'Ooh, I don't know about that,' he said. 'I don't know whether I *am* a unilateralist.' She said: 'He seemed bemused. He almost seemed to be saying to himself, "Am I a unilateralist or not?"' He was last claimed as a member of CND in May 1986, when his name appeared on an advertisement by Parliamentary Labour CND in *Sanity*, the CND magazine. He later tried to draw a distinction between 'mainstream' CND and Parliamentary Labour CND, whereas the only difference was that it had a corporate opt-out from CND's policy of withdrawal from Nato (a 'nuclear alliance'), which conflicted with Labour policy. But Blair's support for unilateralism had certainly lapsed by the time the advertisement appeared: the fact that he was recorded as 'A. C. L. Blair' was proof that the list had not been kept up to date (after his debut as 'Blair, Mr Anthony' in *Hansard*, he had himself amended in January 1984 to 'Blair, Mr Tony').

Friends say he was privately emphatic that the party should drop unilateralism before the 1987 election. Certainly, when Neil Kinnock decided never to defend the policy again after that defeat, Blair was one of the few he consulted before the shift gradually became public. The world was changing. After the Reykjavik summit in 1986 between the Soviet Union's new leader Mikhail Gorbachev and Ronald Reagan there was a gradual thaw of frozen certainties.[10] Kinnock started the retreat on 5 June 1988, saying on BBC1's *This Week Next Week*: 'There is no need now for a something-for-nothing unilateralism.'[11]

When Kinnock finally abandoned the policy in spring 1989, Blair was inevitably part of the supporting chorus again.

Getting ready for take-off

When Blair turned thirty-five in May 1988, he had been an MP for just five years. He had risen faster than any Labour contemporary with the exception of his friend and ally Gordon Brown, who was already in the shadow Cabinet as deputy to the shadow Chancellor, John Smith. Now Blair was poised to join him.

That month, Blair employed a new adviser. Anji Hunter had been a friend since schooldays. She had not really been political until she became, at the age of twenty-nine, a student again at Brighton Polytechnic. She was now married, to Nick Cornwall, manager of Richmond Park, with two small children, and had finally decided to complete her disrupted education. She got a First in History and English. A week after her finals, she started working for Blair full-time, having worked for him since the 1987 election during vacations. For his next six years in the shadow Cabinet, as he rose to the top, she was his 'fixer, charmer and tactician', in the words of another of Blair's small pre-leadership entourage.

Before any of those things, however, she was his Marcia Williams. Ben Pimlott's description of the relationship between the future Baroness Falkender and Harold Wilson applies equally to that between Hunter and Blair: 'Her important role was to be the person who thought about Wilson's needs and cared about his well-being more than anybody else outside his family.'[12] She made Blair's physical projection of himself as a statesman possible. From an unusually early stage in his career he had the self-possessed demeanour of someone who is always on show. He rarely carried his own luggage or wore a coat.

Nor, after he joined the shadow Cabinet, did he often drive. 'One of the worst things now is that I always have to drive,' said Cherie, 'because if something happened while Tony was driving it would probably be splashed across the newspapers.'[13] It was an unusually media-conscious consideration.

The following year, 1989, Hunter's position was secured when Blair made Sylvia Littlejohns redundant. She had worked for Tony Crosland in Opposition and in government, and recognised Blair as another significant Labour politician from the start. 'I could tell he was something special. He had a good brain, and you could sense the inner urge to get to the highest place,' she said. She always thought Gordon Brown had more gravitas, but was 'not as organised' as Blair. Crosland, who was 'very precise, quite a shy man', used to call her 'Mrs B' (she was Sylvia Boulton then) and would ask her to come to his office at 10.42. 'I'd go up to his room and I'd wait for two seconds until it was exactly 10.42 and then go in.' Working for Blair was 'much more fluid', and although he was not as intellectual as Crosland he could 'dictate a beautiful letter, perfectly phrased, very quickly'.

Blair eventually decided, however, that he wanted his own team, personally committed to his vision of Labour's future, and took advantage of a minor mistake to reshuffle his staff. Littlejohns had bought a computer on hire purchase, and claimed the regular payments against Blair's office allowance. She was 'so busy typing thousands of letters' that she forgot to check when the instalments were finished, and discovered that they had continued to claim after the payments stopped. Blair was 'very worried' about any suggestion of impropriety and 'put it right straight away', paying a big cheque to the Fees Office to return the overclaimed money.

A little later, he told her he wanted his secretarial work done in Sedgefield, where Phil Wilson ran his constituency office, and that she would have to find work elsewhere. 'I started crying, and he got very upset. He got his hanky out and gave it to me,' she said.

'I live on my own,' she told the future Prime Minister through her tears: 'When you grow up you'll understand.' In the middle of a parliament, she could not find another MP to share her salary, so she had to leave the Commons, reflecting on the determination of a young man who was going to go far.

Electric Avenue

Blair worked hard in 1987–88 to build up his support among Labour MPs. He had 'Leadership Approved' stamped on his forehead at a time when the parliamentary party was rediscovering the joys of loyalty.

He also acquired a useful platform outside the Commons as his articles for *The Times* became an irregular column, more or less fortnightly, until August 1988. This was a good way to get noticed by his parliamentary colleagues. He wrote in favour of televising the House of Commons on 24 November 1987: 'Politics works through publicity and television is the best form of publicity.' He set out his early views on sound-bite politics, and demonstrated a sound grasp of media handling:

> Our news today is instant, hostile to subtlety or qualification. If you can't sum it up in a sentence, or even a phrase, forget it. Combine two ideas or sentiments together and mass communication will not repeat them, it will choose between them. To avoid misinterpretation, strip down a policy or opinion to one key clear line before the media does it for you. Think in headlines.

He was perfectly capable of making these observations for himself, but they coincided precisely with the Peter Mandelson guide to political communications. 'These are very depressing reflections because they bear heavily on the quality of our democracy,' Blair wrote, going on to offer a manifesto for political evasion: 'The truth becomes almost impossible to communicate because total frankness, relayed in the shorthand of the mass media, becomes simply a weapon in the hands of opponents.'

Over the summer of 1988 Blair had the chance to shine with the financial scandal of the Barlow Clowes affair. He had just arrived in the Members' Lobby on his return from a trip to Japan when he was intercepted by a new Labour whip, Alun Michael. Some of Michael's South Wales constituents had lost money with an investment group. 'We had about a five-minute chat, and he looked slightly glazed,' said Michael.

> I was convinced he hadn't taken it in. But then ten minutes later I got a call from him, saying he'd been thinking about it. The thing that impressed me was that he immediately analysed the situation, came to a conclusion and checked it back, and had gone to the heart of the matter.

Bryan Gould was happy to let his deputy take the limelight in his fight on behalf of pensioners who had lost their life savings through a failure of government regulation. 'Bryan gave Barlow Clowes to Tony and let him get on with it. A lot of shadow Cabinet people wouldn't do that,' said Nigel Stanley, Gould's adviser. Blair's ability to grasp the important facts of a complicated situation was not in doubt, but he showed political sharpness too, embarrassing the government with the evidence that it should have known all along that Barlow Clowes was a dubious investment group. The publicity he attracted was well timed.

In November 1988, he was elected to the shadow Cabinet, coming ninth, while Brown maintained a differential by coming top of the poll. Brown had stood in for John Smith when he had his first heart attack in September, and had been acclaimed for a penetrating assault on Nigel Lawson during a debate on the economy. The Chancellor had decided to discontinue some economic forecasts, Brown noted with stern disapproval: 'Most of us say that the proper answer is not to discard the forecasts of the Chancellor but to keep the forecasts and discard the Chancellor.'[14] It was a parliamentary triumph in which Brown's accomplished skill contrasted with Blair's brittle performances.

Blair heard the result of the shadow Cabinet elections as he was waiting to be interviewed by Emma Udwin for LBC radio, and said he first had to phone to tell his wife. Soon afterwards, he blinked modestly in the limelight of a *Newsnight* profile: 'I'm still young. I've had some good breaks. I've been very lucky, but I'm acutely conscious of the fact that the history of politics is littered with the P45s of those who were supposed to be rising stars and ended up being shooting stars.'[15]

Neil Kinnock wanted to make him shadow Employment Secretary, feeling that Michael Meacher had not been bold enough in revamping this important area of policy. But Meacher still had powerful backing on the left and centre-left. Kinnock said:

> All shadow Cabinet allocation is a jigsaw. And I wanted the jigsaw to come out in a particular way a year before that happened. But because of the disposition of forces in the party I couldn't quite make the jigsaw come out the way I wanted, so I had to put a piece to one side.

Blair became shadow Energy Secretary instead for a year. He was described by *Private Eye* as 'the bright-eyed, innocent energy spokesman wheeled in by Kinnock to replace John Prescott'.[16] He was given a substantial parliamentary job, that of fighting electricity privatisation against Cecil Parkinson. This was a bigger test of the same issue he had faced at trade and industry – the Labour Party's changing stance on public ownership.

Blair started as a traditionalist in his first Commons debate as a shadow Cabinet minister, on the electricity industry, on 12 December 1988: 'We are proud that we took the industry into public ownership. When we come to power, it will be reinstated as a public service for the people of this country, and will not be run for private profit.' This clear pledge to renationalise the electricity industry was absolute, underpinned by 'the stupidity, indeed the impossibility, of an energy policy determined by the interests of the private sector'.[17]

However, he followed what was becoming a regular pattern. The Labour leadership would oppose privatisation, promise to renationalise, but then it would decide that there were more important things to do with the money, and the restoration of public ownership would recede into 'when resources allow' limbo, until – in most cases – privatisation was grudgingly accepted. By the time of the 1992 manifesto, Labour's ambitions for the electricity industry were limited to a pledge to assert 'public control' rather than ownership, and only of the National Grid – the cable and pylon network.

In the meantime, Blair took full advantage of the contrast between him and his government counterpart. Cecil Parkinson had been close to Margaret Thatcher's throne, but his career was now in genteel decline. He lacked the edge and quick wits to exploit his far greater experience. The privatisation of electricity was also a policy full of holes. It would raise money – but allow Blair to argue that the one-off gain to the taxpayer would be used irresponsibly to pay for tax cuts. Despite the rhetoric of promoting competition, the consumer would only be protected by regulation. And it would expose decades of dishonest accounting for nuclear power.

'The Secretary of State says that he is introducing real competition,' said Blair, in an early encounter. 'He kept on mentioning competition during his speech, as if the more he mentioned it the more real it became.'

1. Mary Blair, Leo's foster mother and Tony's 'Granny Blair', campaigning for the Communist Party in Glasgow. Tony's father, Leo, was an active communist in his youth before joining the Conservative Party after the war.

2. Hazel, Tony's mother, around the time of her marriage, at the age of twenty-five, in 1948.

3. 'You are your father's son,' said one family friend: Tony (here aged about three, in his father's arms) inherited Leo's charm and drive.

4. Bill, Sarah and Tony Blair, aged about seven, one and four, when the family lived in Adelaide, Australia.

5. Blair (left) as Captain Stanhope in the First World War play *Journey's End* by R. C. Sherriff at Fettes College, 1971.

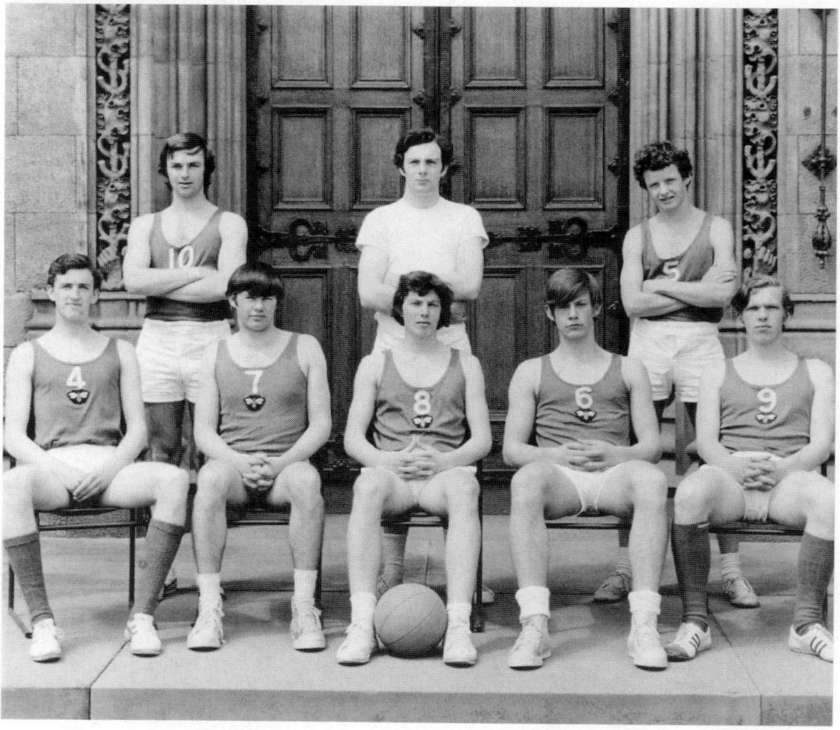

6. A. C. L. Blair (centre), captain of the Fettes basketball team, 1971.

7. Anji Hunter is now Special Assistant to the Prime Minister: when she and Blair first met she was a fifteen-year-old rebel about to be expelled from her school in Scotland.

8. Amanda Mackenzie Stuart, Blair's sixth-form girlfriend, presents a bouquet to the Queen Mother at celebrations to mark the centenary of Fettes, 1971.

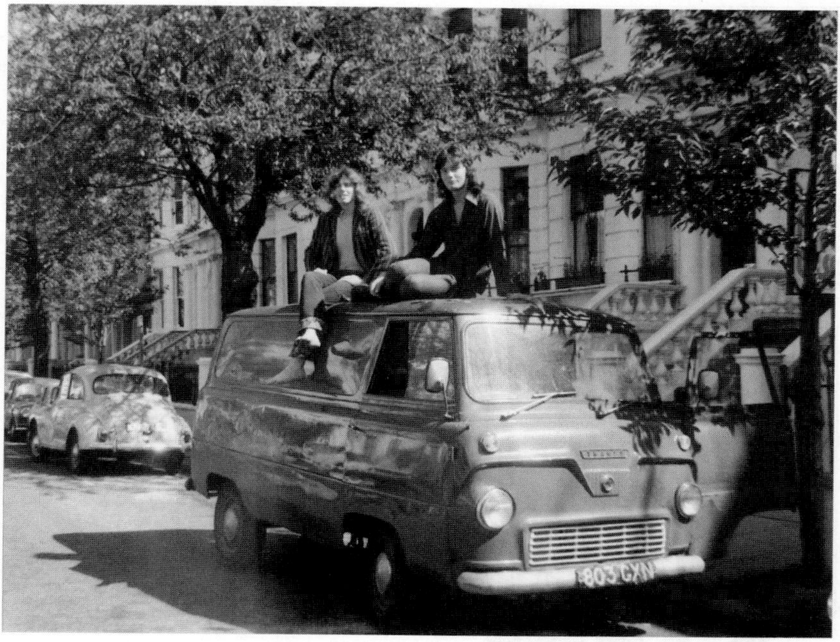

9. Blair and Alan Collenette, his friend and gap-year business partner, in Kensington in the summer of 1972, sitting on their main commercial asset as rock promoters, a Thames van purchased by Blair for £50.

10. Blair and Collenette at the entrance to the crypt of the Vineyard Congregationalist Church in Richmond, south-west London, the main venue for their bands.

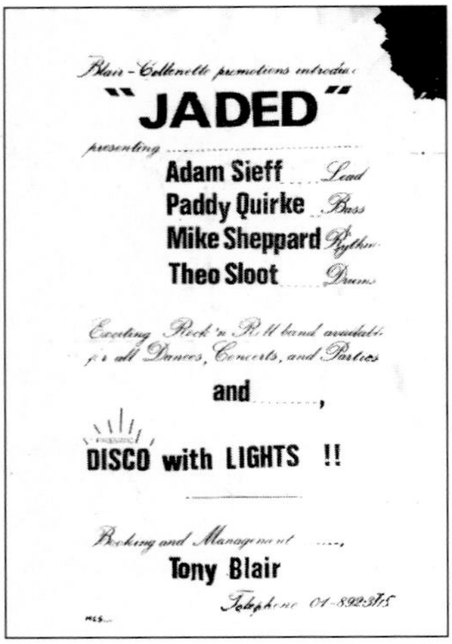

11. Handbill for the band Jaded: Blair was responsible for 'Bookings and Management'.

12. Poster advertising a disco at the Vineyard, November 1971.

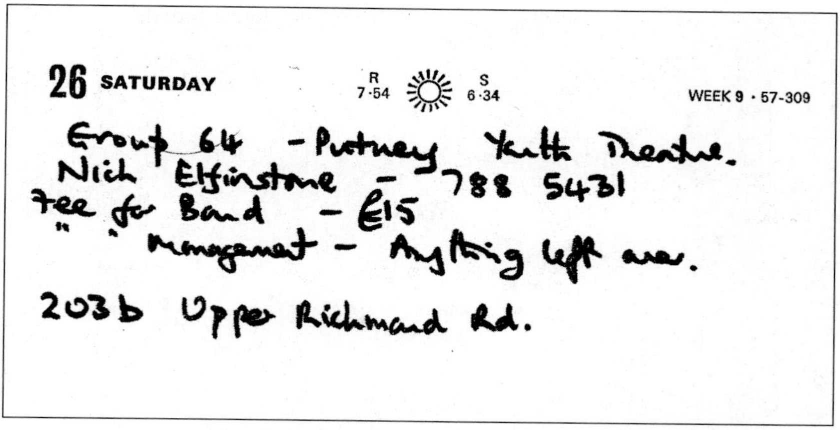

26 SATURDAY R 7·54 S 6·34 WEEK 9 · 57-309

Group 64 - Putney Youth Theatre.
Nick Elfinstone - 788 5431
Fee for Band - £15
" " Management - Anything left over.

203b Upper Richmond Rd.

13. Entry by Blair from February 1972 in the joint diary he kept with Collenette recording the fee for 'Management' as 'Anything left over' after paying the band £15.

14. The strawberries-and-cream brigade: Blair at St John's College, Oxford.

15. Cherie Booth as a girl guide helping with a fancy-dress competition. 'You can see from the photograph that I used to do a lot of badges, mainly non-outdoors. I always fell into the river and got drenched when we went on hikes or to camp.'

16. Last of the summer wine: Blair and Alan Collenette share a bottle of Hirondelle at the Henley Regatta in 1978.

Every time Parkinson intervened, Blair left him limping. He derided the 'sheer, breathtaking irrelevance' of the obsession with privatisation, against the 'real agenda for a modern energy policy' – energy conservation.[18]

'Beautiful person'

Blair's new interest in energy conservation was not wholly spontaneous. In the run-up to the European elections in June 1989, the nation, and especially southern England, went a distinct shade of political Green. Towards the end of the long Lawson boom, the Conservative protest vote was worried about traffic, air quality, dirty beaches and global warming. The merged Liberal Democrats languished in fourth place in the opinion polls behind the Green Party.

Fiona Reynolds, then at the Council for the Preservation of Rural England, lobbied Blair on electricity privatisation. She said he was 'quite different' from conventional Labour politicians, for whom the energy portfolio meant coal and jobs. 'He was not a born-again Green, but he was looking around him and saying, "Where can I build some alliances?" And he saw that Green issues had to figure.'

None of Blair's positions in this period appears to have been sincere. His defence of public ownership, his advocacy of competition and his new-found Green consciousness all bore the marks of expediency. It provided just the excuse that was needed to groom him as one of Labour's front-line faces. Having played no part in the 1987 General Election campaign, he appeared – in a well-cut dark blue suit – in party political broadcasts on 3 May and 12 June 1989, just before the county and European elections respectively. The double campaign was pivotal to the party's strategic plan for the General Election, then at least two years away. The plan was drawn up by Philip Gould, Peter Mandelson's friend who organised a group of volunteers in advertising and marketing known as the Shadow Communications Agency, which ran Labour's opinion research, advertising and broadcasts.

John Prescott resented Mandelson and Gould for promoting what he called the 'beautiful people', but the traditionalists could not accuse Blair of being simply the creation of the image-makers. He paid attention to the detail of parliamentary business, fighting the electricity privatisation Bill with diligence and some creativity. During the committee stage, when the Bill was debated in detail, Blair's oldest child, Euan, then five, was not sleeping: 'It was a hellish time, getting up two or three times in the night to settle him, then going to work next morning.'[19] However, the way he fought the Bill was one of the reasons given for voting for him six years later by Chris Mullin, Tony Benn's chief organiser in the early 1980s. Writing in *Tribune*, which he once edited, Mullin praised his strategic thinking:

> As shadow Energy Secretary, for example, faced with the privatisation of electricity, instead of wasting hundreds of hours on irrelevant trench warfare, he identified the half-dozen or so key issues and arranged for them to be debated at a time when the outside world was still awake.[20]

Mullin was the only member of the left-wing Campaign Group to vote for Blair in 1994, and was later rewarded with ministerial office.

Fiona Reynolds supported his view of Blair:

> He was very unlike anyone I'd ever worked with on a Bill before. Normally what happens is that the government dictates the agenda. He drafted amendments which triggered the key debates and set the timetable. He ensured that each committee session had one point for debate, and one only.

Successful lobbying from Green pressure groups won an amendment to the Bill in the House of Lords requiring the electricity industry to promote energy efficiency for the sake of the environment. Cecil Parkinson had the amendment thrown out again in the Commons, but became irritated when his young opposite number tried to intervene in his speech on 20 July 1989: 'This is not the Old Bailey,' he snapped. 'The Honourable Gentleman is not Rumpole and I am not in the dock. He will have an opportunity to make his speech in a moment.'

With the sale of Nuclear Electric in trouble, it was a confident Tony Blair who addressed a Labour conference for the first time in October 1989. Even after six years of Kinnockite modernisation, shadow Cabinet ministers who were not also members of the National Executive still had to speak 'from the floor', and were allowed three minutes (this had applied in government, as when Chancellor Denis Healey had to defend the spending cuts required by the International Monetary Fund against three minutes of barracking in 1976). But three minutes was all Blair needed.

It was a new kind of speaking for him: rhetorical in style and populist in content, saying of electricity privatisation: 'We do not want it postponed, we do not want it delayed, we do not want it put off, we want it abandoned, here, now and for ever. [Applause.]' He deployed the tricks of alliteration and inversion effectively:

> In place of that tired Tory agenda for the '80s – privatisation, pollution, price rises – we give the country a new vision for the '90s where conserving energy is as important as producing it . . . Under Labour the environment will govern our energy policy, not energy policy govern our environment.

That was the last that was heard of Blair the Green, however. While declaring boldly 'there will be no more nuclear power stations under Labour', he had already alienated more committed environmentalists by accepting the specious argument that there would be an 'energy shortage' if a Labour government did not complete nuclear power stations under construction, including Sizewell B. This argument, which contradicted his stress on using less energy, was close to the heart of 'Nuclear' Jack Cunningham, MP for Copeland (which includes the Sellafield nuclear reprocessing plant) and then shadow Environment Secretary.

Nor was the environment prominent among Blair's priorities afterwards. Nevertheless, his one-year tenure of the energy brief was topped out when, in November 1989, the government abandoned the sale of Nuclear Electric.*

The bottom of the locker

The collapse of the government's nuclear privatisation plans could not, however, entirely conceal the illogic of Labour's position on public ownership. After getting his fingers burnt at the 1987 Labour conference, Bryan Gould was wary of going back into the kitchen, and failed to press the issue in his policy review group, on 'A Productive and Competitive Economy'. Towards the end of the two-year policy review in the spring of 1989, Neil Kinnock feared that Gould had conceded too much to conservative forces in the trade unions. Most importantly, British Telecom was still lined up for renationalisation.

Just as the review group's report was completed, Gould was surprised to find Blair in his office as a member of a delegation from Kinnock, along with Gordon Brown and John Eatwell, the leader's economic policy adviser. According to Gould, Brown and Eatwell told him they were unhappy with the final draft of his policy document. Gould told them it was the result of 'a pretty carefully worked-out compromise' and said he 'sent them away'.

Later that year Gould was moved to Environment, and Brown was given his Trade and Industry brief. Kinnock defended the putsch, which he said 'came from a need that I and others felt to sharpen [our] approach, and not to convey the impression that at the bottom of our lockers somewhere we still had this idea of wholesale recapturing of the denationalised industries'.

---

*It was eventually privatised, as British Energy and Scottish Electric, in 1996.

It was too late to change the wording of the final policy review document, *Meet the Challenge, Make the Change*, which promised to 'return privatised enterprises to the community', subject to 'the constraints of finance and legislative time' – in other words, never, while still giving the damaging impression that Labour wanted to waste taxpayers' money reversing privatisation.

As the two-year policy review turned into a rolling annual revision, the bottom of that particular locker was never really cleared out. One problem was that the government kept filling it up with new, even more essential services, such as the water industry. It was not until the rewriting of Clause IV that the Labour Party's formal attachment to wholesale public ownership was finally broken.

However, when, in October 1989, Neil Kinnock at last put in place the piece of his shadow Cabinet jigsaw left over from the previous year, Blair found himself trouble-shooting another piece of unfinished policy review business, one that had haunted Labour since the Winter of Discontent.

Notes

1. Andy McSmith, *Faces of Labour*, pp. 15–16.
2. BBC2, *Newsnight*, 21 November 1988.
3. Colin Hughes and Patrick Wintour, *Labour Rebuilt*, p. 42.
4. BBC TV conference coverage, 30 September 1987.
5. *Channel Four News*, 25 September 1987.
6. *The Times*, 1 July 1987.
7. *The Times* Diary, 2 December 1987.
8. Article for *News on Sunday*, 1 November 1987; this was an echo of John Maynard Keynes, who said that, when a nation's investment 'becomes the by-product of the activities of a casino, the job is likely to be ill-done', itself quoted by Blair in a speech on 'New Policies for a Global Economy' at the National Film Theatre, London, 27 September 1994.
9. *Hansard*, 11 May 1988, col. 310.
10. For a fuller account, see Hughes and Wintour, *Labour Rebuilt*, p. 111.
11. BBC1, *This Week Next Week*, 5 June 1988.
12. Ben Pimlott, *Harold Wilson*, p. 344.
13. *New Woman*, May 1994.
14. *Independent*, 26 October 1988.
15. BBC2, *Newsnight*, 21 November 1988.
16. *Private Eye*, 26 May 1989.
17. *Hansard*, 12 December 1988, cols 681, 687.
18. *Ibid.*, cols 682, 688.
19. London *Evening Standard*, 16 November 1993.
20. *Tribune*, 8 July 1994.

9

OPEN SHOP

Shadow Employment Secretary, 1989–92

> 'Neil Kinnock was aghast with pride and admiration at the way Tony carried that off.'
>
> —*Jack Dromey, national secretary of the TGWU*

Tony Blair's reward for embarrassing the government over electricity privatisation was to come fourth in the shadow Cabinet elections in October 1989, behind Gordon Brown, John Smith and Robin Cook. Kinnock promoted Brown to Trade and Industry and Blair to Employment. The Brown–Blair gap was closing.

At Energy, Blair had to handle a big Bill which touched on the issue of public ownership, although the main burden of changing the party's stance fell on others. Now he was given lead responsibility for changing another policy central to ideological and presentational renewal – trade union law.

Ever since the unions, led in Cabinet by James Callaghan, sabotaged the Bill based on Barbara Castle's White Paper *In Place of Strife* in 1969, the Labour Party had appeared unable to resist the sectional demands of organised labour. The strife returned, as Callaghan's nemesis, in the winter of 1978. It was clear that there was something rotten in the state of Labour's relationship with the unions.

In Kinnock's first parliamentary term as leader, he was unable to shift the party's policy on trade union law, and found the party trapped by such ill-starred conflicts as the miners' strike, the *Stockport Messenger* lockout and the Wapping dispute, while the government was determined to extract every possible vote from law after new law against unpopular unions.

Kinnock's description of Michael Meacher as 'weak as water' reflected his judgment of Meacher's tenure of the employment brief and of the chair of the policy review group covering trade union law. The group's title, 'People At Work', was applied ironically to the apparent inactivity of its membership. Its final report started to unravel the moment it was finished in May 1989.

Having accepted that industrial relations should be governed by law, an important shift from the orthodox view advanced by Blair in 1983, the report proposed no sanction on unions which broke it. It rejected the sequestration of unions' assets, a means of enforcement which had been developed by the courts, rather than invented by the Conservative government. The courts' powers of sequestration had been extended and used against the miners, the print union NGA and, most controversially at the time, the seafarers' union in its dispute with P&O Ferries.

Blair, as a member of the 'People At Work' group, organised a rescue operation with Charles Clarke, Neil Kinnock's Chief of Staff. With three weeks to go before the 1989 Labour Party conference, Derry Irvine was called in to devise a scheme. He had been elevated to the House of Lords in 1987, as Lord Irvine of Lairg, and was Labour's legal affairs spokesman. He proposed setting up specialist Labour Courts, like the Family Division of the High Court. The idea was sold to Ron Todd, the TGWU General Secretary, as a means of preventing ignorant and prejudiced High Court judges who knew nothing about industrial relations imposing draconian sanctions on unions which tried to stay within the law.

Meacher had to put his name to a 'clarifying statement' adding the Labour Courts idea to his review group's report. Whenever someone issues a clarifying statement you know they are in trouble. Weeks later, Meacher became shadow Social Security Secretary, while Blair knew he had to move quickly to reconstruct the policy before it received any further scrutiny. Before that could be accomplished, however, another gaping hole in Labour's policy on trade union law opened up – and the way it was handled would not only restore the damage caused by Meacher's timidity, it would propel Blair into the category of possible future leaders of the party.

Television coverage of the House of Commons began on 21 November 1989. Blair, who had long supported it, may have had second thoughts a week later, when viewers of the new BBC *Westminster* programme on 29 November saw him fall victim to a fine parliamentary ambush. There he was, speaking confidently in a debate on the latest draft of the Social Charter, just published by the European Commission. Six months earlier, he said, Margaret Thatcher had condemned the first draft as 'more like a

Socialist Charter', and he expounded enthusiastically on why Labour supported the charter and all the rights it would give British workers. But the latest draft of the charter contained some new words. Timothy Raison, a former Conservative minister, intervened to ask a question:

> Will the Honourable Gentleman tell us the Labour Party's view of one right in the charter – the right concerning professional organisations and trade unions: 'Every employer and every worker shall have the freedom to join or not to join such organisations without any personal or occupational damage being thereby suffered by him'? That would put an end to the closed shop. Is that the Labour Party's position?

It was not. The party's new policy document had a whole section headed, 'The right to join a union', but said nothing at all about the right not to join. It said nothing about closed shops, which required 2 million workers to join specified unions in order to get or keep jobs covered by them, and which the government was preparing to abolish.

Raison had hit on precisely the issue that Blair feared. Within days of taking his new post, he had seen the new draft of the Social Charter and spotted the problem. He had talked to union leaders, but they had refused to accept that something had to be done. Blair was forced to stall: 'If it has that meaning, it also has the meaning that one has the right to be a member of a trade union. How the government would justify their position on GCHQ, I do not know' – which drew the chant of 'Answer' from the opposite benches.[1]

After the debate, 'Blair came down to the shadow Cabinet room, and was quite clear about what needed to be done, and then followed it through', according to Neil Stewart, then in Neil Kinnock's office.

Kinnock was obviously supportive, and said he told Blair: 'Whenever you're asked, "Is this Kinnock's view?" say, "Yes". If there are any awkward bits, well, we'll find a way of dealing with that. And that's what he did.'

Charles Clarke, also in the leader's office, said, 'In fact, Tony moved faster on that than I think Neil might have done.'

It was another occasion when he went to see deputy leader Roy Hattersley for advice. Again, it was a way of canvassing support: it was clear to him what he had to do. Having made the Social Charter – which later became the Social Chapter of the Maastricht Treaty – central to its case for Europe, the Labour Party could not reject a part of it. His lukewarm defence of the closed shop in parliamentary committee six years earlier was easily abandoned. 'I think this is the second thing, after his selection, which demonstrates his steel,' said Hattersley.

At the beginning of December, Blair appeared in another Labour political broadcast. It was unintentionally sinister, as some creative mind had decided to make a feature of the front bench's 'shadow' titles. Blair walked out of darkness towards the camera, as the voice-over announced: 'Tony Blair is shadow Minister for Employment.' It was an apposite image, for Blair was indeed about to walk out of the shadows.

With Kinnock and Hattersley squared, Blair went back to the trade union leaders. According to one of them, his approach was quite different from other Labour politicians, who assumed that deals had to be done and negotiations entered into. His approach was not, 'Will you back me?' but, 'I am going to do it and you know it's right, don't you?' Blair's public embarrassment in the House of Commons paradoxically helped his cause: it was a vivid demonstration of what he had insisted, that the unions and the party could not dodge the choice between the Social Charter or the closed shop. Most of the trade union leaders knew it was a change that had to be made, but were not prepared to say so in public. Their unwillingness was the kind of attitude which intensely frustrated Kinnock, who was 'aghast with pride and admiration at the way Tony carried that off', according to Jack Dromey, national secretary of the Transport and General Workers' Union.

Within a week, Blair had spoken to, and neutralised opposition from, all the relevant unions – except the one most opposed, the NGA print union. Advised by Alastair Campbell, the political editor of the *Daily Mirror*, and Peter Mandelson, the media operation swung into action. At a news conference on the Social Charter on 6 December, Blair said he accepted it 'in its entirety'. On 12 December he told the *Financial Times* Labour would not 'pick and choose' from it. These hints prepared the ground for a seven-page statement to his Sedgefield Labour Party on Sunday 17 December 1989, followed by a 'media roadblock' the next day. It was difficult to get through the day without hearing or seeing him, from breakfast television through to *Newsnight*.

His case was simple. Labour supported the Social Charter, and one of the fundamental social rights contained in it was the right not to join a union. In order to secure the right to join, which he attacked the government for failing to guarantee, he was prepared to accept the opposite right.

The NGA and its leader, Tony Dubbins, were beside themselves. The NGA depended on the closed shop more than most unions. It had failed to preserve its closed shops – by illegal mass picketing – at the *Stockport Messenger* in 1983, and at News International which moved overnight from Fleet Street to Wapping in 1986. Almost more than the change of policy, however, Dubbins was enraged by the fact that he had not been consulted, and demanded that Blair come to the union head office in Bedford to explain himself. Blair went, and was subjected to a one-sided screaming match. But the verbal violence was an expression of Dubbins's powerlessness. The deed had been done, and there was nothing he could do.

Stewart, who followed Blair's progress from Kinnock's office, said: 'He faced Dubbins down. That shapes my judgment. It's about managing people – you should be leading people, but with just a hint that you know what you want of people. The question that matters is what happens if people cross him.'

Blair had been nervous about how his move would be received by the rest of the party, but the storm passed quickly. His name was reviled in his absence at the next meeting of the National Executive, for the 'undemocratic' way in which the policy change had been sprung on unsuspecting party and union members. *Private Eye* reported that 'Tony Blair, the smarty-pants in charge of Labour's shadow employment team', was 'savaged' at a meeting of the Parliamentary Labour Party.[2]

At the shadow Cabinet, however, he was surprised to be supported by John Prescott. It was a significant hint of mutual respect to come. A former shadow Employment Secretary himself, Prescott had already thought through the problem. He claimed credit for having moved the party from its historic attachment to the idea that trade disputes should be settled without involving the law, to a model of industrial relations based on legal rights. One such right was that to join a union: 'That implies the right not to join,' Prescott said simply.

There was some – but surprisingly little – grumbling at Blair's coup from the lower levels of the party and the unions. More significant was the private grumbling of the Conservative Party. Norman Fowler, the Employment Secretary, had brought forward his Employment Bill to that week in December, and was disappointed to discover that, with one bound, his opponent was free. Blair taunted Conservative MPs in the Commons: 'There they were, all togged up in their party best, and they put their hands into the magician's hat, hoping to pull out a nice white, bright, sprightly, lively rabbit, but instead find that they are holding a very dead fox.'[3]

The closed shop had never been a high-profile political issue, for the simple reason that for ten years the supposedly virulently anti-trade union Conservative government allowed it to continue. As long ago as 1977, Margaret Thatcher had said: 'We do not think it is right . . . But because we do not like it . . . does not necessarily mean I can pass legislation about it.'[4] Many closed shops existed, as Blair had tried to explain to the Trade

Union Bill committee in 1983, for the convenience of employers, and to prevent 'free riders' – that is, non-members of trade unions who benefited from conditions negotiated by them. They were a relic of an older form of industrial relations, which was in decline but which inevitably appealed to the Labour Party's sentimentality about archaic forms of solidarity. Philosophically, however, they had always been hard to justify, as the starkness of the Social Charter principle made all too clear. Once the government finally brought itself to abolish closed shops, it would have been disastrous for Labour to defend them.

The next leader of the Labour Party

Neil Kinnock's favour immediately began to shine more fiercely on Blair. Harriet Harman recalled the moment, around January 1990, when she realised that Kinnock regarded Blair as a possible successor:

> Neil said, 'Here comes the next leader of the Labour Party,' when he came into a room, and I laughed because I thought he was joking – I didn't mean that it was ridiculous, but I didn't realise he was serious – and I looked at him and I realised he was completely serious. At that point I thought, 'I wonder.'

It is hard to recall the depths of obscurity from which Blair rose in the space of just four years. He was not even one of the thirteen Labour politicians on which the views of party members were sought in an academic survey at the end of 1989 and beginning of 1990.[5] Bryan Gould was on the list and, as one who had basked in the leader's approval in earlier years, he recognised what was happening:

> When I was very much Neil Kinnock's blue-eyed boy, which would have been around '86, '87, and through to '88, when major debates took place in the shadow Cabinet, which wasn't all that often, I would signal that I wanted to speak and Neil would almost always bring me in at the end, before he wound up. He knew, or hoped, as was usually the case around that time, that I would say something pretty helpful to him, and he could then bounce off that into the wind-up of the discussion. But I noticed in more recent years that Tony fulfilled this role, from '90 onwards, say. Tony, as befits someone called on to do that, would usually say something of pretty mind-blowing banality, but supporting the leadership on whatever it was.

Partly by accident, partly by design and partly by patronage, Blair had put together most of the qualifications for the highest office in the party. He was English, by accent and constituency, when the party needed to break out of its Celtic strongholds; he was good on television; he was respected in the House of Commons; he had shown some steel by – in the American phrase – 'speaking the truth to power', taking on trade union vested interests in the party. The closed-shop episode was the significant moment at which he started to close the seniority gap between him and Gordon Brown. When Kinnock's post-election infatuation with Gould faded, he tilted towards Brown as his successor. During his period of post-electoral depression at the beginning of 1988, he jokingly said to Brown: 'Be on hand. The party may need you.' But now Kinnock thought it was Blair rather than Brown who demonstrated the boldness the party needed.

At the same time, Brown, newly appointed shadow Trade and Industry Secretary, was also attending to unfinished policy review business, namely to get rid of the commitment to renationalise British Telecom. The way he set about his task compared unfavourably with Blair's swift strike, according to someone who worked with both:

> He would vacillate and vacillate. He said, 'What are the unions going to say?' Kinnock's office said, 'We'll tell you what the unions are going to say.' And Gordon just wouldn't focus, wouldn't do it, wouldn't take a risk, thought the unions would be against it.

In some ways, Brown fell victim to high expectations. When he first topped the shadow Cabinet poll in 1988, his political modesty was mixed with a genuine foreboding, a shrewd awareness that he might have peaked too early.

Blair did not actually start to overtake Brown for another two years. During this period, his professed long-term ambition was to be Chancellor to Prime Minister Brown; given Brown's deeper understanding of economics that would have been a rather more one-sided partnership than the reversed outcome. However, it was at the turn of that year, 1990, when Blair could start to entertain serious aspirations to the top job himself, and the balance between the 'two bright boys' began to shift.

On the same day that Blair ditched the closed shop, 17 December 1989, another significant event occurred in the Blair story. The party's director of communications, Peter Mandelson, was selected as Labour candidate for the safe seat of Hartlepool, next door to Sedgefield. Blair's close friend in Sedgefield, John Burton, was interested in the Hartlepool seat but having in a sense 'stood aside' for Blair in 1983 he now stood aside for Mandelson. Why? 'Because Tony wanted Peter. He would have supported me, but I knew he wanted Peter. I realised Peter would be a great asset.'

Blair did everything he could to help win the selection for Mandelson, but with a secretiveness which required the telling of blatant white lies. When Andy McSmith, then Mandelson's subordinate as a Labour Party press officer, asked Blair about newspaper reports that his boss was going for Hartlepool, Blair denied all knowledge and, when pressed, 'looked as blank and bland as ever he could and repeated that he knew nothing' – despite the fact that Mandelson was camped out in his daughter's bedroom in Trimdon.[6]

Mandelson won the selection easily in a weak field, and left his job at Labour headquarters the following summer. Neil Kinnock was displeased that he should have sought a seat, and insisted that he could not keep his party job and be a candidate, although Mandelson remained an informal adviser to him. But he was becoming a more important adviser to Blair and Brown.

Howard's beginning

The new year also brought Blair face-to-face with an old sparring partner, when on 3 January 1990 Michael Howard became the first of the 1983 intake to enter the Cabinet, as Employment Secretary. He was a more skilful opponent than either Cecil Parkinson or Norman Fowler, and would get the better of Blair more often than most observers noticed. They were both barristers, both sharp. It was only Howard's self-satisfied manner that prevented his earning more credit from their two-and-a-half-year tussle.

It was a period during which Blair's confidence as a parliamentarian developed, as his speeches gained in assurance and flair. For much of the time his engagements with Howard were a ritual. He would attack Howard for cutting the training budget. Howard would pretend not to be making cuts, and then attack Blair for not promising to restore them. Blair would respond by saying the 'training revolution' would be paid for by a levy on companies which did not provide training. Howard would seize theatrically on this, describe it as a 'jobs tax', and turn forensic in his pursuit of its appearance and disappearance in successive Labour policy documents. Blair would then denounce Howard for not caring about the unemployed. Finally, Howard would retaliate by saying Labour's plan for a minimum wage would destroy up to 2 million jobs.

As they applied their legal minds to dissecting routinely each other's arguments, both were polite and avoided personal attacks, preserving courtroom niceties. One of Blair's distinguishing features as a politician was his absolute aversion to personal insult. He often annoyed his speech-writers by taking out their best lines for this reason.

The worst Blair would say about Howard was that he had been 'biting the wrong mushroom', such was his distorted vision of the paradise of

Britain, overflowing with jobs and training opportunities.[7] Or that he should be called the Secretary of State for Interviews, as that was all he was offering the unemployed.[8]

Like lawyers, they preserved social relations outside the court of Parliament. Early in their duel Howard invited the Blairs to dinner at his London home. It was unusual for a Cabinet minister to dine with his shadow, but Howard and his friend Norman Lamont, also present with his wife Rosemary, were intrigued by Blair. As the dinner revealed, Howard was rather more open-minded than his public persona. Like Nigel Lawson, he and Lamont were genuinely puzzled as to why Blair was in the Labour Party. They found him charming, although Lamont got the impression that Cherie was uncomfortable in the tent of the ungodly. 'She was rather more severe then than she is today and also more left-wing than Tony,' he wrote later.[9]

Howard produced yet another batch of proposed changes to trade union law in July 1991, a Green Paper on giving individuals the right to obtain injunctions to prevent strikes in public services, among a host of minor measures. The purpose seemed to be primarily to embarrass the Labour Party, long after the real imbalances seen by Conservatives in trade union law had been righted. Conservative MPs, welcoming an old theme like a familiar security blanket, cheered Howard on. Sketchwriter Matthew Parris described his opponent's response:

> Mr Blair pitched it just right. With the lightest of touches and complete self-confidence he sauntered through the Green Paper, grinning. He tweaked this, prodded that, inspected the teeth of a clause or two – and pronounced that it did not pass muster. It was all got up for the hustings. He gave examples, seemingly very learned examples, with the winning assurance of a likeable young swell.
>
> His own side barely understood what he was saying, but loved it. Later, Mr Howard painstakingly picked it apart. But Mr Blair won the moment, and that matters in the Chamber. A certain swagger helps, and a public school education provides it. Class still counts for something in the Parliamentary Labour Party.[10]

When Howard counter-attacked by asking for the definition of secondary strike action that would be allowed under Labour, Blair tartly told him that they were debating the government's Bill, not Labour policy documents. Hardly an adequate response but, again, it had the appearance of an effective put-down.

Howard was striking the right target. He knew that Blair was uncomfortable with the policy he had inherited from Michael Meacher. Labour had accepted pre-strike ballots, the most important reform. But Kinnock and Blair still saw the spectre of Scargill escaping through Meacher's form of words. They could see in their minds a re-run of the miners' strike, with flying pickets asking the power workers, lorry drivers, railway workers and dockers to come out in support. The Meacher document would allow sympathetic strikes if a second group of workers had a 'genuine interest in the outcome of a dispute'. Blair's revamp appeared in *Looking to the Future* in May 1990, a policy document on which the next manifesto would be based. 'Genuine interest' was replaced by 'direct interest between two groups of workers of an occupational or professional nature'. This was hardly less broad, because workers at coal power stations could still argue that the outcome of a miners' strike would affect their terms and conditions. But the new formula used the word 'direct', which had the advantage of appearing to rule out secondary – or 'indirect' – industrial action.

It thus allowed Blair to insist that the type of mass picketing and flying pickets that occurred during the miners' strike 'cannot be allowed to happen again – that's why we want to lay this whole area to rest'.[11]

These wordplays may seem rather small beer and sandwiches, but Blair was pushing at the limits of the possible. His document on picketing was rejected by the National Executive in the morning, and then approved when the meeting reconvened after lunch. 'The only way to bring it about was to take advantage of one or two absences and to use some tortuous language,' said Kinnock. 'So that's how it was done. But I was playing poker, and it came out right in the end.' The decisive vote in the afternoon, to 'clarify' the morning's decision, did indeed 'lay this whole area to rest'. The specifics of Labour policy on trade union law were hardly heard of again – not until a debate emerged on the rules for union recognition under Blair's government. Blair had eliminated another negative.

Looking to the future

The Labour Party assembled for its conference in Blackpool at the end of September 1990 in an upbeat mood. Margaret Thatcher had suffered six months of catastrophic unpopularity since the riots provoked by the new poll tax in England and Wales in April. Nigel Lawson's resignation the previous year had exposed deep divisions over Europe, and now Michael Heseltine stalked the television studios, unable to foresee where circumstances might lead him. Labour had completed its policy review and looked forward with some excitement to the next election. The shift in the party's attitude to trade union law was one of the most important and symbolic changes. With shadow Cabinet members finally allowed to address delegates for ten minutes from the platform, here was Blair's chance to identify himself with the light at the end of the tunnel.

As he walked out to the podium, he was, of course, nervous. The conference platform – one of the most striking in recent years – was dominated by a tilted row of four huge photographs of 'real people'. The theme was 'Looking to the Future', echoing the party's 1945 manifesto, *Let Us Face the Future*. In front of Blair lay row upon row of real activists in the Victorian heaviness of the Winter Gardens.

His delivery was shouted and too fast, and at one point he lost his place in his text. It was not his greatest oratorical moment, but just four years later he would be addressing a Labour conference in the same Winter Gardens as leader.

No sooner was the conference over than it was forgotten. That weekend Chancellor John Major and Foreign Secretary Douglas Hurd finally prevailed over a weakened Margaret Thatcher, and the pound joined the European Exchange Rate Mechanism. Seven weeks later, Thatcher was gone. The following year, Blair was to say that 'he viewed the biggest Tory mistake of recent times as the deposing of Margaret Thatcher. A vital sense of direction (even if admittedly in the wrong direction) was lost.'[12] It was a curious judgment, given that Conservative MPs had only been driven to the extreme course of ditching a sitting Prime Minister because of the near certainty that she would lead them to defeat at the next General Election. Blair's view of Thatcher, therefore, had less to do with her election-winning ability in practice than with the cult of personality in theory. His remark was evidence of his growing understanding of the importance in politics of certainty and aggression – a combination usually derided as stridency in Thatcher.

On 27 November 1990 she was succeeded by her Chancellor, a man with 'a quiet, dull grey, low cunning that is all his own' – a soubriquet of Nick Brown's that Blair had described as 'a compliment' in a knockabout debate on the Public Expenditure White Paper earlier that year.[13]

As soon as John Major became Prime Minister, government and opposition were locked in the sumo embrace of the 'Long Campaign'. The Conservatives bounced back in the opinion polls, although Labour remained a little ahead. Major constantly looked for the moment he could call the election, and Labour constantly forced him to postpone it. Labour appeared confident and professional, but the truth was that it was running on autopilot. Its strategy had been designed to fight Thatcher, and was never satisfactorily adjusted to deal with a leader who was at the same time her extension and her opposite – a role which Blair was eventually to fill with rather more gusto. On the central ground of economic competence, Labour's presentation was dangerously weak.

Full employment dropped

As shadow Employment Secretary, Blair had two contributions to make to Labour's claim to be able to manage the economy better than the Conservatives. Neither was successful, although in both cases he shared responsibility with the leading figures in the party. Neil Kinnock described education and training as the 'commanding heights of a modern economy', and yet Blair had no significant training programme planned to back up this claim. Meanwhile, Labour played down the goal of full employment – a goal which could at least have been a symbol of the party's confidence that it could deliver a strong economy.

For many years, the main job of the Opposition employment spokesman had been to sound outraged on television when the monthly unemployment figures were published. It was a role in which Labour's 'Mr Angry', John Prescott, had excelled in the mid-1980s. As unemployment fell during the end of the Lawson boom, from 1986 to 1990, that role fell into neglect, and when unemployment started to rise again in early 1990, Blair's response was muted.

The goal of 'full employment' had been reaffirmed in Labour's final policy review document, *Meet the Challenge, Make the Change*: 'It is a long time since full employment was the objective of government, so long that as a goal it may seem unrealistic. However, as we explain in this report, it is a goal that can be achieved.'

However, in the weeks after the report was endorsed by party conference in 1989, Neil Kinnock and his economic adviser John Eatwell, with shadow Chancellor John Smith and *his* economic adviser Gordon Brown, executed an about-turn on the issue of Britain's membership of the European Exchange Rate Mechanism. Hardly anyone noticed, because Nigel Lawson had just resigned. But certain consequences flowed from this fundamental change in Labour policy.

Once Labour advocated ERM membership, it meant that the overriding objective of its macro-economic policy would be to maintain the value of the pound against the Deutschmark. Critics in the party – such as Bryan Gould, who had been moved to the non-economic brief of Environment – said this meant interest rates and government borrowing would have to be decided by the pound's exchange rate, and could not be set to achieve other objectives, such as full employment.

Brown and Eatwell argued, and Smith agreed, that this was a false trade-off. They concluded that it was not possible simply to cut interest rates and print money to reflate the economy and create lasting jobs. This would suck in imports, cause inflation and lead to unemployment later. Apart from emergency measures to help the people who had been unemployed for a long time, the main ways to create lasting jobs were to raise the skills of the workforce and to encourage long-term investment.

However, instead of arguing that ERM membership was the best way of moving towards full employment in the long term, they, and Blair, ditched the phrase. It vanished from the party's 1990 policy document, *Looking to the Future*, where the goal was downgraded to the 'highest possible levels of skilled and rewarding employment'.

Blair's role in the historic switch in Labour's economic policy was subordinate: as ERM membership gradually became the party orthodoxy, his personal view remained indistinguishable from the party line. Despite being Bryan Gould's deputy from 1987 to 1988, Gordon Brown was his guiding influence. Having argued in 1986 that joining the ERM would be to put the Treasury under the control of the Bundesbank, he now believed that sharing some monetary sovereignty with the Germans was necessary for Labour's anti-inflationary credibility. As Lawson's inflationary 'blip' threatened to run out of control in 1989–90, controlling inflation had – temporarily as it turned out – become more important than tackling unemployment.

There was, therefore, no reference to full employment in Labour's 1992 manifesto, which merely said, 'We are determined to make a swift reduction in unemployment', and suggested that long-term progress depended on Europe-wide co-ordination: 'Unemployment must be tackled by the European Community as a whole.' But both Blair and Kinnock continued to use the term, off text, as a goal they wanted to achieve without setting any targets by which to measure it. 'Caution in targets doesn't relax in the least the objective,' Blair later explained. 'It stems from a desire not ever to get into a situation where we're misleading people.'[14]

This caution served to underscore the party's lack of confidence in the means by which it planned to build a strong economy. Labour's proposed 'training revolution' – rebranded as the slightly more upmarket 'skills revolution' by the time of the election – was more than a slogan, but it lacked the resources and mechanisms to be wholly credible. The contrast with the 'New Deal' five years later is striking: aimed at a specific group, the young unemployed, and paid for by a windfall tax on unpopular privatised companies. Blair extravagantly described his skills package as 'our greatest single priority'.[15] Unfortunately for him, it was not the greatest single priority of John Smith's pre-election shadow Budget.

Most of the resources to pay for training were supposed to come from a levy paid by companies which did not spend at least 0.5 per cent of their wages bill on their own training. But Gordon Brown in particular was sensitive to the Conservative charge that this was a 'tax on jobs', and the 0.5 per cent figure was dropped from the manifesto. Selling a policy with which he broadly agreed in principle, but in the specifics of which he had no confidence, was Blair's peculiar skill, and it was sorely tested in another field.

Minimum wage, maximum trouble

The minimum wage was the only other 'positive' employment policy that the Labour Party possessed. But rather than promote it like a salesman Blair defended it as a lawyer defends a client.

Labour had reversed its position on the minimum wage in 1986, upsetting traditionalists of both its left and right wings. Both preferred that mantra of the 1970s, 'free collective bargaining'. To the old left, the low-paid should be organised in unions, not paid a minimum wage decided and enforced by the capitalist state. To the old right, it was a threat to differentials. For the new unionists, however, a rights-based approach was the most effective way to protect low-paid workers, often working in sectors where unions were poorly organised.

With the help of the Trades Union Congress, Blair managed to stifle the objections of dissident unions in the pre-election period, but he could not shake off Michael Howard, the Employment Secretary, as he hammered away at a single, simple proposition: 'If it means that employers are going to have to pay more than they would otherwise pay, there will be some employers who will not be able to afford to pay that, and they won't offer the jobs.' In fact, the economic effects of a minimum wage are more complex than that, because it can increase spending power and reduce job turnover. But Blair did not sound as if he believed it, in a letter he wrote to the *Independent* on 27 June 1991: 'I have not accepted that the minimum wage would cost jobs . . . I have simply accepted that econometric models indicate a potential jobs impact.'

His real problem was the way the level of the minimum wage would be calculated. It was to be fixed annually in relation to 'median male earnings', a fine combination of labour-movement sexism and statistical obscurantism. Blair managed to abandon the long-term goal of setting the minimum wage at two-thirds of this figure, which did not appear in the

1992 manifesto. But he was still committed to a rate of half median male earnings, then £3.40 an hour. He tried to retreat from this too in July 1991:

> Of course the minimum wage must be implemented carefully and of course we cannot set it at too excessive a level, but we will start the process of having a minimum wage. We shall take care, but we shall introduce it, because it is fair and right and because a society that treats its most vulnerable badly is a society not worthy of the name.[16]

The BBC's industrial correspondent, John Fryer, spoke to Blair several times on the subject during this time. Fryer thought his arguments were unconvincing – although put with obvious skill – and his evidence weak, and asked him why he did not just abandon the policy: 'Although he never moved off it privately, when you looked into the whites of his eyes you detected a lack of true conviction.' This was confirmed in 1994 when, in one of his first decisions as leader, Blair quietly dropped the formula, saying the level of the minimum wage would be set in government. It was eventually brought in at £3.60 in 1999, much lower than the formula required, and lower than the 1992 commitment after taking inflation into account.

During the election campaign, on 18 March 1992, shadow Transport Secretary John Prescott, having been kept off the Labour headquarters 'Key Campaigners' list, was asked about the minimum wage on Sky TV's election phone-in. He admitted that it would lose some jobs: 'I think you have to accept there may be some shake-out in some of the jobs in certain areas, but generally it will be beneficial to the community.'

All Blair's defensive obfuscation had been cut through by Plain-Speaking John. Fryer spotted the discrepancy and spoke to Blair on his mobile phone in Darlington to ask him to come to the BBC studio in Newcastle to comment. 'I'm not having it, John,' said Blair, according to one account of the conversation. 'I'm the spokesman on employment. There's no way you're going to run that story. I can't get up to Newcastle to the studios to defend it. And if you can't pull this story, you'd better let me speak to someone who can.' Blair was in a strong position, because during election campaigns BBC rules are stricter and more cautious than usual – it might have seemed 'unfair' to broadcast that story without an official Labour spokesperson. Blair had not refused to appear, but was merely 'unable' to get to a studio. The Prescott story was not broadcast.

Team player

As the preparations for an election intensified, Blair increasingly took a leading role. The campaign strategy was designed to build up the 'Economic Team' around a leader who was distrusted by the voters Labour needed. For all his strengths as a party manager, it was accepted – even by Kinnock himself – that he had to be seen as surrounded by solid, reassuring competence.

The 'team' were John Smith, Tony Blair, Margaret Beckett and Gordon Brown. They were presented in that order in a party political broadcast on 18 April 1991. It was a fourfold example of a genre known in America as the 'biopic', a thirty- or sixty-second biographical commercial, usually screened at the beginning of election campaigns, to define a candidate in the minds of the voters. The Economic Team broadcast was made by Hugh Hudson, director of *Chariots of Fire* and 'Kinnock – The Movie', the extended 'biopic' of the Labour leader in the 1987 election, and probably the most celebrated British political broadcast.

Over pictures of Blair, in a leather jacket, picking up his daughter Kathryn on a bridge in front of a sunny Durham cathedral, the voice-over said: 'Age thirty-seven. The youngest member of the shadow Cabinet. MP for Sedgefield, Durham. Born in Edinburgh, son of a law lecturer . . .' This was followed by a burst of opportunity chat from Blair:

> There is an immense wealth of talent and potential, and we don't use it, and the reason that we don't use it is that we don't give people the opportunity to develop their own personality, to build their own character, to realise just exactly what they could be – because they could be anything they want to be, provided they get the opportunities. Now, you can't do everything for people, you can't run their lives for them, you can't make all their choices for them. But you can at least give them access to the type of opportunities that I enjoyed, and that many people don't enjoy.

His message, delivered with a taut urgency, seemed to cut through the stasis of Labour politics in that period. It was a significant marker, because it demonstrated his fluency as a mass politician and because it developed the theme, 'Opportunity Britain', which the communications agency under Philip Gould had devised for what was expected to be a General Election year.

Blair was the star of Labour's public opinion research. Although still little-known, he came across better than any of his colleagues in television clips which were regularly tested on groups of floating voters. Researchers recalled only one occasion on which he failed to score highly, when he talked about the problems of having a home in London and another in his constituency, which sounded as if he were complaining about owning two houses.

It was no coincidence that the members of the Economic Team were also the main contenders for the leadership after the 1992 election. John Smith had built himself a commanding position in the party by 1991. Blair consistently told friends in this period that he thought Labour would lose the coming election, because it had failed to change enough. The implication of that, however, is that he must have thought that Smith – or even Brown – would inherit the leadership. Having switched tracks with barely a click between Foot and Kinnock, he was now switching to Smith. This caused Kinnock some frustration, according to his Chief of Staff, Charles Clarke:

> Neil thought they were too loyal to John. There was an economic team of four, which was Smith, Beckett, Blair and Brown – and we [Kinnock's team] always worked with Blair and Brown. But they would never ever come out and really go down the line with Neil. Their loyalty to Smith was greater than their loyalty to Neil during that period.

Kinnock was also infuriated by Blair and Brown's dilatory attendance at shadow Cabinet meetings, which implied they had better things to do with their time. Clarke was once despatched to insist that they turn up. When Blair did come, he always sat at the corner chair by the door so he could arrive late and leave early.

Occasional reports of attempts to encourage Smith to oust Kinnock as leader surfaced between 1988 and 1991. Smith did not deny that he would be a candidate 'if for one reason or another there arose a vacancy for leader of the party'.[17] And he certainly gave vent to his frustrations with Kinnock in private, complaining to his allies Roy Hattersley and Donald Dewar and the less closely allied Peter Mandelson in August 1987 that you never knew where you stood with Kinnock and that his election speeches had been 'froth, pure froth'.[18]

Actually plotting to replace him was a different matter. As long as Kinnock wanted to be leader and, crucially, as long as the opinion polls suggested he had a prospect of forming even a minority government, the party's leadership election system made a challenge impossible. Smith was 'categoric' in rejecting a tentative approach from some of his shadow Cabinet colleagues to put himself forward in the autumn of 1991.[19] Nevertheless, even Kinnock's closest aides were tempted by the thought of changing leader, if only because those same opinion polls also suggested Labour's ratings would improve if Smith took over. Patricia Hewitt, who was central to the election campaign team, said afterwards: 'It's conceivable that with a last-minute change of leader, something akin to the Labor Party in Australia when they elected Bob Hawke as their leader a couple of hours after the election had been called, we might well have won this election.'[20] Charles Clarke, who was rude about Smith's 'lack of leadership qualities', agreed: 'It's just conceivable that if you'd changed leader at the beginning of the campaign itself then it might have been okay.'[21]

By January 1992, Blair's confidant Mandelson – cut off from the leader since he resigned to stand in Hartlepool – had come to the 'tragic' conclusion Labour could not win unless Kinnock stood down.[22] But Blair himself ruled out the possibility dismissively. As long as the polls showed Labour just ahead, who could go to Kinnock and say he would lose? An intriguing hypothetical question is, 'What if the opinion polls had been more accurate before the 1992 election?' Not only might Kinnock have given way to Smith, but Smith might have won and been forced to devalue the pound soon afterwards, as John Major was. In many ways, the Labour Party – and Blair – were fortunate to lose in 1992.

The wager

By the time of the 1991 Labour Party conference in Brighton, Blair was increasingly being talked about as a leadership candidate some time in the future. His speech to the conference rehearsed some of the themes and phrases which were to become the building-blocks of his leadership platform. 'Using the power of all for the good of each,' he intoned:

> This is modern socialism; its means ever changing, its purpose ever constant, founded on the belief that we are more than buyers and sellers in some impersonal marketplace, not merely individuals stranded in helpless isolation, but human beings, part of a community with obligations to one another as well as ourselves.

Condemning the government's record on unemployment, he developed the idea of 'social cohesion' with a classic example of Blair's Middle, the rhetorical device that placed him in the rational centre between two unpalatable extremes: 'No one but a fool would excuse the rioting that disfigured our inner cities a few weeks ago. But no one but a Tory would ignore the social despair in which such evil breeds.'

It was a good speech. It outshone those of the 'big five' – Neil Kinnock, Roy Hattersley, John Smith, Gerald Kaufman and Gordon Brown – who had been earmarked by party officials for prominence in the run-up to the election.

In the five years between the 1987 and 1992 elections the speed and economy of Blair's rise was remarkable. No time was wasted, no years were spent treading water. Starting as an able junior frontbencher, in Year One he made his first attempt at the shadow Cabinet and was rewarded with one of the best positions outside it. In Year Two he was elected to the shadow Cabinet and blooded as a conference speaker. In Year Three he was given one of the important economic posts, and in a single act of political courage and judgment pulled off a coup against the closed shop which made his reputation. In Year Four he was presented as one of the party's leading faces. In Year Five he gave a hint of broader themes of social cohesion, and emerged from the 1992 election as a serious contender for the deputy leadership of the party.

He secured his advancement through ability, charm, loyalty to the leadership, the avoidance of mistakes and – very occasionally – the taking of calculated risks. He was an increasingly surefooted performer in the House of Commons and a potentially outstanding communicator on television.

Some interested observers were even willing to put money on Blair as a future leader. 'How much will you give me for Tony Blair to be Prime Minister by the end of the century?' asked George Elliott of the Sedgefield bookmaker Billy Day in 1991. Elliott, the owner of a local taxi company, regularly ferried Blair and his family to and from the airport and station. He said Day, a former Middlesbrough footballer, replied: 'Don't be silly, man.' When Elliott persisted the next time they met, he offered 500–1, and Elliott bet £10. He said:

> I thought, 'What a good-looking man, to be an MP, which we're not used to in the Labour Party.' He dresses smart and everything, and he comes over well on television . . . I thought, 'Well, if we're ever going to have a chance, there's the man to do it.'

Three years ahead of the deadline, Elliott collected his £5,000.

'Mods'

In order to understand Blair's rise, it is necessary to explain the rise of 'the modernisers'. The term started to be used during the policy review of 1987–89. In the year or so before the 1992 election, Gordon Brown and Tony Blair put themselves at the forefront of an increasingly well-defined body of ideas – a new politics growing within the shell of the old Labour Party. Under Neil Kinnock's leadership, parts of the old husk had fallen off, but the new party was not yet fully formed. Part of the modernisers' problem was that Kinnock himself personified continuity as well as being the agent of change.

The idea of 'modernisation' was a conscious attempt to fill the ideological vacuum on the left of British politics. As such it was rather narrowly based. It did not arise from a social movement outside the party, or from the grass roots or the unions within it. It was synthesised by elements of the parliamentary leadership, drawing on such intellectual forces as the left could muster.

Nor was modernisation a coherent ideology like, say, Croslandite revisionism. Nor would it become one even after Blair gave it the label 'the Third Way' in 1996–97 and it acquired intellectuals such as Professor Anthony Giddens as its disciples. It was as much a process as a prescription. Blair's insistence on a mass membership as the basis of a relationship with the electorate was a way of kicking the party in a certain direction, destination unknown.

One of the modernisers' central beliefs, however, was ideological, even if it took the form of a negative: that the interests of labour and capital are not in conflict, and therefore that the Labour Party should no longer be regarded as the political wing of the trade union movement.

For a long time Blair had borrowed the language of *Marxism Today* to describe the new politics as a 'project', invariably following an 'agenda'. *Marxism Today* was one of the trading posts of the new ideas – its editor and intellectual entrepreneur, Martin Jacques, met Blair in 1991. Blair rang him to suggest an article. Jacques's inclination was to say no straight away, 'But there was something in it that held me off,' he said. He and Blair met, and became friendly. 'The challenge for socialists is to re-establish the agenda for public action without the old failings of collectivism,' Blair wrote in the magazine in October 1991.

The language was abstract and off-putting, but it was an important article. It aimed to bury the notion that public ownership was a necessary expression of socialist values. The state could become a 'vested interest in itself, every bit as capable of oppressing individuals as wealth and capital'. He wrote:

> In the latter part of the nineteenth century, and the early part of this century . . . democratic socialists equated the public interest with public ownership. So that, though their motivation and values were, and remain, correct, and though they correctly analysed the shortcomings of the early capitalist system, they had no developed analysis of the limitations of public ownership through the state as a means of helping the individual.

Since then, capitalism had

> drastically altered with the advent of a modern sophisticated market – the state became large and powerful . . . [and] the majority of people became

taxpayers funding the activities of the state and therefore anxious as to how their money was used.

The role of the state was now 'to ensure a fully competitive market to prevent monopoly and to encourage choice'. Public ownership was not necessarily in the interest of either consumers or workers: 'The task of social or collective action today is not to abolish capital, as part of some war for supremacy between management and labour, but rather to enhance the power of individual employees.'

It is impossible to disentangle the influence of Gordon Brown: such a sentence could have been written by either of them. On economic issues their partnership was so close – or Blair's deference so total – as to give them a joint personality.

If the war between management and labour was over, it was inevitable that the role of trade unions in the Labour Party needed to change. Not only the state but the unions too could be a 'vested interest'. It was only after the election, however, that Blair said: 'The trade union movement is a tremendously important, integral part of British society, *but* it's important that Labour speaks for the whole community.'[23] The implication for the dominance of party policy by trade union block votes was clear.

Notes

1. *Hansard*, 29 November 1989, cols 727–34.
2. *Private Eye*, 2 February 1990.
3. *Hansard*, 29 January 1990, col. 55.
4. News conference, Washington, DC, 13 September 1977, cited by John Campbell, *Margaret Thatcher,* Vol. 1, p. 393.
5. Patrick Seyd and Paul Whiteley, *Labour's Grass Roots*, pp. 153, 246.
6. Andy McSmith, *Faces of Labour*, p. 17.
7. *Hansard*, 21 March 1991, col. 504.
8. *Ibid.*, 5 June 1991, col. 345.
9. Norman Lamont, *In Office*, p. 414; but he dates the dinner to 1983, which may account for the erroneous suggestion that it was part of a plot to persuade Blair to 'cross the Floor' to the Conservatives (*The Times* Diary, 2 February 1999).
10. Matthew Parris, *The Times*, 25 July 1991.
11. BBC1, *On the Record*, 27 May 1990.
12. Interview, the *Fettesian*, December 1991.
13. *Hansard*, 13 February 1990, cols 230–31.
14. Anthony Bevins, *Observer*, 10 July 1994.
15. *Financial Times*, 27 January 1992.
16. *Hansard*, 9 July 1991, cols 799, 826.
17. *Daily Record*, 14 January 1991.
18. Donald Macintyre, *Mandelson*, p. 157.

19. *Ibid.*, p. 227; Andy McSmith, *John Smith*, pp. 181–6.
20. BBC1, *On the Record*, 10 May 1992.
21. Philip Gould, *The Unfinished Revolution*, p. 145.
22. Macintyre, *Mandelson*, p. 226.
23. Interview, 8 June 1992 (author's emphasis).

10

Gordon's Missed Opportunity

The Modernisers Thwarted, 1992

> 'Smithy . . . won't last the course. It's important that you're there to pick up the pieces.'
>
> —*Neil Kinnock to Bryan Gould, 1992*

One of the causes of Labour's pre-election paralysis was the widespread assumption, based on its steady but small lead in the opinion polls, that Neil Kinnock was likely to form a government in a hung parliament. It was not an assumption, however, shared by many of the Labour leadership themselves, including Tony Blair and, increasingly, Kinnock himself. In Blair's case this may have been partly fashionable pessimism, as he had a tendency to describe any adverse situation as hopeless and any setback as the end of his political career. But it also reflected his view that the party had not changed enough.

The tax issue lay like an unexploded mine under Labour's credibility. It was partly detonated by the Conservative 'tax bombshell' advertising campaign in January 1992, but the real explosion did not occur until John Smith presented his 'shadow Budget' in March, responding to Norman Lamont's clever Budget proposing a tax cut skewed towards the lower-paid. Labour had blocked itself when the policy review concluded in 1989 that the only spending promises that were sacrosanct were those to raise the state pension and child benefit. Blair and Brown thought the special status accorded to those two expensive pledges was a mistake. In deciding how to pay for them Labour made another mistake, by proposing to abolish the limit on National Insurance contributions. This was entirely rational and utterly disastrous. For decades there had been an anomaly in the tax system. The contributions which theoretically paid for National Insurance benefits were not charged on earnings above a relatively low amount – £20,280 a year in 1992. The result was that some higher earners were taxed less heavily than lower earners. Labour proposed to levy contributions on all earnings, effectively a tax rise for millions on middle and higher incomes. The hostility of those who lost out (or who could be persuaded by Conservative propaganda that they might lose out) was bound to outweigh the gratitude of those who gained.

When it came to doing something about it, however, Brown and Blair were in an awkward position. Both the spending pledges and the policy on National Insurance were very much the property of the Economic Team. The team member least implicated in the policy was Blair, but loyalty ensured that his and Brown's disquiet was aired only in Smith's room. And at the time they merely argued that the bottom of a recession was not the right time to honour promises agreed during a boom.

Neil Kinnock, meanwhile, had separately identified the problem of the National Insurance ceiling. He recognised the symbolism of bringing in higher taxes at a level of annual earnings as low as £20,280. Although it was well above average earnings, it could be seen, as Bryan Gould described it after the election, as a 'cap on aspirations'. At what was to become a notorious dinner with journalists in Luigi's restaurant in Covent Garden on 14 January, he floated the idea of phasing in the National Insurance change.

Shadow Chancellor John Smith was not pleased. His view was that phasing-in would not have solved the problem, only postponed it. It also drew journalists' attention to a weakness in Labour's policy while under fire from the Conservatives. With two months to go before an election campaign, Kinnock provoked Smith into defending the policy instead of dealing with the problem.

In the election campaign itself, Blair and Gordon Brown, having been 'beautiful people', felt pushed aside. Resentments swirled as Labour politicians manoeuvred behind the scenes of the public campaign to ready themselves for victory or defeat. Blair and Brown, as Smith loyalists, found themselves eclipsed by Smith's older loyalties to his right-wing Labour allies. Roy Hattersley and Jack Cunningham flanked the shadow Chancellor as the heavyweights of Kinnock's ballast. Instead of the 'Economic Team', the leader was bolstered by the 'Right Team', as the leaders of the old Solidarity faction asserted their control – Hattersley because his long-serving adviser, David Hill, was now the party's director of communications, and Cunningham because he was campaigns co-ordinator, the shadow Cabinet post invented in 1985 for Robin Cook.

Blair and Brown wanted Brown to be campaigns co-ordinator, as he effectively became in 1995, and believed the election result might have been different if he had been, although policy commitments and Neil Kinnock's character would have given him little space to move history on to a different course.

With Cunningham and Hill as media planners, and with Peter Mandelson occupied as the candidate in Hartlepool, Blair and Brown were not on television during the campaign as much as they thought they ought to be. In the heated pre-election atmosphere, Brown fell victim to the suspicions of his colleagues because he had set up his own 'secret' campaign headquarters in an office near Waterloo. In fact, the office had been planned as the election base of the Economic Team, led by John Smith, but at the last minute Smith's staff moved into a union office next door to Labour Party headquarters in Walworth Road. His deputy, Margaret Beckett, went with him, while Blair never really based himself there when MPs had to move out of their Westminster offices at the start of the campaign. Brown's large staff of seven (compared with Blair's two)* also contributed to the appearance of a personal power base. This fuelled speculation after the election that Brown had designs on the party leadership, in competition with Smith. Blair, as ever, floated free from any suspicion of intrigue – partly because he was not seen as a threat. But his leadership ambitions were about to become more apparent.

Labour's election campaign was professional and largely gaffe-free, but it was unexciting. The one time Kinnock came to life was to jump about and gee up the audience at the infamous Sheffield rally, a misjudgment which probably had less impact than a series of weak performances, most notably when he said, to a *Granada 500* live studio audience hooting derision, that he had a view on electoral reform but he was not going to tell them what it was. Even Labour's strongest issue, the National Health Service, was not as strong as it looked. The surreal squabble in the media compound over Labour's propaganda use of a girl's ear operation – the so-called 'War of Jennifer's Ear' – did not help, but the NHS alone was never going to win the election.

Blair's pessimism about the outcome was briefly disturbed during the last few days of the campaign. The polls eight days before polling day put Labour up to 7 percentage points ahead, and for a day he allowed himself to dream of a ministerial Rover. But early in the week of polling day he and Neil Kinnock spoke at a rally in Kinnock's constituency. The Labour

*Blair's campaign staff consisted of James Purnell and Roz Preston. Anji Hunter had left his office in 1991 – despite his desperate pleas for her to stay – to spend more time with her young children, but politics had taken hold and she went to work in Neil Kinnock's office during the campaign before returning to Blair.

leader already felt that the election was slipping away, and Blair returned to his long-held view that the party had not done enough to win.

On the day before the election, the party was taken aback by the ferocity of the Conservative newspapers. The *Sun* carried nine pages headed 'NIGHTMARE ON KINNOCK STREET'. The *Daily Express* and the *Daily Mail* carried similar attacks.

All the same, and despite his low private opinion of Kinnock, John Smith left home in Edinburgh for London on polling day saying that when he came back he would be Chancellor of the Exchequer. He had agreed a statement at the Treasury about exchange rate policy, to be issued after the polls closed.[1] But on the night of 9 April 1992, Kinnock and Blair's pessimism was quickly confirmed. Just after eleven o'clock, the result in Basildon was announced. This was an important marginal seat, with a large working-class Conservative electorate. The swing to Labour was miserably small, and David Amess held the seat. 'That's it,' said Kinnock, watching television with his wife Glenys. His dream was over.

Blair, in Sedgefield, increased his majority again, to 14,859. But nationally the party's share of the vote rose just 3.5 percentage points to 35 per cent – barely one voter in three and still a lower share of the vote than in 1979. The Conservatives were way ahead on 41.9 per cent. It was not much consolation at the time, but Labour did better than it deserved to. It benefited from out-of-date constituency boundaries and ran a particularly effective campaign in marginal seats. John Major's majority was only 21, but it was enough, just, to last a full five years. For Blair the result confirmed his belief that Labour needed further change – on a scale which the party's history taught was heroic – and that there was no time to lose.

Vaulting ambition

Neil Kinnock conceded defeat at five o'clock in the morning of 10 April 1992, on the steps of Labour headquarters in south London. The battle for the succession started a few hours later. This was not the campaign to succeed Kinnock – John Smith had more or less wrapped that up months, if not years, before. It was the campaign to succeed Smith which began later that morning, as the BBC's election coverage continued from the night before, trying to come to terms with the largely unexpected result. From the BBC's Newcastle studio just after nine o'clock on Friday morning, Blair launched his bid. He drew attention to the party's limited success in winning seats in the south of England, 'in the south-west and in London, which I think was very important', where Labour would need to win more seats next time and might need someone designed to appeal to the English middle classes.

With his increasingly sure sense of political timing he judged that this was the moment above all, when the rest of the party was exhausted and depressed, to press the case that Labour had failed to win because it had not modernised enough and to promote himself as the agent of further change.

He brushed aside a question about Kinnock's future. 'That is not even on the agenda at the moment. He has our tremendous respect and gratitude and support.' Indeed, the ever-courteous Blair was the only member of the shadow Cabinet to telephone Kinnock later that morning with commiserations.[2] But the only reason the question of the leadership was not on the agenda was because, just as in 1983 and later in 1994, there was no serious doubt about it. It was the deputy leadership that was really at stake, and with it the prospect of inheriting Smith's crown, which Smith himself never expected to wear for long.

A vast amount of ink and angst has been spent on the question of how Tony Blair secured the leadership in the hours and days after John Smith died on 12 May 1994, and more specifically on Peter Mandelson's role in those events. Indeed a central weakness in his government was what Blair described as the 'titanic feud' between Gordon Brown and Mandelson arising from that period. But those looking for the explanation of how Blair secured the leadership ought to focus instead on the hours and days after the Labour Party lost its fourth election in a row in 1992. It is in the conversations and calculations of the key players over the weekend from Friday 10 April to Tuesday 14 April that historians will find the answers.

The jostling for position began long before the 1992 election, as has been seen, not so much for posts in government, which had been settled, but for advantage in the case of defeat. Blair told the novelist and political columnist Robert Harris over lunch in March, just five weeks before the election, that he expected Labour to lose, and left him 'in little doubt' that he expected Gordon Brown to stand for the leadership, that he would be his deputy and that Mandelson would run the media campaign for both of them.[3] Such candid ambition was all the more remarkable for the fact that it was the first time they had met – at Blair's request. Blair must have known, however, that Smith was in a powerful position, popular and respected in the party and in the country and with the backing of the leaders of the GMB general union and the Transport and General. He would have known that the only people with a prospect of challenging him were Brown and Bryan Gould. Brown's position had been strong enough to fuel public speculation the previous autumn that he might run against Smith if Labour lost, forcing Brown to authorise Mandelson to tell journalists on his behalf that there was no possibility that he would do so.[4]

Indeed, whatever discussions Brown, Blair and Mandelson may have had, Brown did not countenance standing against his friend and protector when talking to anybody else. 'I felt I owed a debt of gratitude to John Smith. I felt I had to be loyal. It was for no other reason,' he told his biographer, Paul Routledge.[5] Loyalty apart, however, he was probably right not to do so, if only for the pragmatic reason that Smith had established such a commanding position.

Blair, however, thought this was Brown's chance. 'Tony thought that Brown would have won. You could have presented the argument: "Smith's a nice guy but part of the old order." You could have won the New Labour argument two years earlier,' according to a 'close Blair associate', who sounds like Alastair Campbell, quoted by Donald Macintyre in his biography of Mandelson,[6] and like the 'close aide' of Blair's quoted by Philip Gould in his account of the emergence of New Labour from its chrysalis: 'Tony's view was that the party wanted to be led, it didn't just want to keep sleepwalking and if you sold it an out-and-out modernising message it would take it.'[7]

Another anonymous Blair 'ally' using Campbell's vernacular said Blair felt Brown 'bottled out' of a contest when he had his best chance[8] – although that may be more a retrospective justification of Blair's own later decision to seize the crown from *his* senior friend.

If Brown would not challenge Smith, Bryan Gould certainly would. His reputation in the party had been waning, and he had little support among the unions, but if his campaign had maintained its flying start he might have run Smith close and secured the deputy leadership. Indeed, it was the deputy leadership – and the ultimate succession – that was the real prize.

Kinnock urged Gould to concentrate on the race for deputy leader. Despite his disappointment with Gould over public ownership in the policy review, and his wariness of his Euroscepticism, the outgoing leader thought Gould was essentially a moderniser and had the advantage of 'Englishness', despite being from New Zealand. Robin Cook, who had been Kinnock's campaign manager in 1983 and was now Smith's, also wanted Gould in order to balance the old right. Kinnock's view was that Gould could win the deputy leadership and help keep the modernising 'project' alive. Gould said Kinnock urged him to let 'Smithy' have the leadership: 'He won't last the course. It's important that you're there to pick up the pieces.' Gould did not know whether Kinnock meant Smith would run into political or health problems, but his advice 'certainly proved to be remarkably prescient'.[9]

Blair and Brown knew that Smith would resist Gould as his deputy: their differences over Europe and their personal animosity were too great. Similar arguments ruled out John Prescott. Nor was Brown himself keen to see his rivals promoted to a post he coveted. At some point, Mandelson even drew up a campaign plan for Brown to run for the deputy leadership on a joint ticket with Smith.[10] But a nebulous obstacle emerged. On Saturday in Trimdon, Durham and Newcastle, Blair took part in a series of overlapping discussions with Brown, who had come down from Scotland; Nick Brown, the Newcastle MP who had helped both of them get into the shadow Cabinet; and Mandelson, the new MP for Hartlepool. At a time when Labour was acutely aware of the need to appeal to southern voters, a leadership team of two Scots seemed too narrowly based. In fact, Smith had already decided that the 'two Scots' problem ruled out Brown – already assured of the most senior policy post as shadow Chancellor – as his running mate. However, as the weekend passed he gave no indication as to whom he did want.

From Smith's point of view the choice was between Blair and Margaret Beckett, who both offered a kind of balance to his ticket, one of youth and the south, the other of women and the left. But Smith seemed agnostic between them. 'John sat back,' said David Ward, his adviser. 'He should have spoken to Blair and Brown himself. It was a generational difference – he felt he shouldn't have to chase after these young things. He was waiting to see who would show an interest.'

The *Observer* that Sunday reported that 'Mr Smith is thought to favour Margaret Beckett . . . as his deputy leader'. This may have reflected the views of the leaders of the two big unions, Smith's own GMB and the Transport and General, but later that day Beckett told colleagues and journalists that she would not run for deputy. She even 'suggested to Mr Smith that other contenders, such as Mr Blair or Mr Brown, might be more appropriate running mates for him'.[11] She had, like the four modernisers holed up in the north-east, received no signal from Smith, despite having had lunch with him and other members of the shadow Treasury team on Friday. She may have assumed he was not interested, having calculated, like the modernisers, that the critical factor in the deputy leadership election was his endorsement, overt or implied.

Beckett's withdrawal was Blair's opportunity, and he hesitated long and hard. He knew that being deputy to Smith would be quite different from being deputy to Brown. It would anoint him Heir Apparent, which would mean thwarting Brown, as it turned out, two years before it became necessary. The running north-east caucus went on. One critical question was whether, with John Prescott also preparing to stand, Blair could win under the unreformed electoral college system. Nick Brown, the former fixer for the GMB union's Northern Region, was pessimistic. Although Smith's endorsement would carry Labour MPs, who had 30 per cent of the vote, Blair had little recognition among party members, who had another 30 per cent. Nick Brown also thought that too many of the union leaders who could influence the block votes in the largest part of the electoral college, 40 per cent, were unsympathetic to Blair's policy changes on trade union law, even if they respected him. A further complication was that, if Blair had stood, Jack Cunningham would have been drawn into the race: he entertained serious if unrealistic leadership ambitions himself and would not have tolerated a junior member of the north-eastern group of Labour MPs going ahead of him.

In a soft preview of their later agonised discussions, Blair and Gordon Brown discussed the prospects. Gordon agreed with Nick Brown that Blair was unlikely to win. This was not necessarily a self-serving view, as it coincided with that of the 'Kinnocracy', the circle around the outgoing leader who were disillusioned with Gordon Brown's caution and who were pushing Bryan Gould as the defender of modernisation. Two years later the Kinnocracy would be enthusiastic supporters of Blair's leadership campaign, but now they thought it was too early for him. However, Gordon Brown's advice to Blair not to run was deeply resented by some of Blair's friends, and by Cherie. She never wavered in her ambition for her husband, and wanted him to stand. She thought the two Browns were holding him back so that Gordon could consolidate his position as Smith's undeclared successor. She was probably right.

It is also noteworthy that Peter Mandelson now urged Blair to run. Even Donald Macintyre who generally insists that his subject only reluctantly let go of Gordon Brown's leadership hopes after Smith's death, writes of that weekend: 'Mandelson finally came round to the idea that Blair, if Brown could not do it, might promote the modernisers' cause by standing for the deputy leadership.'[12] By doing so, he must have recognised the threat this represented to Brown's succession.

Other modernisers, including Harriet Harman, urged Blair to break with Brown and put himself forward. An extraordinary letter published in the *Guardian* on Monday 13 April revealed some of the hidden thinking of his supporters. It was written by Colin Byrne, who had resigned as Labour's chief press officer the previous autumn. He was engaged to Kinnock's press secretary, Julie Hall, and had shared a house with her and Mandelson. It exposed some of the private resentments of the modernisers against John Smith, but it also revealed a tilt against Brown, whose loyalty to Smith was paramount:

> John Smith may be a very nice man . . . But what is his record, or that of a handful of centrally-placed right-wing shadow Cabinet members and trade union leaders who are about to emerge as his campaign managers and backers, on the radical reforms Labour has made to its policies and practices – and must go on making if it is not to tread water, sink and die?
>
> What did the right ever do about Militant during the bitter years up to Neil Kinnock taking over? What did they do about reforming the party's relationship with the trades unions and its industrial relations policies? What did they do about Europe? The answer, as I saw for myself during those years of crucial policy review and National Executive Committee meetings, was usually to sit on their hands and let the Kinnocks and the Blairs take the flak.

The use of Blair's name without the other half of the couplet, 'Brown and—', was significant to anyone who followed the 'Kremlinology of the Labour Party'.[13] It was also somewhat propagandist, as Blair was not even a member of the National Executive until later that year. Byrne was reflecting his admiration for Blair's role in private meetings of shadow Cabinet members. But how much did Byrne's rage against Smith represent the views of Blair, or of Mandelson?

Blair, Brown and Mandelson all knew about the letter on Sunday, and all three tried to persuade Byrne to withdraw it, even after he had faxed it to the *Guardian*. 'They believed I was being emotional and not acting in the interests of the party,' said an unrepentant Byrne. Mandelson did not speak to him for three months, although he would later promote him as a candidate for the job of press secretary to Blair as leader. It was not so much the broad sentiments, it was the folly of their being made public which annoyed him.

While the tone and personal nature of the letter was the freelance emotion of a Kinnock-loyalist, there is no doubt that all three – and Kinnock himself – viewed the prospect of Smith's succession with varying degrees of disquiet. Blair was of course personally close to Smith and would never, for example, have attributed to him any weakness in the battle against Militant. After all, it was through Smith that he and Derry Irvine came to defend the party against Militant in 1982. Blair did disagree with Smith over the need for change in the party, and those disagreements were to become sharper over the next two years, although they remained amicable.

And, according to Smith's adviser David Ward, Blair was finally invited by Smith to make that case for change as his deputy on the day Byrne's letter appeared.

Ward said Smith asked him to telephone Blair in Trimdon on Monday to say that Smith wanted him to run for the deputy leadership. Blair said only that he would think about it. Other sources suggest that, on the contrary, Smith made it clear to Blair that his intervention would be unwelcome.[14] Certainly, his delay sent an unenthusiastic signal, and it is possible that Ward's late phone call was an attempt gently to foment tension between Blair and Brown in order to keep them in their place. According to Ward, Blair had always been Smith's preferred deputy, although he admitted it was curious not to have acted on that preference more quickly and to have spoken to Blair himself. But Beckett was less of a threat to Smith, who was playing a similar game of cat and mouse with her. He did not encourage her, either on Friday or by responding to her decision to pull out on Sunday. Tactically, it did not make sense to declare his hand too early, because that would make him the supplicant and give his preferred choice a negotiating advantage.

Meanwhile, earlier that day, Kinnock and Roy Hattersley had announced their resignations as leader and deputy leader. Hattersley was one of the widening circle whom Blair consulted. He advised his protégé not to run:

> I urged him not to stand for deputy because I believed he should be leader of the Labour Party one day . . . I believed he was John's natural successor, more than Gordon. I then assumed that John was going to be leader for two parliaments and we would almost certainly win the coming election, and there was nothing to be gained for him being just deputy. Everybody who's been deputy leader knows it's a rotten job and everybody tells their friends not to do it. Everybody told me not to do it. And I didn't take their advice. Tony did take mine. I think he was very torn.

When Blair called Ward back, he loyally pressed Brown's case. 'We have decided that it should be Gordon,' he said, the 'we' referring to him and Brown. Smith, irritated at having his hand pressed in this way, reverted to Plan B, for Beckett – which probably was his Plan A all along.

As Blair continued to dither, the key question was whether Beckett really meant it when she said she would not stand. Nick Brown was despatched to see her, in order to sound her out on behalf of Blair and Gordon Brown. He made an appointment to meet her at her office in the House of Commons at 10.30 on Tuesday morning. As he arrived, a few minutes early, he met Smith coming out. Smith asked Nick Brown to come into his office, where Robin Cook was waiting. Smith told them: 'Margaret has decided to stand, and I think this is a very good idea.' Cook was horrified, because he was still, like Kinnock, pressing Gould's case. But it was too late. It was too late for Blair, too. He had hesitated too long.

On Wednesday 15 April, Beckett held a news conference to say: 'On Sunday I said I was not stepping forward and that I was at the back of the queue, rather than the front, but I have been moved to the front.' John Prescott also announced he would stand. In Sedgefield, Blair announced that he would not be a candidate and backed Smith and Beckett as the modernising ticket in an interview on BBC TV's *Look North*:

> John and Margaret offer tremendous intellectual leadership, which is very important; they've got immense political experience – both were ministers in the previous Labour government; and, most important of all, they will carry on the process of changing and reforming the Labour Party to make sure that our ideas and organisation fit the age we live in.

Those five days after the General Election were one of the most vital episodes of Blair's rise to the Labour leadership. It is difficult to judge whether he should have stood or not. Charles Falconer said two years later: 'I'm not sure that Tony thought being deputy was necessarily a good thing. Though now he will probably regret not having run.'[15] Blair did affect to believe that the deputy leadership of the Labour Party was a peculiar non-job. But his intense ambition would not quite let the matter go.

His private regrets were outweighed in public by the fact that he would have more time to see his children. Cherie said: 'When it came to whether or not he was going to run for the deputy leader's job, Euan said he was glad that Daddy has chosen to spend more time at home.'[16]

As events turned out, it did not matter. But if he had become deputy leader he would have emerged more strongly as the leadership candidate of the future, the modernisation of the party would have been pushed forward more vigorously, and he would not have become isolated in the way that he did, which would have mattered had Smith lived. On the other hand, his relationship with Gordon Brown would have been strained two years before it needed to be, and possibly broken. His prolonged hesitation also had an important effect in changing the balance of power between him and Brown while preserving the relationship. Most people close to Blair think he genuinely deferred to Gordon Brown until the 1992 election. Now the relationship started to evolve. In the inner circles in which Blair consulted, he emerged as the bolder and more impatient of the two. He appeared keen to put himself forward and stand up for what he believed, whereas Brown seemed less willing to take risks.

That was a pattern which would develop more strongly over the next two years, as Blair put on political weight rapidly. Several times in 1993 and in early 1994 Blair indicated to friends that he would seize the chance to succeed Smith if it came up.

Significantly, Peter Mandelson, the third point of the triangle, had demonstrated – to Blair if not to Brown – that he was prepared to promote Blair's leadership ambitions over those of Brown, if Brown should not be available. He could still argue – as indeed he did in private over the next two years – that he saw Brown as first choice as moderniser candidate for the leadership, but in a foretaste of 1994 he had already encouraged Blair to put himself forward in the teeth of Brown's opposition.

The Smith campaign

John Smith was not a 'moderniser'. He had no record of enthusiasm for internal party reforms, but was convinced that one member, one vote had to come. In the immediate aftermath of defeat, the logic of change was inescapable – not least because John Edmonds, the leader of the GMB, had offended many in the party by going on the BBC's *On the Record* on Sunday to anoint Smith before Kinnock had even resigned. When Bryan Gould launched his leadership bid he said that, if he were elected, it would be the last time a leader was elected by trade union block votes, and Smith was forced to match his pledge. Blair and Brown found he did not need to be persuaded of the modernising case as they seized the chance to define the climate of party opinion.

The debate was quickly framed in terms wholly to the modernisers' advantage, as between 'modernisation' and 'one more heave'. No one publicly argued for 'one more heave' – even the traditionalists argued that the party should change, albeit to restore the verities of its golden age, 1945–51. Although Blair and Brown did not contribute as much as they claimed to Smith's platform for the leadership contest, *New Paths to Victory* – Robin Cook was the principal author – it was undoubtedly a 'modernising' manifesto.

Bryan Gould, having entered both the leadership and the deputy leadership race, ignored the advice both of Smith's campaign manager, Robin Cook, and of his own, David Blunkett, to withdraw from the leadership contest and concentrate on the deputy leadership. As the campaign progressed, he increasingly played to the traditionalist gallery, calculating that his only hope was to swing the block votes of the conservative unions, alarmed by the threat from the modernisers to their power in the party.

John Smith and Margaret Beckett were elected leader and deputy leader of the Labour Party on 18 July 1992. The following morning, the *Sunday Times* colour magazine devoted five pages to a profile by Barbara

Amiel of the 'man Labour missed', Tony Blair. It was an important article, not least because it has been adduced in evidence that Peter Mandelson, who was closely involved in its preparation, was now leaning towards Blair rather than Brown as Smith's successor. However, the idea for it came from *Sunday Times* editor Andrew Neil alone. He had dined with both Blair and Brown, even when the Labour Party was supposed to be boycotting the Murdoch-owned press, and had been increasingly impressed by Blair. It was the longest and most prominent profile article of Blair yet, in which he set out the modernisers' case at length – and it was overwhelmingly favourable. On Mandelson's advice, Amiel was given access to the Blairs over a weekend in Sedgefield, and Mandelson was presumably one if not all of the sympathetic and anonymous Labour MPs quoted by her. 'I think it was a mistake,' said one of them, 'for him not to run for the deputy leadership. Now we don't have a vehicle for our point of view. John Smith was not against him running, you understand, but he didn't encourage him.' Not enough, anyway. 'Another' anonymous MP said: 'The question is, does Blair have the ambition or is he too much of a team player, afraid to risk losing?' It was a question that would wait another two years for an answer.

Mandelson was not, however, responsible for Neil's headline, 'LABOUR'S LEADER IN WAITING', and he continued to promote Brown equally. Nor was he the only part of an operation to advertise Blair as a possible future leader. The same day's *Sunday Express* ran a story by Fiona Millar, partner of Alastair Campbell, Blair's future press secretary, reporting that John Major and many of his Cabinet suspected Blair 'will one day be the man to take them on'. Unlike Mandelson, Campbell and Millar now backed Blair over Brown, as did Philip Gould, the other member of Blair's embryonic leadership campaign team.

Private Eye that month commented waspishly that Blair was

> the latest in a long line of bright young-ish things from the Labour Party front bench to be named sorrowfully as the 'leader Labour missed' . . . Those who have had this treatment in the past include Eric Varley, Richard Marsh, Robert Kilroy-Silk, Brian Walden, Alf Robens, Wilfred Fienburgh, Gerry Reynolds, Tony Crosland, David Owen, Shirley Williams, Roy Jenkins and others too obscure to recall. What they have in common is that they mostly belong to the Tory-minded wing of the Labour Party.[17]

Five days after John Smith was elected leader, on a modernising platform with 91 per cent of the vote, Gordon Brown came top, and Blair second, in the shadow Cabinet elections. Both were rewarded with the posts they wanted: Brown became shadow Chancellor; Blair shadow Home Secretary. The modernisers had won everything but the leadership.

Into the overtaking lane

During John Smith's twenty-two months as leader of the Labour Party, three factors combined to shift the balance of power between Brown and Blair. The first was Brown's promotion to shadow Chancellor. The second was Blair's own performance as shadow Home Secretary. Blair emerged as easily the better communicator of the two, while Brown seemed, if anything, to become more inarticulate. And the third was Blair's greater prominence in the battle for 'one member, one vote' in party decision-making.

Before the shadow Cabinet reshuffle, Blair consulted his mentor, Roy Hattersley, the outgoing deputy leader and shadow Home Secretary. 'He came and talked to me about what job he ought to do, because he very much wanted to do the Home Affairs job,' said Hattersley.

> I told him to take it. It's a rotten job in government. It's a pretty good job in Opposition. What you want in Opposition is a lot of parliamentary work. Also, what you want in Opposition is something that looked like it meant seniority – the shadow of the Home Secretary. In government you're waiting for somebody to break out of prison every day. In Opposition you're hoping that somebody will break out of prison so you can complain about it.

Again, Blair was not asking advice so much as canvassing support. He had fixed on the post for some time. It was natural: Brown would be shadow Chancellor, and he would take one of the other shadow great offices of state. He hoped to be Foreign Secretary in a John Smith government. World statesman he was not, but his passing knowledge of American, Australian and continental European politics was a more than adequate qualification in the modern Labour Party. However, the shadow Foreign Secretary would have to hold a divided party together while the Commons ratified the Maastricht Treaty, while the shadow Home Secretary was staring a great political opportunity in the face. Blair had realised that the traditional role for that post – complaining about prison escapes – did not begin to exploit its potential.

When he became shadow Home Secretary in July 1992, there was surprisingly little evidence in his record as a politician of economic affairs that his views on crime and the family were special. The next two years were to see Blair transformed from deft Opposition politician to potential Prime Minister. At the time of the leadership election in 1994, Blair told one member of the shadow Cabinet he had 'learned as much in the last two years as he learned in the previous ten'. However, it could not be guessed that he was about to bring about a category shift in the Labour

Party's stance on social issues, a shift which invited comparison with its change on Europe.

Gordon Brown's accession to the shadow Chancellorship, meanwhile, was logical and much desired by him, but it was to hold him back. He was running into treacle, defending Labour's adherence to the European Exchange Rate Mechanism up to the moment when the pound was devalued in September 1992. When the pound went down, Brown's reputation dropped with it. He also pursued rigidly the line of 'No New Taxes'. Both policies were arguably right if Labour were to win, but they perplexed party members. Blair recognised the need for political breadth, while Brown seems to have been cautiously following John Smith's route to the top. It was widely assumed that the economic portfolios were the commanding heights of the Parliamentary Labour Party and, therefore, that the shadow Chancellor was effectively the deputy leader. This was not necessarily or even often true. In fact, before Smith, only Gaitskell and Wilson had benefited from economics experience. It did Jenkins, Healey and Shore no good and Callaghan succeeded, after a nine-year gap, despite being Chancellor rather than because of it.

When devaluation happened, John Smith stood by his aboriginal pro-Europeanism, and persuaded the shadow Cabinet and National Executive that the pound's ejection from the ERM strengthened rather than weakened the argument for a single currency. A single currency would, he said, 'guarantee an end to intra-European currency speculation'.[18] This was too much for Bryan Gould, who delivered his resignation letter to the reception desk of the Imperial Hotel in Blackpool on the first day of the Labour Party conference.

It was Gordon Brown who was the lightning conductor for discontent in the party. Perhaps because no one could doubt Smith's European credentials, as one who had defied the party whips to vote to go into the European Community in 1971, Smith was able to take a relatively relaxed and pragmatic attitude to Britain's new-found freedom outside the ERM. It was left to Brown to insist that this could not mean a return to a policy of expansion fuelled by government borrowing, and his communication skills were found wanting. Thus, for the greater good of the party, he unwittingly sacrificed his prospects of becoming leader on the altar of monetary rectitude.

Satirists confirmed Brown's decline. Even before the 1992 election Rory Bremner growled: 'What the people of this country want is lists, long lists, short lists, depressing statistics, disturbing industry results and gloomy surveys.'[19]

The year 1992 was the crucial one in Tony Blair's rise. By the start of it, he was one of the 'Leadership Team', but he was still Gordon Brown's younger brother. Brown and Blair, in that order, were the leading modernisers in the Kinnock team. By the end of the year, they were the leading modernisers in John Smith's team, but Blair had drawn level – although not everyone had noticed. If Smith had died at the end of that year it is impossible to say which of the two, Blair or Brown, would have succeeded to the leadership. There can be no doubt that Blair would have wanted to stand. The only question is whether he could have beaten Brown in the unreformed electoral college. My guess in the first edition of this book that he could have done so has been challenged on the grounds that Brown was much better known among the public, and would have benefited from the block vote system.[20] But the principle of balloting individual party members and trade unionists had been established in the Smith–Gould contest, and Blair had the core of his team around him already, including Alastair Campbell and Philip Gould, and the support of most of those who described themselves as modernisers. Only Mandelson's position would have been even more awkward than in 1994.

Whether or not they thought he could win the deputy leadership there and then, Neil Kinnock and those around him – the Kinnocracy – were firmly of the view that, after John Smith, Blair rather than Brown would inherit the crown. Charles Clarke said:

> I remember after the '92 election, Robin Butler [the Cabinet Secretary] said, 'Who's going to be the leader after next?' and I said, 'Tony Blair.' Not who I thought should be: who *would* be. I think the argument was always going to be, 'Who's going to win the election for Labour?'

Blair was increasingly being noticed among the wider public. In a dry aside in December 1992, *Private Eye* described him as 'the only member of the Labour Party a normal person could ever vote for'.[21] But Brown was certainly better-known and, outside the small clique of modernisers, he was still regarded in the Labour Party as Blair's senior partner. That perception was about to start shifting. In January 1993, Blair unleashed ten words on crime that were to change his world.

Notes

1. James Naughtie, 'A Political Life Observed', in *John Smith: Life and Soul of the Party*, edited by Gordon Brown and James Naughtie, p. 54.
2. *Guardian*, 1 October 1998.
3. Robert Harris, *Talk* magazine, May 2000; Donald Macintyre, *Mandelson*, p. 232.
4. Macintyre, *Mandelson*, p. 234.

5. Paul Routledge, *Gordon Brown*, p. 164.
6. Macintyre, *Mandelson*, p. 233.
7. Philip Gould, *The Unfinished Revolution*, p. 187.
8. Macintyre, *Mandelson*, p. 233.
9. Bryan Gould, *Goodbye to All That*, pp. 253–4.
10. Undated document quoted in Macintyre, *Mandelson*, p. 235.
11. *Daily Telegraph*, 13 April 1992.
12. Macintyre, *Mandelson*, p. 235.
13. Andy McSmith, *John Smith*, p. 288.
14. Andy McSmith, in Kevin Jefferys, *Leading Labour*, p. 202; although the suggestion that Smith and Blair spoke directly by telephone is doubtful.
15. Interview, 6 September 1994.
16. Barbara Amiel, *Sunday Times Magazine*, 19 July 1992.
17. *Private Eye*, 31 July 1992.
18. Labour Party National Executive Committee statement on 'Europe: Our Economic Future', 23 September 1992.
19. BBC1, *On the Record*, 23 February 1992.
20. Andy McSmith, *Faces of Labour*, p. 51.
21. *Private Eye*, 1 January 1993.

II

SOCIAL MORALIST

Shadow Home Secretary, 1992–94

> 'It is the duty of the statesman to create for the citizen the best possible opportunity of living a good life. This is not to degrade morality, but to moralise politics.'
>
> —*Aristotle,* Ethics, *quoted by Tony Blair*

'I think it's important that we are tough on crime and tough on the causes of crime too.' Blair's opening words in an interview on Radio 4's *The World This Weekend*, 10 January 1993, reverberated over the next eighteen months, helping to carry him to the leadership of the Labour Party. Terrible things had become commonplace, he went on to say, and not just in inner-city areas:

> Friday nights made absolutely impossible for people; old people afraid to live within their own home, never mind go out on the streets; young people often intimidated by other young people: these things are wholly unacceptable, and those that commit these types of offences should be detected and caught and punished, if necessary severely. But I think that what we have got to do is recognise that there are two sides to this, there's the side of personal responsibility, which we must enforce against those that are committing crime, but then there's also some of the deeper and underlying causes, which we've also got to address.

His interviewer, Nick Clarke, asked if personal responsibility would mean locking up people as young as twelve, as some police officers had suggested.

> Obviously there will be a category of people who society requires protection from, and they are going to have to be locked up – some of them. Now, on the other hand, if you simply get to the stage where you've locked up the kid, in a sense you've lost. And the re-offending rate for those [who] then come out of these institutions is very, very high indeed. But if for example

> you were to intervene at a much earlier stage with penalties and punishments within the community, then I think that you would have a better chance of deterring them from going further up the scale . . . I do not believe that dealing with them once they've become persistent young offenders is the crux of the issue, the issue is trying to deter them from ever getting into that position.

Unexpectedly, Nick Clarke found he now had only one test of 'firmness' left. Was Blair prepared to see the prison population rise?

> You've got to be prepared to punish those that have committed criminal offences, and, where necessary, that will mean custody. But let's be quite clear, the objective of any sensible Home Secretary is not to increase the prison population.* And you see that is why I say to you that you've got to try to deal with both aspects of this problem . . . The Tories have given up on crime. The best that they can hope for now is to get a few headlines in the newspapers. What we need is a proper national strategy for crime that's both tough on crime and tough on the causes of crime.

Thus ended a perfectly formed, revolutionary interview. The phrase with which it opened and closed came from Gordon Brown. Sources close to both of them confirmed this to the author at the time. It was an example of a distinctively Brownian device, the 'varied repetition', like 'full and fulfilling employment' from Brown's own repertoire.†

A few months later, Brown must have swallowed hard when a shadow Cabinet meeting discussed the problem of getting Labour's message across on economic policy. John Smith teased his shadow Chancellor with a twinkle and a smile: 'Why can't you come up with a slogan like Tony's?' Blair looked embarrassed, but said nothing.

The phrase was borrowed abroad. It was used by Rudolf Scharping, leader of the German Social Democrats, in his unsuccessful campaign for the October 1994 General Election (although it lost something in translation: '*Härte zeigen gegen Über Kriminalität und ihren Ursachen*'). It was adopted by the African National Congress in South Africa's first multiracial local elections in November 1995, which heralded one of the worst crime waves in the world.

---

*The prison population did rise during the first three years of the Labour government, as Blair boasted to the House of Commons (*Hansard*, 14 June 2000).

†It is a device similar to the 'inverted repetition', such as, 'Our aim is not increased opportunities to tax – we will not tax unless we can increase opportunities.' This is also, of course, the John F. Kennedy oratorical style, as in, '. . . ask not what your country can do for you – ask what you can do for your country' (Inaugural Address, 20 January 1961, written by Theodore Sorenson).

Thus Brown contributed to his own eclipse, by enabling his friend to convince the Labour Party that he could defeat the Conservatives on their own ground. But if the slogan itself was Brown's, the thinking behind it was joint intellectual property, brought into focus by a visit they both paid to Bill Clinton's victorious 1992 election campaign team. Blair's *The World This Weekend* interview came just three days after they returned from America.

Lessons from America

One of the ways in which Bill Clinton was 'a different kind of Democrat' was that he was 'tough on crime'. In the United States, of course, toughness goes further than Britain. It means unhesitating support for the death penalty, and it often has a racial dimension. But its critical significance in Clinton's 1992 presidential campaign – the first successful Democratic campaign since Jimmy Carter's in 1976 – was as the key to reclaiming conservative social values. This, above all, was what Blair and Brown were interested in as they talked to Clinton's advisers in Washington in January 1993.

One of Blair's closest associates had already been caught up in the excitement of an ally winning an election campaign from the moment his jaded eyes looked up from Labour's defeat in Britain. In the summer of 1992, Philip Gould, who played a central role in Labour's campaign, flew to Little Rock, Arkansas, to work in the Clinton campaign 'war room'. Another of Blair's future associates helped arrange the trip. Jonathan Powell, the Political Secretary at the British Embassy in Washington, was a Clinton enthusiast. He had followed the campaign closely and reported back to a sceptical Foreign Office in London that he thought Clinton would win.

Blair and Brown met Paul Begala, Clinton's strategist and speechwriter, in the offices of the Transition Team on Vermont Avenue. He explained how, as Governor of Arkansas, Clinton had helped set up a 'modernising' faction called the Democratic Leadership Council after Walter Mondale's defeat by Ronald Reagan in 1984. The DLC saw its tasks as to force the Democratic Party to come to terms with social change, a process it called 'reality therapy', and to give it a 'populist' message that reflected the values of the majority. The DLC became the ideological power base of Clinton's bid for the presidency. Begala explained:

> He had worked for years on a set of ideas as a governor that put personal responsibility back at the centre of an activist communitarian philosophy, requiring responsibility in exchange for opportunity. And that applies to a

> host of issues. It applies to crime, where he was a Democrat who's very tough on crime. It applied to welfare reform where he supported child care, medical care, job training skills for people on welfare – but then after two years you had to get off. You had to demand that sort of responsibility of people. That was a revolutionary breakthrough for a Democrat.[1]

It was a breakthrough, too, for Blair in particular. It meant that elections need not be fought on the issue of tax, on which left-wing Opposition parties would always be at a disadvantage, but could be fought on social issues where the right was vulnerable.

One of the problems the modernisers faced was the dearth of successful left-of-centre parties abroad from which to learn. He and Brown had also travelled to Australia in 1990, to see his old university friends, and to meet Bob Hawke, the Labor Prime Minister and winner of three successive elections. Since Blair's previous visit, to deliver a lecture on the prospects for the British Labour Party in 1982, its Australian counterpart had reinvented itself. The new model Labor Party was described as 'assertively pragmatic, anti-utopian and non-socialist'.[2]

By the time of Blair's 1990 visit, Hawke and his Treasurer, Paul Keating, were pushing a programme of privatisation and deregulation similar to that of the British Conservative government. It was described as 'market socialism', and obstinately opposed within the Labor Party. On the other hand they maintained an Accord – a social contract – between government, employers and unions, which aimed at consensus and social solidarity.

'We should go out of our way to build common cause with other parties around the world in searching out the way forward,' Blair wrote just after the 1992 election defeat. He pointed out that the French and Australian socialists had held on to power, and 'adapted in government, though not without huge internal tensions', while the left in Germany, America and Britain had been in 'long and painful' Opposition. In other words, there was no single model, merely a self-assembly kit of clues. 'There are great movements of history at work here,' he wrote, in his vacuo-Olympian style – the plain conclusion from his survey being precisely the opposite.[3]

It was not until his visit to the United States in January 1993 that anything resembling a 'great movement' became evident, as Blair suddenly gained a sense of perspective, and acquired a language in which to express his latent 'social moralism', a set of beliefs which were to provide him with a distinctive platform for the leadership of the Labour Party.

The trip was controversial in the Labour Party even before Blair and Brown set off, because the lessons of Clinton's victory had already stoked the bitter post-election argument. The week before they departed, John Prescott, the leading 'traditionalist' in the shadow Cabinet, had launched a pre-emptive strike in which the modernisers were accused of pursuing a hidden agenda of 'Clintonisation'. He claimed there were some in the party who were 'obsessed with image', who were 'about to draw exactly the wrong conclusions from Bill Clinton's victory'. Their real aim, he said, 'is to turn Labour into a social democratic party – proportional representation, homage to Maastricht, divorce from the unions'.[4] The links between Clinton, proportional representation and the Maastricht Treaty were tenuous, to say the least. But divorce, or at least amicable separation, from the unions was certainly one of the attractions to Blair of Clinton's attack on 'special interests'.

John Smith was so irritated by the modernisers' visit that he summoned Peter Mandelson as their joint adjutant while they were away. 'All this Clintonisation business, it's just upsetting everyone. Stop boat-rocking with all this talk of change and modernisation. It will just divide the party. If we remain united we'll win. Do just shut up,' was Mandelson's version of Smith's dressing-down.[5] It was a rare conversation, as Mandelson spent the Smith years – his first two years as an MP – out in the cold. When, later in 1993, Smith spoke disparagingly of 'the black art of public relations that's taken over politics', it was Mandelson he had in mind.[6]

Clare Short, an even more outspoken 'traditionalist' on Labour's National Executive, saw the trip as a conspiracy to sell out the deepest values of the party. By the time Blair and Brown returned, she was seething:

> The secret, infiltrating so-called modernisers of the Labour Party have been creating myths about why Clinton won, in order to try and reshape the Labour Party in the way they want it to go. I think they have very little understanding of Labour's traditions, of its strengths. They look at the polls to find out what the weaknesses are. They're willing to rip lots of things up without realising they'd have nothing left.[7]

In its details, however, the argument between modernisers and traditionalists was largely at cross-purposes. Clinton's plan to 'end welfare as we know it', for example, was a clever balance between traditional left-wing carrots (training and government job creation) and modern sticks (time-limiting benefit). But, in the broad picture, Prescott and Short were quite right in their suspicion that the modernisers were up to no good. Blair and Brown were indeed engaged in a half-secret plot to subvert their party. The final paradox being, of course, that both Prescott and Short joined them soon afterwards.

The strategic lesson of Clinton's victory for Blair and Brown was a banal but important one – that all politics is a battle for the centre ground. The idea that a party can win by enthusing its core supporters, who will otherwise become disaffected and refuse to turn out to vote, is a durable one in the Labour Party. It was revived in government in the form of calls for the party to pay more attention to its 'heartlands'. Clinton's campaign manager James Carville put it most graphically: 'Whenever I hear a campaign talk about a need to energise its base, that's a campaign that is going down the toilet.'[8]

Clinton demonstrated that a successful campaign for the middle ground also appeals to a party's natural supporters. British elections have shown the same thing. Parties that win elections win votes in the middle ground as well as in their heartlands. In 1979 and 1983 Labour lost votes not just in the middle ground but also from among its core supporters.[9]

Blair had long argued against Labour being simply the party of the dispossessed, a view expressed passionately in May 1993:

> We play the Tory game when we say we've got to speak up for the underclass rather than the broad majority of people in this country. It's not just an electoral fact that you will lose an election if you allow yourself to be painted into that corner, though you will. It is also that it is false. Because the aspirations that I know from my own constituency unite the majority of people in that constituency, are infinitely more important than trying to divide people up into groups and saying Labour's task is to take those who are on social security benefit and represent those people. They don't want that and they don't need it. What we have got to do is to show how, by giving those people opportunity, we actually assist the whole of society to prosper.[10]

Blair did not simply transplant an ideology from America. He used the similarities between the ideas of the modernisers on both sides of the Atlantic in order to apply some of the Democrats' vivid language to a body of ideas which he had already largely developed.

Four years earlier, Blair had written in *The Times* that the new lawlessness of gangs of young men would not be remedied

> only by stiffer penalties . . . That deals only with the symptoms. To perceive the underlying causes for this violence is more exacting and more troubling in its message. But it surely has something to do with the decline in the notion of 'community', of the idea that we owe obligations to our neighbours and our society as well as ourselves.[11]

Now Clinton speechwriter Paul Begala expressed the same idea, in more forthright language: 'There had been a drift in the past toward a notion that the larger community owed the individual something, and yet there was no reciprocal obligation. That was wrong. It was destructive of the social order.' In America, these ideas were associated with a new school of political philosophy called 'communitarianism'.

Communitarian ideas were not new – the American communitarians had rediscovered the work of, among others, the Scottish philosopher John Macmurray, whose work had inspired Blair at Oxford.[12]

Blair's four days in America marked a turning-point in his development as a politician. He had at last found a populist language in which to express the ethical socialist ideas which had formed his political convictions. Almost overnight he began to talk with the breadth and confidence of a possible Prime Minister, as well as the urgency of a party reformer.

Social morality . . .

Labour has always been seen as a liberal party, but especially so since the great reforms of the 1964–70 government under Home Secretary Roy Jenkins. The abolition of hanging, the easing of divorce and the legalisation of male homosexuality all marked Labour as anti-authoritarian. Race equality law identified the party with regulations to enforce liberal ideas. Those reforms, which Jenkins saw as building a 'civilised society' were associated with the social and political changes leading to what was often called the 'permissive society', and eventually led to Labour being seen as out of touch with public opinion and 'soft' on crime.

Public attitudes, especially to sex equality and divorce, did become more liberal, but the Labour Party found itself carried away far beyond mass opinion. By the middle to late 1980s, the myths of the 'loony left' caricatured liberal attitudes to sex and race. On crime, Labour was seen as hostile to the police, because of the stance of a few MPs and some sections of the left in control of a few local councils. On the family, the party was sometimes seen as favouring lone motherhood over two-parent families, because of feminist arguments against the family as an oppressive institution of the patriarchy.

Blair frequently referred back to an earlier period of Labour's history. 'Some of the strongest speeches you will ever read about crime were made by members of the post-war 1945 government.'[13] In fact, law and order was hardly a prominent issue of the time. The Criminal Justice Bill of 1948 was notable mainly because it abolished birching, and is mentioned little in accounts of the period, with one major exception. Sidney Silverman, a Labour backbencher, proposed an amendment to end hanging for a trial period. Most of the Cabinet, including the Home Secretary, James Chuter Ede, were opposed to the amendment, although Aneurin

Bevan supported it. The amendment was narrowly passed in the House of Commons – in the only serious backbench rebellion of the 1945–51 government. However, the House of Lords struck it out, and the government used the whips to persuade Labour backbenchers not to reinstate it. It was not until 1965 that the death penalty was finally abolished. It was no surprise that Blair the populist found more to commend in the era of Attlee and Ede than that of Wilson and Jenkins.

As shadow Home Secretary, however, Blair held to a liberal line, against the death penalty and in favour of racial equality, equality for homosexuals and a woman's right to choose on abortion. He argued to equalise the age of consent at sixteen for heterosexuals and gay men in February 1994 (the Commons in the end only voted to bring the age of consent for homosexual men down from twenty-one to eighteen). His views on abortion were unchanged since his article on the subject in *The Times* on 19 January 1988. The Commons was then about to vote on the Private Member's Bill introduced by David Alton, the Liberal MP, to restrict abortion to within eighteen weeks of conception (from twenty-eight weeks) unless the woman's life was threatened or the foetus had a 'disability incompatible with life'. He wrote: 'Personally, I have found this an agonising decision. Both my constituents and probably my constituency party would wish me to support the Bill.' Sedgefield has a sizeable Roman Catholic population, dating from Irish immigration to the coalfields around the turn of the century. His parish priest – whose church he attended with his Roman Catholic wife – had also lobbied him. But he concluded:

> The inescapable consequence of the Alton Bill is that a woman will be made, under threat of criminal penalties, to carry and give birth to a child, perhaps severely disabled, that she does not want. I do not say she is right, in those circumstances, to have an abortion. But I cannot in conscience, as a legislator, say that I can take that decision for her.

Once again, he showed his ability to be direct but not confrontational with people who disagreed with him. When he became leader, however, he tried too hard to placate anti-abortionists, succeeding only in raising expectations to dash them. Asked by the *Sunday Telegraph* if 'the dictates of his private conscience would lead him to oppose' abortion, he said, as he had implied in 1988: 'Yes.'[14] This prompted a front-page headline reading, 'BLAIR: I'M AGAINST ABORTION', but his fundamentally non-fundamentalist position had not changed.

Blair's great triumph as shadow Home Secretary was to move the debate on from these traditionally 'liberal' themes to a 'tough' message on crime and the family based on the concept of duty. The argument, which he developed with increasing force during 1993, was simple. In return for society fulfilling its side of the moral bargain by giving people the hope of a better life, people had a responsibility to give something back to the community and to obey its rules. And, because mutual obligations originate in family responsibilities, the family must be strengthened.

Tellingly, it was in the *Sun* that Blair chose to expound his new populism. On 3 March 1993 he wrote: 'It's a bargain – we give opportunity, we demand responsibility. There is no excuse for crime. None.'

The transformation of his stance and his language in just six months is shown by contrasting this with his 1992 conference speech, in which he said, 'There is no excuse for crime. But . . .' Now he seemed to echo the words of Margaret Thatcher when the Brixton riots burst upon a horrified Middle England in 1981: '*Nothing* can excuse the violence.'

Blair's attempt to 'moralise politics' took a dramatic step in the wake of the horrific murder which seemed to link crime with family breakdown – that of two-year-old James Bulger by two ten-year-olds. In a speech he gave in Wellingborough, on 19 February 1993, he described the weakening sense of community in a moral language that had long been lost to Labour politicians:

> The news bulletins of the last week have been like hammer blows struck against the sleeping conscience of the country, urging us to wake up and look unflinchingly at what we see . . . A solution to this disintegration doesn't simply lie in legislation. It must come from the rediscovery of a sense of direction as a country and most of all from being unafraid to start talking once again about the values and principles we believe in and what they mean for us, not just as individuals but as a community. We cannot exist in a moral vacuum. If we do not learn and then teach the value of what is right and what is wrong, then the result is simply moral chaos which engulfs us all . . .
>
> The importance of the notion of community is that it defines the relationship not only between us as individuals but between people and the society in which they live, one that is based on responsibilities as well as rights, on obligations as well as entitlements. Self-respect is in part derived from respect for others.

His speech was of no direct relevance to the Bulger case, but touched a national mood of anxiety over the break-up of morals and families. It was like a Conservative politician's speech, responding to a moral panic induced by an atypical case by condemning a general moral decline. Blair's office was flooded with letters of approval and support.

The next part of his argument – the need for 'strong' families – was expressed by stealing a Conservative phrase: 'It is parents who bring up kids, not governments' (that *Sun* article again). It was the right time to reclaim it. The wave of concern about youth crime meant that both the Labour Party and the country were receptive to a new message.

Blair was emboldened to use not just Conservative phrases, but to lay claim to some of the roots of Conservative philosophy – Edmund Burke's eighteenth-century idea that a nation is built up from 'little platoons', starting with the family. In a speech in Alloa on 25 June 1993, Blair said:

> It is largely from family discipline that social discipline and a sense of responsibility is learnt. A modern notion of society – where rights and responsibilities go together – requires responsibility to be nurtured. Out of a family grows the sense of community. The family is the starting place.

Blair was not consciously plundering Burke; in fact he was returning to the language of John Macmurray: 'It was in the family that society originated; and it is in the family that the habit of social co-operation is learned afresh by every new generation.' It sounds like Blair in the 1990s, but it was Macmurray, writing in the 1950s.[15]

Blair's Alloa speech was also an early instance of his promotion of the two-parent family: 'All other things being equal, it is easier to do the difficult job of bringing up a child where there are two parents living happily together.' He drew attention to the 'fairly appalling' fact that ten years after marriage breakdown, half of all fathers have lost contact with their children.

Despite the Conservative language, Blair did not accept all of the right's case. He specifically took issue with the individualism that was the other strand of Thatcherism, using Burkean arguments to renew the case for collective action. In his Alloa speech, he saw 'strong families' as necessary to produce a 'strong society', but also the reciprocal – a strong society is needed to nurture families: 'If the old left tended to ignore the importance of the family, the new right ignores the conditions in which family life can most easily prosper.'

. . . or social conservatism?

Blair's views were often simply described as socially conservative, but his positioning was cleverer than that. His desire to strengthen the existing institution of the family was undoubtedly conservative, but it was also strongly populist, hence historian Peter Clarke's comparison of Blair's with Gladstone's 'moral populism'.[16] And some of the implications of the obligations that society owes to individuals can be radical or egalitarian.

In part, too, Blair seemed to be merely reflecting a new moral tone introduced into British politics by his leader, John Smith, also a Christian socialist. Smith did not talk much about the family or crime, but he did assert his 'profound conviction that politics ought to be a moral activity' when he delivered the R. H. Tawney Memorial Lecture in March 1993.[17]

Blair joined the Christian Socialist Movement in June 1992, influenced by Smith, a long-standing member. It was a departure for someone who, until then, had been extremely private about his religion. It was also a good time to make political use of long-held conviction. In the Foreword to a collection of Christian socialist essays called *Reclaiming the Ground*, which included the text of Smith's Tawney lecture, Blair went further than Smith in using the militant language of Christianity:

> Christianity is a very tough religion. It may not always be practised as such. But it is. It places a duty, an imperative on us to reach our better self and to care about creating a better community to live in. It is not utilitarian – though socialism can be explained in those terms. It is judgmental. There is right and wrong. There is good and bad. We all know this, of course, but it has become fashionable to be uncomfortable about such language. But when we look at our world today and how much needs to be done, we should not hesitate to make such judgments. And then follow them with determination. That would be Christian socialism.*

Two other members of the shadow Cabinet, David Blunkett and Jack Straw (who was confirmed in the Church of England in 1989) were also members of the Christian Socialist Movement† and shared much of Blair's social moralism, both the Christian part and the realisation of it as a populist political strategy. But it was Blair who finally managed to find the words and themes with which to leapfrog Thatcherism. Before long, he was making off with Conservative words and phrases by the bookcaseful. In so doing, he did not appear to be capitulating to the right but forcing it on the defensive.

Barrack-room lawyers

The first Conservative politician to feel the heat of Blair the Social Moralist was Kenneth Clarke, who was appointed Home Secretary after the 1992 election. Clarke's style was breezy, accusing Blair of 'talking total and utter nonsense', although he was often sharper and better briefed

---

*Chris Bryant, editor, *Reclaiming the Ground*, p. 12. The blunt, unusually short sentences are interesting because they are certainly Blair's own: later it became difficult to distinguish this blunt-preacher style (as opposed to his discursive-seminar style) from Alastair Campbell's famous staccato verbless sentences.

†Gordon Brown joined in 1994.

than his casual manner suggested. From the start, though, Blair generally had the upper hand on the broad themes. He simply had to repeat 'rising crime' and 'thirteen years' before attacking the government for failing to tackle the 'causes of crime'. Clarke only levelled the playing field when they debated specific government proposals. Blair's tactics then were often to drive deep into the small print – 'pedantic nitpicking' Clarke called it, accusing him of making 'barrack-room lawyer's points'.[18]

Blair tried to outflank Clarke over the Labour-bashing ritual of renewing the 'temporary' powers of the Prevention of Terrorism Act. This increasingly cynical charade gave the Conservatives the annual chance to present Labour as 'soft on terrorism', pointing out with satisfaction that the provisions had been introduced by a Labour government in 1974, secure in the knowledge that the popular press would ignore Labour's reasoned argument that the power to detain for seven days without charge was no longer needed. Blair's counter-weapon was his trademark Bipartisan Reasonableness: he persuaded Northern Ireland spokesman Kevin MacNamara to offer the government the chance to discuss an all-party consensus on the issue.

Clarke did not fall for it, but the ploy made him look more than ever as if he was simply playing party politics when he accused Blair of wanting to let terrorists 'melt into the population like snow off a ditch'.[19] It was, as Blair complained, an 'outrageous' suggestion, but the ritual was losing its potency. Matthew Parris mocked Clarke's 'strategy for dealing with the most insidious danger Her Majesty's Government has faced in decades'. Its centrepiece was the 'Prevention of Tony Blair (Exclusion of Sound Bites) Bill (1993)'.[20] The following year, Blair raised the stakes in the same game. John Smith met John Major in secret to propose a bipartisan deal. When Major turned it down, the fact of the meeting was leaked, presumably by the Labour side, although Smith purported to be 'deeply disturbed' by the breach of 'Privy Council terms' of confidentiality. It was not until after Blair became leader that the anti-terrorism trump was finally denied the Conservatives altogether. In March 1996, after fifteen consecutive years of voting against, Blair persuaded his party to abstain in the vote.

Only once did Clarke decisively get the better of Blair, but then he gave him 'the most comprehensive verbal thumping anyone has seen Blair receive' (Parris again).[21] It was their last clash in the House of Commons before Clarke became Chancellor of the Exchequer in May 1993. Clarke announced that he was abandoning the 'unit fine' system, under which standard penalties were translated automatically into cash amounts on a sliding scale according to the means of the miscreant. Someone had just been fined £1,000 for dropping a crisp packet out of a car window. It was a climbdown in broad daylight, an embarrassment in which Blair could have revelled. Instead he made the mistake of demanding a statement on the bugging of the royal family alleged in that day's *Daily Mirror*. Clarke rounded on him: 'I find the Honourable Gentleman's choice of priorities in politics utterly absurd.' Long-dispirited Conservatives cheered Clarke delightedly on as he dismissed Blair as a 'tabloid politician'.[22] A chastened Blair said privately that he thought his speech that day was one of his worst performances in the House.

Clarke was replaced by Blair's old opponent Michael Howard. When they had last faced each other, at Employment, Howard and Blair had been evenly matched. Now Howard, lacking Kenneth Clarke's bounce, was fighting a losing battle. This became all too evident in a strikingly illiberal speech to the Conservative conference in October 1993. He announced 'twenty-seven' new measures, as if the number itself made them tough. But the list had almost nothing to say about the causes of crime, and thus conceded Blair's ground.

When Howard came to enact some of the measures in the Criminal Justice Bill, Blair yet again failed to provide the Conservatives with an easy target. Cutting against the grain of expectations, he persuaded John Smith that Labour should abstain on the Bill's Third Reading rather than vote against it. This provoked howls of outrage from the libertarian left and muted groans of despair from Conservatives. Both disappointed groups wanted Blair to oppose action against outdoor 'rave' parties and the new offence of 'aggravated trespass'. Blair cited other measures in the Bill which Labour supported, including the clause lowering the age of consent for homosexual men.

One of the most controversial measures in the Bill, however, was the restriction of the right to silence. Michael Howard argued that he wanted to deal with the problem of 'ambush defences', when a defendant, having remained silent, suddenly comes up with a story during a trial. When the Bill was debated clause by clause, Blair argued that if ambush defences really were a problem, then the answer was to adopt the Royal Commission's proposal to require early disclosure of both sides' cases at a pre-trial review. Strangely, when Labour was in government, Jack Straw, with Blair's approval, decided that the Royal Commission had been wrong and Howard right, and allowed the courts in some cases to make inferences from a defendant's refusal to answer.

At the time Blair's decision to abstain on the Bill as a whole was simply tactical: Howard was desperate for Labour to vote against a Bill which he could describe as 'tough on crime'; Blair was determined to avoid handing him that propaganda advantage.

A turning-point for Labour?

The redefinition of socialism as being more to do with the moral than the material relationships between people was potentially the most important philosophical change in the Labour Party since it was last in office. It was a change completed and made explicit by Tony Blair. For all Labour's history, the party had been committed to greater economic equality. The problem for Labour leaders has always been how to prevent that being caricatured by opponents as enforced uniformity.

The long-forgotten 'Statement of Aims and Values' of the Labour Party, which deputy leader Roy Hattersley drafted in 1988, sought to do it by identifying equality with freedom. It stated in its first sentence that 'the true purpose of democratic socialism' was 'the protection and extension of individual liberty'. But if people were to be equally free, Hattersley argued, they needed resources, and not merely the absence of restraint, in order to make real choices. Thus he demanded equality of outcome not merely an equality of opportunity.

The nature of equality in Blair's philosophy was different. It was not an equality of material goods, but an equality of respect. Again, this had economic consequences, because too great a disparity of material condition undermines mutual respect, but they were secondary. Socialism required, Blair said in 1993, 'equality of dignity, of treatment of people within society and for the notion of community to have any meaning, then there must be a certain degree of equality of outcome'.[23] Blair's morality judged the quality of relationships, whereas for Hattersley morality lay less in judging what people do – the point of freedom being that individuals can do what they like provided it does not harm others – than in judging the degree of material equality in a society.

Neil Kinnock's views, on the other hand, were always more communitarian. But Kinnock's community was that of post-war working-class solidarity. His famous question in 1987, 'Why am I the first Kinnock in a thousand generations to get to university?', looked back to the post-war welfare state. Like Blair, he sought to express the principle of mutual support for individual advancement. But the example he gave was his own life, his origins in the Welsh mining villages. Blair's life told a different story, of the aspirations of those who started off in comfortable circumstances. Blair's formula was more abstract and hence more universal. He recognised the general aspiration – to 'settle down', 'start a family' – rather than the history of specific communities.

Notes

1. BBC1, *On the Record*, 17 January 1993.
2. Graeme Duncan, *The Australian Labor Party: A Model for Others?*, Fabian Society pamphlet 535, October 1989.
3. *Fabian Review*, 9 May 1992.
4. *Guardian*, 31 December 1992.
5. Donald Macintyre, *Mandelson*, p. 241.
6. *Woman's Own*, 21 June 1993.
7. Interview, 9 January 1993.
8. Mary Matalin and James Carville, *All's Fair*, p. 207.
9. Anthony Heath, Roger Jowell and John Curtice, *How Britain Votes*, p. 158.
10. Untransmitted BBC TV discussion with Roy Hattersley, 26 May 1993.
11. *The Times*, 12 April 1988.
12. See pp. 42–5.
13. *Independent*, 2 July 1994.
14. *Sunday Telegraph*, 27 October 1996.
15. John Macmurray, *Persons in Relation*, p. 192.
16. Peter Clarke, *A Question of Leadership*, p. 348.
17. Chris Bryant, editor, *Reclaiming the Ground*, p. 132.
18. *Hansard*, 2 November 1992, cols 30, 41.
19. *Ibid.*, 10 March 1993, cols 958, 962.
20. *The Times*, 11 March 1993.
21. *Ibid.*, 14 May 1993.
22. *Hansard*, 13 May 1993, cols 941 and 942.
23. Untransmitted BBC TV discussion with Roy Hattersley, 26 May 1993.

12

The Battle Against the Block Vote

One Member, One Vote, 1992–94

> 'Sometimes I feel like I'm on the end of a branch that is being busily sawed off at the trunk.'
>
> —*Tony Blair,* Sunday Times Magazine, *19 July 1992*

While Blair built a reputation with the voters as someone with a 'conservative' message on crime and the family, he built his reputation with Labour members as a party reformer. Both themes had been inspired by – although they did not originate with – his visit to the Clinton campaign team. Bill Clinton's stand against American trade unions and other traditional Democratic Party interest groups steeled Blair's drive to change Labour.

Ten days after coming back from America in January 1993, and a week after launching 'tough on crime', Blair came out fighting for 'one member, one vote' in the party.

In an interview on BBC1's *On the Record* he said, with unusual bluntness: 'We have block votes determining everything. That's all got to go.' He swept aside a compromise which had been gaining ground since the summer, which would give a say in party affairs to trade unionists who were merely Labour supporters, rather than party members, and insisted on the simple principle of one member, one vote for all important decisions in the party. Trade unions should be represented only through their members as full members of the party. 'What I believe that the Labour Party requires is not a process of adjustment, it is a project for renewal.'

After the programme John Smith warned Blair that he might be endangering his chances of ever becoming leader. But the truth was that, on the contrary, it helped assure his ascendancy over Gordon Brown as the candidate of the modernisers in any future leadership contest. 'The succession is decided. The heir is chosen. Step forward Tony Blair. Give way Gordon Brown.' Toby Helm's report in the *Sunday Telegraph*, 28 February 1993, accurately reflected the admiration of most modernisers for Blair's boldness on crime and the block vote: of the core modernising clique, only Peter Mandelson's view was still ambiguous.

Smith was personally friendly with Blair – as witnessed by that openness in discussing his future leadership chances – and seems to have taken an indulgent view of what he regarded as his impossibly modernist ambitions. But it was significant that, in warning him, Smith did not disagree with what Blair had said. For all his apparent daring, Blair knew that he had the leader's backing.

Smith's problem was that the decision on whether to bring in the principle of one member, one vote would have to be taken by the very union block votes whose power was being challenged. His predecessor had been trying for the nine years of his leadership and secured only three minor concessions. In 1987, Neil Kinnock had secured a hybrid system for choosing parliamentary candidates. Party members voted as individuals, but up to two-fifths of the votes were reserved for the block votes of local trade union branches and other affiliated bodies. Then, in 1991, party members voted in a national postal ballot for their seven representatives on the ruling National Executive, previously elected by local party delegates at the national conference. The third change was agreed under Kinnock, but would not come into effect until 1993, when it was agreed that the share of the votes at Labour conference held by the trade unions would be cut from 90 to 70 per cent, an important shift in favour of constituency party delegates.

Immediately after the 1992 General Election, there was a consensus in the Labour Party that the time had come for one member, one vote, pure and simple, and thus Smith publicly committed himself to basing 'our internal democracy on the principle of one member, one vote, and not on the basis of block votes'.

During the leadership campaign, Kinnock took advantage of the resentment against the block vote barons to set up a sub-committee of the National Executive in May to look at abolishing union block votes not just in future leadership elections but in the selection of candidates and in the making of policy at the party's annual conference. Kinnock's authority was fading fast, however, and at the next meeting of the National Executive the trade unions secured most of the places on what became known as the Union Links Review Group.

Kinnock was furious, and became more so when it emerged that Smith did not intend to use his authority as the new leader to bounce his first party conference into accepting reform. Even before he had been elected, Smith gave in to union pressure and said that the internal changes would not be finalised until the following year's party conference in 1993.[1] Smith was convinced he would lose if he pressed the vote at the 1992 conference, and thought it would be easier to win when the union share of the vote was cut to 70 per cent the next year. Instead of the dramatic showdown the modernisers wanted, Smith's first annual conference speech as leader was dull, unheroic – and a tremendous success.

By then, the tectonic plates of British politics had shifted. On 16 September, interest rates were raised from 10 to 12 per cent. Later that afternoon it was announced that they would go up to 15 per cent the following day. Then, just after 7pm, Chancellor Norman Lamont, with the body language of a Eurosceptic lifer let out of prison, announced the 'suspension' of the pound's membership of the European Exchange Rate Mechanism. It was an old-fashioned devaluation crisis and a national humiliation for which the Conservative government suffered a sudden and lasting loss of support. Parliament was recalled, and John Smith was at his unforgiving best in the debate.

Smith now appeared less interested in internal party reform. With the government in disarray and his public standing rising, a protracted conflict with the unions seemed to him unnecessary. But he took one important step which indicated his continuing commitment. Bryan Gould had been a member of the Union Links Review Group and, when he resigned over the party's continuing support for the principle of monetary union, Smith appointed Blair in his place at the end of October.

Blair and Gordon Brown had just strengthened their positions by being elected to the National Executive, along with the former leader, Neil Kinnock, under its new one member, one vote franchise. The result meant there was now a solid block of modernisers on both the shadow Cabinet and the National Executive – and on the increasingly powerful Joint Policy Committee, the 'inner Cabinet' of both overlapping bodies.

Blair was in a good position to argue the case for one member, one vote in the Review Group. All Labour politicians pay lip-service to the need for the party to recruit more individual members, and the centre-left had long regarded it as the key to unlocking the block vote issue. If the party could build up its individual membership, it would not need the unions to provide it with cash and a social base. Sedgefield's 'Famous Five', who had got him into Parliament, now provided him with a platform for the party leadership. By 1992, the Sedgefield Labour Party had one of the largest memberships in the country – 1,200 members, three times greater than the average. The party cut membership subscriptions and contracted with headquarters in London to make up the shortfall from fundraising. They succeeded, and by the time John Smith died the Sedgefield party's membership was 2,000. They had shown it was possible to tap into the large pool of Labour supporters in the unions, the 4 million union members who voluntarily paid a 'political levy', then an average £1.70 a year, on top of their union dues.

When Blair arrived at his first meeting of the Review Group, he was horrified to discover that it was poised to reject one member, one vote. Its draft report endorsed a compromise devised by Tom Burlison, who represented the GMB union. The important thing, he said, was to involve levy-paying trade unionists as individuals in choosing parliamentary candidates. This met half of the modernisers' case, but would create two classes of membership – the full party member, and what Burlison called the 'Registered Supporter', whose votes would be worth less.

Blair set about his task in the same way that he had gone about changing policy on the closed shop. Rather than try to steer a compromise and broker deals, he made his argument and worked hard to persuade individual members of the group. But he arrived in the middle of a debate, and the position of the leader was unclear. In order to keep his options open, Smith allowed himself to be described as 'persuadable' of the merits of the Registered Supporters scheme. Blair remarked ruefully to friends that he was getting no support from Smith on the group, and was pessimistic about the outcome.

His main contribution was to stall for time – his opposition to the Registered Supporters scheme deadlocked the discussion. Eventually, it was agreed to present a range of options – including one member, one vote – instead of a firm conclusion. 'We were on the defensive,' said Nigel Harris, Blair's only committed ally on the group, from the AEEU engineering union. 'The one thing we had to make sure was that our proposal went to the members, to the conference.'

At the beginning of 1993, however, Smith finally decided that the Registered Supporters scheme could not be sold to the general public as a fully democratic system. By the time of his *On the Record* interview, Blair must have known that the leader would throw his weight behind the modernisers. It would otherwise have been reckless to have dismissed the compromise out of hand. When he was asked if he thought there was a way to allow anybody other than full party members to choose candidates, he said: 'No. I believe it should be one member, one vote . . . There should not be two classes of membership.'

Smith digs in

John Smith calculated that the way to win the battle that mattered – on the choosing of candidates – was to give a little ground on another aspect of the reforms, by conceding a trade union role in future leadership elections. He insisted that trade unionists should vote as individuals, and that their votes be counted nationally, rather than cast in blocks, union by union. On this basis, he was prepared to give trade unionists a one-third share of the vote, with one-third for party members and one-third for MPs and Euro-MPs – the old electoral college was split 40/30/30 in the unions' favour. Until this point, Smith had insisted that the vote should be divided 50/50 between party members and parliamentarians, the option favoured by Blair and Brown.

Blair privately described Smith's concession as a 'disaster'. He saw it as not only a dilution of the principle of one member, one vote, but a blow to his hopes of becoming leader. In fact, it was neither. The 50/50 proposal already diluted the principle, because MPs' votes would be worth far more than those of individual party members. And in 1994, although the trade union section did produce the lowest vote for him, at 52 per cent against 58 per cent among party members and 61 per cent among MPs, he still had the majority of the union vote in a three-cornered contest.

Blair and Brown also underestimated the extent to which Smith's compromise would take leadership elections out of the hands of the union bosses and give them to Labour-supporting union members in a 'primary'-style election. The critical principle was that trade unionists would vote as individuals. The GMB would not vote as a block, but GMB members across the country would vote, along with members of other unions, in a direct ballot. In choosing the party leader, the power of the unions' activist and official structures was broken. (It was on this principle that Blair reneged as Prime Minister, when union block votes served his purpose in choosing a leader for the party in Wales.)

Presentational reforms to union block votes at the Labour conference had also been agreed, in order to avoid television pictures of a single union baron posting a ballot worth hundreds of thousands of votes in a box. Henceforth each union delegate would vote individually and the result expressed in percentages rather than in thousands and millions of notional members represented. But the issue of selecting parliamentary candidates remained stubbornly unresolved. On 14 July 1993, the Union Links Review Group assembled in Westminster for its final meeting. At last, having postponed confrontation at the previous year's conference, Smith was forced to act. He arrived at the meeting, unannounced.

Six hours later, he emerged to tell a waiting television crew, who had been tipped off, that he had achieved 'consensus'. Thus was New Labour born – in an Old Labour fix. It was a consensus in the sense that decisions of the pre-Gorbachev Politburo were a consensus. Smith dictated terms. Most union representatives had no authority to accept them, so there was no vote. Nevertheless, a document was drawn up, on one side of A4: one member, one vote for choosing parliamentary candidates; individual voting in three sections for the leadership, one-third of the vote each; and cosmetic changes to the block vote at conference. Much of the six hours had been spent arguing fiercely over Smith's insistence that he and he alone should be permitted to speak on behalf of the group.

Five days later, the 'consensus' package was approved by 20 votes to 7 at a special meeting of the National Executive. But the proposals still had to be passed by the Labour Party conference in September and the votes there were still ranged against the leader. The arm-twisting was about to begin in earnest. The scene was set for a showdown in Brighton.

The entanglement with economic policy

John Smith's leadership was now the issue. The one vote that mattered at the party conference was to be on rule change E, amending the party's constitution on the choosing of parliamentary candidates. As the conference approached, it became ever clearer that John Edmonds was not just taking up a bargaining position – he really was prepared to have his union vote against the leader it had so enthusiastically helped to elect. 'It's our party too,' Edmonds menacingly declared to his union's conference.[2] David Ward, Smith's adviser, said:

> There was a misunderstanding between the two Johns on this. They were both extremely sincere in their positions. Edmonds didn't really believe that Smith believed in his position. And Smith thought that if he levelled with Edmonds, they could do a deal. But Smith had reached the point where he would have to resign if he could not win the vote. If he gave in, people could say this person was leader only so far as he was allowed to be by John Edmonds.

Although he had a steely confidence in his ability to face down Edmonds and the GMB in the end, this was not a position that Smith wanted to be in, and he blamed some of the modernisers for getting him into it. He was irritated in particular with Blair, Gordon Brown, Robin Cook and Peter Mandelson, and relations were cool for some time after the conference.

Meanwhile, Smith tried to convince the unions that he had their interests at heart by moving in their direction on other issues. In his speech to the Trades Union Congress, on 7 September 1993, he made a symbolic shift on economic policy. He restored the goal of 'full employment' to its prominent place in Labour's gallery of slogans, and promised rights for full-time and part-time workers 'from day one' of getting a job.

The 'day one' promise undermined all the cautious dodging of Blair's time as shadow Employment Secretary. Before the 1992 election Blair had said it was 'not yet decided' whether Labour would reverse the extension from six months to two years of the period before employees are protected from unfair dismissal.[3] Alastair Campbell, Blair's proto-press secretary, accused Smith of having 'changed the chemistry inside the shadow Cabinet and widened its splits' in his column in *Today* newspaper.[4]

The upgrading of the goal of full employment, meanwhile, alienated Brown. Full employment had not quite been dropped before the 1992 election, and Smith committed himself to it in his manifesto for the leadership election, *New Paths to Victory*. But now he left out the emphasis on low inflation with which Brown insisted it should always be qualified.

By the time of the Brighton conference, with Smith still heading for defeat by a narrow but clear margin on one member, one vote, Brown's stock in the party had touched bottom. The results of the voting among party members for the National Executive marked the passing of an era, as Tony Benn failed to be re-elected after thirty-one years of continuous service. But they also marked the dawning of a new one. Blair increased his vote, although he only stayed in sixth place, while Brown slipped below him from third to seventh, or bottom, place. The party grass roots were not voting for future leaders – they voted from the heart for David Blunkett, Harriet Harman, Neil Kinnock, Robin Cook and John Prescott above Blair and Brown. But the reversal of positions on the 'Future Leaders' ticket was telling, even if its significance was lost in a more pressing drama.

The Labour conference opened with the votes stacked against rule change E. In the end, Smith's salvation came at the very last minute and from an unexpected source. At lunchtime before the vote, the delegates from MSF, the Manufacturing, Science and Finance union, met to discuss how to cast their block vote. They suddenly accepted a spurious argument that the union's policy of sex equality required them to abstain, because the rule change also contained new rules requiring half of all winnable seats with no sitting Labour MP to choose a woman candidate.

Minutes later, Smith himself opened the debate, and John Prescott wound up on behalf of the National Executive. Prescott's appeal was an instant legend, a windmilling exhortation to back the leadership:

> There's no doubt this man, our leader, put his head on the block when he said he believes, because he fervently believes, of a relationship and a strong one with the trade unions and the Labour Party. He's put his head there, now's the time to vote, give us a bit of trust and let's have this vote supported.

When Prescott talked about the leader's head on the block he was not referring to Smith's threat to resign, which had not then been made public, but to the fact that he had backed the unions' case for full employment, a minimum wage and workplace rights. It is unlikely that Prescott's speech swayed all that many votes, but it was part of the theatre, and confirmed his high place in the leader's esteem. From that moment, Prescott became in some senses the effective deputy leader (he was promoted from transport to employment spokesman after the conference). With MSF's 4.5 per cent block vote abstaining, rule change E was carried by a margin of 3.1 per cent, against the opposition of the two largest affiliated unions, the GMB and TGWU.

If MSF had not abstained, Smith's contingency plan was not to resign immediately, but to appeal to the conference the next day and turn the issue into a vote of confidence in his leadership. Under those circumstances, the MSF and GMB delegations would almost certainly have given way. Smith would have lost a damaging battle, but he would still have won the war. He knew he had to win the vote, and always thought he would – although he thought it might take two attempts to do it.

Smith's ultimate trump card was that the TGWU and the GMB did not have an alternative leader who was not also committed to one member, one vote, despite a bit of cautious trimming from his deputy Margaret Beckett.

Aftermath

Rule change E certainly was a decisive breakthrough, but Blair's satisfaction was tempered by the feeling that Smith had built a bridge across the Rubicon and set up camp on the middle of it. Blair intended that the change should open the way to his real objective: the end of union votes altogether. Behind the cosmetic changes, 70 per cent of the votes deciding Labour policy at its annual conference were still held by the unions. Blair wanted that figure cut to 50 per cent – which he achieved as leader, enabling him to say the unions no longer 'controlled' Labour policy – but at the same time he wanted to bypass the conference altogether. Nor was the issue solely that of block votes cast by union delegates – the constituency party delegates at conference also cast small 'block' votes on behalf of their members, usually without consulting them. Indeed, half of the wider membership never attend party meetings.[5]

Blair had proposed to the Union Links Review Group that it should pursue one member, one vote to its logical conclusion, and consider referendums of party members on policy. Clare Short, his most outspoken opponent on the group, was scathing:

> I've heard him argue it, but whether he will continue, I don't know, because sometimes he does change his mind. But I think it's absolutely crass and stupid. Say you've got a proposal for a housing policy – just one small area of policy – you've got housing for rent, housing for elderly people, mortgage tax relief, all these questions. So you're going to have a long and detailed document that everyone can read . . . How can you then say, 'Are you in favour, yes or no?' and call that a rational, intelligent policy-making process? So I think that's a way of really downgrading the membership's engagement in any rational creative process and giving the power to parliamentary leaders who make proposals and then the passive membership has to say yes. I don't like it at all.[6]

Blair's keenest supporter on the group, Nigel Harris, recalled drily: 'It didn't find much favour . . . That was too democratic for some of them.' The idea was revived soon after Blair became leader, with ballots of party members on the new Clause IV. The ballots were optional, but three out of four local Labour parties took part, and in 1995 Blair took the power to put the party's entire policy programme – a draft manifesto – to a referendum of all Labour members.

The last citadel of union power in the party, the nomination rights to eighteen out of the twenty-nine members of the National Executive itself, was only finally stormed after Labour came to power when in 1998 this was cut to twelve seats out of thirty-two. But by 11 April 1996, Blair was able with some justice to claim to an audience of New York business people: 'We have altered the structure of the party to free it from the excess influence of pressure and interest groups . . . Our relations with the trade unions have been placed on a more sensible and modern footing.'

Blair's two themes in 1993, moral populism and one member, one vote, were linked. According to Blair, the Sedgefield model was 'more than a glorified recruitment drive. I see it as being about actually transforming the relationship of the Labour Party with the broader community.' That was bound to mean adjusting the party's stance on social issues, although the awkward implications of driving policy away from the cherished prejudices of party members and towards those of the wider electorate were smoothed by an attractive rhetoric of a genuine internal democracy:

> If we can't actually trust ordinary Labour Party members with decision-making within the Labour Party, how on earth are we going to go out and try and win support for the Labour Party in the broader community – the vast majority of whom aren't members of the Labour Party? . . . I just think it's so clear, as we approach the twenty-first century and say, 'What does a radical, modern, progressive, left-of-centre party look like?' The answer is, it's got to look like a party in touch with its local community because its local community is part of that party.[7]

The heroic assumption that Labour could reverse the trends of history and become a mass-membership party again was unrealistic, and what was surprising was not that Blair was found out but that he was able to sustain the illusion for so long. For decades, the party's individual membership had been declining, from over 1 million in the 1950s to its low point after the 1992 election of 260,000. This was not simply a product of Labour's failure. The Conservative Party's membership had also declined, from a higher base. Society had changed.

The membership figures shot up when Blair became leader, but this was as much to do with the excitement of impending victory as with the recruitment drive which he ordered or with the innovations of mail order membership. And what was striking about the character of Labour's new members was how similar they were to Labour's old members – indeed, many of them were simply weaker party identifiers who had been members in the past but had lapsed.[8] Blair's disappointment as leader in the quality of his new followers was evident in the cooling of his democratic ardour, just as any schismatic church starts as a New Testament fellowship but eventually acquires bishops.

By the time in 1999 that the party needed a leader in Wales and a mayoral candidate in London, the block vote was back, in an attempt to ensure the 'right' result, and it looked as though Blair had regarded one member, one vote as merely the means to the end of getting himself elected leader.

On a branch, not waving but sawing

The immediate impact of the successful campaign to introduce one member, one vote was paradoxically unfavourable to Blair. Far from strengthening his position in the party, it weakened it. John Smith did not share his view that the internal reforms he had just won were only a part of a wider process of renewal. He was content to 'play the long game', and confided widely that new policies would be unveiled closer to the election.

Meanwhile, he thought, the right stance for the mid-term period was to let John Major get on with making a mess of things. This enabled him to reach an accommodation with the 'traditionalists', led by John Prescott, who had emerged as the darling of the party mainstream. Blair's frustrations grew. Smith, for his part, was exasperated by Blair's desire to push him – as he saw it – into more trouble.

A kind of peace was made when he and Blair met alone for dinner in January 1994. Blair was conciliatory, and said he understood Smith's strategy, which Smith interpreted as a half-apology. Smith seems to have seen the future with unsentimental clarity. Derry Irvine recalled: 'During the last six months of his life, John Smith made it clear to me on several occasions that he favoured Tony as his successor.' If so, he had changed his mind since his holiday in August 1993, when, according to his and Elizabeth's hosts in the south of France, Alan Haworth and Maggie Rae, the issue of who should succeed him was a 'sharp point of disagreement'. As friends of Blair, Haworth and Rae pressed his case, but, said Haworth, 'John Smith would say of Tony that he's indecisive and takes far too much advice.' He also had an ideological preference for Gordon Brown. 'John was, by instinct, a redistributor of wealth,' said Rae. 'If you represented Monklands, you would have to be a redistributor by instinct. And I think he thought that Gordon was more in that mould than Tony. I think he probably is.'

Blair certainly felt isolated. Another friend said: 'I don't feel that Blair was right at the centre of all those day-to-day decisions that were going on, whereas he had been to a much greater extent with Kinnock.' By April 1994, Blair was as gloomy about his and the party's future as he had ever been, telling friends that things looked bleak, and that he did not think Labour would ever be capable of winning.

On Sunday 10 April, a chill ran briefly through the Labour Party when the words 'John Smith' and 'doctor' appeared in the same news agency story. It turned out that he had twisted his ankle climbing his 108th Munro – a Scottish mountain over 3,000 feet – in Wester Ross. A doctor ordered him to rest for a week. Smith's 1988 heart attack was at the back of many minds in the party, but this scare only seemed to confirm how fit he was.

On Monday 9 May, three days before he died, there was a macabre conversation in Smith's office. Smith told his closest adviser David Ward that his press officer Michael Elrick had laid a bet with him to encourage him to lose weight. Smith acknowledged, not for the first time, that he had to look after his heart more carefully. 'You do realise it would be pretty awful if anything should happen to you?' asked Ward.

'What would happen?' asked Smith. Before Ward could change the subject, he had answered his own question. Whatever his personal preference, he saw the future: 'It's got to be Tony, hasn't it?'

Notes

1. *Tribune* debate, 26 June 1992.
2. Speech to GMB conference, 7 June 1993.
3. *Financial Times*, 27 January 1992.
4. *Today*, 9 September 1993.
5. Patrick Seyd and Paul Whiteley, *Labour's Grass Roots*, p. 228.
6. Interview, 9 January 1993.
7. BBC1, *On the Record*, 21 June 1992.
8. Survey carried out by the *Independent*, 2 October 1995.

PART THREE

LEADER OF THE OPPOSITION

13

Blair's Number Comes Up

The Leadership Campaign, 12 May–21 July 1994

'But Gordon has wanted it so much. Much more than I ever have.'

—*Tony Blair to Roy Hattersley, 1994*

Tony Blair heard of John Smith's death on the Great Northern Road in Aberdeen just after 9am on 12 May 1994. He was in the front passenger seat – because of his long legs – of the standard-issue Labour Party red Vauxhall Astra, taking him from Dyce airport to a routine Euro-election campaign visit in a constituency the party did not even expect to win. 'I got up very early in the morning to fly up to Aberdeen and on my way from the airport I got phoned,' he said.

Maureen Smith, the press officer for the Scottish Labour Party, answered the mobile phone in the back and passed it to Blair. It was David Hill, Labour's chief press officer. A hospital was mentioned. 'I thought one of his children had been injured or fallen ill,' said Norman MacAskill, the local party organiser, who was driving.

'John Smith has had a heart attack,' said Blair, when the call was finished. He was immediately on the phone again, to Anji Hunter, his assistant. It may not be so bad, said Maureen, mentioning Michael Heseltine, who had just survived a heart attack. 'I don't think we're in that kind of situation,' said Blair, simply. Two more calls, from Gordon Brown and Derry Irvine, confirmed that Smith was dead.

'It was a cataclysmic event because I was in a state of shock and grief, obviously, over John, who I was very close to and to whom I owed a lot,' said Blair. 'And then – I mean, you know, whatever anyone says – within moments of these things happening, the world just moves on.'[1]

Blair went ahead with his visit, 'on autopilot', said MacAskill. 'It seems strange now, and it was surreal at the time, but we just carried on doing what was on the schedule.' An early hint of the national show of respect for Smith came when Blair and MacAskill were stuck in traffic in Aberdeen on the way from the Labour Party office to the Marine Research Institute. A van driver, recognising Blair, shouted: 'Very sorry to hear about your man Smith. He was a good man.' Outside the nondescript institute on a windy slope of grass, Blair agreed to a short television interview in which he paid tribute to Smith:

> He had this extraordinary combination of strength and authority and humour and humanity, and all of us who knew him closely, personally, will mourn him. I think the whole of the country will feel the loss, and our thoughts and prayers go out to Elizabeth and the family. But it's simply devastating.

No one mentioned the leadership succession until Blair returned to the Labour Party office to be told that the London *Evening Standard* was preparing a profile of him as the next leader. 'He expressed extreme distaste,' said MacAskill. In between engagements, Blair was on the phone in the car and at the Labour Party office continuously. When he was not on the phone, 'He was talking about his children – his first reaction was that he wanted to go home to his family,' said MacAskill. Anji Hunter had booked an early flight back to London, and Blair returned to the airport after a lunch with local party members. He travelled alone to Heathrow – his last forty-five minutes as anything resembling a private citizen.

The golden legacy

On the morning of John Smith's death, Peter Mandelson, reviewing a biography of Neil Kinnock in *The Times*, wrote: 'Politicians often have to wait until they are old or dead before anyone has anything nice to say about them.' Although Smith had been held in high regard inside and outside the party, the grumbling about his leadership was growing. The modernisers in particular were frustrated with his steadiness, which they saw as inaction.

On his death, however, his achievement could be seen more clearly, and by his death he gave Labour an emotional bond with the people. He left the party more united, more popular and more trusted by the British electorate than it had been since the 1960s. Of all the tributes, the most affecting were the many letters received by his wife Elizabeth from people who had never met him. A remarkable number were from people who described themselves as 'lifelong Conservatives' or who said they 'always looked on politicians as people who promise the world but never deliver', but who admired and respected John Smith. The word 'integrity' appeared again and again.[2]

Inside the Labour Party, too, Smith earned the loyalty of those who expected to oppose him. He achieved a balance between modernisers and traditionalists that neither side thought possible. As a moderniser, he transformed the party's internal democracy. As a traditionalist, he restored pride and self-confidence in the party's history. His strategy was to respect all the traditions of the party. Where Kinnock had rubbished the hard left in order to build himself up, Smith neutralised them by making them feel they were a legitimate strand in the party.

Since then, one of the defining questions for the party has been whether Smith would have won the 1997 election. For all Blair's fondness for his former mentor, his own answer was no. On the day before Smith died, Philip Gould gave Blair another of his 'very long' memos urging that the party be rebranded as 'New Labour'. An impatient Blair did not need to read it: 'This is all very well,' he said, 'but as far as I can see Labour will only win when it is completely changed from top to bottom.'[3] The reading of subsequent events is crucial. The common-sense view would be that the scale of Labour's landslide in 1997 rendered the modernisers' argument null: clearly Smith would have won, although not with such a large majority. But there is a romantic moderniser view that the effect of Blair and his New Labour revolution was so transcendent that it made the difference between defeat and overwhelming victory. This seems unlikely: the fundamentals of politics had changed with the pound's devaluation in September 1992. Smith did nothing to detract from Labour's appeal and offered a great deal in reassurance to add to it, even allowing for the exaggeration of posthumous eulogy. His integrity placed him if anything in a better position than Blair to exploit John Major's breaking of his pledge not to raise taxes.

Whatever he would have done had he lived, Smith left an extraordinary bequest to his successor. For a party committed to fraternity, the Labour Party has a remarkable history of fratricide. Smith left a united party, fundamentally reformed. In retrospect, he also made Blair's leadership and the total victory of the modernisers possible. After Kinnock in 1992 the party was not politically ready for Blair, even as deputy leader, and Blair was not personally ready for it. Two years later, everything had changed. This was the second of Blair's remarkable inheritances: the first had been the Sedgefield seat; the third would be the sound economic legacy from the Conservative government.

Support for Blair, half-hidden while Smith was leader, crystallised immediately, just at the moment when Blair and his supporters had become most gloomy about his isolation in the party.

The iron in the soul

The events of the five days after Smith's death have assumed a huge, and partly mythic, significance in the history of New Labour. Since the first edition of this book appeared, a number of accounts of that period have testified to its significance for the central triangle of Blair, Gordon Brown and Peter Mandelson. In his biography of the Chancellor, published in January 1998, Paul Routledge fires a double-barrelled charge on behalf of Brown. First, he says: 'Blair had repeatedly promised Brown he would not stand against him in a future leadership election.'[4] Second, he portrays Mandelson as a schemer who turned against his friend and was working secretly to promote Blair's candidacy from the moment of Smith's death. The first lacks plausibility. The idea that Blair would have given Brown to understand that he would stand aside and support Brown for the leadership in all circumstances makes no sense. There had been an understanding between them, dating from 1992, that it would be disastrous to stand against each other in a leadership election, and in 1992 they shared the view that Brown was in the stronger position. But such an understanding by its nature envisaged that the position might change: it assumed that they both wanted to stand, and favoured whoever was in the ascendant.

As for the second charge, that Brown was betrayed by Mandelson, there is more substance, though Routledge goes too far. Although he thought Blair was better placed than Brown to lead Labour to victory at the next election, he knew too that Brown did not see it that way and he tried to remain loyal to both. What is overlooked in all the recent accounts is the prior fact, which was that the support for Blair at all levels in the party and in the country was too great for any rival to resist. Cynics might conclude from this that Mandelson's ultimate loyalty was to Blair, because he knew from the moment of Smith's death that he would emerge the winner. However, this would be to forget his genuine commitment to the Labour Party and his belief that its electoral prospects would be best served by Blair as leader.

At lunchtime on the day of John Smith's death, outside Holborn tube station, Cherie Booth bumped into their friend Barry Cox, the London Weekend Television executive who had been their next-door neighbour in Hackney. She was on her way to Heathrow airport to meet Blair, and asked Cox if he agreed that he should stand. Cox said: 'Cherie was worried because Tony had always had this view that he shouldn't run against Gordon. That had become looser in the preceding twelve months, but he'd never actually said he would do it. It was always something that was several years away.' Cox said he thought Blair should stand, and Booth asked if she could call on him if necessary to help persuade her husband. It did not turn out to be necessary. Indeed, Blair had made it quite plain to other friends over the previous year that when the time came, he would go for the leadership.* The iron had entered Blair's soul, not in 1994 but in 1992. That iron took human form in Cherie. On each of the occasions when Blair and Brown's interests clashed, in 1992, 1994 and again in 1998 in the kerfuffle over Routledge's biography, Cherie was more aggressive towards Gordon than Tony allowed himself to appear.

Only Blair himself knows what he thought as he sat alone on the flight to London. But he had learned in 1992, when he hesitated over running for the deputy leadership, that decisions taken – or not taken – immediately are the ones that matter. One member of the then shadow Cabinet said: 'Once you hesitate, you then learn the next time that you don't hesitate. So when John Smith died, Tony did not hesitate for one second.'

When he arrived in London, it was as the likely next leader of the Labour Party. Already there the crackle of energy around him which accompanied the rapid expansion of a previously slight and brittle politician to fill most of the space in British politics. He returned to his office in Westminster to find four people waiting. Shadow Cabinet minister Mo Mowlam and three of the 'Kinnocracy' – Adam Ingram, an MP who had been Neil Kinnock's Parliamentary Private Secretary, Charles Clarke, who had been his Chief of Staff, and John Eatwell, a Labour peer who had been his economic adviser – had come to offer to help elect him leader. Blair listened to them, but said only, 'Right; thank you,' well aware that such discussions were inappropriate. Jack Straw came out of his office opposite to offer his support and Peter Kilfoyle arrived to offer his intelligence, as a whip, that Blair's support among Labour MPs was overwhelming. Within hours, the phone calls to Blair's office pledging support confirmed that picture.

One Labour MP cynically observed that Blair's supporters refrained from launching his campaign for a decent period of mourning – 'about twenty minutes'. Most Labour politicians actually conducted themselves, through to the end of the leadership campaign, with a tact and restraint that was rather unfamiliar in the party, and a tribute to John Smith. But over private cabals all over Westminster hung the muttered words, 'It's got to be Blair.'

Harriet Harman, who spoke to Blair that day, said:

---

*See p. 185.

> He had decided, and I was astonished how decided he was. And what he said was he had lots of other things in his life, he didn't actually need to do it for himself, but that he was going to do it. It was like the tiger had jumped out of the pussy cat's skin. And he's been like that ever since.

Another early shadow Cabinet supporter, Chris Smith, said:

> He knew he was going to win and he knew right from the start he had to stand. My reading of it was that there was never any doubt in his mind that he had to be the candidate. And what Gordon decided about whether he was or wasn't going to stand was really irrelevant. Tony was going to stand. He'd made up his mind . . . I never picked up a shadow of doubt. I remember him saying to me something like, 'There are times in life when your ticket comes up with your number on it, and this is one of them.'

His decision made an awkward conversation necessary with Gordon Brown. That was the context in which Blair phoned Mandelson that afternoon to ask if they could meet and talk. Mandelson could not have been surprised at Blair's determination to stand. He recalled to his biographer Donald Macintyre a Sunday morning walk in the park with Blair around the turn of 1993–94 in which 'Blair was hinting that the trio's unwritten assumption of Brown's primacy could not be taken for granted'.[5] Mandelson had already been round to Brown's London flat that morning. Brown clearly expected to be the modernising candidate for the leadership, although he did not say so directly. It seems that Mandelson neither encouraged him nor discouraged him, saying only that they would have to discuss what to do with Blair. Thus was the great myth of Mandelson's betrayal born. Brown misread his friend's careful neutrality as agreement, and was shocked to discover later that Mandelson harboured any doubts about who should be the candidate. This overlooked the fact that it was already far too late for Mandelson – even assuming he possessed the power of dictating newspaper headlines attributed to him – to influence Blair's decision to stand.

Mandelson claimed to have been noncommittal with Blair too, when they met just before 6pm in an empty division lobby next to the Chamber of the Commons, the House having adjourned as a mark of respect for Smith. By his account he told Blair he was 'entitled to consider himself a possible candidate'.[6] Such pomposity sounds strange in such a close friendship, but it fits with Mandelson's mannered style and the high emotion of the moment. It was in effect his blessing, given in the knowledge of Brown's view. Blair did not misinterpret his apparent neutrality. If he were 'entitled' to consider running, then run he would, because he was already sure of victory. And if he was surprised by Mandelson's reticence, he was able to work out the reason for it, namely to preserve their triangular relationship by building up Brown to make it easier for him to pull out.

The more difficult conversation, between Brown and Blair themselves, began that evening, at a secret 'safe house', namely that of Blair's brother Bill in Islington. Blair explained he was coming under pressure to run, sought Brown's advice and kept his options open. What else was said between them that night and at a series of meetings over the next eighteen days, only the two of them know. Even Anji Hunter, who was usually with Blair, and Sue Nye, who went with Brown, had no direct knowledge of what went on while they waited together in various north London kitchens.

The observances of mourning coincided with Blair's need to preserve the relationship with Brown. Outside his closest circle, he pretended to be reluctant. Even by the following Tuesday, Roy Hattersley felt he had to try to persuade him to stand when they spoke on the telephone:

> I said to him he had to do it for two reasons. One was the positive reason, that he would win, that he was the best leader. And the second was that if he didn't, nobody would ever treat him seriously politically again. And I remember what he said to me. He said, 'But Gordon has wanted it so much. Much more than I ever have.' I said to him, 'Well, there are a lot of people who wanted to lead the Labour Party who had to get used to the idea that they're not going to. And Gordon just has to join a rather long and distinguished line.'

As Hattersley himself conceded, Blair's reluctance was feigned: 'I think it was a bit put on. But it was put on for good reasons. I think it was put on for decency. He is very close to Gordon, and I think it was put on for Gordon rather than put on for the world.' Neither Gordon Brown nor his supporters were taken in, which made the continuing conversation difficult for both men. Brown, not best placed to observe the extent to which the landscape had changed over the previous two years, expected more deference from his 'junior' partner, and was bemused and hurt by Blair's ambition.

'It's got to be Blair'

From the moment of John Smith's death, the media turned to Blair with a speed which many Labour Party members felt was disrespectful and undemocratic. Disrespectful because they wanted time to mourn the loss of John Smith; undemocratic because they felt the choice of his successor was being dictated to them. Neither feeling was justified. Media coverage as a whole was justly respectful of John Smith's memory. And journalists were bound, too, to look to the succession and comment on Blair's election-winning strengths, which were real.

Later editions of the London *Evening Standard* carried an article headlined, 'WHY I SAY TONY BLAIR SHOULD BE THE NEXT LEADER', by Sarah Baxter, former political editor of the *New Statesman*. On the BBC's *Six O'Clock News*, Smith's biographer, Andy McSmith, interviewed to pay tribute to his subject, was taken by surprise when he was asked to name the next leader. He said it would be Blair, 'for no other reason than that I did not want to be proved wrong'.[7] Neither were Blair or Mandelson lackeys, merely informed observers of the Labour Party. Nor was Denis Healey, the former deputy Labour leader, who endorsed Blair on *Channel Four News*; although Alastair Campbell, assistant editor of *Today*, who claimed to be surprised by the same question on *Newsnight*, was already the future leader's chief apologist: 'My own view is that it will probably be Tony Blair.'

Campbell's comment prompted an immediate call from Mandelson: 'That was completely out of order; you can't rule Gordon out like that.'[8] Campbell was not surprised by Mandelson's rebuke. Over the previous two years, he and Philip Gould had tried to persuade Mandelson that Blair rather than Brown should be the modernisers' candidate to succeed Smith, against Mandelson's insistence that Brown still had the better claim. However, although his loyalty to Brown was deep-rooted, and his emotional distress at having to choose between his friends genuine, there can be no question that Mandelson could see quite clearly that Blair would win if he stood. And Mandelson knew when he met Blair in the division lobby, if not before, that Blair would stand. All the rest was decoration, politeness and ego-management.

The next day, Friday, Mandelson spent a lot of time in the warren of offices behind the Press Gallery of the House of Commons, which press officers and occasionally MPs patrol. It was a highly visible mission, and many of the political editors he selected for briefing were surprised by how strongly he was pressing Brown's case. He acknowledged that Brown and Blair would not run against each other – a commonplace of internal Labour politics for more than a year – but resisted what was already the conventional wisdom when it was put to him that this meant Brown would have to pull out. 'Don't write Gordon off,' he told them. His message was resolutely even-handed, although to more sceptical journalists this meant heavily stressing the shadow Chancellor's political weight and intellectual force.

Mandelson stuck to the line-to-take all day. When he bumped into

Derry Irvine, in Westminster to make arrangements for John Smith's funeral, Irvine said the leadership was Blair's for the taking, and was surprised that Mandelson disagreed: 'I am not persuaded of that.'

On Saturday, however, Mandelson appeared on Channel Four's *A Week in Politics*. Simply going on television two days after Smith's death was guaranteed to irritate many Labour MPs but, more importantly, what he said opened the rift with Gordon Brown. After a token disclaimer, stating that neither Blair nor Brown had the 'appetite to talk about succession' at that point, he went on to talk about it for them. He listed the contenders in a very particular order: 'Tony Blair, for example, or Gordon Brown, or Robin Cook, or John Prescott . . .' He cannot have been unaware of the significance of naming Blair first. Then he set out the criteria for choosing the new leader:

> Who would maximise support for the party in the country? Who will play best at the box office, who will not simply appeal to the traditional supporters and customers of the Labour Party, but who will bring in those extra, additional voters that we need in order to win convincingly at the next election?

To Brown's people this was transparent code for Blair. 'Peter shows his hand' was the message from one Brown supporter to the electronic pager of the shadow Chancellor's press officer, Charlie Whelan. The illogic and paranoia of the Brown team's reaction speaks volumes for the bruised emotions of their man. The idea that maximising support for Labour should be code for Blair meant, on the face of it, that they accepted Brown would not be such an effective vote-winner. Ultimately, that was their argument: that Blair was a sell-out too far, and that Brown would have defended Labour's core values at an electoral price worth paying. Even if it were true – and the policy differences between Blair and Brown were in fact few – it was an argument that was never likely to run in a party desperate to win.

The fundamental ambiguity of Blair–Brown understanding of 1992 was exposed in the *Sunday Times* the next day. Briefed by Mandelson, political editor Andrew Grice 'revealed' a 'secret pact' between Blair and Brown not to stand against each other. As it was now clear to Brown that Blair intended to stand, he thought this was an attempt by Mandelson to force him out of the race. While Mandelson might have agreed with Brown the line that he and Blair would not run against each other, such was Blair's early dominance that it now had a very different implication. It is difficult to believe that Mandelson had not worked this out, which is what lies at the heart of the Brownites' charge of betrayal against him.

Fourth Estate

On the Sunday after Smith's death the discreet Blair campaign met at the house of his neighbours Margaret and Henry Hodge in Richmond Crescent, Islington. They had long been family friends and she was now the Labour candidate for the forthcoming by-election in Barking, east London. According to one participant, Blair said: 'You have got to understand that the only thing that matters in this campaign is the media. The media, the media and the media.' This was the driving obsession of his campaign not just for the leadership but for the coming General Election. Hence the central roles for Alastair Campbell and, within days, Peter Mandelson, who was not at the Hodges'.

Long before Smith's death, but thereafter with intensity, Blair pursued a deliberate and cynical course of seducing the leading figures of the Tory press – owners Rupert Murdoch, Lord Rothermere and Conrad Black, and writers like Paul Johnson, Simon Heffer and Andrew Neil. Heffer had already written a glowing endorsement of Blair in the *Daily Mail* that Friday, hailing him as a 'devoted and active father, practically rather than theoretically committed to family values', who has 'brought an unselfconsciously moral tone to his pronouncements on law and order'. Margaret Thatcher was their heroine, and they had become disillusioned with John Major, especially over Europe, partly reflecting their readers' low opinion of him. Blair was able, therefore, to step into a great vacuum. It was an opportunity that did not exist for Kinnock and one which Smith was too fastidious to exploit. 'That is the Grade I point to understanding the politics of that era and to understanding the genius of Tony Blair,' said one of the inner circle.

Blair and Brown met again face to face on Sunday. Again, their conversation was painful and inconclusive. According to one of Brown's supporters, Blair was even prepared to concede that Brown was better placed to win the leadership election, but argued that he, Blair, was better placed to win the country at the General Election. By now, Brown knew that he could only run for the leadership by running against his former junior partner.

One decisive factor in securing the leadership for Blair was the reported views of the wider electorate. Three instant opinion polls that Sunday suggested he was well ahead. Opinion polls were so influential in this election that they might be described as the fourth section of Labour's three-part electoral college. A MORI poll of the general public put Blair on 32 per cent, John Prescott on 19 per cent, Margaret Beckett on 14 per cent, Brown on 9 per cent and Robin Cook on 5 per cent.[9]

Philip Gould talked to Blair in his Islington kitchen on Monday. The future leader was already

> thinking about fighting the Tories in a new way. He did not want to get trapped on their ground: he said we should concede and move on – agree with the Conservatives where we could only lose, fight only where we could win.[10]

In his insistence on the positive virtues of compromise, at least, Blair's strategy was consistent with his position twelve years earlier, in his Australian lecture, that political judgment is a matter of 'knowing when to fight and when to accept defeat'. Choosing the ground on which to fight was Blair's hallmark throughout.

Meanwhile, Mandelson was still trying to extricate himself from his sense of obligation to Brown, oblivious to the fact that Brown already thought he was working for the other side. On Monday afternoon, he wrote the letter which, as he observed ruefully after speaking to Brown a few days later, made him 'an enemy for life'.[11] It set out Brown's problem of 'not appearing to be the front runner' candidly and observed, accurately, that it would need a 'massive and sustained' media onslaught which would involve 'explicitly weakening Tony's position' and 'even then, I could not guarantee success'. Having dwelt tactlessly on the many negatives of Brown's position, the letter closed abruptly on the alternative: '. . . or you need to implement a strategy to exit with enhanced position, strength and respect. Will you let me know your wishes?'[12]

The belief harboured by Brown that this letter constituted his betrayal by Mandelson is mistaken. The offer to run Brown's media campaign ('to be effective I think I would need to become clearly partisan with the press in your favour') was hardly sincere, but the larger question is whether Mandelson was duplicitous in pretending to Brown he was on his side while secretly working to promote Blair. He should be exonerated on that specific charge. It was unwise for him to drop large hints of his support for Blair on television on Saturday, and he was largely responsible for his own reputation as a schemer which made it impossible to play the role of honest broker. But it was Brown's failure to see that the lie of the political land had changed since 1992 which meant that the bad news came as such a shock that the bearer of it had to be excommunicated.

Donald Macintyre's telling portrait of the psychology of Mandelson's relationships with both Blair and Brown, drawing on Mandelson's remarkable correspondence, has allowed a better understanding of 'What Peter was up to' in those few days. Mandelson had perhaps been more reluctant than Alastair Campbell or Philip Gould to let go of the possibility of Brown in the 1992–94 period, but he was not blind to the fact that Blair had overtaken his mentor. Furthermore, as Macintyre attests, there was an easier personal chemistry between Mandelson and Blair during 1993 and early 1994 than between Mandelson and Brown. Mandelson was always trailing around behind Blair, coaching him for interviews, and Blair always on the phone to him straight after his performances, whereas Brown had his own press officer, Charlie Whelan, from the start of 1993. Mandelson worked hard for Brown, trying to help present the 'New Economics', but the personal distance between them was growing.

The same was happening between Blair and Brown. In a significant shift in micro-geography, Blair failed to move offices with Brown in 1993 when the shadow Chancellor – along with Mandelson and the Treasury team – moved to the new parliamentary building at 7 Millbank. It was a shrewd piece of tactical inertia on the part of Anji Hunter, and allowed Blair to emerge from Brown's slipstream.

Brown's massive resentment at being denied the leadership sought an outlet. Even Blair, with his legendary tact, was unable quite to finesse that one, although it was Mandelson who bore the brunt. Not for the first or last time, he was Blair's lightning conductor. Four years later, Routledge's well-sourced biography of Brown, by now Chancellor of the Exchequer, suggested that he still thought he had been cheated of the leadership. The evidence in the book is indirect, but Brown's feelings shine through one of the few direct quotations from him in it:

> The newspapers, with a few notable exceptions, did not back me – not least because I was out of fashion. I was never part of the London scene anyway. But that did not in my view mean much, once the campaign started among ordinary Labour Party members and indeed backbench MPs.[13]

This was all the more striking for being at odds with the 'politically correct' view which Brown expressed in an interview just after the General Election: 'That's the way things go. You've just got to keep going and be decent in your relations with people. You never know what's going to happen in the future.'[14] No doubt he had in mind the fact that James Callaghan, the older man, lost to Harold Wilson in 1963 only to succeed him thirteen years later.

But the bitterness would bear fruit in government. It was for this reason that some of Blair's more thoughtful supporters later wished Brown had stood, in order to put paid to his belief that he could have won. Neil Kinnock's former Chief of Staff Charles Clarke, later an MP and a minister in Blair's government, said:

> I started out believing that Gordon should not run for the leadership, but I

> have subsequently come round to the view that it would have been better if he had, and actually been beaten. That would have humiliated him and meant that Tony did not owe him a debt. There was never the remotest chance that Gordon would be elected leader of the party.[15]

That would have been disastrous for Blair, however. His need for Brown, co-worker in the construction of New Labour, was too great to risk his retreating into his tent. But the tension shattered the tightly-knit unity of the New Labour clique. It would poison relations at the top of the party throughout the period leading to the General Election (although it did surprisingly little damage to the campaign), and contributed eventually to the resignations of Mandelson, Geoffrey Robinson and Charlie Whelan. More significantly still, it underlay the growing tension between Brown and Blair themselves, with Brown accused of 'psychological flaws' in his all-too-apparent determination to grasp one day what had been denied him in May 1994.

The funeral service at the Smiths' parish church, Cluny, in Morningside, Edinburgh, on Friday 20 May was broadcast live to the nation, and attended by prime ministers past and present, Edward Heath, James Callaghan and John Major, and the leaders of all the other parliamentary parties. When the shadow Cabinet entered the church, Gerald Kaufman thought that Blair looked different and said to Roy Hattersley: 'The mark is on him already.'

Derry Irvine delivered a tribute. He had known John Smith since they had studied law at Glasgow University in 1959:

> He was then what he remained: a Highlander and so, to a degree, a romantic; a Presbyterian, not a Puritan, reared in the Church of Scotland; and a Labour Party family man. He was driven by a set of moral imperatives which owed everything to his inherited conscience.

Irvine sought to explain the public response to Smith's death: 'He won the respect of the country by saying what he meant and meaning what he said.'

Donald Dewar, another contemporary MA, LLB from Glasgow University, also paid his respects, capturing the national mood: 'The people have lost a friend – someone who was on their side – and they know it.' (It was a phrase recalled on Dewar's own untimely death in 2000.)

That weekend John Smith was buried on the island of Iona on the west coast of Scotland.

Gordon does the decent thing

Gordon Brown's speech to the Wales Labour Party in Swansea on the Sunday after the funeral was a masterpiece of studied ambiguity. It could be interpreted as a graceful concession, or as a statement of claim. Originally, Blair had been listed to speak and Brown had not, but Brown pushed himself on to the agenda, and knew this would force Blair, the weaker orator, to pull out. Brown's behaviour aggravated the tension in his relations with Blair.

The speech took the form of a leaderly appeal for unity and contained one strikingly lyrical passage:

> To everything there is a season, and a time to every purpose. A time to mourn, and a time to renew. A time to reflect, and a time to move forward. A time to challenge, and a time to come together. A time to debate, and a time to unite. For us now more than ever before, this is the time to unite. [Applause.] Because we have travelled too far, too many miles together, for us now to lose sight of our destination. Together we have climbed too high for us not to achieve the summit. And it is near.

As Brown knew Blair intended to run, there was a clear implication to the call to unite. But his advisers did not discourage the newspapers from reporting the speech as the opening shot of the leadership campaign. The speech was also seen as a pitch to the left of the party, which irritated some of Blair's allies. Glenys Kinnock, in the second row, muttered 'that's more money, more money' every time Brown said something that implied public spending. Blair responded by authorising Mandelson to tell *The Times* that he, at least, would not be 'bending this way and that' to curry favour with different sections of the party.[16]

Blair gave his first speech of the non-campaign two days later, on Tuesday 24 May, to a conference on the family and crime, offering a summary of his social moralism, an idea whose time had now come:

> The break-up of family and community bonds is intimately linked to the breakdown of law and order. Both family and community rely on notions of mutual respect and duty. It is in the family that we first learn to negotiate the boundaries of acceptable conduct and to recognise that we owe responsibilities to others as well as ourselves. We then build out from that family base to the community and beyond it to society as a whole. The values of a decent society are in many ways the values of the family unit, which is why helping to re-establish good family and community life should be a central objective of government policy, and that cannot be done without policies, especially in respect of employment and education, that improve society as a whole. We do not show our children respect or act responsibly to them if we fail to provide them with the opportunities they

need, with a stake in the society in which they live. Equally, we demand that respect and responsibility from them in return.

He sounded as different as possible from expectations of a Labour politician. The contrast with Brown's speech was deafening. Brown delivered moving oratory to a labour movement conference in Wales; Blair conducted a seminar among academics in a London hotel, while the subtext spoke of another strength, that of the family man.

It is not clear when Brown admitted defeat to himself. Philip Gould said he spoke to Brown on the phone on the Sunday before the funeral and, when Brown asked for his opinion, told him Blair should be the candidate: 'It was clear to me that he would not, in the last resort, stand against Tony.'[17] But the Swansea speech was clearly made in the fading hope that it would inspire a surge of support.

It did not. That Bank Holiday weekend, 28–30 May, BBC opinion polls suggested Blair had a clear lead in all three sections of the electoral college. Most significant was a Gallup survey of Labour Party members for *On the Record*, which put Blair on 47 per cent, Prescott on 15 per cent, Brown on 11 per cent, Beckett on 5 per cent and Cook on 3 per cent, with Don't Know in second place on 18 per cent.[18] Blair's lead was so substantial that Brown's faint hope of becoming leader (this time) was extinguished. However, despite speaking to each other almost constantly, Blair was still uncertain of his friend's intentions when the two of them met for dinner on Tuesday 31 May, at the minimalist Granita restaurant in Islington.

The 'Last Supper' has been mythologised as a moment of supreme self-sacrifice. In fact, its significance was as the moment Brown chose to bow formally to the fact of Blair's impending victory. One journalist was puzzled by what she misheard as the 'Grim Eater', which might have been right from Brown's point of view. He did not eat much, and was seen later that night in Rodin's restaurant in Westminster enjoying a second dinner with his team.

Brown had in fact finally decided to withdraw at another, secret dinner the night before. On Bank Holiday Monday, he dined at Joe Allen's restaurant in Covent Garden with his non-campaign manager Nick Brown, his press officer Charlie Whelan and Murray Elder, John Smith's Chief of Staff. The discussion was a run-through of what had already been recognised, after Nick Brown's weekend of trying to recruit supporters.

Gordon Brown said he knew he could win only by 'calling on such dark and awful forces' that it would negate the attempt – just as Peter Mandelson had said. It would mean splitting the modernisers by portraying Blair as SDP, non-Labour, anti-trade union. It would have been an unpleasant campaign which might have damaged the party's chances – and thus his own – of gaining office.

Tuesday morning's newspapers saw the paradoxical results of the Joe Allen dinner: a spate of stories in the press alleging that Brown and Blair were level-pegging among MPs and union leaders. This was pure nonsense and a tribute to the joint efforts of Charlie Whelan and Peter Mandelson, still trying to salvage his relationship with Brown. It was too late for Brown to pull out from a position of strength, but the final push was designed to allow him some dignity.

Mandelson's attempts to reinstate himself were negated, however, when he leaked news of Brown's decision to journalists, reinforcing his authority with the press but forcing Brown to bring forward the timing of his announcement. In a press release issued on Wednesday 1 June, the shadow Chancellor said he would not contest the leadership and would support Blair.

The campaign takes shape

The day after Brown's self-sacrifice, Blair sat down to write a plan for his campaign. Until the leaking of two prime ministerial memos in July 2000, it was a unique document in the public record, written by him for the internal purposes of the back room only. It was made public by Philip Gould, one of its recipients, in his memoir *The Unfinished Revolution*. Most of it consists of unexceptional trailers for themes later worked to exhaustion: 'Traditional principles but modern application'; 'honouring the past but not living in it'; 'one-nation socialism'. But it also brings the reader up short with its third-person listing of Blair's own strengths: 'strong convictions based around Christian socialism . . . family; more to life than politics . . . Conviction: Blair believes in what he says; says what he believes . . . on politics – change in style and manner: pluralist, open, inclusive.'[19]

The self-conscious exploitation of his religious beliefs and his family would undercut his later protestation, 'I can't stand politicians who go on about religion,'[20] and his pleas that politicians' children should be kept out of, for example, arguments over education policy. The pluralism and openness of Blair's politics was also more of a public relations contrivance than the real thing.

Meanwhile, it became clear there would be two other candidates – effectively for deputy leader although they both stood for the leadership as well. Margaret Beckett had already eyed John Smith's job when she thought he might resign over one member, one vote at the 1993 conference.

That was a misjudgment, both of the likelihood of Smith going and of the extent of her support. Now she misread the party again, by appearing to think it operated the US vice-presidential principle. The leader was dead; she was the leader.

In the week leading up to the European elections, Beckett firmly decided to put herself forward for the leadership, despite advice to the contrary from every colleague who chose to give it. It was nearly an act of attractive bravery, reminiscent of Margaret Thatcher's in 1975. It might not have mattered that she appeared to stand no chance of winning, but she risked losing her existing post as deputy leader as well. John Prescott had already said he would not challenge her as deputy, but her bid for the leadership allowed him to argue that she had vacated that position. Perhaps she did not want it.

So it was that the first 'primary'-style election for the leadership of a British political party had three candidates for two jobs: John Prescott, Margaret Beckett, who stood for both posts, and Tony Blair, who stood only for the top job. Rory Bremner called them the Lion, the Witch and the Wardrobe.

Before that contest could begin, though, there were other elections to win. The European elections coincided with five by-elections, four of them in safe Labour seats. The day before polling, Alec Kellaway, the Liberal Democrat candidate in one of them, Newham North-East, announced he was joining the Labour Party. He said the imminent election of Tony Blair as Labour leader had convinced him, a former Labour defector to the SDP, that it was time to come home. His was the first in a trickle of defections to Blair's Labour Party.

Labour held all four of its by-election seats with hugely increased majorities, and pushed the Conservatives into third place in Eastleigh, a formerly safe Conservative seat outside Southampton which the Liberal Democrats took with a 22 per cent swing.

The Blair campaign teams

The morning of Friday 10 June 1994 saw the official start of the Labour leadership campaign. John Prescott and Margaret Beckett held consecutive news conferences in a crowded room in the House of Commons. Blair launched his campaign the next day on a clear sunny morning at Trimdon Labour Club in his Sedgefield constituency. The contrast with the enclosed, metropolitan news conferences of his rivals could not have been more marked. Like so many good ideas, it seemed the obvious thing to do once it had been done. It was Peter Mandelson's idea.

After Blair's announcement of his 'candidature for the position of leader of the Labour Party', Peter Brookes, one of the 'Famous Five' who had watched football on television with him in 1983, got to his feet: 'He's never let us down, and he won't let the country down.' The meeting ended, and the hall was given over to a wedding reception.

After this sparkling start, the Blair campaign stumbled. Most outside observers would not have noticed anything amiss, but Blair failed to live up to his own high standards in his first two big tests on television. He made an awkward start to his interview that Sunday with David Frost, who started by welcoming 'the lead guitarist of the Ugly Rumours'.

'Lead singer, actually,' Blair replied, rather flatly. It was hardly worth a second thought, but it seemed to unsettle him as he threaded uncomfortably through the rest of Frost's random questions.

Blair was even more nervous, looking white and ill, before a televised debate with Prescott and Beckett on *Panorama* on Monday. Although he was under par, his par was high, and much of his performance was clear and effective, playing on his distinctive themes of crime and the family. But he was furious with himself for having agreed to take part at all. Immediately afterwards, he telephoned Mandelson, by now firmly campaign adviser-in-chief. There followed a pruning of Blair's media engagements, which allowed time to regroup, and the campaign was more or less technically flawless after that.

The extraordinary fact about Mandelson's role in the campaign is that, officially, he did not exist. The official campaign team had been unveiled on the day of Blair's announcement. Mo Mowlam and Jack Straw were joint campaign managers. The campaign committee consisted of Peter Kilfoyle, Andrew Smith, the fraternal delegate from Gordon Brown's Treasury team, Barry Cox, the television executive and only member from outside Westminster, who was responsible for fundraising, and Anji Hunter, head of Blair's office. The committee met every morning, but the decisions that mattered – about media strategy and speeches – were taken elsewhere.

The central figure in the 'real' Blair campaign was Mandelson. The transparent fiction that Mandelson was 'not involved' was deemed necessary because Mowlam and Kilfoyle were two of many who told Blair that they would not work for him if Mandelson had anything to do with the campaign. It meant an elaborate deception had to be maintained.

Although most Westminster journalists knew about it, Mandelson's role was barely reported until after the campaign. The silence was broken by Blair himself on the day of his election as leader, when he thanked family and friends at his victory party. 'A particular thank-you to a friend of mine called Bobby, who some of you will know. He played a great part and did so well.' Most people in the room were bemused, but thought little of it until the next day's newspapers identified the mysterious friend. Had the secret been revealed earlier, Blair's vote would undoubtedly have been lower, because some MPs would not have voted for him if they had known how much he relied on Mandelson.

'Bobby' was not a nickname, it was an essential codename among the campaign staff who were in the know, used in telephone conversations and messages in Blair's busy office in Parliament Street.*

Blair's semi-public thanks to Mandelson was a curious private joke, as he acknowledged Bobby's secret contribution in front of many MPs who were hostile towards him. He must have known that these MPs would find out who Bobby was, and that the story would appear in the newspapers. Thus he bestowed his special favour, dividing his closest supporters into the 'some of you' who knew, and the others who did not. It belied an arrogance and a disdain for many in the Labour Party.

It begins to make a peculiar kind of sense in the light of an incident at the start of the public leadership campaign which is recounted by Donald Macintyre. Mandelson had briefed Andrew Grice, political editor of the *Sunday Times*, on the themes of Blair's campaign, which produced the front-page headline on 19 June, 'BLAIR REVEALS SDP MARK II'. It was a fair summary, but absolutely not what Blair wanted to read. He thought the party and the trade unions were neuralgic about the parallels with the SDP and went into one of his periodic 'meltdowns', shouting at Mandelson, who was at Blair's Islington home when the first-edition front pages were faxed through on Saturday evening.

Mandelson then did what he had always done best, and in later editions the headline read, 'BLAIR WILL PLEDGE FIGHT FOR A MODERN PARTY'. But he was upset by Blair's outburst and, telling him he was 'fed up' because 'everything I do is wrong', stormed out of the house. The next morning, Blair went round to Mandelson's flat – the one in Wilmington Square in Clerkenwell that was not commensurate with his later status – and sought to reassure him that the *Sunday Times* report was in fact 'very good'. In a scene resembling a melodrama of married man and secret lover, 'a tearful

*Just as President Clinton's unpopular adviser Dick Morris was codenamed Charlie when he was secretly recalled in 1996. George Stephanopoulos, Clinton's official adviser, had been puzzled by the 'Charlie called' Post-it notes by the President's phone in the Oval Office. Like Mandelson, Morris was reviled as a cynical Machiavelli who saw politics as a matter of using opinion polls to find out what people want and giving it to them.

Mandelson, sitting on his sofa in his white dressing gown, appeared inconsolable'. The real cause of his distress was that he was forced to live a secret life and was denied the credit, recognition and limelight he craved. He told Blair he could not bear 'doing these things, in a box, behind the scenes and then you complaining because you don't like the headlines'. Blair sought to reassure him that, once the campaign was over, he would 'legitimise' him and give him his own 'identity'.[21] Indeed, he would later declare: 'My project will be complete when the Labour Party learns to love Peter Mandelson.'[22]

Mandelson would 'resign' or go 'on strike' several more times during the leadership campaign (and later), but each time Blair talked him round and promised to make an honest man of him. But if thanking 'Bobby' at his victory party was meant as the first step in that direction, it was a counter-productive way to do it.

Mandelson's role was initially known only to members of the inner campaign team. They included Tim Allan, who returned to Blair's office from a brief spell as a researcher on Channel Four's *A Week in Politics* and who acted as press officer, and Peter Hyman, a researcher for Donald Dewar, who had been talent-spotted by Mandelson. For policy and strategy, Blair spotted his own talent, bringing in David Miliband from the leftish think-tank, the Institute for Public Policy Research, and Tom Restrick, a former BBC television producer. Both had taken Firsts in Philosophy, Politics and Economics at Oxford. Miliband went on to be head of policy in the Leader of the Opposition's office and then of the Policy Unit in Downing Street; Restrick to become a barrister in employment law.

Cox, meanwhile, had raised enough money to fund a semi-professional campaign, which now employed several staff, rented an office and produced a glossy leaflet for party members and trade unionists. It was called 'Principle, Purpose, Power'. 'Looking back,' said one of Blair's supporters after three years of government, 'one out of three wasn't bad.' The title was the work of Chris Powell, an advertising executive who worked for the Labour Party when Mandelson was director of communications (and brother of Charles, Margaret Thatcher's Private Secretary, and of Jonathan, later to be appointed Blair's Chief of Staff). The text was written by Alastair Campbell, then still on the *Today* newspaper.

One member of both the inner and the broader, publicly acknowledged campaign team was Philip Gould, who now became a consultant to Blair working, on the American model, for a candidate rather than a party. In the style of American political consultants, he boasted that Blair was the dream candidate 'because he does what I say'. This grossly overstated his influence – many of Gould's long memos were filed unread – but contained an element of truth in that Blair was one of the most 'porous' politicians of modern times. If he was given a good line or a persuasive analysis of how best to respond to a situation, he soaked it up instantly. If Gould reported that people in his much-maligned focus groups, small groups of randomly selected voters, were worrying about something, Blair could adjust to it effortlessly in flight.

The final member of the campaign team was Cherie. She was not involved in day-to-day campaign planning, but she had always been ambitious on her husband's behalf. Just before John Smith's death, she said:

> If I didn't actually believe in what Tony was doing it would be far more difficult to cope. But I'm very proud of him. I think that he's got a lot to offer and I really want him to succeed. The fact that Tony's fairly famous and I'm not doesn't bother me at all. I'm well paid and highly regarded in my own field.[23]

As Charles Falconer put it, 'She is utterly committed to Tony's ambitions.'[24] Blair hinted at this when he said of his decision to stand for the leadership: 'Cherie was in no doubt that for the Labour Party it was the right thing to do.'[25]

John Prescott climbs on board

When the twelve-year-old Tony Blair stood as the Conservative in his private school's mock election in March 1966, John Prescott, twenty-eight, was Labour candidate for Southport in the real election. He was organising a dock strike as a member of the National Union of Seamen, and was denounced that summer by Prime Minister Harold Wilson as one of 'a tightly knit group of politically motivated men who, as the last General Election showed, utterly failed to secure acceptance of their views by the British electorate'. He meant they were Communists, which Prescott was not, but he could hardly say so, as Prescott had been an official Labour candidate.[26]

Prescott left Grange Secondary Modern school in Ellesmere Port at fifteen and trained as a chef, before working as a steward in the merchant navy. The experience radicalised him. As the former Conservative minister Alan Clark once said, 'The reason John Prescott became a socialist was probably because he met someone like me when he was a steward on a ship.' But he also had 'modernising' tendencies, which had been overlooked during a long-running personal feud with Neil Kinnock.

Prescott was also a friend of Blair's father-in-law, Tony Booth. In the 1992 election campaign, the two were a popular double-act at union-organised rallies. Prescott would play Alf Garnett, the racist working-class

Tory bigot, while Booth played his character from *Till Death Us Do Part*, Garnett's militant socialist son-in-law.

Even so, Blair and Prescott made an unlikely leadership team, and one which would have been unthinkable only eighteen months earlier. At the end of 1992, they had been locked in bitter dispute about the lessons of Labour's defeat and Clinton's victory. But, as they worked together on the Union Links Review Group, Blair seems to have realised that Prescott's main motivation was a desire to be loved and to have the confidence of the leader, a confidence he repaid with determined loyalty. 'At the beginning of the campaign, if you'd said I would vote for John Prescott, I would have said, "Don't be absurd",' said Roy Hattersley. 'Prescott has grown beyond all belief and nearly beyond recognition.'

Blair was in any case hardly spoilt for choice of deputy leader. For factional Kinnockites the charge sheet against Margaret Beckett was longer. At the famous *Tribune* rally at the 1981 party conference after Tony Benn had been defeated for the deputy leadership, she had vilified Neil Kinnock for abstaining. Unlike Prescott, she never had a following among the 'soft' left. She had been rehabilitated by the resolutely unfactional John Smith when shadow Chancellor, and raised to the deputy leadership by him. For some 'modernisers', her disloyalty to Smith over one member, one vote at the 1993 conference was therefore all the more unforgivable.

Blair privately shared this less-than-generous assessment of Beckett, but had to be prepared to work with her as he was not in much of a position to influence the party's choice. During the leadership campaign, Beckett continued to argue for the trade unions to have a 'collective voice' – that is, block votes – in the Labour Party.[27] On that issue Blair's preference was clear. So the contest was between a traditionalist who had been loyal to John Smith over one member, one vote and disloyal on economic policy, and one who had been the opposite. In making his choice, Blair was under fierce pressure from Gordon Brown in Beckett's favour.

Prescott had engaged in a sustained course of conduct prejudicial to Brown's 'New Economics'. He opposed the Maastricht Treaty and a European single currency. He was also the chief opponent in the shadow Cabinet, with David Blunkett, of Brown's refusal to allow discussion of higher taxes on the rich.

At the start of the official leadership campaign, Beckett was the favourite for the deputy leadership, nominated by Brown and most of the shadow Cabinet. Blair and one of his campaign managers, Jack Straw, remained neutral and did not nominate. But Blair's other campaign manager, Mo Mowlam, was so irritated by Brown's endorsement of Beckett – which could have been seen as the indirect seal of Blair's approval – that she nominated Prescott. Thus a delicate balance was maintained.

The decisive event in tilting Blair privately to Prescott in defiance of Brown's reservations occurred early on, at a hustings meeting held by the Transport and General Workers' Union on 16 June, before its left-controlled executive met to decide whom to recommend to its members. Asked if she would get rid of all Tory employment legislation, Beckett said, 'We have to get rid of the framework put in place by the Tories.' It was a crude appeal to special interests, which secured the union's recommendation, but it also convinced Blair that she would be a liability as deputy leader – especially when she repeated it on the *Today* programme the next morning, saying, 'There could well be a need just to sweep the board clear and start again.'

Blair made his view clear in his first conference speech as leader, four months later:

> I have heard people saying a Labour government should repeal all the Tory trade union laws. Now, there is not a single person in this country who believes that we shall actually do it. No one believes strike ballots should be abandoned. So why do we say it? We shouldn't, and I won't.

This was not the only reason for tilting against Beckett, of course. Prescott's public persona had softened as John Smith drew him into his collegiate leadership, and had become less frightening to the middle classes, while he remained an effective and engaging performer. He ran an energetic campaign for the deputy leadership, aiming his appeal as a mass politician at the 4 million trade union voters with a simple message: full employment.

Blair's preference for Prescott was strong enough for him to utter a significant rebuke to Philip Gould, who told him that Harriet Harman came across well in focus groups and might make a better deputy for him: 'I suggest you go away and refocus your focus groups.'[28] It was not always that Blair would prefer his own judgment to that of 'the research'.

However, the tilt was discreet until the last two weeks of the campaign – in other words, until it became reasonably clear that Prescott was going to win. Was it the right decision? Some senior Conservative strategists privately cheered Prescott on. But the public relations version of the Blair–Prescott relationship passed into conventional mythology – the complementary opposites, middle-class public schoolboy and working-class product of a secondary modern, mod and trad, working in tandem. It certainly helped Blair manage the party in the run-up to the General Election, but he may have paid too high a price for Prescott's loyalty in government, creating the unwieldy super-ministry of Environment, Transport and Regions as well as bestowing the Deputy Prime Minister title on him.

Warm words

Blair's formal campaign was remarkable for two things: the utter blandness of his platform, and the favourable media coverage it received. The second was a tribute not only to the skill and judgment of Peter Mandelson but to that of Blair himself who, despite sometimes appearing to lack confidence, could also act as his own cynically effective spin-doctor. Michael Brunson, then political editor of ITN, has confessed that he cut a deal with Blair when he obtained rare footage of him with his family, and a rare joint interview with him and Cherie, who

> became sufficiently relaxed to look forward to the prospect of life at 10 Downing Street, should it ever happen. Even as she was uttering the words, I could sense Tony Blair's considerable unease that his wife appeared to be mentally measuring up the curtains in the prime ministerial flat, before he had even been elected leader of the Labour Party.

In the street outside their Islington home, as Brunson's crew were packing up, Blair 'quietly suggested a deal – that we could use the pictures of Euan at the piano in return for not using Cherie's remarks about Number Ten'. Brunson agreed, 'judging in my own mind that what Cherie had said about Number Ten was innocuous stuff, even if her husband did not think so, for which it was not worth losing the sequence around the piano'. Thus viewers of *News at Ten* on 6 July were treated to wholesome pictures of Blair playing football in the park with Euan and Nicky, an exclusive joint interview with Tony and Cherie in which they talked about how he did not like being the 'political wife' when she was the candidate for Thanet North in 1983, and pictures of Euan's back as he did his piano practice.[29]

Blair's manifesto for the leadership, *Change and National Renewal*, ran to 5,000 words, but all it did was dress up existing Labour policy in what John Prescott derided as 'warm words'. That was because the campaign was being fought on two levels: in the Labour selectorate and in the wider electorate. If Blair had begun his lurch to the centre during the campaign, it would have frightened the Labour horses, so he kept the blinkers on while wooing Middle England by tone and body language alone.

'Education is at the heart of our project for national renewal,' the document declared boldly. But this promise had been 'liberated', as Blair put it in another context, 'from particular policy prescriptions'.[30] Nursery education 'for every three- and four-year-old whose parents want it' was 'an objective' without a deadline. This was party policy. The document was in favour of good schools and against bad schools (while recognising the 'challenges' of their 'surrounding social environment'). It wanted to 'overcome the debilitating divide between academic and vocational courses', which Harold Wilson promised to do in 1963, and it wanted to 'make a reality of lifelong learning', enhancing the skills of people in work. But it did not say how.

The novelty of Blair himself, however, was enough to distract journalists from a document which had little to say, but said a little about everything, when it was launched on 23 June at Church House, Westminster. Thus Blair won the leadership on a platform of 'change' with only the vaguest outline of what it might involve. Instead, he offered a vision, the 'British Dream', which turned out to be closely related to its American cousin: 'The hope of a better life for your children than you yourself had – that used to be the Labour dream, and will be the Labour dream again.'[31] Such atmospherics were sufficiently well-presented to avoid awkward questions. Blair was hailed as so different from political life as we know it that detailed position papers were unnecessary.

Blair responded to the charge of vacuity with his characteristic chutzpah. It would be a mistake to write the Labour manifesto two or three years before a General Election, he said – 'We've done that before.' And added:

> We shouldn't get bounced by the Tories or a bit of twittering in various parts of the media, who say, 'If you don't produce all your detailed policies then we can't take you seriously.' Rubbish. Out there, what the public actually want is a clear vision of what Britain would look like and a clear set of ideas, and those are the things that I want to set out now. The detailed policy work will come, but it should come within that intellectual and political framework.[32]

In this he was happy to admit to learning a lesson from Margaret Thatcher, whose 'clarity' and 'conviction' he admired a number of times during the campaign. This was a double-edged message, carefully balanced. To the party, it was intended to signal that Blair would fight Labour's corner ruthlessly – 'why can't our leaders fight for our class the way she fought for hers?' – but to the wider electorate it meant leadership and 'putting the great back in Great Britain'.

The chance to serve

On 21 July 1994 at the age of forty-one, Blair was elected the fifteenth, youngest and most un-Labour leader of the Labour Party.* In his

*Tony Blair is technically only the fifth 'Leader of the Labour Party', the title adopted in 1978, replacing 'Leader of the Parliamentary Labour Party', which dated from 1922. Before then, the leader was the Chairman of the Parliamentary Party, starting with Keir Hardie in 1906 – it was for the election in that year that the Labour Representation Committee, founded in 1900, renamed itself the Labour Party.

acceptance speech at the Institute of London, which Gordon Brown in an act of considerable generosity helped to draft, Blair began as he would go on, promising everything and not very much at the same time. He began and ended with a tribute to John Smith, quoting the closing words of his speech on the night before his death. 'A chance to serve, that is all we ask.' He declared: 'Let it stand as his epitaph. And let it be our inspiration. I am ready to serve. We are ready to serve. And together we will make this a turning-point, we can change the course of history and build a new, confident land of opportunity in a new and changing world.'

But Blair also made a significant defence of Fabian gradualism:

> I say this to the people of this country, and most of all to our young people: join us in this crusade for change. Join us. Of course, the world can't be put to rights overnight. Of course, we must avoid foolish illusions and false promises. But there is, amongst all the hard choices and uneasy compromises that politics forces upon us, a spirit of progress throughout the ages, with which we keep faith.

An hour later, Blair gave another speech, much shorter, at the private party in Church House, in the precinct of Westminster Abbey, to celebrate his election. His host was one of the central figures in his career: Derry Irvine, Lord Irvine of Lairg, pupilmaster and patron. Speaking without notes to the people who had worked for his leadership campaign, he thanked his staff, 'particularly Anji Hunter', his parliamentary colleagues, his family, Cherie, her family, 'some people who are down here today from Trimdon, including John Burton and Phil Wilson' – and 'Bobby'. Finally, he thanked all his supporters 'for giving us the chance to build this country again'. Referring to his earlier speech, he switched into his intense, urgent style:

> I meant what I said about wanting to win power, not to enjoy it, but to change the country, to change its place in the world, to make it a country people are proud of again, to make this country of ours a country where *everyone* gets the chance to succeed and get on.

As he paused on the threshold of the ante-room of power, his personal credo in private as much as in public was a commitment to nothing more radical than equality of opportunity, as much a Conservative value as a Labour one – indeed, it was the meritocratic aspiration which inspired Thatcherism.

On 21 July 1994, the Labour Party stepped decisively into the unknown, deciding that it wanted to win the next General Election badly enough to give Blair the benefit of its many doubts. Unlike Foot and

Kinnock, but like Gaitskell and Wilson, Blair's relationship with his members was based on respect rather than affection.

It would be too simple, however, to see his election purely as the act of a party so desperate to win that it entered a Faustian pact with a man it regarded as a Tory. Blair posed a threat to the Conservatives not merely because he offered a competent, fresh, forward-looking and ethically superior version of their own programme, but because he also drew on Labour's historical resources to present himself convincingly as on the side of the people, of 'the many against the few'.

Election of Leader and Deputy Leader of the Labour Party, 21 July 1994

	Total (%)	*MPs and Euro-MPs* (%)	*Party members* (%)	*Labour-supporting trade unionists** (%)
LEADER				
Tony Blair	57.0	60.5	58.2	52.3
John Prescott	24.1	19.6	24.4	28.4
Margaret Beckett	18.9	19.9	17.4	19.3
DEPUTY LEADER				
John Prescott	56.5	53.7	59.4	56.6
Margaret Beckett	43.5	46.3	40.6	43.4
Votes cast (actual)	952,109	327	172,356	779,426
Turnout (%)		98.8	69.1	19.5

*And Labour-supporting members of affiliated socialist societies.

Notes

1. *Independent*, 13 July 1996.
2. Gordon Brown and James Naughtie (editors), *John Smith: Life and Soul of the Party*, pp. 182–206.
3. Philip Gould, *The Unfinished Revolution*, p. 182.
4. Paul Routledge, *Gordon Brown*, p. 204.
5. Donald Macintyre, *Mandelson*, p. 253.
6. *Ibid.*, p. 256.
7. Andy McSmith, *Faces of Labour*, p. 60.
8. Macintyre, *Mandelson*, p. 256.

9. *Sunday Times*, 15 May 1994.
10. Gould, *The Unfinished Revolution*, p. 200.
11. Macintyre, *Mandelson*, p. 262.
12. *Ibid.*, pp. 258–9.
13. Routledge, *Gordon Brown*, p. 205.
14. *Sunday Times*, 11 May 1997: even in this Bowdlerised version there is a hint that Brown found 'being decent' difficult, and had not perhaps been decently treated himself.
15. Jon Sopel, *Tony Blair: The Moderniser*, p. 189.
16. *The Times*, 23 May 1994; Macintyre, *Mandelson*, p. 267.
17. Gould, *The Unfinished Revolution*, p. 195.
18. BBC1, *On the Record*, 29 May 1994: the findings were based on a sample of 472 members in twenty-two constituencies. In the event the survey overestimated Blair's support and underestimated Beckett's, who at that stage did not seem a likely candidate for the leadership.
19. Gould, *The Unfinished Revolution*, pp. 202–4.
20. *Vanity Fair*, March 1995.
21. Macintyre, *Mandelson*, p. 271.
22. Attributed, *Daily Mail*, 13 September 1995.
23. *New Woman*, May 1994.
24. *Daily Mail*, 16 January 1995.
25. *The Times*, 1 October 1994.
26. Ben Pimlott, *Harold Wilson*, p. 407.
27. For example, in the BBC TV *Panorama* debate, 13 June 1994.
28. Gould, *The Unfinished Revolution*, p. 208.
29. Michael Brunson, *A Ringside Seat*, pp. 223–5.
30. Speech to Fabian Society conference, 18 June 1994.
31. Answer to a question at the launch of *Change and National Renewal*, 23 June 1994.
32. BBC1, *On the Record*, 26 June 1994.

14

Social-ism

The Rewriting of Clause IV, July 1994–April 1995

'It is time we gave the party some electric-shock treatment.'
—*Tony Blair, 1994*

Having hung to the left before the leadership election, as soon as the votes were safely counted Blair made a dash to the centre ground. During the campaign, he had worried about being labelled 'SDP Mark II', played down his views on trade union block votes in the Labour Party and dismissed a debate about Clause IV, saying 'no one' wanted it 'to be the priority of the Labour Party at the moment'.[1]

On his first morning as Leader of the Opposition, however, he latched on to the prejudices of what would soon become known as Middle England, knowing he did not need to look over his shoulder to the party and the unions any more. He said in a radio interview that the unions would have no more influence over the next Labour government than employers: 'They will have the same access as the other side of industry . . . We are not running the next Labour government for anyone other than the people of this country.'[2]

That Sunday, Brian Walden pursued the logic of social moralism in a television interview. Blair finally agreed with Walden's statement that 'single parents who have chosen to have children without forming a stable relationship . . . are wrong'. Pressed three times, he conceded: 'Yes, I disagree with what they have done.' Blair was reluctant only because he wanted to avoid offending people who had become lone parents through family breakdown. The danger was illustrated by the novelist Will Self, who attacked him a while later: 'I don't want some pol like you telling me that I represent social disintegration because I'm separated from my wife and children. Mind your own bloody business.'[3] But the gain from the 'family values' constituency of *Daily Mail* readers made the risk worth taking.

The *Daily Mail* – along with the rest of the Conservative press – welcomed his election with more enthusiasm than it has ever expressed for a Labour leader. The editorial in the *Daily Mail* on 26 July said: 'This paper is not in the habit of congratulating leaders of the Labour Party, but then few politicians recently have spoken with the courage and conviction of Mr Tony Blair.' On the same day, the *Daily Telegraph* devoted precious column inches to an interview in which Blair appealed to its readers,

> in their own interests, to consider the alternative – not how we are parodied, but how we are . . . Many of those who voted Conservative are now asking serious questions about their quality of life and living standards and prospects for their children under the Conservatives.

That day he commandeered his shadow Education Secretary's news conference, held to launch a new policy document. Where Ann Taylor was opposed to league tables of school exam results, he said he was in favour of publishing information. In case journalists did not spot the difference, they had been briefed beforehand by Blair's staff that his words would contradict those of Taylor's document, which said: 'Test results and league tables are not acceptable management tools in the assessment of school performance.' On the lunchtime television news Blair was asked what the main points of the document were, and his first point was that unfit teachers should be sacked – another 'tough' message, designed to distract attention from the document itself.

He collected an endorsement from another historic enemy later in the year when Adair Turner, the new Director-General of the Confederation of British Industry, said: 'We were extremely impressed with the way Mr Blair is now talking our language, the language of business.'[4]

As for being the SDP Mark II, three of the Gang of Four who led the breakaway from Labour in 1981 endorsed Blair within a fortnight of his election. Roy Jenkins said he accepted 'even with enthusiasm' that a non-Conservative government 'necessarily involves Mr Blair as Prime Minister', and urged Blair to enter into 'friendly relations with the Liberal Democrats, within whose ranks are many whose thought-out instincts are very close to his own'.[5] Shirley Williams said Labour and the Liberal Democrats 'have a great deal in common and ought to work together towards a common programme',[6] while Bill Rodgers said he hoped Blair would win the next election.[7] The fourth member of the Gang, David Owen, who had endorsed John Major but not the Conservative Party in 1992, kept his own counsel.

The ghost of the Social Democratic Party was certainly abroad. The Blair Bubble was a phenomenon of British politics without parallel since 1981. At the end of that year, the Liberal–SDP Alliance briefly touched 50 per cent in the opinion polls. By the end of 1994, the Labour Party under Blair reached an improbable 61 per cent.[8] As the SDP had done, Blair engaged the moderate leftish sympathies of most individual journalists while satisfying their desire for a 'big story'.

If the newspapers and old-time Social Democrats were delighted by Blair's energetic start in his new job, the leaders of the Liberal Democrats and the Conservatives seemed unable to respond effectively to the threat. Paddy Ashdown took a collection of Blair's speeches on his holiday in France in the summer of 1994, but appeared irritated when he was asked questions about the author of his holiday reading.[9] John Major took a personal dislike to Blair, complaining privately that he found him 'cold', humourless and hard to get on with, contrasting him unfavourably in these respects with John Smith and Neil Kinnock. But he found it difficult to focus his tactics against Blair, uncertain how to deal with such a bold raid on what he thought was his own political territory. 'If you have to choose between a real Conservative party and a quasi-Conservative party, where the Labour Party says one thing but the party's heart and soul is elsewhere, then I believe people will go for the real thing,' he said.[10] This was called the 'Coke' strategy in Conservative Central Office – selling the Tories as the 'real thing' – but it was vulnerable to consumers deciding for themselves that they preferred Pepsi.

The Conservatives' problem was that, though Blair was more like Neil Kinnock than John Smith, their line of attack against Kinnock did not damage Blair. They had accused Kinnock of changing policy out of lust for power. This did not work with Blair, because the message was the man. Blair's rhetorical offensive, on trade unions, social moralism and schools, was a middle-class message delivered by a former self-employed barrister, a family man and an assertive parent of school-age children. Kinnock had used similar language, but did not embody the message, partly because he rarely referred to his family, and gave the impression of reading, somewhat uncomfortably, from a script.

Only Michael Heseltine, then the President of the Board of Trade, was able to land a punch on the new leader. In a variation of the 'Coke' strategy, he attacked Blair's judgment. 'Why should you believe a man who has got all the major judgments wrong in the first half of his life, when he tells you he is going to get them all right in the second half of his life?' he thundered on the *Today* programme in September. He cited Blair's past support for the Campaign for Nuclear Disarmament, and his past positions on trade union reform, privatisation and low taxes. It was a superb performance, which reduced interviewer James Naughtie to squawks of indignation.[11]

Heseltine was obeying the first law of American politics: 'Define your opponent before he gets the chance to define himself.' Many people had still not formed a settled view of Blair, and Heseltine tried to disrupt Blair's control over his image. The attack drew blood immediately, with a Labour official quoted in *The Times* the next day, 16 September, denying that Blair had ever been a member of CND. Three days later this was amended to an admission that he was 'briefly' a member of Parliamentary Labour CND, and Labour officials – incorrectly – repeated their denial that he had ever been a member of 'mainstream CND'.[12] Parliamentary Labour CND was organised by, and its members were members of, 'mainstream CND'.

Another effective attack used by Michael Heseltine was the 'head and body' line, stressing the gap between the leader and his party. The party membership was clearly to the left of and more traditionalist than the leader at its head, while party policy-making and the National Executive were still dominated by trade unions. Blair was only too aware of his vulnerability to the 'head versus body' problem – it was one of the reasons why he launched his battle to rewrite Clause IV of Labour's constitution.

Clause IV

Blair's holiday in the summer of 1994 in the south of France was a working one. He planned his first Labour conference as leader, an event he wanted to be seen as marking a decisive break with the past. He discussed the nature of that break with Alastair Campbell, who finally accepted the job as his press secretary. He had been reluctant when first sounded out during the Labour leadership campaign, enjoying an expanding career as a broadcaster and with a baby daughter born in April. Before being elected leader, Blair also offered the job to Andrew Grice, political editor of the *Sunday Times*, who turned it down. Now Campbell accepted the job for which he might have been born. His first task would be to sell the ditching of Clause IV.

Clause IV has been described by one historian as 'the red lamp which attracted socialist political myth'.[13] The words were drafted in the month of the Russian Revolution in 1917 by Sidney Webb and Arthur Henderson, and adopted in February 1918, before the end of the First World War. It was very much the product of its time, and was already out of date six years later, when the first, minority, Labour government took office. It had no intention of even attempting to carry it out.

The words of Clause IV, Part Four – the 'common ownership' part – first appeared on membership cards only in 1959, the very year when Hugh Gaitskell asked the party to delete it.[14] Only then did it become central to an invented history of the party, which was used to bolster the argument that the party had always been essentially 'socialist', while its leaders had always been temporising pragmatists.

By the 1950s, few in the party read the fifty-six-word sentence literally:

> To secure for the workers by hand or by brain the full fruits of their industry and the most equitable distribution thereof that may be possible upon the basis of the common ownership of the means of production, distribution and exchange, and the best obtainable system of popular administration and control of each industry or service.*

Its defenders tended to advocate neither the abolition of private capital and markets, nor their replacement by a planned, collectively owned economy. For them it meant only there should be more public ownership than now, and it stood for the distant hope of an economic system that was morally different from capitalism. It was a tokenism which Harold Wilson, as a leader of the left, was happy to exploit. 'We were being asked to take Genesis out of the Bible. You don't have to be a fundamentalist to say that Genesis is part of the Bible,' he explained later.[15] It was 'symbolic of values rather than policy', as Blair himself put it in his interview with the *Daily Telegraph* in July, as he tried to keep the press off the scent of change.[16]

In 1959, Gaitskell mishandled the attempt to change Clause IV because his rational mind paid attention to the words rather than to the symbolism. He allowed the party to believe that his response to a third election defeat was to abandon the party's principles, and he was forced to settle for a National Executive statement adopted at the following year's conference to 'reaffirm, amplify and clarify' Clause IV. The statement declared that the Labour Party's 'central ideal is the brotherhood of man. Its purpose is to make this ideal a reality everywhere.' It retained the phrase 'common ownership', calling for an expansion of it 'substantial enough to give the community power over the commanding heights of the economy'. These were Aneurin Bevan's words, inserted as an amendment just after his death in 1960 by his widow, Jennie Lee. But the scope of nationalisation was at least limited: 'Further extension of common

*The words 'distribution and exchange' had been added in 1928.

ownership should be decided . . . with due regard for the views of the workers and consumers concerned.'[17] The statement was a reasonable reflection of the actual beliefs of the party at the time, which were only a little to the left of Gaitskell's, but his real defeat was that Clause IV itself was left untouched.

Both Blair's predecessors, Neil Kinnock and John Smith, had wanted to get rid of Clause IV, which committed the party to the 'common ownership' of the economy, but both had calculated that the time was not ripe.

When John Smith died, he had been preparing a less confrontational initiative on Clause IV. His approach was symptomatic of his wider strategy, to put the left to sleep and allow the voters to forget about them. He made it clear he did not agree with the clause, but described the debate about getting rid of it as 'academic'.[18] Privately, he felt he could not take it on as well as the block vote, and was extremely angry with Jack Straw, then shadow Environment Secretary, for producing a pamphlet calling for Clause IV to be scrapped in the middle of the battle for one member, one vote in 1993. His chief policy adviser, David Ward, said Smith intended to publish a personal statement of values at the 1994 Labour conference, and had consulted Blair about it. 'It would have been a rewrite and purely secular version of his Tawney lecture in March 1993,' said Ward. One of Smith's last acts before he died was to set a date in June 1994 for a meeting with his advisers to draft the statement. The plan was to ask the party to discuss it and then to adopt it – possibly amended – at the following year's conference in 1995. Smith's intention, said Ward, was then to deflect any questions about Clause IV by saying it had been 'superseded' by the new document. The sleeping dogs of the left and the unions would have been left to lie, but Clause IV itself would also have remained. Smith's 'quiet life' approach was defended by Roy Hattersley: 'I have learned, during the forty years since Clement Attlee was Prime Minister, that the party does best when it is at peace with itself.'[19]

Blair decided to go to war instead. Using the authority conferred on him by mid-term elevation, he could smash an idol the party really cared about and hence persuade voters that it had really changed. 'It is time we gave the party some electric-shock treatment,' he declared at a secret summit of the inner modernising clique at Chewton Glen Hotel in Hampshire on 9 September 1994.[20] It was attended by just eight people: Blair, Brown, Campbell, Mandelson and Philip Gould were the core; Colin Fisher, a long-term Labour adviser who ran a management consultancy, paid for the luxury awayday; and two more junior figures were also present, Roger Liddle and Michael Wills. Liddle was a close friend of Mandelson's from 1979 when they both served as councillors on 'red'

Lambeth council, Liddle defecting to the SDP while Mandelson stayed with the unfashionable Labour right. He was still a member of the Liberal Democrat executive, but had been for some time a New Labour 'sleeper' and would return to the Labour fold the following year. Public knowledge of his proximity to the heart of the Blair leadership would have had an incendiary effect on the Labour Party. Wills knew Mandelson well from his time as a producer at London Weekend Television, but was closer to Brown, who was lobbying Blair – unsuccessfully – for him to be made Deputy General Secretary of the party.[21]

Rewriting Clause IV was a risk. 'Few politicians are good at taking the high ground and throwing themselves off it,' said Mandelson, talking about Blair's decision. 'Tony does it, and takes enormous care to bring everyone else behind him. He manages the process of risk-taking with great application to detail.'[22] In this case, however, the work was not done in advance: Blair seems simply to have judged that he would be able to pull it off in the end.

Essential to this exercise, however, was the support of John Prescott, who knew nothing of the Chewton Glen meeting. It was an early test of the deputy's loyalty to the new leader. Prescott knew he was being used to give traditionalist cover to the modernisers' 'project', but there was little he could do. Nor did he disagree in principle with rewriting Clause IV, although he made it tactically known that he had doubts about whether it was the right time to do it. He consented to the idea, on condition that he could assure trade union leaders that there would be no more party reforms before the General Election.

There was a whiff of Gaitskellism in the air in Blackpool as the Labour conference opened on 2 October 1994, revealing the slogan 'New Labour, New Britain' on a 'pistachio' green backdrop. Gaitskell's ally Douglas Jay had suggested changing the Labour Party's name in 1959 (one of his suggestions was 'Radical Labour'). Philip Gould had suggested New Labour under Neil Kinnock in 1989; it had been proposed again and rejected by John Smith.[23] Now Blair made the change.

The more important parallel between 1959 and 1994 was not revealed until the end of Blair's first conference speech as leader. At the 1959 Labour conference, when Tony Blair was six, Gaitskell said it was better explicitly to accept the mixed economy, 'instead of going out of our way to court misrepresentation'. Thirty-five years later, right at the end of his speech, Blair used almost the same words to demand a new Clause IV, to set out Labour's aims in terms 'the Tories cannot misrepresent'.

The announcement was one of the best-sprung surprises of modern party conference theatre. Unusually, most journalists were not given copies of the speech before Blair went to the rostrum. Those who were found their copy had the last three pages missing.

The manner of Blair's request, however, was indirect. Immediately after declaring, 'Let us say what we mean and mean what we say,' he failed to say what he meant. He and John Prescott would propose a new statement of the party's objects to 'take its place in our constitution for the next century'. It was not until after his standing ovation that many delegates realised that he meant rewriting Clause IV – although a vigilant Arthur Scargill was already denouncing Blair's betrayal to journalists under a balcony during the applause.

The press, however, was unanimous in its acclaim. Campbell, in his strange position as a *Today* columnist but already acting as Blair's spokesman, paid barbed tribute to Mandelson's role in planning the coup:

> Many newspapers rightly spotted the hand of Peter Mandelson, legendary MP for Hartlepool and the spin-doctor's spin-doctor, of whom John Smith once memorably said that he was so devious he would one day disappear up his own something or other.
>
> Few people are as capable of arousing strong passions as Peter, who is both admired and loathed.
>
> Having been a close friend of his since the days before he started wearing cufflinks, I have none of the traditional hang-ups about Peter, and fully intend on becoming Blair's press secretary to exploit his expertise which in some areas is second to none.
>
> Speech-writing, however, is not one of them, but such is his ubiquitous appeal that *The Times* yesterday suggested he had helped write Blair's speech.
>
> I know from the days when Peter was a *People* columnist that writing was never his strong point, and that he had to look to his friends to help him out. Know what I mean?[24]

It was the first sign of another rivalry at the top of New Labour. However, that between Mandelson and Campbell would be conducted with greater restraint and good humour than that between Mandelson and Brown.

The campaign to change the party constitution got off to a poor start when, two days later, the conference carried a motion affirming Clause IV by 50.9 to 49.1 per cent.* It was not until December – which was when the new text had originally been promised – that the National Executive agreed a timetable for a special Labour Party conference to vote on the

*The defeat was seen by Blair's advisers as the revenge of Robin Cook, in the conference chair and calling speakers against reform, for not being consulted.

change in spring 1995. This was designed to pre-empt the summer season of trade union conferences, at which activists would try to decide union policies against change – as they did over one member, one vote. At the same time, a survey of local Labour parties by *Tribune* found that 59 of the 61 who had voted on Clause IV had voted to keep it. These were decisions by activist-led General Committees, and Blair intended to encourage ballots of all party members, but the omens did not look good.

The battle had begun. Superficially it was merely a battle over words drafted seventy-seven years before. In reality, it was a battle to change the party's soul. And the suspicions of the traditionalists, now including much of the Smithite mainstream, were stoked by an issue which touched the party's soul more than any other.

The London Oratory

Tony and Cherie confirmed in December 1994 that they would send their elder son Euan to the London Oratory, a traditionalist Roman Catholic state boys' school which had taken advantage of Conservative law to opt out of local council control. The Labour Party went into what Aneurin Bevan once called an 'emotional spasm'.

That the Blairs were considering the school had been reported during the leadership campaign, hardly causing a ripple of interest.[25] Blair had defended the idea at that time in a matter-of-fact way:

> Parents are going to choose whatever is the best choice of school for their kids. We have disagreed with the government opting out schools, but you can't say to parents they then can't choose them – that would be manifestly absurd – any more than you could say with a National Health Service trust that you shouldn't use it.[26]

When the decision was announced, however, it served to crystallise anxieties in the party about its new leader's lack of a 'bottom line'. Euan, then aged ten, suddenly found himself at the centre of a national controversy. Many party members thought it hypocritical of Blair to attack the government for favouring certain schools over others, and yet to benefit from that advantage for his own family. Roy Hattersley urged him to keep the party's pledge to abolish such schools, and deplored Labour's acceptance of Conservative language by which 'parental choice' – which he defined as 'the freedom of the middle classes to talk their way into unfair advantage' – had become a 'canon of democratic socialism'.[27] But Blair was unembarrassed by the contradiction, and used it to make a populist point, rubbing salt into his party's wounds: 'I am not going to make a choice for my child on the basis of what is the politically correct thing to do.'[28]

The Blairs had run up against the conflict between freedom and equality that socialists have sought to sidestep through the ages. If parents can choose between schools, differences will be exaggerated. And where there are only so many 'good' schools, choice for some is opportunity denied for others.

Blair repeatedly stressed that the London Oratory was a state comprehensive, as indeed it was supposed to be, in that it was required to admit children regardless of ability or background, apart from religion. But children had to be interviewed before they were given a place, according to the school's prospectus, to 'assess whether the aims of the parents and the boy are in harmony with those of the school'. The purpose of interviews at church schools was only supposed to be to assess children's 'religious suitability', but they allowed schools effectively to select pupils by ability. The Oratory's admissions criteria were not new, and had been tolerated by the Labour-controlled Inner London Education Authority. But the Catholic Church's own education service complained: 'We are aware of one or two instances where Catholic schools interview parents before determining whether to admit a pupil. This we deprecate and accept that such procedures could give rise to allegations of "selection by stealth".'[29]

As damaging to Blair was that the decision undermined his rhetoric of 'strong communities'. The Oratory, in Fulham, was eight miles from his home in Islington, where there are other Roman Catholic secondary schools. It would not take a philosopher to realise that any real 'community' consisting of real families would have to include schools. Unsurprisingly, Blair construed the word in terms which reduced it to vapid generality: 'The notion of community for me is less a geographical concept than a belief in the social nature of human beings.'[30]

The problem of choice and equity in education may ultimately be insoluble for the left. Blair sought instead to focus attention on immediate measures to raise standards and direct resources to failing schools. He appointed David Blunkett shadow Education Secretary when he moved Jack Straw to take his own brief of home affairs. Blunkett had a bumpy start. On New Year's Day 1995, he thought he was merely repeating the party line in interviews with the *Sunday Times* and *Mail on Sunday* when he said the party was considering charging VAT on school fees. But Blair and Gordon Brown reacted immediately to front-page headlines warning of this 'threat' to private schooling. By lunchtime, Blunkett was on the radio to reverse the position: 'The shadow Chancellor and the leader think it is helpful to rule out that possibility in order to avoid confusion.'[31]

By March 1995, he began to deliver what Blair wanted: a policy aimed at raising standards that would offend the National Union of Teachers. His 'fresh start' plan to close failing schools and re-open them under a new head, new governing body and new name was a Blairist strike which ensured he was harangued and jostled by Socialist Workers' Party teachers at the NUT conference.

Against this background, the battle to replace Clause IV – especially with no alternative form of words yet proposed – seemed to many in the Labour Party an attempt to abandon their basic values. Blair appeared to confirm their fears when he refused to say Labour would renationalise British Rail if it were privatised.

On 10 January 1995, a majority of Labour's Euro-MPs sponsored an advertisement in the *Guardian* defending Clause IV, saying it could be 'perhaps added to, but not replaced'. Blair, in Brussels for a conference, rounded on them, accusing them of 'infantile incompetence' and 'gross discourtesy'. The intemperate language spoke of weakness rather than strength, but the air of crisis spurred Blair's supporters to begin fighting for a new Clause IV. Later that month the National Executive agreed to urge local Labour parties to ballot their members on Clause IV; Robin Cook, an important centre-left figure, came out for rewriting the constitution; and Blair began a tour to meet party members all over the country to argue for change.

It was only then that the debate over Clause IV really began. Blair's shirtsleeved question-and-answer sessions up and down the country set a new model for relations between party and leader. With the defenders of common ownership forced to spell out their arguments, the process immediately turned in Blair's favour. Thousands of party members saw him in person, engaged in dialogue and persuasion rather than edited on television. Face to face, the party was surprised by its new leader, and the leader seemed, not for the first time, surprised by himself. Blair turned a corner, and was on a rising trend up to the special conference in April.

The end of the beginning

At the Scottish Labour Party conference in Inverness on 10 March 1995, Blair cleared the way for a new Clause IV. The party in Scotland is more traditional than the English party, but it also has a history of great loyalty to Labour leaders. With the confidence gained from speaking to party rallies around the country, Blair overcame the ties of tradition. The autocue had broken down, so he was forced to improvise, appealing directly to his audience:

> If we have the courage to change, the country will . . . There will be people voting at the next election who will barely have been born at the time of the last Labour government. When that day comes, the next election is going to be every bit about us as about the Conservatives. Make no mistake about that . . . The question people will ask is, 'Do we trust Labour?' I believe it is essential, for that trust to be won, that we are clear about the values we hold dear. We need the people with us . . . The only thing that stands between us and government is trust. Trust will be gained, not by clinging to icons for fear of thinking anew, but by seizing the spirit without which all thought is barren.

After a debate ringing with scriptural references – 'nothing stands still', said the delegate from the Western Isles, 'not even the authorised version of the Bible' – the conference voted for a Revised Standard Version of Labour's sacred text. But it was only now that the final form of the new Clause IV began to take shape. For months a draft put together by David Miliband had been circulating among shadow Cabinet members and union leaders, one of whom described it as a 'raggedy composite'. It was substantially rewritten by Derry Irvine, and then, in a 'safe house' near Inverness, Blair and his advisers sat down to finalise a text. Returning from the conference in Inverness, on an aeroplane from Glasgow to London, Blair wrote out a near-final draft of the new Clause IV Part One, the paragraph designed to replace the words on the back of party membership cards:

> By the strength of our common endeavour to achieve what we cannot do alone to grant each of us the power to realise our full potential, and all of us the means to create, for this and future generations, a community, in which power, wealth and opportunity are in the hands of the many not the few, where the rights we receive reflect the duties we owe, so that, freed from the tyranny of poverty, ignorance and fear, we may live together in a spirit of solidarity, tolerance and respect.

This handwritten version was close to the final version, unveiled at the National Executive meeting on 13 March, the main difference being that it was then prefaced with the apparently blunt assertion: 'The Labour Party is a democratic socialist party.'

Blair's airborne jottings were far from the spontaneous 'first draft' of the young philosopher king, however. They had been copied out from a typed text – the 'David Miliband' draft – which had been annotated by Peter Mandelson. Mandelson crossed out a disparaging reference to 'private profit' in the economic section and tried – unsuccessfully – to delete any reference to trade unions as allies with whom the party would work. His main contribution, however, was to remove the word 'equality'. The spirit in which the people of Britain had originally been enjoined to live was one of 'solidarity, liberty and equality' – dismissed by Mandelson as an 'old-fashioned mantra'.[32] Thus was the central tradition of the left suppressed, subordinated to the need to find a form of words capable of embracing the widest possible electoral coalition. So diluted a definition of socialism was it that Mandelson felt able to show a copy of it to Howell James, who was a personal friend as well as being John Major's political secretary.

In one sense, the rewriting of Clause IV was an inconclusive symbol. The economics of the old clause were so archaic that little credit can be claimed for doing in 1995 what should have been done in 1959, which is after all when the German Social Democratic Party wrote all traces of Marxism out of its programme at Bad Godesberg.

However, it would be a mistake to underestimate the ideological significance of the rewriting. The very universality of the sentiments of the new Clause IV marked the rejection of all the dominant traditions of socialist philosophy, to leave only the most attenuated system of public ethics as Labour's core belief. In *She* magazine, Blair provided a twenty-four-word summary of the new 340-word clause: 'Social-ism . . . is not about class, or trades unions, or capitalism versus socialism. It is about a belief in working together to get things done.'[33] Blair's lowest-common-denominator definition was so low that most Tories or Christian Democrats could sign up.

Two Labour Party Special Conferences, at Wembley, 24 January 1981, and at Westminster, 29 April 1995, bracketed Labour's wilderness years. The Wembley Special Conference, to decide the form of electoral college which would take the choice of Labour leader out of the hands of MPs, was the high point of Tony Benn's ascendancy, and triggered the SDP breakaway. The Clause IV Special Conference at Methodist Central Hall saw New Labour break away from its past, and summoned the SDP back to the fold. It marked the end of the beginning of Blair's leadership. Curiously, the conference was unconstitutional. There was no provision for it in the Labour Party's rules: the previous special conference in January 1981 had technically been an adjourned session of the 1980 annual Labour conference. It did not matter: after Arthur Scargill, the leader of the National Union of Mineworkers, threatened litigation, the issue was settled by a retrospective vote at the 1995 Labour conference.

Methodist Central Hall was where the original Clause IV was adopted during the First World War. In the very chamber where it was agreed without debate to abolish private capital in 1918, Blair's polite endorsement of 'the enterprise of the market and the rigour of competition' was approved by a 65 per cent vote in 1995. It was an unexpected result. A few weeks before, the public service union, Unison, previously loyal to the Labour leadership, decided without balloting its members to cast its 11 per cent block vote against the new clause. But then the results from local party ballots started to come in, running at an average of 85 per cent in favour of change. The left-wing MP Diane Abbott claimed party members were so keen to win the next election that they would have voted 'for the healing power of cabbage' if the leader had asked them to. It was an insulting and unconvincing explanation of the size of the majority.

After the result was announced, Blair spoke briefly, without notes:

> I wasn't born into this party. I chose it. I've never joined another political party. I believe in it. I'm proud to be the leader of it and it's the party I'll always live in and I'll die in. [Applause.] If sometimes I seem a little over-hasty and over-urgent, it's for one reason only: I can't stand these people, these Tories, being in government over our country.

The vote was a decisive rejection of the judgment of Labour Euro-MP Ken Coates: 'This young man has not the faintest idea of how socialists think, and does not begin to understand the mentality of the party which he has been elected to lead.'[34] In a *Guardian* interview after the vote, Blair conceded that Coates *had* had a point:

> I know the Labour Party very well now. It may be a strange thing to say but before I became leader I did not. The Labour Party is much nicer than it looks. Labour often looks as if it is about to engage in class war, but in fact it is full of basically rather decent and honest people.[35]

It was a curious observation, probably with a double propaganda purpose. First, to reassure Labour members that he quite liked them really; and, secondly, to suggest to the wider public that the Labour Party was different from its stereotype.

Blair turned the Clause IV debate into a personal triumph. He recalled Conservative predictions that he would have to be rescued from a suspicious party by the trade union block vote. David Hill, the party's chief spokesman, produced a long list of quotations from Conservatives saying how significant it was that Labour still had the old Clause IV, and a new list saying how insignificant the change was. Just before his victory on Clause IV, Blair trounced John Major at Prime Minister's Questions. It was 25 April, the day after Major brought the Euro-rebel Conservative MPs back into the party, without any concessions on their part. The contrast with Blair's facing down his (admittedly weaker) Clause IV rebels was sharp, and Major unwisely tried to point out that both parties were divided over Europe. But there was a difference, said Blair: 'I lead my party. He follows his.' Enjoying the smack of firm government-in-waiting,

Labour MPs roared their delighted approval. Major ruefully admitted later that Blair's 'wounding jibe' was 'the best one-liner he ever used against me'.[36]

Attracted by the heady scent of success, the party's membership had risen from 260,000 to 330,000. (In stark contrast to later concealment of decline, the numbers were rising so fast that updates were issued almost monthly during this period.)

Blair's victory created expectations of further change. He played on this in his unscripted speech after the Clause IV vote to make a politically risqué joke: 'I want to say something about the party's name.' He paused, as delegates looked at each other in surprise. 'It's staying as it is.' It was the cheek of a rock star who half-despises his audience, and a bit too close to the bone for John Prescott, who did not look pleased. It is inconceivable that any previous Labour leader could have said the same.

In any case, the name had been amended in practice already, to 'New Labour'.* The real area for change defined itself. The failure of the leaders of the Transport and General Workers' Union and Unison to consult their members before voting against change had once again embarrassed the block vote. And, now that the party's membership had passed the 300,000 level at which it had been agreed under John Smith to 'review' the trade unions' 70 per cent share of Labour conference votes, Blair was asked by journalists when it might be cut to 50 per cent.

Blair was noncommittal, triggering the first of Prescott's semi-public tirades against him (or usually his advisers). Prescott felt Blair had reneged on their deal over the new Clause IV, which he had agreed to support on condition there were no more party reforms before the General Election. In television interviews, Prescott said, 'I personally don't see that change taking place this side of an election,' and warned 'those in victory' of the need to hold the party together.[37] Whether the deputy leader's impotent rage reassured the unions or not, they agreed to cut the block vote to 50 per cent at the autumn annual conference four months later.

In his first nine months as leader, Blair acted on Harold Wilson's famous dictum: 'The Labour Party is like a vehicle. If you drive at great speed, all the people in it are either exhilarated or so sick that you have no problems. But when you stop, they all get out and argue about which way to go.' The initial pace set by Blair as leader caught his opponents in and out of his party off-balance, and left them unable to fix him.

---

*When asked in an *Observer* interview, 10 September 1995, if candidates would appear on the ballot paper at the next election as New Labour or Labour, Blair paused before plumping for Labour.

The new Wilson

Blair's leadership election manifesto, which did not advertise any changes to the Labour Party, turned out to be a misleading prospectus. By the time of the Special Conference, Blair had changed the party's constitution, effectively changed its name and redrawn its policies on tax, inflation, the minimum wage, exam league tables, opted-out schools, Northern Ireland, regional government and the House of Lords. Perhaps the most significant policy shift was the subtle Eurosceptic rebalancing of Labour's position on the single currency.* In each case, policy change moved Labour closer to the Conservatives.

This dazzling display of ruthless electoralism reduced John Major's party to a state of numbed disarray. Blair had shown himself to be an even more impressive Leader of the Opposition than the young Harold Wilson. The similarities between Wilson and Blair were remarked on – not least by Blair himself – when Wilson died in May 1995. The 47-year-old Wilson had been presented as Labour's answer to John F. Kennedy when he succeeded Hugh Gaitskell in 1963. It seemed that the only way the Labour Party could present itself as 'modern' was when a respected leader died in the post and his successor faced a short run-in to the next election. Blair could not resist comparing himself with Labour's longest-serving Prime Minister. 'In the sense that he appeared to embody the desire of the country to move on and address a new age with its technological and economic and social challenges, then there are parallels,' the new Wilson claimed, immodestly.[38] They had in common a love affair with television. In a tribute to Wilson, Blair wrote: 'Communicating with the people, and speaking up for them in public, is a vital part of the politician's role.'[39]

In private, however, Blair was critical of Wilson's governments, and thought he had learned important lessons from Wilson's failures, particularly the 1967 devaluation, the failure to reform trade union law and the neglect of the party. He did not blame Wilson alone. Reflecting on Labour's most golden moment in history, the 1945 General Election, Blair perpetrated another heresy, accusing Clement Attlee of leaving 'fundamental issues of ideology and organisation' unresolved. He said: 'In wartime, these became obscured. But later they reasserted themselves and in the late Seventies and Eighties were almost fatal.'[40]

Blair had acted with speed and decisiveness to prepare the ground for a famous election victory. But he was well aware how ill-prepared he and especially his party were for successful government. With the Labour

---

*See pp. 473–5.

Party not just signed up to a new Clause IV but apparently revitalised by the campaign for a new definition of socialism, Blair's leadership entered a new phase. From now until the General Election, his focus would not simply be on winning that election, but on the one after that. That would require competence, coherence and economic success in government. The excitements of changing a political party gave way to the less exhilarating task of preparing to rule a country. Meanwhile, the Labour Party vehicle slowed down enough to allow several travel-sick passengers to get out and argue about the route.

Notes

1. BBC1, *Breakfast With Frost*, 12 June 1994.
2. BBC Radio 4, *Today*, 22 July 1994.
3. *Independent Magazine*, 3 June 1995.
4. *Sun*, 15 November 1997.
5. *The Times*, 23 July 1994.
6. BBC Radio 4, *Today*, 1 August 1994.
7. *The Times*, 3 August 1994.
8. Gallup polls, December 1981 and December 1994. The two figures are not comparable, however, because opinion polls are not what they used to be: as with by-elections, they are increasingly used as a way of voicing a protest.
9. *Observer*, 25 September 1994.
10. BBC1, *Panorama*, 3 April 1995 (7 April in Scotland).
11. BBC Radio 4, *Today*, 15 September 1994. The same line of attack unnerved Blair in his *Panorama* interview with David Dimbleby at the start of the General Election campaign in 1997 – see p. 308.
12. *The Times*, 19 September 1994; see also p. 103.
13. Roger Eatwell, *The Labour Government, 1945–51*, p. 20.
14. Steven Fielding, 'Mr Benn and the Myth of Clause IV', *Parliamentary Brief*, April 1995.
15. *Listener*, 29 October 1964, quoted by Ben Pimlott, *Harold Wilson*, p. 227.
16. *Daily Telegraph*, 26 July 1994.
17. The statement is reprinted as an appendix in Philip M. Williams, *Hugh Gaitskell*, p. 572.
18. BBC Radio 4, *Today*, 24 February 1994.
19. Roy Hattersley, *Observer*, 15 January 1995. Hattersley later (*Guardian*, 2 July 1996) attributed this sentiment to John Smith himself, in their last talk together 'a week or so before he died'.
20. Philip Gould, *The Unfinished Revolution*, p. 218.
21. Donald Macintyre, *Mandelson*, pp. 273–4.
22. *New Yorker*, 5 February 1996.
23. Gould, *The Unfinished Revolution*, p. 96; and interview with Leslie Butterfield, who handled Labour's advertising during John Smith's leadership. See also p. 225.
24. *Today*, 6 October 1994.
25. *Daily Express*, 21 June 1994.

26. BBC1, *On the Record*, 26 June 1994.
27. *Observer*, 15 January 1995.
28. BBC1, *Good Morning*, 1 December 1994.
29. Letter from Michael Power of the Catholic Education Service to the *New Statesman*, 14 August 1998.
30. *New Statesman*, 28 April 1995.
31. BBC Radio 4, *The World This Weekend*, 1 January 1995.
32. Macintyre, *Mandelson*, p. 277.
33. *She*, March 1995. The user-friendly rendition of socialism in two parts was not original: it was, paradoxically, one of Tony Benn's lines in speeches during the deputy leadership election campaign in 1981. He would complain that opponents spat out the word as if it were an insult: 'But that it not how it is pronounced. It is social-ism.'
34. *Daily Telegraph*, 13 January 1995.
35. *Guardian*, 1 May 1995.
36. John Major, *The Autobiography*, p. 607.
37. BBC1, *On the Record*, 23 April 1995; BBC2, *Westminster On-Line*, 2 May 1995.
38. BBC Radio 4, *The World at One*, 24 May 1995.
39. *Independent*, 25 May 1995.
40. Speech at Fabian Society commemoration of the 1945 General Election, 5 July 1995.

15

Shadow Prime Minister

Preparation for Power, April 1995–December 1996

> '"Vote for Tony Blair's New Labour. We all agree the old one was absolutely appalling and you all know that most of the people in Labour are really the old one, but we've got some who are nothing to do with that – vote for us."'
>
> —*Clare Short, 1996*

After his triumph at the Clause IV Special Conference, Tony Blair's leadership took on a less exuberant tone. The prospect of a Labour victory at the forthcoming election imperceptibly became a settled fact. Within the Labour Party, meanwhile, the shock of the new was beginning to wear off, and the tensions between the leading figures threatened to break into the open. The rumbling feud between Brown and Mandelson was largely kept secret, but spread like a bruise beneath the surface of New Labour. 'Why, oh why, can't my two best people get on with each other?' Blair moaned to his staff.[1] It was a rhetorical question, betraying his impotent irritation that others could not be as self-disciplined in their personal relations as him.

Mandelson wanted to be put in charge of planning for the General Election campaign, saying it 'would help legitimise my role' – referring to Blair's promise to him during the leadership election. Brown disagreed, saying that, as chairman of the daily media meeting, he should chair the planning committee, too: a separate chairman would, he warned, 'institutionalise parallel structures'.[2] Brown, ever jealous of his power base, did not mind Mandelson doing the work as long as he, Brown, remained firmly and formally in charge. Blair did not care as long as the work – of setting up a central 'war room', modelled on the 1992 Clinton headquarters in Little Rock, Arkansas – was done. But this lack of public recognition was precisely what had driven Mandelson to tears during the leadership election campaign.

The plan for 'an operations room/war room' was set out by Philip Gould in March 1995 in his famous memo, 'The Unfinished Revolution', the title of which he later used for his book about the building of New Labour. Originally the idea was that the war room 'should be established in the leader's office', but it was quickly realised that it was not feasible in the Leader of the Opposition's suite of offices in the Palace of Westminster. Instead, Blair decided to set up campaign HQ half a mile upriver from his office, in a huge first-floor space in Millbank Tower, a green 1960s monstrosity constructed, symbolically enough, on the site of Sidney and Beatrice Webb's London house.

The mechanics were dealt with by the appointment of Tom Sawyer as Labour Party General Secretary, a post technically in the gift of the National Executive, which was ready to let the new leader have his man. But the political control of the election campaign was still contested. Gould's memo continued Mandelson's attempt to remove Brown from control. It suggested that the daily media committee chaired by Brown should be 'reconstituted'. It should meet in the leader's office and be 'chaired by TB, or JPow/AC in his absence' ('JPow' being Jonathan Powell, Blair's new Chief of Staff, and 'AC' being Alastair Campbell). This was unrealistic, and what Gould brazenly called the 'daily news management meeting' continued daily under Brown's chairmanship throughout the election campaign.

The memo was one of Gould's more ambitious documents, ranging widely over issues of ideology as well as organisation. (Blair, after receiving one thirty-six-page *tour d'horizon*, gently said he preferred a single side of A4.[3]) But beyond Gould's attention-seeking declaration that 'Labour is not ready for government: it needs to complete its revolution', which was widely reported, the memo's main significance was organisational. It complained that Labour 'does not have the flexibility, capacity for innovation, or directness of decision-making that is the hallmark of a successful political organisation'. And it advocated a 'unitary command structure leading directly to the party leader' to weld 'project, policy and message' into a cohesive, flexible organisation. But the rivalry between Brown and Mandelson was the main obstacle to the creation of such a 'unitary' structure.

The reason the Gould memo became famous was because it was leaked to the *Guardian* before Blair addressed the Trades Union Congress in September 1995. Some of Blair's more factional supporters suspected that Gordon Brown's supporters had a hand in it, hoping to damage Mandelson by association with Gould. They were suspicious of Brown's office, and particularly of Charlie Whelan, the shadow Chancellor's press officer. Blair met him and accepted his assurances that he had not leaked the memo – a meeting for which Whelan said he asked.

In the summer of 1995 Mandelson seemed to concede that Brown would remain in overall charge of election planning, but complained to Blair about being seen as the 'leader's little helper' and wrote:

> There is no question of me ceasing to act as your friend and adviser. I am always thinking of you. I will do anything you ask of me. You are the most important thing to have happened for our party and the country. But we have to face up to the fact that we cannot go on like this.[4]

Suppressing his impatience with the melodramatic tone, Blair wearily talked him round again, and the central New Labour trio managed to 'go on like this' for another year. Still Mandelson felt that he had not been 'legitimised' as promised. Blair had – after a battle of wills with the Old Labour diehards in the whips office – appointed him a Labour whip in the Commons: he was one of six of the 1992 intake who were the first to be promoted to the front bench in October 1994.

But Mandelson resented the fact that he was essentially still in the back room, still 'being Peter', organising election campaigns and offering political advice (although briefing journalists less than before). In July 1995 he ran Labour's cynical and only just unsuccessful campaign for the Liberal Democrat target seat in the Littleborough and Saddleworth by-election, which also acted as a catalyst for a summer of discontent during which an internal backlash against 'New Labour' was allowed to gather a little steam. The winning Liberal Democrat candidate, Chris Davies, had been attacked as 'high on tax and soft on drugs', prompting the *New Statesman* to urge 'socialists' to vote for him.[5] The real significance of the by-election, though, was that it brought home to Blair that, for all his attempt to colonise the centre ground, New Labour could not simply annex the Liberal Democrat part of it.

All the same, the New Labour honeymoon carried pretty much everything else before it. Blair's second party conference, in Brighton in October 1995, went so much according to plan that the leadership was not defeated once – the first time this had happened since the 1960s. Paradoxically, the clean sweep was bought at the price of an old-fashioned deal with the trade unions. Blair agreed to a motion pledging to restore Railtrack – to be sold off the following year – to public ownership. In his speech, he underlined the commitment:

> To anyone thinking of grabbing our railways, built up over the years, so they can make a quick profit as our network is broken up and sold off, I say this: there will be a publicly owned, publicly accountable railway system under a Labour government.

That was what he said, but it was not what he meant. He did not even mean it was a priority. He meant it would be nice to have a publicly owned railway but that there would be a lot of better things a Labour government could do with the money. Indeed, he hinted at this elsewhere in his speech: 'Socialism to me was never about nationalisation or the power of the State.' It was an insincere pledge which Gordon Brown, John Prescott and Clare Short, as transport spokeswoman, spent a year trying, unsuccessfully, to get round. In the end it was simply dropped when the final manifesto was drawn up.

Brighton 1995 was his most sermonising conference address as Leader of the Opposition. Without a *coup de théâtre* like Clause IV, he tried to set out a vision for a morally renewed 'Young Country', and defined his socialism in spiritual terms:

> It is a moral purpose to life, a set of values, a belief in society, in co-operation. It is how I try to live my life; the simple truths. I am worth no more than any other man, I am my brother's keeper, I will not walk by on the other side. We aren't simply people set in isolation from each other, face to face with eternity, but members of the same family, community, the same human race. This is my socialism.

Against this, the main announcement of his speech – a deal with the privatised telecoms company BT – had a touch of bathos. In return for a Labour government giving BT early access to the cable television market (that part of the deal was not mentioned in the speech), BT had agreed 'to connect up every school, every college, every hospital and every library in Britain – for free'. The Conservative government had deliberately kept BT out of the cable television market to stop it using its monopoly power to crush the smaller cable companies. The deal certainly helped Blair present himself as being 'in power but not in office', but he glossed over what the company would get out of it.

Meanwhile, the move to the centre ground was leaving a few people behind. Liz Davies, on the editorial board of *Briefing*, the hard-left journal described as 'scary' by Blair in his 1982 Australian lecture, was drummed out as Labour candidate for Leeds North-East. She and Scargill, off to set up his Socialist Labour Party, marked the sealed border of 'New Labour' to the left, but all week Blair and Alastair Campbell harboured the secret of how open the party was to the centre.

From the moment Alan Howarth, the Conservative MP for Stratford-on-Avon, admitted to his 'pair', Margaret Hodge, Labour MP for Barking and next-door neighbour to the Blairs in Islington, that he was considering joining the Labour Party, Blair and Campbell were in a position to influence the time and place of his defection. They chose the Sunday after the Labour conference and before the Conservative one. And they placed it in the *Observer*, because Blair wanted to maintain good relations with a paper read by his party. It was the first time a Conservative MP had defected to Labour, and the Conservatives hated it.

As John Major's majority dwindled, although not quite quickly enough to cut short his government's life, Blair conducted himself without taking his eyes off the coming General Election for a second. He and Major traded cynicism as Blair avoided a series of more or less blatant electoral traps. Labour gave up its long policy of voting against the renewal of the Prevention of Terrorism Act. Blair offered talks to reach a cross-party consensus on how to deal with the rising number of unfounded claims for political asylum. He ordered his MPs to abstain in the vote to cut income tax by 1p in the pound after the 1995 Budget. And he refused to give a commitment to allow homosexuals in the armed forces.

This was adroit defensive politics, complemented by the thinnest of positive policy programmes. Blair did not believe that politics in the 1990s was about 'the fundamental struggle between diametrically opposing ideologies'.[6] But that meant that, once the fun of smashing Labour's traditional ideological idols lost its allure, attention was bound to turn to the 'tittle-tattle' of personal antagonisms.

Titanic feud

Blair's shadow Cabinet was soundly constructed in that its main personnel kept the same portfolios throughout his three years as Leader of the Opposition and throughout the first term of government. In 1994 he had moved Jack Straw to replace himself at home affairs; David Blunkett took Straw's brief at education; Robin Cook replaced Jack Cunningham at foreign affairs. But the jostling between Blair's three senior lieutenants, Gordon Brown, John Prescott and Robin Cook, was regularly reported. Although they met every week – the so-called 'Big Four' including the leader – before the shadow Cabinet, they could not avoid their differences bubbling into the press occasionally. Cook resented being moved from an economic portfolio at trade and industry, and used his position as chairman of the party's new policy-making body, the National Policy Forum, to challenge Brown's dominance. So did Prescott, who as deputy leader without a portfolio could also drive his tanks across Brown's economic lawns. The tensions were largely personal, although they often took political forms.

The most serious animosity, however, was between Brown and the nominally junior Mandelson, who were politically the closest of all.

Mandelson finally achieved some kind of 'legitimacy' in October 1995, when Blair promoted him to shadow minister for the civil service and publicly made him responsible for election planning. But he still had to report directly to Brown's 'strategy committee'. The party's campaign operations moved into Millbank Tower, but Mandelson felt he was constantly obstructed by Brown. As a peace gesture he had agreed to the appointment of Joy Johnson, a Brown admirer and BBC news editor, as the party's media director in February 1995. Unsurprisingly, the appointment was unhappy and short-lived. Mandelson patently did not trust her, and as a result she did not have Blair's confidence. As Alastair Campbell, Brown and Mandelson gathered in Blair's office to discuss their response to John Major's re-election in his 'put up or shut up' challenge to Conservative rebels in July 1995, she was excluded, left 'storming around' outside while Anji Hunter told her, 'This is how it works.'[7] After she left in January 1996, Johnson revealed that she had been deeply out of tune with the political approach not just of Mandelson but of Blair too: 'The trouble with these people is that they hate the party more than they hate the Tories.'

She testified to Blair's huge estimation of Mandelson's abilities: he once told her Mandelson was responsible for ridding him of the 'Bambi' tag, which enjoyed brief journalistic currency when coined by a Prescott-supporting party official in the early days of the unacknowledged leadership contest. It was a telling example of how the Mandelson myth held sway not just among his enemies but with his closest and most powerful friend: the truth was that Blair shook off the nickname because he showed confidence, leadership and pace, not because of a Mandelsonian word in the ear of influential commentators.

Blair was undoubtedly still heavily dependent on his 'Bobby'. Mandelson had coached him in the empty House of Commons Chamber before his first confrontation with John Major at Prime Minister's Questions in October 1994. MPs meeting Blair in his office on routine business were often nonplussed to find Mandelson in the room, acting as something between a private secretary and a political deputy.

Mandelson's natural skills, which were for organisation and presentation, hampered his attempts to move out of the back room and establish himself as a politician in his own right. His book, *The Blair Revolution*, written with Roger Liddle – by now a member of the Labour Party – was published in February 1996. Instead of setting out, Crosland-like, an intellectual basis for New Labour, it was more noticed for previewing some of the organisational themes of the Labour government, such as its plan for a Prime Minister's Department. Most of the politically interesting ideas were filleted out at an early stage because their ultra-revisionism would have caused problems for Blair, coming from someone still seen as the 'leader's little helper'.

Mandelson felt his attempts to heal the breach with Brown had been rebuffed, and was infuriated by the shadow Chancellor's graceless refusal to speak to him in meetings, and his tendency to respond to him by addressing Blair. The fact that he and Brown's press officer, Charlie Whelan, were engaged in a low-level war of briefing and counter-briefing did not help. The tensions were beginning to affect policy-making.

When Brown announced plans to abolish child benefit for sixteen- to eighteen-year-olds on 19 April 1996 the newspapers were confused about what it meant. Alastair Campbell had given exclusive previews to *The Times* and the *Mirror*, who were told it was a 'tough decision' which showed Labour was prepared to end the provision of state benefits to the middle-class parents of students who did not need it. Whelan, meanwhile, had told the *Guardian* it was an egalitarian measure designed to shift funds to working-class youngsters who did not qualify for child benefit once they were out of full-time education. Either way, it was not only an electorally unappealing idea, but one on which Brown had consulted few of his colleagues. Robin Cook, notionally in charge of policy, interrupted his visit to China as shadow Foreign Secretary to give a radio interview dismissing Brown's plan as only 'an option'. Meanwhile another of Brown's feuds, with Cook's ally Chris Smith, the shadow Social Security Secretary, surfaced when the Sunday papers reported that he too was opposed to the idea.[8]

It was out of a meeting in Blair's office on 9 May to sort out this mess that Mandelson so theatrically stormed. As Mandelson's biographer Donald Macintyre observed, the tensions which came to a head were wholly personal – so much so that few of those present could later remember what the argument was about. Mandelson could only recall that, feeling slighted by Brown and then by Blair's support for Brown, he 'went nuclear, lost all grace'. He left the room, slamming the door, and went back to Millbank, where he wrote Blair a long, emotional letter resigning as campaign manager:

> I am very sorry that your meeting ended as it did, but I think we have to recognise that you and I have reached the end of the road . . . I hope you don't think that *amour propre* is the root of my problem. I have long gone beyond that. But I felt greatly let down by you this morning and embarrassed. I do not want to be in that position again. Needless to say, I will always be available to you in any circumstance to help and advise. Operationally, though, I think we have reached a glass ceiling.[9]

He then left for Prague, to attend a North Atlantic Initiative conference. The turmoil he left behind was intensified two days later when on Saturday 11 May *The Times* led its front page with a report that Blair was trying to get Brown and Mandelson to resolve their differences. That relations between the two men were poor was well-known at Westminster, but few journalists had any idea quite how bad things had become. Philip Webster, political editor of *The Times*, did not know about Mandelson's walk-out, but was obviously confident that matters were serious enough to make a story of it. It is often the case that when the press reports splits and rows among politicians it is accused, as Blair accused it during this period, of retailing 'tittle-tattle' (a Thatcher phrase). Then it turns out that the truth was far worse than was reported at the time. After the *Times* story, the rest of the media piled in gleefully, with reports and analyses of the Brown–Mandelson split, reworking the competing versions of the events immediately after John Smith's death from which it arose. But no journalist could have imagined that, all the while, the protagonists were refusing to speak to each other, slamming doors and writing tear-stained letters to the leader, especially when there were no discernible policy disagreements between them.

As the situation looked briefly to Blair as if it might run out of control, he wrote a reply to Mandelson, parts of which were transcribed by Macintyre, which made it clear that he could not tolerate walk-outs or 'irresponsible' stories like that in *The Times*. He acknowledged that Mandelson had been his 'rock and comforter', that Brown could be difficult to work with, and said he had come to a 'settled view' that there was 'culpability' on both sides. The trouble was that they were both 'more desirous of victory over each other than of trying to make it work'. And he warned:

> We are not players in some Greek tragedy. We have one overriding responsibility to deliver an election victory, and though it may seem pious it is just not fair to all those people who really want such a victory and are working for it, to be casualties of some titanic but ultimately irrelevant personality feud.[10]

It was splendid stuff, written with more than half an eye to how it would look to posterity – in contrast with Mandelson's intemperate and often rather foolish diatribes (although Mandelson obviously had his eye on history too: Macintyre only got to see his letters because he had kept copies). And Blair's underlying message was firm: he would rather accept Mandelson's 'resignation' than risk his own relationship with Brown.

When Mandelson received Blair's reply on his return from Prague on Sunday, he dashed off another emotional letter, in which he responded to the charge that he sought victory over Brown regardless of the cost by reporting that Michael Wills 'says Gordon is "determined to kill me before I destroy him"'. This was a less colourful version of Wills's observation to another friend that Brown and Mandelson were 'like scorpions in a bottle; only one of them will crawl out alive'.[11] Mandelson protested to Blair with magnificent disdain that he had no interest in 'destroying' Brown: 'As long as I enjoy *your* confidence and patronage why should I be bothered by what happens to him?' Then he 'resigned' again:

> Nobody, you included, I suspect, thinks Gordon is going to change and therefore, as the number two [to Brown, presumably], I have to go. You are too nice and too considerate towards me to say this, I know, so I had better say it for you. You have to do whatever you think is right for the party to win and, in everything you decide, I shall make it as easy for you as I possibly can.[12]

The exchange of letters offers an astonishing view of the cauldron of resentments and jostling egos on which Blair sat as he drove the party to increasingly certain victory. It is a reminder of quite how emotional, volatile and egotistical politicians can be. But it also illuminates Blair's talent for retaining the individual loyalty of the scorpions as they circled each other, looking for the chance to strike. Blair managed to avoid either of them deciding that 'my enemy's friend is my enemy'. As Mandelson himself had observed of Blair the previous year, 'he manages to combine firmness and clarity with the political skills that make such diverse individuals as John Prescott and Robin Cook believe they are valued'. This was one of the 'personal insights' which Mandelson promised publishers in an early synopsis of his book before deciding that discretion was the better part of vanity publishing.[13]

Mandelson's histrionics worked in the sense that Blair now summoned him and Brown to his office, which forced Brown to acknowledge the problem and to agree to try to work with Mandelson. Nothing was solved – nor could it be, as Mandelson had pointed out – in the long run. But Mandelson looked forward to Blair giving him a real job in government, publicly dreaming in January 1997: 'When I have the chance to turn my energies and skills elsewhere, to see through to implementation a complex area of policy, that is the day I will feel at long last I have obtained the reward I am due for all these hard labours and abuse.'[14] He had to wait more than a year for that day, and then found he had to wait another ten months when his Cabinet career was rudely interrupted by the backwash of the 'titanic' feud with Brown at the end of 1998.

Suburban populism

If the personal rivalries of his lieutenants were difficult to manage, Blair was good at appearing above it all, and the political themes of his drive towards the election were clear. He had learnt most of his important lessons about politics from the Thatcher period. He was influenced, from his vantage point on a rising escalator at the centre of the Labour Party, by *Marxism Today*'s analysis of how Margaret Thatcher built and maintained her 'hegemony' over Britain. He marked well how she used language to identify her 'common sense' with popular values. As a rhetorician, she understood the need to control the commanding heights of the political vocabulary, laying claim to liberty, aspiration, the right to own, leadership and morality. And Blair noticed the parallels with the lessons the Democrats learnt in the United States, where David Kusnet, later a speechwriter for President Clinton, wrote a book called *Speaking American*, about how the Democrats needed to use language which helped persuade ordinary voters that the party shared their basic values. Blair knew, through bitter personal experience, that the Labour Party had been just as bad at 'Speaking English'.

His strategic objective was to establish his own hegemony over British politics, based on the ruthless cultivation of the consensual centre ground and his own brand of rhetoric, the language of uncomplicated utter reasonableness. With thoroughness and – one suspects – much private holding of nose, he went into the tents of the ungodly but powerful and convinced them he deserved a chance: the media, big business, celebrities, Liberal Democrats, moderate Conservatives and even some immoderate ones. In this he was breathtakingly successful. Whereas Thatcher achieved hegemony in government, Blair secured domination of the entire British political landscape while in Opposition.

The way he played Baroness Thatcher herself was just one aspect of this success. She was dying, politically, and he kept her alive. 'She was a thoroughly determined person and that is an admirable quality,' he said. 'It is important in politics to have a clear sense of direction, to know what you want. I believe I know what Britain needs.'[15] Her gratitude and pride at Blair's seeking her advice, combined with her irritation at the pygmy succession in her own party, made her easy prey for an opportunist of instinctive political genius. In contrast to John Major's sullen resentment at her back-seat driving, Blair put her in the front seat and politely listened to her directions – while steering the vehicle where he willed.

Jonathan Powell's access to Thatcher through his brother was crucial. Blair and Powell met in January 1993 in Washington, where Powell was at the British Embassy. This was just as Powell's brother Charles met

Thatcher herself, whom he served for six years as Private Secretary. Charles (the only one of four brothers to pronounce his name 'Pole') was First Secretary at the British Embassy in Bonn when Thatcher arrived on a visit soon after her election as Leader of the Opposition. Blair appointed Jonathan his Chief of Staff in January 1995. (Another brother, Chris Powell, was appointed to run Labour's advertising, as director of the agency BMP.) The Blair team were initially taken aback by Jonathan's civil service formality, especially the fact that he took minutes, but he soon impressed with his quiet efficiency. His understanding of the civil service was also a strength in managing the transition from Opposition to government.

In the autumn of 1996, someone in Conservative Central Office used a second-hand account of a private conversation with Thatcher in order to engage in some low-key spin, telling the *Sun* she thought the Labour leader was 'creepy'.[16] Jonathan was able to establish quickly that the Lady's favourable view of Blair had not changed – the previous year she had described him as 'probably the most formidable' Labour leader since Gaitskell.[17] Alastair Campbell's zero-tolerance media operation swung into full rebuttal mode, providing the *Daily Telegraph* and the *Independent* with 'a source close to Mrs Thatcher' who said she regarded Blair as someone with 'many admirable qualities'. The source of this source was revealed three weeks later when a series of the Blair entourage's pager messages were intercepted by hackers and published in the press. A message to Campbell read: 'Pls call when you and TB are free. I have a message from Mrs T. – Jonathan.' (Another message was 'Pls do something about the hair', from Anji Hunter to Tim Allan, who was minding The Body at a televised speech at the Guildhall in the City of London.[18])

As the election approached, Thatcher, whom John Major wanted 'destroyed',[19] proved the feeling was mutual when she announced deliberately at dinner in the Reform Club, on 23 January 1997: 'Tony Blair is a man who won't let Britain down.' It was of course a 'private' dinner, but attended by Peter Stothard, the editor of *The Times*, and the identity of the 'very senior Conservative' to whom he attributed the words quickly became known.[20] Blair used the incident in an unnecessarily defensive response to her public description of New Labour (rather than Blair himself) as a 'boneless wonder' during the election campaign.[21] 'Privately, Lady Thatcher has been reported as saying I would not let Britain down,' he wrote in the *Sun*, combining the air of teacher's pet and school sneak.[22] And he left a votive offering at the shrine, still held in reverence by many *Sun* readers, admitting there were things 'the 1980s [code for Mrs

Thatcher] got right'. Confessing the sins of his past life as a backbench MP, he said, as an example, 'Labour was too slow to recognise the importance of trade union reforms.'

Indeed, the themes of Blair's suburban populism owed much to her. In an article in the *Daily Mirror* he parodied Thatcher's famous housekeeping analogy:

> The average family and the average company boss could tell Treasury ministers a thing or two about how to manage budgets. Most families . . . don't stand at the top of a hill with a fistful of fivers and let them fly away in the wind. Yet that is what this government does. With your money.[23]

The idea of the 'average company boss' was an even bigger step in Labour's cultural revolution. The 1992 Clinton campaign, however, with its focus on 'the forgotten middle class', had shown how these themes might be stolen by the left. No sooner had Kenneth Clarke, the Chancellor, mentioned the stresses and strain on people in 'Middle England' during the Labour leadership campaign than Blair, blithely ignoring the sensitivities of Scotland and Wales, stepped in to lift the phrase – which became a staple of political commentary.

In his 1996 conference speech, Blair introduced his party to its target voter, inhabitant of Middle England:

> I can vividly recall the exact moment that I knew the last election was lost. I was canvassing in the Midlands on an ordinary, suburban estate. I met a man polishing his Ford Sierra. He was a self-employed electrician. His dad always voted Labour, he said. He used to vote Labour, he said. But he'd bought his own house now. He'd set up his own business. He was doing quite nicely. 'So,' he said, 'I've become a Tory.'

So was born 'Sierra Man', who had become 'Mondeo Man' by the time of the 1997 election.

The move to the centre ground meant policy changes, and Peter Mandelson's early book proposal revealed that there was plenty more revisionism being considered which Blair judged not worth trying to force on a reluctant party. According to Mandelson, 'what New Labour must do if it is serious about transforming Britain' included workfare programmes for the unemployed and single mothers, no-strike deals in the public sector, and the freeing of all schools from local council control.[24] But another aspect of Thatcher's approach Blair recalled favourably was that the Conservatives 'travelled very light' in Opposition before 1979.[25] He tried to limit his policy battles in the party to the most central and symbolic planks of the platform.

The leak of 'The Unfinished Revolution' memo also drew attention to

Philip Gould's backstage role as opinion polling adviser. Blair once boldly declared: 'I am a politician who works by instinct.'[26] Sometimes he was. But usually his instincts would be strengthened or suppressed by the reports from focus groups or the polling carried out by NOP for the party. There was, for example, a noticeable delay between John Major's declaration of his war of non-co-operation with the European Union over the beef ban in May 1996, and Blair's indication that he supported the government 'with reservations'. Blair's instinct had been not to condemn the non-co-operation tactic outright, which produced one of his weakest performances in the Commons as leader, but he was not confident he had got the line right until the polling told him so.

Gould was at the heart of the election campaign because he was the only person who could consistently and quickly answer the question: 'What do the people out there think of this?' In the run-up to the General Election, he would talk to small groups of floating voters every week. This was not 'numbers' polling but 'feel' polling, designed not to measure how far Labour was ahead (in any case a hazardous and inexact science) but to know the sort of things that real people – that is, those who do not think about politics every waking moment – said about political developments. Before he went to a focus group himself, Alastair Campbell told Gould, 'I thought you were a bit of a nutter, frankly.' But he became a convert: 'The people who were talking were the people who had to vote for us, so you had to listen to what they were saying.'[27]

Gould's defence of modern campaign techniques in his book, *The Unfinished Revolution*, fails completely to rebut the suspicion that they were simply a matter of delivering, not even what suburban England said it wanted, but what Gould said it wanted. But there can be no doubt that any effective political party needs to know, through direct contact with small groups or sample surveys, what voters think. Stan Greenberg, Clinton's polling adviser who joined Labour's Millbank operation, pointed out:

> The institutions that used to be effective in mediating popular sentiment have atrophied, and have lost their ability to articulate. So the trade unions, for example, just don't have the kind of base that they use to have.[28]

The other half of a modern communications strategy was, as Blair said on the weekend after John Smith's death, 'the media, the media and the media'. In July 1995, his courtship of the formerly Tory press achieved its greatest triumph. With Campbell, Blair made a twenty-two-hour journey to Australia as the guest of Rupert Murdoch, to give a speech to the NewsCorp 'Leadership Conference' in Hayman Island, the company's private resort. 'To have turned down the chance to address first-hand the largest media group, not just in Britain but the world, would have shown we weren't serious about winning,' Blair later wrote. 'The idea that we should refrain from putting our case to any section of the press – especially to those previously hostile – is ridiculous.'[29]

It was an ambitious speech, engaging directly with the Thatcherite tendencies of his audience. He said: 'The central question of modern democratic politics is how to provide security during revolutionary change.' The new right, he admitted,

> led the changes in politics in the '80s. It held the political initiative. The Thatcher/Reagan leadership symbolised it. And it got certain things right. A greater emphasis on enterprise. Rewarding not penalising success. Breaking up some of the vested interests associated with state bureaucracy. In that sense Mrs Thatcher was a radical, not a Tory.
>
> But I want to suggest that in the end it was a project more successful at taking on and destroying some outdated attitudes and prescriptions, than it was at building and creating . . . If – and I accept this is the real challenge – the left can liberate itself from outdated preconceptions, strip its essential values out from the means of their application relevant to another part of history, then the modern left of centre is best able to provide security amid change.

Appealing to Murdoch's dislike of the British Establishment, he set out his aim of a 'true meritocracy', complaining that 'our legal system is a nest of restrictive practices', that 'the old boys' network' was in evidence in the City of London, that a 'system of divided education' saw a high intake at Oxford and Cambridge from public schools, and that there was 'still prejudice against success in trade and business'. If Murdoch noticed that this tirade was delivered by a public school- and Oxford-educated lawyer, he did not mind. But Blair also confronted Murdoch's anti-euro views, arguing pragmatically that Britain would be 'driven' into closer European integration in the end:

> You can have it honestly under New Labour, with some chance of influencing the process; or you can have it larded with anti-European rhetoric about 'defending Britain to the death', and arrive there in any event with the Conservatives.[30]

It was a speech into which he had put a lot of work: 'It's one of the speeches I felt most happy about, because I felt it did set out a different agenda for politics and indeed in the Western democratic world.'[31]

The whirlwind trip (he was back to deliver a speech on what was then called the 'information superhighway' in London the next day) also afforded the chance to see Australian Prime Minister Paul Keating, who had been Treasurer, or finance minister, when they last met five years before. Blair flew with him to Hayman Island in his jet. Keating offered two unnecessary pieces of advice. First, he said, it was 'better to have Murdoch on your side than against it'. Secondly, he said, 'no party in the English-speaking world' in modern times had won an election promising to put up taxes.[32]

St Olave's

The grumblings of discontent which surfaced in the Labour Party in the summer of 1995 did not immediately find an issue or a leader. But there was one Labour backbench dissident who could not be dismissed, in Blair's words, as 'flotsam or jetsam'. Roy Hattersley complained with touching naïvety that, since Blair became leader of the party, 'the issues we have articulated most clearly have been the subjects that worry the suburbs'.[33]

Blair responded indirectly in an interview in which he said: 'I am a politician, not a psychiatrist, but if people seriously think that by going back to where we were ten or twelve years ago we are going to win power, then they require not leadership but therapy.'[34] He specifically excluded the former deputy leader from his strictures, but Hattersley took offence anyway, scoffing at the fact that 'people who read R. H. Tawney are deemed to need psychiatric help'.[35] By the spring of 1996, his jocularly bitter asides included the low blow of agreeing with Blair that the policies of the early 1980s were wrong, but adding that, 'unlike him, I was against the policies of 1983 *in* 1983'.[36] While this contained a truth, it was unfair: Hattersley had plainly never been either anti-European or unilateralist, but as shadow Home Secretary at the time he bore more responsibility for the policies of 1983 than Blair, then merely an unsuccessful by-election candidate.

Hattersley, settling into his new job as a journalist and preacher of the political religion of his youth, finally broke with New Labour after the election, at which he retired as an MP. Before he marginalised himself, however, he had one last hurrah. All his political life the childless Hattersley had regarded comprehensive schools as the foundations of the New Jerusalem. Many of his generation shared Anthony Crosland's famously profanely-expressed desire to 'destroy' every grammar school in the country, because their existence condemned the vast majority of the children of working people to second-rate schools.

At Labour conference in 1995, he laid siege to David Blunkett's policy on education. Blunkett had just dropped the pledge to return grant-maintained schools (like the one at which Euan Blair had just started) to local council control, promising only to rename them 'foundation' schools. He had also dropped the pledge to abolish entrance exams in the few remaining formally selective state schools. Blunkett, whose three sons went to the local comprehensive in Sheffield, overcompensated for this retreat by a too-clever-by-half play on the words of George Bush (senior). To thunderous applause, he declared: 'Read my lips: no selection, either by examination or by interview, under a Labour government.' Possibly the stupidest statement Blunkett has made, it was to meet the same fate as Bush's original. While Labour was still opposed to selection in principle, its new policy made clear that the future of existing selective schools would be a matter of 'local agreement'.

Blunkett's words would blow up in his face just three months later. The unhappiness over Blair's choice of school for his son had been only the pre-tremor of a more serious earthquake. The decision by Harriet Harman, the shadow Health Secretary, to send her second son to a selective grammar school was the first time Blair faced a real crisis in his party.

It was not, however, unforeseen. Harman had told Blair of her decision just before Christmas 1995, but nothing was done to prepare for the inevitable storm. When Blair sent Euan to the London Oratory, attended by Harman's elder son (Harman's husband Jack Dromey is a Roman Catholic), the issue of selection was clouded. But at St Olave's in Orpington, Kent, it was crystal clear: it was one of the country's 160 selective state schools. Blair realised he could not ask Harman to reverse her decision, because she had only done what he had done with Euan – put the interests of her child (as she saw it) first. Nor could he sack her from the shadow Cabinet, for the same reason. He was not pleased. 'But I took the view she had not done something *seriously* morally wrong,' he said later.[37]

Blair underestimated the power of the charge of hypocrisy, both in the Labour Party and among the general public, and thought it could be defended as essentially a private matter. Meanwhile, his press secretary, Alastair Campbell, was not interested in getting Harman out of a problem of her own making – as a strong Hattersleyite on education policy he had been unhappy enough with Blair's decision to send his son to the Oratory. If Campbell had wanted to, he could have 'managed' the story during the Christmas recess, by persuading Harman to give a personal interview to say what she later said: 'It's easier to go through the eye of a needle than be a good mother and a good politician.'

As it was, the timing of the disclosure was not under Blair's control. When, on Friday 19 January 1996, Harman learnt from the school's head that the *Mail on Sunday* was about to report the story, she contacted the leader's office. She was told to pre-empt it by releasing the information herself. She telephoned the political editors of the *Daily Mirror* and the *Independent*. Over the weekend, she lay low while the news sank in, but, as Labour MPs returned to the Commons on Monday, they were in mutinous mood. Too late, she appeared on *Channel Four News* to give a reasoned defence of her position, which was that she was opposed to selection, but as long as it existed had to do the best for her child.

In the tariff of ideological crimes in the Labour Party, hers was widely regarded as an automatic sacking offence. Before the comprehensive revolution, Labour Cabinet ministers could happily send their children to private schools, let alone grammars, but afterwards they were under an implied moral obligation to go to 'Labour' comprehensives. The Parliamentary Labour Party gave an emotional shudder and momentarily contemplated revolt, but by Wednesday realised that because Blair had backed her she would have to stay. He used the issue in the Commons to contrast his leadership with John Major's, saying that he 'would not buckle'. In a fully reported speech to a 'private' meeting of Labour MPs Harman apologised for the 'diversion', while Blair attacked the Conservatives. 'I have had enough of yielding to these bastards. They are not going to have a scalp,' he said.

The impact of the Harman affair on Labour's policy was limited. David Blunkett came under pressure to clarify what he would do in government about selective schools like St Olave's. He proposed that their future should be decided by a ballot of parents of children at local primary schools, a compromise which allowed Blair to declare that they would remain selective 'if that is what the parents want', and that a Labour government 'will not close down good schools'.[38]

Despite the strains, Blair and Blunkett had developed a strong working relationship. Blair was impressed with Blunkett's old-fashioned emphasis on basic literacy, numeracy and homework – and sometimes even taken aback by how far Blunkett would go. Blunkett was honoured in that only he and Gordon Brown were publicly promised the jobs they shadowed if the election was won. In return, Blair was grateful for Blunkett's discretion over both the Oratory and St Olave's.

Extraordinary as it seems in retrospect, the row over Harman's choice of school was the worst crisis Blair had to face in three years as Leader of the Opposition. It revealed a thin skin, when Cherie threatened to sue the *Daily Express* for describing her son's school also as selective (the threat was dropped after the *Express* cheekily accepted it was a comprehensive 'in the same way that Number 10 Downing Street is an inner-city terraced house').[39] But it hardly matched up to the scale of subsequent government crises.

The more lasting impact of the affair was on the image of Blair and his party. A central component of Blair's appeal in the two years before he became leader was that he was recognisably a human being, that he did not sound like a politician and did not seem to talk in sound-bites. It was an impression he sought to reinforce after he became leader: 'This may sound like an odd thing to say, but I don't actually feel much like a politician.' Not surprisingly at a time when politicians were held in such low esteem, he said:

> I feel a perfectly normal person. I look at politicians who are older than me and I wonder when was the last time they had their own thoughts to themselves in their own way without feeling they had to programme their thoughts to get across a message. I think you can totally lose your humanity.[40]

The idea that Blair was never 'programmed' to 'get across a message' was of course absurd, and, for many voters, Harman's choice of school reinforced the idea that she and Blair were politicians, who 'said one thing and did another'.

More worrying for Blair was the fact that, although Labour MPs could not have Harman sacked straight away, they looked forward to voting her out of the shadow Cabinet in the autumn. He pre-empted them by bringing the elections forward to July, and persuaded a slew of loyalist hopefuls to stand aside. Those who just missed being elected the previous year – Tony Lloyd, Derek Fatchett, Joyce Quin and Brian Wilson – were assured of Minister of State appointments in government, the tier just below Cabinet level, if they withdrew. Thus Labour MPs were asked to choose between the existing team as a whole, including Harman, and a handful of candidates of the hard left.

The device worked, and Harman was safely retained, in nineteenth place out of nineteen (Blunkett also had his knuckles rapped, dropping to seventeenth). Blair then twisted his heel in the chest of the parliamentary party, announcing a new disciplinary code for MPs when the results were published. With further and counter-productive brutality, he demoted Clare Short from transport to overseas development. She had just provoked him, sensitised by the media-allergic Alastair Campbell, by walking out of a television interview when asked an unscheduled question about the current London Underground strike. She had annoyed Blair at regular intervals over the previous year after grudgingly coming on board 'the project', admitting, with her unique blend of candour and condescension, she had misjudged him:

> I was an outsider to the bandwagon for Tony Blair because it doesn't work for me. I now recognise that I'm a minority, because for most people in the country it does work, a young, very middle-class, upper-middle-class sort of attractive young man.[41]

She had called for a debate on the legalisation of cannabis when Labour attacked a Liberal Democrat by-election candidate for doing the same. She had said people on her kind of salary as an MP should pay more tax, a crime she compounded by telling a journalist about the 'ring Tony at home' messages on her electronic pager which followed. More substantially, she had failed as transport spokeswoman to finesse Blair's insincere pledge of a publicly-owned railway.

However, she held a special place in the Labour Party's affections, and among a wider public, with her plain-speaking humanity. She also knew well – this was Blair's real miscalculation – how to exploit that appeal to make life uncomfortable for him. Blair later admitted to friends her demotion had been a mistake, and Campbell issued a half-apology for having 'overstepped the mark' in briefing against her after her tax interview.[42] In an interview in the *New Statesman* two weeks after being reshuffled, she portrayed 'Tony' as a nice man led astray by his advisers, whom she described as 'the people who live in the dark'. From outside Blair's big tent, she turned her aim inwards:

> These people are making a terrible error. They think that Labour is unelectable, so they want to get something else elected, even though really it's still the Labour Party . . . They are saying: 'Vote for Tony Blair's New Labour. We all agree the old one was absolutely appalling and you all know that most of the people in Labour are really the old one, but we've got some who are nothing to do with that – vote for us.' One, it's a lie. And, two, it's dangerous. I think they're profoundly wrong.[43]

The words 'lie' and 'dangerous' were seized on by the Conservatives, who took full-page advertisements that Sunday in the *News of the World*, *Mail on Sunday* and *Sunday Times*, over the slogan, 'New Labour New Danger'. One of the people 'in the dark', Peter Mandelson, responded with the high-risk tactic of massive escalation. Branding the advert's device of giving a picture of Blair sinister eyes 'demonic', he launched a complaint to the Advertising Standards Authority and encouraged a bishop, Richard Harries, to write an article decrying such personal attacks. He was accused of attracting huge free publicity to the image of Blair, but had judged correctly that it did not chime with public perceptions of him, that it made the Conservatives look desperate and that it distracted attention from Short's important point, which was that the Labour Party had not really changed.

Contract with Britain

In his 1994 conference speech, Blair talked of the need to build trust with a people not just suspicious of the Labour Party but disillusioned with politics itself: 'When we make a promise, we must be sure we can keep it. That is page 1, line 1, of a new contract between a Labour government and the citizen.' Having borrowed so much from the US Democrats, this echoed the language of the Republicans' 'Contract With America' which carried them to a landslide victory in the mid-term elections a month later.

At the 1995 conference, Blair took to the National Executive the power to order ballots of the entire party membership, tucked in a series of minor rule changes. Then in March 1996 he overcame the National Executive's reluctance, to force through the final step in the plan to persuade the electorate that the Labour Party had indeed changed and could be trusted to stick to its new unthreatening persona. The party's draft manifesto, under the ungainly title of *New Labour, New Life for Britain*, would be put to a referendum of all party members. Once again, Blair took his jacket off and took to the road to engage in direct dialogue with the party. His aim this time was not so much to win an argument – when members studied the document, they could not find anything with which they could violently disagree – as to ensure a decent turnout. The referendum was a transparent device, and the question on the ballot paper might as well have been, 'Do you want to win the election?' The 95 per cent Yes vote in November 1996 was therefore no surprise; more important was the respectable turnout of 60 per cent.

The power to ballot the membership had other potential uses, as the rising moderniser Stephen Byers suggested to journalists at an off-record dinner in a fish restaurant in Blackpool at the TUC conference that September. His comment that Blair might use it to ballot party members on breaking the link with the trades unions, if a Labour government were hit by unpopular strikes, soon became not only on the record but prominently so. This helped to explain the eagerness of some union leaders to ballot their Labour-levy-paying members on the early manifesto: they wanted to drive home the point that it was, as GMB leader John Edmonds had said, 'their party too'. They voted by 92 per cent in favour of *New Life*.[44]

The drafting of *New Life* was a big operation undertaken by David Miliband, Blair's head of policy, working with Robin Cook, as chairman of the party's National Policy Forum, and taking advice – a significant indicator of New Labour's core priorities – from Philip Gould.

This process acted, as Blair intended it to, to force him and his senior colleagues to ask some searching questions about Labour's plans, especially on constitutional reform. On the House of Lords he had begun to retreat from the policy of an elected second chamber during his leadership campaign. As shadow Home Secretary he had promised the Labour conference on 30 September 1993: 'We will abolish the House of Lords and replace it with a proper democratically elected second chamber with a new electoral system to go with it.' He singled out hereditary peers, 'in varying stages between life and death', as 'an insult to modern democracy'. During his campaign for the Labour leadership, however, the abolition of the rights of hereditary peers became 'a minimum first step'.[45] By February 1996, he could quote with approval the suggestion from Ivor Richard, Labour leader in the Lords, that 'people of a particularly distinguished position or record' could serve in the Upper House, and said 'the final balance between election and merit' – merit being a better-sounding word than appointment – was something that did not need to be debated immediately.[46]

When it came to Scottish and Welsh devolution, however, Blair left the business of cutting through the legislative and logical complexity of the issue until the last moment before the early manifesto was published in July 1996. At the end of the previous year, he had asked Derry Irvine to chair a secret committee to look at the issue. Irvine was his troubleshooter for complex policy problems.* While he was Leader of the Opposition, Blair called him nearly every day, usually early in the morning – Irvine was at his desk at 6.30. 'What is so impressive about Derry Irvine is that he can peel away the layers of a problem. He has a combination of fierce intellect and a fairly brutal approach to hard work – if you hadn't done the work, there was no point coming into the room,' Blair had said of his mentor in 1991.[47]

The previous Labour government had exhausted itself in passing the Bills to set up a Scottish Parliament and Welsh Assembly only to have them thrown out when referendums failed to meet the thresholds inserted into the legislation. Blair was personally unenthusiastic about devolution, and might have preferred some kind of Grand Committee system, by which Scottish MPs at Westminster would have formed themselves into a subsidiary assembly for Scottish business. But both Labour and the Liberal Democrats, working together on the Scottish Constitutional Convention, had moved far beyond that long before. Both parties also

*He was also his second opinion on appointments, interviewing Jonathan Powell before he became Chief of Staff and, in government, candidates for Cabinet Secretary (Peter Hennessy, *The Prime Minister*, p. 490).

agreed that a referendum was no longer needed, since devolution was the 'settled will' of the Scottish people. Nor did Blair like the presentational downside of the planned power of a Scottish Parliament to raise or cut income tax by up to 3p in the pound. In March 1996 he decided to promise referendums in Scotland and Wales *before* parliament passed the legislation, to make it harder for opponents to obstruct it – and that in Scotland there should be a separate question in the referendum on the tax-varying power. Having made the decision, however, he managed to inflict unnecessary damage on the Scottish Labour Party's strained loyalty, when news of the change leaked in London to the *Independent*, instead of being announced in Scotland as planned.[48]

At the same time as the manifesto was being drafted, Labour's programme was also being boiled down into five 'early pledges', condensed into just 106 words on a credit-card-sized *aide mémoire* which said: 'Keep this card and see that we keep our promises.' It was a clever idea, and as such had many parents. Margaret McDonagh, then the party's Deputy General Secretary, had kept a 'Proposition 186' card from a California state referendum on health care in 1992, which listed the four benefits of voting Yes.[49] The idea was developed by Peter Hyman, one of the more rigorous populists in Blair's office, and the pledges were exhaustively tested by Philip Gould in focus groups: the more modest and simple ones were more credible, and 'if we said how the promise would be paid for, the power of the pledge was enhanced enormously', Gould said.[50]

Eventually, the pledges were – John Prescott memorably forgot them in his winding-up speech at the 1996 conference – to cut infant class sizes, to speed up punishment for young offenders, to cut NHS waiting lists, to get 250,000 young people off benefit and into work, and to 'set tough rules for government spending and borrowing'. Only this last pledge was vague. There was a good reason for that: Blair wanted a specific promise not to raise income tax rates, but Gordon Brown resisted. He wanted to keep open the option of a higher rate on incomes over £100,000 a year, but the argument that swayed Blair was that they should wait until the Conservatives' last Budget in November 1996.

After the wobble over Clare Short's demotion in the summer of 1996, the Blairs went on a family holiday in Italy. It did not seem significant at the time, but they stayed at the villa in Tuscany of a rich backbench Labour MP, Geoffrey Robinson. Robinson had become increasingly friendly with the shadow Chancellor in recent years, helping to fund his office, and had been helpful to Blair in buying the *New Statesman*. (The ownership and editorship of the *New Statesman* had always been a minor preoccupation of Labour leaders in the year or two before an election, even if it did provide Short with a platform for her stab at 'people in the dark'.) But Blair had no idea that Robinson had also just offered – or agreed when asked, depending on whose account one prefers – to lend Peter Mandelson the money to buy a London home commensurate with his imminent status as a government minister.

Returning from Tuscany, Blair threw himself with renewed energy into the long campaign for the General Election, now no more than nine months away. His last party conference speech before the election contained ten vows, a 'performance contract' for the five-year term of a Labour government. These overlapped with the five pledges, and were not quite the same, but the sense was clear: 'This is my covenant with the British people. Judge me upon it. The buck stops here.' Blair's strategy had been set nine months earlier, in January 1996, when he used another tripled mantra to describe it to his inner team: 'Reassurance, reassurance, reassurance.'[51]

The bear hug

Blair had the belt and the braces. Now he added the safety pin. Taking nothing for granted, he wanted to be sure that if he won a small majority at the election, or if the outcome was in the balance, he could fall back on the Liberal Democrats.

On 14 October 1996, Donald Dewar and Archy Kirkwood, the Labour and Liberal Democrat Chief Whips, held a joint news conference to call for an independent investigation into the allegation that the Conservative MP Neil Hamilton had accepted cash in return for asking parliamentary questions. It seemed like a minor piece of inter-party opportunism until Robin Cook and Robert Maclennan, in charge of constitutional policy for their respective parties, held another news conference two weeks later. They announced that the first meeting of a joint committee of the two parties had just been held to discuss a 'common programme' of constitutional reform.

From the start, Blair had adopted the friendliest stance towards the third party ever seen from a Labour leader. Although he and Ashdown were not then on close personal terms, they had already discussed the possibilities of Lib–Lab co-operation in general terms. Now, Ashdown began to move cautiously in his direction. In May 1995, he dropped the policy of maintaining 'equidistance' between Conservatives and Labour, saying it was inconceivable that his party would sustain the Conservatives in office in a hung parliament. Blair, meanwhile, in April 1996, described Labour as 'a party of the centre as well as of the centre-left'.[52]

Part of Blair's motive was hegemonic: the nicer he was to Paddy Ashdown's party the easier it would be to pull over recruits (several middle-ranking Liberal Democrat officials like Peter Mandelson's friend Roger Liddle were already poised to defect), reassure Liberal Democrat voters and isolate the Conservatives. Blair set out his approach most overtly in an interview in the *Observer* in May 1996:

> Politics will alter dramatically in the next few years. But I cannot foresee exactly what shape it will take. There is no doubt that if we continue to occupy the centre ground, if we become the One Nation political party, if we can attract support from the centre as well as the centre-left, then we will be able to benefit significantly.[53]

This was perhaps the most honest guide to Blair's strategy over the next few years: much of the time his views on specific questions such as electoral reform and coalition was wilfully obscure, but the big picture was clear enough. If he sat on the centre ground and kept his options and his lines of communication open, nothing but good could come of it.

A more specific part of Blair's motive, however, was simple insurance: he wanted to bind Ashdown into backing him in case of an inconclusive election result. Based on his experience of the early 1980s, Blair feared that a section of his party would go into internal opposition as soon as Labour won an election. The left was not the ideological force it once was, but if the Parliamentary Labour Party contained forty MPs whom the whips found hard to control, the government's business could become difficult. (As it was, Blair could accommodate a rebellion by sixty-five Labour MPs over Incapacity Benefit in May 1999 and still win the vote by a majority of forty.) One of the secondary purposes of the ballot on the manifesto was also to reinforce discipline among Labour MPs in government: within ten days of the election Peter Mandelson had turned the old left-wing charge against leaders for betraying manifesto promises to New Labour's advantage, when he described the manifesto as 'binding' on MPs.[54]

The central issue between Labour and the Liberal Democrats remained the question of electoral reform. In 1993 John Smith had decided against changing the voting system for the House of Commons, but promised a referendum under a Labour government, in order to keep the option open and to keep the new pluralists in his own party quiet. At first, Blair hedged. His personal opposition to proportional representation remained, although it had become muted. In September 1994 he said he was 'not persuaded' of the case for it.[55] This was a formula – which implied that he might become persuaded after the election – which just about survived his three years as Leader of the Opposition.

On the promise of a referendum, however, he dithered. It was one thing to keep open the option of reform if he needed it; it was quite another to be committed to a referendum in his first term in government whether he needed it or not. He hinted to Labour MPs opposed to electoral reform that he would not stop them if they tried to drop the policy. But he was convinced, by Peter Mandelson and others, and in the context of increasingly warm relations with Ashdown, that dropping the referendum pledge risked closing off the option of reform altogether. The month before the 1995 Labour conference Jack Straw, the shadow Home Secretary, finally took a clear position, against the grain of his own scepticism: 'It would be a breach of faith with the party and the country if we were to overturn the decision to hold a referendum. It would also dishonour the pledge given by John Smith.'[56] It was a choice of words which seemed to set the promise in stone. Blair was keen to take credit, in later conversations with reformers, for the decision to 'save' the referendum pledge – although it later turned out to be insincere.

Blair also appeared to harden his 'not persuaded' line when asked in a *New Statesman* interview in July 1996 whether it meant he was against proportional representation. 'Yes,' he replied. 'I've never been convinced that small parties do not then get disproportionate power.'[57] It caused a minor back-room stir, and Blair had to tell Ashdown he had not meant it to come out quite like that. It had of course been his position ever since he first expressed a view in public in 1987.[58] But now the greater need to tie in the Liberal Democrats supervened.

Blair had already let Ashdown know that he was thinking of offering government posts to a handful of senior Liberal Democrats even if he won a working majority. Mandelson had argued in 1995 that such a post-election pact would be needed to ensure a 'longer-term stable left-of-centre government'. His argument was not from the principle of a new pluralist politics – witness his Littleborough and Saddleworth by-election campaign – but from hard Labour interest and tactical thinking: 'The worst scenario would be to dismiss any idea of a pact, only to be forced to confront it later if the election goes less well than expected. Taking on the issue in advance would be the better option.'[59] The condition of such a deal would be Blair's public support as Prime Minister for electoral reform, and Blair was persuaded that there might be a compromise system he could endorse.

A long struggle behind the scenes ensued, detailed in Paddy Ashdown's *Diaries*, as electoral reformers, led by Robin Cook in the Labour Party and by Ashdown and Roy Jenkins in the Liberal Democrats, fought to tie Blair to the promise to put a 'proportional' system to the referendum.

Blair and Mandelson were convinced that preferential voting, a compromise called the Alternative Vote, would have a better chance of getting through the House of Commons. It would not strictly match parties' seats to their shares of the vote, but it would be more proportional than the existing system, and would keep its single-member constituencies.[60]

The reformers seemed to have triumphed when the final version of the Labour manifesto committed the party to a referendum on a 'proportional' system. The word 'proportional' was vital, because Cook, Ashdown and Jenkins thought it ruled out the Alternative Vote. In return, the reformers were prepared to concede a change which would make it easier to postpone the referendum. The promise was changed with legalistic precision from 'we will deliver a referendum' to 'we are committed to a referendum'. The reformers accepted Blair's argument that it would be counter-productive to tie a Labour government – or a Lib–Lab one – to a referendum if it looked like it could not win a 'Yes' vote. Ashdown and Jenkins had long accepted that, with most of the press opposed and the Labour Party divided, winning would be difficult, which is why they set such store by Blair's personal endorsement.

Blair had been on friendly terms with Jenkins, the leader of the Liberal Democrats in the House of Lords, since at least 1992, when he explained why he had fallen silent in the car taking him to the studio for *Any Questions*: 'Roy Jenkins sits quietly before these shows as well, and once he told me, "Oh dear boy, I am just contemplating the vast expanses of my own ignorance."'[61] But since becoming Labour leader, he had cultivated him just as carefully as he courted Ashdown. Tony and Cherie invited Paddy and Jane to dinner, who reciprocated on Paddy's fifty-fifth birthday in February 1996. Meanwhile it was made known to the journalists who would be impressed that Blair regarded Jenkins as a great authority on modern British history and regularly consulted him.

Jenkins was the co-author of Blair's extraordinary ambition to make the twenty-first century that of 'the radicals' in the way that the twentieth century had belonged to the Conservatives. This idea can be traced back in Blair's thinking to at least 1992, although the division among radicals that he wrote about then was between agitators and pragmatists. In a book review of a biography of Keir Hardie, he took issue with the implied thesis of the author, Caroline Benn,

> that the choice of a radical politician is to be an idealist or a pragmatist, with Hardie commended as the former. But the real choice is between the agitator and the pragmatist. Both can be idealists. Both have their failings. For the pragmatist, the potential tragedy is love of office for itself; for the agitator, it is self-indulgence. Radical politics needs both types and needs

> them to succeed. Because while they fight it out, the conservatives can rule the country.[62]

This analysis took what was to become its more familiar form when Blair rehearsed it in an article in the *Observer* in September 1996, writing of

> the division in radical politics at the end of the last century and the beginning of this, between Liberals and the Labour Party. This distortion, born out of historical forces that are largely now spent, is surely one reason why the last 100 years has been so dominated by Tory governments.[63]

To this end he claimed the radical Liberal tradition for New Labour, via Hobhouse's 'liberal socialism' and the New Liberals. When he spoke at a Fabian Society commemoration of the fiftieth anniversary of the 1945 Attlee government, he paid his respects to the Liberal gods too: 'We must value the contribution of Lloyd George, Beveridge and Keynes and not just Attlee, Bevan or Crosland.'[64]

If this analysis of twentieth-century history were taken seriously, it meant that Blair might want to offer the Liberal Democrats a place in government not just out of short-term interest but in order to try to heal the historic breach between the two traditions. And he did not only share his thinking with Mandelson, a political street-fighter. It was Peter Thomson, guardian of Blair's spiritual and philosophical integrity, who told his friend Boris Johnson in mid-1996: 'They are going to change the whole thing, bring in the Liberals.'[65]

Thus it was that Blair and Ashdown went into the 1997 election campaign in the most coalitionist posture short of coalition itself. Bolstered by some tacit co-operation on the ground, they aimed – and were more successful than they expected – to mobilise the anti-Conservative tactical vote.

Notes

1. Donald Macintyre, *Mandelson*, p. 279.
2. Memo from Mandelson to Blair, 31 January 1995; memo from Brown to Blair, 1 February 1995; quoted by Paul Anderson and Nyta Mann, *Safety First*, p. 439.
3. Philip Gould, *The Unfinished Revolution*, p. 216.
4. Macintyre, *Mandelson*, pp. 280–81.
5. *New Statesman* leading article, 14 July 1995.
6. *Independent*, 27 April 1996.
7. Alastair Campbell, quoted by Macintyre, *Mandelson*, p. 282.
8. *Mail on Sunday*, 5 May 1996.
9. Macintyre, *Mandelson*, pp. 287–8.

10. *Ibid.*, p. 289.
11. *Ibid.*, p. 290.
12. *Ibid.*
13. *Observer*, 24 December 1995.
14. Interview, *New Statesman*, 24 January 1997.
15. *Sunday Times*, 23 April 1995.
16. 'Creepy Blair drives Maggie back to Major', *Sun*, 10 September 1996.
17. Interview, *Sunday Times*, 28 May 1995.
18. *Daily Telegraph*, 3 October 1996.
19. Diaries of Judith Chaplin, special adviser to John Major, *Sunday Telegraph*, 19 September 1999.
20. *The Times*, 8 March 1997; *Tribune*, 13 March 1997; see also Andrew Neil's account of Lady Thatcher saying to Rupert Murdoch: 'Don't you worry about Tony Blair. He's a real patriot.' (*Full Disclosure*, p. xxiii.)
21. *Daily Telegraph*, 1 April 1997.
22. *Sun*, 2 April 1997.
23. *Daily Mirror*, 27 September 1994.
24. Early version of his book proposal, *Observer*, 24 December 1995.
25. Interview, London *Evening Standard*, 21 February 1995.
26. Speech to the British–American Chamber of Commerce, New York, 11 April 1996.
27. Gould, *The Unfinished Revolution*, p. 332.
28. *Ibid.*, p. 333.
29. *Guardian*, 27 July 1995.
30. 17 July 1995; 'new Labour' still had a lower case 'n' in Blair's text.
31. Interview, *Today*, 27 September 1995.
32. Alastair Campbell, quoted in Macintyre, *Mandelson*, p. 326 and p. 286. The second was untrue: see p. 297.
33. *Independent*, 12 August 1995.
34. *Observer*, 10 September 1995.
35. *Guardian*, 18 September 1995.
36. *Observer*, 14 April 1996 (author's emphasis).
37. *Daily Mirror*, 26 January 1996 (author's emphasis).
38. Speech at Didcot Girls' School, 7 June 1996.
39. *Daily Express*, 23 March 1996.
40. *The Times Magazine*, 1 October 1994.
41. BBC2, *The Wilderness Years*, 18 December 1995.
42. Interview, *Guardian*, 17 February 1997.
43. *New Statesman*, 9 August 1996.
44. Turnout among party members, after intensive telephone canvassing, was 60 per cent; among Labour-supporting members of trades unions and socialist societies it was 17 per cent, although not all took part. Turnout in the 1994 leadership election was 69 per cent and 19.5 per cent.
45. Speech in Cardiff, 15 July 1994.
46. John Smith Memorial Lecture, 7 February 1996.
47. *Harpers & Queen*, January 1991.
48. *Independent*, 25 June 1996.
49. Gould, *The Unfinished Revolution*, p. 271.
50. *Ibid.*, p. 267.

51. *Ibid.*, p. 259.
52. Speech to British–American Chamber of Commerce, New York, 11 April 1996.
53. Anthony Bevins, *Observer*, 5 May 1996.
54. BBC1, *On the Record*, 11 May 1997 (he immediately ran into difficulty with the things which were not in the manifesto, such as independence for the Bank of England).
55. *Guardian*, 19 September 1994.
56. *Ibid.*, 24 August 1995.
57. *New Statesman*, 5 July 1996.
58. See pp. 139–40.
59. Early version of Mandelson's proposal for a book, which was published in Bowdlerised form as *The Blair Revolution*; Andy McSmith, *Faces of Labour*, p. 341.
60. Mandelson had supported the Alternative Vote system publicly in February 1996; Blair indicated his support privately to Ashdown the following month (*The Ashdown Diaries*, p. 411), although his public position remained obscure.
61. *Sunday Times Magazine*, 19 July 1992.
62. *Sunday Times*, 25 October 1992.
63. *Observer*, 15 September 1996.
64. Speech at Fabian Society commemoration of the 1945 General Election, 5 July 1995.
65. Conversation recalled by Johnson, who had been a teacher at Thomson's school in Australia, Geelong Grammar, *Daily Telegraph*, 25 July 1997.

16

Not a Landslide Country

Election Campaign, January–April 1997

'Zipped lips, buttoned imaginations and clenched buttocks – a party trapped by its own opinion-poll lead.'
—*Andrew Marr,* Independent, *10 April 1997*

The experience of long years in Opposition drove some assumptions deep into Blair's psyche. On the positive side, he developed a fine understanding of media relations, opinion research and political marketing. On the negative, he learned the reflexes of self-control and pathological risk-aversion, from the time when party was anarcho-democratic.

This defensiveness was unnecessary, but it was understandable. It was a group psychosis that gripped the whole party. It had lost four consecutive elections, and the last when the opinion polls said it would win. This time, no matter how far ahead Labour was in the opinion polls, it would take no chances. It seemed, however, that everyone – apart from Blair – had their bottom line. Most party members took it for granted, for example, that Labour would increase income tax – a little – on the rich. Alastair Campbell had reflected this view in an article criticising John Smith for being too cautious:

> There are few, if any, circumstances I could envisage that would lead me not to vote Labour, but if I thought Labour wouldn't spend more on health and schools, or that they wouldn't adopt a more interventionist approach to the economy, or that they wouldn't raise my taxes, then I'd have to think a bit. This is not an 'irresponsible shopping list'. It is the absolute minimum, surely, that the public will expect of Labour.[1]

That was before he entered the bunker. And in the bunker, tax was regarded as the central issue when it came to maintaining the electorate's trust in Labour – and spending 'more on health and schools' was only the other side of that coin. 'You can't trust Labour' was the Conservative poster with the L-plate launched in January 1992 which struck a chord. The 'tax bombshell' advertisement was another, even more effective. Blair was determined it would not happen again. He chose the same month, January, before the 1997 election to launch his own bombshell on tax.

The debate had engaged Blair, Gordon Brown and their advisers for five years. Blair, Peter Mandelson and Philip Gould were convinced that Labour should make an absolute pledge of no rises in income tax rates. On this, Blair accepted the verdict of Gould's focus groups, which generally thought that higher taxes for the better-off were the thin end of the wedge of higher taxes for them, although the evidence was not as clear-cut as Gould suggested.[2] Brown appears to have been determined to expunge all traces of Labour's tax-and-spend policies – except, possibly, for a new top rate of 50p in the pound on income above a threshold of £100,000 a year.

In keeping open the option of a new top tax rate, Brown had some good arguments on his side. The devaluation disaster of 1992 had already destroyed the Conservatives' reputation for economic competence, and the rises in indirect taxation imposed in the 1993 Budget had done the same for their image as the party of lower taxes. Although a new top rate would raise a relatively small amount in relation to the tax system as a whole – about £1 billion a year – it would help answer the question, 'Where is the money coming from?' And it would play to a core value of the party's which had some populist resonance, that the rich should pay their fair share. Setting the level at £100,000 a year would ensure that it was not seen as a 'cap on aspirations'. Paul Keating, the Australian Prime Minister much quoted by Campbell, was wrong when he said that no one in the English-speaking world in modern times had been elected promising to put up income tax. Bill Clinton pledged an income tax rise for individuals earning over $100,000 a year, balanced by the promise of a 'middle-class tax cut'. Although the tax cut never materialised, the tax increase for the rich certainly did, with amazingly little fuss. In his first budget in 1993, President Clinton put up the top rate of income tax, on earnings above $115,000 a year, from 31 to 36 per cent, and even brought in a new top rate above that, of 39.6 per cent on earnings over $250,000 a year.

Nevertheless, Blair refused to take any risks with the deep-rooted assumption that Labour would raise taxes. For him, it was better for Labour to appear to lack principles than to be saddled with a caricature of the old ones. This was, then, a tactical argument among egalitarians rather than a repudiation of redistribution. Brown's plan for a windfall levy on the privatised utility companies, although it was a one-off, would be enough to sustain Labour's modest promises during an election campaign, and the shadow Chancellor already had a secret plan to raise an extra £5 billion a year by increasing taxes on company pension funds. As for the argument that Labour would have won more votes by adopting a policy more in tune with its tradition, the election result spoke for itself. Supporters of a higher top rate could argue that it would have been worth winning less well in order to achieve a more progressive and more honest tax structure, but that was never an argument Blair would have paused to consider.

Nor was Brown a forceful advocate of the higher rate policy. It was he who had dissuaded John Smith in the autumn of 1993 from confirming that there would be a 50p-in-the-pound rate under Labour. Although they decided that there was no need to say anything about tax rates at all at that stage, they shared the assumption that there would be such a higher tax rate, and that it would apply to the excess on incomes over something like £70,000 to £100,000.[3] During 1993, Brown made some propaganda use of research showing that only those with incomes of over £64,000 a year had benefited from Conservative tax changes since 1979, a figure which appeared in Blair's leadership manifesto. Blair himself said he did not want to add to the tax burden on the 'vast majority' in the *Mirror*, 18 January 1995, which implied he might want to do so on the tiny minority of the very rich.

Over the next two years, both Brown and Blair consistently stressed their desire to reduce the overall tax burden and attacked John Major for his 'twenty-two tax rises'. They did not say where they stood on the question of how the tax burden should be shared among taxpayers. Brown, although he hardly minded press reports that he favoured a 50p top rate which helped cultivate his image as truer to the party's values, readily accepted in private the argument that Labour was boxed in by its history as a party of government which had in the 1970s taxed some 'unearned' income from investments at the marginal rate of 98p in the pound. Slowly, the debate shifted until Brown was simply defending – as a man about to be responsible for the nation's unpredictable finances – his room for manoeuvre. That was not enough to overcome Blair's sense of overwhelming political necessity.

When Brown was interviewed on the *Today* programme on 20 January 1997, it was assumed he would announce the decision that a Labour government would stick to the spending plans set out by the Conservatives for the next two years, on which the newspapers had been briefed. He did, but he also dropped the bombshell that Labour would fight the election pledged not to increase any income tax rates at all. The pledge – which did not of course exclude the possibility of rises in indirect taxes – was backed up by posters with Blair's image and carrying his signature, and by rewriting the fifth promise on the pledge card. The vague commitment to 'set tough rules for government spending and borrowing' was replaced by the blunt guarantee: 'No rises in income tax rates.'

Cherie stands (silently) by her man

Despite Labour's victory in the Wirral South by-election on 27 February 1997, Blair shared the conventional wisdom that the General Election would be closely fought. Clearly, there was unlikely to be a swing to Labour as great as that in the by-election – that would have delivered a 293-seat Commons majority. But the opinion polls in the constituency proved accurate, and on the basis of the national opinion polls Labour was heading for a majority of about 190. Even if the polls were as inaccurate as in 1992, the majority would still be around 80.

The collective state of denial which gripped the Labour Party from its leader downwards was perversely reinforced by each successive evidence that they were heading for a landslide. Partly this was a matter of tactics, in that Blair was determined to avoid the triumphalism which had done so much damage last time. Mostly it was a matter of psychology. For Blair and his colleagues, victory was arduous, to be fought for every inch of the way, and the prospect of it was unmentionable. But defeat was unthinkable. They were Calvinists, certain that they were predestined to be saved, and yet humble, tormented by dark fears that they might not be. Even contemplating the heady pleasures of a landslide was sinful and hubristic.

Blair's pessimism was so ingrained that Labour officials learnt that the best way of gaining his attention was to give him bad news from the opinion polls, focus groups or canvassing returns. Once satisfied that the world was about to end, he would then be able to concentrate on what else was being said to him.

Alastair Campbell's assault on the formerly Conservative press now reached election fever pitch. On the day of the Wirral South by-election, the *Sun* carried the first of a two-part interview with the Labour leader headlined, 'TONY BLAIR OPENS HIS HEART TO THE SUN'. His Everyman tastes were much mocked in the broadsheet papers: he liked to eat 'fish and chip suppers' while watching *Gladiators*, *Noel's House Party* and *EastEnders* on television, before going 'down to the Labour Club for a pint of Fed'. He liked the Beatles, REM, Simply Red – 'and classics too'. It was perhaps too close to the election to allow such self-mockery as when he was asked eighteen months earlier which rock bands he liked: 'All the bands that everybody loves.'*

He told the *Sun*: 'I also enjoy playing the guitar.' During another personal interview with *Bella*, the mass-circulation women's magazine, he had pulled an electric guitar from under a sofa in his study. 'My pride and joy,' he said, saying he sometimes played to unwind after a day's politics: 'I plug it in and give it a little burst.'[4] This cover version of The Who's 'My Generation' was extended in a highly-charged live performance in Stevenage during the election campaign itself: 'I am a modern man, from the rock'n'roll generation. The Beatles, colour TV, that's my generation.'[5]

Only one interview hit a discordant note. An American television journalist called Daphne Barak had been allowed in to 'Myrobella', the Sedgefield house, and Blair's diffidence did nothing to flatter her substantial ego – 'I've interviewed some of the world's most extraordinary people in my professional life . . . Never have I come across anybody quite as frightened, quite as uncertain, quite as eager to please as Tony Blair.'[6] John Major was delighted by the result. 'Have you seen it, have you seen it?' he asked Tory whip Gyles Brandreth eagerly. The Prime Minister had some of Barak's phrases by heart: '"Nervous, boring, empty, at a loss" – that's more like it, isn't it?' he told Brandreth, 'looking positively jaunty'.[7]

In his *Sun* interview, however, Blair was back on safe English ground, combining Modern Man with Thatcherite Man: 'We were never poor but Mum had to run a very tight ship. I think that's why I've probably always hated being in debt.' And, of course, Family Man. 'I do make time for my kids. I love being with them.' He tried to teach them the value of money:

> They don't get whatever they want. We're quite strict about that. For Christmas, Euan got a computer game, Nicky a football strip and Kathryn some clothes and a Barbie doll to add to her collection. It's odd, isn't it, how kids can have these sudden obsessions with things? I don't know where Kathryn got her first Barbie doll from – certainly not me!

He was Everyman for every class. On *This Morning With Richard and Judy* on 6 March, he said he 'sometimes' played the National Lottery, although he was a bit stuck on how he chose his numbers, retreating to the safety of his children's birth dates. In *Museums and Galleries*, 3 March, it turned out that he liked all the painters that everybody likes: Piero della Francesca, Mantegna, Hans Memling, Vermeer,

---

*Although he added, 'Well, maybe not Phil Collins.' Collins had said before the previous election that he would go abroad if Labour got in (Lesley Ann Down, *News of the World*, 29 October 1995).

'Goya (especially the black Goyas) and Picasso's Blue Period . . . the landscapes of Cézanne, especially those of Aix-en-Provence'. He also admired Walter Sickert, Sir Stanley Spencer, Paul Nash ('especially the paintings of both wars'), Francis Bacon, Lucian Freud and Euan Uglow (although he did not say that Cherie had once posed for him). He revealed that he owned paintings by twentieth-century British artists Richard Eurich, C. R. W. Nevinson and Frank Brangwyn.

All these presentations of himself – with the possible exception of *EastEnders* and the definite exception of the Lottery – were authentic. In 1993 he contributed a recipe to an Islington charity fundraising book for 'pasta with sun-dried tomatoes', but like most people he enjoyed fish and chips too. The more interesting question was whether he was misusing his family for electoral purposes. At the same time as detailing their Christmas presents to *Sun* readers, Blair was worrying about the effect of public attention on his children. Politicians had never before allowed their children so much into the limelight. In another long personal interview, with Lynda Lee-Potter in the *Daily Mail* on 22 April, he suggested that this was as much their choice as his. He said Cherie and the children wanted to be part of his public life. 'You're not protecting us by keeping us out of things,' Cherie had told him. 'We just don't feel part of what you're doing. I'm going to be with you, not in any political sense but as your wife.'

In the children's case, this raised an awkward question of informed consent. In Cherie's, it produced the awkward public persona of the silent spouse. And the idea that this persona was imposed on her against her will by wicked spin-doctors is plainly false. Just before she entered her self-imposed public silence when John Smith died, she explained her reasons: 'These days I have to be careful about what I do and say. I can't always say what I think because I don't want people assuming that that's Tony's opinion too. The better known he becomes, the more important that will be.'[8]

She was, said her mother, ready for the challenges ahead: 'She is well prepared and she knows it's going to happen. We Booths are strong women. We have had to be.'[9]

For all that, the intensity of the interest in her as Consort of the Prime Minister in Waiting came as a shock. But she had decided she would not, as Blair put it, 'hide away'.[10] She was not like Norma Major, who thought she had married a banker, or Mary Wilson, who thought she had married an Oxford don. When she and Tony Blair married, one of them was going to be Prime Minister, and the other would be Prime Minister's spouse. That meant an unreal balancing act: she had to be the supportive wife, Blair's domestic anchor, visual representation of his status as Family

Man, guarantor of his humanity and normality; and, because he was Modern Man too, she did not want to compromise her intelligence, independence or her own career. The clothes and hair were the hardest bit to start with:

> I do like clothes, it's one of the nice things about being a woman, but I've never been obsessed by them. I have always thought of myself as a brains rather than a beauty. I'm not a clothes horse or a frilly person. I live in the real world most of the time and don't want to feel like a fairy on top of the Christmas tree. I want people to feel I am approachable.[11]

Although she had an image consultant/press officer from the start, in the form of Fiona Millar, Alastair Campbell's partner, her long pale blue outfit and 1970s hairstyle on the day of Blair's coronation as Labour leader attracted an avalanche of unforgiving comment. As usual, Blair himself was blunter about the effect on her, and more than a little patronising:

> She found it very hard to begin with because people did take her to bits. They criticised what she wore and how she looked. Probably she didn't get the clothes thing right to begin with. But she wasn't supposed to be a fashion model. Then a few weeks into it she just decided: 'This thing has happened. There is no point in running away from it. I'm going to make sure that I look the part.' It's how she operates when she sets her mind on something. She's sorted herself out completely . . . She lost nearly two stones. She started to take more of an interest in clothes than she ever had before. She just got herself psychologically attuned to the fact that life was going to be different. It's what I had to do as well really.[12]

She lost weight 'partly through anxiety', although the *Sunday Times* was forced to apologise for suggesting she had been anorexic.[13] She also started to go to a gym and acquired a personal trainer. The second makeover, with shorter swept-back hair, eye make-up accentuating a thinner face and expensive clothes, was generally judged a success, prompting a (female) *Times* columnist to gush, 'First lady as babe!'[14] Although she was also photographed in the Islington Sainsbury's in civilian clothes – a gaudy patterned sweater which Blair admitted he gave her – in the pre-election period, the general effect was to remove her from the ranks of 'one of us' into the category of celebrity. That would have been inevitable, however, on the strength of her earning power alone.

Her legal career had not really taken off until 1991, when she transferred to the chambers of Michael Beloff, a large set which did a lot of work in the expanding areas of judicial review and European Community law, after Derry Irvine telephoned Beloff to suggest it. 'She was obviously getting restless,' said Beloff. 'I was rung up by Derry Irvine, who said, "I think she deserves to be in a set that's reputed to be better and looks stronger than the set she's presently in."'

Beloff said he was 'bowled over' by her:

> One of the things I find absolutely amazing, and I think her colleagues do here, is that sometimes you get these rather hostile profiles – I think some said, 'She's very chippy, she's charmless' – it's simply incredible. It's like saying Marilyn Monroe is ugly or Linford Christie can't run. She's one of the most obviously charming people that I've ever met.

She was, however, forceful and determined. Beloff said there were 'collisions' over her 'progressive views' about the administration of chambers: she was in favour of computers and modern business methods.

She became a Queen's Counsel, a top-ranking barrister, in April 1995, when she gave one of her rare interviews, emphasising her independent ambition: 'If one day I was asked to be a judge, I would love to be one.'[15] Being a QC meant she could charge higher fees, but being Mrs Blair allowed less time in which to earn them. Mr Blair, meanwhile, was revealingly irritated by the regularly repeated estimate that she earned £200,000 a year. 'The amount Cherie earns is exaggerated to say the least. She doesn't earn a lot more than me,' he told the *Sun*. At the time, February 1997, his salary was £66,123, although he may have had in mind his imminent prospect of a pay rise to £102,000 after the election. 'It wouldn't be fair to say more than that. It doesn't bother me. She hasn't always earned more than me.'[16] (The last tax year in which he would have earned more than her would have been 1982–83, before he became an MP.)

He did not mind the role reversal (much). But Modern Man was not wholly New Man, as Cherie testified in another public outing which did not touch on politics, except of the personal kind. 'He's very good at polishing shoes and has been known to cook a meal – if I am in late, he cooks. I wouldn't say he is intimate with our washing machine, but he does know where it is,' she wrote, as guest editor of the women's monthly, *Prima*, in October 1996.

After running the gauntlet of the fashion editors, Cherie then had to put up with commentators criticising her for playing a mute role by her husband's side. Her work for charities dealing with breast cancer, domestic violence and neglected children was decried as anodyne. Her recreations, listed in her first *Who's Who* entry in 1996, were too saccharine: 'theatre, the arts, keeping fit, enjoying my children'. Barbara Amiel, wife of *Telegraph* proprietor Conrad Black, declared 'I prefer my Cherie sour', and deplored her remake, 're-educating' her into a 'phoney' submissive wife.[17] She at least had some experience of the real Cherie, having stayed in Sedgefield when she wrote her 1992 profile of Blair.

Certainly the real Cherie could be tart. As Blair found when he first met her, she did not have much time for those who had had it easy. Like many intelligent people, she could be impatient with irrelevance. She was also less practised than her husband at concealing her distaste for the Conservative press. When Adam Nicolson was allowed into Myrobella for his *Sunday Telegraph* profile of Blair in 1996, she agreed to be photographed in an apron at the Aga, but said something revealing a 'palpable sense of hostility' towards the *Telegraph* although, said Nicolson, 'I have promised not to quote her.'[18] On this subject at least her father, Tony Booth, may well have been speaking for her when he was rude about '*Telegraph* types' for keeping 'us', the working class, 'enslaved' for 'a thousand years'.[19]

On another occasion, she had exposed her cultural and class assumptions when she was asked at a party by *Sun* columnist Anne Robinson in 1995: 'Do you read the *Sun*?'

'Certainly not,' said Cherie. 'I wouldn't have it in the house.'[20]

Her husband, who had just flown halfway around the world to address executives of Rupert Murdoch's media empire, could not afford such plain speaking. Blair could not expect *The Times* or the *Sunday Times* to support him (although *The Times*'s call for its readers to vote for the candidate most opposed to monetary union slightly blunted its opposition), but central to his election campaign was the aim of neutralising the *Sun* and the *News of the World*. In the event, he did better than that.

The campaign

On 17 March John Major asked the Queen to dissolve Parliament and confirmed the date of the election would be 1 May. Blair started out nervous, still uncertain of success. As arranged in advance, he gave a quick 'doorstep' interview coming out of his house in Richmond Crescent, before being whisked with Cherie to Gloucester, the seat which, on some calculations, was the one Labour needed to win a majority of one.

That morning, he had written an article in the *Sun*, launching an intensive phase of his appeasement of its Euroscepticism. In it he pledged to 'fight any bid to foist on Britain the high social costs which are hampering business on the Continent'. That night, the newspaper repaid him by urging its 4 million readers to vote for him. 'THE SUN BACKS BLAIR,' declared the next day's front page. 'Give change a chance.' But Blair was briefly caught out on *Newsnight* when Jeremy Paxman asked him if he was embarrassed that his article that morning had appeared opposite a topless woman on page three. Blair laughed, automatically, effectively answering

Paxman's question. As Clare Short, who ran a campaign against the *Sun*'s Page Three Girl, observed: 'He could have said, "I don't like it but that's where they put it."'[21]

Instead, Blair said of his endorsement by the *Sun*: 'I was extremely pleased. It was very important.'[22] This was confirmed by academic research after the election: undecided *Sun* readers were less likely to plump for the Conservatives than the readers of the 'Tory faithful' newspapers, the *Daily Mail*, the *Daily Express* and the *Daily Telegraph*.[23] Even the readers of the *Daily Telegraph*, on the day after the election was called, were treated to an appeal so tailored to its audience that it approached parody: 'It is important to recognise that Labour offers a degree of continuity as well as change,' Blair wrote for the forces of conservatism.

Labour's plans had all taken an election on 1 May as their starting-point, but leaned heavily on the destabilising assumption that Major would call it earlier. Thus everything went according to plan, which only reinforced the sense of unreality, the sense that something was bound to go horribly wrong. Even the unexpected bonus of the first two weeks of the campaign being devoted entirely to the issue of 'Tory sleaze' failed to induce optimism. The winding-up of parliamentary business was dominated by the Opposition's complaint that the investigation into the 'cash for questions' affair had not been completed. In particular, there was the problem that the central charge against Neil Hamilton, the former minister and Conservative MP for Tatton, had been neither proved nor dismissed. His cause was not helped when, on 26 March, Tim Smith, the victor over Blair in the Beaconsfield by-election in 1982, and who had admitted taking Mohamed Fayed's cash, announced he would not contest the General Election. But, under the rules of the Conservative Party at the time, Hamilton was able to ignore pressure from Major to stand down, thus opening the way for Labour and the Liberal Democrats to withdraw in favour of BBC reporter Martin Bell, standing as an anti-corruption independent. Nor could Piers Merchant, Conservative MP for Beckenham, be forced out for kissing a seventeen-year-old girl in a park.

The real campaign, with manifestos and battle buses, did not start until after the Easter break. The three Blair buses, with 'Leading Britain . . .' '. . . into the future . . .' '. . . with Tony Blair' on the sides, made their first stop on 1 April. 'Hello Northampton,' said Blair from the movable platform stored under the 'Leading Britain . . .' bus. 'It's a beautiful day. The sun is out and with a bit of luck and your support the Tories'll be out too.' Once they had seen one stop, the journalists had seen them all. On previous occasions, they paid to ride on the same bus as the party leaders, so they could chat to the leader's staff and often the leader too. This time, they were confined to their own bus, corralled and cosseted throughout a controlled and antiseptic election. Blair spoke to 'the pack' who travelled with him only three times, once at a drinks party and twice on the plane known as 'Blairforce One', chartered to supplement the buses.

Like all modern campaigns, Labour's in 1997 was really fought in offices and television studios. Millbank Tower was the hub: Blair moved his office there to join Gordon Brown and Peter Mandelson. The tension between his two main lieutenants continued, but during elections there is plenty for everyone to do and, as long as Labour was winning, the 1997 campaign would look like a model of harmony and good planning. There were a few awkward moments. The failure to anticipate the problem of making up the shortfall from not selling off air traffic control was one; the question of who would resolve disputes about trade union recognition was another.

Blair also fell victim to his own Anglo-centrism, and managed to annoy some Scottish voters with a loosely-worded interview in the *Scotsman*. Neither his nor Alastair Campbell's tenuous Scottish origins had inoculated them against the subtly different assumptions of political culture north of the border. They had mishandled the announcement of the referendum on devolution. Blair had also been caught out in an earlier *Scotsman* interview by not appearing to know about the 'Claim of Right' – the assertion that the sovereignty of Scotland lay with the Scottish people, signed by most Scottish Labour MPs including John Smith in 1989.[24] Now, he appeared to compare the promised Scottish Parliament to a 'parish council'. His point was less inflammatory in the context of the question he was asked, which was whether he would ever deny the Scottish Parliament the right to put up tax: 'The powers are like those of any local authority . . . once the power is given, it's like any parish council, it's got the right to exercise it.' But he also compounded his 'Claim of Right' blunder by saying how he would explain devolution to his own constituency: 'We have devolved these matters to a Scottish Parliament, but as far as we are concerned sovereignty rests with me as an English MP.'[25]

However, the larger failing of the 1997 Labour campaign was caution. As Roy Jenkins had teasingly said of Blair the previous summer, he resembled a curator carrying a priceless Ming vase across a newly polished, slippery museum floor. The voters were already bored by the opening salvoes on the financial and sexual failings of various Conservative MPs, and there was little in the rest of the piece to stir them. Having challenged

Major to a live televised debate, 'any place, any time',[26] Blair now made his excuses when the Prime Minister accepted – or, rather, he asked Derry Irvine to engage in a legalistic negotiation over terms which was designed to fail. 'It was risk minimisation,' said one adviser. 'The whole election campaign would have become focused on it.' Which might have been a good democratic argument for doing it: American experience in 1992 and 1996 had showed that huge television audiences, even in the land of twelve-second sound-bites, would watch presidential debates an hour and a half long. But, as with the leadership election, Blair fought a defensive campaign designed to sit on a big lead in the opinion polls, calculating that it was not worth taking any chances, not with a Ming anyhow.

Labour's manifesto was launched on 3 April. The previous day Blair had been filmed in his garden in Islington writing out his personal ten-point contract with the British people, yet another summary of the full document. He wrote in ink rather than blood, but the implication was clear. 'Education will be the *No. 1 priority*,' was his first point. 'We will increase the share of national income spent on education and decrease it on the bills of economic & social failure (esp. unemployment).'

In contrast to the high drama over finalising Labour manifestos in the past, this one had been approved under a news blackout in conditions of strict secrecy by the joint meeting of the shadow Cabinet and National Executive the week before. At 9.10am on 26 March numbered copies were handed out at the meeting, and Robin Cook allowed twenty minutes for reading it before he started to go through it. Only Dennis Skinner and Diane Abbott raised objections, but as neither seconded each other's proposed amendments, there were no votes. On the retention of Trident nuclear missiles, Skinner asked mischievously, 'That was accepted at conference?'[27] He knew full well it had been. Then the numbered copies were gathered up to guard against leaks. As a result, it was difficult to check the final version against the early manifesto.

Even when the manifesto was published, however, journalists showed relatively little interest in the differences between the two documents. David Miliband had been through it looking for hostages to fortune, while Derry Irvine, as Blair's enforcer, gave it a final once-over with a lawyer's eye. Blair's pledge of a 'publicly owned railway', having proved impervious to fudge, was cut out. The wording of the promise of a referendum on electoral reform was changed slightly to weaken it. And two things were added. The obvious one was the pledge not to raise income tax rates – although it was hardly noticed that this had not been sanctified by the ballot of members. It was not noticed at all that the promise to ban tobacco advertising was also added.

Confidence gained

As the campaign progressed, Blair's self-assurance grew. There was a marked difference between the nervous uncertainty of his first big television interview of the campaign with David Dimbleby on *Panorama* on 7 April, and his swashbuckling aggression on *Question Time*, again presented by Dimbleby, on 24 April, a week before polling day.

On *Panorama*, Blair was slow to get to grips with the opening question: 'Did you believe in Old Labour?' He fell into the trap by suggesting he had always been 'New Labour', although the evidence he cited was thin: 'I was the person who, when I was the Treasury spokesman for the Labour Party, was arguing that we had to stand up for the rights of small investors.' Dimbleby put to him Labour's past support for unilateral nuclear disarmament, the closed shop, its softness on crime and the power of trades unions in the party, and asked: 'So was Britain right not to vote in a Labour government in 1983, in 1987 and in 1992?' Before Blair could regain his poise Dimbleby hit him with some stunning putdowns: 'You're not an old man. You haven't been in politics long.'

Once the interview moved on to why people should vote in a Labour government in 1997, however, Blair gained the upper hand. When Dimbleby suggested he could raise the money to renationalise the railways by putting up taxation, Blair swept him aside: 'Yes, but I don't want to do that.' When Dimbleby asked why he had agreed to spend £15.5 billion on the Eurofighter project, Blair replied: 'Because it's essential for the defence of our country.'

Overall, it was hardly a weak performance, but it was enough to convince Blair's inner team that they had been right to avoid a head-to-head debate with Major. They were worried, however, by the growing complaints from political pundits, who felt increasingly like football commentators watching a team with a 5–0 lead pass the ball around midfield.

There was a dreamlike quality to the campaign, and a sense that Blair was, as he had once accused others of being, 'programmed'. Occasionally, he seemed to rely on the advice of his minders when he might be expected to make up his own mind. On 9 April he was asked by a photographer if he would put his arm round Cherie. He in turn asked Campbell, who said: 'It wouldn't be appropriate at this moment in time.' (It was an attitude satirised in the first *Private Eye* cover of the new era, of Cherie embracing him in front of the door of Number Ten, asking, 'Happy, darling?' to which Blair replies, 'Sorry, you'll have to ask Peter Mandelson.')

This lent credibility to a bizarre and untrue story which nevertheless refused to lie down during the campaign, that Blair wore an electronic

17. Blair on the doorstep in Iver, Buckinghamshire, during the Beaconsfield by-election campaign, 1982.

18. The 1983 General Election campaign: with Cherie, her father Tony Booth and Pat Phoenix, later Booth's wife, at Pat's cottage in Hollingsworth in the Pennines.

19. With four of the 'Famous Five' who helped him win the Labour candidature in Sedgefield, on the day after his election as leader, July 1994: (L to R) Phil Wilson, John Burton, Paul Trippett and Peter Brookes.

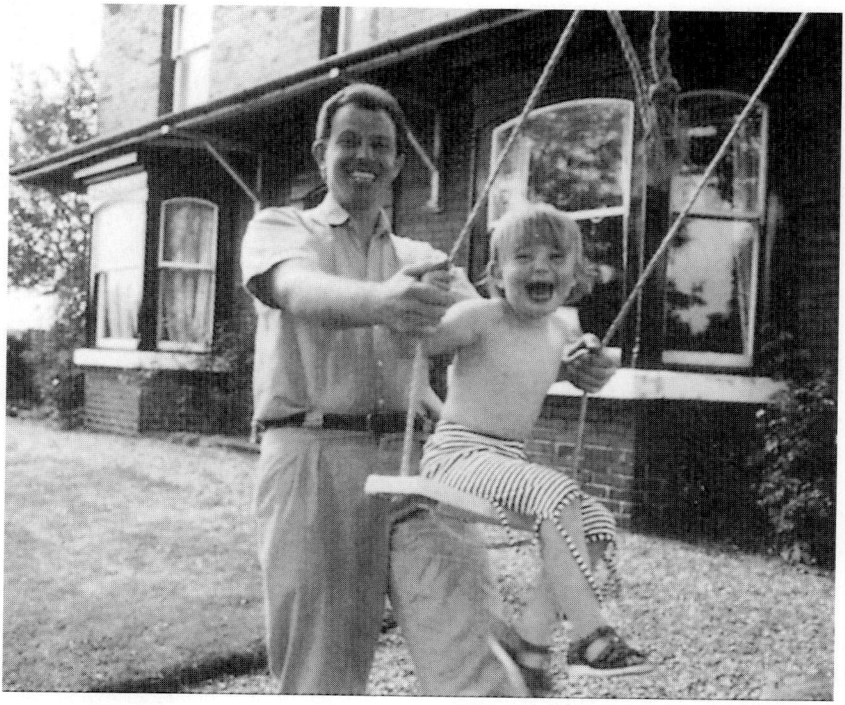

20. With Kathryn in the garden at 'Myrobella', 1991.

21. Charming rather than charismatic: the smile that makes the art of politics possible.

22. 'Two bright boys': with Gordon Brown at a news conference, February 1991.

23. 'The mark is on him already': at John Smith's funeral in Edinburgh, May 1994, with David Blunkett, Roy Hattersley, Glenys Kinnock, Gerald Kaufman and Neil Kinnock.

24. Blair meets the Queen's Lancashire Regiment for a photocall during the 1996 Labour conference. One of his pre-election priorities was to live down his past CND membership and reassure voters that Labour could be trusted on defence.

25. 'I am a modern man. I am part of the rock 'n' roll generation' (speech in Stevenage, 22 April 1997). Blair with Stratocaster in the sitting room of their Islington house in Richmond Crescent.

26. The 1997 election campaign started with a menagerie of attention-seeking animals: in addition to L!VE TV's News Bunny, Tony and Cherie were also pursued by a chicken from Conservative Central Office.

27. If mobile phones are a health hazard, Blair will be among the first to suffer: he is not computer-literate but is well versed in some forms of new technology.

28. Backstage on the last Sunday of the campaign, with David Miliband, head of policy; Anji Hunter, political assistant; and (seated) Alastair Campbell, press secretary.

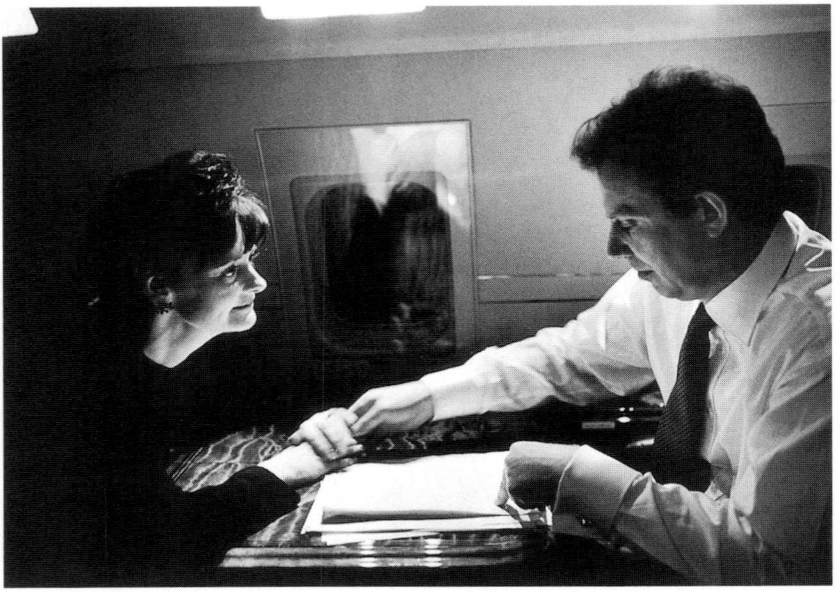

29. On the plane from Sedgefield to London in the middle of election night, 1–2 May 1997. According to Tony later, Cherie is saying: 'Now be strong and realise what a great opportunity this is for you. Make the most of it.' All he could feel, however, was 'a great sense of anti-climax' as he told himself how lucky he was: 'And don't you damn well blow it.'

ear-piece through which he could be prompted during news conferences. It seems to have originated when a local newspaper reporter saw Blair being interviewed at a campaign stop by a television presenter in a remote studio, in which case he would have had an ear-piece in order to hear the questions being put to him. It was similar to another misunderstanding which had excited John Major, that Blair wore make-up at Prime Minister's Questions in the Commons. Major said, 'We need to give that greater currency, don't you think?'[28] As a fellow television interviewee, he should have known that Blair would often have powder on his face from his performances. Now the ear-piece rumour so excited researchers at Conservative Central Office that they spent fruitless hours studying videotapes of Blair answering journalists' questions for evidence that he was being fed his answers by Campbell or Mandelson.

Indeed, Blair had been concerned enough about seeming over-reliant on modern communications technology that he stopped using a prompter – the device which projects the scrolling text of a speech on to glass screens on either side of a rostrum – some months before the election campaign and did not use one during it. (After the election, he returned to the technological prop.)

At his speech in Edinburgh on 17 April, it was decided to go further: that he should put his text to one side and try to recapture some of the spontaneity of his shirtsleeved roadshows with party members for Clause IV and the manifesto ballot. He had been buoyed by the disarray of the Conservative campaign, as a series of junior ministers came out against the single currency. On 15 April, he said to Campbell: 'They can't come back from this.'[29] The next day John Major scrapped his planned news conference and broadcast to beg his party not to 'bind my hands' on Europe. When Blair then stepped away from the rostrum at his Edinburgh speech the impromptu effect was fortuitously enhanced by the failure of the microphone clipped to his tie, which turned the event into an old-fashioned hustings. His performance attracted such favourable notices that he repeated it ('he's going to be spontaneous again', Campbell told journalists) in Stevenage on 22 April.

By the time of his *Question Time* appearance, then, he was entering into the spirit of things. Besieged by a fit-up by Conservative Central Office, which appeared to have briefed the first five questioners on his 1983 views on trade union law, he fought back with fire and implicitly invoked the right to change his mind. 'You could go back and say to Margaret Thatcher, "You closed more grammar schools than anybody else" . . . There's no point. Let's move this political debate on.' To trade union demands for renationalisation and a minimum wage of £4.42 an hour he responded with Thatcherite populism: 'There is a word in the English language and it's called no, and if people make demands upon me that I think are wrong then they'll be refused.'

Ground ceded

The only apparent wobble of the campaign came on the evening of the Stevenage speech, when news began to spread of an ICM opinion poll in the next day's *Guardian*. In contrast to all the other polls, which showed Labour's lead down a little from the start of the campaign but still a huge 18 percentage points, ICM now had Labour only 5 points ahead. Nerves in Millbank Tower were steadied by Labour's private polling, carried out daily by NOP, which showed no change. Early the following morning, however, Blair's entourage were shocked when, as they gathered in his campaign office, the door was kicked open and the leader himself burst in, shouting, 'Come on, Irvine, haven't you finished the work I gave you last night?'[30] It took them a moment to realise that this was a boisterous impersonation of the shadow Lord Chancellor's treatment of his pupil-barrister twenty years earlier.

If Blair's exuberance was supposed to signify confidence, it was still no coincidence that it was the next day, 24 April, that he hit the Conservatives hard with the accusation that they intended to abolish the state pension. It was an unnecessary tactic of dubious morality which undoubtedly scared many old people. The claim was based on a proposal naïvely floated by Peter Lilley, the Social Security Secretary, earlier that year, for a move towards having all pensions paid out of investments. Lilley insisted that those who could not afford to provide for themselves would have their provision topped up by the state to the level of the existing state pension, but that did not prevent Labour generally and Blair personally suggesting that old people were about to have their pension books taken from them. Major was so angry that he said he would rather leave politics than allow it to happen. Blair's defence of his dishonesty was blithely disingenuous: 'The Conservatives are accusing me of planning to surrender the whole country at Amsterdam. That's far worse than anything I've said about them.'*

It was not the only example of cynicism overcoming principle during the campaign, although in most instances this meant giving ground to the

*Whoever won the election would face negotiations in Amsterdam on minor amendments to the treaties of the European Union (Robert Harris, *Sunday Times*, 4 May 1997).

Conservatives rather than attacking them. Early in the campaign, Blair had parried a Tory attack on trade union law by dismissing what had only recently been Labour policy as 'the grossest misrepresentations'. The newspapers had reprinted 'Tory propaganda' as fact, he said, claiming that under Labour 'employees will get full employment rights from their first day. Wrong.' Never mind that it had been 'right' three years earlier under John Smith. Now, wrote Blair in *The Times*, 'The changes that we do propose would leave British law the most restrictive on trade unions in the Western world.'[31]

The most striking example, though, was Blair's pitch to the *Sun*'s nationalism. In a confused way, it was to this that Maurice and Charles Saatchi referred in an untransmitted Conservative party election broadcast – vetoed by John Major – depicting Blair shaking on a Faustian pact with a devilish figure. If anything, it was the Labour Party which had entered into a Faustian compact with Blair, as the wittily accurate backbench Labour MP, Austin Mitchell, observed.[32] In a series of seven articles and two interviews in the *Sun* during the campaign, Blair stretched his ability to tell an audience what they wanted to hear.[33] 'I know exactly what the British people feel when they see the Queen's head on a £10 note. I feel it too. There's a very strong emotional tie to the pound which I fully understand,' he said. He went on:

> Of course there are emotional issues involved in the single currency. It's not just a question of economics. It's about the sovereignty of Britain and constitutional issues too . . . I do understand how passionate people are about the pound. And that is why I would let the people have a final say in a referendum if I, as prime minister, ever decided to join a single currency.[34]

Nervous pro-Europeans, both inside and outside the Labour Party, had already been disturbed by Robin Cook's comment early in the campaign that 'the probability is' that a government which decided not to join in 1999 would be 'looking towards the subsequent parliament' for entry.[35] It was no more than a statement of the obvious, but it was precisely the point on which the Labour government would trip up within months of taking office. No wonder it jangled some nerves – particularly the rather frayed ones of the Chancellor, Kenneth Clarke, desperately trying to keep Major upright as the sceptic blows rained down. Clarke was worried enough to make secret contact across enemy lines through Anthony Teasdale, his special adviser, with Roger Liddle, Peter Mandelson's pro-European friend. He was relieved when the message was relayed back from Labour high command: 'The policy is staying the same.'[36] So it did, despite further pro-European alarm over, in particular, Blair's article in the *Sun* on 22 April. It was, as Blair noted, the day before

St George's Day, 'the day when the English celebrate the pride we have as a nation'. He wrote (or, judging from the concrete and punchy style, Alastair Campbell wrote):

> On the day we remember the legend that St George slayed a dragon to protect England, some will argue that there is another dragon to be slayed: Europe . . . Let me make my position on Europe absolutely clear. I will have no truck with a European superstate. If there are moves to create that dragon I will slay it.

Whatever the squeamishness of the pro-Europeans, however, the article was a masterpiece of mood music which yielded no hostages to fortune. On the single currency, it said 'there are formidable obstacles to Britain joining the first wave if it goes ahead'. But it said Britain should keep its options open, subject to a 'triple lock' of consent by Cabinet, parliament and the people in a referendum. That was the policy set six months before the election.

Of course, there were many, both inside Millbank Tower and outside, who urged Blair to be bolder, to use the platform of an election campaign to claim a mandate, for pro-Europeanism, for liberal values or for more overt egalitarianism. Bill Clinton had had the same argument with Robert Reich, his Labor Secretary, and others, who said it would be harder to move public opinion in a progressive direction after the election without giving a clear lead in the campaign. Blair was unmoved, insisting that Labour had to win arguments from government, and could not win them in Opposition.

On the last weekend of the campaign, *Observer* editor Will Hutton put the Reich argument to Blair, suggesting that the coalition he had built was broad but shallow and could not hold. Leaving Europe to one side, 'the coalition is stable and rational,' Blair replied. 'Remember when Mrs Thatcher built up her coalition, people asked: "How can this be? She has got traditional Labour support coming out for the Conservatives." We are doing the same in reverse.'

The *Observer* interview, with Hutton, political editor Patrick Wintour and Andrew Adonis, who would shortly join the Downing Street staff, produced one of the few significant statements of the campaign from Blair. Just as it was ending, the conversation flickered back into life, as Blair insisted, in passionate, confidential mode:

> I am of the centre-left and I want the left to be part of this project. I want the left to realise that if we win this election, we will have done so without ceding any ground that cannot be recovered. I'm going to be a lot more radical in government than many people think.[37]

This cut directly against his strenuous reassurance of the voters that what they saw was what they would get: the five pledges, the ten vows and the 177 manifesto promises. It may well have been intended to be off the record, a political spin designed to persuade his left-ish interviewers that he was really on their side. (He told his next interviewer, Ian Jack, 'I've just been speaking to three guys telling me how to lose the election.') Indeed, the status of Blair's words was unclear at the time, according to Wintour: 'We weren't quite sure if it was off or on the record, but I went back to Alastair and asked if it was on the record and he said yes.' Wintour admitted that Campbell may not have been paying full attention to the question. But it was too late for the apparent admission that Blair was concealing a 'radical' programme from the electorate to make any difference. The day the interview appeared, Rupert Murdoch's other mass-circulation title, the *News of the World*, came out for Blair. 'Thank goodness for that,' said Murdoch, according to its editor Phil Hall who told him what he intended to do the previous week, 'because I've just spoken to the *Sunday Times* and they're going to say "Vote Tory". It's better to be on the winning side.'[38]

The growing certainty of Labour's victory rendered the morning news conference the next day meaningless, as journalists were unable to think of sensible questions to ask about the campaign. 'This is not a landslide country,' intoned Blair: it was wrong historically (the elections of 1900, 1906, 1918, 1924, 1931, 1935, 1945, 1983 and 1987 were all won by margins of more than 100 seats), and wrong this time, but he had run out of sensible answers to give. Nevertheless, for all their refusal to acknowledge the obvious at the higher levels of consciousness, he and Jonathan Powell worked hard in the last few days on finalising the mechanics of taking office.

Philip Gould, convening focus groups every night and faxing the summaries to Millbank at 1am before arriving himself for the early meeting at 7am, was still not sure that Labour would win on Monday and Tuesday of the week of polling day. He was a prime example of the pessimistic mindset gripping the inner court. Stan Greenberg, the US pollster with a more detached view, never doubted the outcome. He offered to accept bets from all-comers in Millbank on the size of Labour's margin of victory in percentage share of the vote: 'I'll take ten points.' It was not until Wednesday night on the eve of the poll that Gould, after convening a group of eight women in Watford, allowed himself to say that Labour would win. Earlier that day, Blair told John Williams, political columnist on the *Mirror*, who had drawn Labour majorities of 105, 115 and 129 in the battle bus journalists' sweepstake: 'You've no chance with any of those.'[39]

New dawn

Blair was in Trimdon on 1 May, discussing the mechanics of taking office with Jonathan Powell. In mid-morning, he was filmed going to vote across the field at the side of Myrobella with Cherie and the children. It was a clear, warm, sunny day. John Prescott came over from his constituency in Hull to be briefed, among other things, on the plan to make the Bank of England independent, which Blair had already agreed with Brown. After lunch, Blair took a nap in the garden, knowing that he would need the rest that night and the next day, while Cherie and his father Leo rested in the house. When he woke, he resumed discussions with Powell, now joined by Peter Mandelson, who was still lobbying for a job in his own right in government. He once again pressed to be made minister for Europe, a potentially key job outside the Cabinet, as he had at times over the previous year or two, but Blair again refused. He wanted him to carry on 'being Peter' as ministerial troubleshooter and adviser on presentation, but promised him he would be brought into the Cabinet after six months – a deadline which was missed by eight months.[40] The early afternoon discussion was interrupted by a phone call from Philip Gould, who had obtained inside information from the BBC exit poll showing Labour around ten points ahead. According to Mandelson, Blair was 'quite elated', but 'he didn't yell or anything', he just asked: 'God, do you think it could be true?'[41]

When the polls closed at 10pm, and the exit polls predicted a landslide, Blair and his family were sitting talking. 'Nicky had gone to get a bit of kip but the other two wouldn't leave. I thought they should go to bed,' said Blair. But Cherie said: 'I think it's a night they'd like to remember.'

A year later, Blair was able to recall his exact words – 'Fair enough, and it looks as though we're going to make it' – and those of Euan, sticking to the party line: 'You can't take it for granted, Dad.' He reflected:

> Realising that you are about to become Prime Minister is a very strange moment. My dad was fabulous. He was absolutely knocked out by it. He said: 'Mum would have been very proud.' But he read my mood correctly. He kept saying to me during the evening: 'You will do it well.' He understood what I was worrying about.[42]

By the time Blair arrived at his count the early results, including Labour's win in Basildon, were in line with the exit polls. He gave a short speech of thanks, above all to Cherie and his father, and added: 'All that could make this complete was that my mother was here still.' Then he was driven to the Constituency Labour Club in Trimdon, where he remained the calm centre of a storm of adulation. John Major spoke to him by phone to say he was about to make a statement conceding defeat, just before Blair made another short speech. 'You know me, I am never complacent,' he said. 'But it's looking very good.'

The full scale of what was happening did not sink in until Blair took to the air, flying to Stansted in a small chartered jet. During the flight in the early morning of 2 May the results relayed via Alastair Campbell's pager came from the increasingly far shores of Tory England, including Defence Secretary Michael Portillo's famous defeat by Stephen Twigg in Enfield Southgate. Blair had forgotten that he had set Portillo's seat as a target two years earlier. Speaking of Labour's cross-class appeal in the 1945 landslide, he pointed out that the party had 'single-mindedly set out to reach beyond the traditional industrial areas'. Under Clement Attlee, 'outer London swung dramatically to Labour . . . We won Enfield: Michael Portillo take note. And we gained Barnet – the home of Mrs Thatcher.'[43] Her seat, Finchley, fell that night too.

The passenger list for the plane defined Blair's inner sanctum: as well as Campbell, there were Cherie, Peter Mandelson, John Burton, Jonathan Powell, Anji Hunter, a Special Branch officer and Tom Stoddart, the Labour Party's official photographer (and husband of the MP Kate Hoey). Blair said:

> There's a nice picture of us on the plane on the way down where she [Cherie] is really saying to me: 'Now be strong and realise what a great opportunity this is for you. Make the most of it.' But although it may sound absolutely ridiculous, all I could feel was a great sense of anti-climax. I felt that it was such an extraordinary thing to have happened to me. While others did the celebrating I really felt the need to tell myself how very, very fortunate I was, and, 'Don't you damn well blow it.'[44]

The plane was followed by another, larger, thirty-seater aircraft with more staff and family from Sedgefield. From Stansted Blair travelled in a dark green Jaguar, on loan from the car company, with police outriders and followed by a coach. On the way he took a call of congratulation from President Clinton. The cavalcade arrived at the Royal Festival Hall in London, where the election night party had been planned with the same precision as the rest of the campaign. At the last moment, unexpected roadworks blocked their way to the access ramp, causing a delay which meant that, as Tony and Cherie made their way to the platform just after 5am, the sky lightened.

After the noise and elation, Blair's words struck a reflective, quizzical note. 'A new dawn has broken, has it not?'

Even at the moment of victory, a victory of dreamlike wish-fulfilment, he was downbeat. In a short speech, he used a phrase designed to reassure a wider audience, but which probably only puzzled most voters: 'We have been elected as New Labour and we will govern as New Labour.' It certainly meant nothing to the party workers, politicians and celebrity supporters who cheered it mindlessly nonetheless. Beyond reassuring Middle England that he would not suddenly revert to tax-and-spend, trade-union socialism, did Blair know what he meant? As Neil Kinnock embraced him on his way up to the platform, saying, 'Brilliant! Bloody brilliant!', Blair made a self-deprecating joke, 'OK, wise guy: what do we do now?', echoing Bill McKay's words to his chief handler on being elected senator in the 1972 film, *The Candidate*.[45]

Labour won 44.4 per cent of the vote and 419 seats, a majority of 179, greater than Attlee's in 1945, greater than any party's at any election since 1935. The Conservatives, with 31.5 per cent and 165 seats, broke nearly all records in the opposite direction, including their lowest share of the vote since 1832. The Liberal Democrats, meanwhile, on a slightly reduced share of the vote, 17.2 per cent, managed to win their largest number of seats, forty-six, since the old Liberal Party collapsed as a parliamentary force after 1929.[46]

As it happened, the opinion polls were wrong – although not as wrong as in 1992. The unprecedented extent of tactical voting between Labour and Liberal Democrat supporters helped conceal the error, by enabling Labour to take up to twenty-one extra seats from the Conservatives, adding thirty or forty to Blair's majority, while the Liberal Democrats took up to fourteen more.[47]

It was a landslide, but it was a shallow one in two senses. First, Labour's share of the vote was unexceptional. It was a fraction lower than the 44.9 per cent won by the Conservatives under Margaret Thatcher in 1979, which gave her a majority of only forty-three. Tactical voting was one factor, but more important in magnifying Blair's victory was the little-noticed pro-Labour bias in the constituency boundaries. Despite a strong feeling in the Labour Party that the electoral system had been tilted against them for the previous eighteen years, the opposite had always been the case, despite occasional redrawing of boundaries intended to correct for the drift from Labour inner cities to Tory suburbs.*

*If the Labour and Conservative shares of the vote had been reversed in 1997, John Major would have had the same forty-three-seat majority as Margaret Thatcher in 1979 (John Curtice and Michael Steed, in David Butler and Dennis Kavanagh, *The British General Election of 1997*, p. 316).

Secondly, Blair was not carried to Downing Street on a huge wave of positive enthusiasm. It was more a negative vote against an exhausted Conservative government which had only been elected on sufferance in 1992. All the analysis of the election has suggested that the real damage to John Major was inflicted early on by the devaluation of 1992. The healthy performance of the economy since then was not a factor, a phenomenon dubbed the 'voteless recovery'. True, Blair had ruthlessly removed as many reasons as possible for not voting Labour. And a wave of euphoria certainly did sweep the nation, but it came after the election rather than before – even then it was heavily tempered by scepticism: at the Uxbridge by-election three months after the General Election, the Conservatives held the seat with an increased majority.

On the other hand, the opposite mistake is to assume that the 1997 election was evidence of a turning away from politics. The caution and cynicism of the Labour campaign may have been at odds with the rhetoric of the 'new politics', but the sharply reduced turnout, down to a post-war low of 71 per cent from 78 per cent in 1992, was largely explained by the fact that most voters assumed Labour would win, whereas the previous election was thought to be close.[48]

The public mood in which Blair was carried to his largely unexpected landslide was characterised by low expectations and the perception that, as Paul Trippett put it of his quest for the Labour nomination in Sedgefield in 1983, 'Here was a sensible, quiet young man who wanted a chance.' He was given his chance, becoming Prime Minister four days before his forty-fourth birthday, in a stronger position than any of his predecessors in the twentieth century.

Notes

1. *Spectator*, April 1994.
2. Philip Gould, *The Unfinished Revolution*, pp. 289–90.
3. Interviews with David Ward, John Smith's senior policy adviser.
4. *Bella*, 8 January 1997.
5. Speech, Stevenage, 22 April 1997.
6. *Daily Express*, 5 February 1997.
7. Gyles Brandreth, *Breaking the Code*, p. 453.
8. *New Woman*, May 1994.
9. *Daily Mail*, 16 March 1996.
10. Granada TV, *This Morning With Richard and Judy*, 6 March 1997.
11. Sue Evison, *Sun*, 1 May 1997.
12. Lynda Lee-Potter, *Daily Mail*, 22 April 1997.
13. *Sunday Times*, 30 March 1997.
14. Kate Muir, *The Times Magazine*, 6 June 1998.

15. *Channel Four News*, 25 April 1995.
16. Sue Evison, *Sun*, 28 February 1997.
17. *Daily Telegraph*, 24 February 1997.
18. *Sunday Telegraph*, 23 June 1996.
19. *Ibid.*, 20 April 1997.
20. *Sun*, 8 December 1995.
21. *Independent on Sunday*, 6 April 1997.
22. *New Statesman*, 21 March 1997.
23. Pippa Norris and others, *On Message*, p. 162.
24. *Scotsman*, 9 September 1996.
25. *Ibid.*, 4 April 1997.
26. Speech to Labour Party conference, Brighton, 3 October 1995.
27. Janet Jones, *Labour of Love*, p. 40.
28. Brandreth, *Breaking the Code*, p. 479.
29. Gould, *The Unfinished Revolution*, p. 369.
30. Roy Hattersley profile of Derry Irvine, *Observer*, 11 May 1997.
31. *The Times*, 31 March 1997.
32. 'Squashed hedgehog on the road to the manifesto', *New Statesman*, 30 August 1996.
33. Blair articles in the *Sun*, 17 and 25 March, 2, 4, 7, 16 and 22 April 1997; interviews, 17 and 28 April 1997.
34. *Sun*, 17 April 1997.
35. ITV, *Jonathan Dimbleby*, 6 April 1997.
36. Donald Macintyre, *Mandelson*, p. 332.
37. *Observer*, 27 April 1997.
38. BBC Radio 5, 17 December 1999.
39. John Williams, *Victory*, p. 108.
40. Macintyre, *Mandelson*, p. 338.
41. Gould, *The Unfinished Revolution*, p. 388.
42. Lynda Lee-Potter, *Daily Mail*, 17 April 1998.
43. Speech at Fabian Society commemoration of the fiftieth anniversary of the 1945 election, 5 July 1995.
44. Interview, *Mirror*, 29 July 1997.
45. Andrew Rawnsley, *Observer*, 26 April 1998; Carol Thatcher recalled the same scene when her mother seized the Conservative leadership in 1975 and commented: 'My mother knew exactly what to do and embraced the leadership as if it had always been her destiny.' (*Below the Parapet: The Biography of Denis Thatcher*, quoted in John Campbell, *Margaret Thatcher,* Vol. 1, p. 308.)
46. Share-of-the-vote figures for Great Britain (the same basis as that of opinion polls). The equivalent figures for the whole of the United Kingdom, including Northern Ireland, were: Labour 43.3 per cent, Conservatives 30.7 per cent, Liberal Democrats 16.8 per cent.
47. John Curtice and Michael Steed estimated that tactical voting added between thirty and forty-two to Labour's majority, in 'The Results Analysed', the now legendary 'Appendix' to the long-running series of election books by David Butler and Dennis Kavanagh, in this case *The British General Election of 1997*, p. 313. The Referendum Party and UK Independence Party, on the

other hand, cost the Conservatives only six seats. 'For the most part the success of the Referendum Party was not so much a cause of the Conservatives' difficulties as a symptom.'

48. Geoffrey Evans and Pippa Norris (editors), *British Parties and Voters in Long-Term Perspective*, 1999.

PART FOUR

GOVERNMENT

17

We Are the Servants Now

First Hundred Days, 2 May–9 August 1997

> 'For his first hundred days the Prime Minister was a combination of John Fitzgerald Kennedy and Napoleon.'
>
> —*Iain Macleod on Harold Wilson, 1966*

Labour was handed power at a time when, in the words of its election theme song, things could only get better. After a few hours' rest at home in Islington, Tony Blair went to Buckingham Palace where he accepted 'Her Majesty the Queen's kind offer to form a new administration of government in this country', as he told the crowd of Labour Party staff and friends organised by Millbank Tower, waving Union Jacks, when he arrived at Downing Street at 1pm.

At forty-three, he was the youngest Prime Minister since Lord Liverpool, on his forty-second birthday in 1812, unexpectedly succeeded Spencer Perceval, assassinated in the lobby of the House of Commons. Even now Blair maintained a strenuously subdued demeanour, the controlled erasure of triumphalism which had characterised the entire election campaign. The pause for historic words from a new Prime Minister 'on the steps' of Number Ten is a tradition that has only grown up since the war, given particular resonance by Margaret Thatcher's quotation from St Francis of Assisi, an unusual and politically loaded choice. Blair resisted the call of the rhetorical wild. He paid tribute to John Major for 'his dignity and his courage', and repeated that 'we ran for office as New Labour, we will govern as New Labour'. He set the objectives of his government, rather woodenly, starting with 'a world-class education system in which education is not the privilege of the few but the right of the many' (the second part of which had been achieved by the 1944 Education Act, although it was clear enough what he meant). He promised to modernise the National Health Service and create 'the competitive economy of the future'. His would be 'a government that seeks to restore trust in politics in this country, that cleans it up, that decentralises it, that gives people hope once again that politics is, and should be always, about the service of the public'. And it would give the country 'strength and confidence in leadership both at home and abroad, particularly in Europe'.

Against the scale of his electoral mandate, his rhetorical restraint outside his new home was strangely deflating, as he ended:

> For eighteen years, eighteen long years, my party has been in Opposition. It could only say, it could not do. Today we are charged with the deep responsibility of government. Today, enough of talking, it is time now to do.

For all its pedestrian phrasing, his words were well judged for how they would be seen in homes all over the country, where the prospect of a Labour government was still viewed with as much trepidation as hope.

Pausing for photographs with Cherie, and then with Euan, Nicky and Kathryn as well, he sent the children in first and went in through the shiny black door.

Blair had only been in Number Ten once before, for an official dinner with President Clinton in November 1996. 'I remember walking down the corridor of Downing Street for only the very second time in my life,' he said later. 'In a little room just off the Cabinet room,' he met Sir Robin Butler, the Cabinet Secretary, who greeted him with the words, 'Well, you're in charge. What are we going to do, then?'[1]

In a risky off-text preamble to his 1998 party conference speech, Blair said: 'When you become Prime Minister the first thing they do – after telling you how to launch the nuclear bomb – is to take your passport from you, and then the rest of the time trying to get you to travel around the world.' After finding out how to authorise the use of the Trident missiles against which he and many Labour members had once campaigned, he was introduced and shown around. John Major had left a bottle of champagne with a note for him and Cherie saying, 'It's a great job – enjoy it.' Then the new Prime Minister had lunch with his extended family: Cherie, the children, Cherie's mother Gale, his brother Bill, sister Sarah, father Leo and stepmother Olwen.

The first day in Downing Street had been planned in some detail. Blair's Chief of Staff Jonathan Powell had been working on 'the transition' with increasing intensity since the beginning of 1996. He and Blair had seen how not to do it when Blair visited the Clinton team preparing for the presidential inauguration in January 1993. Despite having nearly three months after winning the election to prepare for his inauguration, Bill Clinton's presidency got off to a truly awful start. At the first day's press briefing, live on television, George Stephanopoulos, the President's spokesman, said discrimination against homosexuals in the military would be ended 'probably within the next week'; explained why Zoë Baird would make a good Attorney General despite having employed illegal immigrants and evaded taxes; and defended the decision to bar the press corps from the West Wing of the White House.

'So that's where we were on our first day,' wrote Stephanopoulos,

> managing a crisis before we had functioning computers, before we understood our political opponents and the White House press corps, before we even knew how to work the phones. The President tried to dial out a couple of times, but every time he picked up the receiver, an operator picked up the other end, which he didn't seem to like at all.[2]

Blair's team came in with their own mobile phones, with the first day choreographed by Powell in a 'day one' book, in co-operation with a civil service whose job it is, unlike American political appointees, to ensure a smooth handover.*

The first business was the forming of the government. That too had been considered for some time, including the boldest stroke: forming a coalition with the Liberal Democrats. It would have been a brilliant manifest of Blair's non-tribal reasonableness, the first time that a party which had just won an election voluntarily shared power with another. But the scale of Labour's victory frightened Blair off the idea. He seemed to have been cooling towards it in the days before polling day and defended his failure to seize the moment by saying that, having won the greatest majority since the war, a coalition would have seemed 'slightly quixotic'.[3] The reasons why, when Blair phoned Paddy Ashdown on Friday, it was not to offer him a job are explored further in Chapter 30, but it was true that it was now harder for them to argue that the historic division between their traditions was holding back the progressive forces of British politics. At the same time, mainstream Labour support for electoral reform – the essential condition of a coalition deal – evaporated like dew by mid-morning. Who in the Labour Party would now agree that the electoral system was unfair when it had just delivered such a patently well-deserved and invigorating verdict?

---

*One issue on which Blair was not going to get hung up was gays in the military. That accounted for a bumpy episode in May 1996, when he, John Prescott and David Blunkett failed to vote for a backbench Bill to lift the ban on open homosexuality in the armed forces.

Instead, the new Prime Minister promised Ashdown he would consider the fall-back plan to set up a joint committee of the two parties with Cabinet committee status.

It was not Ashdown, therefore, who followed the 'Big Four', John Prescott, Gordon Brown, Robin Cook and Jack Straw – into Downing Street on the afternoon of 2 May. Blair had decided a long time before that the top team would keep their shadow portfolios in government, with John Prescott taking the title Deputy Prime Minister and the merged departments of the Environment and Transport as reward for his loyalty. It was Mo Mowlam who was the next to make the short walk in front of the cameras, to have her appointment as Northern Ireland Secretary confirmed. Frank Dobson, who had lost Environment, took over Health. Chris Smith, who had clashed with Gordon Brown over public spending, moved from Health to the Department of National Heritage, renamed Culture, Media and Sport.

For all the theatrical surprises there could have been, the lists of ministers issued on Friday, Saturday and the following Tuesday were conservative. The sudden elevation of Frank Field, the heretical moralist, from the back benches to just below Cabinet rank was eye-catching, but was not as dramatic as it could have been. Blair came close to appointing him Social Security Secretary over Harriet Harman, who shadowed the department in Opposition.* The coup of persuading a business leader of the stature of Sir David Simon, chairman of BP, to join the government as a peer was muffled by a premature leak in Saturday's *Financial Times* suggesting he would be minister for Europe – and by the off-note sounded by the use of the House of Lords to bypass the democratic mandate just granted by the British people.

Blair was conscious that he was the first Prime Minister to take office without any government experience since Ramsay MacDonald in 1924. At least MacDonald had Arthur Henderson, who had served in the wartime coalition, in his Cabinet. Blair's was the first Cabinet in modern times to contain no one who had served at that level before. The three members with ministerial experience, Margaret Beckett, Jack Cunningham and Ann Taylor, had served at relatively junior levels in the previous Labour government.† However, Blair was also well aware that Cabinet had long ceased to be the power centre of modern British government.

---

*See p. 374.

†Blair did have one minister outside his Cabinet, John Morris, the Attorney General, who had served in the 1974–79 Cabinet, as Secretary of State for Wales.

Blair's 'transition' was very different from the previous one, which was Margaret Thatcher's in 1979. As far as she was concerned, all the civil service did was 'carefully scrutinise an Opposition's manifesto with a view to the hasty preparation of a new administration's legislative programme'.[4] That was a dismissive description of what had always been a more elaborate exercise, but this time the preparations were longer and deeper than before. As one of his significant legacies, Neil Kinnock had agreed with John Major that contacts between shadow Cabinet ministers and civil servants should begin earlier than in previous cycles. Kinnock had been unhappy with the amount of time his team had had to prepare before the 1992 election. As a result, Blair and Powell met Butler and a group of permanent secretaries in January 1996, nearly eighteen months before the election.

Powell's schedule ran for the first thirty days, rather than a hundred, and was overtaken by events. But before it could start, Blair had to make a human – and surprisingly unplanned – 'transition' of his own.

The removal van

From the start of Blair's leadership of the Labour Party, it was decided that the family would move into the Prime Minister's official residence if he won the election. 'As far as I am concerned we are a family. Wherever Tony goes we all go. If that means Downing Street then so be it,' said Cherie in an interview published the day after her husband was elected Labour leader.[5] It would be the only way to allow him to spend any time with the children.

In secret discussions with the civil service and with Gordon Brown, it was agreed that, if elected, the Blairs would live in the larger flat above Numbers Eleven and Twelve which had traditionally been occupied by the Chancellor of the Exchequer, while Brown would take the one above Number Ten. Partly because detailed planning would have smelt of triumphalism, however, the move from 1 Richmond Crescent was an improvised affair.

Even after three years as First-Family-to-be, the intensity of the media attention took the Blairs by surprise. Richmond Crescent was turned overnight into a semi-permanent media encampment. When Cherie answered the door in her nightdress at eight o'clock on Saturday morning, she found herself blinking in the lights of what had become effectively a film set as she took delivery of a bouquet of flowers from the governors and staff of St Joan of Arc, their Islington primary school. She was mortified, but her mother, Gale, reassured her: 'Don't worry. Everybody will warm to you.'[6] Her husband teased: 'Actually the picture was very Cherie. She's not a morning person. I am, which is one of our outstanding incompatibilities.'[7]

Then on Bank Holiday Monday, 5 May, all the things they would need in Downing Street were carried through the film set to a blue Transit van. For six weeks, the electorate had seen the front of Tony Blair. Now they saw the back, all the intricate workings and support structure. After the Prime Minister himself left the house for Downing Street at 9am dressed in a suit, someone else inevitably carrying his red box (Alastair Campbell in this case), the rest of his wardrobe followed. Only there was no wardrobe. The clothes were carried out on wire coat hangers and hung on a clothes rail in the van in full view of the cameras.

All the ties seen on television, the suits, the jackets with four cuff-buttons were there, along with Cherie's clothes and her shoes. Not one but three hanging canvas shoe-holders, fifty pairs of shoes in total. They took just the essentials. An electric guitar, in its box. An amplifier. An acoustic guitar. The children's toys. A brass bed. (The bed was only a temporary measure: a £3,500 Swedish-made bed was delivered to Downing Street the following month, prompting the front-page headline in the *Sun*: 'THINGS CAN ONLY GET BEDDER'.[8]) The van was too small, and had to go back for a second load after lunch. As it set off, Campbell issued a letter to journalists asking them to allow the Blair children to be 'left to live as normal a life as possible' once they had finished moving into their new home.

It was the first time since Asquith that a Prime Minister had lived in Downing Street with a family of young children: in May 1997 Blair's were thirteen, eleven and nine. In 1908, Elizabeth and Anthony ('Puffin') Asquith, aged eleven and five, used to play with Megan Lloyd George, the Chancellor of the Exchequer's daughter, also five, who lived next door. No other twentieth-century Prime Minister had a primary-school-aged child on coming into office, although Ramsay MacDonald's daughters, Joan and Sheila, aged fifteen and thirteen in 1924, were said to have been allowed to practise their golf chip shots in a corridor at Number Ten, and Harold Macmillan's grandchildren sometimes stayed there, prompting the Prime Minister to put up the probably apocryphal notice, 'No roller skating: Cabinet meeting today'.*

The move into Downing Street allowed *Private Eye* finally to get to

*The other youngest children in Number Ten were: Megan Lloyd George, who was fourteen when her father became Prime Minister in 1916; Attlee's daughter Alison, fifteen in 1945; Wilson's son Giles, sixteen in 1964; and Major's son James, fifteen in 1990.

grips with Blair's character, launching 'The St Albion Parish News' on 16 May, featuring the Rev. A. R. P. Blair, the vicar who wants to be called Tony, and his church warden P. Mandelson. 'We didn't have to spend any time at all thinking this one up,' said Ian Hislop, editor of the *Eye*. 'I just looked at him moving in to Downing Street with his guitar and I thought, "Hello, I know what he reminds me of".'[9] The column, following in the tradition of 'Mrs Wilson's Diary', the 'Dear Bill' letters of Denis Thatcher and 'The Secret Diary of John Major Aged 47¾', was an instant success.

The publicity attracted by the move convinced Tony and Cherie to sell the house in Richmond Crescent, which they originally intended to keep as a second London home. It would provide little seclusion and the security measures would be expensive and irritating to neighbours. It was sold in July 1997 for about £615,000, and the rest of the contents, including a piano, were moved to Myrobella, their house in the Sedgefield constituency.* That meant they were hit by the new higher rate of stamp duty (property sales tax) imposed in his first Budget by Gordon Brown on houses worth more than £250,000. They still had a mortgage on Myrobella, however, which allowed Blair to pretend to feel the pain of interest-rate rises: 'I deeply sympathise with people who have got problems.'[10]

By Tuesday, Blair had settled in. Coming through the connecting door from the Cabinet Office to Number Ten with Sir Robin Butler, he saw Phil Wilson, one of the 'Famous Five' who had helped him win the nomination in Sedgefield, sitting in the office of the political staff. 'I hear you've got a new job,' said Wilson, who was now working for the Labour Party at Millbank.

'Something to do with running the country,' replied Blair, offering to show him round. He took Wilson to his 'den', the 'little room' to which he had been taken when he arrived. John Major had used the famous pillared Cabinet room itself as his office, which did not suit Blair because it did not have a sofa and armchairs in it, so Jonathan Powell had allocated him to the side office which had belonged to Major's Political Secretary, Howell James, and, longer ago, to Marcia Williams. Now, as they sat there alone, Wilson remembered driving around Sedgefield in Blair's brown Mini Metro fourteen years earlier – 'six in the back and four in the front' – scrounging for votes. They looked at each other, and Blair raised

---

*The Richmond Crescent house had been valued at £375,000 when it was bought, for £175,000 in cash and part-exchange of the house in Stavordale Road, in 1986, and had had about £20,000 spent on improvements, according to the *Mirror*, 12 July 1997.

his arms and stretched them out wide, as if to say, 'Who would have thought it?' They burst out laughing.

'How's it going?' asked Wilson.

'Oh, it's working for a living.'

Week zero

An incoming Labour government would not have, Blair said in a radio interview in 1995, 'some grand programme – in the first hundred days, you do these thirty or forty things. I think that type of politics usually does end in tears.'[11] That turned out to be the flat opposite of the truth. Not the Kennedy of Camelot nor the Wilson of White Heat, nor even the Roosevelt of the New Deal, whose legislative activism in his first three months gave rise to the 'Hundred Days' phrase, had put on such a dazzling show to introduce themselves to an astonished and grateful populace.

The first announcements were well trailed: signing up to the European Social Chapter and recognising trade unions at the GCHQ intelligence centre. On Tuesday 6 May, however, the new Chancellor, Gordon Brown, took the country by surprise when he announced – after putting up interest rates by a quarter point to 6.25 per cent – that he was handing future such decisions to the Bank of England. The Bank was instructed to set interest rates in order to achieve the government's 2.5 per cent target for underlying inflation. Its instructions were also, 'without prejudice to this objective, to support the government's economic policy, including its objectives for growth and employment'.

That legalistic 'without prejudice' was the final end of the Keynesian road. When Blair set out the publicly tentative plan to give the Bank 'greater operational responsibility' in his Mais lecture in May 1995, he had quoted approvingly Callaghan's disavowal of deficit spending in his 1976 Blackpool conference speech: 'I tell you in all candour that option no longer exists.' As Blair said, it 'sounded the death knell of the post-war Keynesian consensus'. Margaret Thatcher administered the last rites; now Blair and Brown laid flowers on the grave. As a 23-year-old new member of the Chelsea Labour Party, Blair must have been struck by Callaghan's speech: even in the socialist fundamentalism of his Australian lecture in 1982 he was forced to acknowledge that 'a reflation of the economy that is unplanned would lead, almost for a certainty, to inflation'.

By 1995 it had long been taken for granted that Britain should not borrow and spend its way out of recession if that meant taking risks with inflation. Blair took a hard line on inflation within that consensus: 'The idea that inflation can be stabilised at around 5–10 per cent, with permanent benefits to growth, is pure and dangerous fantasy,' he said.[12] The Bank of England decision had effectively been taken by Brown and Blair then: Brown was supported by his economic adviser, Ed Balls, who had previously advocated it as a *Financial Times* journalist; Blair by his, Derek Scott. But it had been tentative, and only became firm after Brown discussed the arguments with Alan Greenspan, the chairman of the Federal Reserve, the United States independent central bank, on a visit in March 1997.[13]

Independence for the Bank of England was widely hailed as a masterstroke and lent substance to the post-election euphoria of an electorate retrospectively delighted with its decision. A fresh face and a basic level of competence was enough of a contrast to induce a heady change of national mood. Most parties get a post-election 'bounce' in opinion polls, as interviewees selectively recall voting for the winning side, but New Labour, having broken all polling records in Opposition, now soared to undreamt-of heights in government – and stayed there. Blair's approval rating was up an unprecedented twenty-five points two months later.[14] The residual shadows of trade union domination, hidden leftism and simple unfamiliarity fled in the light of the new dawn.

The City approved of Bank of England independence. Long-term interest rates instantly fell, on the assumption that inflation would be more rigorously controlled in future, despite the fact that Kenneth Clarke had recently been vindicated in resisting the advice of Eddie George, the Bank's Governor, to raise interest rates. The press hailed 'Flash Gordon', with only the hard-line Eurosceptics muttering about central bank independence being a condition of joining the single currency. It was hardly noticed that the move had not been endorsed either by the party or the people in the manifesto, which had said only: 'We will reform the Bank of England to ensure that decision-making on monetary policy is more effective, open, accountable and free from short-term political manipulation.' Nor that the new Cabinet had yet to meet. A decision of momentous importance for the future of the nation's economic policy and arguably the sovereignty of parliament had been taken – Brown proposing, Blair disposing – within the tiny inner core of New Labour in Opposition.

On Wednesday, Blair addressed his huge new parliamentary party on the morning before the new parliament assembled. Nick Brown, the Chief Whip, was forced to find a new venue at the last moment, because the Institution of Civil Engineers hall which had been booked in advance was not big enough for the 418 new Labour MPs – the 419th, Betty Boothroyd, had stood as Speaker and would that afternoon be re-elected to the post. The only place in Westminster big enough was the Church of England's synod chamber, so it was in this ecclesiastical setting that the new Prime Minister made a speech of biblical humility: 'We are not the masters. The people are the masters. We are the servants of the people.' This inverted the much-misquoted motto of triumphalism from the other Labour landslide, 'We are the masters now,' proclaimed by Clement Attlee's Attorney General, Sir Hartley Shawcross, in 1946.*

On Thursday, the new Cabinet met for the first time. 'The first Cabinet meeting could not have been more different from the last shadow Cabinet meeting. All the relationships between Tony Blair and Cabinet ministers were transformed. They turned like sunflowers to the sun,' according to one of those present. The deference shown to the first Labour Prime Minister to win a working majority for thirty-one years was not reflected in the next day's newspapers, which seized on Alastair Campbell's comment that the new Cabinet operated on first-name terms. According to the *Sun*, 'Tony Blair brushed aside the traditional formality of Cabinet meetings, telling colleagues: "Call me Tony." And he ordered ministers to call each other by their first names, not titles, ending a centuries-old tradition.' In fact, although Alex Allan, the Prime Minister's principal private secretary, had worried aloud about the formality of modes of address, Blair had simply suggested in passing that 'we' should continue to use first names, as an Opposition. This was not much of a change: John Major did the same when speaking to his ministers, although they usually called him 'Prime Minister'.

While Campbell briefed journalists on what had not happened at Cabinet, he also failed to tell them about what had happened, namely the decision, bounced by the Prime Minister, to set up a 'joint consultative committee' with senior Liberal Democrats. The Cabinet also approved the Queen's Speech, which would the following week set out the planned legislation for the coming parliamentary session.

The first week was all about presenting the new administration as dynamic – despite few policy differences with its predecessor – which also meant taking early and decisive control of the machinery of presentation. On Friday the week was rounded off by the announcement that, when parliamentary routine resumed after the debate on the Queen's Speech, the Prime Minister would make himself available to answer questions for thirty minutes every Wednesday instead of fifteen minutes on both Tuesdays and Thursdays. The twice-weekly jousts had set the

---

* *Hansard*, 2 April 1946, in fact records Shawcross – a moderate who later acquired the unshakeable tag of Sir Shortly Floorcross – as saying: 'We are the masters at the moment.'

weekly rhythm of the House of Commons since they were regularised as an experiment under Harold Macmillan in 1961.

Blair found Prime Minister's Questions a draining enough ordeal in Opposition, when all the rules favoured him. The Leader of the Opposition held the initiative by asking the questions, while the Prime Minister had to anticipate them; he could only ask three, while the Prime Minister had to answer as many as could be fitted in from other MPs as well; and he had nothing better to do with his time than think up clever questions, while the Prime Minister had a country to run. But Blair also knew, because every recent ex-Prime Minister had said so, that preparing for the twice-weekly duel of wits took up a great deal of time in government. Margaret Thatcher and John Major had both considered the idea of a single session and rejected it.[15] As early as in the middle of 1995, prompted by the Procedure select committee's inquiry into reform of Prime Minister's Questions, Blair asked Jonathan Powell to investigate the possibility of change. The select committee suggested that MPs should be required to give notice of more questions, a proposal which got nowhere, but Paddy Ashdown in his evidence to the committee suggested a single thirty-minute session, divided by subject into three ten-minute parts.[16]

Like independence for the Bank of England and a joint committee with a rival party, it was the kind of coup which could only be carried out by striking quickly. It had been agreed with Sir Robin Butler at his meeting with Blair in Islington at the start of the election campaign. Major opposed the change, and Betty Boothroyd was reluctant, rightly recognising it as a diminution of the power and prestige of the Commons. But the brute fact was that the timetabling of Commons business was ultimately controlled by the majority party.

Blair argued that he would be accountable to the House for exactly the same amount of time each week – more, in fact, because the ritual of MPs standing up to announce the number of their question before asking their 'supplementary' was abolished. Statistically, he did answer more questions in the Commons in his first seventeen months than Major did in his last eighteen.[17] He also spent more time than Major in the Chamber answering questions after his more frequent statements. But the frequency of Question Time rather than its length was an important factor in allowing the House to hold Prime Ministers continuously to account.

'They have done everything right while we did everything wrong in the first week,' said an admiring George Stephanopoulos, no longer at the White House and now in London to share in the victory of his ideological cousins.[18]

Bathed in limelight

Nor did the pace slow much in the second week. Blair walked from Downing Street to the Palace of Westminster, instead of being driven the 300 yards, to hear Her Majesty deliver Her Speech on Tuesday 14 May. Derry Irvine, now Lord Chancellor and therefore not only a Cabinet minister and head of the judiciary but also the presiding officer of the House of Lords, handed her the text and walked down the steps backwards. Much of the speech was about 'modernisation', but some rituals had been more modernised than others.

On 16 May, Blair went to Northern Ireland to show his commitment to the stalled peace talks. 'John Major had an incredible amount of concentration on the peace process. We knew of course that Tony Blair was going to carry it on,' said John Alderdice, leader of the cross-community Alliance Party, 'but the amount of his commitment at a personal level we couldn't be sure of – how could we be?' Blair cleverly sought simultaneously to reassure the Unionists that they would remain part of the United Kingdom for the lifetime of 'even the youngest', while not mentioning the point on which the talks had stuck: whether the IRA should disarm for its political wing, Sinn Fein, to take part.

It was not until 20 May that the General Secretary of the Trades Union Congress, John Monks, was allowed into Downing Street, a meeting so successfully downplayed that it was not even reported in the newspapers until two days later. If he noticed the ghosts of Frank Cousins, Hugh Scanlon and Joe Gormley coming out as he went in, he did not say so. He was followed by a more substantial ghost, when on 22 May Baroness Thatcher dropped in for a courtesy call. Again, the fact of the visit was suppressed, but this time only so that Alastair Campbell could give it to the Sunday papers in order to maximise the publicity. Once again, Blair had breathed new life into the legend to his own advantage. If there was anything in her handbag this time, it was Essence of National Leadership, and she anointed yet another 'chosen successor' with it. The meeting sent a signal to a large section of the electorate who admired her, who voted for Blair this time and on to whom he intended to hold. It was all part of New Labour's professional after-sales service.

Other ghosts rattled their chains. Lord Rothermere, owner of the *Daily Mail* and the London *Evening Standard*, took his seat in the Lords – on the Labour benches – on 21 May. 'This government is doing all the things the last one should have done and failed to do,' he said. He had hinted at his conversion before the election when he said: 'Tony Blair is a very capable, very charming, very astute man, full of enthusiasm and drive. He unquestionably comes from the British middle classes, as does his wife.'[19]

When Lord Rothermere died the next year, Blair attended the funeral and spoke, as did Thatcher, at the memorial service.

Blair's association with Thatcher did not speak only to Lord Rothermere's readers, it sent a signal overseas. The British landslide had prompted a frenzy of interest in the new alchemy of how to win elections, which suddenly made him the most popular boy on the international block. At his first European Union summit at Noordvijk, in the Netherlands, on 23 May, international interest in him was at fever pitch. That ensured a wide audience for his message of a new 'third way' in European politics, a phrase he had used before the election in relation to New Labour's economic policy but which he now deployed on a wider canvas.* It helped to make sense of the paradox of a social democrat who used some of Thatcher's language and who appeared to carry her endorsement. On 27 May he was in Paris to sign a security pact between Nato and Russia, which in retrospect laid the basis for stopping President Milosevic of Yugoslavia in Kosovo. Two days later, President Clinton and his wife Hillary came to London. The Cabinet's new status as audience rather than players was underlined when the US President spoke to them in Downing Street and they applauded.†

Blair's new overseas admirers were also reminded of Thatcher's handbag when, at a meeting of fellow-socialist leaders of EU countries at Malmo, Sweden, on 6 June, Blair warned them to abandon 'old-style' left-wing ideas of 'more spending or regulations'. He lectured them with the supreme self-confidence of someone who had just won a huge parliamentary majority:

> As I said to the British Labour Party a few years ago, we modernise or die . . . We have come here to share ideas, but yes certainly to provide leadership. I may say that people are now looking for who can provide leadership for this new block of people sharing the same values, who can now shape Europe.

It was arrogant and they hated it, especially Lionel Jospin, Prime Minister of France, who thought he had rehabilitated the 'old-style' ideas rather well. Blair even presumed to lecture his uneasy ideological colleagues on monetary union, from the standpoint of a country which had opted out of it and showed no sense of urgency about wanting to opt back in: 'Whether it looks like a weak currency or a strong one, if it masks unreformed economies, the strains in the system risk being too

---

*See p. 431.

†The event was not unprecedented, however: Richard Nixon had attended a meeting of Wilson's Cabinet in 1969.

great. There is no comfort in size alone.' They smiled with gritted teeth: this was not quite the emollient crowd-pleaser they had expected. Was it wise? It played well at home, asserting that Blair would not be a pushover in Europe, and it made his colleagues at Malmo realise that they would have to argue for their assumptions: they would not simply be taken for granted. But the speech was unnecessarily abrasive, and meant Blair had to work harder than he otherwise would have done to maintain a common front with his European allies during the Kosovo war, for example.

There was another big European Union get-together on 16 June, when the grand ambition of a new treaty to rewrite, simplify and democratise the Maastricht Treaty ended as a bureaucratic tidying-up exercise at the inter-governmental conference in Amsterdam. Blair proved himself both an adept negotiator and a shrewd showman. Through pushiness and chutzpah he managed to commandeer an environmental stunt on bicycles and emerge out in front for the cameras (the twenty-stone Helmut Kohl opted out of that one), and later reinforced the image of youthful vigour when he was filmed running between meetings.

Then it was off to Denver on 22 June for a meeting of G7, the world's seven largest industrial nations, plus Russia, which made what had started as an informal G3 the G8 international circus. Blair travelled by Concorde, chartered at a cost of £250,000 in a deal with British Airways to save flying time, some of the cost being recouped by charging journalists £3,700 each for the round trip.[20] Returning via New York for a United Nations summit on the environment, Blair rediscovered the thin green thread in New Labour's rich tapestry, and used his family to shield himself from any suggestion of opportunism:

> My three young children in London complain I am never at home. But if there is one summit they would want me at, it is this one. They know our decisions here will have a profound effect on the world they inherit. So I speak to you not just as the new British Prime Minister, but as a father.

The hard choices, however, were left to others, as he criticised the United States for failing to meet the targets set at the 1992 Rio de Janeiro summit on global warming. (The United Kingdom, by a fortuitous combination of recession and the switch from coal to more efficient gas for electricity generation, was on course to meet its target.) John Prescott had boasted on the *Today* programme soon after the election that he was going to be greener than John Gummer, his predecessor as Secretary of State for the Environment, which was harder than it looked because Gummer was at odds with his Cabinet colleagues in his commitment to the environmental cause. Prescott worked hard to help secure agreement on a legally-binding treaty to limit the 'greenhouse effect' of burning fossil fuels at the Kyoto summit in Japan in December 1997, identifying the awkward parties and criss-crossing the globe to be solicitous towards them beforehand. Even the United States signed the agreement, although it was not ratified by Congress. Blair took credit for Prescott's achievement when speaking to Labour Party or environmentalist audiences, but with only a limited sense of real engagement.

At the end of June there was a delicate piece of unfinished business, as Blair handed over Hong Kong to China, an event which had been agreed in 1898: when the music stopped, the parcel had only just been handed to him. He had not yet quite got the hang of looking solemn at these occasions, and so appeared nervous and uneasy as he met the Chinese leadership. But he succeeded in his aim of getting through the ceremonials with the minimum of fuss, in order to avoid awkward questions about Margaret Thatcher's betrayal of democratic rights there, or Britain's continuing obligations towards Hong Kong people who wanted to leave. Once again, he used his family as a credential of his integrity. 'My sister-in-law is Hong Kong Chinese,' he told American television, referring to his brother Bill's wife, Katy Tse.[21]

New Prime Ministers always find themselves swept up in foreign affairs more than they expect. Inevitably, some of Blair's staff felt he had been captured by the civil service and run around the world when he should have been back at base, driving forward the domestic machine, which had started well, but which was beginning to hit some obstacles and soft patches of inertia. Although Blair chose to make his first big speech as Prime Minister at the Aylesbury Estate, in Southwark, south London, on 2 June, because 'for eighteen years the poorest people in our country have been forgotten by government', it was clear that no one had any idea what was meant in practice by the 'radical reform of the welfare state' of which he blithely spoke. The refurbishment of the apartments of the new Lord Chancellor, Derry Irvine, including expensive authentic wallpaper, had been first reported on 12 June. And Gordon Brown's first Budget had been delayed by unexpected complexities.

When the Budget came on 2 July, however, it was hailed a triumph despite an unexpected tax rise amounting to £5 billion a year from the abolition of tax relief on the investment income of company pension schemes. This was rather more significant than the windfall tax, which amounted to a one-off charge of the same amount, accepted with good grace by the privatised utilities on which it was levied. The Conservatives pointed out in vain that Blair had said before the election that he had 'no plans to increase tax at all'.[22]

Beyond that, there was relatively little for Brown to announce. One of the reasons for the delay was that he wanted to announce his Working Families Tax Credit, which he saw as an important incentive to move people 'from welfare to work', modelled on the Earned Income Tax Credit in the United States, but the scheme needed too much work and he was forced to postpone it until his second Budget. That did not prevent him claiming his measures were historic: 'You have got to look back to the creation of the welfare state in 1908 and 1911 under Lloyd George, and then to the Forties and the changes that were brought about in the welfare state then, and say that this is the next link.'[23] He named Lloyd George, a Chancellor who became Prime Minister, as the predecessor he most admired. Blair encouraged him in his ambition: 'He is one of the cleverest people in British politics in a very long time and we are lucky to have him. He has the qualities of Lloyd George, tremendous drive and ability and humanity as well.'[24]

The British people shared the Prime Minister's high opinion of him, and the Chancellor's high opinion of himself. According to a Gallup poll in the *Daily Telegraph* on 5 July, this was the most popular Budget since opinion polling began.

Personal lives

Towards the end of the hundred-day period, Blair gave simultaneous personal interviews to the *Sun* and the *Mirror*, on 29 July. The pro-Murdoch bias of the pre-election period was moderating, although the bias towards self-parody increased. To the *Sun* he said: 'Sometimes I forget I'm Prime Minister. To me, I'm just Tony Blair.' To the *Mirror*, he declared:

> For me the important thing is to keep in touch with the people all the time. Every week I like to go out and just spend time with people in all parts of the country. I like to talk to people and make them feel I'm approachable and that their concerns are the concerns that I have too.

Indeed, one of the justifications for reducing the frequency of his exposure to questions in the Commons was the promise that he would take questions from the general public once a month. In Worcester on 13 June, he had fielded questions in threes from an invited audience, using the 'jacket off' format of the Clause IV and manifesto ballot road shows among Labour Party members. Blair genuinely relished these sessions, a hybrid of seminar, chat show and evangelical study group. It was a forum that suited him, in which he came across as persuasive, sincere and human. There was a good democratic case for them as a form of direct popular accountability, if a fair way of admitting a representative cross-section of people could be devised. However, the promise of a monthly 'People's Questions' was insincere. The pressure on prime ministerial time meant they became an irregular fixture, revived at moments when the public or the party needed to be persuaded of the case for welfare reform, Alun Michael or Frank Dobson. Nevertheless, Blair was entitled to claim to be the first Prime Minister to hold such sessions so often, and the grass-roots voter contact was a useful supplement to the ritual point-scoring of the House of Commons.

Two days after he declared to the *Sun*, 'You must never forget that what the public giveth, the public can take away,' the public in Uxbridge took away a little of Blair's shine. He had been persuaded to ditch the convention that Prime Ministers do not campaign in by-elections by Philip Gould, his polling adviser. Sir Michael Shersby held the formerly safe Conservative seat with a majority over Labour of just 1.8 per cent at the General Election and when he died soon afterwards Gould's focus groups in the constituency suggested the momentum of post-election euphoria would deliver the seat for New Labour. His professional pessimism had been overthrown on 2 May. But if there is one thing voters dislike it is being taken for granted, and they preferred the rootedly local candidate John Randall, owner of the Randalls of Uxbridge department store, to Andrew Slaughter, the loyalist Labour candidate imposed from London on a reluctant local party.

At the end of Harold Wilson's first hundred days in January 1965, Labour lost the Leyton by-election. Iain Macleod mockingly said of that period that 'the Prime Minister was a combination of John Fitzgerald Kennedy and Napoleon'.[25] Blair's only electoral setback at the end of his first hundred days, by contrast, was to fail to win a seat from the opposition.

The period ended on an ambiguous note. The day before the Blair family set off to Geoffrey Robinson's villa in San Gimignano – the full import of their destination had yet to make itself felt – Alastair Campbell was the bringer of bad news which the *News of the World* was planning to publish that Sunday. Robin Cook's affair with his assistant, Gaynor Regan, was about to become public. Campbell has since been unfairly accused of issuing the Foreign Secretary with an ultimatum, telling him that he must choose between Gaynor and his wife, Margaret. However, Cook accepted responsibility for making a decision he had already avoided for too long, attempting to conceal the relationship long after it was an open secret in internal Labour circles. Campbell got through on a mobile phone to Cook in a car travelling between terminals at Heathrow and sitting next to Margaret, with whom he was about to embark on a 'patch-it-up' holiday. Campbell's words were to the effect that 'clarity in news management' was the only way through. Margaret remembered, in retrospect, that her husband became 'very still and very silent'. It was obvious that his choice could not be postponed for more than a few hours. On arriving at Terminal Four he ordered various staff out of the VIP lounge and told his wife: 'I am afraid there won't be any holiday, Margaret. It's cancelled. The *News of the World* is running the story of my affair with Gaynor on Sunday. I can't leave the country. I think you and I should part.'[26] Margaret knew about Gaynor, but had assumed the affair was over and hoped the holiday would be a chance to rebuild. According to his biographer, Cook 'knew he could not go on with the holiday with Margaret' and 'nor could he ditch Gaynor'.[27]

It was a difficult situation, with which Blair seemed deeply uncomfortable. He too had known about Regan for some time. He may have been relieved that the relationship had not become public before the election, but he must also have guessed that disclosure could not be postponed for ever. When he spoke to Cook in the VIP lounge after he had cancelled his holiday and his marriage, Blair merely reassured him that his job was safe.[28] He then wrote a letter to Margaret which, for once, misjudged its recipient. She paraphrased it as saying he was 'sorry that the press continues to harass you' and that 'Cherie and I are thinking about you', and was deeply offended that it failed to express any sadness about the ending of her marriage. 'It was a dreadful, unfeeling letter,' she said, which 'grated like sand on raw skin'.[29] She dashed off an angry reply, which produced an immediate telephone call from Peter Mandelson, who had been left with the delicate task of damage limitation while Blair and Campbell were both on holiday in Italy. He was solicitous and tried, ultimately without success, to dissuade her from taking revenge on her husband, which she did in a book published eighteen months later.

The crisis further damaged Cook's standing, while having little lasting effect on the government. It did, however, expose the ambiguity of Blair's advocacy of 'family values' which would also shortly come into awkward proximity with Bill Clinton's private parts.

Great expectations

Blair arrived in Downing Street uniquely well-placed to exploit the potential power of the Prime Minister's office. In the Cabinet he was, like Harold Wilson in 1964, unencumbered by potential threats to his leadership. Gordon Brown's ambition was fierce but could only be advanced through loyalty. The views of party members may have been more traditionalist than his, but they had signed up to 'New Labour', their expectations were numbed and there was no alternative parliamentary leader of the status of Aneurin Bevan or Tony Benn.

To an unusual extent, Labour's election victory had been his alone, with Brown the only member of his Cabinet who had also been a member of the inner core which planned and executed it. Although ministers like Jack Straw and David Blunkett were supremely well-prepared in their policy areas, and were well supported by the civil servants in their departments, they were no match for a Prime Minister who entered office with a plan to take unprecedented power over policy and presentation to the centre.

In the House of Commons, of course, Blair's huge majority gave him a dominance so total that the change to Prime Minister's Questions was only a small part of an inevitable diminution of the Chamber's significance. The election of William Hague as Conservative leader on 19 June, by the surprisingly large margin of 92 votes to 70 over Kenneth Clarke, had contradictory effects. Hague was a brilliant Commons performer who repeatedly embarrassed Blair at Questions, although less so in debates. On the other hand, Clarke would have been – assuming he could have held the Conservative Party together – a more serious and confident challenger for the middle ground which Blair had made his own.

Such early success was bound to conceal dangers. Paradoxically, Blair's very modesty begat a form of arrogance. Because the party had refused to conceive of such a huge victory, the election when it came was interpreted as the more miraculous. There was a danger that he might think, like other successful leaders before him, that he had a transcendent and infallible understanding of 'the people', although it was a danger which Blair mostly resisted in his first few years in government.

His success also invested some of his more extravagant rhetoric with a weight it could not bear. Rhetorically, the scale of his ambition was unlimited: to remoralise British society; to refound the welfare state; to create a coalition of political forces that would dominate the whole of the twenty-first century; to secure peace in Northern Ireland; to provide modernising leadership for the whole of the European Union; to make Britain a 'beacon to the world';[30] and even to eliminate world poverty.[31]

Against those ambitions, the inevitable restoration of politics as usual, which began with the Bernie Ecclestone affair in November and the Labour Party rebellion over the cut in lone parent benefit in December, was bound to be more disappointing than if his majority had been smaller. His decisiveness on coming to office had been planned for a closer outcome. Not surprisingly, perhaps, he failed to adjust to the greater leverage he held as a result of the most stunning election victory since 1945. He could have had the Liberal Democrats in his Cabinet and left out more or less who he liked. He could have started to prepare the ground of public opinion on the euro earlier – instead of letting the issue lie until the autumn, when emergency remedial work was needed. And he could have taken more care to ensure that the rhetoric of humility, of service and of propriety in public life would not be so easily undermined by carelessness or worse.

Notes

1. The Beveridge Lecture, Toynbee Hall, London, 18 March 1999.
2. George Stephanopoulos, *All Too Human*, pp. 108–20.
3. Robert Harris, *Talk* magazine, May 2000.
4. Margaret Thatcher, *The Downing Street Years*, p. 18.
5. Fiona Millar, *Today* newspaper, 22 July 1994.
6. Lynda Lee-Potter, *Daily Mail*, 6 January 1999.
7. *Ibid.*, 17 April 1998.
8. *Sun*, 24 June 1997.
9. *Independent*, 31 May 1997.
10. Interview, *Sun*, 29 July 1997.
11. BBC Radio 4, *The John Humphrys Interview*, 8 June 1995.
12. Mais lecture, 22 May 1995.
13. For a good account, see Hugh Pym and Nick Kochan, *Gordon Brown*, pp. 5–16.
14. Peter Kellner, *Observer*, 6 July 1997.
15. Dennis Kavanagh and Anthony Seldon, *The Powers Behind the Prime Minister*, p. 235.
16. Peter Riddell, *The Times*, 17 July 1995.
17. Kavanagh and Seldon, *The Powers Behind the Prime Minister*, p. 272.
18. Speech to Institute of Public Relations, 12 May 1997.
19. *Financial Times*, 27 April 1997.
20. *Daily Telegraph*, 5 June 1997.
21. Interview on ABC television, 22 June 1997.
22. In answer to questions at a 'Business Breakfast' organised by the Birmingham Chamber of Commerce, 20 September 1995.
23. Interview, *Sunday Telegraph*, 6 July 1997.
24. *Mirror*, 29 July 1997.
25. Speech in the Commons, March 1966, quoted in Robert Shepherd, *Iain Macleod*, pp. 419–20.
26. Margaret Cook, *A Slight and Delicate Creature*, pp. 2–3.
27. John Kampfner, *Robin Cook*, p. 154.
28. Cook, *A Slight and Delicate Creature*, p. 3.
29. *Ibid.*, pp. 279–80; Kampfner, *Robin Cook*, pp. 164–5.
30. Speech to Labour Party conference, Brighton, 30 September 1997.
31. Department for International Development White Paper, 'Eliminating World Poverty', November 1997.

18

Blair and the Crown

Death of Diana, 31 August 1997

> 'I am from the Disraeli school of Prime Ministers in their relations with the monarch.'
>
> —*Tony Blair, 1997*

By August 1997, after a hundred days in office, it seemed Blair's honeymoon with the electorate must come to an end soon. Instead, it went on and on. The strategy of drawing every centre of power or influence into the New Labour net was paying rich dividends. This was the product of Blair's ambition – pursued after the election as vigorously as before – to establish his own 'hegemony' over British society, a centrist version of Margaret Thatcher's dominance of all areas of national life. His was the biggest tent pitched on the field of British politics in time of peace and relative economic well-being.

Anyone with any purchase on public life was invited into Blair's marquee: business leaders; newspaper proprietors, editors and what the Americans call big-foot columnists; pop stars, sports stars, architects, fashion designers, celebrities, rich people; Liberal Democrats, soft Conservatives – and some hard ones, including Baroness Thatcher; foreign leaders; the churches; and the royal family. Long before the election, Blair had captured this citadel, a house divided against itself which had long ceased to be an efficient part of the constitution and was rapidly ceasing to be dignified either, but which still – as Diana's death showed – held a power of symbolism and sentiment.

Blair and Prince Charles first met when Blair was Labour's spokesman on employment. After he became leader, he was invited to dinner at St James's Palace. They had in common the search for popular policies on the 'non-political' centre ground, and the Prince had used the word 'stakeholder' in his speeches long before Blair made his speech in Singapore. They talked about education and the work of the Prince's Trust, running homework clubs and schemes for the young unemployed. In the summer of 1996 they spoke again when the Prince came up with a plan to rewrite the monarchy's Clause IV. Charles's group of advisers sketched out plans to modernise the monarchy over the longer term – by implication, when he succeeded his mother. Blair had to strike a balance in his relations with a fellow moderniser and with the Queen.

This was easy, however, compared with holding the ring of Charles's failed marriage. One of the more delicate problems facing the incoming Prime Minister was Charles's evident desire to marry Camilla Parker Bowles in the teeth of public hostility. The loser in the public relations battle with Diana – who gave her *Panorama* interview in November 1995 – was bound to want to hitch himself to New Labour's bandwagon. No wonder, then, that Charles should have appeared to endorse the new Prime Minister in a television interview after the election; in particular, he welcomed the government's emphasis on school standards.[1]

Typically, Blair kept lines open to both camps (although Cherie privately took Diana's side against Charles, according to a friend). Diana had controversially shared a platform with Jack Straw before the election at a conference on homelessness. After the election she was invited to Chequers for lunch with Prince William, who played football in the grounds with Euan and Nicky. In August 1997, Blair satisfied her desire for some kind of public role by appointing her a roving 'ambassador' for humanitarian causes. She repaid him with a party-political attack on the record of the previous Conservative government on landmines as 'hopeless', in an interview at the start of a trip to France with her boyfriend Dodi Fayed.[2]

The new Disraeli

At two o'clock in the morning of Sunday, 31 August, the Prime Minister was woken by the telephone. It was the duty clerk at Number Ten, with the news that Diana had been seriously injured in a car crash in Paris. He was at his constituency home, Myrobella, in Trimdon. He did not go back to sleep and was still awake when the phone rang again at three-thirty. It was a Private Secretary calling from his home to say Diana, Dodi Fayed and their driver were all dead. Alastair Campbell, who had been wakened in his house in London, was the next on the line. 'This is going to produce real public grief on a scale that is hard to imagine,' Blair told him.[3] They both immediately recognised it as the kind of moment which tested a Prime Minister. He was due to go to church in Sedgefield later that morning. The television cameras would be there. He would have to speak for a nation unable quite to believe what it was hearing.

Most of the Prime Minister's entourage had returned to London the night before, after a party meeting in neighbouring Darlington, happy to take the weekend off. One secretary, one of the Downing Street 'garden girls', stayed behind at Myrobella. Blair asked her to call Phil Wilson, one of the Famous Five who had helped him win the seat in 1983. He had been woken early in the morning by his young son, puzzled by the lack of children's cartoons on the television, so he was expecting the call. The Prime Minister would need someone to go on ahead and talk to the journalists at the church, could he come over? Wilson put on a black tie and grabbed a spare in case Blair had not got one. When he arrived at Myrobella, he was about to burst into Blair's study as he had been so used to doing in the past when the secretary stopped him. 'He's on the phone,' she said.

'Yeah?' said Wilson.

'It's the Queen,' the secretary explained. Wilson waited in the hall. When Blair emerged, Wilson offered him the spare tie.

'I think I'll have the one you're wearing, Phil,' said Blair, absently. 'Have you any cufflinks?' Wilson took off his tie and phoned another member of the Famous Five, Paul Trippett. Trippett had been up late the night before and had heard of the car crash.

'What, is she dead?' he asked, after cursing Wilson for waking him.

'Yes,' said Wilson, urgently. 'Have you got any cufflinks?'

When Blair emerged from his car outside St Mary's church a little later, suitably attired, he showed just how surefooted he and Campbell were in judging the public mood. In between his telephone conversations with the Queen and Prince Charles, the two of them had rehearsed the words and style of Blair's address. Campbell said: 'It was both of us going back and forth. A dialogue. You have to remember we both knew and liked her very much. It was shocking. We'd both break off. "How could this have happened?" It was an important moment.'[4]

Four months after becoming Prime Minister, Blair spoke for a nation about to go into unusually demonstrative mourning:

> I feel like everyone else in this country today. I am utterly devastated . . . People everywhere, not just here in Britain, kept faith with Princess Diana. They liked her, they loved her, they regarded her as one of the people. She was the people's princess and that is how she will stay, how she will remain in our hearts and our memories for ever.

The 'people's princess' was the phrase that stuck in the mind, cleverly deploying the adjective used by the 'people's party' during the election campaign. It later emerged that Campbell had suggested it. 'Tony had to say something that united and settled the country and articulated what people were feeling,' Campbell said. 'It was Tony who said it.'[5] In fact, he may have picked it up subliminally from Julie Burchill, of all people, who had applied it to Diana when she was alive.[6]

It was a strange moment. Campbell's claim that he and Blair 'knew and liked her very much' was based on little contact and less meeting of minds. It was no doubt genuine enough on a personal level, but it was mocked by the Ghost of Campbell Past, who until 1994 had filled his column in the *Today* newspaper with republican invective based on the simple thesis: 'The class system, with the royal family at its apex, is wrong.'[7] In those days he was often exuberantly rude towards Diana: 'She is the reasonably pretty, not very bright, very manipulative separated wife of our adulterous future king.'[8]

Between them, however, Blair and Campbell used the strange public mood of the next few weeks to strengthen the bond not just between the new Labour government and the people but between it and the monarchy. It was a dangerous time for the Queen and Prince Charles: they had been seen as Diana's oppressors, and the wave of emotion released by her death threatened a quasi-republican backlash. For a time the Downing Street machine effectively handled public relations for the royal family as well as the Prime Minister, and saved the monarchy from sinking into eighteenth-century ridicule and contempt. Blair lent them his huge democratic mandate and his media management skills. He was there at RAF Northolt when Diana's body was flown back from France. He made a statement outside Number Ten insisting – in the face of tabloid newspaper condemnation of the Queen for failing to rend her garments and wail in public – that the royal family shared 'our' grief over Diana. And he was there in Westminster Abbey for the funeral a week after her death, reading the 'when I was a child, I spoke like a child' passage from Corinthians with such quivering emotion that it was later reprinted in a collection of 'speeches that changed the world'.[9] It was a remarkable appropriation of a national event for partly political purposes.

The Spencer family had wanted a private funeral and the Queen was inclined to let them. But Blair, with Prince Charles's support, negotiated a 'unique funeral for a unique person'. A 'war room' was set up in Buckingham Palace, and daily planning meetings were attended by Campbell, Anji Hunter or Hilary Coffman, who had worked in the press office of four successive Labour Party leaders and who had helped organise John Smith's Westminster Abbey memorial service. Blair tactfully advised the Queen to fly the flag at half-mast over Buckingham Palace as demanded by the tabloid newspapers, regardless of protocol, and to extend the route of the funeral procession to allow more people to see it.

The reaction to Diana's death prompted a great deal of comment on how the traditionally repressed British had discovered how to express their emotions in public. What was more certain was that the British had discovered a Prime Minister who knew how to express their emotions in public, and that the royal family was now deeply in Blair's debt.

Campbell was not the only late convert to the monarchist cause among Blair's close political friends. Peter Mandelson had been so unmoved by the public display of royalist fervour on the day of Charles and Diana's wedding on 29 July 1981, that he went on a 'Republican Away-Day' to France with, among others, Alan Haworth, Harriet Harman and Jack Dromey, all friends of the Blairs in Hackney.[10] By the time Blair became Prime Minister, however, Mandelson was an occasional guest of Prince Charles and Camilla.

Blair's own anti-Establishment instincts had been sublimated for even longer. The only hint of defiance came from Cherie, who did not curtsey when she and her husband went to see the Queen at Balmoral after Diana's funeral – nor, more publicly, at the funeral itself.* Her husband, on the other hand, told the Queen in a fawning speech at her fiftieth wedding anniversary celebrations three months later: 'I am from the Disraeli school of Prime Ministers in their relations with the monarch.' He presumably meant to refer to the One Nation Tory's personal admiration of Victoria rather than to his reputation for wily flattery for political ends. 'You are our Queen. We respect and cherish you. You are, simply, the best of British.'

The object of flattery is always grateful, and the Queen responded with a speech which, apart from reminding him he had 'inherited' a sound economy, endorsed New Labour: 'I believe that there is an air of confidence in this country of ours just now.'

Antidisestablishmentarianism

One of the subjects on which Blair and the Queen agreed was that the Church of England should remain the country's established church, with

---

*After her failure to bend a knee was noted in the press, she started to curtsey at public events, such as the Millennium celebrations at the Dome, but continued to stand up straight in private meetings.

the monarch as its head. Before the election, Blair had defended establishment and indicated to Chris Bryant, who was then chairman of the Christian Socialist Movement, that if Labour won the Church of England would remain established as long as he were Prime Minister.

His conservatism on this issue was surprising in the light of the fact that he was married to a Roman Catholic and that he was, as he described himself, 'an ecumenical Christian'.[11] Like Prince Charles, he was careful of the sensibilities of other religions which had significant followings in Britain, emphasising the common ground between what he once called the 'Abrahamic' religions, Judaism, Christianity and Islam.[12] However, he argued that the fact that the Church of England was supposed to be for everyone embodied the principle of inclusiveness.

He was similarly reluctant to press the other elements of modernising church–state relations which had been encompassed by Prince Charles's advisory group. As well as proposing at some point in the future ending the monarch's status as 'Supreme Head and Governor' of the Church of England, the group wanted an end to the bar on marrying a Roman Catholic and on elder daughters succeeding to the throne.

Blair had no deep or organic attachment to the idea of a monarchy, but recoiled instinctively from the political and administrative complications of an alternative. In order to put sand on the slippery slope, therefore, he resisted even the most limited of further reforms. Lifting the ban on the monarch marrying a Roman Catholic would be 'complex in the extreme', he concluded in a letter explaining that he had 'no plans' to change the law.[13] In a written answer in the Commons a little later, he remembered to add that 'the government have always stood firmly against discrimination in all its forms, including against Roman Catholics, and will continue to do so'.[14]

In his relations with the Crown, then, Blair showed himself to be a conservative, and all the more effective for the veneer of radicalism. His true views on the monarchy were as elusive as on almost everything else. The assumptions of his friends – and of his wife – tended towards moderate republicanism. His own ecumenical religious belief – and his wife's Roman Catholicism – might have prompted him to question the Queen's place at the head of his own Church of England. But he took the politically convenient line, and ignored the glaring logical contradictions this presented.

Notes

1. BBC1, *Breakfast With Frost*, 15 June 1997.
2. *Le Monde*, 27 August 1997.
3. *Sunday Times*, 7 September 1997.
4. *Guardian*, 4 April 1998.
5. *Ibid.*
6. Peter Oborne, *Alastair Campbell*, p. 7.
7. *Today*, 28 April 1994.
8. *Ibid.*, 8 April 1993.
9. 1 Corinthians 13:11; Owen Collins, editor, *Speeches that Changed the World*, HarperCollins, 1998: other contributors included Moses, delivering the Ten Commandments, and Nelson Mandela.
10. *Mail on Sunday*, 15 November 1998.
11. *Sunday Telegraph*, 7 April 1996.
12. Interview, *Daily Telegraph*, 20 October 1999.
13. Letter to Lord James Douglas Hamilton, Conservative whip in the Scottish Parliament, 29 October 1999.
14. Parliamentary written answer to Roseanna Cunningham, 13 December 1999.

19

Vicar of St Albion

The Church's Nominations Rejected, September 1997

'Jesus was a moderniser.'
—*Tony Blair, 1996*

A Prime Minister who did not usually attend Church of England services, Blair caused a Trollopian flurry in September 1997 by rejecting both of the candidates put forward by the Anglican Church to succeed David Sheppard as Bishop of Liverpool. Margaret Thatcher had caused friction by twice insisting that the Church's second preference be appointed, but no prime minister had rejected *both* the Church's nominees since 1977, when James Callaghan set up the system by which the Church proposed and the Prime Minister disposed.*

As Prime Minister, Blair usually went with his family to the Church of the Immaculate Heart of Mary, a modern redbrick hut in Great Missenden, near Chequers, or to Westminster cathedral if they were in Downing Street at the weekend. 'My wife is Catholic, my kids are brought up as Catholics,' he once explained. 'I have gone to Mass with them for years because I believe it's important for a family to worship together. I wouldn't want to go to an Anglican or Protestant church when my wife and kids are going to a Catholic one.'[1]

It was an important part of Blair's attempt to lead as normal a life with his family as possible, he said:

*Thatcher insisted on Graham Leonard for London in 1981 and Mark Santer for Birmingham in 1987 (Hugo Young, *One of Us*, p. 422); after this the Church ceased to rank its candidates in order of preference.

> When we first started going to Chequers, someone said, 'We'll get a vicar to come in and take a family service so you don't have to go out.'
>
> I thought, 'He must be joking. Going to church is one of the few times we get out and actually mix with people.'[2]

Blair saw no reason why this desire to be with his family should require him to give up the Church of England. Nor would it be required by what must be assumed to be Cherie's liberal or even radical Roman Catholicism.*

When asked if he would convert to Catholicism, Blair said: 'I am not proposing to do that.'[3] Asked the same question on another occasion, he said: 'Surely, being a Christian is what is important.'[4]

His extreme ecumenicism in both politics and religion certainly makes him an unlikely convert. Even if there is an element of political opportunism in his openness to all denominations and keen interest in all main religions, there is a seriousness to his study which is unmistakable and impressive. He is the first Prime Minister since Gladstone to read the Bible habitually. 'As a private individual, I find prayer a source of solace and I read the Gospels. They are compelling texts, and a most extraordinary expression of sensitive human values. I also read the Old Testament, which is in some ways more detailed and vivid than the New Testament.'[5] The positive write-up for the part shared with Judaism was at a tangent to his own Jesus-centred faith, but would go down well with religious Jews.

He was the first Prime Minister to have read the Koran, which he has done three times, including once on holiday in Portugal in January 2000. He told *Muslim News*: 'If you read the Koran, it is so clear . . . the concept of love and fellowship as the guiding spirits of humanity.' He described Islam as 'a deeply reflective, peaceful, very beautiful religious faith'.[6] It took some chutzpah to tell Muslims what their religion meant, but he interpreted the central truths of all major faiths as the same: Christianity, for example, was 'full of mercy and compassion'.[7]

This broadmindedness led to conflict with more doctrinal Christians. Blair had taken communion with his family at the Roman Catholic Church of St Joan of Arc in Islington since they moved there in 1986. The sacrament of the eucharist, taking bread and wine as the body of Christ, was important to him, although he held that it was a universal

---

*One of the few clues to the nature of Cherie's religious beliefs was her comment that 'a good primary school is worth a Mass' to a Labour MP who knew Blair well in the mid-1980s. Given the universal description of her as 'devout', however, this should be put down to self-deprecation rather than cynicism.

Christian service rather than the rite of a particular church.* He liked to quote Mark: 'Sabbath was made for man, not man for the Sabbath.'[8]

A new priest arrived at the church in 1996, however, an event which coincided with new guidance for Catholic churches in the British Isles on who was allowed to take communion. Even for inter-church families, the new rules forbade non-Catholics from taking part except in cases of 'grave and pressing spiritual need', or on special occasions such as the confirmation of children in mixed-denomination families.

The fact that the non-Catholic in this case was likely to become Prime Minister prompted the issue to be referred upwards. Cardinal Basil Hume, the head of the Roman Catholic church in England and Wales, wrote to Blair in June 1996 and asked him not to take communion at his family's church. It was all right to do so when in Tuscany for the summer holidays, said Hume, as there was no Anglican church nearby, but there were plenty in London.

Blair had no choice but to accept the Cardinal's ruling, but made it plain that he did not agree with it. He wrote back to say he would refrain from receiving communion if it really caused a problem for the Catholic church. But, he added, 'I wonder what Jesus would have made of it.'

His letter revealed a theological presumption greater even than Margaret Thatcher's lecture to the Assembly of the Church of Scotland in 1988. It was also interesting as a pointer to the rootedness of Blair's faith in the historical person of Jesus, which in turn sheds sceptical light on the assumption, encouraged by wishful-thinking Catholic converts, that Blair is really One of Them. The style of religious thought which discusses Jesus the man tends to be Protestant, while Catholics who lay a similar emphasis on the humanity of Christ tend to be dissidents, such as Hans Küng, the Swiss theologian whom Blair admired. Al Gore, a Southern Baptist, said when running for promotion to President in 2000, that he often asked himself: '"WWJD?" for a saying that's popular in my faith, "What Would Jesus Do?"'[9]

Despite lecturing Cardinal Hume on what Jesus might have thought of the rules for church services, Blair seemed to be on good terms with him. Unlike previous Roman Catholic leaders, Hume was not afraid to speak out against what he saw as the social damage inflicted by Conservative policies, especially under Margaret Thatcher. Before he died in 1999, Tony

*Blair asked for the ecumenical service at the start of Labour conference in 1997 to include for the first time the celebration of the eucharist, and representatives of Anglican, Roman Catholic and Methodist churches took part (Alan Wilkinson, *Christian Socialism*, p. 236).

and Cherie were among the last visitors to pay their respects on his deathbed.

Pontius Pilate on the road to Damascus

Nor was Blair's brush with Cardinal Hume an isolated excursion into theological debate. Over dinner with A. H. ('Chelly') Halsey, the distinguished sociologist and custodian of the tradition of English ethical socialism, in 1995, Blair described Pontius Pilate as 'the second most interesting character in the New Testament'. Professor Halsey objected that socialists ought to prefer the Good Samaritan, but Blair 'begged me to understand that the powerful were also deserving of our political sympathy'.[10] It was a theme he developed in one of his most extraordinary articles, a personal reflection on the meaning of Easter published in the *Sunday Telegraph* the following Easter Sunday, 7 April 1996:

> One of the things that lends power to the Gospels is that the characters are so real. Pilate is fascinating because he is so obviously human and imperfect, torn between principle and political reality. Were the Gospels simply a didactic tale, his choice would be remembered as a simple one. But it is not described in this way.
>
> The intriguing thing about Pilate is the degree to which he tried to do the good thing rather than the bad. He commands our moral attention not because he was a bad man, but because he was so nearly a good man. One can imagine him agonising, seeing that Jesus had done nothing wrong, and wishing to release him. Just as easily, however, one can envisage Pilate's advisers telling him of the risks, warning him not to cause a riot or inflame Jewish opinion. It is a timeless parable of political life.
>
> It is possible to view Pilate as the archetypal politician, caught on the horns of an age-old political dilemma. We know he did wrong, yet his is the struggle between what is right and what is expedient that has occurred throughout history. The Munich agreement of 1938 was a classic example of this, as were the debates surrounding the Great Reform Act of 1832 and the Corn Laws. And it is not always clear, even in retrospect, what is, in truth, right. Should we do what appears principled or what is politically expedient? Do you apply a utilitarian test or what is morally absolute?

After such an audacious sweep of historical references, he could safely avoid answering either of these questions. However, among the bland generalities which were Blair's great strength, the meditation on Pilate was jarringly unexpected.

The *Sunday Telegraph* article had started life as a tape-recorded conversation with Matthew d'Ancona, a columnist on the newspaper. Blair then made minor amendments to the transcribed version. It was during these discussions about the text that he let slip the highly suggestive observation: 'Jesus was a moderniser.'*

In the text of the article itself Blair observed that the Gospels were characterised by a restless searching after truth: 'Jesus challenged, he changed, he asked why.'

The extent to which Blair identifies his political practice with his religious belief is unusual among twentieth-century Prime Ministers. Even with Thatcher, there was a sense that her Methodism was like a recovered memory, part of an invented internal architecture which helped present herself as consistent.[11] Most other Prime Ministers, and all four previous Labour Prime Ministers, were agnostics or atheists.†

Blair shares his Christianity with three Labour leaders, Keir Hardie, George Lansbury and John Smith, all of whom explicitly identified their religious with their political missions and none of whom became Prime Minister. In his Easter 1996 *Sunday Telegraph* article, Blair said: 'My view of Christian values led me to oppose what I perceived to be a narrow view of self-interest that Conservatism – particularly its modern, more right-wing form – represents.' There was an outcry from Conservative politicians and press who accused him of claiming that Tories were un-Christian. Which, in effect, he had.

The difficult question was always going to be how to put 'Christian values' into practice. In his article, Blair had hinted at the direction in which he wanted to go when he talked about sin – a word which 'seems old-fashioned today', he admitted:

> Yet the concept is simple and important. In theological terms, it is alienation from God. In everyday terms, it is the acknowledgement of right and wrong. It is the rejection of a purely libertarian ethos. This is an area that will become of increasing importance in politics.

Aware that this begged a few questions, he went on: 'I don't mean "sin" in the sense of personal morality, but there is a desire in the modern world to retrieve and re-establish a sense of values, of common norms of

---

*The off-the-record comment was revealed by Dominic Lawson, editor of the *Sunday Telegraph*, in a long personal article entitled, 'Mr Blair does not deserve our faith', on 27 April 1997, just before the election. Lawson took offence that Blair should have 'identified himself, however unwittingly, with the Messiah'.

†Stanley Baldwin and Alec Douglas-Home were serious and sincere believers, Harold Macmillan less serious. Ramsay MacDonald was not an obviously religious man. Clement Attlee told his biographer, Kenneth Harris, he had no faith. Harold Wilson claimed to be a believer, although as his wife, Mary, commented: 'Religion was part of his tradition.' Kenneth O. Morgan says of Callaghan: 'he lost his religious views altogether' when he left home (*Callaghan*, p. 15).

conduct.' This only raised further questions – all morality is by definition social. If he were trying to get away from the old problem of seeming 'judgmental' about divorce, abortion or homosexuality, these were frowned on precisely because they broke 'common norms of conduct'. He ended up saying either nothing very much, or got himself into precisely the same difficulties as the moralists of the right from whom he attempted to separate himself.

Those difficulties were illustrated when his personal choice, James Jones, finally took over as Bishop of Liverpool in November 1998.* Jones had already criticised Robin Cook over the break-up of his marriage, declaring: 'You cannot with moral consistency say, "I will not break my promises to the electorate but it is okay for me to break my promises to my wife."'[12] And he marked his installation with an appearance on BBC2's *Newsnight* welcoming the government's Green Paper on the family for its declaration that 'marriage is still the surest foundation for raising children'.

However, the document also asserted that 'this does not mean trying to make people marry, or criticising or penalising people who choose not to. We do not believe that government should interfere in people's lives in this way.'[13]

Blair himself had tried and failed to elucidate that contradiction in an article in that morning's *Sun*: 'I know that some people choose not to marry,' he wrote (his press secretary, Alastair Campbell, who presumably had a hand in drafting the *Sun* article, was one of them):

> That is their right, and it is not for the government to tell them what to do. But for the majority who think marriage is for them, it is right for government to help. This does not mean tax breaks to bribe people to marry. Or penalising people who choose not to. It means supporting those who choose to marry.[14]

In other words, the government must encourage marriage but must not discourage non-marriage.

Jones ignored the second half of the message, and continued to disagree with the government over, for example, repealing the ban on the 'promotion' of homosexuality. But Blair had chosen him precisely because he thought a wishy-washy liberal leftie would be wrong for Liverpool.

---

*Blair continued to take an interest in the appointment of bishops, for example choosing his old college chaplain Graham Dow to be Bishop of Carlisle in May 2000. However, after William Chapman succeeded the conservative John Holroyd as the Downing Street appointments secretary in 1999, it became less likely that the Church would propose candidates he would find unacceptable.

Christian optimist

Blair's Easter 1996 credo was a direct response to that other theologian-premier in her famous address to the Church of Scotland in 1988. Margaret Thatcher had quoted Paul's second letter to the Thessalonians: 'If a man will not work he shall not eat.' Blair rejected her interpretation:

> This injunction by Paul should never be used to justify the withdrawal of support from the helpless. We must always be willing to assist the vulnerable and disadvantaged. But what I think Paul meant was that: that everyone had a duty to get on and work for the common good. To participate in the benefits, they had to give as well as take . . . Unless each of us accepts personal responsibility, the community in which we live suffers as a result.

In other words, however, if the poor do not make an effort, they do not deserve to 'participate in the benefits'. The difference between him and Thatcher was narrower than he was trying – at this point – to suggest. She was more pessimistic about human nature, but in the end Blair did not come up with different answers to the next set of questions: How is a sense of duty to be encouraged in those who lack it? How is a community to protect itself from the irresponsibility of any of its members? His attempt to open up clear pink water between him and Thatcher was elegant, but not wholly convincing:

> I recognise that people can by their own volition exert themselves to become better, more decent people. Human beings have free will, the choice to act well or badly. What distinguishes me from Conservatives is that I believe people are more likely to act well and improve themselves in a society where opportunities are offered to them to do so; which strives to be cohesive and treats people as of equal worth. This, I think, is the crucial difference between my own position and the Marxist and Tory extremes.

This may be the real divide between the theology of the right and the left: that the right regards humanity as fallen, essentially wicked, and the function of politics as being to minimise the damage, while the left is ever hopeful, looking for the best in people.

Blair went on: 'Christianity is optimistic about the human condition, but not naïve. It can identify what is good, but knows the capacity to do evil. I believe that the endless striving to do the one and avoid the other is the purpose of human existence. Through that comes progress.'

The difference between him and Thatcher, therefore, was essentially one over whether the glass of human virtue was half full or half empty. She thought people would behave responsibly if threatened with punishment (but should be rewarded with 'entitlements' if they meet their 'obligations'). He, on the other hand, thought people would behave responsibly if given fair opportunities (but should be punished if they did not).

Notes

1. Interview, *Daily Record*, 6 March 1998.
2. Linda Lee-Potter, *Daily Mail*, 17 April 1998.
3. Interview, Birmingham *Evening Mail*, 13 June 1997.
4. Interview, *Daily Record*, 6 March 1998.
5. *Sunday Telegraph*, 7 April 1996.
6. *Muslim News*, 31 March 2000.
7. *Sunday Telegraph*, 7 April 1996.
8. *Ibid.* (Mark 2:27).
9. Interview, *Washington Post*, 12 July 1999.
10. A. H. Halsey, *No Discouragement*, p. 120.
11. See John Campbell, *Margaret Thatcher*, Vol. 1, pp. 15–18, 29–31; Jonathan Raban, *God, Man & Mrs Thatcher*, especially pp. 67–71.
12. York diocesan newsletter, quoted in the *Daily Telegraph*, 12 March 1998.
13. Home Office, *Supporting Families: A Consultation Paper*, November 1998.
14. *Sun*, 4 November 1998.

20

New Labour and Money

The Ecclestone Affair, November 1997

> 'It would have been bizarre if a bloke had been in a worse position as a result of donating to the Labour Party.'
>
> —*Tony Blair, 1997*

The first sermon preached by the vicar when he took up his new parish was his lecture to Labour's new MPs in Church House on Day Six. 'You are not here to enjoy the trappings of power,' he told them. 'What the electorate give, the electorate can take away.' The biblical tone implied that the Cabinet would shortly give away all worldly goods and hold everything in common. In the event, most of them were only bounced the next day into giving up £16,000 a year to take £87,000 of the salaries to which they were entitled, while Blair gave up £41,000 to take £102,000. John Prescott was sufficiently irritated to tell Blair he was behaving like 'Jesus Christ'.[1]

It was six months before the halo slipped. Blair has good cause to remember 5 November, 1997. His government, it was reported that day, had changed its policy on the arcane matter of the sponsorship of racing cars by tobacco companies. No earthquake and no one hurt, until it emerged that the change came in response to a request from a rich business person who had given the Labour Party £1 million. The new Prime Minister's personal integrity was called into question because not only had party benefited from Bernie Ecclestone's generosity, but Blair himself had been entertained by him. It was not exactly the trappings of power – for one thing, Blair was still in Opposition at the time – but a spin round the track at Silverstone for him and his children with Damon Hill, Britain's star racing driver, was a treat for the few not the many.

The subject matter of Blair's first real setback in government could not have been predicted. But that it might have involved money, big business and a casual attitude towards conflicts of interest could perhaps have been discerned beneath the promise of the 'highest standards of honesty and propriety in public life' in his first Queen's Speech.[2] A product himself of a new politics in which internal party elections became well-financed campaigns in the national media, Blair showed an early insouciance about the ethical implications.

When he began his campaign for the Labour leadership in 1994, he realised he would need money. The party was in transition from a cashless model of internal politics to a quasi-American one, in which candidates for public office first fight rivals of the same party in 'primary' elections for that party's nomination. Under the old model, internal party elections were conducted on the basis of ideological 'slates', by making speeches and through personal contact. This started to change in 1992, when the spread of ballots of party members and trade unionists expanded the potential electorate in the Labour leadership election, which once consisted of a few hundred MPs, from several hundred activists to 4 million individuals. John Smith produced some colour leaflets, but otherwise ran a conventional campaign. The 1994 leadership election was the first time that a candidate Prime Minister had been selected on a one person, one vote franchise.

The Blair campaign was small in scale relative to America, where the cost of buying television advertising time dominates the political process. Newspaper advertising was unnecessary and might in any case have been counter-productive because it was alien to the culture of the old model (those constraints fell away by the time, in 2000, when Ken Livingstone and Frank Dobson contested the Labour nomination for London mayor). The main expenses were staff, offices and leaflets.

The task of fundraising was entrusted to Barry Cox, millionaire London Weekend Television executive and former neighbour in Hackney. 'It wasn't difficult to raise the money,' said Cox, because many donors were eager to back the favourite.[3] But, in analysing their motives, support for an inspiring national leader was impossible to separate from a desire to secure first-mover advantage in currying favour with the likely Prime Minister.

According to the accounts he submitted to the National Executive, Cox raised £88,000 and spent £79,000, considerably more than Margaret Beckett's £17,000 and John Prescott's £13,000. The bulk of Blair's money came from rich individuals, including Greg Dyke and Melvyn Bragg who, like Cox, had become millionaires at London Weekend Television, David Puttnam and David Sainsbury, the former SDP benefactor who had forgotten, if he had ever known, that Blair once mocked David Owen's rump party as 'the political wing of Sainsbury's'.[4]

Bragg said: 'I don't want to be pious, but no one is in this for the gongs.'[5] Nevertheless, he, Puttnam and Sainsbury all became life peers. Sainsbury did even better, being appointed a minister in 1998, but Blair showed no sign of understanding that he might appear to be selling government office.

This unfortunate appearance also applied to Geoffrey Robinson, a backbench Labour MP who had spent the political exile of the early 1980s making money from a niche engineering company spun off from his previous career as chief executive of Jaguar Cars. He had generously invited the Blair family to spend their summer holiday in 1996 at his villa in Tuscany, and again the following summer after Blair became Prime Minister.

These holidays did not have to be registered, being technically unrelated to Blair's being an MP, and they were in any case heavily publicised. But Blair did not appear to pause to consider the ethical implications. He should have been alerted during the leadership campaign when the Conservatives dredged up his Concorde trip to the United States on all-party business in 1986, which probably ought to have been declared in the Register of Members' Interests. He had seemed cavalier about the requirements of the Register more recently, too. He had declared in the Register that some of his 'research assistance' as shadow Home Secretary until 1994 had been funded by 'non-affiliated trade unions and others'. It was not until the incompleteness of this entry was raised by a Conservative MP that Blair's spokesman revealed the 'others' were David Evans, chairman of Centurion Books, but not the identity of the unions, or why others was plural, or why they had not been identified before. It was only said the funds donated were 'very small', which was irrelevant. Evans became Lord Evans of Watford in July 1998.

Nor did Blair see all the dangers for him of laying Major, a man of blameless personal integrity, on the rack for failing either to disclose the sources of his party's funding or to recognise the potential conflicts of interest thrown up by MPs' outside earnings. When the Nolan committee recommended a complete ban on payments to MPs acting as 'advocates' for a cause, and full disclosure of all earnings 'connected with their being MPs', Major accepted the first part but rejected the second. It was one of his weakest decisions, fiercely denounced by Blair, who declared that the Prime Minister had changed his mind because of the 'squalid monied interests of the Conservative Party'.[6] It led to a humiliating defeat in the Commons in November 1995, when twenty-three Conservatives did not see why they should suffer politically for the greed of their colleagues and voted with Labour.

Blair fulfilled the minimum requirements to mount an effective attack on the Conservatives. He ended the practice of trade union sponsorship of MPs, a hollow legacy of the party's origin, and diverted the small sums concerned into general party funds; he announced that the Labour Party would publish the names of donors giving more than £5,000 in a year; and that the party would refuse foreign donations. But the danger of a generalised attack on 'monied interests', combined with a demand for greater openness was that such openness would merely make it easier to see who Blair's rich backers were and to suggest conflicts of interest. The commingling of financial and sexual 'sleaze', its enthusiastic exploitation by Blair and his high moral rhetoric, occasionally Gandhian in tone, implied that Labour ministers had taken vows of both chastity and poverty.

Blair recognised, too, that there was a potential problem over the funding of his own office as Leader of the Opposition, but the device he chose to overcome it, a blind trust, turned out to be flawed. The idea was adapted from the Industrial Research Trust used by John Smith to supplement the state funding of his office.[7] It was 'blind' in that the recipients were not supposed to know who had given money and so could not be accused of being influenced by donors.[8] It was run by Simon Haskel, an industrialist friend of Smith's who was made a life peer in Smith's first honours list.

When Blair began to attract substantial amounts of money – both for his own office and for the Labour Party – he wanted a fund of his own. Three other Labour peers were appointed as trustees of a 'Labour Leader's Office Fund': Margaret Jay, Brenda Dean and Merlyn Rees. Neither Blair nor anyone in his office was supposed to know the identity of any donors, but the arrangement ran counter to the assumption behind disclosing donations to the party, which was that openness was the only sure safeguard against apparent impropriety. Henry Drucker, who was hired by Blair as a fundraiser for the party, argued against it unsuccessfully and resigned after a few months. He said the problem with a blind trust was that Labour leaders by definition could never say that the public had been told everything: 'A blind fund is just not a good idea . . . it undermines their integrity.'[9]

Drucker's criticism may have been sharpened by the personality clash between him and Michael Levy, the millionaire music promoter who first started to exploit Blair's big-money pulling power. Blair met Levy, who made his money by turning Shane Fenton into Alvin Stardust and had raised large amounts of money for Jewish charities, shortly after becoming leader. Levy offered to help raise funds for him. For a while Blair was an occasional tennis partner at Levy's north London home; when he became Prime Minister Levy was elevated to the peerage and acted as his personal envoy to the Middle East. (In 2000, he was embarrassed by the disclosure that he had paid just £5,000 in income tax in 1998/99.[10])

Drucker was right, and Blair was forced effectively to admit as much when the blind trust was wound up at the end of 1996, having raised £2 million. Lord Nolan's successor as chairman of the Committee on Standards in Public Life, Lord Neill, eventually declared after the General Election: 'Blind trusts should be prohibited as a mechanism for funding political parties, party leaders or their offices, Members of Parliament or parliamentary candidates.'[11]

In any case, the identities of several donors became known in a press report in November 1996 which was not denied: Sir Emmanuel Kaye, founder of the Lansing Bagnall fork-lift truck company was said to have given at least £50,000; Sir Trevor Chinn, chairman of Lex Service, Alex Bernstein, the former chairman of Granada, and Bob Gavron, who made his money in the printing business (and who was also a public donor to the party) were also identified.[12] The blind trust device was unsuccessful in another respect, in that one of its trustees, Margaret Jay, later became a member of Blair's Cabinet as Labour leader in the House of Lords, thus taking into government the very knowledge that Blair himself was not supposed to have.

There was a wider problem with Blair's ambition to present Labour as a pro-business party. The political imperatives were clear. They were partly a matter of collecting celebrity endorsements to identify the party with business success, but also a matter of re-positioning the party ideologically. 'I want a situation more like the Democrats and the Republicans in the US. People don't even question for a single moment that the Democrats are a pro-business party. They should not be asking the question about New Labour,' he told the *Financial Times* on 16 January 1997.

This was an explicit adoption of one of Margaret Thatcher's aims, which had once been regarded as wholly hostile to the Labour Party. A few months after Blair entered parliament in 1983, she said that she wanted an Opposition party which had 'a different way of achieving the same objective . . . more like Democrats and Republicans. In the United States, you have two parties based on free enterprise, freedom and justice. Here the two main parties have two fundamentally different philosophies.'[13]

Blair used his pro-Europeanism to win over the leaders of big business who were worried about being excluded from the euro zone. He used his shirt-sleeved can-do style to impress former Thatcherites like Alan Sugar and Richard Branson. Other business people, more pragmatically, were keen to engage with what was seen, even two years out, as the incoming government. For his part, he was slow to recognise special pleading from them, as for example when he proclaimed his deal with BT from the platform of the 1995 Labour conference.* In Opposition, however, keeping business sweet was all a matter of words. In government, there were tough choices to be made, and some of them touched on the interests of Labour's new business friends.

Formula 1 million

The Ecclestone story began in July 1996, when the Blair family were entertained at Silverstone, home of Formula 1. It was a routine day's work for a modern politician, a photo-opportunity with fast cars and a national sporting hero, combined with a little light lobbying by the Fédération Internationale de l'Automobile (FIA), a world-wide association of motoring clubs (including the AA in Britain) which is both the governing body for Formula 1 racing and a pressure group for motorists.

As with all good tragedies, there were warning signs, only the principal character did not see them. It was plain that the event should have been logged in the Register of Members' Interests. The FIA, a well-funded interest group, had helicoptered Blair and his family to the circuit and given them a special day out. What Blair failed to notice, presumably because it did not occur to him, or to any of his advisers, was that this could create the kind of conflict of interest on which the Labour Opposition had crucified John Major's administration. It was not until the drama was over, and under the pressure which it created, that Blair finally recorded the FIA's hospitality in the Register in February 1998.[14]

It was at Silverstone that Blair first met Bernie Ecclestone, the man who made Formula 1 into a billion-pound business and who was therefore a suitable stage villain for a morality play. The small, high-octane meeting in Ecclestone's mobile home, which was parked at the trackside, had been set up by David Ward, John Smith's adviser who was now working for the FIA. Also present were Ecclestone's friend and colleague Max Mosley, president of the FIA, and Bernd Pischetsrieder, chairman of BMW

---

*See p. 270.

which had bought Rover, Britain's last volume car maker, in 1994. They did not discuss motor racing: instead they talked about Europe. Pischetsrieder urged Blair to ensure that Britain joined the single currency, while Ecclestone, a sceptic, disagreed. Blair defended his middle position, pro-euro but with conditions, with his usual tact and skill.

Ecclestone, whose prejudices about the Labour Party were unmodernised, was pleasantly surprised by Blair. When, the following January, Gordon Brown announced that a Labour government would not raise income tax rates, Mosley teased and chivvied his friend into donating £1 million to the party. Like most rich people, Ecclestone, who earned £54 million the previous year, had assumed that Labour would put up the top rate of income tax from 40p in the pound to 50p. Mosley, a Labour supporter, pointed out that Brown had just saved him £5 million.

In order to make the plot work, the gods ensured that the timing of the donation was just wrong. If it had been made a month earlier, it would have fallen into the Labour Party's 1996 accounts, and would have been made public, under the party's new policy of openness, in September 1997 – just in time to avert trouble. Instead, the donation would have remained secret until September 1998.

Meanwhile, the question of Labour's policy on the tobacco industry lay dormant. At the previous election in 1992 the party had been committed to a radical policy, a total ban on tobacco advertising. Curiously, this was dropped from the early manifesto on which party members had been balloted in 1996. It was then reinstated in the final document, probably to give some substance to a rather thin section on health policy. Thus the manifesto on which Blair was elected in 1997 declared ringingly: 'Smoking is the greatest single cause of preventable illness and premature death in the UK. We will therefore ban tobacco advertising.'

Chris Smith, Labour's health spokesman, had always been careful not to spell out the extent to which a ban would apply to sponsorship, but during the 1997 election campaign he accepted that, in order to protect British motor racing, snooker and darts, tackling sports sponsorship 'might take longer and require a separate measure'.[15]

It seems unlikely, however, that Ecclestone made his donation in the hope of influencing Labour policy on tobacco sponsorship. His wealth came from the sale of television rights to Formula 1 races. Compared with his television interests, the threat of a ban on sponsorship was at worst an irritant. It would impoverish the performers in the impresario's show: the money from the cigarette companies went directly to the teams, who used it to build increasingly high-tech cars and to inflate the salaries of their drivers.

His own later explanation of his motives was most plausible, partly because it was self-interested in a different way:

> I pay a lot of taxes. So, I invested a million quid. They could have got in, changed all the tax structure, my tax bill could have gone up by five or six million, so it seemed like a good idea. I didn't want to see the Labour Party in a position where they were going to be influenced by the trade unions to the extent that the trade unions would be controlling the government.[16]

However, Mosley and Ecclestone certainly saw themselves as representing the industry as a whole, lobbying for its interests, albeit from a relatively detached position. It was not a view of themselves that was widely shared. Indeed, the negative assumptions about their motives, especially in the press and at the Department of Health, was the final spring needed to unfold the tragi-comic saga.

'Third-rate behaviour'

The ban on tobacco advertising seemed straightforward and cost-free, so legislation was promised in the first Queen's Speech. Thus the new Health Secretary, Frank Dobson, was able to promise in the Commons just two weeks after the election to produce a draft Bill to ban 'all forms of tobacco advertising, including sponsorship' – on condition that sports which were 'heavily dependent on tobacco sponsorship' were given 'time and help to reduce their dependency'.[17]

In July, however, the action suddenly moved to Brussels when Padraig Flynn, the European Union social affairs commissioner, managed to resurrect a proposed EU law against tobacco advertising which had been blocked ever since it was first drafted eight years before. Flynn unexpectedly persuaded the Netherlands and Greece to switch sides, which meant, with the change of government in Britain, that a ban on sponsorship after four years' grace could be agreed at the next health ministers' meeting in December.*

The FIA had not been too worried about a ban in Britain, where tobacco advertising on racing cars was already restricted by voluntary agreement to colours and geometric shapes (the Marlboro chevron, for example). But a complete ban across the EU within four years, Max Mosley argued, would add to the pressures already pushing Formula 1 to

---

*The directive, still opposed by Germany, required only a 'qualified majority' to pass, as it had been tabled as a measure needed to complete the European single market – a legal basis later successfully challenged by the tobacco companies in the European Court of Justice.

stage more races outside Europe. Mosley's argument was never tested; nor was the FIA's offer of an alternative, to reduce sponsorship world-wide. But his advice was hardly impartial, even if it may have been less self-interested than Department of Health officials assumed it was. When Mosley met Tessa Jowell, in the new post of Minister for Public Health, and sports minister Tony Banks on 23 September it was clear he had made no progress.

Back at the FIA, David Ward said: 'We felt we had to see Tony Blair.' A meeting with Mosley, Ecclestone and Ward was arranged. Jonathan Powell and a civil service private secretary were the only others present. Agreeing to the meeting was a disastrous misjudgment, for which Powell bore some responsibility, although the buck stopped with Blair himself. He and his family had enjoyed the FIA's hospitality and, not only had Ecclestone given the Labour Party £1 million, but Blair knew that since the election the party's 'high value donors unit' had sought further donations from him. And the explicit purpose of the meeting was to lobby for a change in government policy towards Ecclestone's business interests.

When it took place at Downing Street on 16 October, the Prime Minister seemed to accept Mosley and Ecclestone's arguments with alacrity. Blair later published the private secretary's note of the meeting, in order to counter 'this suggestion that I somehow – which is the implicit suggestion – said, "Well, this is a sort of dodgy meeting, don't take a note or a minute of it"'.[18] He seemed blithely unaware, however, that the record of the meeting confirmed that he was open to special-interest lobbying. It recorded his saying, '[I] don't need persuading about [the] basic case in favour of Formula 1,' but adding that he was 'also in favour of a ban on tobacco ads'. He asked sharp questions: 'Why do other countries not see the problem?' and 'Do other sports have the same scale of dependence?' but did not challenge the central claim that the directive would push Formula 1 racing out of Europe.* He sent his guests off by saying he recognised the problems and 'would think about what they had said'.

Not recorded in the private secretary's note were Ecclestone's parting words to Blair, as they were being shown out. Adopting the manner of the impartial adviser, he said: 'Don't hang yourself on this.' That, of course, was precisely what the Prime Minister proceeded to do. The next day he sent

*Some commentators argued that the concentration of expertise and specialist small suppliers would keep the industry in Britain (see, for example, Martin Jacques, *Observer*, 9 November 1997); certainly Downing Street, defending the decision later, repeated unconvincing figures produced by the motor racing industry for possible job losses.

a memo to Frank Dobson asking him to look for a way to 'protect the position of sports in general and Formula 1 in particular'.[19]

The request was acted on with an excess of zeal. On 3 November, David Ward took a call from Number Ten, the first contact he had had since the meeting, to tell him that Tessa Jowell was writing to EU health ministers proposing that Formula 1 be exempted from the directive. 'But that isn't what we wanted,' he protested, well aware that exempting a named sport altogether would look terrible. He was told it was too late: it had already been done.

That Jowell was seeking an exemption for Formula 1 was made public on 4 November and reported in the press the next day. She was quickly forced on the defensive when it was recalled that her solicitor husband was legal adviser to, and a former director of, the company running the Benetton Formula 1 racing team. It was immediately clear that the financial interests involved in the decision would be subjected to scrutiny. The press noticed that Ecclestone had just had an audience with the Prime Minister, and it could not be long before the fact that he had also given the party a large amount of money would leak out (it took two days).

Only now was it realised in Downing Street that it might look as if Ecclestone's money had secured a change in government policy. The first response was to do what should have been done much earlier, as a Labour official wrote to Ecclestone on 5 November to say that, in the light of the decision, the party could not accept any further donations from him.[20] Meanwhile, as the Downing Street press office stalled journalists' inquiries, there were heated discussions over what to say about the donation already made, not due to be disclosed for ten months, and then only as being 'more than £5,000'.

Alastair Campbell claimed later that he argued for a policy of complete openness from the start.[21] Blair and Jonathan Powell were not persuaded and took advice from Gordon Brown and Derry Irvine. The Chancellor suggested consulting Sir Patrick Neill, who was to take over from Lord Nolan as the new chairman of the Committee on Standards in Public Life the following Monday. On Friday 7 November, after an Anglo-French summit with President Jacques Chirac at Canary Wharf, Blair approved a letter, drafted by Powell in the name of Tom Sawyer, the Labour Party general secretary, designed to lead Sir Patrick into ruling that Labour could keep the £1 million, but that it should refuse further donations from Ecclestone – which it had just done.

Blair later asserted that Sir Patrick's advice had been sought before journalists became interested in the story, and implied it had been sought as soon as the decision to seek an exemption for Formula 1 had been taken. 'We did it without any compulsion whatever, before any press inquiry had been made whatever.'[22] This was simply untrue.

Nor was the ploy successful. If Blair hoped that Sir Patrick would have been caught unawares before his feet were under his new desk, he was disappointed, when over the weekend the wise former Warden of All Souls, Oxford, advised the party to return the money it had already received. It was advice which Blair had no choice but to accept. It was the right advice, because it was only by returning the money that Blair could hope eventually to shut down the story. It was too late to avoid suspicion of his initial motives, but it allowed the affair to be closed because, whatever policy emerged from the government's negotiations in Europe, the Labour Party would not benefit.

It also meant that when the party admitted on Sunday 9 November that it had received money from Ecclestone, it was able to say also that it had decided to pay it back. This looked considerably more principled than the full story, which continued to emerge in embarrassing daily instalments. It was only on 11 November, when a Labour spokesman, sailing close to the wind of untruth, dismissed a *Times* report that the donation had been £1.5 million as 'wild and seriously inaccurate', that Ecclestone himself revealed the true amount, apparently spontaneously, when buttonholed by journalists. Asked how much he had given, he demanded to know how much the reporter was paid. The reporter said he was happy to tell him, he was paid £54,000 a year. Ecclestone, bluff called, still refused to say how much his donation was. A minute or so later, however, he interrupted an answer to another journalist to say: 'One million pounds is your answer.'

In fact, the disclosure had been agreed between Campbell and a reluctant Ecclestone, who said later he would have been happy for his donation to be public in the first place but, having been sworn to secrecy, was furious at being put at the centre of a media storm by 'those clowns' in Downing Street. It was, he said much later, 'third-rate behaviour'.[23]

The crisis for Blair only began to abate when William Hague, facing an open goal with the ball at his feet, 'walked up to the penalty spot and booted it over the bar' – to use Blair's crude footballing analogy – at Prime Minister's Questions on 12 November. Hague asked, too cleverly for the football-terrace atmosphere of the Commons, if Blair would meet representatives of billiards and snooker on the same terms as Formula 1.

The crisis was finally defused when Blair made an apology – although only for the way he had 'handled' the affair – in his first long television interview as Prime Minister on BBC1's *On the Record* the following

Sunday. His skill at answering questions he had not been asked was deployed to the full. John Humphrys asked why he had met Ecclestone. 'Nothing actually new was said really on either side,' he replied. The implication was that he would have changed the policy anyway: a non-answer which had the paradoxical effect of implying that he had simply used Downing Street as the setting for American-style donor solicitation.

Blair continued wilfully to miss the point. Asked if he should have refused a meeting, he said: 'It would have been bizarre if a bloke had been in a worse position as a result of donating to the Labour Party.' The point was that Ecclestone appeared to be in a *better* position by virtue of being a donor. Not everyone who disagreed with government policy was allowed twenty minutes to make their case in Downing Street.

Blair's skill at blanding over tricky situations, which had served him well in Opposition, just managed to get him through his first real setback as Prime Minister. In the end, he was forced to draw on some of his political capital as a fresh face deserving the benefit of the doubt:

> I would never do anything either to harm the country or anything improper. I never have. I think most people who have dealt with me think I'm a pretty straight sort of guy, and I am . . . In the end, the country's got to look at me: it's got to, in a sense, decide whether the person that they believed in is the same person they've got now, and it is.

Meanwhile, the sub-plot of Labour's manifesto promise to ban tobacco advertising nearly lost itself in a further series of twists and turns. When the European directive was agreed, the idea of a specific exemption for Formula 1 was dropped. Advertising would be banned throughout the European Union by 2000; sponsorship of sporting events would continue under stricter controls until 2003; with an extension for a 'handful' of events deemed to be especially reliant on sponsorship until 2006. It stretched the manifesto pledge a little, but at least the issue seemed settled. Then the tobacco companies succeeded in June 2000 in getting the directive thrown out on the grounds that the European Union did not have the authority to ban their advertising under the powers to complete the single market. As a result, a new British Bill had to be brought in, only just in time to ban print and poster advertising by the end of Blair's first parliament.

The ban on tobacco advertising, which had seemed one of the simplest and cheapest manifesto promises at the start, ended up as anything but, seriously damaging Blair's image of probity, and costing the Labour Party £1 million (when the Ecclestone donation was returned, Robert Earl, the owner of the Planet Hollywood restaurant chain, stepped in with a replacement, but he would presumably have donated about that much anyway at some point). Nor would the manifesto pledge be met in full, although Chris Smith had said before the election – in rather small print – that sports sponsorship was a special case.

Holier than they

Although the issue at stake in the Ecclestone affair may itself have been minor, the flaws in Blair's conduct were significant. In a different political climate towards the end of a premiership rather than the beginning they could have been terminal. They were serious in relation to his own implied standards, especially the standards implied by his attacks on the previous government.

Against Major, the charge was usually one of the *appearance* of a *potential* conflict of interest, and it was usually levelled against his ministers, as when David Mellor had to resign for accepting a holiday from the daughter of the treasurer of the Palestinian National Council. With Blair, who changed policy in response to lobbying from a party donor and provider of personal hospitality, the charge was one of an actual conflict of interest, and it was levelled at the Prime Minister himself.

He should have registered the Silverstone trip, although it was well-reported. He should not have met Ecclestone, Mosley and Ward, and, whether he met them or not, he should not have changed the policy; although whether he should have been committed to banning tobacco advertising in the first place is arguable.

Naturally, Blair insisted on his own probity throughout the Ecclestone affair. 'I would never, ever . . . change a policy because someone supported or donated to the Labour Party . . . I have honestly done what I thought was best for the country all the way through,' he said.[24] He cannot have intended to give Ecclestone a more sympathetic hearing because of the donation. But he did. 'Inexperience', and a shrug of the shoulders, was his private explanation for the error of judgment: a little like a burglar putting the fact that he was caught down to lack of practice.

Blair's petulant tone in response to criticism over Formula 1 diverted from a genuine argument he made in his defence, which is that if parties are to raise significant funds – whether from trade unions, companies or rich individuals – then they are likely to come into contact with donors' interests in government. The only solution to this would be to restrict political donations to small sums, for example making £5,000 the annual limit rather than threshold for disclosure. That would force parties to rely on large numbers of small donations, and may ultimately be where the logic of conflict-of-interest avoidance leads. Blair appeared to suggest it in his *On the Record* interview, but nothing was heard from him about it afterwards.

Meanwhile the high-mindedness – or sanctimony – of Blair's moral populism contrasted with his overlooking the possibility of influence-buying. When he blundered into impropriety, as with Ecclestone, what annoyed him was the automatic assumption that the Labour government 'can't be as good as it looks'. He protested: 'There's been a desire to say right from the word go: "They're all the same. The Tories were sleazy, Labour's not different." I don't believe we're like that at all.' He insisted, 'I said I would deliver something different and I can do it', as if mere words would make it so.[25]

In some important senses, of course, Labour was different. Conservative Party donations had always been completely secret. But Blair's instincts hardly went with the grain. Despite leading the charge in Opposition against John Major under the banners of openness, disclosure and transparency, he more than once failed to register personal benefits which, in the words of the rules, 'might reasonably be thought by others to influence' his actions as an MP.[26]

Although the Ecclestone affair barely dented Blair's high standing in the opinion polls, it marked a change in attitudes among the media, the Labour Party and the electorate. Journalists realised he could blunder and became more aggressive in seeking out mistakes. It sensitised both media and party to the rumbling row over the cut in lone parent benefits. It hinted at a dark side to the honeymoon: like the first quarrel in a love affair, it hardly bruised the shiny surface of optimism, but underneath serious damage was done because the 'bond of trust' he had claimed existed between him and the people had been broken.

Notes

1. Or so he claimed to a group of grumbling Cabinet ministers, 23 September 1997: Janet Jones, *Labour of Love*, p. 121.
2. *Hansard*, 14 May 1997.
3. *Independent on Sunday*, 2 October 1994.
4. Diary, *London Review of Books*, 29 October 1987: this was after Owen refused to join the merger with the Liberals; Sainsbury remained a funder of the recusant SDP.
5. *Independent on Sunday*, 2 October 1994.
6. Rendered as 'squalid monetary interests' in *Hansard*, 2 November 1995, col. 388.
7. The state funding is called Short money after Ted Short, Harold Wilson's Leader of the House 1974–76, who introduced it.
8. *Independent on Sunday*, 14 May 1995.

9. BBC Radio 4, *The World At One*, 20 October 1999.
10. *Sunday Times*, 25 June 2000. He explained it by saying all his capital was in 'two very, very nice residences'.
11. 'The Funding of Political Parties in the United Kingdom,' Fifth Report of the Committee on Standards in Public Life, Cm 4057, October 1998.
12. *Sunday Times*, 17 November 1996; Kaye was later reported also to have given £10,000 to Michael Howard's Conservative leadership campaign in 1997 (*New Statesman*, 27 February 1998).
13. *Director* magazine, September 1983.
14. Blair was required to register the visit by an adverse ruling by Sir Gordon Downey, the Parliamentary Commissioner for Standards, on 26 February 1998, upheld by the select committee on Standards and Privileges, Fourteenth Report, Session 1998–99, 19 March 1998; Sir Gordon described Blair's view, in a letter to him, that the visit was non-registrable because it was undertaken in an official capacity as Leader of the Opposition as 'mistaken'.
15. *Financial Times*, 22 March 1997.
16. *Daily Telegraph*, 22 December 1997.
17. *Hansard*, 15 May 1997.
18. Blair interview, BBC1, *On the Record*, 16 November 1997.
19. Blair's oral paraphrase, *ibid.*
20. Blair interview, *ibid.*
21. Patrick Wintour, *Observer*, 15 November 1998.
22. BBC1, *On the Record*, 16 November 1997.
23. *Sunday Times*, 26 March 2000.
24. BBC1, *On the Record*, 16 November 1997.
25. *Ibid.*
26. 'The Code of Conduct, together with The Guide to the Rules Relating to the Conduct of Members', approved by the House of Commons, 24 July 1996.

21

Welfare Reform

Lone-Parent Benefit Cut, December 1997

> 'The welfare system in Britain isn't working. We are spending more money and more poverty is there.'
> —*Tony Blair, briefing for international press, 2 February 1998*

It was like a scene from a film. The politician at the rostrum, delivering a speech to her party conference, defending her government's unpopular decisions, finds herself reading words she does not recognise on her scrolling prompter. It happened to Harriet Harman in Brighton in October 1997: 'All these unfamiliar words started coming up on the autocue. I couldn't go back to my notes, and just had to carry on. I realised that Gordon Brown had made the changes to delete all my references to spending plans.'[1]

This vivid vignette of modern politics suggested that the Secretary of State for Social Security had lost control of her brief after just five months. The reality was more complex: it showed how closely she worked with the Chancellor. Her fundamental problem was that she was caught in a bigger struggle between the Prime Minister and the Chancellor over the future of the welfare state. Blair was the Christian moralist, Brown the secular economist. Blair saw a welfare system which weakened family ties and personal responsibility; Brown took a technician's view of the incentive effects which discouraged people from working. In practice, both views overlapped – Brown's presbyterian work ethic was no less Christian, or moralistic – but they became caught up in a simpler struggle for Whitehall territory, Brown seeking suzerainty over all economic ministries, Blair asserting his primacy over the key political battlegrounds. Those tensions were then intermixed with a set of disastrous personal relationships among the supporting cast which ensured that things went wrong.

Blair's mistake was to appoint Frank Field as Harman's deputy. Or, at least, that was not a mistake in itself: the error was to appoint him without understanding his plans for reforming the welfare state and without any intention of letting him carry them out. It set back welfare reform by two years. It could have been worse: Blair hesitated until the last moment over whether or not to give Field the top job. According to Field, Blair told him a year before the election, 'I hope to make you Secretary of State.'

It would certainly have been a brave appointment, but both Brown and Peter Mandelson advised against it, and Field was instead given the honorific titles of Privy Counsellor and 'minister for welfare reform'. This puffed up the symbolism of endorsing Field's radical plans without giving him the authority to carry them out. When Alastair Campbell compiled a chronological list of the government's achievements at the end of the year, the sole entry for 3 May was: 'Frank Field appointed to look after the long-term reform of welfare.'[2]

It was bound to end in tears: Blair did not have the courage of Field's convictions. He did not even know what they were, but he liked the sound of them. Like many Conservatives, he was impressed by Field's Christian emphasis on the destructive moral effect of benefit dependency, but rarely paid attention to the small print, which proposed an expensive shift from means-tested to universal benefits, which Field believed should be paid for by higher taxes on the better-off.

Field's appointment suggested that Blair had not read the minister for welfare reform's slim volume, *How to Pay for the Future*, published in October 1996, and that, if any of his advisers had read it, they did not take it seriously. Brown, on the other hand, was well aware of the implications of Field's scheme. It involved the better paid being required to make contributions to a pension fund of their own on top of the state pension, but also provided for more generous pensions for those who could not afford it. In all, taxes and compulsory contributions would rise by £3 billion a year, with everyone earning less than £15,000 a year – below average earnings – gaining at the expense of those above that level. Whatever the rhetoric, the effect was similar to that of John Smith's shadow budget of 1992, only more so.

One of Field's main concerns was with poverty in old age. Most Britons are well-provided for by private-sector pension funds, certainly in comparison with continental Europeans who have state schemes which rely on the generosity of future taxpayers. But a large minority in Britain has no prospect of retiring on anything more than the state pension, which is worth less than state benefits. Focusing state help on the poor creates a 'thrift trap' – people with modest savings find themselves no better off than people who have not saved at all, especially if they need long-term care. But the alternative, a generous universal scheme, is expensive, and Brown thought it more important to focus resources on getting more people into the labour market in the first place, so that more could make their own provision.

As a result, Field found himself frustrated by Treasury obstruction and deliberate inaction. After one fruitless meeting, Brown rounded on him and said, 'Why did you disagree with me? I thought you were my friend.'

To which Field replied: 'Gordon, I disagreed with you *because* you're my friend.' The idea that Brown, who hates meetings, might welcome open debate in the name of friendship was a measure of Field's naïvety. Unfortunately for Field, he had no friends in his own department either. Patricia Hollis, the social security minister in the House of Lords, regarded him in October 1997 as 'a disaster. He is not a team player. He produces nothing workable and creates trouble. He is meant to be having radical thoughts'. All his evidence was 'anecdotal', and 'he knows little about how the whole thing works'.[3]

The idea of fundamental reform of the welfare state therefore remained what it had been before the election: a cloud of radical-sounding words that was almost entirely content-free. The only matters of substance, those of improving incentives for the poor to work, had been planned by the Treasury team in Opposition and were the Treasury's territory in government. It was notable that there was no one in the incoming Number Ten Policy Unit responsible for welfare reform, a subject which was allocated to one of the unit's civil service members, Sharon White.

Thus there was no 'big picture' to draw the eye away from some of the unexpected detail in the foreground. These details included a number of awkward decisions inherited from the previous government which had not been implemented by the time of the election. The most controversial initially was not the cut in lone-parent benefits, but the cut in housing benefit for single people aged twenty-five and over. It was intended to cover the cost for single claimants of renting rooms in shared accommodation, rather than a flat of their own. Harman was lobbied on the issue by Labour MPs. She, Brown and Blair had been careful before the election not to promise to reverse any of the Tory cuts, because Labour had undertaken to keep to the public spending totals planned by the Conservatives for the first two years after the election. But, when she arrived in government, the civil service offered her a little room for manoeuvre by suggesting that money could be saved by restricting the backdating of benefit payments: she chose to use it to revoke the change in housing benefit.[4]

The cut in lone-parent benefits, however, stood. Harman's predecessor, Peter Lilley, had been driven to it partly as a gesture to please Conservative conference, and partly simply to save money.* The benefits system had for a long time recognised the additional costs of bringing up children alone, and there was no evidence that this was a cause of the doubling in the numbers of lone parents since the early 1980s. This was a fundamental social change which happened under the nose of Margaret Thatcher, who – much too late, not that it would have made the slightest difference – advocated restoring the stigma of birth out of wedlock by putting single mothers in hostels.† It did not matter that only a tiny minority of lone mothers intended from the start to bring up their children without the father – the category of which Blair had said, 'Yes, I disagree with what they have done.' The extra benefit for lone parents hardly acted as a visible brake on social change, and nothing could shake the conviction of the simpler nostalgics that the tax, benefit and council housing systems were a conspiracy against the traditional family.

Blair, uncertain about the politics of cutting lone parents' support, torn between *Daily Mail* populism and common-sense compassion, was tilted towards the *Mail* by Brown's desire to sharpen work incentives. The Chancellor was aware that lone mothers, often out of the labour market until their youngest child was sixteen, were the fastest-growing group of benefit dependants. But neither considered the dangers of provoking an unnecessary revolt in the Labour Party. Harman had accepted the cut on the basis that her department's spending limit was fixed, but in his first Budget on 2 July 1997 the Chancellor produced extra money for health and education. That meant she was left defending a cut which was now required purely for the purposes of political machismo. Indeed, the one thing worse than making the cut and later restoring it through Brown's plans to increase child benefit, as far as Blair was concerned, would have been to retreat from it once Labour MPs started to make a fuss about it.

Which they did, loyally and privately at first and then with increasing impatience, because it made no sense. The cut set up new perverse incentives, because it applied only to new claimants, meaning that if existing claimants took a job they would go onto the lower rate if they lost it again. After the measure was through the Commons, Blair said he would

*There were two elements of the cut: the abolition of one-parent benefit and of the lone-parent premium in income support rates.

†Or, rather, 'some sort of supervised accommodation provided by a voluntary or charitable body with other single parents under firm but friendly guidance' (Margaret Thatcher, *The Path to Power*, p. 562).

not have done it if he had had the money: 'If money was no problem, we would not have had to do it, but it would have cost this government over £300 million to keep with the current system.'[5] That figure was disputed, but it ceased to be the real reason early on: after the July Budget it was clear that money, for a compromise at least, could have been found.

The real reason was that Blair did not want to appear to 'bottle out' in the face of an internal revolt – the phrase he used in a *Channel Four News* interview two days before the vote in the House, while Brian Sedgemore denounced the whips, engaged in rounding up the doubters and applying the traditional methods of persuasion, as 'arm-twisters and goolie-crushers'.

When the vote came, on 10 December 1997, it cut a swathe through the Parliamentary Labour Party, stripping it of its first layer of post-electoral innocence and prompting the first resignations from office. Malcolm Chisholm, a Scottish Office minister, resigned along with two parliamentary private secretaries, Gordon Prentice and Mick Clapham; and two others, Alice Mahon and Neil Gerrard, were sacked. In the vote itself, forty-seven Labour MPs voted against the government; fourteen did not vote but were present, a form of public abstention, with a further twenty-five or so unaccounted for. With a majority of 179, it was a scale of revolt in which the rebels could safely indulge without changing anything, but as the first parliamentary rebellion, it was an ill-chosen battle because it was unnecessary.

Afterwards, an older and wiser Harriet Harman reflected on the episode with the sort of clarity that had not been possible at the time:

> We were at the beginning of the first Labour government for the best part of twenty years, we had a huge majority, but the biggest fear people had was that we would go off the rails in managing the economy. And reversing the lone-parent benefit cuts could well have been the issue that took the pin out of that grenade. It wasn't an objective or rational thing, it was a mood thing. I didn't want to be responsible for unravelling people's sense that we were going to control public spending, keep to Tory spending limits, which is what we'd pledged to do.[6]

In retrospect, there was no reason why the government should not have satisfied both right and left. What was required was to raise child benefit for everyone by enough to compensate lone parents for the loss of their premiums. That is, more or less, what eventually happened. But there was a gap during which benefits for new lone parents were cut before the child benefit increases announced in the following Budget, in March 1998, came into effect. Had Blair not been so eager to appease the 'family values' lobby, he could have waited to eliminate the lone-parent premium by levelling up, which still would have allowed him to sell the message, as he did, that lone-parent benefits were being 'aligned' with those for two-parent families, while targeting extra help on children regardless of family circumstances, and increasing the incentive to work.

On the road

Blair's response to adversity was to take to the road, speaking and taking questions from party members in Dudley town hall on 15 January 1998. As with the last time he was in Dudley, trying to sell a new Clause IV that had not been written, he was a salesman without a product. One or two other engagements were dubbed part of the 'welfare reform roadshow', but it soon fizzled out, because there was no end point to the campaign and no purpose to it beyond the presentational one of selling the proposition that no one should be afraid to change the present system.

By the time Blair hit the road, the prospect of anything resembling an overarching plan for welfare reform had evaporated completely. The crisis over the cut in lone-parent benefit provoked a bout of intense shadow-boxing over the future of disability benefits. Two days after the lone-parent benefit vote, a memo from Harman, telling her colleagues she intended to make further cuts in disability benefits, was leaked. This was most inconvenient, as Blair and Brown had not decided what to do, but it was well-known that incapacity benefit had been used during the Conservative years to take middle-aged men in particular off the unemployment count. The budget for disability benefits had tripled over the previous fifteen years, when the underlying health of the population seemed unchanged: an obvious target for the energetic welfare reformer. Unfortunately, that reformer's name was Peter Lilley, and he had already brought in a significant tightening of the eligibility test.

Meanwhile, the premature publication on 9 January 1998 of Paul Routledge's biography of Gordon Brown, revealing the Chancellor's continued resentment against Blair for snatching his crown four years earlier, provoked a wider crisis in relations between Numbers Ten and Eleven Downing Street. Thus the only substantive announcement that the Prime Minister had to make when he arrived in Dudley was that he was setting up a Cabinet committee to oversee reform of the welfare state, chaired by himself.*

Frank Field, who had been trying for some time to persuade Blair to assert his personal authority over welfare reform, was emboldened by

*The committee was not, in fact, a sub-committee of the Cabinet, but a less formal 'ministerial working group'; nevertheless, it spawned a large network of sub-committees.

Brown's reverse and made a speech on the same day in which he appeared to pave the way for compulsory second pensions in order to top up the state pension – the foundation stone of his grand scheme. But he had already destroyed any chance of support from Number Ten: that day Alastair Campbell sent an identical fax to him and to Harman: 'I see from today's papers that no matter how much we urge silence, congenital briefing goes on about who is responsible for what.'

The following month, Campbell sent another joint fax instructing them to 'enter a period of pre-Budget purdah' and urging 'extreme caution in relation to lunches'. That to Harman also said: 'I should also be grateful for an explanation on why the interviews with the *Guardian*, *Woman's Hour* and *World at One* were not cleared through this office.'[7]

Neither Campbell nor Blair can have been pleased by Field's attempt to laugh off the faxes when they were leaked to the *Sunday Express*: 'My first reaction was it's quite serious when somebody as senior as Alastair feels it is necessary to write such a letter. I thought of correcting some of the English and sending it back. That was my second reaction to it.'[8]

When Blair was asked if Campbell were allowed to go around issuing instructions to Cabinet ministers, he said:

> He acts with my authority absolutely. I hope I'm perfectly pleasant to people and well-mannered to them, but they've got to know I'm running the show. If people aren't doing what they should be doing, then it's an obligation on my part to say: 'I'm afraid this is what's going to happen.'[9]

It was an unusually blunt admission of his use of Campbell as his bully boy, one of the ways in which Blair managed to insulate himself from the dirty work of politics.

Meanwhile, Field was allowed to publish a Green Paper called, grandly, 'A New Contract for Welfare', which had nothing to say because Brown would not allow him to say anything and Blair had no idea, apart from repeating the rhetoric of responsibility, of what it should say. Field had been frustrated enough during the lone-parent benefit episode that Blair would not simply say it was wrong to pay lone parents more.

From 'thinking the unthinkable' – the glib sound-bite which had done for Chris Smith when he was first to handle the social security brief under Blair in Opposition – Field was now holding the untenable. In the Cabinet reshuffle in July 1998, he and Harman were both despatched to the back benches,* and Alistair Darling, a technocrat who can do political arithmetic, was brought in to sweep up the broken crockery. Harman's fate

*Field was offered a sideways move to the Cabinet Office as Jack Cunningham's deputy, which he refused.

contained an element of rough justice: she was the scapegoat for Blair's indecision, and yet remained conspicuously loyal to him.

Field, on the other hand, made a resignation statement in the Commons, for which Blair and Brown courageously left the Chamber, bitterly attacking Brown: 'If the last fifteen months have taught me anything it is that the whole Cabinet – especially the Chancellor – must share common beliefs on the biggest of all reforms.'[10]

The departure of Field allowed Gordon Brown's soundly-based policy instincts to prevail over Blair's straining for rhetorical effect, despite the Prime Minister's trumpeted chairmanship of the welfare reform committee. Field had in no way been responsible for the mistaken cut in lone-parent benefit, but his moralistic tone and its association with Blair's desire to impress the *Daily Mail* by sweeping away the 'dependency culture' ensured maximum confusion arose from the decision.

By the end of 1999, with the Working Families Tax Credit and the Welfare Reform Act, there was a coherence to the government's policy which would have looked refreshing and sensible had it not been so grotesquely over-sold in advance. It had nothing to do with 'thinking the unthinkable', 'ending welfare as we know it' or a 'New Beveridge'. It was to increase child benefit, improve work incentives and increase targeted support for pensioners. The increases in child benefit reversed the cut in lone-parent benefit and seemed to operate in a different moral direction: they were value-free about marriage, and indeed partly paid for by the abolition of the Married Couples Allowance in the March 1999 Budget. The only new element, the Working Families Tax Credit, made it more worthwhile for parents to take a low-paid job. It had the added advantage, by replacing a social security benefit with an Inland Revenue tax credit, of switching money for accounting purposes from public spending to tax revenue forgone, thus flattering Gordon Brown's books. For the long term Darling promised, in a Green Paper in December 1998, a more generous state pension for the poorest third of the population and a bigger National Insurance contributions rebate for people making provision for themselves. It was the opposite of Field's idea that the state should offer universal, redistributive provision in return for compulsory contributions; it was boring, unrevolutionary and made sense.[11]

It was a mark of Darling's surer touch that he was able to sit out two parliamentary revolts even larger than over lone-parent benefit without sustaining serious political damage. Sixty-five Labour MPs rebelled over cuts in incapacity benefit when they were voted on in May 1999, with an after-shock of fifty-four voting against the Welfare Reform Bill as a whole in November. Far from being a landmark of social legislation, the Bill was a tidying-up exercise, bringing in compulsory interviews for lone parents and restricting entitlement to incapacity benefit. Tellingly, Blair praised Darling as a 'quiet revolutionary'.[12]

Central to the quiet revolution was the focus on the welfare of children regardless of value judgments about their parents. Higher child benefit combined with 'making work pay' for parents and especially lone parents made credible the Blair's promise in his Beveridge lecture at Toynbee Hall on 18 March 1999 to end child poverty in twenty years. But that one piece of justified hyperbole had been fatally undermined by the emptiness of the rhetoric which preceded it. Abolishing child poverty within a generation seemed like mere words, setting a target sufficiently far in the future to ensure that the speaker would not still be in Downing Street to eat them – even with the interim objective set of halving the numbers of children in poverty within ten years.[13] But with poverty defined as living in a household with below half average income, both targets are technically quite achievable and setting them was highly significant in pre-empting the shape of future public spending. If this were the real end point of Blair's welfare revolution, then cutting lone-parent benefit was the wrong place to start.

Notes

1. *Sunday Mirror*, 3 October 1999.
2. *New Statesman*, 30 January 1998.
3. Janet Jones, *Labour of Love*, p. 123.
4. *Hansard*, 30 June 1997.
5. *Sun*, 12 December 1997.
6. Interview, 17 July 2000. The *Daily Mail* certainly welcomed the announcement of the cut in a leading article on 5 July 1997, after the Budget, as evidence that Gordon Brown 'does seem determined to bring state spending under control'.
7. Fax dated 26 February 1998, *Sunday Express*, 29 March 1998.
8. BBC1, *On the Record*, 29 March 1998.
9. Interview, *Daily Mail*, 17 April 1998.
10. *Hansard*, 29 July 1998.
11. Alistair Darling, *Hansard*, 15 December 1998.
12. Interview, *Mail on Sunday*, 14 November 1999.
13. Speech at Centrepoint charity for the homeless, 16 December 1999.

22

NEIGHBOURS

'Psychological Flaws', 18 January 1998

'With a little understanding you can find a perfect blend.'
—*Theme tune of television soap opera*

George Galloway, the dissident Labour MP for Glasgow, Hillhead, bought a copy of Paul Routledge's biography of Gordon Brown at Glasgow airport and did what most MPs would do – looked himself up in the index. The book referred to an incident in 1981 when Galloway, as a leader of the hard left in Scotland, clashed with Brown over a motion of censure on the party leader, Michael Foot, passed by the Executive of the Scottish party.[1] Galloway thought Routledge's account was inaccurate and complained about it to Seumas Milne, the *Guardian*'s left-wing labour editor. Milne, who realised that the book had not yet been published, asked to borrow Galloway's copy which, it turned out, had been put on the bookshop shelf in error.

Routledge's book would have caused trouble whenever its contents had been made public, but the timing of Milne's front-page report in the *Guardian*, on 9 January 1998, conspired against calm and considered media management. Blair was in Japan, and distance in these cases often serves by a form of Chinese whispers to increase suspicion.

Brown tried to disown Routledge, whose flyleaf boasted that the book had been written with his 'full co-operation', and suggested that in any case the *Guardian* – 'How Blair broke secret pact' – had sensationalised its contents. But Routledge had worked closely on the book with Brown's press officer Charlie Whelan and his economic adviser Ed Balls, and Brown had given him one interview in which his resentment against 'the London scene' which had carried Blair to the leadership in 1994 shone through.[2]

For Blair and Alastair Campbell in Japan the book was a provocation too far, faithfully reflecting as it did the delusion shared by Brown and his entourage that the Chancellor had somehow been cheated of the premiership by his ruthless younger brother. Blair and Campbell had already been annoyed by Brown's failure to conceal his brooding, restless ambition and by what they saw as his responsibility for a string of embarrassments. Individually, the charges laid against Brown were petty. He allowed a television documentary to be made about his role in Labour's election victory which turned into a showcase for his advisers, Charlie Whelan and Ed Balls.[3] He allowed Whelan to suggest to journalists that he regarded himself as prime minister to 'president' Blair, or chief executive to Blair's chairman. He refused to get rid of Whelan when Blair tried to persuade him his press officer was doing him more harm than good in a long phone call on election day.[4] He chose to co-operate with Routledge. Blair and Campbell also blamed a series of presentational foul-ups on him – the confusion over euro policy,[5] the fuss over Geoffrey Robinson's offshore trust and the revolt over lone-parent benefit.

Although Blair's first term as Prime Minister was free from the actual plotting against his leadership which dogged Attlee from the start of his 1945 government and Wilson from three years into his 1964–70 administration, Brown's heavy-footed positioning was already a significant irritation. When Blair and Campbell returned from Japan, Blair was determined to assert his authority over his Chancellor. He felt he had been too polite in tolerating Brown's self-promotion for the sake of a harmonious personal relationship, and that a price, both in terms of making tensions in Downing Street more public and of his working relations with Brown, was worth paying.

Campbell made it clear enough that Blair's chairmanship of the welfare reform committee, with John Prescott deputising in the Prime Minister's absence, should be seen as a snub to Brown. But then a 'senior source inside Downing Street', told Andrew Rawnsley, the columnist on the *Observer*, that it was time for Brown to get a grip on his 'psychological flaws'.[6]

The author of this famous remark, 'someone who has an extremely good claim to know the mind of the Prime Minister', cannot have intended it to be quite so incendiary. Indeed, if it had been phrased differently it could have been a commonplace observation. The Chancellor's obsessive, jealous and grudge-bearing personality certainly made some of the business of government difficult to transact. There was no doubt that the thinking reflected Blair's own. Someone as practised in interpersonal dynamics as Blair can only have been irritated by Brown's unwillingness even to pretend to get on with people, his petulant refusal to talk to those he thought were against him and his allergy to meetings.

However, the whole point of Blair's Brown management programme was not to allow this irritation to show in public. A firm hint of prime ministerial supremacy, as in Blair's admittedly ineffective assertion of control over welfare reform, combined with a gentle admonition for Brown's 'daft and ill-advised' co-operation with Routledge's venture – the commentary offered to Simon Walters on the *Sunday Express* – seemed much more the dressing-down that had been intended. It seems inconceivable that either Campbell or Blair intended the 'psychological flaws' phrase, in all its unavoidable colour, to appear on the front page of that Sunday's *Observer*. However, there is some evidence that it was not an accidental over-expression of genuine frustration: the phrase was also used that week in a column written by John Williams of the *Mirror*.[7]

It was extraordinary – and potentially disastrous – that the tensions between Numbers Ten and Eleven should have reached such a pitch so early on in the administration. Such a pitch that Blair calculated it was better to expose division at the heart of his government (even if he did not intend to lay it quite so bare) than to allow Brown's self-promotion to go unchallenged. It was all the more surprising given that Blair and Brown had both witnessed the devastating parliamentary effect of John Smith as shadow Chancellor reciting the words of the theme song from *Neighbours* to exploit the tensions between Thatcher and Lawson.[8]

The 'psychological flaws' phrase was a barb too far. Blair acknowledged as much by going immediately into reverse spin, publicly praising Brown that evening: 'He is my Lloyd George. Gordon has the intellectual firepower of eighteen Ken Clarkes.'[9] But the damage was done. *Private Eye* captured the moment with a memorable cover headlined 'PEACE TALKS RESUME' (a reference to the run-up to Good Friday in Northern Ireland) which had Blair saying to Brown, 'I am prepared to work alongside you,' and Brown responding, 'Neither am I.'*

---

*The same edition of *Private Eye* (23 January 1998) contained the classic guide in Janet-and-John style to mutual loathings in the Cabinet: 'Gordon hates Robin, John, Derry and Peter. He also doesn't like Mo and he wants Tony's job.

'Robin hates Gordon and John hates Gordon too. Gordon likes Margaret, but John does not. Robin and John hate Harriet because she can't count up, but Gordon likes Harriet because she can't count up. Gordon is the only person who likes Harriet.

'Robin really wants Gordon's job, but Gordon will not let him have it. Alistair pretends to like Gordon *and* Tony, although no one likes Alistair, especially since he shaved his beard off. Gordon, Robin, Jack and John hate Derry and Derry hates them. Gordon, Robin, John, Jack, David, Chris and Clare hate Peter. Peter hates everyone except Tony, Derry and Rupert who delivers the newspapers.'

Four months later, Routledge also found himself at the rough end of Blair–Campbell summary justice. He had been due to join the *Express* as political editor in May 1998, following its new editor, Rosie Boycott, from the *Independent on Sunday*. Instead, the offer was abruptly withdrawn and Anthony Bevins appointed instead.* There was no doubt that the switch was made at Downing Street's instigation, although the roles played by Clive Hollick, owner of the *Express*, Labour peer and donor, special adviser to the Department of Trade and Industry, and by Philip Gould, consultant to and business partner of Hollick, friend of Boycott and adviser to the Prime Minister, remain obscure. Two weeks later, Routledge was hired by the *Mirror*, then embarking on an unrelated feud with Campbell and thus setting itself up as a trouble-making cheerleader for Brown. Routledge was already sitting on a big story about Peter Mandelson's house.

It was not until the reshuffle in July 1998, however, that the imbalance of power between Downing Street neighbours was restored. Reshuffles are always the most naked moment of prime ministerial power, and Blair used his first brutally. Peter Mandelson, Stephen Byers and Margaret Jay were brought in to the Cabinet; Jack Cunningham and Ann Taylor promoted. None was close to Brown, who was actively hostile to both Mandelson and Cunningham.

Brown's favourites, meanwhile, were done down. Nick Brown, most visibly, was moved out of the Chief Whip's office which he enjoyed into the Cabinet, to serve in the Siberian Ministry of Agriculture. As Chief Whip, he had been unstintingly loyal to both Blair and Gordon Brown, but paid the price for being Gordon's campaign manager in 1994 and for sticking to the story that his candidate could have won when interviewed by Routledge for his book.† Another of Gordon's allies, Margaret Beckett, was moved from the Department of Trade and Industry and made Leader of the House of Commons – the government's business manager in Parliament. Meanwhile, from the lower ranks of the ministeriat two Brown partisans, Nigel Griffiths and Tom Clarke, were sacked.

One of the reasons for Blair's put-down of Brown in January was that there had been a dangerous sense developing among MPs of two camps,

---

*Bevins is a quirkily free-thinking journalist, then serving his second stint at the *Independent* where he had been founding political editor, but he was also an open admirer of both Campbell and Blair.

†It was the same story he told me in 1994 for the first edition of this book, and was presumably intended to protect Gordon's dignity, but it offered Blair a scapegoat for the Routledge episode.

with a sense that being in the Chancellor's was more likely to deliver political advancement. The perception had been, for example, that one of the Chancellor's supporters, Douglas Alexander, had secured the Labour nomination for the safe Labour seat of Paisley South for the by-election in October 1997 over Pat McFadden, a member of the Number Ten Policy Unit. The idea that being identified as a Brownite was the key to promotion was now decisively killed off. Geoffrey Robinson's survival was, paradoxically, an added humiliation, as the Chancellor was forced to plead with Blair to keep an ally whose business affairs still had plenty of potential to embarrass the government.

The reshuffle also put an end to the notion that Brown had secured an explicit concession from Blair, as the price of withdrawing from the leadership race in 1994, that he would have the right of veto over all important economic appointments. Although by May 1997 Brown had removed his Cabinet-level opponents from all the main economic and spending departments, and held a dominant position in the making of policy, this was only because Blair felt that what was good for Brown was good for New Labour. He accepted Brown's view that Chris Smith should be moved from health, and he was talked out of making Frank Field Social Security Secretary not just by Brown but by Mandelson, whose political antennae sensed trouble. He also resisted Brown's desire to see his ally Andrew Smith in the Cabinet as Transport minister, the job he had shadowed in Opposition – Smith was only let into the Cabinet in 1999 in order to balance Mandelson's return.*

The hidden struggle for the succession

Gordon Brown's career strategy was based on being the natural successor to Blair. This ensured that, whatever the tensions between them, and whatever the unspoken suspicions about each other's motives, they were bound together. At the same time, Brown wanted to preserve his left-wing credentials, as almost the entire selectorate for the party leadership – MPs, party members and trade unionists – saw itself as to the left of Blair. The tensions were therefore of tone and tactics rather than of policy substance.

---

*Brown was certainly powerful: Cook, by comparison, was unable even to choose his junior ministers. When he saw Blair on the day after the election he asked for Clive Soley or Peter Hain as minister for Europe, and was told the next day it would be Doug Henderson (John Kampfner, *Robin Cook*, pp. 127–9). Peter Hain became a Foreign Office minister in 1999.

Although Brown was widely accepted as the 'bus' candidate throughout Blair's first parliament, who would take over if Blair suddenly ceased to be Prime Minister, it was never as clear-cut as that. Unlike the Conservatives, whose MPs could elect a new leader within a matter of days, Labour required several weeks to organise its ballot among its wider franchise. Almost unnoticed amid the drama over the introduction of one member, one vote at the 1993 Labour conference, new rules were laid down to cover what would happen in government if a Labour leader became 'permanently unavailable' – resigned in a huff, died or went mad. The deputy leader of the party would not automatically stand in until the election of a successor. Instead, the Cabinet would choose a new prime minister from among its number, who would enter the leadership campaign with a big advantage, and Brown's tendency to make enemies made him vulnerable to the Cabinet uniting behind a 'Stop Gordon' candidate. Several Cabinet ministers were contemptuous of his reliance on advisers, bringing at least one to meetings they would attend alone, and where Ed Balls would further irritate colleagues by whispering in Brown's ear. If Blair had failed to turn up for work on any morning during his first term as Prime Minister, the Cabinet would probably have ended up choosing between Brown and, successively, Mo Mowlam, Jack Straw and David Blunkett.

Rather better for Brown would be an orderly handover, by which Blair would announce his resignation, but stay on while his successor was chosen. But the repeated suggestion that Blair might stand down in Brown's favour in the middle of a second term should be read in the context of his need to keep Brown's hopes up. Blair refused three times to say he would serve a full term as Prime Minister if he won a second election on BBC Radio 2's Jimmy Young programme on 9 February 1999, saying only: 'I am very pleased to carry on being Prime Minister at the moment.' But if he had genuinely planned to retire half-way through his second parliament, for example after winning a referendum to join the euro, he was unlikely to want to advertise the fact in advance. Impending devaluations and resignations are two subjects on which politicians are allowed to lie. If he did resign, no one would protest, 'But you said you would stay as Prime Minister for a whole parliament.' The only purpose, therefore, of his coyness about the future was in order to avoid sending a public message to Brown that he intended to go 'on and on'.

The dangers of that were well illustrated when Alastair Campbell gave an affirmative answer when asked at his briefing for the Sunday newspapers if Blair intended to serve a full term if elected next time. This was rendered on the front page of the *Mail on Sunday* as 'Blair to Brown:

You'll never be PM now'.[10] Blair was obliged to pay an extravagant tribute in a television interview that morning:

> It's not for me to choose my own successor but you know what I feel about Gordon, how strong and close we are and all the rest of it. I know people are always trying to make mischief between us but they never will – and he is someone with every quality to be a great British Prime Minister. But whether he's Prime Minister or I'm Prime Minister or all the rest of it depends on the British people.[11]

Just as Blair had not agreed a deal on policy or personnel in 1994, he had not agreed to stand aside and let Brown take over after six years of the premiership.* But it did him no harm to allow Brown to think that this might happen.

Prudence and boldness

Blair owed a great deal to Brown's soundness of political judgment and to his steadiness of economic management. Brown in turn owed much to his good fortune in coming into office five years into the longest economic boom in British history, the junior cousin of its American equivalent, which also began in 1992. However, for a Labour government to avoid making a mess of economic management was a significant achievement. Prudence had damaged Brown's standing in the Labour Party in Opposition, and 11 Downing Street did not appear a promising base for him, as Roy Jenkins and Denis Healey might testify. But prudence enhanced Brown's standing in government and, by exorcising the ghosts of past Labour Chancellors from Philip Snowden on, he ensured that his time may yet come.

Blair generally deferred to Brown on economic policy, well aware of his own infirm grasp on the subject. Back in January 1996, he had tried to exploit the popular vogue for Will Hutton's surprise bestseller, *The State We're In*, by lifting its watchword in a speech in Singapore on 'the Stakeholder Economy'. Blair told Hutton stakeholding would be 'our big idea', but Brown insisted it raised expectations that 'stakeholders' such as employees as well as share-owners would be given a say in the running of companies, and the slogan was diverted into the cul-de-sac of mere rhetoric.

As nearly all the big economic questions were also political, such as the

---

*For what it was worth, Brown denied that Blair had promised to stand aside for him in the second term when asked directly on BBC1, *On the Record*, 26 September 1999: 'No, this is all gossip.'

single European currency and the allocation of public spending increases, this gave Brown more influence at the top of government than any Chancellor since Lloyd George. There was an element of truth in Brown's portrayal of himself as the chief executive, with Blair as chairman, although a more accurate analogy would have been that of one of those successful business partnerships where one is the organisational and financial genius, the other the confident and persuasive frontman.

Clearly, the relationship between Brown and Blair was not as good as pretended. But there were limits to the damage Brown's ambition could cause Blair. In particular, the suggestion that Brown's obvious reluctance to commit himself to joining the euro was dictated by his desire to be Prime Minister is misplaced. The idea that Brown hoped Blair would hold a referendum and lose so that he, as a sceptic, could take over is absurd. If the government recommended joining, the Chancellor would have to support that recommendation whole-heartedly and, more than anyone else in the Cabinet, would have to argue for it publicly by the Prime Minister's side.

Brown's holding back was therefore genuine, although, despite the neo-scepticism carefully cultivated with journalists by Brown's economic adviser Ed Balls, there remained no difference between Brown and Blair over the desirability in principle of joining the monetary union. However, Brown's tactical arguments for putting off joining the euro were powerful ones (as explored in Chapter 29).

Indeed, in most of the areas in which a policy difference was discernible between Blair and Brown, the evidence tends to back the Chancellor's judgment over the Prime Minister's. Brown was a sceptic, not just about the dash for the euro, but about coalition with the Liberal Democrats (he pointedly never attended the joint Cabinet committee with Paddy Ashdown), the Dome and the wilder shores of welfare reform. In each case, it could be argued that Brown either saved Blair from being 'bold' or it would have been better if he had.

Notes

1. Paul Routledge, *Gordon Brown*, pp. 93–5.
2. See Chapter 13, p. 232.
3. Scottish Television, 'We Are the Treasury', 30 September 1997.
4. According to Charlie Whelan, Blair told Brown, 'We don't want Charlie Whelan involved in government': Channel Four, 'Confessions of a Spin Doctor', 25 September 1999.
5. See Chapter 29.
6. *Observer*, 18 January 1998.

7. The article was not published, partly because Williams was engaged in an internal feud with the editor, Piers Morgan, which prompted Williams to leave soon afterwards; it was reported in the *Mail on Sunday*, 9 July 2000.
8. *Hansard*, 7 June 1989, col. 249.
9. *Mirror*, 19 January 1998.
10. BBC1, *Breakfast With Frost*, 26 September 1999. As the election approached, however, Blair could not avoid a direct answer to David Frost's question, 'When you stand, you stand for a whole term?' To which Blair replied: 'Absolutely' (7 January 2001).
11. *Ibid.*, 26 September 1999. Note that Blair omitted the role of the Labour Party in this decision.

23

Government by Headline

'The Twenty-Third Member of the Cabinet', April 1998

> 'Strip down a policy or opinion to one key clear line before the media does it for you. Think in headlines.'
>
> —*Tony Blair,* The Times, *24 November 1987*

When Tony Blair spoke to Romano Prodi, the Italian Prime Minister, on 18 March 1998, he asked him what he thought of Rupert Murdoch's £4 billion bid for Mediaset, the television, newspaper and publishing company owned by former Prime Minister Silvio Berlusconi. Prodi said he would prefer it to be bought by an Italian company, a fact which Blair then relayed to Murdoch. It was a short exchange during a twenty-minute phone call but, when it was reported a week later,[1] it touched a nerve among those on the lookout for signs of a pay-back for the support of the *Sun* and the *News of the World* at the election.

Murdoch's bid was rebuffed by Mediaset two days after the Prime Ministers spoke, but Prodi's preference for an Italian purchaser was a factor in persuading him not to make a higher bid. Murdoch thought there was nothing wrong in asking Blair to find out if the Italian government was likely to try to block the takeover: 'This was a perfectly innocent request for information which I would expect from any British business needing help from their government in European-wide investments.'[2]

That was not how others saw it. Roy Hattersley, by now a graduate critic of New Labour, mocked 'the Prime Minister's new role as European sales representative for Mr Rupert Murdoch'.[3] Alastair Campbell, cornered by journalists at his briefing for the parliamentary Lobby, described the suggestion that Blair had lobbied for Murdoch's business interests as a 'complete joke', 'baloney' and 'c-r-a-p'. As irrelevant proof of his non-denial, he said the phone call had been made by Prodi, not Blair.

Blair himself said: 'I treat Mr Murdoch no differently from anybody else in respect of any business with British interests.' That was a more accurate description of NewsCorp than the attempt by Murdoch, an Australian and American citizen, to pass it off as a 'British business'. But it was difficult assertion to judge, Murdoch's dominant position in the politically-sensitive media market putting him in a different category from other 'businesses with British interests'. There was already a sense in the air, which Blair had cleverly ensured could never be pinned down, that Murdoch had escaped legislative action to curb his cross-media ownership on account of his calling off the dogs. Andrew Neil, the former editor of Murdoch's *Sunday Times*, recalled that Blair once told him: 'How we treat Rupert Murdoch's media interests when in power will depend on how his newspapers treat the Labour Party in the run-up to the election and after we are in government.'[4]

Bricks and bottles

Gerald Kaufman was only trying to be helpful when, two weeks later, he rose to the defence of Campbell at Prime Minister's Questions. As a former press secretary to the Labour Party, Kaufman took offence on Campbell's behalf to Conservative jibes about Blair's phone conversation with Prodi. The press, feeling that Campbell had misled them with his vigorous dismissal of a story which turned out to be essentially true, had savaged him, although neither of Blair's Conservative questioners that day, William Hague and Howard Flight, had in fact mentioned the Prime Minister's spokesman: they had both mocked Blair himself. Kaufman took umbrage anyway, asking the Prime Minister:

> In responding to such attacks, will my right honourable friend take into account the fact that Conservative members . . . are the party of Sir Bernard Ingham, who misused a letter from Law Officers against the right honourable member for Henley [Michael Heseltine], who described a member of the Cabinet as a 'semi-detached member of the Cabinet', and who was described by John Biffen as 'the sewer rather than the sewage'?[5]

Blair went too far in his reply: 'There is one reason why the Opposition attack the press spokesman: he does an effective job of attacking the Conservative Party.' That crossed a constitutional trip-wire: although he was no ordinary civil servant, Campbell was not supposed to engage in offensive action for the Labour Party. But it took a little while for the balloon to go up.

Meanwhile, Paddy Ashdown prompted Blair to defend his strategy of cosying up to media moguls. 'Surely the real issue is not who said what, when and to whom,' said Ashdown, 'but whether the Prime Minister understands why there is so much widespread concern about the seemingly unstoppable growth in media power and political influence of Mr Rupert Murdoch.'

Blair replied soothingly: 'Of course I understand the concerns that people have.' But he went on:

> As for newspaper proprietors, I meet all of them regularly; I know all of them. I regard that as a sensible part of being the leader of a major political party. As a matter of fact, I have no illusions about any of them. They are all highly able, highly ruthless and dedicated to the success of their businesses, as I am dedicated to the success of mine.

It was a revealing answer, just as his defence of Campbell had revealed a little too much of how he saw his spokesman's real role. Campbell was not bound by civil service rules relating to impartiality. He had ended the tradition – rather a threadbare one in the case of Joe Haines under Wilson and Bernard Ingham under Thatcher – of prime ministers' press secretaries being civil servants. He was a special adviser, licensed to be party political, with a special contract which allowed him executive authority over civil servants.* When Christopher Meyer ceased to be the Prime Minister's chief press secretary in early 1996, John Major considered a political appointment, but decided against it, saying he thought it constitutionally improper.[6] Meyer was replaced by another career civil servant, Jonathan Haslam.

However, Blair had gone too far. Although special advisers are allowed to give ministers party-political advice, Campbell remained bound by the rules of the Government Information Service, which he headed, drawing a distinction between presenting ministers' policies, which 'may have the effect of advancing the aims of the political party in government', and the defence of those policies 'in party political terms'. It was not allowed directly to 'attack (though it may be necessary to respond to in specific terms) policies and opinions of opposition parties and groups'.

Campbell was summoned to give evidence to a select committee about his role as the Prime Minister's Official Spokesman, and told a Conservative questioner: 'What would be wrong is if I were using that position to promote and further the interests of the Labour Party by abusing that position constantly by attacking your party.'[7]

---

*See p. 535.

In fact, the rules made no sense. Campbell's position was more honest than that of some of his predecessors, but Sir Richard Wilson as head of the civil service had a spot of bother trying to explain this 'grey area' when challenged about the Prime Minister's words: 'The point he was making,' he said, was that Alastair Campbell had been very effective in attacking the Conservatives when Labour were in Opposition. In government, he was entitled to respond to party-political points, but 'I do not think his job is to go over the top and attack the Opposition with bricks and bottles'.[8]

It was only after Blair's praise of Campbell's 'bricks and bottles' qualities that the Conservatives cottoned on to the fact that he regularly attended Cabinet meetings, and launched an attack on him as the 'twenty-third member of the Cabinet'. It was not without precedent for the Prime Minister's press secretary to attend as an observer. Campbell's immediate predecessor, Jonathan Haslam, had been entitled to attend, but had only done so as deputy press secretary at the crisis meeting of the Cabinet in the House of Commons before the vote of confidence on the European budget in November 1994. Given the brisk formalism of Blair's Cabinet meetings, what was even more significant was that Campbell attended the smaller groups in which the Prime Minister's real business was done, above all the 'war cabinets' for Iraq and Kosovo, and that he was so intimately involved in the negotiations in Northern Ireland over the Good Friday Agreement.

Campbell's presence in these meetings was a significant constitutional change. It ensured that there was 'one truth' about any meeting, making it harder for other participants to put out rival spin. In that sense, Campbell was the real 'Cabinet secretary', because what matters in modern politics is not what the minutes say but the version that is given to the media.

The Tories' discovery that Campbell attended Cabinet drew attention belatedly to his significance at the heart of a government which took media management more seriously than any before. By now, Campbell's influence as one of Blair's principal advisers rivalled that of Peter Mandelson and, when Mandelson was occupied in a Cabinet job as Trade and Industry Secretary from July 1998, would exceed it.

The web they wove

Despite overwhelmingly favourable press coverage of the new government, Blair, just like Harold Wilson before him, began to complain about the newspapers at an early stage. Wilson frequently devoted considerable amounts of the Cabinet's time to lectures about confidentiality. Only three months after the 1964 election, he circulated a memo to Cabinet ministers warning them against leaking.[9] Blair was more sensitive: he circulated a personal minute to Cabinet ministers on 'Press Handling' just three weeks after the election, on 21 May 1997. 'An interesting idea injected into the media will be taken as a statement of government policy,' he said. 'All new ideas or statements of this sort must be cleared with No. 10,' and he reinforced the point with a hand-written note at the end: 'It is essential we act on this.' Inevitably, the 'gagging order' was leaked within days.[10]

Blair's management of the media was more sophisticated and effective than his Labour predecessor's paranoia, however, which drove Wilson to lay down unenforceable rules: 'Ministers should not give press interviews, whether attributably or unattributably, except in the presence of a reliable witness such as a Public Relations Officer; and a careful note of such interviews should be made.' Wilson had been infuriated by an article by Anthony Howard in the *Sunday Times* the previous day which 'purported to describe a conflict of view between the Department of Economic Affairs and the Treasury about the direction of economic policy'.[11] For all the assumption that Blair's obsession with media management meant that policy was unimportant, he had ensured that his government observed the first law of good public relations, namely that communications should reflect reality. With Chancellor Gordon Brown dominant over economic policy there were only personality differences and disagreements over tactics for the press to report.

Nor did Blair, however, rely on memos and bans on unchaperoned contact with the Fourth Estate. He ensured tight control over 'the message' by according a central role in the new government's hierarchy to Alastair Campbell. This was another facet of the paradox of simultaneous devolution and centralisation. While the government was pluralistic to the point of promiscuity in seeking allies and supporters from all the power centres of society, it retained rigid control at the centre over presentation.

Campbell's assertion of his control over Whitehall press officers was bound to attract the charge of 'politicisation', and the memo he wrote on 26 September 1997 urging the Government Information Service to 'raise its game' certainly lacked any sensitivity towards the civil service culture of impartiality: 'Four key messages . . . should be built into all areas of our activity. 1: This is a modernising government . . . 2: The government is delivering on its promises. 3: Its policies are in the mainstream . . . 4: The government is providing a new direction for Britain.'[12]

Campbell could argue that, as he was the Prime Minister's Official

Spokesman, and as 'the overall political strategy, direction and style of the government is set by the Prime Minister',[13] he was responsible for presenting everything, party political or not. There is, of course, a fine line between the promotion of government policy, and the promotion of the governing party's policies – a line so fine it hardly exists. Some newspapers became so excited about the Labour Party 'using the civil service to achieve its political objectives' they forgot that was what the civil service was for.

Campbell's political centrality was bound to attract trouble eventually. What was surprising, and a tribute to his brutal charm, was how long it took for him to begin to offend the journalists with whom he dealt every day. He was generally contemptuous of his former colleagues in the parliamentary Lobby – the journalists granted access to the House of Commons, and in particular the Members' Lobby, who were also entitled to attend the twice-daily briefings by the Prime Minister's spokesman. But, as Campbell's biographer Peter Oborne pointed out, this meant he was 'moderately even-handed in his dealings with political journalists'. Peter Mandelson, on the other hand, made the mistake of thinking of journalists as friends and 'when they let him down – in other words did their job – he felt in some sense personally betrayed'. Campbell expected journalists to let him down and, 'when they did so, he therefore felt none of the special rancour that overcame Peter Mandelson'.[14]

The relationship between Campbell, as the new Prime Minister's press secretary, and Lobby journalists started off in high spirits, although with an undertone of menace on both sides. On 25 November 1997 the preposterous saga of Humphrey the Downing Street cat reached high farce, with both of the day's Lobby briefings dominated by questions about what had happened to him. Cherie had already been forced to pose for the cameras with the wretched creature, a stray adopted by Number Ten staff under the previous regime, in order to counter reports that she wanted to get rid of him. When Campbell told Lobby journalists the cat had moved to a quiet suburban place he was asked, 'Is it a cemetery?' He then thought it important enough to squash speculation that he arranged for a photograph to be issued of the cat at an undisclosed south London location sitting on that day's newspapers – in the style of a ransom demand.

It was Campbell's favouritism towards the Murdoch press which caused some of the early bad blood. The Downing Street press machine turned out an astonishing quantity of journalism under the Prime Minister's by-line, making Blair the most prolific journalist–Prime Minister in history, with an average of one and a half articles in the national press per week in his first year. Of seventy-six articles, twenty were for the *Sun* and a further four for the *News of the World*.*

After the second Cabinet reshuffle in July 1999, Campbell unwisely taunted journalists by handing out mock awards for wrong predictions at a Lobby briefing, including a CD by a band called Garbage to the *Daily Telegraph* for its forecast that Paddy Ashdown would take Mo Mowlam's job in Northern Ireland. As the press warmed to the theme that this was a government of spin and spin-doctors, he countered by boisterously lecturing the Lobby on his thesis that journalists were the spinners who deliberately slanted their reporting to suit their own prejudices.

In early 2000, he annoyed them further by allowing Michael Cockerell, the BBC documentary-maker, to make a film of his work, which included filming the Lobby briefing. Journalists variously resented the favouritism shown to Cockerell, or complained they were being used as extras for a propaganda exercise. Campbell was caught in a dilemma, as every attempt to make the business of presentation more open and to try to communicate directly with the people not only offended the squabbling, jealous press pack but exposed him more and more as a personality in his own right. It is one of the laws of media management that when the press officer 'becomes the story' it is time to get a new press officer, as Charlie Whelan had by now discovered to his cost.

Most newspapers started to attribute statements by Campbell to him by name in March 2000, despite his protests that what he said was only important because he was speaking on behalf of the Prime Minister and that therefore the PMOS formula made sense.† In June, he retreated from giving the daily briefings, letting his civil service deputy, Godric Smith, take the front-line role. Every time there was a spat over the government's use of 'spin', however, such as when the millionaire novelist Ken Follett attacked Blair for allowing off-the-record briefing against

---

*Not only did the machine produce homogenised Campbell-imitation prose in Blair's name, but it also contracted out its services to foreign leaders. Campbell advised the Japanese government on the style of an article published in the *Sun* in the name of the Japanese Prime Minister which expressed regret for the treatment of British prisoners of war in the Second World War, and on 'the way such an article might be expressed' (letter to *Daily Telegraph*, 16 January 1998).

†The title 'Prime Minister's Official Spokesman' had been adopted as a result of the report by Sir Robin Mountfield, outgoing permanent secretary at the Cabinet Office, 27 November 1997: it replaced the impersonal 'Downing Street' which had developed when John Major's government ended the convention of pretending that official briefings for Lobby journalists did not exist.

ministers, Campbell could not resist re-entering the fray – with bricks and bottles (he accused Follett of a 'self-indulgent rant').

Follett had struck a sharp blow to the government's weak point. His motive was suspect – he had been dropped by Blair in a rare case of unnecessarily making an enemy back in 1994, and his wife, Barbara Follett, the MP for Stevenage, had failed to become a minister. But his charge resonated and was, by its nature, irrefutable. Campbell probably had not been rude about Mo Mowlam in private, as Follett alleged, but he may well have expressed unattributable irritation with Gordon Brown and had admitted briefing against Clare Short in Opposition. After she was demoted from Transport in the summer of 1996, he accepted 'we overstepped the mark' – although he was careful to make clear that the 'we' meant him and Blair jointly: 'Anything that I do and say is because Tony wants it done or said,' he said in the same interview.[15]

Such was the corporate personality of Blair–Campbell that, although Campbell was the subsidiary, the spokesman and the adviser, and Blair the ultimate boss, theirs was a remarkably equal relationship. Campbell's bullying, joshing tone often teasingly suggested that the Prime Minister did as he was told, but it would be far-fetched to suggest, as Oborne occasionally does, that Campbell was the 'dominant' partner. That overlooks the extent to which Blair played dumb when it suited him.

Spun done

When Blair said before the election that he would 'govern by headline', it seemed he was setting out Alastair Campbell's central role in a new kind of government, that would not be the passive object of journalists' attention but would manage the news cycle aggressively in order to maintain its hegemony. It was a double-edged ambition, however, because of the narrow line between trying to dictate the headlines and being dictated to by them.

The single word 'spin' had become, by the middle of 2000, the most devastating weapon against the government, as 'sleaze' became for John Major. A short, headline word which summed up all the complaints about the Blair style, it was, like 'sleaze', too imprecise to shake off. At Westminster, it meant the dark arts of media manipulation, for which New Labour had gained a dangerous reputation in Opposition. For most voters, however, it signified the gap between rhetoric and delivery: the fact that the government was claiming huge amounts of money spent on hospitals and schools and that nothing appeared to have changed. This was the perception which did the real damage: the truth was that New Labour was not – and probably could not be – as good at media management in government as it had been in Opposition. Despite the fearsome reputation of Blair, Campbell and Mandelson, the government was dogged from the start by a string of failures which were largely presentational, from the row over tuition fees, through the early chaos over policy on the euro, to the Ecclestone affair and the lone-parent benefit cut. But none of these had much effect on the government's post-election honeymoon with the voters, and it was not until the government was nearly three years old that the idea of 'spin' started to corrode the opinion-poll ratings. It was only then, when the voters began to expect to see visible and concrete delivery of better public services, that serious disillusionment started to set in and William Hague finally gained some traction on the electoral mountain facing the Conservatives, deriding Blair as 'all spin and no substance'.

Notes

1. *La Stampa*, 24 March 1998.
2. Raymond Snoddy, *The Times*, 27 March 1998.
3. *Guardian*, 2 April 1998.
4. *Observer*, 29 March 1998.
5. *Hansard*, 1 April 1998.
6. Anthony Seldon, *John Major*, p. 685.
7. Select committee on Public Administration, Sixth Report, 29 July 1998, paragraphs 25 and 27.
8. Answer to Andrew Tyrie, Minutes of Evidence, select committee on Public Administration, 16 June 1998.
9. Memorandum, Cabinet Papers, 19 January 1965.
10. *Daily Mail* and *Daily Telegraph*, 2 June 1997.
11. Minute, Cabinet Papers, 22 February 1965.
12. *New Statesman*, 24 October 1997.
13. Cabinet Office memorandum on Government Information and Communication Service to select committee on Public Administration, 6 August 1998.
14. Peter Oborne, *Alastair Campbell*, p. 139.
15. *Guardian*, 17 February 1997.

24

HAND OF HISTORY

Northern Ireland, Good Friday, 10 April 1998

'You have to be tough, you have to be informed, you have to have ambition, you have to have a political vision.'

—*Gerry Adams, 1998*

When John Major became Prime Minister seven years before Blair did, he looked at the situation in Northern Ireland with the bemused eye of an outsider, the negotiating instincts of a whip and the desire to make history. 'For a long time, I thought it was silly that we weren't making progress on Ireland and people just seemed to assume the status quo was right,' he said. 'The thought kept running through my mind that if the killing was happening in Surrey it wouldn't be acceptable.'[1] His lack of sentiment allowed a great deal of progress to be made; he ended the media ban on Sinn Fein, the political wing of the Irish Republican Army, and allowed ministers to meet its representatives face to face. But his uneven momentum was snagged almost accidentally on a point of principle: he thought – any reasonable person would – that terrorists should give up their guns and bombs before their representatives took part in democratic government.

Major was persuaded by the government's secret contacts with the IRA, which started under Margaret Thatcher, that the republican movement was genuinely looking for a way to end its 'war'.[2] He sought to assist them by saying in the Downing Street Declaration in December 1993 that the United Kingdom government had no 'selfish strategic or economic interest' in Northern Ireland, a curious formula intended to disclaim any notion of British colonialism. When the IRA announced a three-month ceasefire on 31 August 1994, however, he insisted it should be declared permanent before Sinn Fein would be allowed to join all-party talks about Northern Ireland's future. It was a perverse response to the IRA's historic decision, and one which helped to ensure that the ceasefire, although it lasted longer than three months, turned out not to be permanent. Given the divisions within the republican movement, and its mythology of British treachery, the urgent need was at least to start to admit Sinn Fein to the democratic mainstream in order to reinforce the course of non-violence.

Sinn Fein's leaders finally met ministers in May 1995, only to be told they could not join all-party talks until the IRA had disarmed. Meanwhile, the main elements of what were to become the Good Friday Agreement were sketched out in a long and stuttering series of discussions with successive Irish prime ministers Albert Reynolds and John Bruton and, separately, with the constitutional parties in Northern Ireland. Those elements were: a devolved assembly for Northern Ireland, unionists and nationalists both wanting, for their different reasons, an end to direct rule from London; the end of the Irish Republic's claim to the north; the release of prisoners convicted of terrorist offences; and some form of disavowal of violence.

Major appointed George Mitchell, recently retired from the United States Senate, to chair an international body to oversee the decommissioning of arms – the word 'disarmament' being too close in meaning to 'surrender' for republican sensibilities. On 22 January 1996 Senator Mitchell proposed that 'parallel decommissioning' should take place at the same time as all-party talks. Major accepted it, but clouded the issue by making alternative proposals as well. The IRA had already decided that his government would not give its political leaders the status and influence they sought, and had begun planning the previous autumn for a big attack on the financial centre of London.[3] At 7.01pm on Friday 9 February 1996 it ended its ceasefire by exploding a bomb in the London Docklands near Canary Wharf, murdering two people.

Major kept trying, but he had run out of time, and neither the republicans nor the Unionists would give him any room for manoeuvre. David McKittrick, the *Independent*'s fine Ireland correspondent, compared his dedication to that of Gladstone or Lloyd George, but felt it was misapplied: 'The criticism is not one of lack of commitment but lack of a compass.'[4]

When Tony Blair became Prime Minister his instincts were similar to his predecessor's, but he had a better feel for the psychology and tempo of the situation. In contrast to Major, he had shown an astute understanding of the big themes in his own response to the IRA ceasefire, which came just six weeks after he became Labour leader. Within an hour of the announcement, he was on the radio welcoming the 'opportunity' it provided, and using it as a chance to ditch the idea that Labour sought a united Ireland. Labour's Northern Ireland spokesman, Kevin MacNamara, got as far as the BBC studio in Hull to give his reaction, only to be told that the leader would be speaking for the party on the issue. The next day, Blair effectively dropped Labour's policy of supporting Irish 'unity by consent', a logically-challenged compromise forged in 1980 to stave off the republican left who saw the IRA as a national liberation movement. He emphasised 'consent', and made it clear that the Labour Party did not see itself as a 'persuader' for a united Ireland. 'The important thing is not that the government takes up the role of pushing people in one direction or another, but that they allow the wishes of those in Northern Ireland to be paramount.'[5] MacNamara, long distrusted by the unionists, was replaced by the open and unplaceable Mo Mowlam two months later.

Blair developed close relations with David Trimble, who became leader of the Ulster Unionist Party in 1995. Trimble's roots were in the quasi-paramilitary fringe which regarded the main unionist party as too soft. He won the party leadership by putting himself at the head of fundamentalist Orange demands to march down the Garvaghy Road at Drumcree, forcing the government to back down for fear of violence. This gave him the necessary credibility with the unionist population, who were ready for compromise, but perpetually suspicious of their leaders. He was also, however, a recognisably modern politician, having once said that he would have joined the SDP had he lived on the other side of the Irish Sea at the time. And he was a 'moderniser': one of the reasons he admired Blair was that he felt Blair had done for Labour what he needed to do for the Ulster Unionist Party.

Blair also understood the shift in the thinking of republicans, prepared to postpone Irish unification in return for a show of respect to their tribe. Moreover, while both he and Major recognised the importance of the US, Blair was able to make use of his personal 'special relationship'. His Chief of Staff, Jonathan Powell, as a former political secretary in the British Embassy in Washington, knew all about the cover provided for republican fundraising by the powerful Irish vote, which was wielded on the basis of Irish surnames, sentiment and an appalling ignorance of the realities of modern Ireland. The supply of American money gave President Clinton power. In January 1994 he granted Sinn Fein president Gerry Adams a visa, which infuriated Major but strengthened Adams's argument for ceasefire. Blair's closeness to Clinton would now provide him with an invaluable 'call a friend' service whenever any of the participants seemed less certain than he of the promptings of destiny.

Above all, however, Blair had seen how Major had allowed the process to be blocked on the question of weapons, and he was thus determined to avoid making the mistake of taking a stand on an issue of principle.

An early trip to Northern Ireland formed part of Jonathan Powell's plan for the first thirty days, although no date had been fixed. Two weeks after taking office, on 16 May, Blair made the first journey in what would soon feel like a regular shuttle on an RAF plane from Northolt in north London to Aldergrove air base outside Belfast. He used a tired metaphor, 'the settlement train is leaving', to get the talks process moving again. It sounded as if he were being tough on Sinn Fein – they were told they had to get on board because otherwise the talks would go ahead without them – which, given that the whole point was to end IRA violence, was patently false. He also made a pledge of sorts to the Union, phrased in such a way as to achieve maximum emotional impact with the unionist majority without gratuitously offending the nationalist minority. Speaking at the Balmoral show, he said: 'None of us in this hall today, even the youngest, is likely to see Northern Ireland as anything but a part of the United Kingdom.' Given that the new republican strategy was itself to see a united Ireland as a long haul, it was perhaps more important that Blair omitted from his speech any reference to the decommissioning of IRA weapons as a condition of Sinn Fein's taking part in talks. It was enough to secure a new IRA ceasefire two months later.

The other important decision, which Blair had taken before the election, was to set a deadline. By chance, the legislation specifying which parties were entitled to take part in the talks expired in May 1998. Now Blair drew attention to this date and suggested that a conclusion should be reached by then. All-party 'proximity' talks began in September – modelled on the Dayton talks which had secured a peace settlement in Bosnia, by which the parties did not negotiate directly with each other but through government officials. The talks started without Ian Paisley, of the nay-saying unionist tendency, but included, crucially, both Sinn Fein and the Ulster Unionist Party. Blair first met Gerry Adams in October, and they shook hands away from the cameras – a pressing of flesh that had been prepared for more than in any Mills & Boon novel. Adams was publicly fulsome in his praise for the new Prime Minister: 'You have to be tough, you have to be informed, you have to have ambition, you have to have a political vision. I think he clearly has all of those and he understands the Anglo-Irish situation better than one would presume.'[6]

Meanwhile, Trimble chose not to use his veto. The General Election had been significant for him, too, in that his party had held its share of the vote and gained a seat, despite being denounced by Paisley for taking part in the peace talks. The change in the atmosphere on both sides of the sectarian divide was reflected in the warmth which greeted Mo Mowlam's human touch – a vivid contrast with the style of her patrician predecessor as Northern Ireland Secretary, Sir Patrick Mayhew. She also made the kind of decision which is only called brave if it works, to visit loyalist terrorists in the Maze prison to try to maintain their support for the talks after the murder there of Billy Wright, leader of the Ulster Volunteer Force in December 1997. But it did work and, after a short, tragic interlude of tit-for-tat killings which saw both Sinn Fein and the loyalist Ulster Democratic Party briefly suspended from the talks, the process ground on towards its deadline.

By March 1998, Senator Mitchell, who was now talks chairman and had been asked by Blair to stay on, took stock. He felt an agreement was in sight. Deep animosities had been worn down: the Unionists still refused to talk directly to Sinn Fein. When Gerry Adams tried to speak to him outside the meeting room, the Unionists' security spokesman Ken Maginnis told him, 'I don't talk to fucking murderers,' and walked away. But in discussions in small groups, the eight parties and two governments had made progress. Mitchell calculated that the end of May would be too late, however, because any agreement would have to be ratified by referendums in Northern Ireland and the Republic and followed as quickly as possible by elections to a new Northern Ireland Assembly. All that would have to happen before the marching season in July, when the annual struggle over the symbols of Protestant supremacy takes to the streets of Northern Ireland. He chose Easter weekend as a new deadline. 'It has historical significance in Ireland,' he said with typical understatement.[7] The Easter Rising against the British in 1916 saw the birth of the Republic – and the beginnings of Partition. He set midnight on 9 April, the day before Good Friday in fifteen days' time, as the cut-off. Crucially, however, he secured the consent of all the parties to the new deadline. At a news conference on 25 March, he said:

> This is not a matter of time. We have been at this for two years. It could be discussed for another two years or for another twenty years. It isn't that there hasn't been enough time for discussion, it is that there has not been a decision required and the only way to bring this to a conclusion is to require a decision. I believe the time for that is now.

Principled compromise

Did Blair know, when he arrived in Belfast on 7 April 1998, that a deal was as good as done, or did he use his public optimism as a way of putting pressure on reluctant Unionists? Certainly, his famous mock-Churchillian phrase was delivered with the conversational modesty of a man who believed that destiny was on his side: 'A day like today, it's not a day for sound-bites really, we can leave those at home, but I feel that – I feel the hand of history upon our shoulder, in respect of this.'

On the other hand, it was also designed to increase the price of failure that would be paid by whichever party ended up with the blame. The calculations behind Mitchell's timetable had already been disrupted the previous week when Blair and Bertie Ahern, the Irish Prime Minister, took longer than expected to agree the 'north–south' issues in face-to-face talks in Downing Street – only to have their long list of all-Ireland bodies that would co-operate across the border rejected out of hand by the Unionists.

'As soon as Tony Blair arrived – they came in a bit like the A-team – it changed the whole thing,' said John Alderdice, leader of the cross-community Alliance party and a key intermediary in the talks. The team included John Holmes, the Private Secretary whom Blair inherited from John Major who could remember all the wording and rewording of all the drafts and documents which had cycled through Downing Street in the previous two years; Alastair Campbell, whose role as considerably more than a press secretary was confirmed by his active part in negotiations; and Jonathan Powell, who saw a settlement in Northern Ireland as his chance to make a mark to match that of his brother Charles under Margaret Thatcher.

Mitchell's assessment of the Prime Minister was crisp: 'Blair possesses the elements of effective leadership in our era. He is intelligent, articulate, decisive and photogenic.' He felt reassured by his presence. 'He was making a total commitment, personal and political, to this negotiation.'[8]

For the next three days, Blair was closeted in Castle Buildings, a characterless 1960s office block in the grounds of Stormont, Belfast. In a Herculean episode of prime ministerial attention to details, he went out only once for a short walk with Campbell, in between endless meetings with all the parties, drafting forms of words with his shirtsleeves literally rolled up, sustained by bacon sandwiches, Twix bars, bananas and cups of tea. His informal style, often with his feet up on the table, belied his skill with the written word. 'When he himself was deeply involved in the text it was at its best. But when he said, "I'm away to bed", and let someone else handle it, it wasn't as tight,' said Alderdice.

Mitchell was unstinting in his praise:

> He understands the extent to which both communities see themselves as victims, and he has a remarkable ability to identify with and calm their fears.

> From what I saw I will say this: if I had an important interest, public or private, that was subject to negotiation, I'd be happy to have Tony Blair representing me.

When Blair and Ahern finally settled the north–south bodies on terms acceptable to both the Unionists and Sinn Fein on Thursday 9 April, Mitchell described the breakthrough as, 'in the very best sense of the words, a principled compromise'.[9] It was an apt choice of words, which could have been applied to the entire process. In the end, the Agreement included compromises for both sides which would have been utterly unacceptable had they not been part of the principled whole. The nationalists accepted that Northern Ireland would remain part of the United Kingdom as long as that was the wish of the majority there, a majority artificially created by the border of 1921. The unionists accepted that they would share power with Sinn Fein. And those on all sides who believed in the rule of law accepted that convicted criminals would 'get out of jail free'.

None of these compromises was unconditional, however, and the precise wording of the text of the agreement was endlessly difficult. The midnight deadline on Thursday came and went, but when Blair appeared on the steps in the early hours of Good Friday, to say that progress was being made, it seemed that a settlement was not far off. Nor was it, but Blair's appearance for the television cameras had a tactical element in raising the stakes to deter any last-minute wrecker. That turned out to be Jeffrey Donaldson, the angry young man of the Ulster Unionist Party, who threatened to lead a revolt against the emerging agreement, adopting the same pose that Trimble himself had struck twenty-three years earlier. After a breakthrough at 5am finally settled the constitution of the proposed Northern Ireland assembly, Trimble went to bed and slept soundly for five hours. 'Trimble was calm,' said Alderdice. 'His attitude was, "I've done my best." It was not that he was totally confident about it, but he was not wracked by self-doubt.'

When the full Unionist delegation met on the mid-morning of Good Friday, however, Donaldson insisted that Trimble re-open the question of IRA disarmament. With the other parties ready to assent to the final draft of the text at a plenary session at midday, they were forced to wait in mounting frustration as the heated Unionist meeting dragged on. When groups of Unionists started to cross the corridor to continue their internal disputes in an empty office opposite, they were intercepted by irate delegates from other parties who told them they could not go back on the text now.

Trimble and Donaldson asked for another meeting with Blair, and met him with Jonathan Powell and Alastair Campbell at 3.20pm. IRA disarmament was the point on which the whole agreement turned. The unspoken basis of the agreement had always been that disarmament would not be a prior condition of Sinn Fein's entry into the government of Northern Ireland. Nor could an agreement explicitly bind the IRA or the loyalist paramilitary groups. But equally it was understood that Sinn Fein could not remain in government without IRA decommissioning. Donaldson pointed out two problems. The first was that the agreement did not set a date by which the paramilitaries were expected to *begin* to decommission their arms, except that decommissioning should be *completed* by May 2000. The second was that the expulsion of Sinn Fein, if the IRA failed to decommission, would be decided by a voting procedure in the Assembly requiring cross-community support. In effect, that meant John Hume's constitutional nationalist Social Democratic and Labour Party would have to vote to expel Sinn Fein. For the Unionists, that was an unreliable safeguard.

Blair refused to consider amendments: 'This is what is going into the plenary and this is it. If we renegotiate on one front, the nationalists will renegotiate on another.' Campbell pleaded: 'If you don't accept this document, we will all be crucified. People will not understand.' But Blair agreed to provide a letter which would give Trimble further assurances.

A few minutes later, Jonathan Powell was despatched with the letter to the Ulster Unionist Party office, only to find that the door had been locked to stop the endless interruptions. Eventually he was admitted and handed the letter to Trimble, who then passed it round. This was the moment on which the talks turned. Such was the state of tiredness and haste that it was not until he returned to Blair's office that Powell realised he had not kept a copy, and he later had to ask the Unionists to photocopy it. On the question of excluding Sinn Fein from the Northern Ireland executive, it said that, if Sinn Fein broke the Agreement by failing to persuade the IRA to start decommissioning in the first six months of the Assembly, 'we will support changes to these provisions to enable them to be made properly effective in preventing such people from holding office'. On the timetable, Blair wrote: 'I confirm that, in our view, the effect of the decommissioning section of the agreement . . . is that the process of decommissioning should begin straight away.' The 'process', however, could mean merely that the independent committee should begin talks with representatives of paramilitaries, and the letter contained no sanction on Sinn Fein if the IRA chose not to do even that. The letter did not satisfy Donaldson, who now left Stormont in disgust, but it was enough to keep the rest of Trimble's MPs on the premises, which was all that mattered at that stage.

Blair also asked President Clinton, who had been following the talks through the night in Washington, to make a final call to Trimble, although it was unnecessary. At 4.45pm Trimble phoned Mitchell in his office to say: 'We're ready to do the business.'

History was made when Mitchell, chairing the plenary session, asked each of the parties in turn if they accepted the document that would become known as the Good Friday Agreement. Receiving positive answers from them all, he adjourned the session at 5.26pm, triggering a media scrum as Blair and Irish Prime Minister Bertie Ahern proclaimed a deal well done to the cameras outside.

The Agreement was an extraordinary achievement for all the participants, including, at the end of a telephone line, the President of the United States. As the contrast with John Major suggests, a part of the credit must be taken by Blair's sheer political cunning, his ability to use language to reconcile the irreconcilable, testing his skills of smoothing and telling people what they want to hear to the limit. He was able to build on the courage of John Hume and David Trimble, joint winners of the Nobel Peace prize the next year, while chivvying and charming the whole constellation of interests and egos towards their rendezvous.

It is likely to be remembered as a decisive turning point, which underpinned long-lasting ceasefires from all the main paramilitary organisations and laid the foundations for the normalisation of Northern Irish life and politics. It would have been unimaginable at any other time point since 1921 – despite its superficial resemblance to the Sunningdale agreement of 1974. Deputy SDLP leader Seamus Mallon's description of it as 'Sunningdale for slow learners' contained a truth, but not the whole truth. The important point about Blair's sense of the hand of history on his shoulder is that he managed to shake it off. No one who felt the burden of Ireland's past could have thought the Agreement possible.

Dead lines

The Good Friday Agreement was locked in by means of simultaneous referendums north and south of the Irish border on 22 May 1998. Blair deployed his full arsenal of personal campaigning weaponry behind the Yes vote. In an act of bipartisanship without precedent in British politics, he and John Major held a shirtsleeved question-and-answer session with students in Belfast. He even pulled off some nice lines in self-deprecation. 'I'll take the easy ones, he'll do the hard ones,' he said at the start.* When

*Another line lifted from Gordon Brown, with whom Blair had staged a similar double act a few weeks earlier on 19 March after the Budget. At the end, Blair invited people to write in with further questions. Brown interjected: 'Difficult questions to Number Ten.'

Major answered the first question instead of taking them in threes as suggested, Blair shrugged and said: 'You're the boss.' He wrote articles in the *Sun* and the *News of the World*, and issued five handwritten 'personal pledges' to the people of Northern Ireland, derived from Philip Gould's focus groups there.[10] Finally, he had Alastair Campbell stretch the envelope of the black arts with a personal appeal from President Clinton in the *Mirror* and the *Sun* two days before polling. It turned out that the task of ghost-writing the President's stirring words – 'You can do nothing to change the past but you can do everything to build the future' – had been sub-subcontracted by Campbell to the *Mirror*'s political editor, Kevin Maguire, who was furious to discover that his words were also running, as an 'exclusive', in the first edition of the *Sun*. Campbell insisted that the *Sun* version was different from Maguire's draft – it was in fact hardly changed – and anyway he 'did it for peace'.

The referendums put the seal on the Good Friday Agreement: 71 per cent of those voting in Northern Ireland endorsed the Agreement including, crucially, a narrow majority of unionists; while in the south 94 per cent voted to renounce the Republic's claim, enshrined in its constitution, to sovereignty over the whole of the island of Ireland. The rhetoric of 'consent' was now mobilised behind a complex constitution of checks and balances which reaffirmed Northern Ireland's status as part of the United Kingdom, but with a system of devolved government containing guarantees of representation for the nationalist minority, and a set of all-Ireland talking shops. As Blair put it a few months later, the 'essential dilemma' of Northern Ireland, whether it should 'remain part of the UK so long as a majority there want it', had been resolved in the unionists' favour. 'In return there will be co-operation North and South, provided both sides agree.'[11]

Now, however, the politicians of Northern Ireland had to deliver on the Agreement's fundamentally ambiguous terms. In June, they were elected to a new Assembly to do so, but the hard part was forming an executive 'cabinet' in which, under the rules of proportional representation in the Agreement, Sinn Fein would be entitled to two seats.

Blair must have felt optimistic as he went on holiday to France in the summer of 1998. The triumph of Good Friday had endowed the many 'Blair's first year' retrospectives – which would anyway have tended to be positive – with a truly golden glow. Then on 15 August, in one of the most tragic acts of terrorism yet in Northern Ireland's awful history, a small IRA splinter group opposed to the Good Friday Agreement managed to kill twenty-nine shoppers – nine of them children, most of them Roman Catholic – in the town of Omagh. Blair broke off his holiday to visit the town and to hold a joint news conference with Bertie Ahern promising to co-operate to find the killers. The bomb cast doubt on the darker calculations behind the Good Friday Agreement. The only justification for the moral compromises involved was pragmatic: that fewer people would die in sectarian violence if the largest terrorist organisations were brought to the negotiating table. Over the previous twenty-five years of sectarian violence, an average of about 120 people had been killed every year. The terrible death toll in a quiet town hitherto relatively untouched by the Troubles threatened to upset that calculus.

Blair's initial response was sombre and restrained. Despite intelligence identifying some of the few active members of the so-called 'Real' IRA, there was not enough evidence for an early criminal conviction. Still on holiday, Blair wrote a thoughtful article for the *Observer* on 23 August in which he argued against simply 'taking out' the Omagh bombers, even though 'the names of many are known to us'. In awkward contrast with his support for President Clinton's raids on Sudan and Afghanistan two days earlier, he insisted 'we must be democratic in the means we deploy'. Such high-mindedness did not last long, however. Two days later, he flew again to Belfast to announce the recall of Parliament to pass anti-terrorist measures of what he called a 'Draconian and fundamental nature'. The Criminal Justice (Terrorism and Conspiracy) Act, rushed through in two days in September 1998, which gave senior police officers extra powers to detain people suspected of belonging to terrorist groups, was illiberal and unnecessary. There was no groundswell of popular outrage: the Conservative Opposition restricted itself to repeating its demand for prisoner releases to be stopped. Its main purpose seemed to be to strengthen Ahern's position in the Republic of Ireland, where he had already announced that his parliament would be recalled to pass the kind of anti-terrorist law which republican sympathies there had always blocked.

At least the new British law was not used. The Omagh bomb had a more damaging effect in reinforcing Unionist objections to dealing with terrorists – offset a little by Gerry Adams's historic condemnation of it and his statement on 1 September that violence was 'a thing of the past, over, done with and gone'.

As the months dragged on, the timetable set in the Good Friday Agreement started to slip. David Trimble, who had been elected First Minister, ready to take up his post when the Northern Ireland Assembly assumed its formal powers, continued to refuse to consider sharing office with Sinn Fein until the IRA started to disarm. This represented a significant move since the pre-Agreement position that Sinn Fein required years of 'quarantine' after disarmament, but there was still a long way to go for the Unionists to accept that the destruction of a few weapons would not affect the IRA's capacity for violence and that what mattered was, in John Hume's luminous phrase, the 'decommissioning of minds'. As Blair wrote: 'Powerful and necessary though decommissioning is as a symbol of change and confidence, it is – again, a blunt truth – a deception to claim there is a finite amount of weapons that once decommissioned can never be replaced.'[12]

On the other hand, Blair was certainly disappointed that Sinn Fein and the IRA failed to respond to the historic fact of the Agreement to make what would be, as he suggested, only a symbolic gesture. As ever, the mirage of IRA disarmament shimmered over the next range on the horizon, namely Sinn Fein's entry into the government of Northern Ireland.

As the first anniversary of the Good Friday Agreement approached, Blair tried to force the Unionists and Sinn Fein to bridge the remaining gap between them. The parties were by now used to negotiating with each other, Trimble having first met Adams in September 1998. The gap concerned the exact sequence of events leading to and including IRA decommissioning and the entry of Sinn Fein into executive office. But the magic of Good Friday was beginning to wear off, and Blair was personally overstretched. At the same time as he tried to re-create the atmosphere of the previous year in five days of intense negotiation at the end of March 1999, the bombs started to fall on Yugoslavia. On 31 March, for example, Blair returned from Northern Ireland, answered Prime Minister's Questions in the Commons, chaired a meeting of the Kosovo war cabinet, and then went back to Hillsborough castle, Mo Mowlam's official residence in Belfast, for a twenty-hour session of talks. Only a week earlier, on 25 March, he and Gordon Brown had been up all night negotiating the European Union budget at the Berlin summit.

A draft text was produced at Hillsborough which proposed a 'day of national reconciliation' on which the IRA would verifiably destroy some weapons, and after which the Northern Ireland government and the north–south bodies would begin to operate. The Hillsborough deal was accepted by the Unionists and rejected by Sinn Fein. Each failure eroded a modicum of Blair's negotiating capital. He annoyed both sides at Hillsborough by telling them that the other side had already agreed when they had not.

Blair's personal relations with Adams had also become strained. Blair was irritated by Adams's endless history lessons, Adams by Blair's insistence that 'we are here not because of the past but because of the future'. But Blair thought Adams was sincere when he said he could bring the republicans no further, and therefore decided that the next inch of movement would have to come from the Unionists.

Blair and Ahern now set another arbitrary deadline – 30 June – which was perilously close to the Orange marching season. As ever, the marching season dictated the rhythm of Trimble's flexibility. Each year, he was hard-line in July, flexible in winter. 'We have one last chance to push for peace in this process,' Blair declared.[13] But everyone knew that, just like John Major, if he failed he would start again. The credibility of the midnight deadline on 30 June was not helped by a notice in the canteen at Castle Buildings, Stormont – where the parties returned to the scene of their Good Friday deal – saying it would be open until 3am. The scene in the restaurant in the middle of the night was bizarre. One of the participants commented: 'All you needed to do for internment was close the doors. They were all there, the terrorists and gangsters with their floozies.' The talks in fact adjourned at 4am and reconvened at noon the next day.

Blair spoke of 'historic, seismic shifts in the political landscape of Northern Ireland', meaning that he believed Martin McGuinness, the Sinn Fein number two, when he gave him an assurance, 'speaking now for the IRA', that the republican movement would deliver on decommissioning if the rest of the Good Friday Agreement were implemented. Blair interpreted McGuinness as saying that his and Adams' argument now prevailed among the proverbial 'hard men' of the IRA's active service units. In fact, the position was more nebulous than that: the Adams–McGuinness position rested on a gamble, namely that, once they had secured government positions, the psychology of the hard-liners in the IRA would shift.

Blair and Ahern calculated that Trimble was bluffing when he warned them that 'jumping together' was as far as he could go – an act of decommissioning at the same time as Sinn Fein joined his administration, not afterwards.

That was a mistake, as was the repeated imposition of artificial deadlines. On 2 July, the two Prime Ministers produced a document called *The Way Forward*, which set a date for the start of devolved government in Northern Ireland, 16 July, giving the Unionists two weeks to decide whether or not to take part. The only reason the original Good Friday deadline had worked was because everyone accepted it from the start. The excuse for naming 16 July was that it was the day when formal powers would be transferred to the new Scottish Parliament and Welsh Assembly, but it was no substitute for all-party commitment. And the best that the Canadian General John de Chastelain, the new chairman of the international body to oversee the decommissioning of arms, could produce by way of a timetable to follow devolution was to say that the IRA would make a public declaration of intent 'within weeks'.

In the Commons Blair was hailed, prematurely, as a miracle-worker in some unlikely quarters. As the only remaining MP who was a member of the Cabinet which, thirty years before, had sent the troops into the streets of Northern Ireland, Tony Benn offered his

> sincere congratulations to the Prime Minister on the time, effort, patience and imagination that he and my right honourable friend the Secretary of State have shown and for which there is absolutely no precedent from any previous Prime Minister.[14]

Ulster Unionist Party leaders, however, took just fifteen minutes to reject the Blair–Ahern *Way Forward* package on 14 July. A few days before, as it became clear that Trimble was not bluffing, Blair's 'last chance' language was suddenly replaced by the idea the talks would be 'parked' while the Unionists were given more time to come round. Indeed, Trimble's robust 'No' helped him claw back some ground among the unionist population – for many of whom the pace of events had been too fast. For all that the climate of opinion had changed, he was only too aware that unionist leaders who run too far ahead of unionist opinion are quickly deposed.

Call for Peter

As so often in politics, it was an innocent bystander who took the blame. The chief victim of the collapse of the *Way Forward* deal was Mo Mowlam, who had had next to nothing to do with it. Her breach with Trimble had occurred earlier, during the Good Friday negotiations, when he became irritated by her lack of grasp of detail – one of the reasons he admired Blair was because he had a legal mind similar to his own. During the Hillsborough talks, Mowlam found herself excluded from the real negotiations, which were conducted on the government side by Blair, Jonathan Powell and Alastair Campbell. The fact of the rift was suppressed until the *Way Forward* negotiations, when Trimble called for her resignation as another way of shoring up his support among Unionist hardliners, who regarded her as too sympathetic to the republicans.

Blair was unable to move Mowlam in the botched reshuffle at the end of July, because he was still hoping to persuade her to run for London mayor, and waited until October to offer her up as the apparently pointless but necessary human sacrifice. Peter Mandelson's return to the Cabinet marked a change in Blair's approach to Northern Ireland. It recognised that too much of his prime ministerial capital had been committed. Not only had it taken up too much of his time over the spring and summer of 1999, for no reward, but he was in danger of being too identified with the zigzagging from one side to the other as the ball was batted between the Unionist and republican courts, at a cost to his credibility with both sides. He needed to regain some distance and deniability from the detailed negotiations, so that any deal could be presented as emerging from the parties themselves rather than being imposed on them by the two governments. At the same time, he needed to convince both sides that he remained personally engaged. Whatever the arguments about the leniency of Mandelson's ten-month exile from the Cabinet, and his return directly to the top table rather than to a more junior post, his appointment was vital to the peace talks. Although Blair was no longer his own Secretary of State for Northern Ireland, he had his 'alter ego' in the post.

For all Blair's tactical errors, Trimble shared his essential insight, which was that the republican movement was split and that the peace faction was the dominant one. 'I believe that the leadership of the IRA, or Sinn Fein/IRA, are prepared to give up violence for good,' Blair said as negotiations resumed within days of Mandelson's appointment. But they were not ready to decommission arms yet, he said, 'because, in order for them to persuade their people that actually democratic politics can deliver justice and equality, they need to know that they really will be able to share power if they embrace democratic policies, and that is why I say the issue is fundamentally one of trust.'[15]

Senator Mitchell, restored to his role of emollient facilitator by the withdrawal of the two governments, arranged two weeks of secret face-to-face talks between Trimble and Adams at Winfield House, the US ambassador's residence in London:

> I insisted that there not be any discussion of issues at the meals, they chatted informally about families, vacations and sports, so that they could come to view each other not as adversaries but as human beings and as people living in the same place and the same society and wanting the same thing.

This approach built personal trust between the two sides, although Trimble may have already calculated that he could not lose by letting Sinn Fein into government. If the IRA started to disarm, he would be a hero; if it did not, the republicans would take the blame. The difficulty was to persuade his fellow Unionists that instead of 'jumping together' with the republicans they should, as one Assembly member put it, 'jump in the dark and from a very great height'.

Back at Stormont on 11 November, Mandelson urged Unionist Assembly members, in comments caught on a BBC microphone in the lobby, to force Sinn Fein's hand: 'Put these people on the spot. Call their bluff a bit. They say they are going to deliver. Let's see if they are going to deliver.'

The Assembly members remained unmoved, either by Mandelson's entreaty or by a statement from the IRA supporting 'full implementation' of the Good Friday Agreement. Nor were they impressed by mutually respectful statements issued by Trimble and Adams, each using the other side's traditional phrases. Adams spoke of unionists as his brothers and sisters, admitting that 'all of us are managing our constituencies', and that he had to be aware that 'everything I say has to be heard within unionism'.[16] Trimble was only just holding the majority-unionist bus on the ledge. He had to dissociate himself from a statement by five of his ten Ulster Unionist Party MPs who, along with a narrow majority of his party in the Assembly, were opposed to the deal outlined in the report publicly unveiled by Senator Mitchell on 18 November, recognising it as essentially the same package as *The Way Forward* which they had rejected in July.

Now, however, Trimble appealed over their heads to the party's 800-strong ruling body, the Ulster Unionist Council. The Council was generally considered more conservative than the MPs and Assembly members, but as the body which chose the party leader was also more susceptible to a personal appeal from him. On 27 November the Mitchell report was backed by a 58 per cent majority – although Trimble had to promise at the last moment that if there were no progress on the decommissioning of IRA weapons by February the party would withdraw from the power-sharing government.

The Unionist vote at last triggered the sequence of events prefigured by the Good Friday Agreement. On 29 November the Assembly met to nominate the ten ministers who would govern Northern Ireland from Stormont. Most strikingly, Martin McGuinness, the former IRA terrorist, took the education portfolio. Power was formally devolved from the United Kingdom Parliament at midnight on 30 November and the next day the ministerial cabinet met for the first time, although the two Democratic Unionist ministers stayed away. On the same day, Northern Ireland ministers met their counterparts from the Irish Republic on the North–South Council, and the articles of the Irish Republic's constitution claiming the North were formally revoked. On 2 December, the IRA appointed its interlocutor to talk to the de Chastelain commission.

Unfortunately, the interlocutor had little new to say to the commission. The IRA used the Unionist threat to pull the plug on the executive as an excuse to stall on the specifics of how and when its weapons would be put beyond use. Meanwhile the Unionists were able to say they had given the IRA the chance to deliver. There was no way in which Trimble could escape the condition forced on him by the Ulster Unionist Council, and when February arrived with no progress made he told Mandelson his party would have to pull out of the executive, which would mean the end of devolved government. In order to avoid it looking as if one side were responsible for collapsing the institutions, Mandelson stepped in to suspend the Assembly himself and restore direct rule from Westminster on 11 February 2000, the day before the Ulster Unionist Council was to meet. The executive had lasted only ten weeks, but that it had assumed the government of Northern Ireland at all was enough of a surprise to prepare the ground for the one last heave.

History made

The suspension of the executive was a critical moment because it helped force the seismic shift in republican thinking which Blair proclaimed the previous year. The deadline set by the Good Friday Agreement for the achievement of its two main objectives – devolved government and the decommissioning of arms – was 22 May 2000. As it grew closer, all the pressure was now on the republican side. The ten-week life of the executive proved that devolved government was possible, but in practice there was not enough in it for ordinary unionist people to feel it was important to restore it – in stark and paradoxical contrast to republicans, whose enthusiasm for holding seats in an assembly explicitly representing a part of the United Kingdom was greater than ever. Meanwhile, the prospect of Sinn Fein gaining seats in the Parliament of the Irish Republic increased that enthusiasm further. The republicans also took the 22 May deadline seriously, having signed up for it in good faith two years before, while it meant much less to the unionists, who had already delivered once on their part of the bargain, a power-sharing assembly.

On 6 May, the IRA issued the statement that many people, nationalist and unionist, thought it never would. 'The IRA leadership has agreed to put in place within weeks a confidence building measure to confirm that our weapons remain secure,' the statement said. 'The contents of a number of arms dumps will be inspected by agreed third parties who will report that they have done so to the international independent commission on decommissioning.' The inspectors were named as Martti Ahtisaari, the former president of Finland who had brokered Slobodan Milosevic's surrender after the Kosovo war, and Cyril Ramaphosa, the former general secretary of the African National Congress, having been approached by Downing Street and agreed only the day before. The ANC was the ideal background for a mediator: once condemned by Margaret Thatcher as a terrorist organisation, it had followed the path from armed struggle to democratic triumph which anointed its leaders the world over as secular saints.

The IRA offer was flawed, in the sense that the unionist demand for partial disarmament was flawed, because it could easily open three dumps for inspection while keeping enough explosive to start a small war hidden elsewhere. But it was, although the word was becoming overused, historic. It was just enough to persuade the crucial twenty-five delegates to the Ulster Unionist Council to vote to restore the Northern Ireland executive. Trimble held off the meeting of his party's ruling body until the week after the Good Friday Agreement deadline, calculating that to hold the vote before then would look like an attempt to force the issue before a date which now meant more to the other side than it did to unionists.

The deadline was missed, then, but the 53–47 per cent vote to support Trimble on 27 May, without conditions attached this time, meant that the devolved government at Stormont resumed its powers on 30 May.

The restoration of devolved government was carried out without fanfare and in subdued mood, yet its importance is difficult to overstate. It by no means solved all the problems and conflicts of Northern Ireland. Reform of the Royal Ulster Constabulary had been simply pushed aside, and the issue would return. Although the risk of the IRA returning to violence had become vanishingly small, the threat of violence from dissident republicans remained. The IRA had been the dissident – 'Provisional' – republicans once, but support for violence among republicans generally continued to erode. The threat of violence from the loyalist side, and the use of it in rioting in response to the banning of several marches, including the most sensitive at Drumcree, also remained, but to the extent that it was essentially a reaction to the perceived threat of republican violence it too would decline.

On the basic issue of Partition, the unionists had won, although many were too suspicious to realise it, and Trimble was too tactful to celebrate it. Balancing this was the fact that Roman Catholics no longer felt such an oppressed minority: they were increasingly well-off, decreasingly discriminated against and through differential birth rates had become less of a minority, growing from one-third of the population to more than 40 per cent. This allowed Trimble to share power in a devolved government with Gerry Adams in 1999–2000 when he – along with most unionists – had refused to share power with John Hume in 1974. On the crude calculus of the body count alone, even the tragedy of Omagh could not detract from the Agreement as one of the great achievements of Tony Blair's first term as Prime Minister.

Was he simply lucky to be in Downing Street at the right time? He was certainly lucky that the conditions and the personalities were right. The republican mood had changed, and Hume for the constitutional nationalists had seen that opportunity, while Trimble was the right leader of the unionist majority to seize it; while the new leaders of the loyalist parties had slipped the chains of their past and attitudes in the Irish Republic were also constructive. Certainly, too, John Major had come close to reaching a settlement, and it was under him that most of the terms of what was to become the Good Friday Agreement were hammered out. Had he, in a parallel universe, won the 1997 election, perhaps he could have achieved what Blair achieved. But Senator Mitchell's view was that 'there would not have been a Good Friday Agreement without the involvement of Tony Blair and Bertie Ahern'. Blair brought his own gifts and his own luck to the issue which has broken Prime Ministers and governments before. His relationship with Bill Clinton was one, but his negotiating skill, his ability to finesse issues of deep principle which Major, with his party's unionist assumptions, found difficult, and his unnatural personal persuasiveness were his unique contribution.

Notes

1. Anthony Seldon, *John Major*, p. 263.
2. Many terms in Northern Ireland are loaded or contested. Historically and broadly speaking, republicans are nationalists who support(ed) the use of force to expel the British from Northern Ireland, while constitutional nationalists, primarily represented by the Social Democratic and Labour Party (SDLP), advocate exclusively peaceful and democratic means. Similarly, loyalists are unionists who support(ed) the use of force in their cause, while Unionists with a capital U means a supporter of one of the constitutional unionist parties: the largest is the Ulster Unionist Party, formerly the Official Unionist Party, and the second-largest, which opposed negotiations with republicans, is the Democratic Unionist Party.
3. Seldon, *John Major*, p. 625, and footnote 103.
4. *Independent*, 25 April 1996. Many of David McKittrick's excellent articles from this period were collected in *Through the Minefield*; this one is on p. 4.
5. BBC Radio 4, *Today*, 1 September 1994; it was a form of words which echoed Margaret Thatcher's on the Falkland islanders, which Blair derided at the time; see p. 82.
6. David McKittrick, *Independent on Sunday*, 7 December 1997.
7. George Mitchell, *Making Peace*, p. 143.
8. *Ibid.*, p. 169.
9. *Ibid.*, p. 175.
10. Profile of Philip Gould, *Sunday Times*, 24 May 1998.
11. *Observer*, 23 August 1998.
12. *Ibid.*

13. *Hansard*, 23 June 1999.
14. *Ibid.*, 5 July 1999.
15. *Daily Telegraph*, 20 October 1999.
16. BBC2, *Newsnight*, 18 November 1999.

25

An Uncertain Sound

Hoo-Ha Over a Far-Away Country, May 1998

'We will make the protection and promotion of human rights a central part of our foreign policy.'

—*Labour Party manifesto, 1997*

Prime Ministers always run their own foreign policy, a fact of British political history which often makes the Foreign Secretary's one of the more difficult of the great offices of state to hold. For Robin Cook this was compounded by his exclusion from the inner core of Tony Blair's decision-making. Despite the fact that Blair respected the sharpness of his intellect and Cook's formal position as head of Labour's policy-making machinery, the Foreign Secretary arrived in Whitehall as passenger rather than pilot.

With policy on Europe – such as it was – in the hands of Blair and Gordon Brown, and relations with the United States a matter of buddy-politics between Prime Minister and President, Cook only had the rest of the world to deal with. Nor was he solely responsible for that: as a manifesto promise that would resurrect the career of Clare Short, she joined the Cabinet at the head of a new department, for International Development, to underline the Labour's commitment to relieve world poverty. The new department took the Overseas Development Administration out of Cook's barony at the Foreign Office.

Cook immediately set out to undermine what authority remained to him by launching an ill-considered 'ethical foreign policy' in a grandiose mission statement ten days after the election. In the Locarno room in the Foreign Office on 12 May, after a video extolling Britain's role in the world which had stiff diplomatic service lips curling in disdain, Cook declared: 'Our foreign policy must have an ethical dimension and must support the demands of other people for the democratic rights on which we insist for ourselves.'

As it happened, the statement itself did not use the word 'ethical', promising only, as the fourth of four objectives, 'to spread the values of human rights, civil liberties and democracy which we demand for ourselves'. It raised expectations that the new government would cancel the sale of Hawk trainer aircraft to Indonesia which had been approved by the Conservative government the previous year.

Cook had said in Opposition that he thought the export licences for the Hawks should be honoured, but gave to understand that he had argued with Blair in government that they should revoke the contract.[1] If that was the case, he was overruled, and the Hawk contract was given the go-ahead at the end of July 1997.[2] Douglas Hurd, Cook's immediate predecessor, warned that 'if you alter the course of policy by 2 or 3 degrees and pretend that you are altering it by 180 degrees, you achieve some immediate applause from those who know little about the matter', but store up trouble when claims to a 'superior morality bump into the roughness of the real world'.[3]

British interests in Indonesia had long been promoted by a policy of 'constructive engagement', designed to draw the Suharto regime towards democracy and respect for human rights by trade and co-operation. This policy had produced no softening in the regime since President Suharto had come to power in 1967, with the blood of thousands of 'leftists' on his hands, and with the support of the US and Britain. He had invaded the former Portuguese colony of East Timor in 1975, an annexation not recognised internationally, and pursued a brutal but ultimately unsuccessful policy there of forced assimilation since then. Now he was old and his government corrupt and tottering, but Cook not only allowed the Hawk contract to go ahead but continued the policy of constructive engagement. In August 1997 he visited the region and shook hands with the old dictator himself, just as the Indonesian economy started to go down the drain.

Unwisely, a photograph of the handshake was used in the government's first annual Human Rights Report in May 1998. The Foreign Affairs select committee of MPs observed tartly:

> In the event, the Indonesian people had less patience with their leadership than did the government: following prolonged and violent protests against his regime, President Suharto was forced to resign his office less than four weeks later.[4]

The Hawks issue came back to haunt Blair when another consignment of jets was delivered at the height of the Indonesian-backed terror campaign which followed the vote of the people of East Timor for independence in the 1999 referendum.[5]

Special relationship

Bill Clinton had long been central to Blair's political strategy. Not only did his election in 1992 provide a blueprint, but Blair regarded Clinton's re-election in 1996 as critical to making New Labour seem mainstream rather than backwater, in the run-up to the British election.[6] The personal relationship between the two men was tenuous – they had met once, when President Clinton visited London in November 1995, and had spoken on the telephone a few times. But Blair was determined to exploit their shared image as leaders of the younger generation in order to revive that flag of convenience of British–American diplomacy, the special relationship, and Clinton was happy to share in some of Blair's reflected electoral glory.

As any Briton who has read American newspapers or watched American television knows, the special relationship survives in folk-memory and official communiqués rather more than in the day-to-day business of US foreign policy. But Blair knew from the Reagan–Thatcher years about the power of the idea as a presentational device, so he hastened to build on Clinton's flying visit to London of 29 May, by suggesting a series of think-ins on the 'Third Way' to bind the ideological ties between them.[7]

Meanwhile Iraq, where the Gulf War coalition against Saddam Hussein had resolved into a purely British–American alliance, emerged as the theatre in which Blair was most likely to authorise his first military action. Saddam continued to test the restrictions imposed on Iraq by the United Nations after the Gulf War in 1991, dodging and harassing the UN inspectors charged with ensuring that he did not develop weapons of mass destruction. It was symbolically important to the Labour government generally and to Blair personally to be seen as 'strong' on defence. Blair was aware that he had to exorcise the demon of unilateralism, both for the party and for himself. While his opt-out from the school cadet force at the age of fifteen hardly carried the resonance of Bill Clinton's attempt to dodge the draft while maintaining his 'viability within the system',[8] his past membership of CND, however token, lay like an unused weapon in the hand of the Conservative Opposition. He and the US President had jointly to live down the suspicion that left-of-centre governments were squeamish when it came to issuing orders to military top brass.

Clinton had had some trouble learning to salute properly in his first meetings with US military officers,[9] and inaugurated his presidency with a damaging row over his promise to give equal rights to homosexuals in the military. Not only that, he had to extricate US Marines from a disastrous peace-keeping mission on behalf of the United Nations in Somalia, which George Bush had ordered just before leaving office. But by June 1993 he was already authorising military action himself, ordering a cruise missile strike on Baghdad in retaliation for an Iraqi attempt on the life of former President Bush on a visit to Kuwait.

Saddam took advantage of Russian–French attempts to broker a compromise in the dispute over access by expelling the UN weapons inspectors in November 1997. Blair took the hardest line possible, with a hint of acting out the role of 'strong leadership'. He told the Commons: 'It is absolutely essential that he backs down on this, that he be made to back down . . . If he does not, we will simply face this problem, perhaps in a different and far worse form, in a few years' time.'[10] Just in case anybody missed that echo of moral certainty, Alastair Campbell let it be known that Baroness Thatcher had been in Downing Street, for a half-hour discussion of foreign affairs and Iraq in particular, the week before.

This was an ethical foreign policy of a brutally simplistic kind: Saddam was a Bad Thing; UN resolutions were a Good Thing; if the baddie will not obey the good law, we must bomb his lights out. This was a justifiable policy, although it would have benefited from a little more finesse in execution. Appearing to follow the US so slavishly was a problem: partly because of the anti-American sentiments of Middle Eastern peoples whose governments were needed as allies against Saddam; partly because, once the Monica Lewinsky scandal broke, Clinton's foreign policy seemed too driven by the vagaries of his domestic preoccupations. If military action against Iraq were right and justified under international law, it did not need a special relationship between the United Kingdom and the United States to reinforce it. Indeed, Blair failed during his Washington visit in February 1998 to use the UK's presidency of the European Union, which started in January, to press for a wider consensus on Iraq. As a result, other European countries were further alienated and, when the bombs did start to fall on Baghdad in December 1998, they fell only from American and British planes.[11]

It was not only the continental Europeans who were offended, however. The Blair strategy of uncritical support for Clinton, even as he dissembled and stalled before Kenneth Starr's investigation, was too creepy for many fastidious British tastes. But it paid handsome dividends in the peace talks in Northern Ireland. If there was a special relationship between the United Kingdom and America, there was also one between the republics of America and Ireland. Blair met pro-Republican Congress leaders including Edward Kennedy in February and had them, like most of his audiences, 'eating out of his hand'. This mobilisation of the Irish–American lobby, source of most of the IRA's funds, behind Gerry Adams's strategy of peace was critical to the breakthrough on Good Friday, 10 April 1998.[12]

From such a pinnacle of achievement, Blair's cynical assumption of the role of caddy to the President – they played golf near Chequers during an EU–US summit in London in May 1998 – also plumbed the ethical depths. When Clinton ordered cruise missile strikes against 'terrorist' targets in Sudan and Afghanistan on 20 August 1998, Blair issued an immediate statement of strong support, having been told two days before, by Vice-President Al Gore, that military action was 'imminent'. Despite US claims that the aspirin factory in Al Shifa, Khartoum, was making chemical weapons, no evidence was ever forthcoming, reinforcing the belief that the attack was a crude attempt to distract public opinion from Clinton's broadcast admission on 18 August of a relationship that was 'not appropriate' and 'wrong' with Lewinsky.

Blair continued to insist, six months later, that he had been right to back the US action, although the reasons for doing so had shifted. He effectively admitted that there was no proof the factory was making weapons of mass destruction: 'The US told us at the time of the strike on Al Shifa that it had compelling evidence that the plant was being used for the production of chemical weapons materials,' he said. His defence of the action now rested on the fact that 'no one was killed in it' and that by it 'we gave a very clear signal – and I think the right one – to those who engage in international terrorism that we are prepared if necessary to take action in retaliation'.[13] The contrast with the Gladstonian moral purpose of Blair's policy in the Balkans was stark. Here, in order to conceal the brute politics underlying his support for Clinton's action, Blair was forced to invent the Doctrine of the Clear Signal: it did not matter what was hit, so long as nobody was killed and terrorists got the right message.

Sierra Leone

Blair made an equally unsteady start in the first test posed by an unexpected event for the instincts and direction of his foreign policy. Only three weeks after the election, the elected government of the West African state of Sierra Leone was overthrown. Blair's response had, as Robin Cook had promised, a strong 'ethical dimension'.

Sierra Leone was an ambivalent relic of Britain's colonial past. Freetown was established by the British in 1787 as a settlement for liberated slaves. It later became, with its hinterland, the colony of Sierra Leone. It became independent in 1961 and followed the familiar post-colonial course of becoming a one-party state subject to occasional military coups. John Major refused to help the government in 1991 when rebels started a civil war with help from the rogue dictator of neighbouring Liberia, Charles Taylor. But it was not until 25 May 1997 that dissident army officers led by Major Johnny Koroma, in alliance with the Liberian-backed rebels, ousted President Ahmad Tejan Kabbah, who had been elected the previous year.

No country recognised the Koroma regime and Britain sponsored a resolution at the UN Security Council imposing an arms and oil embargo on the country. It was the wording of this resolution that caused what Blair called the 'hoo-ha' which erupted the following year, because it was ambiguous. Its evident purpose was to prevent arms going to the Koroma government, but it appeared to ban military help to anyone in Sierra Leone, including forces loyal to deposed President Kabbah. Blair, meanwhile, took up Kabbah's cause, entertaining the exiled leader as his guest at the Commonwealth summit in Edinburgh in October 1997 and praising him as the rightful, democratically-elected ruler of the country.

Kabbah was restored to power in March 1998 in a counter-coup led by Nigerian forces, assisted by the British High Commissioner, Peter Penfold and a company called Sandline. The company, headed by Lieutenant Colonel Tim Spicer, a former British army officer, provided advice and mercenaries with Penfold's knowledge and approval. Penfold was hailed as a hero on the streets of Freetown, but the murkier elements of a plot worthy of a good thriller, combined with a knee-jerk journalistic response to 'sanctions-busting', naturally dominated the story at Westminster.

By a combination of incompetence and cover-up, the Foreign Office managed to turn a minor if flawed effort to do the right thing in one of the poorest countries in the world into a crisis which further 'took its toll' on the Foreign Secretary's standing, as Cook himself admitted.[14] The Foreign Office had presented the UN resolution as applying sanctions only to the Koroma junta, while the Order enacting it in British law clearly banned arms supplies to anyone in Sierra Leone.[15] This discrepancy seems to have been the result of simple confusion, but hardly suggested that the Sandline operation had the open and unashamed backing of the British government. To make matters worse, the operation was led by General Sani Abacha, Nigeria's military dictator. Nigeria itself was subject to both European Union and Commonwealth arms embargoes on account of its appalling human rights record.

As the press struggled to work out what had happened, Cook and his officials sought defensively to prove that they did not know what their High Commissioner was up to. Cook's insistence that his officials did not know and if they did had not told him smacked too much of the distinction between operational and policy matters for which Home Secretary Michael Howard had once been crucified by the Labour Party. Blair was finally forced on 11 May 1998 to sweep aside Cook's obfuscation, saying simply that 'the UN and the UK . . . were quite right in trying to do it', namely to restore Kabbah to government. 'That is the background and people can see that a lot of the hoo-ha is overblown,' he said.

Alastair Campbell backed him up in terms of tabloid simplicity: 'The good guys have won,' he told journalists. It was too late, however, to stop a parliamentary and press paperchase through who knew what and when. Blair set up an inquiry under Sir Thomas Legg on 18 May, and then published its report on 27 July, on the same day as his first Cabinet reshuffle – a crude piece of news management which hardly spoke well for his confidence in the rightness of his case.

In essence, though, the story was as simple as Blair said it was. However briefly, the 'good guys' did win. The problem was with the cavalier approach to the due proprieties and processes of international law. Once the Nigerians withdrew, however, the 'good guys' proved no match for the rebel Revolutionary United Force, funded by diamonds from the mines its gangster army controlled, which resumed its reign of terror over most of the Sierra Leonean people – the amputation of limbs its trademark punishment. In July 1999 Kabbah was forced to sign a peace agreement which gave government office and pardons to the RUF. It also brought in United Nations peacekeeping forces. Blair defended the deal as the best hope of peace in the country, but this was belied by the collapse of the deal in April 2000 when several hundred UN soldiers were taken hostage by the rebels.

Blair then took what the *Financial Times* described as a 'huge gamble' to deploy paratroopers to secure Freetown airport.[16] The gamble paid off in the short term because, while they were notionally there only to help with the evacuation of British and other nationals, their presence stabilised the situation and helped in the arrest of Foday Sankoh, leader of the RUF, who could then be tried for crimes against humanity.

Blair's confidence now assumed Thatcherite proportions, as he declared: 'We can be very, very proud of our armed forces and what they have done in Sierra Leone.' He stopped short of calling them 'our boys', but went on: 'I believe that they should have been able to perform their task without some of the carping and quibbling from Conservative Members.'[17]

China

Just as morally ambiguous was Blair's policy towards China, as its economic importance started to catch up with its superpower status. He effected a rapprochement, shifting from the attitude of official disapproval which had prevailed since the Tiananmen Square massacre in 1989, and which had been reinforced by Chris Patten's lectures as the last Governor of Hong Kong on China's refusal to perpetuate Britain's deathbed conversion to the cause of democracy there. In March 1998, the US and Britain, acting as the presidency of the European Union, agreed not to sponsor a resolution at the United Nations condemning China's human rights record. When Blair met Zhu Rongji, China's new Prime Minister, the following month, he hailed him as 'a moderniser if ever I met one'.[18]

The co-option of the Chinese leadership to New Labour, a little like Mao Zedong's adaptation of Marxism–Leninism to Chinese circumstances, was unconvincing. The real issue with China was geo-political, or geo-economic, in that it had emerged stronger from the regional slump which, from August 1997, hit Thailand, South Korea, Indonesia and Malaysia, and reinforced the stagnation of the Japanese economy. When Blair visited China in October 1998 it provided the opportunity for another clever move to secure control of the centre ground at home, with the appointment – announced on the first day of the Conservative Party conference in Bournemouth – of Michael Heseltine to chair a Sino-British trade forum. But it also allowed an exchange of cultural idiosyncrasies designed to promote constructive engagement. When he got to Beijing, Blair learned that pro-democracy dissident Xu Wenli had been detained and intervened with the authorities, who then released him – a sequence so choreographed it resembled a play. Bringing the equally curious customs of New Labour to his hosts, an article appeared over Blair's name in the *People's Daily*, and he recorded an interview with state-controlled Chinese television, of which only thirteen minutes were transmitted, with references to Tibet and to Zhu as a moderniser cut out.

The compromises required by a policy of constructive engagement were made vivid by the Tiananmen-style efficiency and presentational insensitivity of the Metropolitan police force's handling of pro-democracy demonstrators during the visit of President Jiang Zemin to London the following year.*

Saving the world

The other new emphasis in the government's foreign policy, and a strong component of the 'ethical dimension', was that on the war against global poverty. Clare Short declared in her first speech as Secretary of State on 27 May 1997 that it supported the target of halving world poverty by 2015.[19] This startling ambition was no passing rhetorical gesture to please the aid organisations which were the Department for International Development's main immediate client group. It was set out formally as an objective of government policy in Short's first White Paper in November 1997, and then as a mere staging post on the road to 'eliminating world poverty' – the title of the White Paper – altogether.

The White Paper borrowed an arbitrary definition of 'extreme' poverty, an income of less than $1 a day, from the United Nations Development Programme, without any analysis of how effective a measure of deprivation it might be. This definition included nearly a quarter of the world's population, 1.3 billion people.

This was morality on a grand scale, and Short was eager to wrap herself in the phrase Cook never used, asserting in the White Paper that the government had 'already made clear its commitment' to 'a more ethical foreign policy'. Blair let it go through. Meeting the target (and a series of subsidiary ones such as 'universal primary education in all countries by 2015') relied on the contribution of many other rich – and poor – countries, even assuming he, at sixty-one, would still be around to spread the blame for not achieving it. But the ethical dimension did appeal to him. There was an element in him which thought it right to set the highest and most pious objectives, and he shared some of Short's muscular moralism which attempted to drive the government machine by force of words towards being 'more ethical' than its predecessors.

Constructive engagement

Like most prime ministers, Blair was thrown into a series of foreign summits, negotiations and minor crises which absorbed a great deal of time and made it difficult to establish anything coherent enough to be

*A Metropolitan Police inquiry later accepted that the policing of the visit had been inappropriate.

described as a foreign policy. Beyond his policy towards the European Union, he started with little more than a resolute pragmatism, an unformed ambition to do good in the world and a determination to stick as closely as possible to the President of the United States.

As he tried to find a story to tell, the expectations raised by Cook's 'ethical foreign policy' were an unhelpful distraction because, in a policy vacuum, the phrase implied the moral purity of neutralism on the model of Sweden or CND-style unilateralism. Blair's instincts were more aggressive and more engaged with the complexities of interdependence than that. But it was precisely a strong moral basis for his policy which he sought. In Sierra Leone, as in so much else, the intention was good, if the execution rough-edged. The real dilemma, in cases like Indonesia and China, was over the age-old question of constructive engagement: when should the 'international community' trade and negotiate with regimes which abuse human rights in the hope of breaking down the economic and cultural bases of despotism, and when should it isolate them? In Indonesia, Blair was too indulgent towards the Suharto regime. In Iraq, he leant too far the other way. On China, the dilemma was particularly finely balanced.

All the same, as he stumbled through the rubber rope maze of international organisations and treaties, Blair was working towards the clarity of Kosovo. By the end of 1998, he was beginning to assert a principled stance in foreign affairs, heavily if unevenly tempered by expediency, through a series of compromises in the various theatres of international co-operation, towards a more morally-based world order. With the end of the Cold War, conflicts which had been seen largely in terms of competition between the superpowers were now viewed differently. International affairs were increasingly managed by regional groupings of states, usually with some form of blessing from the United Nations and under an increasingly developed body of international law. This allowed more scope for the principles of human rights and self-determination, although the situation in Iraq was too intractable for the common front with the US against Saddam to allow Blair yet to lay convincing claim to an ethical foreign policy. However, the grounds for that claim had been laid in October 1998, when the Serbian dictator Slobodan Milosevic backed down in the face of Nato authorisation for the use of force against his campaign of 'ethnic cleansing' in Kosovo.

Notes

1. John Kampfner, *Robin Cook*, p. 143 and, for a fuller treatment of the issue, pp. 133–52. For the suggestion that he had opposed the sale, see the *Scotsman*, 25 June 1998.
2. Robin Cook, parliamentary written answer, 28 July 1997.
3. *The Times*, 24 November 1997.
4. 'Foreign Policy and Human Rights', First Report of the Foreign Affairs Select Committee, 21 December 1998.
5. After the weakened government conceded a referendum in East Timor, the result was a 79 per cent vote for independence, which prompted militia backed by the Indonesian armed forces to run rampant. It took two weeks to assemble a United Nations peacekeeping force led by the Australians to secure the scorched earth left by the militias.
6. Martin Kettle, *Guardian*, 25 October 1999.
7. See pp. 432ff.
8. Bill Clinton used this phrase in a letter written in Oxford, 3 December 1969, as he sought a place in a Reserve Officers Training Corps unit in order to avoid being called up to serve in Vietnam; see Martin Walker, *Clinton*, p. 124.
9. George Stephanopoulos, *All Too Human*, pp. 132–3.
10. Reply to Tam Dalyell MP at Prime Minister's Questions, *Hansard*, 19 November 1997.
11. See pp. 515–16.
12. See p. 402.
13. Reply to Tam Dalyell MP at Prime Minister's Questions, *Hansard*, 10 March 1999.
14. Interview, *New Statesman*, 13 November 1998.
15. Foreign Affairs select committee, Second Report, Session 1998–99, 'Sierra Leone', 9 February 1999.
16. Editorial comment, *Financial Times*, 15 May 2000.
17. *Hansard*, 17 May 2000.
18. *Daily Mail*, 3 April 1998.
19. Speech at the School of Oriental and African Studies, University of London, 27 May 1997.

26

Third Way

Egalitarianism by Stealth, September 1998

'Blair is a classic one-play quarterback – he fakes to the right and he moves left.'

—*Haley Barbour, former chairman of US Republican Party, 1998*

It is unusual for Prime Ministers to write works of political philosophy while in office, and the publication of Tony Blair's Fabian pamphlet, *The Third Way: New Politics for the New Century*, on 21 September 1998 prompted one commentator to compare him with Gladstone.[1] As with the idea that Blair personally wrote every newspaper article that appeared under his name, the idea that he was a philosopher-prince was overblown. Much of the text was written by David Miliband and Geoff Mulgan in the Policy Unit – the ideas factory upstairs at Number Ten rather than the word factory in the press office downstairs. It was little more than an extended speech, but it was nevertheless a thoughtful and significant attempt to set out and justify what Blair meant by the Third Way.

He had first used the phrase, a natural extension of one of his favourite rhetorical devices, the middle way between two extremes, to describe Labour's policy on the health service, neither a fragmented internal market nor rigid central control, in 1995: 'We propose an NHS that is locally-based and patient-led. It is a sensible third way for the future.'[2] During the run-up to the 1997 election, he used it to describe his economic philosophy, first as the third way between the unregulated free market and the mass of Brussels regulations, then as that between a prejudice for privatisation and one for nationalisation.[3] It was only after the election that it was improvised as the label for his entire political philosophy, a conveniently neutral and flexible term for Blairism. He wanted to suggest that the landslide in Britain was part of a worldwide movement of renewal and modernisation across the left and centre of politics. European social democrats listened politely, but it was initially in the United States that the idea was taken seriously.

While Hillary Clinton was on a tour of Europe without her husband, she and Blair jointly chaired a seminar on the Third Way at Chequers on 1 November 1997; it was agreed to reconvene with President Clinton in Washington in February. Meanwhile, in January 1998, the world first heard of an intern in the White House called Monica Lewinsky, and the Clinton presidency entered a year-long period of weightlessness, floating free in the opinion polls and yet, unhappy and distracted, unable to engage in any sustained way with the business of governing. Suddenly, Clinton was even more grateful for support from Mr Squeaky Clean, although Blair squirmed awkwardly when asked his view of the morality of adulterous affairs.

It was more than simply a courtesy call, therefore, when Blair phoned Clinton, on the day of the State of the Union address, 27 January 1998, to say he was thinking of him. Clinton reciprocated by using the phrase 'the third way' in the address, claiming to have found it between 'those who say government is the enemy and those who say government is the answer'.

When Blair arrived in the US he was taken aback by a hysterically warm welcome at a Washington school which he visited with Clinton on 5 February 1998. It was partly because the school was called Blair High School (after the Civil War general Senator Francis Blair, who also gave his name to Blair House, the government residence where his namesake stayed), and partly because American crowds treated their President like a pop star, Lewinsky or no Lewinsky. The next day, Blair's joint news conference with Clinton was a more difficult engagement. One of the President's advisers, Rahm Emanual, turned to Blair shortly before the press filed in and said: 'You! Don't fuck this up!'

According to another Clinton staffer, Paul Begala, 'Blair sort of looked at his aides, looked over at Clinton, and they both busted out laughing.'

The news conference was dominated by questions about Lewinsky, but Blair's mere presence was important to the President. His then press secretary, Mike McCurry, said later: 'Clinton was so relieved that this guy who he had some rapport with didn't come in and act like he had cooties.'*[4]

In the afternoon, an exhausted Clinton kept falling asleep during the

*US slang for head lice or, more generally, 'the lurgy'.

four-hour seminar on the Third Way at the White House, but came back to life after drinking several large mugs of black coffee. The British team of policy 'wonks', led by David Miliband, head of the Number Ten Policy Unit, included ministers Jack Straw, Alan Milburn and Helen Liddell, and from outside government Gavyn Davies, chief economist at Goldman Sachs, and Professor Anthony Giddens, director of the London School of Economics. The themes were a blancmange of generalities. There was a session on the new economy, 'how to combat inequality and insecurity in the labour market'. There was one on 'One Nation, building cohesive and inclusive societies, tackling social exclusion'.[5] And finally a session on the politics of building a new and enduring electoral coalition. Distracted as he was, Clinton still showed flashes of his huge grasp of policy detail, threaded in and out of an eloquent monologue of political insights. It was indicative, however, that the observation which most hit home with Blair was one of political tactics: 'Never stop addressing the people who voted for you for the first time.'[6]

Back in Britain, Blair followed up the White House event with a seminar in Downing Street which attracted some mockery. Roy Hattersley sarcastically welcomed it 'for the very good reason that, since the Prime Minister believes in the Third Way, it is important for him to find out what it is'. But he also recognised that the concept had an ideological content, describing the seminar as 'another step towards the creation of a new party – cuckooing in the nest as we used to say about the Militants'.[7]

The critics were strengthened by Blair's attempt, like an over-enthusiastic marketing director, to sell the Third Way franchise to unsuitable agents in some overseas markets.

Brazil was a plausible enough recruit to the international Third Way club. Blair had been delighted to discover that the president, Fernando Henrique Cardoso, had written the introduction to a collection of his speeches. He had it translated from Portuguese and was 'really amazed when I realised that this guy was talking the same language. It was straight-down-the-line New Labour.'[8] Cardoso had been a famous sociologist and anti-capitalist colleague of Professor Giddens, who had some claim to be the Third Way's intellectual originator.[9]

Blair's attempt to include China, however, reduced the idea to parody:

> I know it sounds a strange thing to say, but if you sit down with the Chinese Prime Minister and you start to look at the problems of their public sector – I mean, OK, it's completely different – but some of the ideas and principles are basically the same. I mean you're trying to make for an efficient set of public services that doesn't end up in a situation where you're spending large sums of money on things you don't need to spend it on.[10]

Nevertheless, Blair's pamphlet in September 1998 suggested that there was some substance to the concept after all. The most important statement was: 'The Third Way stands for a modernised social democracy.' This marked an end to the 'radical centre' – although not completely to Blair's use of the phrase.* It was the end of the idea that the Third Way was simply located by a process of triangulation mid-way between left and right. 'Triangulation' had been the watchword of Clinton's arch-pragmatist adviser, Dick Morris, in securing the President's re-election in 1996, but it was not where Clinton's policy instincts lay. Equally, for Blair, paying rhetorical homage to the right was part of the marketing strategy for winning elections, but it did not reflect the balance of policy objectives.

The Third Way was certainly willing to co-opt some of the ideas of the right, especially on economics. Of 'the Thatcher government', Blair wrote: 'Some of its reforms were, in retrospect, necessary acts of modernisation, particularly the exposure of much of the state industrial sector to reform and competition.' It was also unembarrassed to be populist, with Blair defending the use of focus groups and opinion polls: 'In a mature society representatives will make better decisions if they take full account of popular opinion and encourage public debate on the big decisions affecting people's lives.' Above all, it was highly pragmatic. 'Our approach is "permanent revisionism", a continual search for better means to meet our goals, based on a clear view of the changes taking place in advanced industrialised societies.' That phrase, an ironic echo of Trotsky's 'permanent revolution', is impossible to imagine in the mouth of any other Labour Prime Minister. But it was a principled pragmatism in that it was in the service of egalitarian values – of 'a fair distribution of the benefits of progress'.

That muted affirmation of the essential purpose of socialism – or social democracy, at least – contradicted the early implication of the Third Way as merely centrist, but was easily overlooked in the bustle of daily politics. Blair's pamphlet was published as he headed for New York for another seminar on the Third Way, just as President Clinton's video testimony to the Starr grand jury on the Lewinsky affair had been released. In New York for just twelve hours, and looking hunted as he avoided being asked about Clinton's personal morality, Blair delivered a speech to the United Nations General Assembly, another to the New York Stock Exchange and met mayor Rudolph Guiliani. The Third Way seminar, at New York

*Originally made famous by Roy Jenkins in his 1979 Dimbleby lecture.

University, was televised, with Clinton, Blair, Romano Prodi, the Italian Prime Minister, and Petar Stoyanov, the President of Bulgaria, in red leather armchairs around a wooden table, with an antique globe to their left, in front of an audience which included Hillary Clinton in the front row. Clinton was described as 'awesome in his eloquence, grasp of detail and ability to go to the heart of the problem'; but the discussion was hardly profound and Blair's contribution was unexceptional.[11]

Six days later came the real breakthrough for the Third Way: the election of Gerhard Schröder's social democrats in Germany. Not only did the removal of Helmut Kohl tilt the balance in Europe decisively from centre-right to centre-left, Schröder had – unlike Lionel Jospin in France – explicitly modelled his 'new centre' (*Die Neue Mitte*) approach on Blair's. Their joint declaration in June 1999, *Europe: The Third Way/Die Neue Mitte*, marked the high point of Blair's attempt to present himself as the exemplar of an international political tendency.*

The stealthy revolution

Blair was regarded with distaste by traditionalists of both right and left within the Labour Party as an interloper whose only interest in the party's history was in junking it. Roy Hattersley and Arthur Scargill used identical analogies to explain their opposition to New Labour. The miners' leader, explaining his decision to leave the Labour Party, said: 'If the church to which you went decided to stop worshipping God and started worshipping the devil, you would have second thoughts.'[12] While the former deputy Labour leader commented at the end of the government's first year: 'If Christians sat down to invent a new religion and decided that the Sermon on the Mount was incompatible with the global economy we would conclude that they had ceased to be Christians.'[13]

Conservative endorsements of Blair, from Margaret Thatcher downwards, only confirmed the fears of Labour members that their party had been invaded by an ideologically-alien body-snatcher. However, not only does such a reading come close to asserting that it is impossible to retain

---

*Lionel Jospin responded to the pamphleteers with a waspish rebuke to some of the confusions of the Third Way in an essay entitled 'Modern Socialism', published by the Fabian Society, November 1999: 'If the Third Way lies between communism and capitalism, it is merely a new name for democratic socialism peculiar to the British . . . If, on the other hand, the Third Way involves finding a middle way between social democracy and neo-liberalism, then this approach is not mine . . . There is no longer a role for such a politics of "in-betweenism".'

left-wing principles and win elections, it makes the mistake of taking the New Labour marketing exercise at face value. In arriving at the Third Way, Blair made compromises on policies which he saw as obstacles to Labour's election. He even jettisoned some core elements of Labour ideology, such as public ownership and the special role of trade unionism, but he retained its deeper values – the philosophically prior goal of a more equal society.

Just because a substantial body of opinion in the Labour Party still harked back to a more left-wing version of socialism, primarily in economics, and distrusted Blair because of his mannerisms and his failure to pay his respects to the household gods, that did not make him a Tory in disguise. The party has since its foundation been suspicious of its leaders and eager to accuse them of betrayal. Blair understood that and sought to head it off by his peculiar combination of pre-emptive directness and ideological evasion. Soon after the publication of his *Third Way* pamphlet, he said:

> If you define socialism as old-style, traditional state control and nationalisation then I am not a socialist. If you define socialism as a set of values based around a belief in society and community, if you define it in a more ethical sense, then that is the reason why I am in the Labour Party.[14]

Some on the right saw Blair more clearly. He was 'a classic one-play quarterback – he fakes to the right and he moves left', according to Haley Barbour, the former chairman of the US Republican National Committee brought in by William Hague to advise the Conservatives how to deal with him.[15]

Essentially, Barbour was right and Scargill and Hattersley wrong. The rhetorical feints to the right concealed a moderate egalitarianism which dared not speak its name, confusing Blair's opponents on both left and right. Words like equality and redistribution had been edited out of the New Labour lexicon, to be replaced by anaemic formulae such as tackling 'social exclusion', slogans such as 'welfare to work' and technical policy changes such as the Working Families Tax Credit.[16] The Social Exclusion Unit, set up in December 1997, was a creditable attempt to work across departments on what would have been known in the old days as the problem of poverty. Blair could also, when speaking to Labour Party audiences, demand to know 'what Tory government would have introduced'[17] a familiar list of policies: the minimum wage (introduced with neither fuss nor job losses at the rate of £3.60 an hour in April 1999); child benefit increases; the restoration of free eye and teeth tests for pensioners; and, later, the increases in spending plans on health and education.

He could also, however, when speaking to other audiences, balance each item on that list with something that did not sound left-wing at all: independence for the Bank of England; a cut in the standard rate of income tax from 23p to 22p in the pound in April 2000; cuts in corporation tax rates; cuts in lone-parent and disability benefits; and cuts in support for asylum seekers.

The problem with this approach, however, was that it meant there was a disjunction between rhetoric and policy, especially during the first two years of the government, which produced only confusion. The strategy of trying to please everyone in order to keep the broadest possible coalition in Blair's big tent began to run into the danger of satisfying no one. The introduction of tuition fees for university students was an early example of a policy which was quintessentially Third Way: its objective was egalitarian, but it was delivered in a pragmatic way which offended those who were attached to the traditional egalitarian policy of free tuition and grants to cover living costs for all. It is worth analysing, because it was one of the policies for which Blair was, and is, hated.

Tuition fees

Neither Labour nor the Conservatives saw any advantage in making the question of student finance an election issue. If student numbers were to continue to expand, the money would have to be found from somewhere. With New Labour allergic to general tax increases, the logic that the beneficiaries of higher education, who generally earn more, should contribute to the cost was inescapable. That was the direction in which the Conservatives were moving too, so Blair agreed to refer the issue to a committee set up under Sir Ron, later Lord, Dearing in May 1996, on the understanding that it would not report until after the election. Labour's manifesto said bluntly that the necessary expansion of higher education 'cannot be funded out of general taxation', although it was coy about the alternatives.

Dearing reported on 23 July 1997, recommending that students should pay a fee of £1,000 a year, covering about a quarter of the cost of the average degree, for which they could take out a loan which would not start to be repaid until they were earning £10,000 a year.

This was not what Blair and Gordon Brown, as guardian of the new government's financial chastity, wanted. Contradicting the unspoken assumption of his brief, not to mention Labour's manifesto, Dearing had come up with a scheme which required substantial extra funds from the Exchequer, at least over the medium term. As student numbers rose, so would costs, while the loan repayments would not start to come in for some time.

David Blunkett, the Education Secretary, therefore bulldozed the report, 'accepting' it in a statement to the Commons three hours after it was published but replacing its recommendations with something he had prepared earlier. The tuition fees would be means-tested against the income of the parents of students, he said, not paid for by loans. Fees would be paid 'up front' and in full by one-third of students, in part by another third and waived altogether for those with the lowest-income parents. Meanwhile, government grants to cover living costs – replaced by loans for all but the poorest students under the Conservatives – would be abolished altogether: students could borrow from a new loan scheme instead.

The scheme bore the hallmarks of haste. It was not discussed at Cabinet,[18] and its presentation was woefully mishandled. There was an outcry over the ending of 'free' higher education. Ted Short, Lord Glenamara, the former Education Secretary and deputy Labour leader, threatened to leave the party over the issue. In the fuss the fees issue and loans were widely confused, with most people assuming that students would be loaded up with debt to pay tuition fees. In fact the fees would only be paid by better-off parents, while the loans would not have to be paid back unless the student could afford it, under more generous terms than the Conservative loan scheme. Blair's line of defence at Prime Minister's Questions that day, that 'people simply would not tolerate' using taxpayers' money to expand university education, seemed off the point.

Meanwhile, it emerged that, in bringing in the new scheme in the autumn of 1998, students taking a gap year between school and university had been forgotten. Were they to be penalised by being forced to pay fees? Over the summer, the government backed down: gap-year students would be treated as if they were starting university in 1997.

The objective, across the political spectrum including the Conservatives, was the same: to widen access to higher education in the name of equality of opportunity. The nub issue was how to pay for it, and where the Third Way differed from 'unmodernised' social democracy was in its sensitivity to higher taxes. 'One of the strongest claims of the Third Way is that tax must be kept under control and that all public spending is "money for results and reform",' Blair wrote in his pamphlet.[19] In effect, his tuition fees policy imposed a deferred tax on those who benefited from higher education and, as a kind of down-payment against their future earnings, a disguised tax on their parents. There was an element of rough justice, or rough social justice, in this, but that had been true of the grants system, which had also been paid according to parental means.

The counter-argument, that graduates who earned more paid more in taxes anyway, did not answer the point that expansion would require higher taxes from current taxpayers, of whom a fairly small minority had been to university. The counter-argument carried more weight in Scotland but, despite some minor concessions won – and paid for – by the devolved parliament, it did not prevail even there.[20]

The real risk was that potential students from working-class families would be put off going into higher education for fear of getting into debt, despite the fact that the debt would be a 'soft' loan and future earnings capacity would be considerably higher. In practice, this did not happen, although more might have been encouraged if the government's message had not been so confused.

Equality

The Third Way was, then, hardly a grand departure in political philosophy. It was more an attempt to reflect the extent to which the Labour Party in Britain shared its response to the social changes of the final quarter of the twentieth century with left-of-centre parties in other countries. The property tax revolt in California in 1978 was a marker of a widespread phenomenon. There was no absolute level of taxation which triggered the turn away from tax and spend. In Sweden, for example, the share of national income taken and spent by the state briefly touched 71 per cent in 1993. In Britain under Blair, the figure was 40 per cent, having peaked at 45 per cent during the 1974–79 Labour government.[21] But the insight that, in societies which had become more 'middle class', higher taxes, however progressive, were no longer the main instrument of greater equality, was hardly unique to New Labour.

The period of the taxpayers' revolt coincided with a reversal of the post-war trend towards more equal societies in most of the rich countries of the world, a change which also demanded a different response from the left. The main factors responsible for the rise of inequality in Britain between 1976 and 1997 were the widening of earnings differentials and the changing pattern of employment: both the extent of unemployment but also the distribution of work among households. The significant trend was the growth of the 'workless class', a phrase Blair used in his first speech as Prime Minister, meaning households with working-age adults but without jobs, including lone-parent households and couples who are both unemployed.[22] Similar factors, although not as marked, operated in the United States and, less marked still, in Western Europe.

Inevitably, the ability of governments to influence these trends is limited. The policies of the Thatcher and Reagan governments had contributed to greater inequality, but differentials had widened as a result of global competitive pressures which squeezed demand for unskilled labour, and the social changes occurred independently of government policy. Equally, the responses of Clinton and Blair could have little impact in the short term, although Blair, operating the direct levers of 'elective dictatorship', was able to achieve more in a shorter time than Clinton, operating the indirect levers of a constitution of checks and balances. The effect of tax and benefits changes in each of Gordon Brown's Budgets was sharply redistributive, but such changes play only a small part in the overall distribution of income and wealth, and the government was embarrassed by official statistics which continued to show inequality rising. Even the growth in employment, which has a more important effect on equalising the distribution of income, failed to overcome the effect of continuing strong economic growth in which the rewards were skewed, as they had been since the mid-Seventies, to 'them that hath'.

Blair's achievement was also concealed, especially in his first two years, by a double gap between words and actions: first by his use of right-wing rhetoric; and second by the time lag between announcement and implementation. This second effect was reinforced by the adherence to Conservative spending plans for the first two years of the Blair government. But the central plan of the first term, decided by Blair and Brown long in advance, was to turn a corner in the middle of the parliament. Blair had always been explicit about his ambition to reverse the traditional pattern of Labour governments, which was higher spending followed by retrenchment. The first half of what was always likely to be a four-year term would be dominated by reassurance and stabilisation, while the second half would see higher public spending, underpinned by 'modernisation' of the public services. It would only be in this second phase that it would be safe to be more explicit about the egalitarian values of the Third Way.

The shift in the trend of public spending was announced in July 1998, in Brown's first Comprehensive Spending Review, but the increased spending did not start until the start of the next financial year in April 1999. This was the fulcrum, half-way through the period. After taking inflation into account, total government spending fell, albeit by less than 1 per cent, in the first two years, from April 1997 to April 1999. Brown kept to the overall figures set by the Conservatives, but because unemployment was lower than expected was able to shift money out of the social security budget into health and education, which just managed to stay ahead of inflation. Spending on the health service, which has to cope with the rising costs of an ageing population and medical technology, rose by 2 per cent in the first year and 3 per cent in the second; education spending rose by less than 1 per cent each year. In the third year, however, spending on these two key public services started to rise markedly. Although total government spending was effectively unchanged in relation to inflation, as unemployment continued to fall spending on health rose 7 per cent in real terms and on education 3 per cent (it was supposed to be more, but spending on capital projects was slow to start). The real boost came in the fourth, pre-election year from April 2000 to April 2001. Total spending was planned to rise 7 per cent faster than inflation, with nearly 8 per cent in real terms for health and a huge 10 per cent for education.[23] In the second Spending Review in July 2000, increases in spending of 5–6 per cent a year in real terms on both health and education would be sustained for a further three years after the likely date of the election, producing a five-year period of planned expansion which was sharply different from the record of the previous twenty (eighteen plus two) years of Conservative spending plans.

Tally-ho! Attack on 'the forces of conservatism'

In his pamphlet, Blair defined the enemies of the Third Way as 'cynicism and fatalism, prejudice and social exclusion'. Even during the honeymoon phase a more specific group of enemies were mustering themselves. At first they seemed a tiny vociferous minority, the defenders of an unpopular cause, fox-hunting. But by Sunday 1 March 1998 a mass movement of 'the countryside' had marched on London in the largest numbers since the CND rallies in the early 1980s, and with a list of grievances long enough to frighten the new government.

Livestock farming was in crisis, with the ban on beef exports unresolved and Labour having additionally banned beef on the bone at home. Rural shooters did not like the ban on handguns Blair had promised, and delivered, as a response to the shooting of schoolchildren in Dunblane. Landowners did not like the promise of the 'right to roam' on uncultivated land. The nouveaux gentry worried about the pressure for house-building in the green and pleasant bits of south-east England, another unresolved problem inherited from the previous government. Less well-off country-dwellers worried about the running-down of rural bus services and the lack of jobs and homes for young people, while no one liked the closure of village post offices. It was an incoherent coalition of interest groups, united only by a strong sense that a government of urban and suburban England did not understand them.

Blair had tried to pitch his tent wide enough to take in most of the countryside, being filmed before the election in green wellingtons, not knowing whether to pat a calf, and giving a transparent interview to *Country Life*. 'I wouldn't live in a big city if I could help it. I would live in the country. I was brought up there, really.' This was not true, 'really', or even at all. His main childhood home was in an estate of private houses on the outskirts of Durham city. Conveniently reflecting opinion polls showing nine out of ten people would rather live in the country, he said: 'Bringing up children in the country is a million times better than in towns. For small and obvious reasons: the facilities are far better.'[24]

In government, he sought to appease the grievances, allowing the Private Member's Bill to ban fox-hunting to fail a few days after the Countryside March. This left him in a curious position. As he rightly pointed out, the Labour manifesto had only committed him to allow a free vote on the issue in the Commons, which he had done. The Labour MP Michael Foster's Bill had been carried overwhelmingly by 411 votes to 151 on 28 November 1997, but the government did not provide parliamentary time for the Bill to complete its stages. Thus public opinion supported a ban by a margin of two-to-one, the House of Commons supported a ban, Cabinet ministers supported a ban (except for Robin Cook, who opposed it, and Jack Straw, the Home Secretary, who said he had no strong feelings either way), and even the Prime Minister said: 'I do think hunting is wrong and I will vote in favour of a ban in the House of Commons.'[25] Yet the ban did not happen. It was the most striking example so far of Blair's unwillingness to be straight with people. He was happy to vote for a ban, provided it was simply a gesture. He had a reasonable defence, and yet managed to use it to make himself seem even more unprincipled. The fact was that the Bill stood no chance of getting through the unreformed House of Lords (and little of getting through the half-reformed House either, but that is another story). But Blair, jumping one stage ahead of the argument, publicly said that the reason the Bill had failed was because it had been blocked by the Lords, whereas it had never got that far.[26]

Trapped between a passionate minority of animal welfare campaigners, which overlapped with the Labour Party's activist constituency, and a passionate minority of 'countryside' campaigners, which aligned even more closely with the Conservative Party's base, Blair scuttled for cover and managed to annoy both sides. In a small footnote to the Ecclestone affair, it could be argued that this demonstrated his sea-green incorruptibility, in that the anti-fox-hunting lobby had donated £1 million to the Labour Party before the election.*

However, Blair made it clear that fox-hunting would eventually be banned when he said on BBC's *Question Time* on 8 July 1999 that he would 'try to find time in the upcoming session or the one after that' for a Bill.†

So the Countryside Alliance was out in force for the Prime Minister's third Labour conference speech in Bournemouth, 28 September 1999. The backdrop read in his own handwriting 'Labour . . . for the many not the few. Tony Blair'. He started his speech with one of his unspontaneous off-the-cuff lines: 'I'm sorry I'm a bit late, but it's all those hunting horns outside the window. Still, here goes. Tally-ho.' It was a typically ironic rallying cry for the new version of the class war.

Adopting a serious tone, he tried to separate fox-hunting from other 'countryside' issues: 'We know farming is in crisis and we are trying to help. But I don't believe that the future of rural Britain depends on fox-hunting.'

The speech's wider significance was as the moment when he came out fighting against 'the forces of conservatism', a formula which rolled up the Conservative Party with small 'c' conservatives wanting to defend the pound, traditional social values along with 'fox-hunting, Pinochet and hereditary peers: the uneatable, the unspeakable and the unelectable'. It would be up to 'us, the new radicals, the Labour Party modernised', to undertake the historic mission

> to liberate Britain from the old class divisions, old structures, old prejudices, old ways of working and of doing things that will not do in this world of change. To be the progressive force that defeats the forces of conservatism. For the twenty-first century will not be about the battle between capitalism and socialism but between the forces of progress and the forces of conservatism. They are what hold our nation back. Not just in the Conservative Party but within us, within our nation.

The speech had a provocative effect on the Eurosceptic press, which was reverting to its basic Conservative outlook, even if it kept its distance from William Hague. The attempt to continue the populist attack on

*The donation was made in 1995 by the Political Animal Lobby, the campaigning wing of the International Fund for Animal Welfare, specifically to reinforce Labour's pledge of a free vote on hunting with hounds.

†Although the issue was further delayed by setting up a committee headed by Lord (Terry) Burns which reported in the summer of 2000.

privilege, 'the old élites, establishments that have run our professions and our country too long', failed to catch the eye of the Murdoch papers. The *Sun* the next day picked up the tame passage on the euro to headline its report 'SURRENDER – Blair gives in to Europe and says we're sunk if we don't dump the pound'.

This might explain why Brown and Blair tried to return to the theme of élitism later. One of the crimes of 'the old order' in Blair's speech was that they 'keep our bright inner-city kids from our best universities'. Brown made this charge rather too specific in May 2000, when he seized on a report in the *Sun* and *Daily Mail* that a comprehensive school pupil from North Tyneside had been rejected to read medicine at Magdalen College, Oxford, and had accepted a place at Harvard instead. The Chancellor used the case of Laura Spence to criticise the 'old-boy network' of the 'old school tie', but found himself in difficulty when it emerged that the college had a good record of attracting state-school pupils.* It was interesting that it was Brown not Blair who took up the case. Blair almost never associated himself with individual cases, and was wary of attacking named institutions. On a similar theme he had once declared that the hereditary peers were unrepresentative because half of them went to Eton, before adding quickly: 'Not that I have anything against people attending Eton, don't get me wrong.'[27]

The Bournemouth speech was significant, however, for its response to the charge that 'big tent' politics meant a lack of direction, public uncertainty and a lack of committed supporters upon which to fall back.

The most important line in the speech, therefore, was Blair's declaration: 'The class war is over. But the struggle for true equality has only just begun.' It was the first time he had used the word equality so prominently, without attaching 'of opportunity' to it, since his first speech in the House of Commons in 1983.

Beyond Majorism

While the Third Way seemed initially to be a rather familiar mix of illiberal social policy, free market economics and steady growth in public spending on health and education – in other words, an attempt to reconcile the Labour Party to Majorism – by the middle of 1999 it had taken on a more starkly egalitarian character. It had originally seemed to be a

*Brown's initiative attracted much mockery, such as a *Private Eye* cover (2 June 2000), with Brown saying to Blair: 'I'm sick of these public school Oxford types getting the top jobs.'

rejection not just of state socialism but of Croslandism, the belief in the redistribution of the fruits of growth through progressive taxation and public spending which had been the closest thing the Labour Party had to an ideology before the economic crisis of the Seventies. But by the mid-point of Blair's first parliament the Third Way had evolved into a modernised Croslandism, albeit with a greater sophistication about the business of 'stealth' taxes on the better-off.

This was certainly more in tune with Blair's own core beliefs, as was the parallel shift around the same time towards a more positive stance on joining the euro. However, as with Clinton in 1995–96, as soon as Blair faced a fight for re-election against a strengthening Opposition, his instinct seemed to be to offset these shifts by striking 'tough' poses on conservative social issues. By the spring of 2000 the series of leaked memos suggested he was lurching to the right again – only he did not need to sell out his principles as much as Clinton because the temper of the British people is basically more social-democratic than that of the American.

In the long run, the Third Way response to global economic changes was to prioritise higher educational standards. 'The main source of value and competitive advantage in the modern economy is human and intellectual capital,' said Blair in his pamphlet. Although the main emphasis of his policy was on standards in schools, the mishandling of tuition fees blunted the message that education, and especially higher education, was the passport to competitiveness in the increasingly global economy.

The Third Way was never designed as a vote-catching slogan. It was a flag of convenience when sailing among academics and foreigners. Although it was a meaningless phrase in itself, which was partly why Blair chose it after trying out and discarding labels such as 'stakeholder', he gave it a meaning which, for all its evasions, was substantial. For the first two years of his government, that meaning was obscured by a rhetoric of pleasing all of the people all of the time, and by spending constraints, but, especially after the declaration of war on the 'forces of conservatism' in September 1999, it became clear that Blair's description of it as 'modernised social democracy' was about right.

Notes

1. Robert Harris, *Sunday Times*, 20 September 1998.
2. *Daily Mail,* 30 June 1995.
3. Speech to business leaders in Paris, 15 November 1996; speech in the City of London, 7 April 1997.
4. Begala and McCurry were quoted by David Margolick, *Vanity Fair*, July 2000.

5. Alastair Campbell, briefing for the international press, 3 February 1998.
6. Patrick Wintour, *Observer*, 22 February 1998.
7. *Guardian*, 14 May 1998.
8. Martin Kettle, *Guardian*, 7 February 1998.
9. The idea of the Third Way at least was implicit in the title of Giddens' 1994 book, *Beyond Left and Right*, although it proclaimed the importance of environmentalism; he published a more on-message book, *The Third Way: The Renewal of Social Democracy*, at the same time as Blair's pamphlet in September 1998.
10. Martin Kettle, *Guardian*, 15 May 1998.
11. Andrew Marr, *New Statesman*, 2 October 1998; see also E. J. Dionne, *Washington Post*, 25 September 1998.
12. *Guardian*, 4 May 1996.
13. *Ibid.*, 14 May 1998.
14. Speech, Westminster Central Hall, 5 November 1998.
15. Address to Conservative MPs, Eastbourne, 12 October 1998. Compare conservative theorist David Frum's approval for President Clinton, 'The left gets words, the right gets deeds,' *Weekly Standard*, February 1999, quoted disapprovingly by Christopher Hitchens, *No One Left to Lie to*, p. 86.
16. The term 'social exclusion' had been borrowed by the tone-deaf wordsmiths of Downing Street from the European Union, where it was Commission-speak, no doubt translated from Finnish via Portuguese, for unemployment, poverty and discrimination.
17. Speech, Labour Party conference, Blackpool, 29 September 1998.
18. According to Ivor Richard: Janet Jones, *Labour of Love*, p. 107.
19. In his joint paper with Gerhard Schröder, *Europe: The Third Way/Die Neue Mitte*, he was more specific: 'The biggest part of the income must remain in the pockets of those who worked for it,' implying a maximum marginal tax rate of 50 per cent.
20. See p. 457.
21. Average public spending 1997–2001 was forecast to be 39.4 per cent of gross domestic product, the lowest figure since that for the Macmillan government, 1957–63. The figure for Thatcher, 1979–90, was 43.0 per cent, and for Major, 1990–97, 41.4 per cent. Analysis of Treasury figures by Tony Travers at the London School of Economics, *Guardian*, 25 August 1999.
22. Speech, Aylesbury Estate, Southwark, 2 June 1997.
23. I am grateful to Carl Emmerson at the Institute for Fiscal Studies for these figures, which were updated in July 2000 to take account of actual spending 1997–2000 and plans for 2000–2001.
24. *Country Life*, 26 September 1996.
25. Letter to Roseanne Mills, aged eleven, a junior member of the RSPCA, made public 13 March 1998.
26. For example, BBC1, *Question Time*, 8 July 1999.
27. Interview, *Sunday Telegraph*, 14 February 1999. David Sainsbury, government minister and paymaster general of the Labour Party, went to Eton.

27

Unfinished Business

Scotland, Wales and the House of Lords, November 1998–November 1999

'I am still pondering the consequences of my own generosity.'
—*Tony Blair, 1999*

Tony Blair was expecting William Hague to ask a question about European taxes at Prime Minister's Questions on 2 December 1998. The new Social Democrat finance minister in Germany, Oskar Lafontaine, was keen to stop rich Germans using Luxembourg as a tax haven, and his push for harmonised Europe-wide taxes on investments handed the British Eurosceptics a rod with which to beat Blair and Gordon Brown.

Instead, Hague asked: 'Can the Prime Minister confirm that he is happy to see nearly a hundred hereditary peers continue to sit in the House of Lords?'

Most MPs on both sides of the House had no idea what Hague was talking about. Labour had promised to get rid of hereditary peers and was expected to bring in a Bill soon to do just that. Why should some of them be allowed to survive?

Blair replied: 'I am delighted to hear the Right Honourable Gentleman's question,' meaning he was surprised to hear it, because he thought the deal he had reached a week earlier before with Robert Cranborne, the Conservative leader in the House of Lords, was still secret. He was puzzled, too: he had expected Hague to be annoyed with Cranborne, but could not believe he would advertise the split between the Conservative Party in the Lords and in the Commons. So, he went on, he assumed Hague's question was 'an indication that he is now prepared to agree to what would remove hereditary peers altogether, in the two stages, in the House of Lords'.

Hague had indeed been 'extremely upset', in Cranborne's words, when Cranborne told him about the deal, an hour or so before Question Time.[1] Cranborne urged him not to raise it in the Chamber because he would only make a fool of himself, but Hague recognised the deal as a fundamental threat to his authority and publicly disowned it, as surprised Labour MPs tried to work out what had been going on.

'Although we welcome the huge climbdown on his part,' he told the Prime Minister, 'we are not prepared to acquiesce in that change, because we are not prepared to join forces with him on major constitutional change that is based on no comprehensive plan or principle.'

'That is extremely interesting,' replied Blair, meaning, 'I can't believe my luck.' He confirmed that he had agreed a two-stage plan, under which 'one in ten' of the hereditary peers would stay in the first stage. The Liberal Democrats had agreed. 'His party in the House of Lords has now agreed. It is clear from this exchange that the Right Honourable Member for Richmond, Yorks [Hague] no longer speaks for the Conservative Party in the House of Lords.'

Hague replied testily, amid rising uproar: 'The Prime Minister need be in no doubt who speaks for the Conservative Party,' and attacked Blair's 'total lack of principle and his horse-trading'.

It was an unusual exchange, as Hague attacked Cranborne's deal without having any alternative of his own. His position was, 'No reform without knowing where it is going,' he said. 'What we know is that the Prime Minister intends to turn the House of Lords into a house of cronies, and that he is now prepared to engage in any horse-trading that is necessary to achieve that end.'

Blair for his part defended the deal as the common-sense way to 'get the thing done with as little fuss and as easily as possible', knowing that he had the votes of the Tory peers behind him. He observed sadly: 'I cannot prevent the Right Hon. Gentleman from engaging on a kamikaze mission. I can only tell him that even his cronies in the House of Lords agree with me that we should try to get this reform through.'

Labour MPs were a little uncomfortable as they absorbed the terms of the deal, and Hague would have, if not the last laugh, some satisfaction by the end of the parliament. The House of Cronies tag would stick to the Prime Minister, while the Leader of the Opposition's temporary embarrassment would be forgotten.

Minutes after Prime Minister's Questions was over, Hague sacked Cranborne as Conservative leader in the Lords. Viscount Cranborne, a hereditary* schemer at the top of British politics as descendant of William Cecil, Lord Burghley, Elizabeth I's Lord Treasurer, apologised to Hague for 'running in like an ill-trained spaniel', and said that if he had been in Hague's position, he would have sacked himself too. Blair's conviction that he had the Tory peers squared was borne out when John Mackay turned down Hague's invitation to replace Cranborne. Hague was then forced to appoint Thomas Strathclyde, Cranborne's Chief Whip, who accepted the Tory leadership in the Lords only on condition that he could continue to support the deal. Blair taunted Hague at the following week's Prime Minister's Questions: 'Lord Cranborne said to the Leader of the Opposition, "Back me or sack me," and the Right Honourable Gentleman succeeded in doing both.'

Cranborne's coup

Unlike the devolution of power to Scotland and Wales, unfinished business from the Labour government in 1979, reform of the Lords was unfinished business from the Liberal government in 1911. It was, as Blair would sometimes comment, remarkable that, at the end of the twentieth century, people should be entitled to make the laws of the country by an accident of birth. At the rostrum at Labour conference, he struck an unconvincing pose as a rabble-rouser: 'I say to the House of Lords: we have the votes of the people, you have the votes of nobody.'[2] Asquith had limited the power of the Lords to block legislation in the Parliament Act of 1911, and subsequent governments had filled the upper house with life peers who increasingly dominated legislative business.

Harold Wilson tried to remove the hereditary peers in 1969, but was thwarted by the unholy alliance of Michael Foot on the left, who did not want a second chamber at all, and Enoch Powell on the right, who defended the existing arrangement. The Labour government of 1974–79, driven from one crisis to another, left the issue alone.

Thus, when Blair came to power, the House of Lords still consisted of

---

*This is the grammatical form enshrined in legislation. An amendment to the Lords reform Bill moved by Earl Ferrers to change 'a' hereditary peer to 'an' throughout was defeated in the early hours of 29 April 1999. When Margaret Jay reported this at a Cabinet meeting later that morning as an example of Tory wrecking tactics, Clare Short interrupted to say it should be 'an', to murmurs of support. Blair moved quickly to suppress a Cabinet rebellion, and it became agreed government policy, enforced by collective Cabinet responsibility, that it was 'a hereditary peer' (*Financial Times*, 30 April 1999).

790 hereditary peers, overwhelmingly Conservatives, and 402 lifers. One of Blair's pre-election adjustments had been to drop Labour's pledge of a directly-elected second chamber to replace the Lords, so that his only commitment was that 'the right of hereditary peers to sit and vote in the House of Lords will be ended' – in other words, a return to Wilson's position of twenty-eight years before.

Labour's manifesto declared disingenuously that this would be the 'first stage in a process of reform to make the House of Lords more democratic and representative', while the second stage was sent deep into the long grass with the promise of 'a wide-ranging review'.

Derry Irvine, co-author with Blair of Labour's simplified plan for reform, privately made the Prime Minister's intentions clear to Ivor Richard, Labour's leader in the Lords, within months of the election. Irvine and Richard clashed repeatedly like bull elephants.[3] Irvine was effectively Blair's representative in the Lords, as well as being Lord Chancellor and thus the speaker of the upper house. Richard had helped negotiate Blair's retreat from a directly elected second chamber, and had assumed that Blair's attachment to his compromise plan for a part-elected, part-appointed assembly was genuine. He was surprised to discover that Irvine's brief was apparently to 'clear out the hereditaries. No elections. An appointed chamber.'[4]

Richard was authorised by Blair to open negotiations with Cranborne, who had a better understanding than Hague that the hereditary principle had become politically indefensible. Richard and his Chief Whip, Denis Carter, met Cranborne and 'Tommy' Strathclyde for lunch of egg mayonnaise and cold pheasant at Cranborne's house in Chelsea on 21 January 1998. Cranborne and Strathclyde said they would accept the end of hereditary peers and a Lords two-thirds elected, one-third nominated, which Richard proposed, but he said he could not go further without the go-ahead from Blair.[5]

Richard was then frustrated by what he thought was Blair's failure to focus on the issue and to make a decision. Irvine appears to have shared this view, from Richard's report of his saying of the Cabinet committee on Lords reform in March: 'I'm fucking sick of this. The fucking Prime Minister won't make any decisions.'[6] It is more likely, however, that there was a simple disagreement between Richard and Blair, which the Prime Minister did not yet want to acknowledge.

Blair had in fact made two decisions. The first was to sack Richard in his first reshuffle on 27 July 1998. According to Richard, the exchange was abrupt.

'Sit down,' said Blair. 'There's no easy way to do this. I want a change.'

'Why?'

'I want somebody else.'

'Who?'

'I have to speak to the person concerned.'

'As you will, Prime Minister.'[7] Richard was obviously one Cabinet minister who did not 'call him Tony'.

Blair's other decision was to authorise Irvine to re-open negotiations with Cranborne, on the basis of an interim House of Lords with no directly elected element at all. The only issue in these discussions, which began before Richard was sacked, was how many hereditary peers would be allowed to stay on in the first-stage reform. Irvine's opening bid was fifteen; Cranborne asked for 100. Irvine said fifty; Cranborne said he would put it to Hague, who was the only one on his side who knew about the negotiations. From the evidence of what happened later, Hague can hardly have encouraged Cranborne, but Cranborne continued to haggle with Irvine nevertheless. By the time Richard was replaced by Margaret Jay – herself a hereditary peer of sorts, as the daughter of James Callaghan – Cranborne had got the figure up to seventy-five, which Irvine thought might be acceptable because it was only 'one in ten'.

Cranborne suggested a further fifteen officers of the House. Irvine said, 'I'll ask the Prime Minister.' He came back 'by return', according to Cranborne, and said, 'Done.' Cranborne cheekily said that, 'of course', the deal would include the Earl Marshal and some other panjandrum. Irvine commented: 'So he got the figure up from seventy-five to ninety-two. And good luck to him. But he didn't get a hundred.'[8]

In order to be able to sell the deal to the Labour Party as the first stage towards the 'more democratic and representative' Upper House promised in the manifesto, Margaret Jay announced in October 1998 that the government would set up a Royal Commission to make proposals for a reformed chamber.

Cranborne met Blair over a glass of whisky at Number Ten to seal the deal on 26 November. Their discussion was mostly about the timing of its announcement. Blair was concerned that when Hague discovered that Cranborne had concluded it without consulting him, he would denounce it publicly. Cranborne assured him that Hague was unlikely to do that because he and Strathclyde were confident the Tory hereditary peers would support it, because they saw it as their best chance of salvaging something from the inevitable. Blair suggested Cranborne should meet Alastair Campbell to discuss it, which he did on Monday, 30 November. Two days later, Cranborne told Hague. A few hours after that, he was sacked. In the longer view of his family's 400-year political history, however, he had saved at least some element of the hereditary peerage.

Nearly a year later, on 26 October 1999, the House of Lords quietly declared itself 'Content' to pass the Bill to abolish the right of hereditary peers to sit and vote, with the Conservatives abstaining. The Labour cause was greatly assisted by the demonstration by the Earl of Burford, as the son of the Duke of St Albans not even a member of the House, who shouted: 'Stand up for your Queen and country – vote this treason down.'

The result was one of the more bizarre votes in the history of elections when, on 5 November, the hereditary peers, divided into party groups and crossbenchers, chose seventy-five of their number to represent them in the new House. Cranborne's final triumph came just before the vote when, in addition to the seventeen hereditary peers qualifying by virtue of their office to stay in the House, the Prime Minister nominated a further ten hereditary peers – including Cranborne himself – for life peerages.

All told, then, Cranborne got two more than the 100 he originally sought from Derry Irvine. Irvine accepted the deal was a breach of the manifesto, but defended it on the grounds that it was nine-tenths of what Labour wanted, and meant the rest of Labour's programme went through unscathed, making time for additional legislation: 'I claim a huge success in getting rid of nine-tenths of the hereditaries with legislative peace.'[9]

Even the most cursory examination of Labour's past record on constitutional reform should support Irvine and Blair in their assessment of the importance of getting legislation through by consensus as much as possible. Reform of the Lords in 1969 and Scottish and Welsh devolution in 1978–79 were both lost to procedural guerrilla warfare in parliament which, in the case of devolution, disrupted the government's ability to carry its other business. Blair himself, on the relatively minor issue of the voting system for European elections, suffered six defeats in the House of Lords before he finally prevailed.

His achievement was, therefore, historic, but it was also substantially negated by the inadequacy of the wholly appointed house which replaced the mostly hereditary one. The 'House of Cronies' jibe may not have been strictly accurate. Labour peers continued to be in a minority in the new House: one of the first votes after the expulsion of the hereditary peers was to approve Blair's third Queen's Speech, on 24 November 1999, by just 168 votes to 164, a result obtained by what Labour Chief Whip Denis Carter described laconically as 'precision whipping', and with the support of Liberal Democrat peers. Even a further twenty Labour life peers created in March 2000, to add to the twenty-two created the previous year, only brought the government's total up to 202, as against 236

Conservatives, 63 Liberal Democrats, 161 crossbenchers and 26 bishops. And Blair continued regularly to lose votes in the Lords, with even his own creations going native. Helena Kennedy, the celebrity lawyer and quintessential 'Tony crony', led a revolt against restricting the right to trial by jury in January 2000.

However, the 'interim' House of Lords remained a spatchcocked insult to democracy, as it continued to provide red-leather seats in Parliament to an assortment of Labour donors, prime ministerial favourites and worthies. Blair compounded the weakness of his claim to be a constitutional reformer by overclaiming, as ever. He described 'the influence of hereditary peers in our democracy' as 'gone for good', when ninety-two of them were still amending, revising and delaying legislation on the basis of who their ancestors were.[10]

The crowning act of cronyism was the appointment of Dennis Stevenson as the chairman of the House of Lords Appointments Commission in May 2000. This was the body which would propose 'independent' peers in addition to the political nominations submitted by the party leaders, and was the basis of Blair's claim that 'this supposed control freak will be the first Prime Minister to remove from himself the sole power of patronage in appointing peers'.[11] Stevenson was a donor to Blair's Labour leadership campaign fund in 1994, and had been Peter Mandelson's employer as boss of SRU management consultancy before the 1992 election. He was also chairman of Pearson, which owned the *Financial Times*, and a director of BSkyB and Manpower recruitment agency, two companies which sponsored the Millennium Dome. He was made a peer in 1999, sitting as a crossbencher, and chaired a task force on how to get computers into schools.

Another monument to Blair's lack of principle was the report of the Royal Commission on the future of the House of Lords, setting out the options for the second and final stage of reform. Contrary to Harold Wilson's dictum that Royal Commissions 'take minutes and last for years', this one, chaired by John Wakeham, the Conservative fixer and former Cabinet minister, was appointed in January 1999 and reported exactly a year later. But the report, proposing three options for a mostly-appointed House with a small minority of elected members, was widely described as 'dismal', and there was no timetable attached.[12] It dismissed the idea of a directly elected second chamber as a recipe for conflict and deadlock with the rival democratic mandate of the House of Commons, but ignored alternatives which would reduce the power of party whips, such as having members elected on long, non-renewable terms.[13] It was an intellectually shabby attempt to produce what the Prime Minister wanted, and left all the big questions of how to create a second chamber of Parliament that is democratic, legitimate and efficient to Blair's successors.

Home rule for Scotland and Wales

'The Scottish Parliament, which adjourned on 25 March 1707, is hereby reconvened.' The words of Winnie Ewing, the Scottish Nationalist stalwart sworn in as the first Member of the Scottish Parliament for 292 years, were greeted with applause on 12 May 1999.[14] As the oldest member, she took the presiding officer's chair temporarily until a permanent occupant – the former Liberal leader Sir David Steel – was elected that afternoon.

Just as with the House of Lords, Derry Irvine's rigorous preparation had ensured that the business was done, even if some noses were put out of joint. It is striking how, in the case of devolution, Blair picked up in 1997 almost precisely where Callaghan left off, rerunning the unsuccessful and sabotaged referendums of 1979 in 'new, improved' format eighteen years later, and this time obtaining the 'right' answer. The pre-legislative referendum in Scotland on 11 September 1997 produced a 74.3 per cent Yes vote on devolution, with 63.5 per cent voting Yes to the Scottish Parliament having tax-raising powers. The referendum in Wales a week later was by contrast a close-run, apathetic thing, with No in the lead throughout the count until the last returns from Carmarthenshire tipped the result, 50.3 per cent Yes, 49.7 per cent No.[15] The legislation was then delivered without incident, in time to hold elections in May 1999.

Despite Blair's difficult relationship with the land of his birth,[16] he had safely delivered what the moderate consensus in Scotland had wanted since the eruption of the Scottish National Party as a serious electoral force in 1974. Nor did the nation of Scotland immediately embark on the slippery slope to independence, as the unionists in both the Conservative and Labour parties had feared and the separatists in the SNP had hoped. Indeed, despite the beginning of limited home rule being a prosaic anti-climax for the passionate supporters of devolution in both the Labour and Liberal Democrat parties, it quickly became the settled political landscape. The ruling Lib–Lab coalition was an uninspiring creature, and yet the SNP opposition sank into introspective lassitude rather than seizing its moment.

With the same party in power in Westminster as in Edinburgh and Cardiff, devolution did not expose the tensions between different parts of the United Kingdom, however, so much as the contradictions within the

Labour Party, between Blair's desire for discipline and the logic of devolution. In Scotland the contradiction was suppressed because – despite some havering from Robin Cook – it was as much the 'settled will' of the Scottish people that they should have a devolved Parliament as that Donald Dewar, Blair's Secretary of State for Scotland, and Jim Wallace, leader of the Scottish Liberal Democrats, should be its inaugural First and Second Ministers.

Cook ruled himself out of contention in January 1998, and Dewar was elected Labour leader north of the border unopposed. In Wales, the leadership was a trickier issue. Blair's Secretary of State, Ron Davies, was a machine politician with enough of a record on the left to come out on top of Welsh Labour politics so long as it was not too democratic. Blair and Davies had a problem, however, in the shape of Rhodri Morgan, the engaging MP for Cardiff West, who was more popular with grass-roots party members and shop-floor trade unionists. That meant that the 'one member, one vote' system which had elected Blair leader of the national party could not be relied on to deliver the right result, so an electoral college of trade union block votes and local party delegates was put together instead. Blair's apparently illogical preference for Davies was explained by an unusual instance of his allowing a personality clash to cloud his judgment. Morgan had been his deputy energy spokesman in 1987, and Blair felt he was unreliable. It was a costly error, which led Blair to go back on his professed principles. Fortunately for him, few people noticed when, on 4 August 1998, the electoral college elected Davies rather than Morgan as leader of the Wales Labour Party. The Prime Minister, who had made his reputation in the Labour Party as an advocate of one member, one vote, was on holiday. He seemed to have got away with it, until Davies went for a walk on Clapham Common.

'Moment of madness'

Ron Davies resigned as Secretary of State for Wales on 27 October 1998, after having his car stolen the night before. Downing Street was told of the theft by the police and Blair summoned Davies to explain what had happened. He chose not to do so, although he admitted to an error of judgment in accompanying a stranger to his flat from the south London park, which is a known rendezvous for homosexuals. Alastair Campbell coined the phrase 'moment of madness' which has ever since described the end of Davies's political career.

Blair compounded the error he had made in blocking Rhodri Morgan in August by promoting another of his former deputies, Alun Michael, to the Cabinet to take Davies's place. Michael, who had impressed Blair as a safe pair of hands as his number two when shadow Home Secretary, 1992–94, was now reluctantly and unhappily press-ganged into standing for the leadership of the Wales Labour Party.

This time, Blair had a real fight on his hands, as he tried to install his puppet against the popular and independent-minded Morgan. In February 1999 the Labour Party in Wales managed to reproduce the worst features of undemocratic, activist-led block voting, only this time it was Blair rather than the Bennites who was the beneficiary. Labour Party members, voting 65 to 35 per cent for Morgan, were steamrollered by the votes of MPs and Welsh Assembly candidates, with the block votes of three trade unions, the engineers, transport workers and GMB general union, decisive.[17] Michael was elected, by a margin of 53 to 47 per cent over Morgan.

The means could not even be justified by the ends. So great was Michael's devotion to home rule for Wales that he had not even stood as a candidate for the Assembly: he had to be parachuted in at the last minute to the list of top-up candidates in the only region where Labour was likely to qualify for a top-up Assembly Member. In the Assembly elections themselves, on 6 May 1999, Labour fell short of the overall majority it was expected to secure, winning only twenty-nine of the sixty seats. For the first time, Plaid Cymru, the Welsh nationalist party, emerged as the recipient of substantial protest voting in the South Wales valleys, where Labour loyalty used to run as deep as the seams of coal, and won Rhondda and Islwyn.

As soon as he was installed at the head of Labour's minority administration, Michael repaid Blair's confidence by putting a vegetarian in charge of agriculture and a non-Welsh-speaker in charge of Welsh language teaching. After less than a year, Michael was forced to resign, lacking the political skill to build bridges to the Opposition parties, which united against him on an obscure issue of European Union finance. Even the manner of his going caused Blair further embarrassment, as he resigned just before losing a motion of no confidence while the Prime Minister was on his feet in the House of Commons, eight minutes into Question Time, having just said, 'I believe that the Welsh First Secretary is doing an excellent job.'[18] Conservative MPs, who had the news of Michael's resignation relayed to them on their electronic pagers, noisily failed to contain their mirth.

It was the first time Blair had reason to regret Paddy Ashdown's departure as Liberal Democrat leader, because his successor, Charles Kennedy, had refused to help prop Michael up, despite the Prime Minister's personal plea. Blair was forced, therefore, to bow to the inevitable, and Rhodri Morgan, who promised to work with the Liberal Democrats, was confirmed as First Secretary of Wales the next week. Just a month later, Michael resigned from the Welsh Assembly and admitted that he really saw himself as a Westminster MP. Morgan was soon considered to be doing a good job (he sacked the vegetarian agriculture secretary after a decent interval in July 2000). Blair admitted: 'He's doing a very good job. He's exercised real leadership and I have to say I got that judgment wrong. You've got to exercise discretion. You've got to know the battles to fight and the battles not to fight.'[19] However, he went on to make the same mistake on a larger scale when it came to blocking Ken Livingstone as Labour's candidate for London mayor.

Meanwhile, devolution also proved troublesome in Scotland, although the conflict with London was less acute than some had predicted. Blair had been alarmed to discover, two weeks before polling day, that the terms of the coalition deal between Labour and the Liberal Democrats in Scotland had not been finalised: the sticking-point was tuition fees, to which the Liberal Democrats were strongly opposed, and no deal was possible until after the election, when it could be fudged by referring the issue to a committee. As John Reid, Dewar's successor as Secretary of State for Scotland, commented graphically: 'When we put blood into frozen limbs there will be problems.'[20]

When the tuition fees issue was eventually settled, more than a year later, the compromise introduced some strange inconsistencies – students with better-off parents living in England would continue to pay fees, while those in Scotland would have their fees paid out of an additional loan scheme. But the whole point of devolution was that laws could be different north and south of the border.

An accidental revolution

Devolution has rightly been described as Blair's inheritance rather than his passion. Unlike John Smith, whose life embodied Scotland's separateness within the United Kingdom, and unlike Neil Kinnock, famously one of the left-wing opponents of Welsh devolution in the 1970s, Blair tolerated strictly limited home rule because Labour, the Liberal Democrats and most of the local media were so committed to it. This was obviously more the case in Scotland than in Wales, which lacked a national legal and education system, or a national media and culture, so the Welsh Assembly had fewer powers. But it did have 'a £7 billion-odd budget to decide,' as Blair put it. 'In anybody's language that's pretty big potatoes.'[21]

Blair claimed it was a 'myth' that he was less committed to Scottish home rule than Smith. 'I supported it in the 1970s, when it was quite fashionable in large parts of the Labour Party to disagree with it.'[22] This was unconvincing, not least because the opponents of devolution in the 1970s Labour Party were a minority. He has claimed to have made speeches in the 1980s setting out his vision of a devolved United Kingdom, but they are not easy to find. He was, however, prepared to confront directly one aspect of devolution which had made Labour uncomfortable in the past. He accepted that it would mean that Scottish and Welsh over-representation in the House of Commons would have to be ended. It was a conclusion Labour had often balked at, because this was one source of its electoral advantage under the existing voting system. But Blair's politics was predicated on making the Labour Party the sort of party that could win majorities in England without needing to rely on the Celtic fringe.

Whatever else, though, he did not sound like an instinctive sharer of power. On the day the new Scottish Parliament first met, he told Peter Luff, the Conservative MP, that when it came to the proportional voting system which ensured that the Tory party had some seats at Edinburgh, 'I am still pondering the consequences of my own generosity in that respect for his own political party.'[23] This was taking the idea that subsidiary authorities in the United Kingdom only hold such power as the House of Commons delegates to them a little far, and a little personally.

Blair's substantial programme of reform of the institutions of British democracy did not form a coherent whole, and did not seem to be animated by a desire to 'let the people decide' – as opposed to a desire for him, as Prime Minister, to decide how much power might be temporarily leased from the centre.

The idea that the people of Scotland – or Wales, or London – claimed the right to decide for themselves how they should be governed was lost in referendums which were a matter of legislative tactics. The idea that Parliament might pass better laws if its revising chamber had some democratic legitimacy was lost in an unprincipled deal to remove its built-in Conservative bias. Just as the idea that the people as a whole might have the right to decide for themselves what kind of voting system they preferred for the House of Commons was lost in the short-term need to string the Liberal Democrats along.

The ruling assumption of the liberal left, developed in response to the 'elective dictatorship' of the Thatcher years, meant little to Blair. The idea of direct rather than representative democracy which dominated the thinking of the New Labour inner core cut against the idea of a grand plan to re-engineer the institutions of the British state to make them more democratic. For Blair, true democracy is delivered by a party which is electorally successful because it is in tune with what people want, because it is sensitive to opinion polls, focus groups and popular culture.

Thus it was that Blair delivered a historic set of changes to the British constitution in the unheroic posture of a technocrat fixing unrelated faults in a basically sound machine. Most of the hereditary peers went; Scotland, Wales, Northern Ireland and London all acquired their own governments of different kinds; and various forms of proportional voting systems were introduced in all of them, as well as in elections to the European Parliament. All in the space of two and a half years. Had it been sold as a connected programme of reform, it might have been hailed as a democratic revolution, the greatest constitutional upheaval since votes for women; instead, the nation shrugged and moved on.

Notes

1. BBC2, *The Lady in the Lords*, 6 February 2000.
2. Tony Blair, to Labour conference, Brighton, 30 September 1997.
3. As early as 3 June 1997, according to Richard's wife's diary, Derry was muttering under his breath when Richard interrupted him in meetings. '"If you want to insult me Derry, at least do it audibly," Richard told him' (Janet Jones, *Labour of Love*, p. 78).
4. Diary entry for 2 December 1997, Jones, *ibid.*, p. 142.
5. Jones, *ibid.*, p. 165.
6. Diary entry for 13 March 1998, Jones, *ibid.*, p. 198.
7. Jones, *ibid.*, p. 273. Blair's answer to the 'Why?' question was at least more tactful than Clement Attlee's famous: 'Not up to it.'
8. Cranborne and Irvine were interviewed by Michael Cockerell, BBC2, *The Lady in the Lords*, 6 February 2000.
9. BBC2, *The Lady in the Lords*, 6 February 2000.
10. Speech, Labour Local Government conference, Blackpool, 6 February 2000.
11. Speech, Labour Party conference, Blackpool, 29 September 1998.
12. Under Model A, one in nine members of the Lords would be selected from regional lists according to votes cast at general elections; under Model B, which the commission leant towards, one-sixth would be elected from regional lists at European Parliament elections; under Model C, this proportion would be raised to one-third.
13. The Conservative former Lord Chancellor James Mackay proposed electing 'senators' on fifteen-year, non-renewable terms in his rather good report, 16 April 1999.
14. *Scottish Parliament Official Report*, 12 May 1999, col. 5.
15. Turnout in Scotland was 60.4 per cent; thus even the 1979 threshold of 40 per cent of the electorate voting Yes was satisfied with 44.9 per cent doing so. Turnout in Wales was 50.1 per cent.
16. See p. 306.

17. One union, the public service workers, Unison, balloted its members and 74 per cent of them backed Morgan; independent polls suggested the members of other unions supported him by a similar margin.
18. *Hansard*, 9 February 2000.
19. *Observer*, 9 April 2000.
20. BBC1, *Panorama*, 28 February 2000.
21. Interview, *Financial Times*, 14 January 1999; the Welsh for 'pretty big potatoes' is *tatws go fawr*.
22. *Ibid.*
23. *Hansard*, 12 May 1999.

28

PURER THAN PURE

Mandelson's Home Loan, December 1998

> 'Ministers should avoid accepting any gift or hospitality which might, or might reasonably appear to, compromise their judgment or place them under an improper obligation.'
>
> —A Code of Conduct and Guidance on Procedures for Ministers, *drawn up by Blair, 31 July 1997*

Tony Blair stepped outside Number Ten just after 10pm on 16 December 1998 to announce the launch of air strikes against Iraq. It was the first time he had ordered British armed forces into action, and when he stepped back inside he was unsurprisingly absorbed in following the progress of Operation Desert Fox. On the afternoon of the next day, Thursday, he was to make a statement to the House of Commons about the bombing. As he worked on the statement at lunchtime, he was therefore more preoccupied than usual when Alastair Campbell interrupted to say that a story was about to break in the press, and they needed to decide how to handle it. Peter Mandelson, who had been Secretary of State for Trade and Industry for five months, had secretly borrowed £373,000 from Geoffrey Robinson, then a fellow-MP and now a fellow-minister, to buy his Notting Hill house in 1996.

What must Blair have thought at that moment? He later said privately that he realised the moment he learned of the loan that Mandelson would have to resign. That would have been the correct reaction, but he did not tell Mandelson so until six days later, after the story became public and on the third day of the media firestorm which followed. The impression is that he waited to see how bad the public reaction would be and only then fired the ejector seat.

But what did Blair feel about being betrayed by his friend and counsellor of twelve years? He was entitled to know about the loan, which might have given the appearance of affecting Mandelson's advice about ministerial appointments in 1997, and which was clearly material to the Department of Trade and Industry's well-publicised and already embarrassing investigation into Robinson's business affairs. Blair had not asked Mandelson how he had managed to afford such a dramatic step up from a flat in Clerkenwell to a house in Notting Hill – perhaps Mandelson managed to suggest in passing, as he did to others, that he had inherited money when his father died some eight years earlier (he did, but it was only £55,000: the house cost £470,000).

There can have been no doubt in Blair's mind that Mandelson had broken the rules on the disclosure of financial interests, and he immediately asked Sir Richard Wilson, the Cabinet Secretary, to look into it in relation to the DTI investigation.

Whether or not Blair had been unbalanced by Mandelson's revelation, he stumbled uncharacteristically seven or eight times in his statement in the Commons.

There was no time before going to the Commons to dwell on these questions, but Blair had every reason to be alarmed. Robinson had not only been generous to Mandelson: he had also lent Blair his villa in Tuscany for holidays and had been 'happy to support' Blair's office as Leader of the Opposition.[1]

Indeed, Blair was one of four members of the informal core of New Labour who were in hock to the man who was to take the unfortunate title of Paymaster General in government: Gordon Brown for some of the costs of his private office, Peter Mandelson for his house and Anji Hunter for the loan of a flat in the Grosvenor House hotel during the election campaign. This impressive inventory of generosity was open to misinterpretation, particularly in the cases of Mandelson and Brown because of its unnecessary secrecy.[*]

Afterwards, he seemed in no hurry to act. The excuse that he was distracted by the Iraqi crisis could only apply until Saturday, when the bombing campaign was suspended. It was not until then that he spoke to Mandelson, and then he only 'firmly advised' that the loan should be paid off.[2] That would hardly have lessened Mandelson's error in failing to

---

*Mandelson and Robinson both suggested that the other had wanted to keep the loan secret. 'Geoffrey Robinson asked for confidentiality and I respected that,' said Mandelson in his statement to the *Guardian* confirming the existence of the loan, 22 December 1998. Robinson said later: 'I think Peter should have declared it, that's the only problem there, and I'm allowed to lend money to whom I want.' (BBC Radio 4, *Today*, 26 January 2000.)

declare the loan in the first place. As in the Ecclestone case, it seems Blair's first concern was presentational: he was trying to soften the impact of the story rather than to do the right thing. It was in any case already too late to repay the loan: the story was in the hands of the *Guardian* and publication was imminent. Furthermore, as Mandelson admitted to him on Sunday, he could not raise the funds to repay Robinson 'immediately'. Even this was less than the truth, which was that there was barely a better prospect of Mandelson paying off the money 'immediately' than there had been when it was lent – against the security of Mandelson selling his memoirs or inheriting his half share of the family home in Hampstead Garden Suburb from his 77-year-old mother.

Another alarming aspect of the news for Blair was the question of how the story was about to reach the public domain. Although the precise route or routes was obscure, the motive seemed to lie in the feud between Gordon Brown and Mandelson, dating from the 1994 leadership contest. Although Robinson was friendly with both men, and with the third point of the triangle, Blair, he was closest to Brown. Indeed, he was a central member of the small group of Brown loyalists, one of whom, Michael Wills, said Brown was 'determined to kill' Mandelson before Mandelson destroyed him. The two of them, said Wills, were 'like scorpions in a bottle: only one of them will crawl out alive'.[3] In such a climate, and with the information known within the group, it was not surprising that it was given to Paul Routledge, the political editor of the *Independent on Sunday* and a friend of Brown's press officer, Charlie Whelan. Routledge decided to follow up his admiring biography of Brown with a hostile one of Mandelson. If not necessarily on Brown's instructions or with his knowledge, it seems one of his zealous lieutenants sought to bring down the Chancellor's enemy. (Nor would Robinson have authorised the disclosure, as it should have been obvious that it would damage him as well.) However, Routledge was denied the satisfaction of delivering the knockout blow after someone opened a package containing proofs of his book when they were delivered in error to his old *Independent on Sunday* office in the House of Commons on 2 December, before being sent on to him at the *Mirror* office. As a result of this interception Mandelson's assistant Benjamin Wegg-Prosser was tipped off by a sympathetic journalist about the contents of the book, while the same information reached the *Guardian*.

With Operation Desert Fox over and the Prime Minister at Chequers for Christmas, it was not until Monday 21 December that Derry Irvine, Charles Falconer and Alastair Campbell convened in crisis session at Downing Street to discuss what to do. They agreed to advise Mandelson to confirm the facts the *Guardian* had put to him, and make a full statement including the precise amount of the loan. The first edition of the newspaper that evening launched Mandelson on a thirty-six-hour fight for his job. But it was not until he spoke to Blair on the phone at 10pm the following night that Mandelson mentioned the possibility of resignation, saying – as Blair would recall the next day in his reply to his letter of resignation – they could not seem to be 'like the last lot'.[4] Blair told him to sleep on it. When they spoke again, just after 10am on Wednesday morning, Blair said his long-term prospects would be best served by resigning. By now, however, Mandelson's position had become so exposed that he was coming to the same conclusion. This was hardly the behaviour of a Prime Minister determined to ensure the highest possible ethical standards in his government. It had only the modest advantage of presentational competence over John Major's repeated attempts to resist press outcries.

Mandelson asked more than once if Blair thought that if he resigned now he could 'return to the front rank' in due course. Blair said he thought he would.[5] Having thus secured his return ticket out of the Cabinet, Mandelson's resignation was announced with the now-traditional publication of the exchange of letters. Less traditional was the fact that both letters were drafted by Alastair Campbell. Mandelson also wrote a private, handwritten note 'congratulating Blair for being such a decisive and strong leader'.[6] Robinson's resignation was announced a few hours later. Blair's letter to him was not so solicitous, acknowledging only that 'you have felt these past months hounded by the campaign against you'. Whelan, who denied being the source of the story, resigned two weeks later.

Mayfair and Park Lane

Blair appointed two business people as ministers in May 1997, and both spelt trouble. Geoffrey Robinson was already an MP, although his elevation straight from the back benches to Minister of State level at the Treasury came as a surprise. Sir David Simon's elevation was even more dramatic, moving straight from the boardroom of BP, where he was chairman, into government, also at Minister of State level at the Department of Trade and Industry, via a life peerage in the House of Lords.

The new Lord Simon, like Geoffrey Robinson, was rich enough not to draw a ministerial salary. When in London, Robinson lived in a penthouse flat at the Grosvenor House Hotel on Park Lane. Simon, as a successful business executive at the head of one of Britain's biggest companies, had built up a rather smaller fortune, mostly in his shareholding in BP, worth £2 million. The rules on the private interests of members of government, *Questions of Procedure for Ministers*, were clear: 'A minister should, upon assuming office, review his or her investments and, if it seems likely that any of them might give rise to an actual or apparent conflict of interest, they should be disposed of.' Although it was unlikely that BP might make an unexpected killing from changes in government policy for which Simon was responsible, 'competitiveness in Europe', it was hard to think of a subject under that broad heading in which the company did not have some kind of interest, and the test was only one of an 'apparent' conflict.

The usual practice had been for ministers to put their shares in a blind trust – the same imperfect device as Blair had used in Opposition to raise funds for his office. Simon consulted his permanent secretary, Michael Scholar, to explain that he did not think he could do that. The difficulty was that the trustees would be obliged by trust law to sell most of the shares in order to invest in a more balanced portfolio. Simon thought he would fall foul of the City's ethical rules against insider trading which would not allow him, as a director with inside information, to trade in the company's shares until after its quarterly results were announced. Putting the shares in a blind trust would effectively be to sell them while he still possessed privileged information. He was being far too fastidious: when Sir David Sainsbury made a similar translation from company chairman to minister the next year, he put his much larger shareholding in Sainsbury's straight into a blind trust without any fuss. But Scholar and Sir Robin Butler, the Cabinet Secretary, agreed Simon should hang on to his shares until the end of the year. Meanwhile, anything which touched specifically on BP's business would not be allowed across his desk. Blair, whose party had feasted on the Conservatives' relaxed attitude towards ministers going straight from the Cabinet room to the board room, had given no thought to the awkward and technical issues involved in traffic in the opposite direction. Thus John Redwood, the aggressive Conservative trade spokesman, was able to knock some of the shine off the new government's ethical gloss.

Simon's case meant the rules had to be rewritten, at greater length and with a longer title, *A Code of Conduct and Guidance on Procedures for Ministers*, published on 31 July 1997. The requirement of the new code to 'dispose of any financial interest giving rise to the actual or perceived' conflict of interest now had an escape clause: 'or take alternative steps to prevent it'.[7]

By a quirk of fate, it fell to Peter Mandelson as a minister at the

Cabinet Office to announce the new code with words which can only have mocked him with the secret funding of his London home as he uttered them:

> It's going to be tighter and it's going to make life harder for ministers and that's quite right. There will be new limits on gifts and hospitality received by ministers, advice on organising their financial affairs and there will be stricter rules on the accountability of ministers to parliament . . . We have said that we will observe the highest standards of propriety in government. That's what this new ministerial code is about and that's what we will do.

Only five days later, Simon announced that he had sold the shares after all. BP's quarterly results had been published, showing a 21 per cent increase in profits. Instead of holding the shares for two quarters, as Simon had originally suggested, he and Blair agreed it was time to limit further presentational damage. Blair had just had the unpleasant experience of being made to look foolish by William Hague in the Commons the previous week. For the first time since the election, he had no better response than to sulk petulantly, 'I really think that the Right Honourable Gentleman should go away and grow up and ask more sensible questions', and said that if Hague thought Simon had broken any rules he should say so outside the Chamber, where, without parliamentary privilege, he could be sued for defamation.[8]

However, the new code maintained the same high moral tone as the old in declaring that 'ministers should avoid accepting any gift or hospitality which might, or might reasonably appear to, compromise their judgment or place them under an improper obligation'.[9] Blair simply could not see that these were words which could be turned against him. Three months later, they were, as Bernie Ecclestone's donation became public.

No sooner had Blair managed to drive on from that disaster than it emerged at the end of November that Geoffrey Robinson had a beneficial interest in a £12 million discretionary trust in Guernsey; it was, in a twist that would destroy the credibility of any novel, a bequest from a rich Belgian lady friend, Joska Bourgeois. Presentationally, this was awkward, as Robinson, number three in the hierarchy of Treasury ministers, was responsible for scrapping tax-privileged savings accounts, PEPs and TESSAs, on the grounds that they allowed the better-off to avoid tax. A Guernsey trust was, of course, the sort of legal tax-avoidance device open only to the very rich.

Just as that embarrassment subsided, an accounting irregularity came to light at a company controlled by the crook Robert Maxwell, of which Robinson had been chairman. According to the accounts of Hollis Industries, an engineering company, Robinson was paid £200,000 as chairman in 1990, a payment that was not declared in the Register of Members' Interests. Robinson said the payment was not made and the accounts were inaccurate. He escaped censure from the parliamentary standards commissioner for lack of evidence, but Blair's holiday arrangements started to haunt him, allowing William Hague to observe cuttingly that 'the Paymaster General hangs on to his job because he has villas in high places'.[10]

The Mystery of Robinson's Missing £200,000 was referred to the Department of Trade and Industry, just in time for Mandelson's arrival as Secretary of State on 27 July 1998. Meanwhile the one-week wonder of Derek Draper's big mouth did more to distract Blair from potential ethical problems than to deal with them.

Draper, a self-described New Labour 'fixer', is an engaging character, partly because of his streak of utter irresponsibility. As Mandelson's assistant before the 1997 election, he was on friendly terms with many of the cadre of bright young things in the fluid hierarchy of Downing Street. As a lobbyist, Draper claimed to be 'intimate with every one of' the 'seventeen people who count'. Blair himself sustained only collateral damage when, on 5 July 1998, the *Observer* published the results of its sting, by which American journalist Greg Palast persuaded Draper he worked for a US energy company seeking business openings in Britain which depended on the form of government regulation of the industry.

The damage caused by the article was in its exposure of the fringe of former advisers to New Labour politicians who were now plying their trade as lobbyists, the trade which had so plagued John Major. Hague was able to conflate Draper, Robinson and others as Blair's 'feather-bedding, pocket-lining, money-grabbing cronies',[11] causing the Prime Minister to suffer another sense-of-humour failure.

The only issue of real substance was whether Roger Liddle, in the Downing Street Policy Unit, had offered to make calls and arrange meetings on Draper's behalf. Liddle was a veteran special adviser from the Callaghan government but an honorary 'teenybopper' – John Prescott's term for Downing Street's gilded youth – and also a pre-election business partner of Draper's at the lobbying firm Prima Europe. Liddle denied offering to act on behalf of Draper's company, Palast did not have a tape recording, and Blair was able to ride out the storm by promising to 'strengthen' the rules governing contacts between special advisers and lobbying firms: 'Anyone found breaching them will be out on his ear,' said Blair, with unconvincing bravado.[12]

While Mandelson said gently only that Draper was a 'show-off', Blair commented:

> We have to be very careful with people fluttering around the new government, trying to make all sorts of claims of influence, that we are purer than pure, that people understand that we will not have any truck with anything that is improper in any shape or form.[13]

The 'purer than pure' phrase was, once again, a rhetorical excess which would prove unsustainable. As Blair retrospectively admitted by tightening the rules on special advisers, he had failed to insist robustly that nothing should be allowed which would undermine his humble ambition to be given, in the words of John Smith's epitaph which he often quoted, 'the chance only to serve'.

Ministers and their money

The key issue in Peter Mandelson's secret loan was not, however, the appearance of a conflict of interest in the DTI investigation of Geoffrey Robinson's business affairs. In order to avoid one minister having to investigate another, the civil service had ensured that Mandelson was insulated from the investigation anyway. But there was no doubt that Mandelson had broken the code of conduct for ministers. Elizabeth Filkin, the Parliamentary Commissioner for Standards, issued her ruling to that effect in July 1999, and was irritated by the decision of the Standards and Privileges Committee not to impose any penalty, not even requiring him to apologise to the House.[14]

Equally, as Blair said, this aspect of Mandelson's misdemeanour was not an 'earth-shattering event', like losing pilots over the Gulf:

> We both took the view that, in the end, even though there had been nothing wrong in the sense of any interference with the inquiry into Geoffrey Robinson, none the less it was a serious misjudgment, it was a mistake and it was wrong not to have told the permanent secretary at the time of this arrangement and therefore it was right that he go.[15]

Blair's defence was disingenuous, however. The real problem was not the appearance of a conflict of interest but an actual conflict in Robinson's appointment as a minister. Blair had to duck this point because it implicated him, and was able to do so because it was not covered explicitly by the ministerial code.

By accepting Robinson's loan, Mandelson had put himself under an obligation to someone who wanted ministerial office. Although Mandelson had no constitutional role in his appointment, the reality was that his role as counsellor to Blair gave him considerable potential power. Blair, too, was in Robinson's debt: his only defence was that, although he had not registered his friend's hospitality, it was front-page public knowledge.

30. On the threshold of doing rather than saying: with Cherie, Nicky, Kathryn and Euan, 2 May 1997.

31. With father Leo, stepmother Olwen and Cherie at Labour conference, Brighton, September 1997.

32. Blair stands by Bill Clinton: news conference dominated by questions about Monica Lewinsky at the White House, February 1998.

33. Bold yet tentative: creeping around a tree on the way to a news conference in the garden of Number Ten on the results of Scottish, Welsh and local council elections, 7 May 1999.

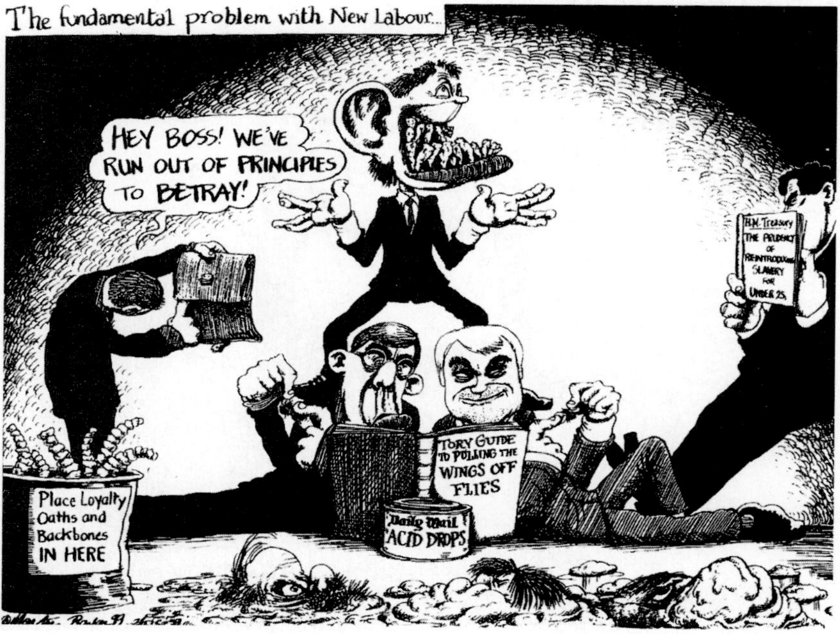

34. The limits of 'permanent revisionism' as seen by Martin Rowson in the *Guardian*, May 1999.

35. 'We will not let you down': Blair's promise to the Kosovo Albanian refugees was backed by a visit to those stranded on the Macedonian border, May 1999.

36. The Kosovo war transformed Blair's caricature from the woolly vicar of St Albion to a righteous zealot: Steve Bell in the *Guardian*, June 1999.

37. 'I feel your cold': empathising with the northern core vote in the Manchester drizzle, December 1999.

38. One of the stiffest tests of the job is looking authoritative in native gear: Blair and Japanese Prime Minister Yoshiro Mori in local shirts at the G8 summit in Nago, July 2000.

39. The Prime Ministerial Mug: as a man whose lack of eccentricity is quite eccentric, this is the nearest thing he has to a foible, carried into Cabinet meetings and clutched – this one with a photograph of his three elder children printed on it – when he announced the birth of number four to the cameras waiting in Downing Street, May 2000.

40. Blair cradles Leo as he and Cherie leave Downing Street a week later for a fortnight's parental leave at Chequers.

41. 'Being a Prime Minister can be tough, but being a parent is probably tougher' (a line borrowed from Bill Clinton). On the BBC's *Question Time* the day after Euan, sixteen, had been arrested for being drunk and incapable in Leicester Square, July 2000.

42. End of an era: Blair had Peter Mandelson sit next to him in the Commons the day he sacked him, January 2001: note the unbridgeable four-inch gap between them.

Thus the decision to appoint Robinson, straight from the back benches to Minister of State rank, could have been influenced, indirectly and secretly through Mandelson, and directly and publicly through Blair himself. If the Prime Minister had been genuinely concerned to maintain the 'highest standards of honesty and propriety in public life', as pledged in his first Queen's Speech, he would not have accepted either of Robinson's invitations to holiday at his Tuscan villa. Or, having accepted the first, he would not have made him a minister.

For his part, Robinson insisted: 'I would never think to use the existence of the loan – or any contribution I made to the Labour Party or leaders' funds – to gain influence or advancement.'[16]

Conflicts of interest were not confined to the case of Robinson. Blair did not merely continue the charade by which honours looked as if they were being sold for party donations, he introduced a new variation, by which generous party donors became ministers. At least Robinson was elected by the voters of Coventry, whereas David Sainsbury was chosen by Blair alone. As well as giving to Blair's leadership campaign in 1994, Sainsbury had donated to the party before the election. Then, a year after being appointed Minister for Science in July 1998, he announced he would give the party a further £2 million. Reaction was muted, partly because the situation was so unusual, partly because it was difficult to put a finger on what was wrong. Sainsbury himself was clearly straight and public-spirited, but did he have to be a minister to fulfil his desire for public service? It was not until the unexpected furore blew up over genetically-modified foods that the Tories could sense a conflict of interest and call for his resignation. Sainsbury was an enthusiastic advocate of genetic science, and his family company had an interest in the technology.

The second issue for Blair arising from Mandelson's home loan was whether he reacted properly to the revelation. If Blair had really been 'purer than pure', he would have insisted on Mandelson's resignation as soon as he had established the facts. But his six-day delay was nothing compared with John Major's common pattern, which was to stand by ministers out of misplaced loyalty until their position became completely untenable and only then to bow to the inevitable.

Blair continued to be considerate on a personal level, inviting Mandelson and his boyfriend Reinaldo Avila da Silva to Chequers to stay the night on the day he resigned, 23 December. He wrote out some advice on how Mandelson should rebuild his career, an opportunity gently to draw attention to his friend's political weaknesses: he should spend time 'reconnecting with the public' and get round the party, 'talking to and learning from party members'; he should sell the house and get a flat;

spend more time in Hartlepool; 'mix more in Parliament and be a team player'; and he should be open about his relationship with Avila da Silva.[17]

Mandelson was also lucky to escape unscathed from the revelation, the Sunday after Christmas, that he had accepted but not declared free flights from American businesswoman Linda Wachner. Elizabeth Filkin ruled that he did not have to register them, because they were 'offered to him as a personal friend rather than in his capacity as a Member of Parliament', but, she added, 'by August 1998 Mr Mandelson was Secretary of State for Trade and Industry and since Ms Wachner had a business operating in the UK it would have been wise for him to have registered the benefit'.[18]

Mandelson managed to maintain a low profile in exile, and largely avoided the temptation to brief journalists, although humility did not come naturally. Six months later he joked: 'I have only just got out of the habit of jumping into the back of cars and wondering why they don't move off.'[19]

The coda to this part of the story was that it finally enabled Blair to get rid of Charlie Whelan, Gordon Brown's excessively partisan press officer, who was widely but not necessarily correctly assumed to have given the loan story to Paul Routledge in the first place. It was noticeable that, with both Whelan and Mandelson away from the front line over the next year, there were far fewer reports of differences between Blair and Brown in the press.

Then there is the question of whether Mandelson's mere ten months out of the Cabinet was sufficient penance to pay. Ten months was certainly an indulgent sentence, but his return was vindicated – for the moment, at least – by the extra momentum it gave the Northern Ireland peace talks.

Blair's standards of conduct were more driven by presentation than purity of motive, but if he had not made such extravagant claims to higher morality, his actions might have been welcomed as a refreshing, pragmatic improvement on what went before.

Notes

1. Geoffrey Robinson, *The Unconventional Minister*, p. 7.
2. Donald Macintyre, *Mandelson*, p. 442.
3. *Ibid.*, p. 290; Macintyre's account of this unedifying saga is the most authoritative.
4. *Ibid.*, p. 445.
5. *Ibid.*, p. 446.
6. *Ibid.*, p. 447.
7. Paragraph 117, *A Code of Conduct and Guidance on Procedures for Ministers*, 31 July 1997.
8. *Hansard*, 30 July 1997.

9. *A Code of Conduct and Guidance on Procedures for Ministers*, paragraph 1, vii, 31 July 1997.
10. *Hansard*, 8 July 1998.
11. *Ibid.*
12. *Ibid.*
13. Speaking at launch of homelessness initiative, 7 July 1998.
14. Standards and Privileges Committee, Ninth Report, Session 1998–99, 1 July 1999; Filkin pointed out to the *Sunday Times*, 4 July 1999, that Teresa Gorman and Robert Wareing both had to apologise to the House for offences of comparable gravity.
15. Interview, BBC Radio 4, *Broadcasting House*, 27 December 1998.
16. Robinson, *The Unconventional Minister*, pp. 7–8.
17. Macintyre, *Mandelson*, pp. 447–8.
18. Memorandum to Standards and Privileges Committee, published in its Ninth Report, Session 1998–99, 1 July 1999.
19. Speech to AEEU conference, Jersey, 30 June 1999.

29

Regrets

Launch Party for the Euro, 31 December 1998

'To be in or not to be in, that is the question.'
—*Tony Blair, 1998*

Gordon Brown was not there when the finance ministers of eleven of the fifteen countries of the European Union sipped champagne and watched school children dressed in euro-capes release 3,000 balloons into the Belgian drizzle. They were celebrating the signing of the legal agreement which would, at midnight that night, lock their currencies together. The euro did not yet exist in notes and coins, but now it could be traded, replacing eleven national currencies on the computer screens of the foreign exchange markets.

Britain was the only EU country not to be represented by a minister at the meeting. Denmark and Sweden, which also chose not to take part, despite qualifying to do so, and Greece, which failed to qualify, had sent ministers to observe and express solidarity.[1] Brown sent Sir Stephen Wall, the British ambassador to the EU, instead.

For Germany, giving up control of the Deutschmark, the event was important enough to send Gerhard Schröder, the Prime Minister's opposite number. 'Our future begins on 1 January 1999,' he declared. 'The euro is Europe's key to the twenty-first century. The era of solo national fiscal and economic policy is over.' That, of course, was a large part of the reason why the British were absent guests at the party. Blair's government, twenty months old, was not yet ready to tell the British people that the euro was their future too.

Under John Smith, and under Neil Kinnock before him, Labour had opposed the British opt-out from the single currency negotiated by John

Major at Maastricht in 1991. Smith wanted Britain to join the single currency at its launch (when he died that could have been as early as 1997 but was already more likely to be 1999) and intended to hold an early referendum to endorse that decision in government.[2]

Blair had made a subtle shift during the leadership election campaign in 1994, preferring the negative formula of being 'not opposed in principle' to joining the single currency over the simpler position of being 'in favour in principle'. By the time he was elected Labour leader, he said only that there were 'potential benefits' in joining and was starting to set conditions.[3]

He was well aware that if he became Prime Minister, history was likely to judge him, at least in part, for how he disposed of the European question. How could he not be, when such figures as Roy Jenkins told him this was his test of greatness? He was 'plainly a proper European', as the Jenkinsite Hugo Young observed, recounting nine private conversations between 1993 and 1996.

Nor was he simply telling Young what he wanted to hear. Dominic Lawson, the Eurosceptic editor of the *Sunday Telegraph*, commented: 'I can surely not be the only editor who has been told, over the years, by Mr Blair, that the single currency, and Britain's membership of it, is a historic inevitability.'[4] There can be no doubt about Blair's fundamentally pro-European outlook, but, unlike Jenkins, Young and John Smith, he was not an enthusiast. He was too young to have been inspired by the 'Never Again' post-war idealism of the early crusaders for Britain's membership of the European club.

That idealism was in any case much weaker in Britain, which emerged from the war convinced it was the exception in Europe. Almost no one in Britain would have proposed a single currency had the idea not emerged on the continent. While it was the logical next step towards a single European market, which certainly promised greater prosperity, there were also good economic arguments against it which counted for more in Britain in the absence of a consensus for 'ever closer union'. The most persuasive was that if countries or regions became depressed, they would not be able to use their exchange rate as a mechanism of adjustment. In the United States, this problem is met by migration: people simply move to another state in search of work. In Europe, with its different languages, cultures and institutions, this is harder.

The core nations of Germany and France, however, had resolved the balance of factors in favour of currency union, partly for reasons of history, partly because they had achieved a significant degree of economic integration. Most of the peripheral nations wanted to join because monetary stability and modernity demanded it. But for Britain, with its different experience of the Second World War and more American orientation, culturally and economically, the temptation was always to ask, 'Why?' Blair had resolved that question for himself: his answer was essentially, 'Because it's there', and if it were going to happen it would almost certainly be successful and Britain would be better off and more influential as part of it. The problem was how to sell that message into the prevailing scepticism of British opinion, a question he addressed in a memo, 'Standing up for Britain', in December 1999.[5] He said it came down to 'a brute argument about power and influence', and argued that Labour needed to present itself as patriotic, tough and strong on defence.

His first priority as Leader of the Opposition, under cover of his ruthless exploitation in the Commons of the government's open divisions on Europe, was to back off Labour's commitment to monetary union from its start. Blair firmly endorsed Major's opt-out – indeed it was the basis of his policy: that a Labour government would decide whether or not to join on the basis of a series of conditions. Robin Cook hardened those conditions in December 1994, requiring a politically accountable central bank and convergence on employment and growth as well as on inflation and public borrowing. As these were not in the Maastricht Treaty, they nullified support for the single currency 'in principle'. The new line brought together most of the divided Parliamentary Labour Party, allowing Blair to present a united front throughout the time when the Conservative Eurosceptic rebel MPs had the whip removed.

The name of the currency was decided, and the 1999 start date confirmed, at the Madrid summit in December 1995. While Blair and John Major played grandmother's footsteps over who would first promise a referendum on the issue, Blair kept the option open of joining the euro from the start, or soon afterwards, without tying himself down to a target date.

It was not until the spring of 1996 that Major finally overcame fierce resistance from his Chancellor, Kenneth Clarke, to commit a future Conservative government to a referendum if it were to recommend joining. And it was not until November that year that Gordon Brown promised that a Labour government would do the same. Brown and Blair were both reluctant to promise a referendum, not least because the difficulties of winning a Yes vote seemed so formidable. When Harold Wilson won the referendum on EEC membership in 1975, Britain had already been a member for two years and was therefore voting for the status quo. Even in France, where the assumptions of the élite were overwhelmingly behind currency union, the 1992 referendum on the Maastricht Treaty, which committed the country to it, had only been won by a margin of 51 to 49 per cent.

Yet Blair recognised not only that he had to match the Conservative pledge, but that it would be disastrous for a Labour government to attempt to join the single currency without holding a referendum. The difficult issue was always going to be one of timing. The start date for monetary union would be less than two years away when Labour came to power, and there was nothing cowardly or Eurosceptical about the calculation that the odds were heavily against winning a referendum in time to allow for the preparations to join by then.

This was a calculation that Blair and Gordon Brown made at least two years before the election. If Britain were not going to be in at the start, then the likely date for entry receded beyond a second General Election. A referendum in the second half of the government's first term might prejudice Labour's chances of re-election. But the possibility of early entry had to be kept alive in order to sustain the argument that 'the national interest' was the only test of whether Britain should join. Although Blair considered ruling out joining monetary union for the life of a parliament – and no one knows what he might have done had the election seemed genuinely close – it would have made no sense to have adopted a more hostile stance than John Major.

As the election approached, it became clear that a Blair government would not try to take Britain into the first wave of monetary union. The *New Statesman* ran a mock obituary on 8 November 1996 for Britain's hope of being in at the beginning. But Blair and Brown also sought to prevent the option of joining at the start – or soon afterwards – being closed off, laying plans to make the Bank of England independent, also a condition of joining the single currency.

During the 1997 election campaign, Blair's basically pro-European stance was phrased in the most negative form possible. His government would be 'not opposed' in principle to joining, would wait for convergence and would hold a referendum if it wanted to join. He decorated this with the sceptical curlicues of slaying the dragon of the European superstate and his patriotic feelings about the Queen's head on the currency. But, as was noted in Chapter 16, and to use Blair's own words, this was done without ceding any ground that could not be recovered.[6]

He moved quickly to start recovering the ground even before the polls closed. On election day, his Chief of Staff, Jonathan Powell, telephoned Sir David Simon, chairman of BP, to ask him if he would be a minister. Sir David had been one of a secret group of four pro-European knights convened by Blair to advise him in Opposition. The others were Sir Michael

Butler and Sir David Hannay, former ambassadors to the EU, and Sir Robin Renwick, Powell's former boss as ambassador to Washington. They met, in Blair's office, only three times, but Blair was struck by Simon's insistence that the euro was going to happen and that it would intensify competitive pressures on the British economy, whether it was in or out. Overruling Margaret Beckett's reluctance to have someone in her department who had 'never stood at a despatch box',[7] Simon was appointed Minister for Trade and Competitiveness in Europe on the Tuesday after the election – the same day the Bank of England announcement was made. Simon moved into his office in the Department of Trade and Industry eager to begin the twin tasks of raising business awareness of the likely impact of the creation of a monetary union of 290 million people in the rest of Europe and of preparing for Britain's entry, possibly within two or three years.

Outlook unsettled

Blair's early strategy in government, such as it was, was to let the issue lie, in the hope that the Eurosceptic tide would ebb as the Conservative civil war receded from the headlines. Meanwhile, he hoped to change the dynamics of the EU. By playing a leading, constructive role he hoped, rather as Major hoped before him, to diminish British perceptions of Brussels as a threat.

However, the formula which had seen Labour through the election campaign turned out to be unstable in government. The imminence of the start date for monetary union, and the fact that Britain's joining then had not been ruled out, meant that the markets were sensitive to suggestions that there might be a last-minute dash to join.

Thus the lead report in the *Financial Times* on 26 September 1997, that ministers were considering 'early' entry to monetary union, lifted share prices and depressed the pound. It was a somewhat speculative use of the pink paper's front page, but, because neither Blair nor Brown had clarified the policy since the election it was open to interpretation, both by ministers and by journalists.

Furthermore, because it was possible to suggest that either Brown or Blair wanted to join at the launch of the single currency and that the other wanted to put it off until after the next election, or for even longer, the *FT* report prompted a stream of 'Brown–Blair split' reports in the press. Thus it was decided that Brown should give an interview to *The Times* to show that he and the Prime Minister were united. What followed was a comedy of errors as Brown tried to clarify a position that had not yet been decided. He, Blair and Robin Cook had taken one formal decision, not to seek to join monetary union at the start, but they had not yet agreed when to announce it, which Brown could not do in a press interview: it would have to be announced to Parliament first, which was not sitting for another week. Informally, they also understood that joining had been put off until after the next election, but had not agreed a form of words.

Unsurprisingly, then, Brown's 'interview', conducted in the form of faxed drafts, made no sense when it was published on 18 October. The substantive passage was this: 'If we do not join in 1999, our task will be to deliver a period of sustainable growth, tackle the long-term weakness of the UK economy and to continue to press for reform – in other words to make sure the British tests are being met.' Contradicting this blatant ambiguity, Brown went on to assert:

> I am determined that we will not fall into the trap which the Conservatives fell into over the Exchange Rate Mechanism saying they would join when the time is right and implying in doing so that it could join the next day or the next month, allowing that possibility to dominate every waking hour and week of the government.

The only way he could do that was to allow his press secretary to interpret his words for him. 'What it means in effect is that we won't be going in in this parliament,' Charlie Whelan said, encouraging *The Times* to put a headline on its interview, 'BROWN RULES OUT SINGLE CURRENCY FOR LIFETIME OF THIS PARLIAMENT', without any visible means of support in the text.

On his mobile phone in the Red Lion pub across the road from the Treasury, Whelan confirmed to other journalists the interpretation put by *The Times* on the interview. He was overheard by two Liberal Democrat press officers who gleefully exposed the mechanics of New Labour spin, then still a relative novelty, but on this occasion he was guilty only of an over-emphatic version of the agreed government line. Indeed, his version was a more faithful rendering of what Brown and Blair really thought than the policy which Brown was now forced to spell out in detail, when he made a statement to the Commons when it returned a week later.

David Simon was incensed by what he saw as Blair and Brown's chaotic approach to the issue. Speaking at ten o'clock two days after the *Times* interview at North London University, he said he had a speech on the euro written for him, 'but I'm not going to read it out because they finished drafting it at nine o'clock and the policy has probably changed by now'.[8]

Simon's appointment and disappointment – he left the government after two years – were symptomatic of Blair's approach. Like Frank Field, he had been appointed partly for symbolic purposes, and yet neither he nor Field was allowed to pursue the mandate they thought their appointment implied. Simon recognised that his was intended to send a strong pro-euro signal, but thought he had also been given the job of preparing for conversion to the euro. When Blair and Brown were finally forced to pay attention to the question of his job description, in the days after the *Times* interview, they were only prepared to grant him the more limited role of preparing businesses for the fact that their trading partners in Europe were going to convert to the euro. Simon was responsible for the television advertisements the following year in which a Shakespearian actor played the part of a company boss haranguing surprised workers and fellow passengers about the imminence of the single currency.

The process of agreeing a statement in the Commons, however, at least required Blair and Brown to negotiate a precise joint position. Under pressure from Simon and the pro-euro Peter Mandelson, Blair insisted that the option of joining during the parliament be kept open, however nominally. This was purely symbolic, however, a sop to the Jenkinsites.

Brown's statement on 27 October 1997 confirmed that Britain would not be seeking to join the single currency at its launch, or for some time afterwards:

> Barring some fundamental or unforeseen change in economic circumstances, making a decision to join during this parliament is not realistic. It is therefore sensible for business and the country to plan on the basis that, in this parliament, we do not propose to enter a single currency.

However, this was balanced by a statement of intent which lent a pro-euro colour to the whole: 'We are the first British government to declare for the principle of monetary union,' Brown said, and he laid out the five economic conditions for joining behind which the government could shelter for the rest of the parliament.* He declared unconvincingly: 'The time of indecision is over. The period for practical preparation has begun.'

The media paraphrase of the statement was the opposite of the *Times* headline: 'Brown says "Yes but not yet" to the single currency' was the headline on *News at Ten*, while on *Newsnight* on the evening of his statement the Chancellor lapsed into ordinary English and said with a

---

*The conditions were entirely subjective. The main one was whether British and other European business cycles and economic structures were 'compatible'; two others related to inward investment and the future of the City as a financial services centre; and the last two were general: whether there was 'sufficient flexibility' to deal with problems; and overall whether joining would 'help to promote higher growth, stability and a lasting increase in jobs'.

directness which Blair would spend nearly three years avoiding: 'We would like to join.'

The statement was undoubtedly a significant moment. When Brown's words sank in, they did change the national psychology. The assumption that Britain would join the single currency became palpable. Surveys soon showed that, although most people still said they would vote against it in a referendum, they expected it to happen. For all his caution, Blair had taken some kind of stand against public opinion, although it was hardly a form of leadership that would have been recognised by his alleged role model, Margaret Thatcher. This was the kind of leadership that nudges the crowd in the right direction and puts oneself in the middle of it.

False dawn

At the beginning of 1998, the strategy seemed to be working. Blair told the Japanese employers' federation that 'most recent opinion polls' indicated that there had been 'a big change in public attitudes towards Europe' since the election. He said Britain would not be part of the currency at the start, 'but we are making preparations so that we can be there shortly thereafter'.[9] But the polls turned sour and it was not until a year later, after the launch of the euro, that Blair announced the 'National Changeover Plan'. This was not a plan for Britain to introduce the euro, it was only a plan to begin preparations in order to keep alive the possibility of deciding to do so later:

> If we wish to have the option of joining, we must prepare. The sheer nature, scale and complexity of the arrangements require considerable time for such preparation. Joining the euro is, for example, far more detailed in its consequences than decimalisation. If we do not start to face this reality now, we will simply not have the practical means necessary to make a choice.[10]

So much for 'shortly thereafter', then.

The other part of his strategy, to be seen at home to be playing a leading role in Europe, was always going to be a tricky test of his diplomatic skill. The British presidency of the EU during the first half of 1998 provided the opportunity, but it was difficult to show leadership while not taking part in the most important business, namely preparations for the launch of the euro. He made use of one of his personal assets, namely fluent French, to address the French National Assembly in its own language on 24 March 1998. The contrast with previous British prime ministers' unwillingnesss or inability to speak good European – Thatcher's flat rendition of her neighbours' tongue at the signing of the Channel Tunnel treaty in 1986 for example – was music to French ears.

His attempt to present Britain as the honest broker of the launch of the euro was foiled, however, by an unseemly wrangle over the appointment of the first president of the European Central Bank, the body charged with maintaining the stability of the new currency. The main business of the EU summit in Brussels on 2 May 1998 went smoothly, as it was formally agreed which countries would be part of the monetary union. But the French would not abandon their candidate for the ECB, and blocked Wim Duisenberg, the former head of the Dutch central bank, until he was finally prevailed on to make some unminuted 'spontaneous remarks' around midnight to the effect that he did not wish to serve the full eight-year term. Satisfied that the former head of the Bank of France, Jean-Claude Trichet, would start an eight-year term after four years, the French conceded. But Blair's reputation in Europe as a negotiator was dented when Duisenberg said the next day he might stay the full term if his health held up.

There was a delayed reaction to Blair's role as midwife to the euro from the Eurosceptic press in Britain. At the summit in Cardiff on 15 June marking the end of his six-month presidency, Blair said that the success of the single currency was 'crucial to high levels of growth and employment'. Rupert Murdoch, in London for the funeral of former *Daily Mail* editor David English a week later, took his new editor of the *Sun*, David Yelland, to task for missing the significance of Blair's tiptoe step towards abolishing the pound. So it was not until 24 June that the famous *Sun* headline hit the newsagents: 'IS THIS IS THE MOST DANGEROUS MAN IN BRITAIN?' It was a full-blooded attack on the euro, complete with a picture of Blair in a mask as the 'Tone Danger' recalling the 'demon eyes' Tory poster, a picture of Helmut Kohl and a list of the 'twenty perils of the euro'.

The treatment confounded Peter Mandelson's happy prediction two months earlier that Murdoch would eventually come round: 'If the whole project has been established successfully, it's got under way, everyone's flocking to it and we are losing out economically and financially by being apart from it, he as a pragmatist would say: "OK, we've got to go in."'[11]

Somehow, though, it was like the history of the 1992 'Nightmare on Kinnock Street' repeated, if not as farce, at least as post-modern irony. The *Sun*'s offensive lacked real viciousness, not least because it was inconsistent with its support for Blair only a year before. And the very next day it carried an article by the very same (questionably) most dangerous man in Britain, the Tone Danger himself, praising the bravery of the police as a curtain-raiser for the newspaper's own awards ceremony that evening.

Later in the year, however, the Conservative press rediscovered some of its anti-European aggression with an assault on the new German finance minister, Oskar Lafontaine. The *Daily Mail* warned of the 'March of the Euro Tax Man', threatening to impose taxes from Brussels. The *Sun*, pleased with its line, asked, 'Is this the most dangerous man in Europe?' While a *Daily Telegraph* editorial was headed simply, 'The German Menace'.[12]

Blair's gentle observation that 'there is a section of the British newspapers that are vigorously hostile to Europe and who always want to say Britain is totally isolated in Europe' marked the beginning of a more combative relationship with the press.[13]

At the beginning of 1999, he consulted pro-euro business leaders, ministers (like Lord Simon and Mandelson) and cross-party heavyweights (Paddy Ashdown, Kenneth Clarke and Michael Heseltine) over his statement on the Changeover Plan, but he resisted their pressure to make a clear declaration of intent to join the euro. Instead he used the phrase, 'both intentions and the conditions are genuine'.[14] The frustration of the euro-supporters was increased as Blair resisted their entreaties that he put himself at the head of the embryonic all-party Yes campaign for the referendum. Companies had already stumped up the money to set up an organisation called 'Britain in Europe', but they wanted to know what the government's position would be, and above all what Blair's position would be, before they launched it.

If Blair hoped that the passage of time itself would erode public suspicion of the European Union in general and the single currency in particular, he was, by the middle of 1999, frustrated. The euro fell steadily in value against the dollar and the pound from the moment of its launch, starting at $1.18 and falling below $1 by the end of the year. In March 1999 the entire European Commission resigned after an independent report found evidence of nepotism and incompetence. In June, Labour received a drubbing in the elections to the European Parliament.

Then, in July, it seemed that patient, constructive negotiation had finally achieved a resolution of the beef crisis, as the new European Commission ruled that the risk of BSE was over and the ban on exports of British beef was lifted. It was not until after Blair had extravagantly boasted of a triumph for his policy of being nice to foreigners in their own language that it emerged that several European countries, most blatantly France, which had been the biggest market for British beef, were refusing to lift the ban. Several months later, the British government was finally forced to begin legal action in the European Court.

By now, the prospect of having to fight a referendum soon after an election in 2001 seemed uncomfortably close. Blair finally agreed in June 1999 that he would preside over the official launch of 'Britain in Europe', provided its aims were brought in line with government policy. The launch was delayed until October and, instead of being an all-party campaign to join the euro, it would now be an all-party campaign to join the euro if the government's conditions were met.

Change in the weather

Just as it seemed in the middle of 1999 that the prospects of a referendum were sliding towards the third term, Blair tentatively started to nudge the supertanker of government, accompanied by its flotilla of pro-European interests, out of the harbour towards a decision to recommend joining the euro early in his second parliament.

He gave an important speech at the London Business School on 27 July, declaring: 'To be in or not to be in, that is the question.' He was talking about being 'in' the EU rather than the monetary union, but now the one clearly implied the other. The dithering Hamlet seemed at last to have found his resolve:

> In the end, we have always chosen to be in. Any British government, governing for the true national interest, always comes back to the same place. It is not weakness, or the beguiling embrace of European allies; it is stark reality, good old-fashioned British pragmatism that brings us there.

On the euro itself, he tightened up the wording another tiny notch: 'We will recommend Britain joining providing the economic conditions are met.'

The next day, however, David Simon was off. He resigned in the reshuffle, saying he had done his twin job of preparing for the start of the euro in the rest of Europe and preparing for Britain's presidency of the EU: 'The reason I stopped when I stopped was that those jobs were done.' He refused to say he was disillusioned. He admitted that 'our leadership has not consistently been leading', but he recognised that, 'politically, the problem with saying we are harmed by being out is that you are out there painting defeat for your country'.

If he was not disappointed, there were others who were. Roy Jenkins now had to accept that his alleged protégé would not be making a sudden, exciting dash for a referendum before the election. A few months later he looked back at the young prince who had failed to seize his moment:

> It is no good just waiting for the weather of public opinion to improve. It is no good just going down in the morning, looking at the rain, gloomily tapping the barometer and saying we cannot do anything today. The great Prime Ministers, those who leave a mark on history, are those who make

the political weather and not those who skilfully avoid its storms and shelter from its downpours.[15]

Jenkins attended the launch of the 'Britain in Europe' campaign on 14 October 1999. It was a strangely unhistoric event in the IMAX cinema at Waterloo, which looked like a television studio. The grand old men of British Europeanism, Ted Heath (ushered to his seat by Peter Mandelson), Jenkins, Heseltine and Clarke, joined Blair, Gordon Brown and Charles Kennedy. Richard Branson was there on video, but he was the only business supporter who was a household name. Blair took questions from the floor and was asked if a commitment to Europe required joining the euro in the long term. He said he did not understand the question, asked for it to be repeated and waffled his way through the answer. Heseltine had to take over, saying technically no, but it was a matter of judgment.

It was precisely the question that was not supposed to be asked. The plan for the first phase was to make the basic case for Britain's membership of the EU – our 'destiny', Blair had called it in his party conference speech two weeks earlier – and only then to argue that joining the euro was necessary to fulfil it.

Time was short, however. He had been in government for more than two years and public opinion was going backwards. He was bound by the policy laid down as a hasty compromise in October 1997, and did not want to make an explicit shift for fear of provoking all-out war with the Eurosceptic press. Relations with the press generally had become more difficult as the government's opinion-poll ratings fell and Alastair Campbell's role became the focus of attention. Increasingly, Blair, Campbell and Peter Mandelson openly and pointlessly criticised the anti-European press for distortion and the pro-European press for cowardice.[16]

Blair was also constrained by the growing jealousy with which Gordon Brown guarded his right to interpret the economic conditions, which accompanied the Chancellor's tactical reluctance to become locked in to a timetable for an unwinnable referendum. Brown was displeased when, in January 2000, Blair suggested in a television interview that he alone would decide whether the conditions had been met: 'I will decide the issue of monetary union – I'm the Prime Minister who's got responsibility for it – according to the British national interest.'[17]

Brown responded six months later with an assertion whose grammatical oddity reflected the war behind the words: 'The tests, for which this government and this Treasury is the guardian, are real,' he told the City.[18] In the intervening period, Blair had allowed Peter Mandelson and Robin Cook – who had become an ardent advocate of monetary union, swinging like a repelling magnet to oppose Brown – to say warm things about the euro, and the press noticed the contrast with the Chancellor.

Blair had decided to make his move. 'We cannot avoid this debate on Europe,' he wrote in a memo called 'Standing Up for Britain', written in April 2000 and leaked as part of a job lot that summer.*[19] 'On the euro, we need to be firmer, more certain, clearer. The truth is that the politics is overwhelmingly in favour: but the economics has to be right; and at present it is not. It would be far better to be open and up front about this.' However, he needed to choose his moment to be so. He needed someone to create a diversion to distract the press. Then, on the evening of 5 July, his son Euan was found lying on the pavement in Leicester Square, and was arrested for being drunk and incapable.

With a coolness bordering on the emotionally chilly, in the middle of a hoo-ha over government spin and media management, he used Euan's embarrassment as cover for making an audacious leap towards the euro in July 2000. Appearing on BBC1's *Question Time* the next day, when Euan's excessive exam celebration was reported, he won sympathetic applause for his performance as blushing but supportive parent. He was also asked about the euro and for the first time predicted that the conditions would be met and his government would recommend joining within a few years. The economy was running well, he said: 'If we carry on in this way then I believe we will be able to make a recommendation early in the next parliament.' That implied a referendum by 2003.

He simplified the conditions: 'The test for me is, "Is it good for jobs and mortgages and industry?" If it is, I will lead that referendum fight and recommend to the British people joining.' He even rather transparently took his script from the Jenkins school of critics: 'Even though it is unpopular with certain people – and I know it's unpopular, I can sense that from parts of the audience here tonight – sometimes it's up to a Prime Minister to tell you even the things you don't want to hear as well as the things you do.'[20]

The shift was noticed – it coincided with Robin Cook's description of Britain's membership of monetary union as 'inevitable' – but Euan's story dominated the front pages the next day.

---

*The memo was linked to another, also leaked, in which Philip Gould and Stanley Greenberg analysed the Labour Party's opinion-polling evidence on the prospects for a Yes campaign in a referendum. It suggested shifting the argument from Britain playing a leadership role in Europe to exploiting Britain's unique ties with the US as the gateway to Europe, but admitted that support for the euro was likely to remain 'contained and vulnerable to attack . . . One will never create anything like a national consensus on the euro, except perhaps after joining the single currency.'

The drift towards destiny

In his first two years Blair was condemned to have Churchill's caustic 1936 description of the passivity of Chamberlain's government at the approach of war thrown at him: 'So they go on in strange paradox, decided only to be undecided, resolved to be irresolute, adamant for drift, solid for fluidity, all-powerful to be impotent.'[21] It is difficult to find fault with Blair's basic strategy, however. Obviously, the opponents of the euro could not approve. But there was a hollowness in the case argued by the Jenkinsites, who thought it would be attractively brave if Blair risked everything on holding a referendum within a year of the election on the question of joining monetary union at its launch.

What would it have done for Blair if he had tried and lost? It would have made him look inept; it would have robbed him of his place in history; it would have united, revived and vindicated the Conservative Party. The criticism is therefore, as ever, a tactical one: that public opinion would have been readier to join if he had been more open about what he wanted; but that too is arguable. Certainly his posture was unedifying. For the election, he adopted the most sceptical position compatible with wanting in principle to join monetary union, which itself marked a significant step – of principle rather than practice – towards further European integration from the position of the Major government. To the extent that the British public were not in favour – either in principle or in practice – this was a policy of surreptitious courage. The Jenkinsites were disappointed that he did not immediately after the election declare that he believed it was the nation's destiny to join as soon as the economics came right. Jenkins himself complained that he regarded the election win as a store of value to be hoarded rather than capital to be spent.

It would, however, have appeared dishonest to say something so significant after the election but not before. The criticism that counts is one of failing to develop the argument more openly after the election. There was a perfectly good economic case against joining the single currency at its launch. Ireland provided a test case: its economy was aligned with the British economic cycle rather than the continental one, and so low euro interest rates fuelled a rapid boom and pushed inflation up to 6 per cent within eighteen months of the euro's launch. But as time passed, the economic arguments for staying out would weaken, as interest rates would start to converge. And, although Blair carefully nudged the official language forwards when no one was looking, it was not until July 2000 that he finally came clean about what had been his aim all along: to fight a winnable referendum soon after a second election if he could.

In order to have a chance of shifting public opinion, however, it was not enough simply to allow the perception to grow that joining the eurozone would become inevitable. Blair had to explain how Britain could retain its national identity in a giant economic bloc that was not a superstate. Not only were the fundamental economic and constitutional issues of the euro suppressed in his public appearances, they were never discussed at Cabinet and indeed 'Europe' ceased around mid-1999 to feature as a regular item on the Cabinet's agenda.[22]

It could be argued that Blair should not have allowed himself to be so boxed in by the Eurosceptic press and his Chancellor. The delay in making the case in his first two years may have made a referendum early in the second parliament harder to win, although the timing was always going to be awkward: the best time would probably be some time after euro notes and coins were introduced in what were now, with Greece, the euro twelve at the start of 2002.

Blair recognised the potential significance of that date when he was asked in early 2000 if it was not getting too late to turn around public opinion. 'I don't, as a matter of fact, accept this,' he said.

> If we decided to make a recommendation to people, the whole dynamics of the argument would change, because the circumstances would have changed. And when people are asked now whether they want to go into the euro, they're asked as of now. Well, the government's position 'as of now' is not to go into the euro, so it's hardly surprising people say, 'Well, no'. But I think when you get underneath it people want to keep the option open. They understand that we live in a different world today, the world's moving closer together. From the first of January 2002 the euro notes and coins are going to be in circulation. So they'll make up their mind on sensible British grounds. They always do.[23]

It is quite likely that Blair will shy away from an early referendum during his second term, however, if only because it will still be too early for the fatalistic majority of the electorate to feel that they are losing out by being outside the euro. He is now making what might turn out to be a dummy run for it. Although he does not show the passion that might be expected, his fondness for portentous language of the nation's 'destiny' when speaking of it suggests that he hopes to have Britain's joining the euro as one of the historic achievements of his premiership, although he may have to settle for being the Prime Minister who paved the way.

Notes

1. Technically, Sweden was ruled not to have qualified as it was not entitled to opt out, unlike Britain and Denmark.
2. Interviews with David Ward, chief policy adviser to John Smith.

3. BBC2, *Newsnight*, 12 July 1994.
4. *Sunday Telegraph*, 28 June 1998.
5. It was one of a batch, including two written by Blair, leaked to News International newspapers between May and July 2000.
6. See pp. 311–12.
7. Ivor Richard, Janet Jones, *Labour of Love*, p. 57.
8. *Observer*, 26 October 1997.
9. Speech, Tokyo, 10 January 1998.
10. *Hansard*, 23 February 1999.
11. Channel Four, *Blair's Year*, 19 April 1998.
12. 24, 25, 26 November 1998.
13. BBC Radio 4, *Today*, 11 December 1998.
14. *Hansard*, 23 February 1999.
15. *Independent*, 9 February 2000.
16. Campbell posted a rant on the Number Ten website against the press for making a 'real, sensible and mature debate very difficult' on the euro, 1 July 2000; on the same day Mandelson wrote a close textual analysis of the differences between British and continental press reporting of the same events in the *Independent*.
17. BBC1, *Breakfast With Frost*, 16 January 2000. A year later, on the same progamme (7 January 2001), Blair accorded Brown a joint role: 'I very much hope it will be both of us together.'
18. Mansion House speech, 15 June 2000.
19. *Sun* and *The Times*, 27 July 2000.
20. BBC1, *Question Time*, 6 July 2000.
21. For example by Martin Wolf, *Financial Times*, 10 January 2000.
22. Peter Hennessy, *The Prime Minister*, p. 481.
23. Section of an interview with Robert Harris, 17 February 2000, cut from his article for *Talk* magazine, May 2000, and published in the *Guardian*, 23 May.

30

Why Lib–Lab Coalition Didn't Happen

Paddy Bows Out, 20 January 1999

'I know some of you are a bit nervous about what I am doing with the Liberal Democrats.'

—*Tony Blair, to 1997 Labour conference*

Paddy Ashdown's dream of a Labour–Liberal Democrat coalition faded in the first light of 2 May 1997, but it did not die.

Blair half-planned, from near the beginning of his leadership, to offer him a seat in the Cabinet. As the likely size of Labour's majority became clear, however, Blair drew back. He has since said privately he regretted not having brought Ashdown into his Cabinet on the Friday morning after the election, although he may have been telling his listeners what they wanted to hear. That may explain why he told Ashdown 'he wished it had been done then', according to a leaked extract of Ashdown's diary from six months after the election.[1] Speaking publicly, he suggested that he would only have offered Ashdown a coalition if Labour's majority had been insecure:

> Supposing you'd ended up with the situation of a hung parliament – everyone would have accepted it. In a situation where we'd had a very small majority, people would have understood it easier. In a situation where you had the largest majority any British political party had had since the 1832 Reform Bill, it seemed slightly quixotic, I suppose.[2]

Quixotic or not, he could have done it. At that moment of supreme power, he could have done almost anything. But that did not make it a good idea. The practical need for coalition fell away as it emerged that the Labour left would have no leverage in Parliament, while the costs to Blair remained high. A single Cabinet seat would not have been enough for the

Liberal Democrats. He would have to give up two posts, for which there would have been a heavy price to pay in his own party.

In any case, the underlying assumptions sustaining a deal were swept aside by the sheer size of Labour's landslide. The idea that the Labour and Liberal traditions, divided for nearly 100 years, needed to be reunited to keep the Conservatives firmly out of office for more than one parliamentary term vanished in the morning. Within the Labour Party, the case for electoral reform, which would be the price of any coalition deal, was fatally weakened.[3] The referendum needed to endorse a new system would further divide the party and could easily be lost.

Catch-22

The 1997 election exposed the fundamental contradiction between the aim of a proportional voting system and Blair's ambition of historic realignment, to make the twenty-first century 'the century of the radicals' in the same way the twentieth century had been dominated by the Conservatives.[4]

First, Blair's thesis, derived from Roy Jenkins, that the Conservatives had ruled in the twentieth century because of the breach between Labour and Liberal traditions was a gross simplification. The Conservatives may have held office for sixty-eight years of the century, but sixteen of those were in coalition governments.[5] And their opposition may have been divided, but it was divided for different reasons at different times. The Conservative dominance of 1922–40 was built as much on the 1931 split in the Labour Party as that between Labour and the Liberals. The dominance of 1951–64 occurred while the Liberals were an insignificant parliamentary force.[6] Again, in 1979–97 the division was as much one within the Labour Party – the SDP breakaway – as one between the Labour and Liberal traditions. As the century drew to an end, the scale of Blair's own landslide had rendered the thesis counterintuitive if not wholly wrong, however much he professed to keep his mind on the figure for Labour's share of the vote, which at 44.4 per cent fell some way short of overwhelming.

Second, the Conservative mastery of the twentieth century was achieved not by an alliance of parties but by one pragmatic, hegemonic one, using coalition as a weapon for capturing the parliamentary leaderships of rival parties – Lloyd George and then MacDonald – before absorbing them. If there were a lesson from the electoral history of the century, it was that a flexible, big-tent party could rule on its own for decades under the existing voting system. It was an argument for Lib–Lab merger and keeping the twentieth-century voting system, not for coalition under a proportional system. The point about proportional systems, as Blair himself had always argued, is that they tend to require parties to form coalitions in order to represent a majority of the votes cast. If the Liberal Democrats are seen as a middle party, rather than a long-lost sibling of the Labour Party, then they are likely to hold the balance of power. They are also likely to use that position to switch allegiance between the larger parties. That may or may not reflect the true wishes of the electorate at any given time, but it has nothing to do with achieving the hundred-year rule of 'the radicals'. Only merger between Labour and the Liberal Democrats would achieve that. Merger, however, was never possible. This was not simply because the parties competed so fiercely on the ground and in local government, but because it would fall victim to the electoral reformer's catch-22. In order to merge, the parties would have to join first in a coalition. And the price of coalition was a proportional voting system, which would render merger unnecessary.

Once he was in Downing Street, Blair no longer needed to wrestle with that conundrum. Ashdown was not, therefore, invited to be Secretary of State for Northern Ireland or Defence. He was invited to sit in a talking shop which was given the purely honorific status of a Cabinet committee, even though the Prime Minister chaired it. Ashdown concealed his bitter disappointment until after his resignation as Liberal Democrat leader, when he said of Blair's failure to do a deal: 'I'm not sure it was the right decision but he will have to speak for himself.'[7]

The curious thing, however, was that Blair did not abandon the plan for a Lib–Lab coalition, even though its moment seemed to have passed. Instead, he suggested that he and Ashdown should think about reviving the idea later in the year, linking it to the setting up of the commission charged with devising the proportional voting system to put to the referendum. Indeed, there followed at least two intense but ultimately fruitless bouts of negotiation, in the autumn of 1997 and again in the autumn of 1998, which Ashdown certainly believed brought his party to the threshold of sharing power.

It's good to talk

Ashdown's disappointment at the door of the church on 2 May 1997 was a rude jolt after a long and largely clandestine courtship. He had hoped for a hung parliament at the 1992 election, when Neil Kinnock would have been prepared to concede electoral reform as the price of a coalition. But little work had been done in advance on the precise terms of a deal.

'Kinnock is a very nice man, but we never really hit it off,' Ashdown admitted. Nor did he hit it off with John Smith: 'We got on perfectly adequately as party leaders, but we were not bosom friends.' By chance, however, he and Smith had a practice run through the negotiations when they and the late Sir Robin Day were left with a bottle of brandy at the end of a dinner held by the Other Club, at the Savoy Hotel in London. 'And Robin Day decided to behave as Robin Day and to interview us in a mock interview in which basically the terms of a coalition which would have occurred after a hung parliament in 1992 were very plainly laid out,' said Ashdown.

The Other Club, a secret dining club founded by Winston Churchill and F. E. Smith, the Conservative Lord Chancellor and Secretary of State for India, was part of the hidden wiring of the British Establishment, an opportunity for high-powered name-dropping and confidential cross-party networking. Ashdown, Blair and Gordon Brown all became members in 1991.*

Smith's attitude to doing deals with the Liberal Democrats was purely pragmatic, however. According to Ashdown,

> John's view was always that, 'If I have to do a deal with the Lib Dems, I am sufficient of a realist to prepare for it.' Tony's view was always that, 'The Lib Dems are part of what I see as my project.' So John's view was a passive, 'We'll talk about this after the election' one, very practical, realistic, down to earth, and Tony's was, 'I'm going to make this happen.'

As soon as Blair became leader, he and Ashdown, and other sympathetic figures in both parties, opened a series of secret discussions about possible forms of co-operation. These were made public in October 1996, six months before the election, with the formation of a joint committee of both parties to work on a common programme of constitutional reform.†

For a new political alignment capable of dominating the twenty-first century, however, the Joint Consultative Committee announced on 22 July 1997 was a modest beginning. It was certainly a constitutional innovation: a subcommittee of the Cabinet, chaired by the Prime Minister, five of whose

---

*Its membership lists were leaked to John Lloyd, *The Times*, 29 July 1997. Lord Hartwell and Sir Nicholas Henderson were honorary secretaries; William Whitelaw, Robin Day and, later, Derry Irvine presided; other members included Edward Heath (1960), Roy Jenkins (1964), Roy Hattersley (1971), Prince Charles (1976), Robert Cranborne (1981), Peter Shore (1981), Jack Cunningham (1984), Chris Patten (1986) and John Smith (1986). Peter Mandelson joined in 1998, according to 'Peterborough', *Daily Telegraph*, 18 March 1998.

†See pp. 289–93.

members still sat on the Opposition benches in the House of Commons. Not that the Liberal Democrats offered much opposition in the honeymoon days. Ashdown had successfully bounced most of his party into voting for the Labour Queen's Speech on 20 May, which was carried by a 270-vote majority.*

Novelty and the symbolism were all. Tony Benn was eager to denounce the Joint Consultative Committee as 'the beginning of the end of the Labour Party',[8] and the majority of Liberal Democrats, at all levels in the party, regarded it with deepest suspicion. In order to ease its birth, Blair allowed the newspapers to suggest that the Cabinet was split on whether to adopt a proportional voting system for the 1999 European Parliament elections,[9] so that the change could be presented as a Liberal Democrat triumph gained through the joint committee. Certainly many of the Cabinet personally opposed the idea, but the manifesto was clear: 'We have long supported a proportional voting system for election to the European Parliament.' In any case, the legislation was agreed by the Cabinet on 17 July, before the joint committee was set up.

For the rest, the remit of the committee was 'To consider policy issues of joint interest to the government and the Liberal Democratic Party', which in effect meant being told what the government was doing in a consultative tone of voice by Labour ministers in Downing Street or Whitehall, instead of in a confrontational one at the House of Commons, and a few days before the media were told instead of afterwards. The committee discussed Scottish and Welsh devolution, House of Lords reform and the question of changing the voting system for the House of Commons, but in no case did the government appear to be influenced by its deliberations. Indeed, the form of proportional representation decided for the European elections, the 'closed list' system, was the one the Liberal Democrats least wanted and was, they felt, a deliberate attempt by Jack Straw to discredit the very idea of electoral reform.

Nor did the Liberal Democrats have anything to show for an extensive range of secret meetings, called 'bilaterals' to make them sound important, which took place between their spokesmen and ministers under the committee's auspices. Alan Beith and Bob Maclennan had a series of fruitless meetings with Straw to try to persuade him to adopt an 'open list' voting system for the European Parliament. Maclennan spoke to Derry Irvine about devolution and reform of the House of Lords. Maclennan

---

*Four Liberal Democrats abstained. The Liberals also supported the Queen's Speech in 1977 but that was under the terms of the formal Lib–Lab pact between David Steel and James Callaghan.

and Nick Harvey spoke to Dick Caborn (John Prescott's number two, as the Deputy Prime Minister himself did not want to take part) about regional government. Simon Hughes talked to Nick Raynsford, minister for London.

As Liberal Democrat scepticism deepened, Ashdown urged his party to keep its eye on the bigger prize, namely Labour's manifesto promise of the 'early' appointment of an independent commission 'to recommend a proportional alternative' to the existing voting system for the House of Commons, which would then be put to the people in a referendum. That Roy Jenkins would chair the commission was agreed early on – Jenkins dined at Downing Street with Blair, Ashdown and Peter Mandelson on 12 June, six weeks after the election. It was remarkable enough that the Prime Minister was willing to entrust the design of a new voting system to someone who was at the time the leader of a rival party in the House of Lords. More remarkable still, however, were the negotiations which now took place over the appointment of two or three Liberal Democrats to the Cabinet in the next reshuffle.

Over dinner in Downing Street again, on 21 October, the four men reconvened, with Blair's Chief of Staff, Jonathan Powell, to discuss what Ashdown archly referred to in his diary as 'TFM', The Full Monty, or coalition. Blair said he was 'really worried about the reaction from his party', according to Ashdown's diary. As a result, he thought he might try to 'prepare the ground a bit' by saying he 'didn't see any reason in principle why the Liberal Democrats shouldn't be in the government' when he announced Jenkins's appointment. Despite the fact that 'all his instincts were to go early', Blair suggested May the following year as the earliest he could bring Ashdown into government. At this stage Ashdown thought he could deflect criticism from his own party by not taking a Cabinet post himself straight away. He suggested Alan Beith, his deputy, and Menzies Campbell, his foreign affairs spokesman, instead. 'If the public just sees this as the way an old man can get his foot into the Cabinet door,' it would not work, he told OMF (Our Mutual Friend, or Blair), before adding that he would like to become a Cabinet minister in a later reshuffle.[10]

After another secret meeting with Blair, Ashdown returned to his office in the Commons to declare excitedly, 'We could be in government this time next week,' according to a surprised colleague who was there. Not for the first time, though, Ashdown's enthusiasm was premature. He had assumed that the sticking point of electoral reform had been settled. It had not. The coalition deal was predicated on the Prime Minister committing himself in advance to Roy Jenkins's recommendation. But, as drafts of the terms of reference for the Jenkins commission batted back and forth between Downing Street and Ashdown's office, it became clear that Blair was determined to refight the battle over the word 'proportional' which Ashdown and Jenkins thought they had won before the election. Of course, Blair's reluctance was phrased in terms of what his party – in the convenient form of John Prescott – would accept, and what he thought he could get through the House of Commons. But Blair had not given up on the idea of minimal reform in the shape of the Alternative Vote system.

The great advantages of the Alternative Vote, for Blair, were that it was (a) simple and (b) not very proportional, although it would tend to give the Liberal Democrats more seats. It would require only a small change in the law, allowing voters to mark the ballot paper with numbers to put candidates in order of preference. If no candidate wins a majority of first-preference votes, unsuccessful candidates drop out and their votes transfer to the voter's next choice, ensuring that every MP has the support of more than half the voters in their constituency.*

The problem for Blair was that something else had happened during the early hours of 2 May 1997. Before all the votes had even been counted, Professor John Curtice of Strathclyde University produced his estimate for the BBC of what would have happened had the election been held under the Alternative Vote system. The result would have been even more skewed in Labour's favour, and Blair would have won a majority of 213 seats rather than 179.[11] It seemed a rather hypothetical statistical exercise, but it was to have a critical effect on what followed. Some of Blair's advisers thought that the Alternative Vote could be presented as a proportional system, because it would almost always produce a *more* proportional outcome than the existing system. The trouble was that the 1997 election was one of the few when that was not the case. Jenkins insisted that – as he later wrote into his report – the Alternative Vote 'on its own' was 'unacceptable' because it would be unfair to the Conservatives.

When Jenkins's appointment was finally announced on 1 December 1997, therefore, there were no friendly words from Blair about Liberal

---

*It was a change which was passed by the House of Commons in the Representation of the People Bill in 1931, but it fell with the Labour government. The government initially proposed the Supplementary Vote, a form of the Alternative Vote giving the voter only a first and second preference, but this was amended in committee. The Supplementary Vote was also recommended by the Labour Party's Plant Commission in 1993, and was adopted by the Blair government in the London mayoral election in May 2000.

Democrats in government, while the terms of reference for the commission were flatly incompatible with each other. In the end, it was charged with observing 'the requirement for broad proportionality, the need for stable government, an extension of voter choice and the maintenance of a link between MPs and geographical constituencies'. As Jenkins drily remarked, 'They are challenging in the sense that you cannot have absolute regard to all of them.'[12]

Blair nevertheless wanted the commission to support the Alternative Vote as a first stage, with a more proportional system as a possible second stage. The first stage would not necessarily have to be put to a referendum, while the second stage need never happen. Jenkins refused, however, and he was backed by Ashdown. The Alternative Vote was 'ruled out absolutely as the final position', said Ashdown, although he tried to use it as a bargaining counter, saying that, 'if you were in a dynamic situation, the Alternative Vote could have been until quite late the means by which you got from where we are to where we want to be'.

Among senior Liberal Democrats, only Matthew Taylor, then environment spokesman, was a strong advocate of accepting the Alternative Vote as a downpayment on full proportional representation. More significantly for the long term, however, was the fact that Charles Kennedy, who had been excluded from Ashdown's inner councils, took a relaxed view of incremental change.

Jenkins, identified as TGPB, 'The Great Pooh-Bah', in Ashdown's diaries, stood firm. It did not matter that the Alternative Vote would only have been biased against the Tories in 1997, 'the point was the perception that it was a conspiracy against the Tories', said Ashdown.

After ten months' careful deliberation, Jenkins came up with a compromise which, despite being written in his colourful and flowing prose, satisfied no one and failed miserably to justify itself. His report, published on 29 October 1998, proposed a system which it called 'Alternative Vote Plus', which was essentially the same as the top-up system about to be inaugurated in the new Scottish Parliament and Welsh Assembly. Most MPs would be elected in single-member constituencies, using the Alternative Vote, but some extra MPs would be elected for an area covering between four and ten constituencies in order to 'top up' under-represented parties to make each party's share of seats as close as possible to its proportion of the votes cast.[13]

A fully proportional system could have been defended as a radical change which would end forever the prospect of a single party holding power on a minority vote, and which would require a new way of doing politics. Equally, the Alternative Vote could have been defended as improving the existing system by ensuring MPs were elected by majority votes in their constituencies and generally giving fairer representation to large minority parties like the Liberal Democrats. The Jenkins compromise, on the other hand, had no clear purpose. It would not have affected the outcome of the 1979, 1983 or 1987 elections – the series which had converted so many in the Labour Party to the cause of reform.* Yet its cumbersome design, creating two kinds of MP and requiring a procedurally complex method of electing 'top-up' MPs from party lists, offered no substitute attractions.

The key feature of the Jenkins scheme was that it required a redrawing of constituency boundaries which, added to the time needed for a referendum, gave Blair the excuse he needed to break his manifesto promise to hold one in his first term.

The Prime Minister welcomed the report 'warmly', but weakly, as a minimal change rather than full proportional representation:

> It's very much a modification of the existing Westminster system rather than any full-blown PR system as practised in other countries. It addresses some of the weaknesses in the present system, such as the complete absence of Conservative representation in Scotland and Wales and the comparable Labour under-representation that occurred in parts of the south during the 1980s.

Apparently caught unawares in a *Newsnight* interview a month later, however, he refused to say he liked it. 'I want to wait and see how the range of constitutional change settles down', he said, and disagreed when Jeremy Paxman suggested it could not be sold to the public. 'I don't think it's impossible to sell at all.'[14] But it was clear that the New Labour sales force would be flogging everything else in the shop first.

Meanwhile, Blair's isolation within the government was evident. John Prescott made little attempt to disguise his opposition and Gordon Brown was a significant block on co-operation. He refused to attend meetings of the joint Cabinet committee, and got on badly with Malcolm Bruce, the Liberal Democrats' Treasury spokesman. Even Blair occasionally allowed his irritation with Ashdown to show. Ashdown claimed that government spending on education was being cut, and accused Blair of statistical manipulation that would 'make Arthur Daley blush', at Prime Minister's Questions on 22 April 1998. It stood out because he was usually

---

*The Jenkins commission estimated that the effect of the Alternative Vote Plus on post-war elections would have been to turn majorities for Wilson (1964), Heath (1970), Wilson (October 1974) and Major (1992) into hung parliaments.

supportive. Blair accused him of being 'utterly irresponsible' and 'not serious'.[15] Afterwards Ashdown wrote to him disputing the figures, to which Blair responded with a letter saying huffily: 'I will not have the record of my government traduced.'

The second round of coalition negotiations, before the publication of the Jenkins report, also came to nothing, despite Ashdown's coded boast in a television interview in July 1998: 'I intend to make sure . . . that we deliver this party into government.'[16]

By the end of the year, with no rationale for reform, and now no timetable for it, it was clear to Ashdown that the realignment of British politics would not happen for many years. In retrospect it should have come as no surprise when, three months after the Jenkins report, he announced he would retire as leader of the Liberal Democrats. He had led the party for eleven years and brought it to a high watermark under the 'first past the post' electoral system, but the prospect either of a change in that system or of a place in government had receded beyond the next election.

Blair's response to Ashdown's announcement was intriguing, a signal that he was ready to play the same game of secret enticements with his successor. He said the next day, 'I've no doubt at all that co-operation will continue', because the people 'don't want parties stuck in rigid tribal boundaries'. And he inserted a line in a speech to voluntary organisations containing a curious play on words, identifying the existing voting system with Thatcherite materialism: 'If everyone shared that first-past-the-post, me, my, mine philosophy then there really would be no such thing as society.'[17]

Radical century

Charles Kennedy knew little or nothing of Ashdown's negotiations with Blair at the time, and when asked about them on becoming leader said they 'belong to history'. Which was true in one sense, except that having held a dress rehearsal Blair would find coalition easier to negotiate next time.

Was this a great missed opportunity? Did Blair lack the courage to use the huge authority conferred by the 1997 election to change British politics for good? The judgment here is similar to that on the euro, in that it all depends on one's standpoint. He certainly could have done a deal after the election, but should he have done? There was a logical flaw in Blair's coalitionist rhetoric, his ambition to shape 'a century of progressive politics after one dominated by Conservatives',[18] because he did not believe in proportional representation on its own merits. So what would he have gained by coalition? It would certainly have deflected criticism of him as a control freak. It would have split the Liberal Democrats, but Blair would have had to haggle with the 'Ashdown Liberals' over tuition fees, education spending and, possibly, genetically-modified foods. In return he might have had to commit himself to something like the Jenkins 'Alternative Vote Plus' for the election after next.

The most cynical reading of Blair's motives, therefore, seems justified. Before the election, he used coalitionist language in order to appeal to the centre ground and prepare the ground for a deal in case his parliamentary majority was small. The moment he was sure that Britain was a landslide country after all, his focus immediately shifted to the election likely to be in 2001. He needed to prepare the ground in case he had a small majority then. Contrary to what he pretended to Ashdown when discussing The Full Monty, therefore, his instincts, from the moment the votes were counted in 1997, were for delay and obfuscation.

Blair's expressions of regret that he did not bring some Liberal Democrats into government on 2 May need to be read in the context of his careful handling of Ashdown's sensibilities. More telling indicators of his real views are his known opinions of the defects of full-blown proportional voting systems and the absolute lack of any genuine pluralism in his style of governing. His desire to embody a new 'style and manner' of politics, 'pluralist, open, inclusive', set out in private at the start of his leadership, was purely presentational. More authentically Blair is the style of stringing people along and keeping options open, while waiting to see what happens and whether anything falls into his lap. In this, he is a politician of instinct, of 'feel' for the weaknesses of others. It was how he played the Conservative hereditary peers: he sensed they were looking for a deal in return for going quietly and simply waited until the turkeys had persuaded themselves to vote for Christmas. It was how he played Margaret Thatcher, and it was how he played Ashdown.

The way he handled Ashdown was not merely cynical but brutal as well. It seems likely that Ashdown's diary entry for the crucial dinner in October 1997 was leaked on Blair's behalf: Ashdown had given him a copy as an informal minute of what had been discussed. Once Ashdown had stood down and started looking for a publisher for his diaries, Blair would have been concerned about such a significant story coming out in a blaze of publicity closer to the election.

Blair was not wholly cynical, however, in that he was prepared to see the Alternative Vote brought in. He admired Ashdown's political qualities and sincerely thought the Liberal Democrats should be part of the progressive consensus. It was Ashdown and Jenkins who made the serious strategic error in rejecting the Alternative Vote option. As a result of their purism, they lost the chance of a partial reform which would have almost certainly given the Liberal Democrats a fairer share of seats.

Ashdown suggested that eventually Blair 'understood' that the Alternative Vote 'couldn't be sold to the electorate, because it would hurt the Tories'. But he understood no such thing. He allowed the Jenkins report not merely to gather dust but about six inches of topsoil, while keeping the option of the Alternative Vote alive, knowing that Ashdown's successor, Charles Kennedy, would not take such a hard line against it.

When Kennedy was elected Liberal Democrat leader on 9 August 1999, by a margin of 57 to 43 per cent over Simon Hughes on the fourth count, Blair in Tuscany phoned him in the Bahamas for what Kennedy was keen to stress was a 'very brief' chat: 'It was very much on the basis of, "Are you having a nice holiday?"'[19] Blair had known Kennedy since they both appeared on *Newsnight* as youngest of each party's new intake in 1983, when Kennedy, an SDP MP, was just twenty-three. Since then Blair had often used Kennedy as an example of how close his thinking was to that of some Liberal Democrats. And he continued to do so, saying in May 2000:

> The truth of the matter is that people like myself in the Labour Party today and people like Charles Kennedy in the Liberal Democrats, we basically are driven by the same value systems. There may be differences of policy but that's . . . almost the accident of being inside different political parties . . . So it's important that we move closer together. I've never given up on that goal.[20]

As Blair continued to tie the Liberal Democrats to Labour policies, securing for example Kennedy's guarded endorsement of the NHS Plan in July 2000, achieving the goal of realignment would continue to be more a matter of suction than coalition.

Notes

1. Diary entry for 21 October 1997, *Sunday Telegraph*, 28 November 1999; Blair was responding to Jonathan Powell's comment that 'he couldn't understand why the pair of us had let that moment slip'.
2. Robert Harris, *Talk* magazine, May 2000: it was in fact the largest majority since 1935; the Conservative share of the vote was the lowest since 1832.
3. Patrick Seyd and Paul Whiteley found that support for proportional representation among Labour members fell sharply after the 1997 election, but that a narrow majority still supported it: PR was supported by 41 per cent of

Labour members in 1999, down from 57 per cent in 1989–90, with opposition up to 38 per cent from 31 per cent; *Guardian*, 11 January 2000.

4. Labour Party conference speech, Brighton, 30 September 1997.
5. This includes eight and a half years in wartime coalitions, 1915–19 and 1940–45, and a further eight years in which Conservatives served under Prime Ministers of other parties, Lloyd George, 1919–22, and Ramsay MacDonald, 1931–35.
6. There were only six Liberal MPs elected at each of the 1951, 1955 and 1959 elections, and the party's share of the total vote was under 6 per cent, although the party contested only between one-sixth and one-third of the seats, and its average vote where a candidate stood was between 15 and 17 per cent.
7. BBC Radio 4, *Resigning Issues*, 16 November 1999.
8. *Observer*, 27 July 1997.
9. For example, 'Cabinet split on PR for Euro-elections', *Sunday Times*, 13 July 1997.
10. *Sunday Telegraph*, 28 November 1999.
11. John Curtice and Michael Steed, in David Butler and Dennis Kavanagh, *The British General Election of 1997*, p. 319. Later research, using further evidence of how voters might have used their second preferences, suggested an even more exaggerated result.
12. *Birmingham Post*, 8 March 1998.
13. *The Report of the Independent Commission on the Voting System*, HM Stationery Office, Cm 4090.
14. BBC2, *Newsnight*, 24 November 1998.
15. On the facts, Blair was right and Ashdown was wrong – see the *Independent*, 8 April 1998, and letter from David Blunkett, 9 April 1998.
16. BBC1, *Breakfast With Frost*, 19 July 1998.
17. Speech, National Council of Voluntary Organisations, 21 January 1999.
18. Reaffirmed in his Labour Party conference speech, Bournemouth, 1999.
19. GMTV, *Sunday*, 5 September 1999.
20. Robert Harris, *Talk* magazine, May 2000.

31

Education, Education, Education

Only Excellence Will Do, 22 March 1999

'Give us two terms in power and you will be able to send your kids to a local secondary school.'
—*Tony Blair to fellow Islington resident Anne McElvoy, 1996*

The difficulty of delivering what had been presented as the first, modest instalment of the new educational Jerusalem highlighted the dangers of having raised the state of the nation's schooling to the highest place in the ambitions of the new government. At his most messianic, in his speech to the pre-election Labour Party conference, on 1 October 1996, Blair had declared: 'Ask me my three main priorities for government, and I tell you: education, education and education.'* He emoted with treacly sentimentality: 'The first wonder of the world is the mind of a child.' And underpinned the priority with the statistical specificity of the first of his ten vows to his country: 'I vow that we will have increased the proportion of our national income we spend on education.'

Fulfilling that promise would have to wait until the money became available after two years of Conservative spending plans. Meanwhile, as with the cut in lone-parent benefits, the priority was to reassure those voters who had voted Labour for the first time. The most significant was the 'naming and shaming' of 'failing' schools – an exercise of doubtful validity which undermined teacher morale and encouraged middle-class flight from schools slipping into 'sink' status. 'For the first three or four

*A sound-bite which has been attributed to Jonathan Powell, Blair's Chief of Staff, who would have been familiar with the dictum of US political consultant Roger Ailes that in modern American elections 'there are only three things which matter: television, television and television'.

months it was necessary to establish that we meant business,' David Blunkett, Blair's Education Secretary, admitted a year later. 'Then we could talk about more positive things.'[1]

The more positive things were a series of generally well-prepared programmes for raising standards, especially in primary schools, and tackling underachievement among below-average-ability children, while producing enough headline-driven initiatives aimed at brighter children to keep the press happy. All this increased the stream of paper flooding teachers from central government, but gradually opinion swung behind the changes. The literacy and numeracy hours – a whole two hours each day devoted to reading, writing and 'rithmetic in all state primary schools – were initially regarded as too prescriptive, but were accepted surprisingly quickly. They were introduced gradually and cleverly blended the best elements of 'trad' and 'trendy' educational thinking, and indeed language, rebranding the three Rs.

Less well liked by teachers was the intensification of the testing regime introduced by the Conservatives. One effect of testing, or, rather, of publishing test results, was to increase the pressures driving informed and motivated parents away from schools at the bottom of league tables. Meanwhile, the assisted places scheme, by which the state paid for some 30,000 children to go to private schools, was phased out with less fuss than might have been expected.* Even less attention was drawn to another issue which had proved troublesome in Opposition, that of 'grant-maintained' schools, those state schools like the London Oratory attended by Blair's sons which had opted out of local council control. The devolution of all school budgets to headteachers and governing bodies, started under the Conservatives and continued under Labour, meant that their formal return to the aegis of local government made little practical difference.

The related issue of the future of the 166 selective state schools was also handled in such a way as not to provoke the *Daily Mail*. It was not until November 1998 that Blunkett produced the legal rules for conducting ballots of parents, and not until March 2000 that the first ballot was held, on the future of Ripon Grammar School, in which there was a two-

*It was not until two years later that Blunkett and Blair were hauled to embarrassing account in the courts over some of their looser wording in Opposition. They had both said that pupils currently on the scheme would be allowed to finish their education – but said in government this did not apply to 1,500 children in private junior schools attached to secondary schools. A judge found in July 1999 that they had broken their promises but not the law.

to-one majority for keeping it selective. This more or less ruled out the possibility of any remaining selective schools going comprehensive. It was only now that Blunkett was forced to repudiate his foolish 'read my lips' pledge to the 1995 Labour Party conference of 'no selection'. He was reported as saying his words had been 'a joke'. He denied that, saying he had described the pledge as a 'parody', admitting: 'In retrospect I should have said "no further selection" in my 1995 speech.'[2] It was personally embarrassing, but politically harmless – the damage he suffered among Labour supporters of comprehensive education had already been done.

What was most impressive about Blunkett's performance in the first two years of government was the extent to which he was able to begin to raise standards without significant extra funding. Although for electoral purposes the pledge to cut infant class sizes to a maximum of thirty was to be 'paid for' by the abolition of the assisted places scheme, this saved a negligible amount of money. The class-size pledge – like the waiting-list pledge for the health service – thus distorted priorities by pre-empting what additional funds there were. Like the waiting-list pledge, it also proved remarkably difficult to deliver. Unlike the waiting-list pledge, however, Blunkett managed to avoid a political backlash. Although it had originally been described as an 'early' pledge, it was only delivered in time for a 2001 election by forcing schools to have more mixed-age classes.

It was not until April 1999 that, after two years of sticking to the previous Conservative government's plans for negligible growth, Gordon Brown increased spending on education by significantly more than inflation. But the gaps between announcement and cash (and then between cash and classroom), and between spin ('£19 billion' reached by cumulating the increases over three years) and substance (significant but unspectacular rises),[3] meant that further spin was required to try to draw the public's attention to the moment when the cash started to flow.

Thus Blair himself launched a scheme for selective extra tuition for the most able 10 per cent of pupils in 'inner city' comprehensives on 22 March 1999. Visiting a school in east London, he took off his jacket, like an enthusiastic new headteacher, and wrote 'Only excellence will do' on a whiteboard. The scheme was part of a series of measures designed to deal with the problem of middle-class flight, particularly acute in inner London, but replicated across the country in any urban area with pockets of poverty. Blair knew about it because he was part of it. His own former borough of Islington was one of the sixteen in London taking part in the 'Excellence in Cities' initiative, in which a quarter of schools would become specialist schools, in non-traditionally academic subjects such as the arts, technology, sport or languages by 2003.

'I know all too well how education dominates conversations in this city. I know parents believe standards in too many schools are too low. I also know they are right,' he had written in that day's London *Evening Standard*. 'It means a real movement of parents with secondary age children from London to the Home Counties or families, often reluctantly, sending their children to private schools.' That included most of his friends and most of the journalists to whom he spoke. He and Cherie, of course, had taken the third way: sending their children across London to another borough. Roman Catholicism was the cover story, although there were Catholic secondary schools in Islington, and this wore a little thinner when the Blairs looked at a Church of England school in Hammersmith, west London, for Kathryn before settling on the Catholic Sacred Heart High School, also in Hammersmith, where she started in September 1999.

He had been challenged by fellow Islington resident and journalist Anne McElvoy at the end of 1996 about whether she could expect, if she had children, to be happy sending them to the local state schools he had avoided. 'Give us two terms in power and you will be able to send your kids to a local secondary school,' he replied.[4]

By the summer of 1999, however, a quarter of that time had already elapsed. In January 1998 Blair had acknowledged that the government was in its 'post-euphoria, pre-delivery' phase.[5] Both he and the government continued to float free in the opinion polls – his approval ratings were still over 60 per cent and Labour was still generally above 50 per cent – but there was a worrying feeling that they were like cartoon characters who had run off a cliff and had not yet realised that there was no solid ground under their feet. It was time to stop annoying the teachers and to apply the charisma booster, to return to the old roadshow format to try to win them round. Now, he needed teachers to help sell the 'delivery' phase: they would notice the new money first.

He took a question-and-answer session at Valentine's School, Redbridge, outer east London, televised on *Newsnight*, on 19 July 1999. It was a turbocharged performance. He took off his jacket and, as with previous sales offensives for the new Clause IV, the draft manifesto and welfare reform, successfully sold two messages simultaneously: offering the shining city on the hill while warning that Rome was not built in a day.

He deflected the charge that schools were increasingly becoming selective by stealth, posing the false choice between a 'rigid comprehensive system' and 'dividing children into successes and failures at the age of eleven'. But then he was forced by an attack on his own family's decisions to make the real argument, which was that forcing people to send their children to the local school 'won't work . . . If you say people have got to go to a certain school, people just move to different localities.' (Although he was only asked that leaders should show an example.)

He tried to turn the charge of hypocrisy against him around by using his family as a testament to his sincerity: 'I think I would be the first British Prime Minister that there's been that has sent all my children through the state education system.' The audience, which consisted mostly of teachers, were sent away reasonably satisfied.

Blair's claim was true, although it was not simply a device of hesitant authenticity when he qualified it with 'I think', because the case of James Callaghan was not entirely clear-cut.* Callaghan's daughter Margaret Jay, Blair's leader in the House of Lords, provoked scholarly dispute in May 2000 when she claimed to have gone to a 'pretty standard grammar school'. This excited the Conservatives, who pointed out that most of the pupils at Blackheath High School were fee-payers. But Margaret Callaghan was not: it was a direct grant school and she was a state pupil who had passed her 11-Plus. Her brother Michael, however, went to Dulwich College – again, the Callaghans did not pay fees because he went on a Greater London Council scholarship, but it was undoubtedly a private school and the scholarship was the equivalent of the assisted places scheme.

Blair did have the best claim of any British Prime Minister, therefore, to be personally committed to the state education system. He also could claim to have made possible the longest period of sustained increases in funding since the first half of the 1970s in the plans to raise spending by an average of 6 per cent a year in real terms over the five years from 1999 to 2004.[6] Blunkett's reforms, and the device of channelling some funds directly to schools rather than through local councils, offered some prospect that the extra money would feed directly into improvements in schools rather than leaking into fat layers of bureaucracy. The thinking behind the targeted pay rises for teachers introduced in September 2000

*John Major's children went to private secondary schools, and all previous Conservative Prime Ministers' children were privately educated. Harold Wilson's sons went to University College School, the private school near his home in Hampstead. Clement Attlee's son, now the crossbench peer Earl Attlee, went to Millfield. Although Ramsay MacDonald's children were educated before the 1944 Education Act set up universal state education, his son Malcolm, who served as a minister in the pre-war National Government, went to Bedales.

was also sound: to get the basics right first and then pay good teachers significantly more to stay in the classroom rather than move into administration. The teachers' unions complained of form-filling and divisiveness, while their members took the money. But would it make Islington schools fit for the children of the McElvoys and Blairs of 2005?

Engine of the new economy

When Blair delivered the Romanes lecture on education at Oxford University on 2 December 1999, he offered an overview of the history of British education from the time of Gladstone, who had delivered the same lecture in 1892. Gladstone's theme, the excellence of Oxford and Cambridge, was symptomatic of much that was wrong with British education throughout the nineteenth and twentieth centuries. Blair praised Arthur Balfour as 'the only Prime Minister before Jim Callaghan to take much interest in state schooling' – which was a little unfair on R. A. Butler, whose Education Act of 1944 was described as only a 'half-step forward', because universal secondary education 'came with the 11-Plus, consigning the majority of teenagers to secondary modern schools which were soon a by-word for failure'.

Stepping deftly over the wreckage of the Wilson and Heath governments' response to that weakness of the 1944 Act, Blair arrived in the mid-1970s. Thus he was able to ignore the deep dilemmas of Tony Crosland's forced collectivisation of British education, a policy as ambivalent as its parallel in Russian and Chinese agriculture, and attribute the failure of British education policy simply to ministerial inattention: 'I regret to say it was Labour's Reg Prentice who had this to say of his fifteen months as Education Secretary in the mid-1970s: "We had very little education policy when I was there, and what there was meant very little to me."'

And he praised Callaghan, not so much for doing anything but for launching the Great Debate in his 1976 speech, also in Oxford. 'Read today,' said Blair,

> the speech is remarkably tame. The sensation was caused not so much by what he said, but the fact that he was saying it. For the first time ever, a Prime Minister was placing national school standards high on the political agenda and suggesting that government should give a firm lead and take proper responsibility.

Callaghan had taken as his text R. H. Tawney's observation that 'the endowments of our children are the most precious of the natural resources of the community', a rhetorical commonplace even then, but now central to the economic policy of New Labour and the Third Way. The centrality of education for Blair was not simply as a means of egalitarian social engineering but as a source of national competitive advantage in the world economy.

> The old dispute between those who favour growth and personal prosperity, and those who favour social justice and compassion, is over. The liberation of human potential – for all the people, not just a privileged few – is in today's world the key both to economic and social progress. In economic terms, human capital is a nation's biggest resource.

Hence Blair's decision to keep the departments of Education and Employment merged, a step John Major had taken partly because Conservatives thought of the old Employment department as the representative in government of the trade union movement, but partly for the same Third Way reasons of linking education to economic advantage.

In his Romanes lecture, Blair repeated that the education budget would remain the tautological 'number-one priority', although the underlining had faded under pressure from the competing pressures in government: 'Let me make it absolutely clear. Education will continue to have the first call on public resources in return for a step-change in standards.' In fact, the health service gained larger increases in spending in Blair's first term, and larger planned increases for the second term, with Blair possibly calculating that he could get a bigger electoral bang for the taxpayer's buck in the NHS.*

In education it was difficult to make the sort of progress that parents – or employers or universities – would notice without a huge mobilisation of resources. More so than in the health service, the lead times for improved outputs are longer than the electoral cycle. Against that background, and working uphill against the strong forces of parental choice polarising schools between the oversubscribed and the sinking, Blair and Blunkett made some progress. It was only undermined, as ever, by rhetorical overkill. In many ways Blair's millennial language implied that he was about to lead a campaign of national mobilisation comparable to that in the Second World War. Instead he oversaw a period of steady, incremental improvement which, it must be suspected, will not reverse middle-class flight from Islington state schools until some time after Blair has ceased to be Prime Minister, if then.

---

*Education spending increased by 14 per cent more than inflation between April 1997 and April 2001, while NHS spending increased by 20 per cent (Institute for Fiscal Studies).

Notes

1. *Guardian*, 28 April 1998.
2. *Sunday Telegraph*, 11 March 2000; letter, *Independent*, 15 March 2000. See also *Hansard*, 15 March 2000; and p. 282.
3. Brown set out plans to increase education spending by £3 billion in real terms in 1999–2000, amounting to £9 billion over the next three years; a further increase of £3.5 billion in 2000–2001 would add £7 billion over two years; and the third year's increase would add another £3.2 billion in 2001–2002, producing the £19.2 billion total (a similar calculation produced a £20 billion figure for health spending over three years). These figures were later revised (see pp. 440–41).
4. *Daily Telegraph*, 3 February 1997 and 30 December 1996.
5. BBC1, *Breakfast With Frost*, 11 January 1998.
6. Institute for Fiscal Studies.

32

Better Angels

Kosovo War, 24 March–3 June 1999

'Those that can act, must.'
—*Tony Blair, 1999*

It was only with the ending of the Cold War that the idea of military intervention in defence of human rights became thinkable. Attitudes on the left, which had often been confused with pacifism during the twin peaks of CND activism, 1959–62 and 1979–81, were revealed as a form of moral nationalism, a belief that Britain had an obligation to act beyond its national interest to save the world.

This became evident during the 1990s in Labour's attitude to Bosnia-Herzegovina, the multi-cultural Balkan republic torn apart by ethnic warlords after the break-up of the Yugoslav federation in 1991. Under John Smith's leadership, Jack Cunningham as foreign affairs spokesman followed a non-interventionist line, broadly supportive of the Conservative government's policy of attempting, unsuccessfully, to mediate. He came under increasing pressure, however, to take a harder line against Serbia which, under the leadership of Slobodan Milosevic, was clearly the principal aggressor. In the Commons, Labour was being outflanked by the muscular righteousness of Paddy Ashdown, who added to his credibility as a soldier a growing knowledge of the history and geography of the region. Younger Labour MPs in particular were also agitating for a more interventionist line. This was one of the generational shifts which Blair's leadership exemplified.

Changing the policy on Bosnia was one of the calculations behind Cunningham's replacement by Robin Cook when Blair became leader. Where Cunningham had been a junior minister in the last Labour government, with its largely pragmatic foreign policy, Cook's origins on the left of the party were imbued with internationalist idealism, and he immediately began to demand forceful action against Milosevic. Opposition parties had little impact on government policy, however, and Major felt under more pressure from Margaret Thatcher, who made the use of force against the Serbs a personal crusade. The real pressure came from public opinion, which responded to television pictures of Serb concentration camps and mass graves with the inchoate demand that 'something must be done'. The same pressure applied in the United States, although with much greater reluctance to commit troops on the ground to do it. Eventually Nato launched air strikes accompanied by the use of ground artillery in August 1995, which immediately produced peace talks in Dayton, Ohio. For the interventionists, the settlement came too late: many thousands had died and decades of peaceful co-existence had been destroyed by extensive 'ethnic cleansing'. The lesson of Bosnia for Blair was simple: that Milosevic was a tyrant who would only be deterred by the early and decisive use of force. In fact, Milosevic had partly exploited the air strikes to bring his Bosnian Serb warlords into line, and in order to secure the end of Western sanctions.

It should have been obvious at Dayton that Kosovo was next. Milosevic had come to power in Serbia seven years earlier using Kosovo to exploit anti-Albanian sentiment and to whip up Serb nationalism. Kosovo was the site of Serbia's defeat at the hands of the Ottoman Turks in 1389 and of many Serb Orthodox Christian holy places. Noel Malcolm makes clear in his definitive *Kosovo: A Short History* that this symbolism was largely synthetic. Ethnic Serbs had always been in a minority in the province.[1] The Serbs who remained felt isolated, and Milosevic used their supposed 'plight' to light the fuse of Serb nationalism in the rest of Serbia. In 1989 he put the autonomous province under martial law, and it was his savage repression of Kosovo Albanian protests which prompted Slovenia and Croatia to leave the Yugoslav federation.

Milosevic's policy had already sounded enough chilling historical echoes before the term 'ethnic cleansing' began to be widely used of Serb expansion in Bosnia. Strict physical segregation of Albanian and Serb children was enforced, including separate school lavatories, along with the invention of the 'verbal crime' of insulting the 'patriotic feelings' of Serbian citizens.[2] Ethnic Albanians were stripped of their jobs in the public sector; the Albanian language was suppressed; and 25,000 Serb police were transferred to the province to enforce a series of arbitrary decrees and, increasingly, to engage in simple beatings, torture and theft. After Serbia went to war with Croatia and then in Bosnia, it adopted a policy of settling Serb refugees from both war zones in Kosovo, with the aim of 'reclaiming' the province for Serbs.

Although Western leaders knew all this, they responded noncommittally to pleas from the leader of the Kosovar majority, Ibrahim Rugova. A pacifist intellectual – a structuralist literary critic by trade – Rugova pursued independence for Kosovo with the total support of the ethnic Albanian population. Both before and – more disturbingly – after the war in Bosnia, the West agreed that Kosovo was an 'internal' matter for the rump Yugoslav republic dominated by Serbia. This was part of a trade-off designed to get Milosevic to the negotiating table over Bosnia, but it was to have tragic consequences.

The most important was to undermine Rugova's authority among the Kosovo Albanians, and to strengthen the hand of those who argued that it was only by arming themselves that the people of Kosovo could free themselves from Milosevic's reign of terror. 'For many years the Serb media had referred to Albanian "terrorism", usually meaning students throwing stones,' wrote Malcolm.[3] Now a genuine Albanian terrorist movement was born. In April 1996, the world first heard of an organisation called the Kosovo Liberation Army, the KLA or (in Albanian) UCK, when a fax to the BBC claimed responsibility for a series of attacks on Serbian forces.[4] Some of the KLA's leaders calculated that if they provoked the Serb military into acts of increasing brutality, it would force the Nato alliance to intervene. Equally, however, Milosevic calculated that, as long as he avoided atrocities, Nato would be more reluctant to intervene than it had been in Bosnia, not least because the basis for such action in international law would be doubtful. Whereas Bosnia was a republic within the Yugoslav federation which, like Slovenia, Croatia and Macedonia, had declared itself independent, Kosovo was only a province of the Serbian republic, albeit one which had enjoyed 'autonomous' status until Milosevic abolished it in 1990.

Kosovo was already on the new Labour government's radar, but right out at the edge of the screen. Tony Lloyd, the Foreign Office minister responsible for the Balkans, reading from his civil service brief in a debate on Bosnia in the Commons on 18 June, mentioned in passing 'the need for progress in Kosovo' in a debate on Bosnia as one of the 'other problems' in the region to which the new government needed to attend.

Meanwhile, one of Blair's earliest foreign policy decisions could almost have been designed to give the new Prime Minister the image of himself as a gun-slinging enforcer of international law. In July 1997, British troops in Bosnia identified two alleged Bosnian Serb war criminals, living openly in their sector. Blair, in Madrid for his first Nato leaders' summit, was asked to approve a mission by the Special Air Service to seize them. Four days later, British soldiers arrested Milan Kovacevic and killed their other target, Simo Drljaca, when he opened fire. Kovacevic died of heart failure in the custody of the war crimes tribunal at The Hague a year later.

The roads to war

Kosovo remained peripheral to the new government's foreign policy concerns, while other problems framed the context which would make eventual war against Milosevic more likely. Nato's continuing responsibilities in Bosnia provided a reminder of the dangers of Serb nationalism, while the growing crisis in Western relations with Saddam Hussein provided a template for military action.

Saddam repeatedly obstructed the United Nations inspectors charged with making sure that Iraq was not making weapons of mass destruction. But by February 1998, Saddam's refusal to allow them free access to 'presidential sites' meant that American and British air strikes seemed imminent. The civil service machinery moved smoothly into action, setting up a 'Prime Minister's Group on Iraq'. It was a war cabinet consisting of Blair, Robin Cook, Defence Secretary George Robertson and the Chief of the Defence Staff, General Sir Charles Guthrie – plus three officials, Jonathan Powell, Alastair Campbell and the Prime Minister's foreign affairs secretary, John Holmes. It was smaller than Margaret Thatcher's famous Falklands war cabinet, which consisted of five politicians in addition to the Chief of the Defence Staff: the Prime Minister, Foreign Secretary Francis Pym, Defence Secretary John Nott and Conservative Party chairman Cecil Parkinson.[5] In a way, Campbell took the role of Parkinson, whose membership of Thatcher's war cabinet as party-political creature prompted raised eyebrows. But, said Thatcher, he was a trusted confidant 'who not only shared my political instincts but was brilliantly effective in dealing with public relations'.[6] New Labour can hardly be said to have invented the idea of wartime media management: the one significant difference was that Campbell was not an elected politician.

Despite his quickly acquired reputation as a reluctant parliamentarian, Blair asked the House of Commons to vote on 17 February 1998 on the use of force against Iraq. It was an historic event, characteristic neither of Blair nor of Prime Ministers generally, the first time parliament had been asked directly to approve military action since 1945. As Peter Hennessy, the constitutional historian, commented, it was 'something denied to the House by Clement Attlee over Korea, Sir Anthony Eden during the Suez affair, Margaret Thatcher at the time of the Falklands crisis and John Major in the run-up to the Gulf War'.[7] Winston Churchill, as Leader of the Opposition in 1950, had argued for a vote on Korea, despite the danger that 'false impressions may be created abroad by a debate prominently occupied by a handful of dissenters'. He said: 'It is better to have a division so that everyone can know how the House of Commons stands and in what proportion.'[8] It cannot have given Saddam much comfort when Blair secured his mandate for bombing by 493 votes to 25.[9] However, Blair was displeased that twenty-three Labour MPs had opposed the government, and resolved not to give them the chance to do so again.

Saddam yielded to the threat of force by allowing the inspectors to resume their work, and the crisis did not flare up again until the end of 1998. What was significant about Blair's preparations to join Clinton in launching air strikes against Iraq was that they would not have been authorised explicitly by the UN. While under the UN Charter the use of force can only be justified in self-defence or in fulfilment of a resolution of the UN Security Council, Clinton and Blair argued that they were entitled to enforce the terms of the earlier Security Council resolution which ended the Gulf War, even if Russia or China vetoed a further resolution explicitly authorising the use of force to do so.

When Kosovo started to move towards the centre of Blair's radar screen in February 1998, there seemed to be a disjunction between international law and plain morality. If Nato would use military force to protect Bosnian Muslims from Serb 'ethnic cleansing', why should it not do so to protect Kosovo Muslims, just because theirs was a province of Serbia? On 28 February, Serb forces reacted to a KLA ambush in which two police were killed by shooting sixteen Albanians. Another sixty died over the next week, including women and children. The killings, and the funerals which followed, attracted attention around the world. European Union foreign ministers expressed 'growing concern' and urged restraint on all parties.

Milosevic blithely ignored international ultimatums, knowing they were not backed by the threat of force. By 7 April 1998, Robin Cook could only tell the Commons: 'We are determined that Belgrade should stop behaving as it is in Kosovo.' It was not until the beginning of June, when Milosevic launched a major military offensive against the KLA, which drove as many as 50,000 Kosovo Albanians from their homes, that Western leaders threatened the use of force against Serbia. Britain, representing the EU, sought UN authorisation for Nato air strikes. There was no chance of gaining such approval, because of the Russian veto. But

Cook stepped up the verbal war which he and Blair would carry through by asserting: 'Mr Milosevic should back down and he should back down now. This is his last warning.' Although Milosevic scaled down his operations in Kosovo, he did not withdraw his forces from the province.

Blair and Cook tried to cajole the various overlapping international bodies in which they worked towards making good their threat. The problem was that it was by no means clear – to Milosevic as much as anyone else – that public opinion in Nato countries would support the use of force. No Nato country had a direct national interest at stake, only an indirect interest in 'stability' in the Balkans, and, although Nato's own constitution as a defensive alliance had been breached in Bosnia, several countries were reluctant to go further, in particular Germany, Italy and Greece. Air strikes seemed punitive, simple and relatively free of the risk of casualties but, from an early stage, the difficulty of committing ground troops loitered in the background. It was a fixed point of US foreign policy under Clinton that he would not deploy forces in combat on the ground in Europe.

Blair, meanwhile, began to realise that a credible threat of force against Milosevic had to be backed up ultimately by a willingness to fight on the ground. General Guthrie assessed the prospects of invading Kosovo as 'difficult, but quite possible'. He had seen the Serbs operating in Bosnia: 'They were a gangster army, good at killing old women and children. But doing formed-up training and battle – I don't think they would have been any good at that.' Blair warned the European members of Nato, at the summit marking the end of the British presidency in Cardiff on 14 June, not only that air strikes might have to go ahead without a UN mandate, but that ground troops might be necessary too.

That was going too far, too fast. Simply to get Nato governments to agree to air strikes alone required a further upsurge in violence in August and UN Security Council resolution, number 1199, passed on 23 September, demanding an end to Serbian action by security forces against civilians in Kosovo. The resolution did not authorise military action but the moral pressure on the reluctant members of Nato was such that, when 200,000 Kosovo Albanians fled into the forests to escape a renewed Serb crackdown in October, they finally agreed to action. Nato decisions have to be unanimous, which meant the alliance operated with the forcefulness of the most reluctant member of its sixteen-strong council. But the North Atlantic Council now issued an 'activation order' on 13 October putting 500 aircraft under the command of Wesley Clark, Nato's Supreme Allied Commander Europe, to enforce it. Hours later, Milosevic backed down.

US special envoy Richard Holbrooke negotiated a ceasefire with the Yugoslav president, who agreed to reduce troop numbers in Kosovo and to allow 2,000 unarmed observers into the province under the auspices of the Organisation for Security and Co-operation in Europe (OSCE), which included Russia. Blair had argued that Nato should insist on 'lightly armed' troops being deployed to protect the observers, but Milosevic would not have accepted it and in any case the US and Germany would not consider it. Indeed, in order to secure the activation order, the impatient Clark had to accept the politicians' ruling which forbade him from even working on plans for a ground invasion. But the activation order, once passed in a fleeting moment of agreement, was set in stone, and provided the authority for bombing five months later. Blair said later: 'I was always in the forward end of the troop on this because I always foresaw that if we didn't intervene sooner we would have to intervene later, and that is the lesson from Bosnia too.'[10] However, the OSCE observers had a restraining effect on the Serb forces, and Kosovo quietened while attention switched back to Iraq.

At the end of October 1998, Saddam Hussein provoked a new crisis by ending co-operation with UN inspectors, whom he accused of being American spies. On 14 November, US and British aircraft were recalled when some were already on their way to Iraq, when Saddam backed down at the last minute. Having seen the threat of force succeed twice in a month, Blair's frustration with the unnamed leaders of 'other countries' grew:

> When he [Saddam] finally saw, correctly, that we were ready to use force on a substantial scale, he crumbled. I hope that other countries more dubious of the use of force may now see that Saddam is moved by the credible threat of force. He has exposed the fact that his fear is greater than his courage. Let us learn the lesson of that.[11]

Blair continued to use the stridently uncompromising tone which would become familiar in the Kosovo war: 'If he again obstructs the inspectors' work, we will strike. There will be no warnings, no wrangling, no negotiation and no last-minute letters. The next time co-operation is withdrawn, he will be hit.'

In a joint US–British operation, with no question of deploying troops on the ground and with no European Nato doves to persuade, carrying out that threat was a straightforward matter when, on 16 December 1998, Richard Butler, the senior UN weapons inspector, reported that Saddam was still in breach of UN terms. The bombing of Iraq, Operation Desert Fox, was announced by Blair outside 10 Downing Street just after

10pm, a few minutes before President Clinton made his announcement. It was a sombre moment, the first time that Blair ordered servicemen and women into military action. 'I feel that responsibility, tonight, profoundly,' he said. He gave currency to a new military euphemism, saying the aim of the bombing was to 'degrade' Iraq's capability to build and use weapons of mass destruction and to threaten its neighbours, a term which would recur in the Kosovo war.

The timing of the strike was far from ideal in presenting the Clinton–Blair partnership as reluctant enforcers of international law. Butler's report had been delivered on the day before Congress was due to begin debate on the draft articles of impeachment against President Clinton over the Monica Lewinsky affair. (The debate was postponed for a day and, after Clinton was charged on two counts of perjury, the bombing stopped.)

This led George Galloway, the Labour backbencher, into a passionate denunciation of 'a new crusade, led not by Richard the Lionheart but by Clinton the Liar', in the emergency Commons debate on the bombing on 17 December. Blair shook his head sadly: 'I simply want to say to my honourable friend – to be honest, I think that I am sort of past anger – that I find it curious that he should attack President Clinton personally and mention not a word of condemnation of Saddam Hussein.' This time, the government did not table a motion for a vote and, when Labour left-wingers tried to force a vote on a motion of their own, resorted to the procedural trick of failing to put up tellers to count its own votes, which meant the division could not take place. This avoidance of formally recorded dissent extended to a self-defeating manoeuvre on the Labour Party's own National Executive, when it voted by 19 to 5 on 26 January 1999 not to discuss a left-wing motion regretting the bombing.

Although these pointless evasions rather undermined its force, Blair's 'ethical foreign policy' was beginning to take shape, and quite a different one from that conjured up by Robin Cook when he first gave the phrase currency. Blair defended the bombing of Iraq in the Cape Town Parliament on 8 January 1999, speaking in the same room where Harold Macmillan made his 'wind of change' speech in 1960. Employing his distinctive conversationally blunt mode, Blair said: 'People say – and I understand – you can't be self-appointed guardians of what is right and wrong. True – but when the international community agrees certain objectives and then fails to implement them, those that can act, must.' It was an embryonic form of the doctrine which he would develop in relation to Kosovo: there too the UN Security Council had passed a resolution demanding restraint from a monstrous dictator but failed to authorise the means to enforce it.

A week after the Cape Town speech came the massacre at Racak in Kosovo on 15 January 1999, which demonstrated to the world what anyone with an informed interest should have known, that unarmed observers could not prevent Serb brutality. On a hillside above the village, a fleeing column of forty-five people, including three women, a twelve-year-old boy and several men over sixty, were shot and hacked to death by Serbian Interior Ministry police and paramilitaries. With OSCE observers and television cameras at the scene within hours, the horror of Serb 'ethnic cleansing' was held up for the world to see. The Serbian forces were now fighting a full-scale guerrilla war against the KLA, and there were atrocities on both sides, but the moral balance was now tilted even further than it had been for the previous ten years of Serb oppression.

With the position of the OSCE observers increasingly precarious, Robin Cook presented Milosevic with a new ultimatum on 30 January. Representatives of the Yugoslav and Serbian governments (there was by now little distinction between the two), reluctantly attended a peace conference at Rambouillet outside Paris a week later, with Rugova and representatives of the KLA. While the talks went on, Nato forces in Macedonia were built up, ready to be deployed in Kosovo if there were an agreement. For three weeks, Milosevic's negotiators managed to stall. They refused to agree to a Nato force in the province, or to a referendum on Kosovo's future after three years of interim government, even when watered down to a vague commitment to 'review' the status of the province.* Milosevic calculated that limited air strikes would strengthen his position in Yugoslavia, and that Nato members would not have the stomach for a sustained assault. He was nearly right.

The diplomacy now entered its final phase, with Richard Holbrooke making what turned out to be the penultimate 'final' appeal to Milosevic.

---

*Conspiracy theorists later became obsessed with 'annex B' of the draft agreement, which they claimed was designed to drive Milosevic to war by giving Nato forces access to the whole of Yugoslavia. But the talks broke down because Milosevic would not allow Nato access even to Kosovo, and never got as far as the detail of annex B, which had been drawn up by lawyers in the widest possible terms, using the Dayton accord which Milosevic had signed in 1995 as a model, to give Nato forces permissive legal authority. Given the isolationism of American opinion, the refusal to deploy US troops on the ground and Clinton's hesitation even over air strikes – not to mention the fragility of a Nato alliance in which each member had a veto on military action – the conspiracist view is unsustainable.

The Yugoslav president said angrily that he and his military could 'clean up' the KLA 'in one week if it weren't for the restraint imposed on him by the October agreements,' Holbrooke said. 'I reported back to Washington immediately that this was the most chilling conversation I'd ever had with President Milosevic because the "one week" scenario meant . . . massive refugees [and] great tragedy.'[12]

Neither the White House nor Downing Street was focused on the consequence of air strikes, however, because they were struggling to preserve the Nato mandate for them which had been agreed but not used the previous October.

The moral force of Blair's arguments was strengthened when Poland, Hungary and the Czech Republic became members of Nato on 12 March. They had not expected to take part in Nato's first European war within two weeks of joining, but all three supported military action against Milosevic. This was most significant in the case of Hungary, which shares a border with Yugoslavia.

The OSCE mission pulled out of Kosovo on 19 March, and Serb paramilitaries began to run amok in the province as soon as their backs were turned. At the presidential palace in Belgrade on the afternoon of Tuesday 23 March, Holbrooke asked an intransigent Milosevic if he understood what would happen next. 'Yes, you will bomb us,' came the reply. As the US envoy climbed onto his plane, a journalist asked if bombing might not simply accelerate 'ethnic cleansing' in Kosovo. 'That is our greatest fear by far,' Holbrooke said. 'By far.'[13]

That was not, however, the general view. Blair in particular was oblivious to the risk. In his prime ministerial broadcast on 26 March, two days after the start of bombing, he said: 'Fail to act now, and . . . we would have to deal with . . . hundreds of thousands of refugees.' The next day, the exodus started. Thousands – and soon hundreds of thousands – of ethnic Albanians began to pour into Albania and Macedonia. 'What we never expected was a wholesale expulsion of people from the country,' Wesley Clark admitted candidly later.[14] Although the unexpected crisis made Western leaders look foolish, their response was swift. Macedonian objections were overcome and Nato troops began building the camp that would be known as Stenkovec on Sunday 28 March. By Monday night it held 25,000 people. However, even if Blair had known that hundreds of thousands would have left Kosovo within days, he would not have decided differently. The choice was stark. The OSCE observers could not have stayed: their lives were in danger. 'Ethnic cleansing' would have gathered pace, not as quickly as it did, but with no end in sight. In the year before the bombing, as many as 100,000 ethnic Albanians had fled the province.* As a consequence of the war, nearly half of the province's population of 2 million was driven out, but almost all of them went back. There were casualties, but the war was overwhelmingly supported by the Kosovo Albanians, because it meant an end to Serb oppression.

The hesitation over ground forces

While Holbrooke was in Belgrade on 23 March, Blair made a statement in the Commons that air strikes were imminent. He was forced to admit that there was no plan to use ground troops to force the Yugoslav army out of Kosovo. He did not say that there could be no such plan because Nato commanders had been forbidden to draw one up, but he was open about the general political constraint. 'Let us be clear: we are not going to send in 100,000 or 200,000 ground forces with the consent of other countries, for no such consent exists,' he told the Commons.

The US chiefs of staff had already sought to cover their backs by putting in writing their conviction that the war could not be won from the air alone. They thought it could be won by overwhelming force on the ground, which was their policy in the Gulf War, by which they meant 200,000 troops. But before the bombing began and for some time afterwards, Clinton calculated that he could not sustain support for air strikes among the American public and in Congress unless he ruled out the possibility of escalation involving troops on the ground.

The failure to keep the option open at the start of the conflict was the biggest mistake of the campaign and it allowed Milosevic to persist in his belief that Nato lacked the will to finish what it had started.

The bombing of Yugoslav air defences began at 7pm on 24 March. Blair gave his final approval the day before. As in Iraq, only more so, there were likely to be civilian casualties, and he was later asked if he lost sleep over his decision:

> Of course I felt for the innocent who died. In a war innocent people die as well as guilty ones and that is a terrible responsibility. But there were twenty or thirty thousand innocent Kosovar Albanians who died as part of systematic racial genocide. If we had not fought to restore their land to them then hundreds of thousands of them would have died. And never forget that

---

*Nato claimed 200,000 to 300,000, but estimates are hard to substantiate, as are those for the numbers driven out of their homes who remained in Kosovo. Robin Cook, the Foreign Secretary, justifying the bombing in the Commons (*Hansard*, 25 March 1999), said: 'Since March last year, well over 400,000 people in Kosovo have at some point been driven from their homes.'

> when we didn't act in Bosnia, 250,000 people died and we had 3 or 4 million refugees, with a million of them in the European Union.[15]

Wesley Clark, meanwhile, the American charged with responsibility for the Nato campaign, faced the more immediate problem that he had been closely restricted – much too closely, he thought – in the range of targets he was allowed to hit from the air. Indeed, the entire campaign was fought under the most extraordinary rules of engagement designed to minimise the risk of Nato casualties, rules which meant Kosovo was the first sustained armed conflict in which one side sustained no casualties in combat at all.

As soon as the war started, Clark resumed his efforts to persuade Nato foreign ministers to allow him to attack a broader range of targets. It was quickly clear that Milosevic would not back down within days. And the huge outflow of refugees allowed the Nato hawks, led by Blair, to rally the alliance – even those members who thought they had made a terrible mistake – behind the objective of returning the displaced Kosovars to their homes. In a classic illustration of the way in which war always expands its initially limited objectives, the logic of escalation was thus entrenched. On 27 March, the European 'doves', Germany, Italy and Greece, agreed to escalate to 'phase two', which allowed Nato to bomb supply bases in the rest of Yugoslavia.

In a statement on television news on 3 April, Blair spoke of keeping up the pressure on Milosevic 'with total resolve', and promised the Albanian refugees: 'We will not let you down.' That can only have meant that if ground troops were needed to restore them to their homes, they would be deployed. He wrote an article for the *Sunday Telegraph* on 4 April, which the newspaper headlined, 'Tony Blair insists that Nato will not send ground troops', which was precisely what he carefully avoided doing. He wrote: 'Many people say we should send in ground troops to help, but that misses the point. A Nato invasion force is not an alternative, because it would take weeks to assemble, during which time the emptying of Kosovo would continue.' That did not, however, rule it out in the future. At the same time, Alastair Campbell had briefed some other Sunday newspapers that the Prime Minister was preparing for a 'four-year war'.

It was puzzling, therefore, that Blair should have categorically ruled out the use of ground troops the next day, 5 April, in an article in the *Sun*. 'There is no question of Nato ground forces being sent in unless it is to police an agreed political settlement,' he wrote. This sentence allowed the article to be headlined prominently, 'I won't send our boys in', in a newspaper which had been strongly opposed to deployment. But it made no sense in the context of the rest of the article, which began with a jolting statement of moral absolutism: 'This is now a battle of good against evil . . . It is a battle between civilisation and barbarity, democracy against dictatorship.' The implication was, as Blair had said explicitly in his *Sunday Telegraph* article, that Nato would do 'whatever is necessary' to achieve its goals.

The simplest explanation is that the 'no question' phrase was a mistake, drafted for Blair in haste, because he showed no other signs of trying to manage public opinion in the same way as Clinton in the US. On the contrary, he delivered a populist tough message about Milosevic on ITN that evening: 'We will drive him back out of Kosovo.' It had been clear by the end of the previous week that public opinion was swinging behind the deployment of troops on the ground, an understandable reaction to pictures of thousands of lost souls in the Macedonian mists. Even in America, the pictures of refugees, and those of three captured and bruised US soldiers paraded on Yugoslav television on 1 April, helped harden the minority in favour of ground forces.

From then on, the possibility of shifting the position on ground troops dominated much of the discussion of the war's tactics. Blair toughened his language significantly on 19 April, telling Milosevic:

> You will be made to withdraw from Kosovo. There will be an international military force that will go in to secure the land for the people to whom it belongs. The dispossessed refugees of Kosovo will be brought back into possession of that which is rightfully theirs. Our determination on these points – the minimum demands civilisation makes – is absolute.[16]

Two days later Blair set off for Washington for a commemoration of Nato's fiftieth anniversary, which became a council of war and was a turning point in the Kosovo campaign. Before he arrived in America, Blair secured leverage which turned out to be decisive when Javier Solana, the Nato Secretary-General, agreed to carry out a 'review' of all options. That was the formula which finally broke through Clinton's reluctance, and ultimately the threat of a land invasion – for which Clinton started preparing with no intention of carrying out – was probably decisive in forcing Milosevic to agree to Nato terms.

Campaign

The conduct of the Kosovo campaign was marred by errors, and lacked the heroism of a more equal contest. 'It was not the most dangerous operation,' said General Guthrie. 'It was not the most confused. But it was immensely difficult.' Much of the difficulty of the campaign lay in the need to keep nineteen allies together. 'A lot of my time and I know a lot of his time was spent talking to our allies on the telephone,' Guthrie said of Blair. It also achieved its objectives more completely than even its most committed supporters could have hoped. It was fought predominantly by Americans, as Blair acknowledged, with a surreal *Wizard of Oz* reference: 'The vast bulk of this military operation is being carried out by US forces, although Kosovo is a very long way from Kansas.'[17] The British contribution was the next most significant, and Blair's direction of the war won him unstinting admiration from the forces. 'I thought it was helpful that he made his mind up and gave direction,' said Guthrie. 'That's what military people like. They like to be listened to and they like people who make decisions.'

Unlike previous governments' war cabinets, which had met in the Cabinet room, the Prime Minister's Group on Kosovo, like that on Iraq, met in his study just after nine on most mornings. Guthrie and the politicians sat on the sofa and armchairs, with the officials in a horseshoe around the edges of the room. Sir Richard Wilson, the Cabinet Secretary, often took the minutes on his knee, perched on the arm of the sofa. The informality of style – the Prime Minister sometimes eating an apple during proceedings – belied Blair's firm grasp of decision making. Once or twice a week the group met, with the addition of Clare Short and Jack Straw (to discuss the refugee and asylum crises) and a Treasury minister, as the larger and more formal Defence and Overseas Policy (DOP) committee of the Cabinet, around the Cabinet table. Membership of both groups was fluid, not just from day to day but during meetings: Short sometimes attended the smaller war cabinet; the Attorney General, John Morris, was also a regular attender, with the basis for the bombing in international law and the legality of specific targets being continuous questions.

The war tested Blair's physical as well as his moral resources: it was fought at the same time as important and often all-night negotiations in Northern Ireland and over the EU budget. Apart from the war cabinet, the daily timetable of war was strung between media requirements. The early line to take had to be established at the Ministry of Defence by eight o'clock to make sure that the *Today* programme was covered. After the war cabinet Alastair Campbell would brief Lobby journalists at eleven. The rest of the day was taken up with diplomacy and constant dialogue with Nato and Nato member states, with an occasional impromptu meeting of the war cabinet at about five o'clock.

The paradox of the campaign was that it was criticised for being driven by the needs of media management and yet in that respect it was a mitigated disaster. Nato commanders released video footage from a guided missile attack on a railway bridge in order to show that the bombardier could not have seen a civilian train in time to abort: broadcasters then showed the footage in slow motion which gave the opposite impression. Then the technological difficulty of telling a tank from a tractor from three miles up in the sky was illustrated when a column of Kosovo Albanian refugees was hit. Instead of promising to investigate, Nato's first response was to accuse Serbian forces of staging the incident to make it look like a Nato mis-hit. Most reprehensible, because it was deliberate, was the bombing of the Yugoslav state television station, hit on 23 April, killing several civilians. This was evidently not a 'strictly military target', even if it were used for military communications, and seemed outside the restriction of the use of force in international law to what was necessary and proportionate. Blair defended the attack as being on an arm of Milosevic's military machine. He approved the decision to bomb the station, as was made clear by General Guthrie after the war:

> It was most unfortunate that there were civilians there, and a number were killed, but it was chosen very carefully at the time. Tony Blair would certainly have known we were going to do this. I can't remember whether he – I imagine he approved it, I can't remember the detail of this, but tremendous trouble was taken to make quite sure that the building would be as empty as it possibly could be.[18]

It was not until 19 April, however, that parliamentary opposition to the war in Britain was formally recorded. Backbench Labour rebels finally forced a vote, nearly four weeks after the bombing started, allowing thirteen MPs to register their opposition.[19] They had been denied a vote at the end of the debate on the day after the bombing started, when the Deputy Speaker, Sir Alan Haselhurst, declared, 'I think the Noes have it', and moved on before Tony Benn had time to protest. This allowed Benn to remount his high horse and lecture the nation on how the fiction of Crown privilege gave the Prime Minister of the day the power to wage war. He was right but irrelevant, in that there was no doubt that, if the House as a whole had been asked to authorise military action, it would have done so. However, for a just war of civilisation against barbarity, as Blair described it, an early vote could only have strengthened his moral argument.

The Kosovo war exposed deep divisions on the left, expressed in passionate language on both sides. During the vote Clare Short lost her temper and shouted at the dissidents, 'You are a disgrace to the Labour Party'. In a radio interview the next day, she accused them of being 'like those who appeased Hitler'. She was a rather wild exemplar of the way in which, for many on the left, righteous interventionism superseded anti-Americanism.

Blair's dislike of opposition to the war being expressed democratically recalled not just Thatcher's spat with the BBC over its reporting of 'our boys' during the Falklands War but Major's during the Gulf War in 1991, when BBC reporter John Simpson first got it in the neck from the government. Then, he stayed in Baghdad; this time he stayed in Belgrade and reported on what the war looked like from the other side. For observing truthfully that the bombing had initially strengthened Serbian resolve and Milosevic's grip on his people Simpson was rewarded with oblique insults from Alastair Campbell. But Blair was as oblivious as his Conservative predecessors to an essential point: a just war fought by democracies or an alliance of democracies should enjoy and be strengthened by the support of their peoples, regardless of what is truthfully reported from the war zone. If his judgment was awry on this, it was the product of two factors shared by his predecessors in their wars: absolute certainty in the moral rightness of his cause and close personal involvement in directing the campaign.

Inviting comparisons with Macmillan's closeness to Kennedy during the 1963 missile crisis, Blair seems to have been involved in the US President's deliberations almost as a member of his National Security Council. It was a different kind of special relationship from that between Thatcher and Reagan, and it was certainly rather different from Thatcher's with George Bush – to whom she delivered her famous ticking-off on the telephone, 'George, this is no time to go wobbly', during the build-up to the Gulf War – although the sense of that exchange may have been similar to that of the conversation between Blair and Clinton in armchairs in the Yellow Oval Room in the White House on the evening of 21 April.[20]

Over Diet Cokes, chocolate chip cookies and pastries, the two leaders planned for Nato's fiftieth anniversary summit, due to open on Friday 23 April, with Madeleine Albright, Clinton's Secretary of State, and Sandy Berger, his National Security Adviser. Blair took Clinton through his understanding of the logic of a credible threat against Milosevic, which meant that if Nato were threatening the use of force it had to be prepared to use it, and to follow through with whatever it took to prevail. It had taken time and the unfolding of events to bring Blair to his present position, as he stressed the critical importance of keeping the option of ground troops on the table. 'Well, we've agreed to that,' Clinton said. But Blair now wanted the President's backing for Nato to issue a more forceful threat. He wanted Nato to begin planning for troops to be deployed in what he now called a 'semi-permissive environment' – in which Serbian forces were so battered and demoralised that they could not offer much resistance. Clinton was not persuaded, and Berger believed the Solana review would only confirm that ground troops were a bad idea. Clinton's real view remained obscure. But he agreed to an intensification of the air campaign, and they made a list of the other seventeen Nato leaders and divided them up: Clinton would lobby half and Blair would take the other half.

'You lead, we die'

Blair's forceful seizure of the leadership of Nato was startling. The sudden ferocity of his moral conviction was quite out of character: until this moment, he had always been a highly cautious politician, and even on those occasions when he took risks he did so, as Peter Mandelson said, with great care and attention to detail.

On Kosovo, on the other hand, he took a high moral tone from the start, saying on the day the bombing started: 'Justice is all that those poor people, driven from their homes in their thousands in Kosovo, are asking for, the chance to live free from fear. We have in our power the means to help them secure justice and we have a duty to see that justice is now done.'[21]

Then, when the refugees started to pour out of Kosovo, he recklessly committed himself to an objective which was not wholly in his power to deliver: returning them to their homes. That required a Serbian retreat and Nato occupation of the province. He pledged himself to that aim at a time when he could not have been sure whether the Nato alliance would hold – and most importantly whether Clinton would stay the course. Despite his political and personal closeness to the President, he had no idea whether Clinton or the sceptical State Department could be levered into a more robust position.

Politicians are always keen to leave themselves a way out. Blair was no exception, and must have understood Clinton's reluctance to be dragged by the logic of escalation into sustaining casualties in a place so obscure that it required him to devote a television broadcast to a geography lesson. The accounts by Clinton's former aides George Stephanopoulos and Dick Morris of how the President ordered military action in Haiti, Bosnia and Iraq do not inspire confidence that the right decisions on Kosovo were always taken for the right reasons. In September 1994 Clinton had complained about the planned invasion of Haiti which had full UN backing and succeeded in forcing the dictator Raoul Cedras out of power: 'I can't believe they got me into this . . . How did this happen? We should have waited until after the elections.'[22]

However, the Clinton administration's obsession with opinion research set the seal on a shift in American foreign policy from one of defending 'vital' national interests to one of defending human rights. Stephanopoulos wrote that the White House tested various arguments for invading Haiti in focus groups: 'Our polling showed that the American people were more moved by altruism than naked self-interest. [They were] more willing to use our power to protect innocent civilians from torture and terror.'[23]

Blair had always been careful to give himself an exit before. But not in this case. 'Success is the only exit strategy I am prepared to consider,' he said to applause in the most important speech of his first two years as Prime Minister. Like most important speeches, his address to the Economic Club in Chicago on 22 April 1999 was as much the product of the needs of the moment as of thoughtful philosophical reflection. The need of the moment was his single-handed campaign to influence American opinion in favour of a more vigorous conduct of the war, a campaign which he launched in the city which had been at the heart of US isolationism in the years before the Second World War. Although it was a speech of the moment, it was, unusually, not written on the plane or finished at five o'clock on the morning it was delivered. It had been written – mostly by Blair, in longhand – in London on the day before he left for Washington. In it, he developed the theme set out in Cape Town in January, in which he sought to establish the legal and moral basis for military intervention in 'other people's conflicts', which he rather self-consciously called 'a new doctrine of international community'.

The principle of non-interference was an important one, he said, but it must be qualified. 'Acts of genocide can never be a purely internal matter,' he said, before moving to anticipate the criticism of his moral activism with characteristic fluency.

> Looking around the world there are many regimes that are undemocratic and engaged in barbarous acts. If we wanted to right every wrong that we see in the modern world then we would do little else than intervene in the affairs of other countries. We would not be able to cope.
>
> So how do we decide when and whether to intervene? I think we need to bear in mind five major considerations.
>
> First, are we sure of our case? War is an imperfect instrument for righting humanitarian distress; but armed force is sometimes the only means of dealing with dictators. Second, have we exhausted all diplomatic options? We should always give peace every chance, as we have in the case of Kosovo. Third, on the basis of a practical assessment of the situation, are there military operations we can sensibly and prudently undertake? Fourth, are we prepared for the long term? In the past we talked too much of exit

> strategies. But having made a commitment we cannot simply walk away once the fight is over; better to stay with moderate numbers of troops than return for repeat performances with large numbers. And finally, do we have national interests involved? The mass expulsion of ethnic Albanians from Kosovo demanded the notice of the rest of the world. But it does make a difference that this is taking place in such a combustible part of Europe.

The doctrine was a thoughtful attempt to bridge the gap in international law between declarations of 'fundamental' human rights and mechanisms to enforce them.

On the day after the bombing began, Defence Secretary George Robertson had restated the formula agreed by the Nato allies the previous autumn: 'Our legal justification rests upon the accepted principle that force may be used in extreme circumstances to avert a humanitarian catastrophe.' This may have been an 'accepted principle' of pragmatic morality, such as that which approved Vietnam's invasion of Cambodia to overthrow Pol Pot in 1978, or Tanzania's invasion of Uganda to overthrow Idi Amin in 1979, but it had not been codified in international law. Robertson tacitly accepting the bombing of Serbia broke new ground as 'an exceptional measure', in support of purposes laid down by the UN Security Council, 'but without the Council's express authorisation'.[24]

In the Chicago speech, and in a series of interviews with the US media, Blair developed the idea (also used in the case of Sierra Leone) that regional groups of states, such as Nato, could take action to enforce international law, such as that against genocide, without express authorisation from the UN, provided the action were consistent with the UN Charter.

The importance of putting Milosevic in the dock of history along with Hitler led to Blair's coinage, on the mass audience *Larry King Live* television show, of the tautological 'racial genocide' to describe the Serbian leader's policy towards the Kosovo Albanians. It secured an overwhelmingly favourable response from American commentators and from many political leaders, such as Republican congressman John McCain, who castigated Clinton's weak and vacillating policy. The cautious State Department was less impressed however, Deputy Secretary of State Strobe Talbott remarking acidly in private that 'Winston' Blair was 'ready to fight to the last American'.

The Nato summit was deadlocked, therefore. It produced the 'Washington Declaration', which expanded Nato's aims beyond the purely defensive provisions of the 1949 Treaty. This had been intended retrospectively to acknowledge Nato's role in Bosnia, although it now applied with some force in Kosovo. Blair did not get the hardening of the line against Milosevic he wanted, but Solana's 'review' of the military options kept the possibility of escalation alive.

That, however, was all Blair needed to ensure that Nato would prevail. The organisation's credibility was now at stake, as he explained in the Commons on his return:

> If Nato succeeds, the next time someone tries such a policy and we make a threat it will be credible. Were we to fail – which we will not and must not – the opposite would happen: people would know that, when Nato threatened, it would not be a threat to be taken seriously. That is why people do not talk about Nato's credibility in some abstract sense; it is a necessary part of building peace and security for the long term.[25]

Meanwhile, Blair was hailed not just in America as a great war leader. The *Sun* on 24 April praised his 'superb leadership' and declared: 'With true moral courage, Blair has seized control of Nato and made himself a giant of the free world.' Less than a year after asking if he were the most dangerous man in Europe, the *Sun* now promoted him above the goddess of leadership herself: 'Victory in what has now become a moral crusade of good against evil will transcend even Margaret Thatcher's triumph in the Falklands.'

Now that Nato was effectively locked into a 'victory or bust' stance, Blair's crusade was raised to its most strident level, replete with a range of historical references from Charlemagne to Gladstone. He and Cherie toured Stenkovec No. 1 refugee camp in Macedonia on 3 May to chants of 'Tony, Tony'. He spoke to the refugees:

> Our commitment to defeating this policy of ethnic cleansing, our commitment to allowing these people to return to their homes in peace – that commitment is total . . . This is not a battle for Nato, this is not a battle for territory; this is a battle for humanity, it is a just cause, it is a rightful cause.

Cherie's tears featured on the front pages back home the next day, and she and Blair used horror stories of their visit to lobby Hillary Clinton, in London for a Childline conference with Cherie on 13 May, over tea at Downing Street. Earlier in the day, Blair had delivered a speech in Aachen, Germany, on accepting the Charlemagne prize for European achievement. He spoke with the verbless bluntness which occurred when his moral certainty coincided with Alastair Campbell's prose style: 'There can be no half measures' in dealing with the brutality of Milosevic, he said. 'No compromise. No fudge. No half-baked deals.'

Four days later, he toured the 'front-line states' Bulgaria and Albania. At Sofia University he told the Bulgarians that William Gladstone was 'one of my political heroes'. He was big on 'opposing the persecution of the Bulgarians in the 1870s', which made him a useful role model:

> The parallels between then and now are all too tragically clear. Today we face the same questions that confronted Gladstone over 120 years ago. Does one nation or people have the right to impose its will on another? Is there ever a justification for a policy based on the supremacy of one ethnic group? Can the outside world simply stand by when a rogue state brutally abuses the basic rights of those it governs? Gladstone's answer in 1876 was clear. And so is mine today.
>
> Then, as now, it would have been easy to look the other way; easy to argue that bigger strategic issues were at stake than the fate of a few hundred thousand people in the Balkans. Some people made exactly that argument. Some do today. They were wrong in 1876 over Bulgaria; and they are wrong in 1999 over Kosovo.
>
> Nato's success in Kosovo will be the biggest deterrent to tyrants the world over; and the biggest rallying call for democracy. That is why, whatever it takes, we must succeed; and the policy of brutal savagery that is ethnic cleansing must fail and be seen to fail.

Of course, there were parallels between the moral populism of Blair and Gladstone, who in the Midlothian campaign curdled the blood of the Liberal electorate with tales of Turkish atrocities against Orthodox Christians in Bulgaria. But the differences were perhaps more interesting. Gladstone spoke with the imperial confidence of Britain as the pre-eminent power in the world. Blair's moral ambition, on the other hand, was tempered by the political need to coax a coalition of powers into doing the right thing. Gladstone's morality was coloured by anti-Islamic sentiment, while Blair's morality was mobilised in defence of Balkan Muslims against Orthodox Christian persecution.

The next day, mobbed in a refugee camp in Albania, he was welcomed with the arresting placard, 'You lead, we die'. It was not criticism but hero-worship.

Endgame

Towards the end of May, the Russian foreign minister Viktor Chernomyrdin and Finnish president Martti Ahtisaari, as envoys of Russia and the EU, sensed that Milosevic was looking for a form of words to cover his retreat. Clinton immediately raised the stakes, agreeing to send further troops to Kosovo's borders. On 25 May, Nato approved the deployment of 50,000 troops to the region, and Blair used an active verb to describe their role: 'It is important to ensure that we have sufficient ground forces – we will need them on any basis – to do the job of getting the refugees back home.'[26]

It was then sufficient for Clinton merely to make public on 2 June the fact that he would be meeting his joint chiefs of staff the next day to discuss the military options – including ground troops – and Milosevic effectively conceded all Nato's demands. If he thought Chernomyrdin had promised there would be a 'Russian' sector of a partitioned Kosovo, he would be quickly disabused.[27] When the Serbs started to withdraw on 10 June, the bombing campaign was halted, eleven weeks after it began.

Blair was again hailed by the British press as the hero, including 'WHO BLAIRS WINS' headlines in stereo in the mass-market *Sun* and *Mirror*.[28] But he wisely eschewed triumphalism, commenting on the steps of Downing Street: 'We began this air campaign with reluctance but resolve. We end it with no sense of rejoicing.' This was in stark and intentional contrast with Margaret Thatcher's injunction to journalists asking awkward questions about the bloodless recapture of South Georgia at the start of the Falklands War: 'Just rejoice at that news.' Although rejoicing would have been more justified in this instance, it was just as well Blair adopted a plain tone because the next day Nato's victory was coloured by farce when two hundred Russian troops rushed to Pristina airport from nearby Bosnia. Coolness on the part of the British commander, Michael Jackson, in the face of a successfully provoked Wesley Clark, prevented a military embarrassment turning into a disaster, however. The tiny Russian contingent were eventually talked out of their freelance adventure while Nato forces secured the whole province and the refugees started to return.

One of the extraordinary facts about the Kosovo campaign is what little pay-off there was in terms of domestic popularity as a result of Blair's success. Although his stance had been generally supported by the British public, there was no hint of the fierce heat of patriotic pride which so burnished Margaret Thatcher's public image during the Falklands War, because it was not British territory that was at issue, and 'our boys' were not engaged and taking casualties on the ground. His moral certainty which blazed so brightly, and which was vindicated so completely, brought him fifteen minutes of tabloid adulation followed almost immediately by sullen complaints about traffic jams and trains not running on time. An attempt to capitalise on his 'strong leadership' in a party election broadcast for the European Parliament elections on 10 June fell embarrassingly flat. Whereas the 'Falklands factor' produced an instant electoral reward for Thatcher in local elections – and in the Beaconsfield by-election – in May 1982, the Kosovo war had no effect in averting a dismal 28 per cent vote for Labour, 8 points behind the Conservatives, on a profoundly apathetic 23 per cent turnout.

The verdict on the Kosovo conflict remains sharply divided. The war's opponents on left and right simply did not share the moral assumptions on which it was fought. They continued to point to the failures of the post-conflict administration in Kosovo as if they undermined the entire venture. Most of the Serb minority fled and it was difficult to protect the few who were left from the predictable desire for revenge. The critic with the greatest authority was Nelson Mandela, who argued that Nato should have sought to overcome the Russian and Chinese vetoes on the UN Security Council by persuasion: 'Tony Blair is a young man I like very much. But I am resentful about the type of thing that America and Britain are doing. They want now to be the policemen of the world and I'm sorry that Britain has joined the US in this regard.'[29]

Blair's conduct of the Kosovo campaign earned him great respect with many other world leaders, however. He had earned the right to be a full member of their club. Until Kosovo, too, his meetings and phone conversations with Baroness Thatcher had been ceremonial occasions of Disraeli-like flattery for presentational purposes. He hardly needed her advice on the loneliness of leadership, and on the importance of sticking to one's beliefs, but the gravitas of war lent substance to her admiration of him. The armed forces were impressed too. 'He was robust and courageous,' said General Guthrie. 'It was a brave thing to do, because you never quite know where a campaign like that is going to end up. It is not like a theatre script, with people speaking their lines and staying with their part.'

In Kosovo, Blair passed his first real moral test. 'Two thirds of what we do is reprehensible. This isn't the way a normal human being acts,' says the Bill Clinton character, Jack Stanton, at the end of the presidential election campaign in *Primary Colors*. He justifies the necessary compromises of politics by saying that Abraham Lincoln too sold his soul, 'just so he'd get the opportunity, one day, to stand in front of the nation and appeal to "the better angels of our nature"'.[30] Over Kosovo, Blair appealed to the better angels not just of the British electorate's nature, but of that of the whole 'international community'.

Judging that it was one of those moments which justified the compromises, he behaved out of character, risking humiliation for no significant political gain. If it had not been for his insistence that Nato's determination was total and that all military options were open, Milosevic might have succeeded.

Notes

1. Noel Malcolm, *Kosovo*, pp. 329–33.
2. *Ibid.*, p. 349.
3. *Ibid.*, p. 355.

4. Misha Glenny, *The Balkans 1804–1999*, pp. 652–3.
5. Michael Havers, the Attorney General, also 'always attended' but only to advise on international law, not as a full member (Margaret Thatcher, *The Downing Street Years*, p. 189).
6. Thatcher, *The Downing Street Years*, pp. 188–9.
7. Matt Lyus and Peter Hennessy, 'Tony Blair, Past Prime Ministers, Parliament and the Use of Military Force', Paper on Government and Politics No. 113, University of Strathclyde, 1999.
8. *Hansard*, July 1950, quoted in Lyus and Hennessy, *ibid.*
9. *Hansard*, 17 February 1998.
10. *Washington Post*, 21 April 1999.
11. *Hansard*, 16 November 1998.
12. BBC2, *Newsnight*, 20 August 1999.
13. *The Times*, 15 July 1999.
14. BBC2, *Newsnight*, 20 August 1999.
15. Paul Routledge, *Mirror*, 27 September 1999.
16. Speech to European Bank for Reconstruction and Development, London, 19 April 1999.
17. *Observer*, 16 May 1999.
18. Interview, 15 December 1999.
19. Tony Benn, Jeremy Corbyn, Tam Dalyell, George Galloway, Neil Gerrard, John McDonnell, Alice Mahon, Robert Marshall-Andrews, Bill Michie, Alan Simpson, Llew Smith, Robert N. Wareing and Audrey Wise.
20. Thatcher, *The Downing Street Years*, p. 824.
21. Statement in Berlin, 24 March 1999.
22. George Stephanopoulos, *All Too Human*, p. 305.
23. *Ibid.*, p. 309.
24. *Hansard*, 25 March 1999.
25. *Ibid.*, 26 April 1999.
26. *Ibid.*, 26 May 1999.
27. Zbigniew Brzezinski, former US national security adviser, assessed the evidence for a partition plot that went wrong, *Prospect*, November 1999.
28. 4 May 1999.
29. Interview with Anthony Sampson, *Guardian*, 5 April 2000.
30. Anonymous (Joe Klein), *Primary Colors*, p. 364. For a brilliant exposition of how Lincoln produced the 'better angels' phrase in his first inaugural speech by rewriting 'the guardian angels of our nation', the leaden draft provided for him by his Secretary of State William Seward, see Garry Wills, *Lincoln at Gettysburg: The Words That Remade America* (New York: Simon & Schuster, 1992), p. 158.

33

Getting Stuff Done

'Scars in My Back', 6 July 1999

> 'It is far harder to change the way a public service works because it doesn't have the great engine that the market is always creating for change in the private sector.'
>
> —*Tony Blair, 1999*

Blair's ability to adopt a demeanour that would make an audience think he was one of them got him into trouble when he gave a speech to the British Venture Capital Association. Entrepreneurship was something of which he had little first-hand experience, apart from organising some rock concerts and trying to sell Beecham a recipe for lemonade. But, like many full-time politicians, he admired the charisma and risk-taking of successful business people. He sometimes fancifully stretched his experience as a beneficiary of restrictive practices to fit the role of capitalist frontiersman. Soon after he was elected Labour leader, he told a *Panorama* audience that, as a former self-employed barrister, he knew all about economic insecurity.[1] He told the venture capitalists at the London Intercontinental Hotel that he understood the joys of 'being your own boss'.

In his speech, he adjusted a theme derived from Alastair Campbell, the anti-intellectual assault on snobbery, to the purposes of the moment:

> All my political life, Britain was forced to choose between a rather stuffy Tory élite that supported big business but ignored social injustice and a Labour Party that focused on social injustice but regarded wealth creation as inimical to it. Both showed a certain snobbery towards people who had an idea, developed it and went out and made money.

He wanted, he said, to change attitudes in schools so that children 'have the thought put in their minds that you can go out and be entrepreneurs', which put a thought in his mind that he started to develop, putting his text to one side.

> One of the things I would like to do, as well as stimulating more entrepreneurship in the private sector, is to get a bit of it in the public sector as well. People in the public sector are more rooted in the concept that if 'it's always been done this way, it must always be done this way' than any group I have ever come across. You try getting change in the public sector and public services – I bear the scars in my back after two years in government. Heaven knows what it will be like if it is a bit longer.

It was partly a rhetorical flourish to keep his audience nodding along, but partly a flash of real frustration at not being able to get things done. It contradicted directly what he had said a few months earlier in order to get a different audience nodding in agreement, as he handed out Charter Mark awards to public servants:

> In the last twenty-one months, I've met many people across the public sector who are as efficient and entrepreneurial as anyone in the private sector, but also have a sense of public duty that is awe-inspiring. Most of them could be earning far more money in business. But they don't and you don't.
>
> Why not? Because of a commitment to public service. Because helping a five-year-old to read, coaxing a patient out of a coma, convicting a burglar is fulfilling in a way that money can't buy. This country needs its wealth-creators, but it needs its social entrepreneurs as well.[2]

The 'scars in my back' phrase was just too striking, however, to be easily smoothed over. 'I didn't say that,' Blair said on *Newsnight* two weeks later. 'What I said is that the public sector is often very hard to change. I wasn't criticising public sector workers.'[3] But he was: he said 'people in the public sector' were rooted in resistance to change. It was unusual for him to have to backtrack on words. One of his great strengths was the care with which he spoke.

Surprisingly, however, he did not back off the sentiment, lending it an even harder ideological edge in an interview two months later: 'It is far harder to change the way a public service works because it doesn't have the great engine that the market is always creating for change in the private sector. You don't want the health service to be turned into a marketplace, but you've got to look at ways of pioneering change.'[4]

Strong centre

All Prime Ministers want to build a machine around them which will allow them to drive their sleek vision of executive efficiency through the morass of bureaucratic inertia that is modern government. Wilson intended to make Number Ten the 'powerhouse' of his 1964 administration, but it was a tiny-engined contraption to drive change in a government in which power still lay in the departmental baronies.

Although by the time Blair came in the number working in 10 Downing Street, hidden behind the Tardis-like façade, had doubled from seventy at the end of Wilson's first government in 1970, there was a consensus among both John Major's staff in government and Blair's in Opposition that the Prime Minister's office was underpowered. It had the advantages of small size, short lines of communication and flexibility, but the Prime Minister lacked political support and, although its civil servants were Whitehall's cleverest rising stars, as an executive office it had been left behind by the computer revolution.

Blair and his Chief of Staff, Jonathan Powell, moved swiftly in the weeks after the 1997 election to establish a firm political grip on the centre of government. While Cabinet and ministerial appointments were being announced, the engine room in Downing Street was hurriedly stripped and rebuilt. Peter Hennessy, the constitutional historian, has described the process as 'the special adviserdom coming into its kingdom'. Special advisers – that is, political appointees employed by the taxpayer – were only invented by Harold Wilson in March 1974, when they were more honestly called 'political advisers'. Wilson introduced them as an 'experiment' in his second administration in response to the pressure of work on ministers and the narrowness of the backgrounds of the permanent civil service. He wrote:

> The political adviser is an extra pair of hands, ears and eyes and a mind more politically committed and more politically aware than would be available to a minister from the political neutrals in the established civil service. This is particularly true for a radical reforming party in government, since 'neutralism' may easily slip into conservatism with a small 'c'.[5]

Margaret Thatcher restricted Cabinet ministers to one each, but then acquired a handful herself. Under Blair, most Cabinet ministers had two and some had more, but the real expansion occurred in Downing Street, where the new Prime Minister's large personal entourage was translated wholesale to special adviser status.

For two of the most important jobs in Downing Street, the head of the civil service, Sir Robin Butler, insisted on the creation of a new constitutional hybrid, the 'executive special adviser'. Special advisers could only offer advice and could not issue instructions to civil servants, so Butler suggested at a meeting in Blair's house in Islington in early 1997 that Jonathan Powell and Alastair Campbell should have special contracts giving them executive authority. This was achieved by means of orders being passed by the Privy Council, now a largely honorific body.

Butler's insistence on formal proprieties added to Blair's impatience with him, and he was due to retire within nine months of the election. What had not been decided before the election was Powell's precise role and title in government. Butler was determined to preserve the civil service's control of the linchpin role in Downing Street, that of Prime Minister's principal private secretary. Butler thought Blair wanted Powell to have the job. As obstructive as the Sir Humphrey caricature, he insisted that the role, central to power and status of the Whitehall mandarinate, could not be carried out by a party-political fixer. After all, the principal private secretary dealt with the Palace and advised the monarch in the event of hung parliaments. In their pre-election discussions it had been agreed that when John Major's principal private secretary, Alex Allan, moved on, as he was due to do that summer, the title would be taken by John Holmes, the Prime Minister's foreign affairs private secretary. Powell may have coveted the title which had been held by his brother Charles under Thatcher, but he would have quickly realised, and his brother would have been able to confirm, that the title did not matter so much as a personal relationship with the Prime Minister and physical proximity to him. He continued, therefore, to be called Chief of Staff.

As a result, the new more political staff at Number Ten were headed by a triumvirate, two of whom were political appointments. Where previous Prime Ministers had one civil service bureaucrat at their elbow, Blair had three – Campbell, Powell and the principal private secretary, Holmes, and all of them attended Cabinet and Cabinet committees.

In Opposition, Peter Mandelson had spent some time thinking about how to translate the 'unitary command structure' of New Labour into government. In his book, *The Blair Revolution*, written with Roger Liddle in 1996, he set out a plan for the Cabinet Office to be strengthened as a Prime Minister's Department. Technically, the Cabinet Office, which backs onto Number Ten and has a connecting door, existed to support the Cabinet as a whole. When he was appointed Minister Without Portfolio, based at the Cabinet Office but answerable to the Prime Minister rather than to his Cabinet minister, David Clark, Mandelson redefined its role as being 'to support the Prime Minister'.[6] Later on, Blair reinforced the Cabinet Office, describing it 'as the corporate headquarters of the civil service'.[7] There was no need to add to accusations of a presidential style of government by renaming it the Prime Minister's Department.

Staff numbers at Number Ten quickly rose by more than half, from 130 before the election to 199 in the mid-term, twenty-five of whom were special advisers.[8] The Policy Unit, another Wilsonian innovation, was expanded under David Miliband – whom Blair had appointed at the age of twenty-nine as his head of policy the day after he became Labour leader. The press office, under the strong political management of Alastair Campbell, was reinforced at the end of 1997 by the setting up of a Strategic Communications Unit. The Political Office, created by Marcia Williams in Wilson's first government in order to fight the 1966 election when Labour scraped in with a majority of five in 1964, was headed by Sally Morgan, who had overseen the partially-successful attempts to secure last-minute selections of Blairite Labour candidates in safe seats before the election.

Marcia Williams had been called the Prime Minister's Political and Personal Secretary, because the civil service had once again jealously protected the 'private secretary' title which she had held in Opposition. 'I accepted the new title reluctantly,' she said.[9] The 'personal' half of her role was now taken by Anji Hunter, who adopted the American-sounding title of Special Assistant to the Prime Minister. Although Powell's power grew as the election approached, Hunter had remained the guardian of Blair's personal space. She was, in American parlance, closest to The Body. She organised Blair's schedule, decided who went in which car, and often decided whom he had time to see and whom he did not. In government, her role changed, just as Williams had found Wilson's diary was taken over by the civil service machine. But Hunter remained a trusted and loyal adviser who could act as the Prime Minister's personal eyes and ears.

The eclipse of the civil service 'private secretarydom' was confirmed after a year in government when the geography of power in Downing Street was re-arranged over Easter 1998. Blair moved from the 'den' by the side of the Cabinet room to the grander office at one end. It had been the 'inner private office' occupied by Jonathan Powell and the principal private secretary, both of whom now moved into the 'outer private office', with the economic affairs private secretary, while the rest of the 'outer' private secretaries were pushed upstairs, next door to Hunter.[10] Thus all but two private secretaries were further away from The Body, while special advisers crowded closer in: the 'den' which Blair had vacated was taken by Miliband.

Meanwhile, the Prime Minister began to feel the difficulty of imposing his will beyond Downing Street. In an early hint of his 'scars in my back' complaint, he said, after just nine months in office: 'One of the most frustrating things about coming into government is the time it takes to get stuff moving through the system.'[11]

The business model of government

Blair not only admired business people, he also adopted a lot of their management-speak. John Browne, the chief executive of BP, had challenged him to approach government like a business, setting out his 'performance contract' for his customers. This Blair did in his 1996 Labour Party conference speech, making his ten vows and inviting the voters to judge him on his fulfilment of them. As part of the trust-building exercise before the election, all 177 manifesto promises were underwritten with the same contractual language.

It was largely a public relations exercise, as Blair underestimated the extent to which it would create hostages to fortune. It was also partly designed to insulate the government from pressures within the Labour Party for more spending. He stuck to the contractual model in government, however, bringing in performance agreements between departments and 'the centre' and presenting an annual report to the 'customers', the electorate. Introducing the first annual report on 30 July 1998 in the garden of Number Ten in front of the 'senior staff' of ministers and civil servants, the Prime Minister declared that changing a government 'is like sweeping away the entire management of a company'.

Having strengthened Number Ten, Blair then moved to enforce its power over Whitehall departments, particularly after Sir Robin Butler was replaced as Cabinet Secretary by Sir Richard Wilson in January 1998. Sir Robin, who had served under Margaret Thatcher, noticed that Blair operated differently:

> It's a great contrast with Margaret Thatcher. Tony Blair would be very happy to say, 'Look, this is where I want to get to in a year's time, you boys go off and deliver it for me and really don't bother me more than you have to with the details.' Margaret Thatcher would absolutely be worrying about the details the whole time, too much.[12]

Blair had learnt to delegate from an early mistake in Opposition. He was frustrated when Jack Straw found himself unexpectedly trashed by Michael Howard in a debate on prisons policy on 10 October 1995. He tried prompting Straw against his old opponent and on his old turf, but Howard noticed and challenged him to stand up and speak himself, which he foolishly did, humiliating Straw and conspicuously failing to land a punch himself.

Blair delegated details, but wanted to keep a tight grip on the big picture. Like a chief executive setting targets for his subsidiaries, Blair introduced a new system of targets which would be agreed between departments and 'the centre'.* Instead of conducting business at Cabinet or even Cabinet committees, he did an unusual amount of business in 'bilaterals' – two-sided meetings with his secretaries of state. If he were the chief executive, however, he had to deal with an over-mighty finance department. In an unacknowledged tussle with the Treasury – whose boss thought of himself as chief executive under 'chairman' Blair – the Prime Minister set up a new unit, the Performance and Innovation Unit, to monitor departments and deal with inter-departmental issues. As both those functions had traditionally been the Treasury's, the PIU could be seen as an instrument of asserting Number Ten's control. Or, as Blair put it, 'It will complement the Treasury's role in monitoring departmental programmes.'[13]

New technology offered scope for closer, faster and more precise monitoring than in the past. The Internet revolution had been one of the trends which for all Blair's white-heat futurology he had underestimated in Opposition. Despite being personally 'virtually phobic' about computers, he nevertheless presided over a step change in their use in Downing Street, at a time when government as a whole was rapidly going on-line. 'One of the things I used to have to do was I had to wait for all the telegrams from all the foreign embassies round the world to come into me and I'd read them,' he told GMTV in a live broadcast from his office in Number Ten on 6 December 1999. 'But we have a thing now you can just call up on the computer and you get into them all that way.' His well-advertised phobia was partly for the purposes of encouraging people to learn computer skills, although he continued to prefer to draft things in fountain pen.

Despite these changes, it still proved difficult to obtain the sort of differences on the ground that the voters would notice. 'If there is one thing I have learnt in government, it is how long it takes to get things done,' he told Labour Party members in January 2000. Three of the five central promises (once described as 'early' pledges) turned out to be heavy going in practice: cutting health service waiting lists, limiting infant class sizes and speeding up sentencing for persistent young offenders.† ('No increase in income tax rates' took care of itself, while the buoyant economy took care of the 250,000 young people who had to be moved off benefit and into work.)

---

*Blair described 'the three principal parts of the centre' as 'my own office, the Cabinet Office and the Treasury', *Hansard*, 28 July 1998.

†When Jack Straw first discussed the target with Home Office civil servants after the election, one of them, inadvertently slipping into Sir Humphrey caricature, described it as 'interesting' before hastily adding: 'But we'll do it, we'll do it.'

Whereas Blair did not get as involved in the detail of delivery as Thatcher, there were few enough of these pledges for him to devote his attention fully to them. For the other 172 manifesto promises, however, he was forced to rely on his Cabinet ministers to deliver.

The end of Cabinet government

Blair's management style ushered in a new low in the history of Cabinet government in Britain. That style was 'hub and spoke' rather than collegiate, reducing most meetings of the Cabinet to just forty minutes of approving decisions already taken elsewhere, parish notices and short speeches either delivered by the Prime Minister or vetted by him in advance. The usual agenda for Cabinet meetings was 'stunningly unrevealing', according to the doyen of constitutional historians, Peter Hennessy, consisting only of three regular items, Next Week's Business in Parliament, Domestic and Economic Affairs, and Foreign Affairs (for the first two years there was a fourth, 'Europe', which was subsumed in the second and third items from mid-1999), and an attachment known in New Labour language as The Grid – a plan drawn up by the Strategic Communications Unit of events and ministerial announcements for the coming week.[14]

The trend away from the Cabinet as a decision-making forum had been evident for most of the twentieth century, however. Lloyd George and Chamberlain virtually dispensed with Cabinet meetings in their time and Thatcher famously asserted the primacy of an office which had long ceased to be 'first among equals'. Nigel Lawson said of his period as her Chancellor: 'I used to look forward to Cabinet meetings as the most restful and relaxing event of the week.'[15]

It was not surprising, therefore, that Blair's Cabinet rarely engaged in meaningful debate about policy. Nevertheless, the list of critical decisions not even reported to Cabinet is startling, beginning with independence for the Bank of England, the postponement of joining the euro, the cut in lone-parent benefit and the deal on the future of hereditary peers. There was a 'discussion' of welfare reform at Cabinet on 18 December 1997, but only *after* the revolt on lone-parent benefit. And when some issues were debated at Cabinet, such as the Millennium Dome, a decision was railroaded through against the majority view. But even this was not new: Wilson would not let his Cabinet discuss devaluation and Thatcher bounced the Westland decision through when Michael Heseltine might have mustered a majority against her.

Cabinet government was not dead, of course; it was only sleeping. It could clearly reassert itself if the Prime Minister's authority and popularity slipped, as it did over Thatcher in 1990. As a body, the Cabinet's authority derived from its potential power – of two kinds: its power to block the Prime Minister and its power to influence the choice of successor. This second power was greater in a Labour Cabinet than a Conservative one, where the choice of John Major over Michael Heseltine had been decided by Conservative MPs as a whole. Under Labour Party rules, in the case of a sudden vacancy the Cabinet would choose an interim leader and therefore Prime Minister until a full leadership election could be held.*

The power of a Prime Minister, on the other hand, is more immediate and more continuously used. Notionally, a Prime Minister has no executive authority in domestic policy, except the power of appointing and sacking the ministers who carry it out. Blair used that power sparingly but without sentiment. He allowed himself to be bound by one of the rules thrown up by the Bennite revolution, which required an incoming Labour Prime Minister to translate the entire shadow Cabinet, elected by Labour MPs, into the real thing. The rule had become unsustainable, as there were by 1997 more members of the shadow Cabinet than the twenty-two places available in government. Blair wielded the knife with restraint. Out went Derek Foster, his parliamentary neighbour in Bishop Auckland. In order to allow Blair to tighten discipline by choosing his own Chief Whip, Foster had given up the post, to which he was elected by Labour MPs, in July 1995 in return for what he thought was the promise of a Cabinet job. Out, too, went Michael Meacher, never respected by the modernisers, who accepted a job as environment minister outside Cabinet with good grace and went on to make a modest success of it. And out went Tom Clarke, spokesman on disabled rights, who served for a year as Minister of State in the Department of Culture, Media and Sport. But Blair did not take advantage of the surplus to dispense with the rule altogether and make wider changes.

In his first reshuffle, in July 1998, he brought Peter Mandelson into the Cabinet, conspicuously curbed Gordon Brown's supporters, and sacked Harriet Harman, a close personal friend of nearly twenty years' standing. Thatcher claimed to hate sacking people, and sometimes put off doing it longer than was politically expedient, while John Major became well-known for failing to sack ministers such as David Mellor and Norman Lamont long after their best-before dates. Alastair Campbell has described the Blair style of termination:

---

*See p. 387.

> He knows he must do it, and he tries to be tactful . . . I have been with him when he has sacked people, and he even has a charming way of doing it, being aware of the impact he's having. But then, you know – I wouldn't necessarily want to see this in print with my name to it – once he's out of the room, he's on to the next thing.[16]

According to John Garrett, one of the ministers sacked in the next reshuffle in July 1999, Blair's style was one of clichéd banality: 'I'm going to have to let you go.' Blair said something about making way for a younger generation and asked, 'Do you mind if I ask you how old you are?' When Garrett, taken aback, told him he was sixty-seven, Blair said: 'You look brilliant for your age.'

That reshuffle was mishandled because the only change at Cabinet level was to bring in Paul Murphy to replace Alun Michael as Secretary of State for Wales. Inevitably dubbed 'The Night of the Short Knives', it succeeded in offending John Prescott, Mo Mowlam, Margaret Beckett, Frank Dobson and Jack Cunningham, all of whom had to endure press speculation about their futures which, in all but the first case, proved well-founded when the real reshuffle took place in October (Mowlam and Beckett were moved against their will, Dobson was out and Cunningham sacked). The problem was largely one of timing, with unfilled vacancies for Nato Secretary-General and Labour's London mayoral candidate holding up the sequence. The Nato decision to appoint George Robertson, the Defence Secretary, came the day after the reshuffle, while Dobson did not finally bow to pressure to fight the doomed fight until the beginning of October. However, on Harold Wilson's dictum that you make twenty enemies every time you sack someone – the victim and nineteen people who think they should have got the job – Blair minimised the damage.

If Cabinet was not the locus of decision-making, however, this was not because Blair had an alternative centre of power, an informal kitchen cabinet of associates. Although in the political and physical geography of power Alastair Campbell and Jonathan Powell were closest to him, there was no cohesive inner group of trusted courtiers. The model often used of concentric circles around Blair of people arranged in diminishing tiers of influence is not useful, because all of his key relationships were with individuals rather than groups. Ranking them in order of influence is also an imprecise science, because different relationships mattered at different times and in any case served different purposes which cannot easily be compared. But if there were, as Derek Draper suggested plucking a number at random, 'seventeen people who count', they were by mid-2000: Tony Blair, Gordon Brown, Alastair Campbell, Peter Mandelson,

Ed Balls (Brown's economic adviser), Anji Hunter, David Miliband, Derry Irvine, Jonathan Powell, Charles Falconer, Cherie Booth, Philip Gould, David Blunkett, Alan Milburn, John Prescott, Richard Wilson and Jeremy Heywood (Blair's principal private secretary).

Some Cabinet ministers were central to Blair's government. The relationship with Gordon Brown, however flawed, was the main one, underpinning the basic strategy of taxing, spending and economic management. David Blunkett was trusted to deliver the government's avowed priority of raising educational standards. Alan Milburn, appointed Health Secretary in the October 1999 reshuffle, quickly gained Blair's respect in delivering a second vital public service.

Others had different kinds of relationship. Peter Mandelson was Blair's envoy in overseeing the concluding stages of the Good Friday Agreement in Northern Ireland, but he retained his role as 'Bobby', Blair's personal counsellor and Brown's rival. Derry Irvine's influence declined as the pressures of government crowded in, especially after devolution and House of Lords reform were dealt with.[17]

John Prescott was absorbed in his sprawling department, most of whose policy areas concerned Blair only sporadically, but he was one of the seventeen by virtue of his independent power base in the Labour Party as deputy leader.*

Robin Cook's position as chairman of the party's National Policy Forum did not give him the same leverage. His adoption of euro-enthusiasm, siding with Blair against Brown's perceived scepticism, was less an indicator of his influence than the lack of it. Blair handled most of these relationships adroitly. Mandelson had once offered his unguarded 'personal insight' into how Blair 'manages to combine firmness and clarity with the political skills that make such diverse individuals as John Prescott and Robin Cook *believe they are valued*'.[18] Although Blair's ability to distance himself from the dirtier business of politics began to wear thin when ministers complained that 'teenyboppers' in Downing Street (Prescott's phrase) were undermining their good work, the Prime Minister himself smiled sweetly and looked blank.

Outside the Cabinet, the only minister with a close personal relationship with Blair was Charles Falconer, who had taken over Mandelson's role as his progress-chaser on Cabinet committees – and as impresario for the Millennium Dome. Falconer's progress-chasing role was like a spooling programme on a computer, to work in the background on things the

*Blair could sack him as Deputy Prime Minister but not as deputy leader of the Labour Party, an elected post which gave him the right to sit on the party's National Executive.

Prime Minister could not focus on immediately. He described his role thus: 'Politicians tend to concentrate on one thing at a time. My concern is with things which are not presently in the foreground.'

Although a lot of the business of government continued to be done in Cabinet committees, the key decisions tended to be 'bilateral', between Blair himself and key ministers. The only other people, therefore, with access to the full picture, the Blair's eye view of government and the world, were Campbell, Powell and the apex of the civil service, John Holmes and then Jeremy Heywood, successive principal private secretaries, with Sir Richard Wilson usually one step back from the fray. Holmes played an important role in the negotiations leading to the Good Friday Agreement in Northern Ireland, before moving on to Lisbon as ambassador to Portugal. The Blairs stayed with him on a short holiday in January 2000, and Cherie took a break there with her mother Gale and baby Leo when Euan was arrested after celebrating the end of his exams in July 2000. He was succeeded by Heywood, the economic affairs private secretary, in February 1999. Heywood had been Norman Lamont's private secretary as Chancellor before the 1992 election, when he was credited with the plan for a new 20p starting rate of income tax which destroyed the credibility of John Smith's shadow budget. He was in post when the pound was forced out of the European Exchange Rate Mechanism later that year, so had close and bruising experience of the issue of monetary union.

Although Blair's style was more informal than that of his predecessors, only two of his most important advisers were not incorporated into the official structure. Apart from being paid by the Labour Party for his focus group research, Philip Gould had no official status at all, although it was common enough for prime ministers to rely as heavily, or more so, on free-floating advisers. Finally, there was Cherie, who held the quasi-constitutional role of Prime Minister's spouse and acquired an office in her own name in Downing Street, but whose advice was most informal, and most unknowable, of all.

Managerialism

The centre of government was more of a 'unitary command structure' (Philip Gould's phrase describing the pre-election Labour Party organisational model) than at any time since the war. But the sources of policy advice had also been diffused out beyond the former Whitehall baronies to a network of temporary task forces.

Despite Blair's declaration in his pre-election party conference speech that he would put 'the quango-state in history's dustbin where it belongs', his new government set up new task forces and advisory groups at the rate of more than two per day for several months from early May 1997. By the end of 1998, there were 295 of them, with nearly 2,500 members.[19] They included the Cowboy Builders Working Group, the Creative Industries Task Force, the Hedgerows Regulations Review Group, the Leylandii Working Group and the Review of the List of Nationally Important Sporting Events Which Must be Made Available on Free-to-Air Terrestrial TV Channels. The spread of the term task force was an intriguing linguistic development from the military use, made most famous in politics by the one sent to the Falkland Islands in 1982.

It was easy to be cynical about the roll-call of nearly everyone who thought they were important who were recruited to sit on these bodies. Ken Follett on literacy; Michael Brunson on citizenship; Richard Branson, Paul Smith and Alan McGee on creative industries; David Puttnam on school standards; David Mellor on football; Terence Conran on competitiveness; Bill Morris and Rodney Bickerstaffe on welfare-to-work; Greg Dyke on the health service; John Birt on crime.

But the author of the fullest independent study of the 'task force revolution', Anthony Barker, concluded that 'task forces do create a more inclusive and focused advice-gathering process than previous practice'. He was careful to distinguish between the new, informal and short-lived bodies and executive quangos (quasi-autonomous national government organisations) charged with dispensing public money, which had been the main target of Labour attacks while in Opposition. The task forces usually reported and then disbanded, and only a handful (twelve by November 1999) were made permanent and became, formally, advisory quangos, subject to the ethical rules of the Committee on Standards in Public Life. Barker thought that the charge of Labour 'cronyism' was 'not . . . justified by current practice'.[20] One explanation for the growth of task forces was the spending constraint on the new government in its first two years, which meant that setting up reviews was the main way of appearing to be doing something about interest group concerns.

Politically, there was a price to pay for the strong element of tokenism in the exercise. Alan McGee, discoverer of Oasis and donor of over £100,000 to the Labour Party before the election, was furious when the government paid no attention to his views, as a former addict, on drugs: 'Looking back, I can now see that I wasn't really there to provide advice or expertise. It was much more important that I was there in the right photographs.'[21]

The business model of government worked reasonably well, however, as Blair combined the preachy character of the marketing front man with the smart-casual style of the breezily dynamic managing director of a medium-sized German manufacturing company. Running government by targets was criticised on two counts. One was that it was bound to distort priorities, as the class-size and waiting-list pledges had done in education and health, although the answer to that was to choose better targets. The other was a political criticism, that some targets, especially genuinely challenging ones that would impress commentators and voters, were bound to be missed and this failure would then be used against the government. But, as any business handbook would say, setting targets is essential, because it focuses managers on clear objectives. If targets are missed, managers are forced to explain why – and either the target can be changed or the manager.

However, against Blair's obsessive ticking-off of manifesto promises, and his insistence that, 'trust matters; in all walks of life, people act as consumers, not just citizens', his attempts to gloss some of the promises smacked of the sharper end of commercial practice.[22] The referendum on electoral reform was postponed; tobacco advertising was not completely banned; some hereditary peers were allowed to stay in the Lords. None of these would have mattered much if fulfilling every dot and comma of the manifesto had not been made such an article of faith.

The managerial approach also risked a lack of clear direction and a tendency to strain for rhetorical effect when dealing with second-order issues. On subjects such as genetically-modified food there was a conflict between Blair's technocratic reasonableness and simple populism. He was caught flat-footed on the issue by William Hague at Prime Minister's Questions, on 3 February 1999: he chose reasonableness and was rewarded with a *Mirror* front page portraying him as Frankenstein's creation headlined 'PRIME MONSTER' two weeks later. His cast of mind had been set by the beguiling economic promise of biotechnology which, until overtaken by the hype of the Internet, had been a 'white heat' hope of Britain's future. But the questions refused to go away: whether farm trials of genetically-modified crops would cross-pollinate unmodified crops, when commercial growing might be allowed and how genetically-modified ingredients could be identified to keep them out of food sold as non-GM. He condemned media 'hysteria' over the issue at Cabinet on 27 May, but Prince Charles repeated his view that genetic modification 'takes mankind into realms that belong to God, and to God alone'.[23] The 'Prime Monster' was undermined by doubts closer to home, as it was reported (and not denied) that Cherie had expressed her reservations. He now adjusted his approach and declared he had an 'open mind' about the risks.[24]

The real test of Blair's ability to deliver change was in the two public services central to New Labour's attempt to reclaim the case for state spending by modernisation. Education had been central from the start, but, until the winter of 1999, the health service had been neglected.

Winter frost

It would be going too far to suggest that the names of Mavis Skeet and Robert Winston will go down in history as having saved the National Health Service, alongside that of Aneurin Bevan who founded it. The Labour government would have increased health spending anyway, but they pushed Blair into making an earlier and possibly more extravagant commitment than he intended. Mrs Skeet's throat cancer operation was postponed four times and in the second week of January 2000 it was declared inoperable (she died six months later). It was the sort of individual tragedy which the Labour Party had used in the past to condemn Conservative stewardship of the NHS. Her operation had been cancelled because all the intensive care beds in Leeds General Infirmary were taken by 'flu patients, underlining the gravity of the winter crisis and reinforcing perceptions that nothing had changed in the health service since the new government took over.

Then Professor Winston, the fertility doctor and Labour supporter raised to the peerage by Blair, provided an expert second opinion to back up this view, saying Labour had been 'deceitful' over NHS reform and that the quality of care was deteriorating.[25] It was one of the more serious moments of Blair's government so far: the Prime Minister himself would have to be seen to respond. He was due to appear on BBC1's *Breakfast With Frost* that Sunday, 16 January, and the urgent need was to announce large amounts of new money for the NHS. This led to some rough handling between Numbers Ten and Eleven Downing Street, and between Blair and Brown personally in their discussions on Saturday: the broad outline of future spending plans had been agreed the previous autumn, but the precise figures had not been finalised.

In the interview with David Frost, Blair took responsibility for the case of Mrs Skeet, explained that 'substantial extra resources' were going into the health service that year and the next (which was true),[26] but said it would take time to turn it round. He held out the hope that, 'if we run the economy properly', health spending would rise by 'almost 5 per cent' a year in real terms for the three years after next year. But the figures did not mean much to most viewers: he needed an easily understood indicator which could persuade people that Labour really would make a difference to the NHS over time. If those increases could be achieved, he went on, 'then at the end of that five years [2003/04] we will be in a position where our health service spending comes up to the average of the European Union. It's too low at the moment, so we'll bring it up to there.'

To set a target in relation to other EU countries was unprecedented. Brown was unhappy about it for three reasons. First, he did not want his Spending Review, not due to be announced for another six months, so inescapably pre-empted: such a large pledge severely curtailed his room for manoeuvre in other areas of spending. Secondly, accepting a European comparator could set a precedent for other spending bids. Thirdly, the arithmetic on which it rested had a back-of-envelope feel.

The most recent 'official' figure for average EU health spending, 1997, was 8 per cent of national income, as against 6.9 per cent for the UK.[27] After Downing Street confirmed that these were the figures on which the Prime Minister's calculation was based, defects in the way this figure was calculated were pointed out, suggesting that a more meaningful EU average would be significantly higher.[28] In a way, that did not matter: the EU comparison was simply a way of dramatising a target. The important point was that spending would have to rise by at least one third in real terms over five years in order to meet it.[29]

As it was, the 8 per cent figure turned out to be on the edge of the possible. Brown was forced to bring forward the plans for health spending, announcing them in his March Budget instead of the July Spending Review. Once the Treasury had been through the numbers properly, the best that could be achieved was 7.6 per cent of national income, including private spending, by 2003/04. That could be rounded up to 8 per cent, but depended on a number of factors outside the government's control.

Nor was the increase quite as unprecedented as Blair claimed. In his statement in the Commons after the Budget he described it as 'the biggest sustained investment for the health service'.[30] Spending over the five years from 1971 to 1976 had in fact risen slightly faster. However, the plans for the five years from 1999 still represented a huge and prolonged increase in spending, and a profound shift in policy compared to the previous twenty years.[31]

On Roy Jenkins's 'lighthouse' principle – that a Prime Minister can only shine the rotating beam of his or her attention on one issue at a time – it was only now that Blair focused on the reforms needed to translate higher spending into better health care. In March 2000 he set up a Cabinet committee on Health Performance and Expenditure (called PHX) chaired by him 'to agree and monitor the standards of service and improvements that people can expect by the end of the financial year

2003/04', and began work with Alan Milburn, who had replaced Frank Dobson as Health Secretary in October 1999, on the 'NHS Plan' to be published in July.

Although Dobson was considered unexpectedly successful, and managed to get the NHS through the two lean spending years without political damage, organisationally his time had been dominated by the struggle to deliver the pledge to cut waiting lists. They were not the best target or indicator of performance: as the Conservatives found, the faster the barrel was emptied at the bottom, the faster the water went in at the top. Blair admitted towards the end of the first year in government, when numbers had risen: 'Waiting lists have proved to be the hardest pledge on which to make quick progress.'[32] But progress was made and it became possible to shift attention to more meaningful targets.

It was not until Milburn arrived, however, that the aggressive case for modernisation started to be made. Milburn was a subtle political operator who, like other ambitious newcomers (he was only elected MP for Darlington, next door to Sedgefield, in 1992) hitched his career wagon jointly to Brown and Blair. He started by restating the case for the NHS as a tax-funded state-run service free at the point of need. Blair declared: 'It is a fantastically liberating thought that you can get your health care irrespective of your ability to pay. But the practice on the ground has got to match the elevated nature of that principle.'[33] This marked the rejection of the fashionable 'bottomless pit' view of health service demands on public cash, which often prompted vague musings about 'radical' reforms of funding and delivery. That radicalism had been tested to destruction by Margaret Thatcher's review of the NHS, which had reluctantly ended up at Milburn's starting point. The Thatcher review produced the internal market as a mechanism for greater efficiency, but not the money to keep up with popular expectations. The Milburn–Blair approach was to combine organisational change with extra resources.

The 'radicalism' of their approach was confined, therefore, to innovations of management and delivery within an expanding public service. NHS Direct was announced – by Milburn, then a junior health minister, in an article in the *Sun* – in December 1997, as a limited pilot scheme starting in March 1998.[34] It slowly emerged as a harbinger of a stealthy revolution.*

When the NHS Plan was unveiled on 27 July 2000, it combined the

*Not without setbacks: in February 2000 it was embarrassed by a report that staff pretended to be answering machines, intoning, 'Please try later', when overwhelmed as a result of a computer problem.

language of state planning – made more credible by the computer revolution – with commercial management jargon. It contained targets for everything, and, instead of the internal market, a system of 'earned autonomy' by which high-performing units would be left to manage themselves while the centre would intervene in low performers. Only in one small respect did it adopt a radical Third Way, egalitarian in ends but pragmatic about means, and that was the promise that, by 2004, if an operation were cancelled and could not be carried out within twenty-eight days, the NHS would pay for it to be done in the private sector. Even this move had been resisted by Frank Dobson, whose hostility to private medicine ran deep.

The slowness of achieving change in such a large, complex organisation was illustrated by the target for getting rid of 95 per cent of mixed-sex wards by 2002 – total abolition had been a promise made and betrayed years before by the Major government. The main constraint on delivery would of course be staff numbers and the time it took to train new nurses and doctors. One of the main weaknesses of the NHS was the low numbers of doctors per head of population compared with other EU countries. But the delegation of less-skilled tasks down the chain from doctors to nurses to ancillary staff could produce more immediate improvements. Central to the NHS Plan, therefore, was that it had been drawn up in intensive – and this time genuine – consultation with health staff, most of whose professional bodies signed the statement of principles at the start of it.

The revitalising of the health service could be an historic achievement of Blair's second term, although the slow speed of change may mean that the electoral dividends are limited. What the Prime Minister had achieved by seizing control of the Treasury's spending plans on the Frost programme in January 2000 was to lead the charge in reversing the terms of political trade on public spending. Where he and Gordon Brown had gone into the 1997 election accepting Conservative spending cuts and, by implication, the tax-cutting ambitions that went with them, the tables had now been turned. By the summer of 2000, when Labour's spending plans beyond the next election were set out, Blair started to look happier at Prime Minister's Questions, taunting the Tories about where the spending cuts implied by their tax promises would fall. This prompted Michael Portillo, the shadow Chancellor, on 12 July 2000 to force William Hague to abandon his 'tax guarantee' which promised that taxes would be cut as a share of national income whatever the circumstances.

The change in the political weather was illustrated when *The Economist*, once the house journal of the neo-liberal right, complained after the

July Spending Review that two years of squeeze followed by five of plenty was 'no way to conduct an investment programme'.[35] This was almost identical to the complaint from the left that, by sticking to Tory spending plans for two years, the government had lost valuable time in rebuilding public services, and equally ignored the politics of the situation before the 1997 election in which the pledge had been made.

Although there may have been friction between Blair and Brown over the timing and calibration of the health spending pledge, and Blair's aggressive identification of himself with it (recalling the phrase from the leaked Touchstone Issues memo written in April 2000, 'I should be personally associated with as much of this as possible'), they remained joint architects of the strategy. It was set to ensure that they would fight the next election on the centre-left ground of their own choosing.

Sofa politics

On the surface, Blair's way of working as Prime Minister was more informal than any of his predecessors. Where John Major held most of his meetings in the Cabinet room, Blair always had his in his study. He also did more business at Chequers than his predecessors. Weekends at the Prime Minister's country home would generally produce rough jottings of his thoughts for the coming week which would be faxed to Anji Hunter and Alastair Campbell. Hunter's husband, Nick Cornwall, would announce the arrival of the fax with an irreverent, 'Here comes your Sunday night stream of consciousness.' The notes would form the backbone of the agenda for the start-of-week meeting in Downing Street.

Blair had scribbled notes to himself for some time. 'I go back and write it down all the time, just for myself. I write notes on how these things must be achieved,' he said just before the 1997 election.[36] Alastair Campbell gave an impromptu idea of the form of the 'Sunday night stream of consciousness'. At the time, in early 2000, it would say something like, he said:

> Spain – where are we on this? Foreign policy – AC speak to me. Northern Ireland – I'm really worried about this, Trimble needs shoring up. Adoption – why does it take six months before a couple gets to know the result of something? Business – three times last week people were complaining to me about too much regulation; do we have a grip on this? London mayor – when should I go and do something?[37]

Blair had always shown a remarkable ability to focus intently on an issue for a short time, absorb the important points and move on. His mental style was well suited to the modern premiership, in which the most precious resource is the Prime Minister's time. 'The reality is different from anything that you might have anticipated,' he told Robert Harris. 'The reality is more intense and more endless, even though in theory you would have anticipated that it would indeed be intense and relentless.'[38]

There was a telling vignette of Blair's lifestyle in January 1999 after Peter Mandelson's resignation from the Cabinet, when Blair decided the reshuffle of the junior ministerial ranks on a satellite phone in a dinghy off the coast of the Seychelles, where he and his family were supposed to be on holiday – he had gone further offshore from his hired yacht to get a better reception.*

That intensity, however, partly reflected Blair's own energy and desire for control. If he had wanted to, he could, like Churchill in his second term, have taken naps in the afternoon, or, like Macmillan, have read Jane Austen. The civil service and political machine would have filled the gaps.

One of the members of the Downing Street Policy Unit, Andrew Adonis, was asked if he thought Blair worked harder than Gladstone:

> He does different things. Lots of time on planes, in meetings and doing media interviews – but little time in the House of Commons and virtually no debating. [He] also has a staff, where Mr G had two private secretaries. But that doesn't affect my point – that the weight of the premiership is no heavier than in the past, and that the difference between prime ministers lies in personal temperament and ambition, not the weight of the office *per se*.[39]

Blair was a control-freak, driven Prime Minister, operating a 'command premiership'. But again this was not exceptional. This century Chamberlain, Heath and Thatcher all operated a similar centralised style. Even Major's promise of a more collegiate style was increasingly belied by the reality of a hyperactive and engaged Prime Minister.

'Command premierships have a terrible tendency to end in tears,' Peter Hennessy observed to a Conservative who had resigned from Mrs Thatcher's Cabinet, as they considered the style of a Blair government.

'Yes, but you can get away with it for a very long time,' came the reply.[40]

*The reshuffle had to wait while he 'rescued' a Danish tourist swimmer who had been taken about 1km out to sea by the currents. Unfortunately this everyday tale of prime ministerial heroism unravelled when the swimmer, Hans Joergensen, said that he had not been drowning but waving, that he had hitched a lift because he was 'lazy', and that the idea that Blair had saved his life was 'absurd and ridiculous'.

Notes

1. BBC1, *Panorama*, 3 October 1994.
2. Speech at Charter Mark Awards, Methodist Central Hall, London, 26 January 1999.
3. BBC2, *Newsnight*, 19 July 1999.
4. Andrew Rawnsley, *Observer*, 5 September 1999.
5. 'The "Political Advisers" Experiment', statement to the Commonwealth Heads of Government conference, Jamaica, May 1975, reproduced in Harold Wilson, *The Governance of Britain*, pp. 202–5.
6. Speech, 16 September 1997.
7. *Hansard*, 28 July 1998.
8. Charles Falconer, Cabinet Office minister, Lords *Hansard*, 13 December 1999. The Foreign Office in Whitehall at the zenith of the Empire in the mid-nineteenth century had a staff of forty-five.
9. Letter to the *New Statesman*, 25 October 1996. It was Williams, now Baroness Falkender, who first described Blair as 'a control freak', in the run-up to the 1997 election, when she enviously contrasted Wilson's private office in Opposition (consisting of her and two typists) with Blair's huge personal apparat, funded by taxpayers' money and the Labour Leader's Office Fund (interview, Ben Pimlott, *Sunday Times*, 3 November 1996).
10. See Dennis Kavanagh and Anthony Seldon, *The Powers Behind the Prime Minister*, pp. 11, 260.
11. Question and answer session on poverty, Sheffield, part of the welfare reform 'roadshow', 30 January 1998.
12. Interview with Donald Macintyre, 1998.
13. *Hansard*, 28 July 1998.
14. Peter Hennessy, 'The Blair Style', lecture at the University of Exeter, 8 May 2000.
15. Nigel Lawson, *The View from No. 11*, p. 125.
16. Warren Hoge, *New York Times Magazine*, 14 May 2000.
17. Irvine's replacement by Margaret Beckett in July 1998 as chairman of the Cabinet committee on legislation (known as LEG) marked the end of his initial phase of overseeing and prioritising the new government's Bills, but he retained the chair of the more important QFL committee on future legislation and Queen's Speeches.
18. From the early version of Mandelson's book proposal, *Observer*, 24 December 1995 (author's emphasis).
19. Anthony Barker, *Ruling by Task Force*, p. 16; his list does not include two royal commissions, on long-term care for the old and on the House of Lords.
20. Barker, *Ruling by Task Force*, p. 10.
21. *Independent*, 17 July 2000.
22. Speech at launch of first annual report, 30 July 1998.
23. First posted by the Prince of Wales on his website in February 1999, and repeated in an article in the *Daily Mail*, 2 June.
24. BBC1, *Breakfast With Frost*, 6 June 1999.
25. *New Statesman*, 17 January 2000 (published 12 January).
26. A 6.6 per cent increase in real terms in 1999–2000 and a 7.5 per cent increase in 2000–2001 (Institute for Fiscal Studies).

27. Total expenditure on health as a percentage of GDP, *OECD Health Data 99*, Table 1. Public health spending in the UK accounted for only 5.8 points of the 6.9 per cent total, with the difference made up by private health spending.
28. The 8 per cent was an unweighted average, taking no account of the size of different countries: the weighted average was 8.7 per cent. Blair's pledge demonstrated other uses of innumeracy, in that if Britain increased its health spending, the EU average, which included Britain, would rise. The logical pledge would have been to match the weighted average of the EU excluding Britain, but that would have been 9.1 per cent. (Institute for Fiscal Studies.)
29. By the time the NHS Plan was published in July 2000, the pledge had become less specific. Blair wrote in the preface: '*Over time*, we aim to bring it [NHS spending] up to the EU average.'
30. *Hansard*, 22 March 2000.
31. The real average rate of increase in NHS spending was: 6.4 per cent a year 1971–76; 3.1 per cent a year 1979–97; 2.2 per cent a year for the first two years of the Blair government, 1997–99; and 6.2 per cent a year planned for 1999–2004 (Carl Emmerson, Christine Frayne and Alissa Goodman, *Pressures in UK Healthcare*, Institute for Fiscal Studies, May 2000, p. 4).
32. *Mirror*, 20 February 1998.
33. Sky News, *Sunday With Adam Boulton*, 23 July 2000.
34. *Sun*, 9 December 1997.
35. *The Economist*, 22 July 2000.
36. Lesley White, *Sunday Times Magazine*, 20 April 1997.
37. Warren Hoge, *New York Times Magazine,* 14 May 2000.
38. Robert Harris, *Talk* magazine, May 2000.
39. Peter Hennessy, 'The Blair Style', lecture at the University of Exeter, 8 May 2000.
40. Peter Hennessy, 'Patterns of Premiership', The Mishcon Lecture at University College, London, 18 May 2000.

34

Big Tent Politics

Millennium Celebration at the Dome, 31 December 1999

'This is Britain's opportunity to greet the world with a celebration that is so bold, so beautiful, so inspiring that it embodies at once the spirit of confidence and adventure in Britain and the spirit of future in the world.'

—*Tony Blair, 1998*

It all started to go wrong for Blair at the beginning of the new millennium.* After all the millennarianism of New Labour – Blair's awful line in his pre-election party conference speech about 'a thousand days to prepare for a thousand years' – the arrival of the round number itself was bound to be a disappointment.

Although it was not until April 2000 that Blair and Labour really started to slide in the opinion polls, things started to unravel when the great, the good and the editors of national broadsheet newspapers found themselves trapped at Stratford Tube station in east London queuing for hours to get the Underground to the Dome.

When they got there, the Archbishop of Canterbury, George Carey, led them in the Lord's Prayer, introducing a disorganised jumble of symbolism. Blair mumbled through 'All You Need is Love', although Cherie sang along cheerfully. At the stroke of midnight television viewers waited expectantly for a river of fire, which turned out to be a loose expression meaning a sequence of fireworks. Blair mouthed embarrassedly to a dire

*If the third millennium did not technically start until 1 January 2001, as pedants argue, that is a bit like saying the 1960s did not start until 1 January 1961, and that the year 1960 was in the '50s.

version of 'God Save the Queen' as he stood next to her, while Cherie belted it out *con brio*. Then there came what looked like a Venezualan brothel floor show, a visual spaghetti on television which at least cheered up the VIPs in the Dome, followed by 'Auld Lang Syne'. Having recently launched his attack on 'the forces of conservatism', now the Prime Minister was holding hands with them. The Queen was so conservative she did not cross her arms, limply holding hands with Blair on one side and Prince Philip on the other, while on Blair's other side Cherie and Charles Falconer entered boisterously into the spirit of the party.

Afterwards Blair wanted to visit St Thomas's hospital, but it was too busy and he had to make do with police and fire services. Instead of the dawn of a brave new world the next day, he found himself plunged into a crisis in the health service, unable to cope with an outbreak of 'flu.

Even his special millennium New Year Honours went wrong. There were supposed to be 2,000 names on the list, but two refusals, one of them Channel Four newsreader Jon Snow, spoiled Blair's attempt to synchronise with the date.

Heseltine's wok

If the test of a politician is to be found in those issues on which they take a stand against the grain of public opinion, then Blair has chosen some strange causes to fight. While assailed by pro-Europeans pleading with him to use his communication skills and huge electoral mandate to educate the British people in the idealism and interest in joining the euro, he chose instead to defy the opinion polls on only two significant issues: the Millennium Dome and Ken Livingstone.* The mistake in the first case was more understandable than the second, although in both cases the initial error was compounded by overblown language. The Dome was dreamt up in the vacuum left by the thwarting of Michael Heseltine's ambition and Blair gave the nod to the idea of bipartisan support when he was not concentrating. As the election approached, a firmer commitment from the Opposition was needed to keep the construction workers on the site and Blair gave it, although he and Heseltine negotiated hard over terms. Blair was worried about the 'eyes of the world' argument, about not having anything to show of a nation's confidence in the future at a moment of popular symbolism.

*Strangely, the two mistakes are connected in the person of Simon Jenkins, the former editor of *The Times* who helped persuade Blair of the merits of directly elected mayors and, as a member of the Millennium Commission, pleaded with him to save the Dome.

After several days of fraught bargaining in the shadow Cabinet room at Westminster which allowed Blair to feel that he was in government already, he reached agreement with Jennie Page and Simon Jenkins, of the Millennium Commission, and with Heseltine, the Deputy Prime Minister, on the phone. At one point, Blair said, with 'no swagger', that Heseltine 'must understand that I am perfectly prepared to walk away from this whole thing'.[1] But he was not in fact keen to do so. He had allowed Jack Cunningham, as national heritage spokesman, to support the project from the start, and so the discussions were essentially only on the terms of Labour's continued support. The statement agreed on 17 January 1997 declared:

> The Opposition remain enthusiastic about the proposed exhibition at Greenwich. They will want, if elected, to review all aspects of the project delivery, to ensure it is cost effective and properly implemented, so that it will come within the existing budget.[2]

The important part of that budget, that which was to be met out of public money from the Lottery, was at that time £200 million. By the time the incoming Labour government had 'reviewed' the project, it had escalated to £400 million. The word 'review' in the agreed statement gave the impression that the project's future was more open than it was. However, cancellation was still a realistic option after the election, politically and financially, and on 10 June the Home and Social Affairs committee of the Cabinet discussed a paper from Chris Smith, Secretary of State for Culture, Media and Sport, proposing that the scheme should be scrapped or scaled down. Smith was supported by Gordon Brown, although his opposition to the scheme was muted. Peter Mandelson, who had been put on eleven of the initial nineteen Cabinet committees by Blair, insisted they try to save it. He was supported by Jack Straw, Ivor Richard and John Prescott, the committee's chairman. Mandelson, who would later be appointed to oversee the project, was undoubtedly influenced by his grandfather Herbert Morrison's role in pushing through the much-criticised but ultimately successful Festival of Britain in 1951, and by the desire to have a concrete – or in this case steel and plastic – project to get his ministerial teeth into.

The decision was Blair's, however, and all the more so because there was a majority in the Cabinet against the scheme. When the issue came to Cabinet on 19 June, it was bounced through. Blair announced he was in favour of the Dome, and then left the meeting. Prescott chaired the ensuing discussion, described by Ivor Richard, Labour leader in the House of Lords, as 'a shambles! A disgrace! . . . The worst kind of parish council meeting.'[3] With the majority opposed, the meeting ended with only the most grudging acceptance that the Prime Minister should have his way. Almost as soon as the meeting was over and before the opponents could confer, Downing Street announced that the Dome had been saved, and Blair hauled Prescott, Chris Smith and Mandelson, appointed to oversee the project, to tour the site for the cameras that afternoon. It was one of his less confident decisions, and the one which can most convincingly be described as his biggest mistake in this early period. He was fortunate, however, that Cabinet discipline prevailed, and that the halo effect of the post-election honeymoon made any challenge to his authority unthinkable.*

Having made the decision, however, he tried to present it with as much certainty and brio as if it had been his own brainchild. When a preview of the Dome's contents was unveiled at the South Bank on 24 February 1998, he declared:

> This is Britain's opportunity to greet the world with a celebration that is so bold, so beautiful, so inspiring that it embodies at once the spirit of confidence and adventure in Britain and the spirit of future in the world.

This excess was perhaps trying to compensate for his initial hesitation. The reasons for giving the go-ahead seem to have been essentially negative. He invited the doubters to imagine that he had decided differently:

> Suppose we gave in to the cynics and the snipers. Suppose for a second we allowed pessimism to drive out ambition. Suppose we told Richard Rogers not to build his great building in this country but to move it elsewhere. Then when the eyes of the world fell on Greenwich, people would see a derelict site and a signpost in the ground reading: 'Britain: Year 2000. Nothing doing.' Wouldn't those same cynics feel just a bit unsettled? Wouldn't they feel that Great Britain had missed an opportunity?

The Dome was funded out of Lottery money, the embarrassingly large mountain of cash from the tax on dreams which, in a grotesque reversal of the principles of raising and spending public money, had to be spent on something. Pointless and unwanted schemes to mark the new millennium sprang up all over the country, none more empty and undesired than the Dome. Of course, it was not taxpayers' money, Blair repeatedly insisted, as if that made the waste of such a vast sum all right. He himself had

*It was not until 12 November 2000 that the civil servants' verbatim notes of the 19 June Cabinet meeting were leaked to the *Mail on Sunday*. As Professor Peter Hennessy said, this was a 'Grade One Listed' leak, even if all it added to what was already known about the Cabinet's opposition was that Gordon Brown had been rather less opposed than he pretended.

already blown that distinction by magicking £1 billion of Lottery money during the election campaign into a 'modernisation fund' for health and education, thus enabling the taxpayer to foot the bill by failing to win a fortune every week instead of by paying income tax.

One of the trickier consequences of the decision to go ahead was the need for Blair to put his government's integrity behind the operation to raise the private-sector sponsorship needed to complete the project. The potential for collisions of interest between the government and the Dome's sponsors – the four main ones were confirmed in February 1998 as BT, Manpower, Tesco and Rupert Murdoch's BSkyB – had simply not been thought through. When Mandelson became Secretary of State for Trade and Industry in July 1998, taking responsibility for the Dome with him, senior officials in the department expressed unease. But they stopped short of advising Mandelson to stand aside from deciding on the sale of British Airways slots at Heathrow on the grounds that BA was a sponsor and BA chairman Bob Ayling was also chairman of the Millennium Experience company which ran the Dome. 'Some junior civil servants felt privately that their seniors had let the department down,' reported Donald Macintyre.[4] Neither Mandelson nor his successor Stephen Byers stood aside from adjudicating BSkyB's bid for Manchester United either: if Mandelson had been inclined to allow the bid, it was fortunate for Blair that Byers ruled the other way. Blair was also lucky to escape with the coincidence that Tesco stumped up its £12 million at about the same time that the government decided to drop a plan to tax supermarket car parks. Nemesis was only delayed, however, and Mandelson's phone call on behalf of Srichand Hinduja, who with his brothers had provided £1 million in sponsorship for the Faith Zone, finally brought him down and weakened Blair in January 2001.

More damaging, the Dome was an easy object of satire, an obvious metaphor for 'big tent', content-free politics.[5] The building was commissioned before it was decided what it was for, or what was going to go in it. It was a monument to straining for effect.

When it opened, the commentators hated it but the paying customers thought it was good. Good, but not 'so bold, so beautiful, so inspiring . . .' It failed the hubristic 'Euan Test' Blair had set for it: that children would demand to be taken to it. If it had not been so grotesquely oversold, it might have been remembered as a modestly successful, if slightly worthy, science fair. Instead, as visitor numbers stayed at around half the level needed to break even, it was bound to be remembered as a failure. It almost did not matter what was in it. The fundamental problem was that it was impossible not to imagine a better use of £750 million.

Notes

1. Lesley White, *Sunday Times Magazine*, 20 April 1997.
2. Virginia Bottomley, written answer, *Hansard*, 20 January 1997.
3. Janet Jones, *Labour of Love*, p. 86.
4. Donald Macintyre, *Mandelson*, p. 413.
5. The use of the 'big tent' phrase in politics is usually attributed to Lee Atwater, Republican party consultant and later national chairman, who ran George Bush's 1988 campaign against Michael Dukakis.

35

Forward March of New Labour Halted

Mayor Ken, 4 May 2000

> 'Sometimes I think the experiences in the Labour Party in the early '80s almost sort of scarred me too much.'
>
> —*Tony Blair, 2000*

The question is not why Blair hated Ken Livingstone so much, but why that hatred so clouded his judgment that he made one of the worst mistakes of his premiership. Blair's experience of London Labour politics between 1980 and 1983 made a deep impression on him, and he blamed Livingstone personally for the damage the 'London effect' had on the party's image nationally. But he had such contempt for the left that he failed to recognise that Livingstone was a charismatic populist with a wide appeal beyond the Labour Party. He retained a memory of the early 1980s in the gory technicolor original rather than the later Disney rewrite, starring the People's Ken.

So much did he believe that direct democracy would favour pragmatic, dynamic technocrats like himself that it did not occur to him that someone who had seized power on the Greater London Council by caucus politics and internal coup in the activist layers of the Labour Party could adapt himself to a different environment.

However, from the moment in April 1996 when Frank Dobson, Labour's local government spokesman, launched a policy document which contained a directly-elected mayor for London as an option, Livingstone was always going to be best placed to fill the post. Dobson did not like the policy at the time – although not nearly as much as he was going to dislike it later on – but it was one of Blair's few personal schemes so he gave it a fair wind: 'My guess is that Londoners will actually go for this idea and that we will get an elected mayor.'

The policy was firmed up and was one of those added to the final version of the Labour manifesto after party members had voted on the draft.[1] London would have a directly elected authority and mayor, the final manifesto said, 'following a referendum to confirm popular demand'. When the referendum was held on 7 May 1998, it did more to confirm popular apathy. Although there was a 72 per cent Yes vote, the turnout was only 34 per cent.

By this time, the threat from Livingstone was already clear. The previous summer he had defeated Peter Mandelson who, in the post-landslide delusion of New Labour invincibility, had stood in the ballot of party members for the National Executive. It was the first election Blair had lost, albeit by proxy, since the Beaconsfield by-election in 1982. Opinion polls showed Livingstone was the clear favourite with the public, too. This was just 'name recognition', Blair's advisers told themselves uncertainly. Blair began to be asked awkward questions about who he would like to see as mayor. He pretended he had a plan in the increasingly desperate hope that one would turn up.

The plan had been to draft a big-name business leader. Richard Branson had been courted but, after taking a good look at the prospects, said he might like to be mayor at some time in the future.[2] A bewildering series of ministers were canvassed, including Glenda Jackson, but only Mo Mowlam had the kind of appeal in the party that could reliably see off Livingstone, and she would have none of it. The Independent MP Martin Bell was approached, but it would make no sense for him to run as a Labour candidate and he turned it down 'without thinking'.[3]

Frank Dobson, who had already refused several times, was Blair's only viable option. It was made brutally plain to him that his days as a Cabinet minister were numbered, and in October 1999 he did the decent thing. If the Prime Minister asked him, he told journalists, he would consider standing as Labour's candidate for London mayor. Nine days later, the procedure for choosing Labour's candidate was unveiled.

It had been widely assumed, not least by Blair, that the Labour candidate would be chosen in a one member, one vote ballot of party members in London. But that was just after the election. Since then, he had wanted to fix the selection of Labour's leader in Wales, and so Margaret McDonagh, the General Secretary of the party, had devised a three-section electoral college. Superficially, it looked like the system under which Blair had been elected leader but there was one critical difference, in that it retained trade union block votes rather than balloting trade unionists as individuals. This was now adapted to London, with the added device of including, in the section for Labour candidates for the new Greater

London Assembly, all the MPs and Euro-MPs representing London constituencies.

That was the section of the electoral college which delivered the nomination to Dobson on 20 February 2000. He won by 51.5 per cent to Livingstone's 48.5 per cent. Livingstone won 60 per cent of the vote among party members, and 72 per cent of the trade unions (so much for the block vote), but was overwhelmed by the 86.5 per cent vote for Dobson among candidates, MPs and Euro-MPs.[4] The result was overwhelmingly seen as a fix, and an instant opinion poll the next day found 60 per cent of the London public thought Livingstone should run as an independent, while 51 per cent said they would vote for him.[5]

Blair had devoted a surprising amount of prime ministerial time and credibility to trying to persuade the party not to take the risk. 'My worry about Ken Livingstone,' he said, 'is that the extremism he stood for in the 1980s he hasn't left behind.' The 60 per cent figure suggested there was a large minority in the party which shared Blair's distrust or were prepared to respond to appeals to party unity. But Blair had over-reached himself by saying before the selection that he thought Livingstone would be 'disastrous' as mayor, which served no purpose except to poison relations when the inevitable happened.

Stage one of the inevitable occurred when Livingstone declared as an independent candidate after two weeks of orchestrated suspense. Blair issued a statement repeating his view that 'I believe passionately that he would be a disaster – a financial disaster, a disaster in terms of crime and police and business,' and adding: 'At least in a sense he is not my responsibility any more and it is up to the public to decide who they want to vote for.'

Stage two occurred on 4 May 2000, when Livingstone won 39 per cent of first-preference votes over Steven Norris (the Conservative candidate after Jeffrey Archer dropped out the previous November) on 27 per cent. Frank Dobson came third on 13 per cent, just ahead of Susan Kramer, the Liberal Democrat, on 12 per cent. Livingstone won by 58 to 42 per cent in the run-off against Norris. One of the main motives of the electorate in voting for Livingstone was surprisingly similar to that of Labour Party members. It was perhaps the oldest democratic impulse of all: they wanted to tell Blair not to get too big for his boots.

Fix or fight?

What should Blair have done? The first answer, as in the old joke, was not to have started from here. Directly-elected mayors were one way to try to revitalise local democracy, but they have the drawbacks, as American experience suggests, of personalising campaigns and concentrating power in a single individual. As a matter of brute politics, furthermore, it was folly to create such an important post without having a credible candidate lined up for it. An alternative way of dealing with 'unrepresentative' factions gaining control of Labour councils through the apparatus of the party would have been proportional representation, forcing parties to rule in coalition. Certainly, if the Greater London Assembly had stood alone, with its proportional system of electing members from top-up lists, Livingstone would never have emerged at the head of what would probably have been a Labour–Liberal Democrat coalition.[6]

Having decided on a directly-elected mayor for London, however, how should Blair have handled Livingstone? He considered appointing him a minister in 1997, but ruled it out on the grounds that it would just give him a position from which to resign in a blaze of publicity over an issue of principle.

Therefore the questions which, much too late, occupied Downing Street and Labour HQ at Millbank were: what procedure should be used to select the Labour candidate and should Livingstone be excluded from it? Sally Morgan, Blair's political secretary in Number Ten, wanted Livingstone kept off the short list. Margaret McDonagh, worried about the effect on party morale and the loss of members, especially in London, thought it better to try to tilt the electoral college against Livingstone.

She was nearly right. With the benefit of hindsight, it can be guessed that Livingstone would have lost in a fair ballot, because his vote in the trade unions would have been lower if it had been by one person, one vote, while if the MPs and Euro-MPs had been left out, the Greater London Assembly candidates would still have been strongly opposed to him. The fatal mistake was to try to fix the outcome for Dobson: if Livingstone had been allowed to run and denied the chance to present himself as the victim of a biased ballot, he would have found it harder to run as an independent. But Blair could not take the risk of his becoming the official Labour candidate.

The only leverage Blair had over Livingstone was Livingstone's desire for Blair's job. Livingstone had been forced out of the 1994 Labour leadership contest because he could not muster the thirty-four nominations from MPs needed to take part, but the fire of ambition burned still. Livingstone acknowledged as much when he met Blair at Chequers on the day before the result of the Labour ballot was announced, saying sardonically that he had been converted to the idea of directly-elected mayors – there were only two jobs he would find more interesting. 'But I don't think you'd give me the same leeway as Gordon, would you?'[7] But Livingstone seemed to accept that he had no realistic prospect of government office. Although he lobbied to be allowed back into the party as soon as he left it to run as an independent, he announced soon after he was installed as mayor that he would stand down from the House of Commons at the next election.

Blair, unable to decide whether to try to fix him or fight him in a fair and open argument, did both and got the worst of both worlds. It mattered a great deal to him, but it was in truth a small consolation because he would still have to trade with him, that at least Livingstone was forced out of the Labour Party and was not Blair's responsibility any more.

The party

The London disaster exposed the gulf between Blair and the party he led. For all his claim to be a moderniser of the Labour Party, he failed to change its culture and ethos. Although the party membership had always had a strong pragmatic streak, it remained fundamentally 'old Labour' in its attitudes. The creation of 'almost literally a new party' ran little deeper than the ruling clique, despite the membership's formal assent to the new Clause IV and the draft election manifesto. Membership increased sharply before the election, although Blair blunted the achievement by frequently claiming it had 'doubled'[8] whereas it had increased by a little more than half (54 per cent), from 259,639 in June 1994 to 400,465 in December 1996, before starting to fall again after polling day.

Despite being the first leader to engage semi-systematically and directly with party members, in the 'roadshow' format first devised for the battle for Clause IV, he continued to alienate them. Despite giving them the election victory they wanted more than anything, and a landslide at that, and the prospect of two full consecutive terms in office, party members did not trust him, nor he them.

The betrayal of his apparently brave pre-leadership stand for the principle of one member, one vote began soon after the 1997 election. Not only had he allowed Jack Straw to devise a system of proportional representation for the 1999 European elections which prevented the voters choosing between individual candidates, but Labour Party members would not be able to choose their candidates either. The Liberal Democrats and even William Hague's suddenly-democratised Conservatives would decide the all-important order of candidates on their lists by a one member, one vote ballot. But Labour would fix the order on the list in meetings of regional officials.

From the rhetoric of the outward-looking mass party, part of its local communities, its members trusted to make mature and pragmatic decisions, Blair swung to a more Machiavellian model of politics as a continuous process of image management. The superstructure of politics has always been controlled by small cliques, but in the past they tended to rest on institutions with a social base, such as trade unions or business interests.

The weakness of Blair's attempts to create a party in his own image had been highlighted before the election by his relative lack of success in attracting a higher quality of Labour candidate. A series of older Labour MPs were persuaded by offers of peerages to stand down just before the election, allowing the National Executive to draw up short lists for selection ballots at the last minute. But Charles Falconer, Blair's former landlord, failed to make the list for Dudley North, vacated by John Gilbert, later a defence minister in the Lords. Falconer had 'always hoped to be an MP in a vague way' but never did anything about it because he was 'active in the Eighties when I wouldn't have been attractive to London Labour parties'. He was not attractive to the National Executive panel in the Nineties either, because his children were at private schools. He followed Gilbert into government via the Lords instead, although he admitted it was not the best route: 'I could not think of a sillier way of doing it.'

The greatest change in the composition of the Parliamentary Labour Party, the huge rise in the number of women MPs, came about by a mechanism which Blair did not like, the policy of drawing up all-women shortlists in half the seats defined as 'winnable'. He dropped it with a just-audible sigh of relief when an employment tribunal in Leeds ruled in January 1996 that it constituted unlawful discrimination against men.* When David Frost asked him if it was convenient someone else had got rid of the policy for him, Blair smiled: 'Well, you said that, not me.'[9] He was happy to take the credit, however, for the step forward in women's representation which the policy produced.

His management of his MPs, once they were safely elected, was surprisingly effective, considering the scope such a large majority gave for boredom and irresponsibility. Many MPs knew they had little hope of

* Although the tribunal's ruling was widely regarded in the Labour Party as capricious, and Blair came under some pressure to appeal, it was well founded: Cherie Booth, an eminent employment law QC, later advised the Liberal Democrats that even its more balanced policy of alternating men and women on the lists of candidates for the Scottish Parliament was contrary to European law on equal treatment.

advancement and that rebellions posed little threat to the government. But Blair was the first Labour leader to hold regular meetings with groups of his MPs, which continued from Opposition into government. His parliamentary private secretary, the decent and self-effacing Bruce Grocott, MP for the Wrekin, was an astute choice for the job of keeping him in touch with backbench opinion.

The weakness of New Labour, however, was the lack of committed 'Blairites' at any level in the party except the very top.

Losing the plot

How had Blair so badly misjudged his party in Wales and London? He himself confessed: 'Sometimes I think the experiences in the Labour Party in the early Eighties almost sort of scarred me too much.'[10] This psycho-emotional explanation is persuasive. How else does one explain the paradox by which Blair conjured into existence precisely that which he had devoted his political career to negating? Livingstone was an empty husk, distrusted by his fellow MPs, even on Labour's hard left, whose only asset was a plausibly rogueish manner on television. Just as Blair breathed life into Thatcher, although to opposite effect, Blair breathed life into Livingstone. The parallels between Blair and Livingstone are striking: they were both intensely ambitious, ruthless and populist. As were the differences, by which each of them ended up as his opposite: Blair became the manipulator of internal party democracy, disdainful of public opinion; while Livingstone was the figure who could unite the party with the electorate, as a pluralist and coalition-builder.

Livingstone continued to play this role once he was installed as mayor, playing 'big tent' politics as cleverly as Blair had ever done. He persuaded his defeated Tory and Liberal Democrat rivals to join his administration, along with members of all parties on the Greater London Assembly.

Blair's basic problem in mishandling Livingstone, however, was that he had ceased to see politics the way ordinary people see it, which had been one of his great strengths. This was part of his wider crisis of confidence in the spring of 2000, which he set out in a memo headed 'Touchstone Issues' written at Chequers on 29 April, the Saturday before the London and local elections. There was, he said, 'a clutch of issues' on which a sense had been allowed to develop that 'the government – and this even applies to me – are somehow out of touch with gut British instincts'.[11]

Until that point, New Labour had marched in step with public opinion, but now it had lost the populist rhythm on four 'seemingly disparate' issues 'that are in fact linked': the family, asylum seekers, crime and 'standing up for Britain'. Blair described them, in the American phrase, as 'on your side' issues. They were precisely the territory which he started to steal from the Conservatives when he was shadow Home Secretary and to which he had laid claim as leader of New Labour, before and after the 1997 election. The case of Tony Martin, jailed for life on 19 April 2000 after fatally shooting a young burglar on his property, had been taken up by much of the tabloid press and on 25 April by William Hague. Before that, Hague had joined in the tabloid hue and cry over the government's failure to get a grip on the rising number of applications for refugee status, and in the *Daily Mail*'s evergreen theme that the government was undermining the institution of the family. The ending of the tax allowance for married couples, a process begun under the Conservatives, was one of the main grievances. But it was the Martin case, 'and the lack of any response from us that appeared to emphathise with public concern and then channel it into the correct course', which, Blair admitted, crystallised the perception that he was out of touch.

It had prompted a *Daily Mail* leading article published on the morning he wrote his memo, which listed the same issues (treating Europe and defence separately, which he lumped together). The 'Touchstone Issues' memo rendered a striking impression of Blair as a fearful, headline-driven politician. The obsession with the need to appear 'tough' and the plaintive demand for initiatives that would convey the right 'message' betokened a hollowness at the centre. 'We should think now of an initiative, e.g. locking up street muggers. Something tough, with immediate bite which sends a message through the system,' he wrote. A few weeks later he proposed the fatuous and still-born scheme under which drunken young men who annoy people by shouting and throwing traffic cones would be taken to the nearest cash machine by the police and ordered to pay an on-the-spot fine.

Blair's sense that the press were beginning to combine issues in a way which was dangerous to the government was confirmed on Bank Holiday Monday, 1 May, when the *Sun* took up some of the *Mail*'s themes with the front-page headline, 'MAYDAY, MAYDAY', which attacked the Prime Minister over the threatened closure of the Rover Group as well as over crime and asylum.

Blair's response was panicky, and it showed. Still at Chequers, he copied out by hand – in order to give it more personal authenticity – a 950-word reply to the *Sun* which the Downing Street word factory had produced. All of Alastair Campbell's favours were forgotten now that Murdoch's press could smell blood, and the paper rewarded Blair's copying out his lines by printing them with another front-page headline the next day: 'RATTLED'.

The forward march of New Labour maintained its momentum so long as it had the speed, flexibility and cynicism to beat its rivals in responding to popular sentiment as reflected and intensified by the popular press. But in the spring of 2000 Blair was halted by Livingstone, a left-wing populist, on one side and by Hague, a right-wing populist, on the other.

Notes

1. The early version of the manifesto promised only to 'create a directly-elected strategic authority for London' and to 'explore the role in the large cities for elected mayors, with executive powers, through pilot projects'.
2. BBC2, *Newsnight*, 28 April 1998.
3. *Independent*, 12 May 2000.
4. Figures after transferring the 4 per cent of first-preference votes for Glenda Jackson.
5. ICM poll for the London *Evening Standard* (21 February), which found only 15 per cent thought Dobson had won 'fairly'.
6. Labour won 9 seats in the first Assembly elections, the Conservatives 9, Liberal Democrats 4 and Greens 3.
7. *Guardian*, 22 February 2000.
8. For example, in a speech to Labour local government conference, Nottingham, 8 February 1997.
9. BBC1, *Breakfast With Frost*, 14 January 1996.
10. Robert Harris, *Talk* magazine, May 2000.
11. Leaked the day before the Spending Review, *The Times* and *Sun*, 17 July 2000.

36

Running on Empty

Fuel Protest, September 2000, and Peter Mandelson's Final Fall, January 2001

> 'We hope within the next twenty-four hours to have the situation on the way back to normal.'
>
> —*Tony Blair,* 12 *September* 2000

It was not that Blair had failed to see the fuel crisis coming. Philip Gould, his opinion research adviser, had been worrying about voters' anger over petrol prices from the start of the year 2000. In his Budget in March Gordon Brown had hit the emergency stop button on the fuel duty escalator – the automatic device installed by Norman Lamont in 1993 to increase the tax on petrol by 5 percentage points more than the rate of inflation every year. Blair himself had devoted part of his column in the *News of the World* on 2 July to the argument that, if the government cut fuel duty, it would have to raise taxes elsewhere or cut spending: 'We are not anti-car. But we are pro-hospitals, pro-police, pro-jobs.' As Charles Kennedy observed, he made no mention of the environmental rationale which – ostensibly – lay behind the tax rises in the first place. There was a simple reason for that, which was that the idea that high petrol prices might make a tiny contribution to reducing climate change in future melted no ice with Gould's focus groups. Nor did they care that the rise in petrol prices since the Budget had been driven by the world oil market, rather than tax. They were angry and insisted something must be done.

Blair had no idea, however, that a tiny group of protesters could bring the country to a halt within forty-eight hours by picketing the refineries which delivered fuel to petrol stations around the country. Nor did anyone else, not even the protesters themselves. They were a short-lived coalition of self-employed hauliers, for many of whom the rise in the price of diesel was the last straw in a cut-throat market, and 'countryside' campaigners whose primary resentment was over the crisis in farming or the threat to hunting, but who saw high petrol taxes as yet another attack on rural people forced to rely on their cars. They had tried to organise a 'Dump the Pump' day, calling on motorists to boycott petrol stations on 1 August, a demonstration which had no prospect of success but which was opportunistically backed by William Hague. He, like Blair, sensed the strength of public opinion on the issue.

Over the summer, French fishermen took direct action, blockading several ports in protest at high diesel prices. Their beleaguered industry was already so heavily subsidised that diesel for fishing boats was exempt from duty, but the French government nevertheless opened talks about ways in which it could soften further the impact of the rise in the world price of oil. Blair, and most British commentators, looked on pityingly at this craven and distinctively Gallic way to run a country.

The French fishermen had given the British fuel protesters an idea, however. The first pickets appeared outside refineries on Friday 8 September. To everyone's surprise, they were almost entirely successful in persuading oil-tanker lorry drivers to stop their deliveries to petrol stations. In retrospect, this was not so puzzling. While there was some intimidation, and while the oil companies employing the drivers were, from Blair's point of view, frustratingly passive, the real reason why the drivers refused to cross picket lines was because they drove cars when they were not driving lorries and, like 82 per cent of the population, they agreed with the pickets that the government should cut petrol taxes and that direct action was the only way to force it to do so.[1]

The pickets' success attracted nationwide publicity over the weekend, which prompted pre-emptive petrol buying, and, by Monday evening, 11 September, petrol stations in much of the country had run dry. Ever since the oil shortages of the mid-1970s, the industry had been free of distribution problems or labour disputes and had grown used to operating on low forecourt stocks and efficient, just-in-time delivery. By the time Blair arrived (by car) in Hull that evening for a celebration of John Prescott's thirty years as an MP, it was obvious that the government was facing its most serious domestic crisis.

The following afternoon, Blair gave the first of three news conferences in Downing Street on consecutive days. This was a shaky, unconfident performance, as he stuck carefully to a prepared text which had been argued over all day. He had recognised the significance of the moment, seeing it as a test of his firmness. With the parallel of Margaret Thatcher's confrontations with the miners in mind, he regarded the protesters and – more doubtfully – the tanker drivers as his 'enemy within'. His instinct was to order in troops to drive the lorries, accompanied by a propaganda offensive in support of getting fuel supplies to hospitals which would paint the protesters as irresponsible. But he was aware that the level of public support for the protest was far greater than it had ever been for the miners' strike, and was persuaded that the deployment of soldiers would be counter-productive. One of those urging caution was Prescott, who with all the authority of a former strike organiser argued against inflaming the situation, and who was working through the Transport and General Workers' Union to try to persuade its members among the drivers to resume normal work.

Blair's statement was, therefore, a compromise. 'We cannot accept as a government or as a nation that policy should be dictated by illegal blockades, pickets or direct action,' he said, while adding that he understood the strength of feeling about high fuel prices. It lacked conviction, and satisfied no one, while the 'twenty-four hours' phrase invited that most dangerous of threats to a leader's command of events: ridicule. No one noticed the second half of his sentence: '. . . though it will take longer than that to be fully back to normal'. But after forty-eight hours, on Wednesday 13 September, the tide started to turn. The argument that essential services might be threatened started to come through and it became clear that the protest had nowhere to go. Hague missed his chance, proposing a cut in duty of 3p a litre which was both too little to make an appreciable difference and too much simply to be wished out of thin air without saying where the money would come from. On Thursday, most of the protesters declared victory and called off their blockades, saying they gave the government sixty days to make a significant cut in fuel taxes.

The effect on Blair's standing was immediate and brutal, but short-lived. Over the next ten days the polls showed the Conservatives leading Labour by up to 8 points – for the first time in the eight years since the devaluation of the pound in 1992.[2] Michael Portillo cleverly called it a 'taxpayers' revolt', but this was to lend it more ideological coherence than was justified. Although 79 per cent declared themselves dissatisfied with the way Blair handled the fuel price issue that week, 72 per cent said their lives had been affected 'not very badly' or 'not at all' by the shortages and 55 per cent said the government would be right to use the military to force through fuel deliveries if the shortages threatened the supply of food in the shops.[3]

It was a burst of steam escaping from the boiler of anti-political rage, which vanished with a hiss almost as quickly as it had appeared. By the end of the month, Labour was already back in the lead in the opinion polls.[4] By the time Gordon Brown managed to dress up a package of further concessions to the haulage industry as an incentive to use the cleaner fuel it was already using in his pre-Budget report in November, no one could tell if he was giving in or standing firm. And, once the price of oil on international markets had fallen again over Christmas, no one really cared.

Once again, Blair's desire to show leadership had been subordinated to risk-aversion, and that was probably a good thing. Typically, he retreated into his own version of Bill Clinton's 'feel your pain' politics. 'I totally understand the concern of people about the price if it is costing £50 or more to fill your tank. It is over £50 for the car we have,' he told the *Mirror* on 1 November.* It was a risky moment for his government and an attitude of conciliatory obstinacy, while lacking clarity or glory, enabled him to sit tight until the spasm had passed. Had he held strong views on transport policy, he might have held his nerve better by persuading the voters that he knew what he was doing. Instead, his approach to the issue was entirely pragmatic and electoral: calculating that transport was never likely to be a vote-winner, his aim was to prevent it becoming too much of a vote-loser. That meant stifling John Prescott's enthusiasm for charging motorists for using congested routes, which might be an economically efficient way of allocating a scarce resource, namely road space, but which was electorally poisonous.

When he opened the Heathrow Express rail link to the airport from Paddington station on 23 June 1998, Blair rambled:

> I used to live in London, just by the Arsenal, and when I used to fly up to my constituency in Teesside, virtually every weekend, I would get on the Tube at the Arsenal Tube station and it would take about an hour to get to Heathrow. And I used to sit there and, whenever I had a vision of what a transport policy should be like, I used to think, 'Well, what it should be like is to be able to get to Heathrow quickly.' That was my vision for a twenty-first-century transport policy.

It was a revealingly banal meditation, almost a parody of 'if I were Prime Minister I'd make a law against not being able to find anywhere to park'. It was nonsense, too. The Heathrow Express would hardly make the journey from 'the' Arsenal to Heathrow much quicker. More importantly, King's Cross station, with fast trains to Darlington, was just three stops down the Piccadilly line from Arsenal: any sensible twenty-first-century transport policy, let alone a green one, would focus on improving high-speed rail services.

---

* The 'car' he had then was a Chrysler people-carrier.

This lack of understanding meant that Prescott was allowed to use grand rhetoric without anything to back it up, which had already proved to be electorally corrosive before the fuel protest: any commuter in a traffic jam or on a stuck train could demand to know what had happened to an 'integrated transport policy'.

Post-natal depression

Growing public dissatisfaction over fuel prices, congestion and unreliable public transport was – until September – only background noise during the long slide from one setback to another for Blair's government during 2000. After the loss of London in May, opinion poll ratings both for Blair and Labour continued to drift.

The birth of Leo on 20 May had failed to generate the anticipated gush factor in Blair's favour. Instead of bringing Blair closer to Everyman, the birth of the first child to a serving Prime Minister since Francis Albert Rollo, son of Lord John Russell, was born on 11 July 1849 served to emphasise how untypical Blair's family was.* The Blairs' membership of the nanny-employing class had already been advertised by Cherie's legal action in March against their former nanny Ros Mark over her attempted memoir.

Tony Blair's family had been central to his success, from the time he defeated Gordon Brown for the Labour Party leadership in 1994. He is certainly the first Prime Minister with a recognisably modern attitude to fatherhood, right down to the post-feminist jousting between the sexes. 'When the kids were very young, it was my job to get up to them. Cherie is a complete dynamo when she's up, but when she's asleep, she really is asleep. When the children were four, two and nothing, I was up virtually every night and usually two or three times a night,' he said, in a rare joint interview he and Cherie gave before they knew about Leo.

Cherie retorted: 'Well, he was a really supportive father, but as I was breastfeeding, it's not entirely true. I would lie very still when the baby was crying because I knew he'd crack before I did. Then the baby would be plonked on me in bed. But he was very good – and he's still good with them.'[5]

---

* Only three other Prime Ministers had children while in office. Viscount Goderich, who was only Prime Minister for six months, had a son, George Frederick Samuel Robinson, born in 10 Downing Street itself on 24 October 1827. Lord North had two children while Prime Minister: Charlotte, born in 1770, and Dudley, who died aged one month in 1777. Robert Walpole, usually regarded as the first Prime Minister, had one, Maria, born in 1725, legitimised when he married her mother, his second wife, in 1738.

Blair's rootedness in his family is genuine, even if his use of his image as a family man is quite deliberate. He referred to them constantly, especially just before and just after the 1997 election. He told nearly every personal interviewer that children 'drive you mad but keep you sane', and wrote their interpretation for them: 'I think I function better as a politician because I lead such a normal life.'[6]

At the pre-election Labour Party conference, he spoke 'as a father, as a leader, as a member of the human family'. During the election campaign, he was seen in Molly Dineen's Labour broadcast helping the children with their homework, and joked that David Blunkett would give them more if Labour won.

The month after the election, he told a United Nations summit on the environment in New York: 'My three young children in London complain I am never at home. But if there is one summit they would want me at, it is this one. They know our decisions here will have a profound effect on the world they inherit. So I speak to you not just as the new British Prime Minister, but as a father.'

As he readied public opinion for air strikes against Iraq, he wrote in the *Sun*: 'I'm not just a politician. I am a father with children of my own.' He ordered the Millennium Dome organisers to pass the 'Euan Test', to make sure that his then thirteen-year-old would demand to go. And when he pledged to end child poverty in twenty years, at the 1999 Labour conference, he did so, again, 'not just as a politician, but as a father'.

Unlike some children of politicians, his do not lead neglected, isolated lives. Until he was elected Labour leader, he was home probably at least as often as most modern fathers. Cherie was working full-time, but they employed a nanny to look after the children at home rather than sending them off to boarding school, and relied heavily on the extended family: Tony's brother Bill and sister Sarah lived nearby in Islington; so did Cherie's sister Lyndsey, and her mother Gale was often around. Gale moved into Downing Street with them and continued to help with child care, especially after Leo's birth.

The children were brought up in the public eye more than any political leader's since John F. Kennedy's. Cherie had had some experience of the phenomenon as the daughter of a famous actor, Tony Booth, often in the news for the equivalent of being found on a pavement in Leicester Square: 'I grew up with a famous father and although a part of you is very proud, part of you cringes. But then, most teenage children cringe at their parents – and it doesn't help if your dad is the Prime Minister.'[7]

By the time of Leo's arrival, however, Blair had become more fiercely protective of his children's privacy. He referred to them less often, and media access had been restricted to an annual royal-style photo-call at the start of the summer holiday, in return for the press sticking to its Code of Conduct, which prevents interviewing or photographing children simply because their parents are famous.*

After Leo's birth Blair returned to work from two weeks' 'holiday mode' paternity leave at Chequers to give a poor speech to the Women's Institute at the Wembley Arena. It was 'too political', they complained, with the heckling and slow hand-clapping starting when he began to explain how much the government was doing to improve the NHS. The real damage was done by television pictures of Blair floundering, embarrassed, turning to the chair in the hope that she might rescue him. Within days that image was reinforced by the leak of a note from Philip Gould commenting on the text in draft: 'This is a speech that looks once again like TB pandering, lacking conviction, unable to hold a position for more than a few weeks.'[8]

This was only part of the advance guard of a series of leaks, including the 'Touchstone Issues' memo written by Blair himself as he took stock during his paternity leave, in which he worried that he appeared 'weak' on the family, 'soft' on crime and 'insufficiently assertive' on defence.[9]

The impression given by Blair's summer of discontent was that of a politician who was both empty and out of touch. The panic in his eyes when faced with the WI and the cynicism of postures designed to look 'tough' suggested a radical lack of confidence. But Euan's drunken excess in July – the first evidence that his children would take on a life of their own rather than obligingly provide a backdrop to his own career – had the opposite effect to Leo's birth, bringing him closer to people, making him seem human and fallible again.

The release of public anger over the fuel protest also seemed to have a cathartic effect, both on public opinion and on Blair himself. Even the resumption of what the press called 'transport chaos' after the Hatfield train crash in October did not prevent Blair regaining his composure. He was more certain of the ground on which he would fight the coming election, namely as the party of public spending against the party of spending cuts, as it became clearer that William Hague's tax-cutting plans did not add up. Paradoxically, the fright he was given by the fuel protest helped convince him that the Conservatives were not a real threat.

---

*In July 2000, Blair and Campbell clashed with the press over photographs of Leo outside the church before his christening: the annual holiday photo-call was briefly cancelled before John Wakeham, chairman of the Press Complaints Commission, intervened to persuade Blair and his press secretary that a running feud with the press was not in their interest.

Mandelson resigns again

Blair's recovery of poise and confidence was threatened in January 2001 when a sudden crisis developed over whether or not Peter Mandelson had spoken directly to the immigration minister, Mike O'Brien, two and a half years earlier to pass on an enquiry about the effect of a change in government policy on the possibility of Srichand Hinduja obtaining British citizenship. Hinduja and his brothers, Indian businessmen, later paid £1 million to sponsor the Faith Zone in the Millennium Dome, which was then Mandelson's ministerial responsibility.

Mandelson was forced to resign, for the second time in just over two years, after what Sir Anthony Hammond's official enquiry called a 'muddle' arose over exactly what had happened.

At first, after the initial shock had worn off, Blair was praised for his speed and decisiveness in requiring one of his closest friends and advisers to make the short walk across Downing Street to explain to the waiting cameras that he was leaving the government. Later, however, when Sir Anthony found that Mandelson had behaved perfectly properly in the way in which he had dealt with Hinduja's query, questions were asked about whether Blair had panicked and rushed to judgment.

Certainly, decisions were taken at great speed and it is at least arguable that Blair should have allowed more time to establish the facts. But Mandelson himself was reported to have acknowledged later that 'I think I would have fired myself' if presented with the same case, and to have accepted the presentational difficulties of Blair's delaying a decision and being accused of 'protecting his best pal'. The Prime Minister's ruthlessness did him no harm in the court of public opinion, with the press furore dying as quickly as it had arisen and the opinion polls barely registering a blip.

Blair did look silly when the Hammond report was published in March and he failed to answer the question of why Mandelson had had to resign, saying that it was 'over and done with', that he was very pleased that Peter had been cleared of any impropriety, and that he hoped he would be able to get on with rebuilding his life. But that was a minor and temporary embarrassment. The public's attention moved quickly on to the outbreak of foot-and-mouth disease, another high-speed rail crash and Gordon Brown's pre-election Budget.

The lasting effects of Mandelson's second – and probably final – departure from the Cabinet were less damaging to Blair: it even strengthened his government by removing an opportunity for the press to comment on its internal tensions, above all between Mandelson and the Chancellor of the Exchequer.

Nor did the loss of his Northern Ireland Secretary prove that Blair's controversial decision to bring him back into government was the wrong one. Mandelson's tenure at the Northern Ireland Office had seen a devolved power-sharing government set up and the historic move by the IRA to allow independent inspection of its arms dumps. That had to be counted a success, and it is at least possible that it might not have happened without Mandelson's assiduousness and political skill.

Nevertheless Mandelson's re-resignation marked the end of a personal and political era for Blair. His relationship with Campbell had – as Mandelson's departure itself emphasised – become stronger than that with Mandelson himself, especially since 1997, and even more so since Mandelson's first resignation at the end of 1998. The revelation of Mandelson's loan from Geoffrey Robinson inevitably increased the emotional distance between Blair and his counsellor, even as he continued to value Mandelson's advice. William Hague, in his Commons valediction to the Northern Ireland Secretary, taunted Blair for his 'dependence' on his friend and ally, but it was an out-of-date description of the relationship. More than anyone else, Mandelson had helped construct Blair's public persona as the 'Labour moderniser' and Blair's attention to his promptings for the ten years from 1985 to 1995 was devoted. As he neared government, however, and more so after he had assumed power, Blair was surer of his self-presentation and needed Mandelson less – or others more. Now, Mandelson would not be running the general election campaign and it would be difficult to recover and sustain his past close role as an informal adviser. That phase of Blair's career was over. It seems a fitting point to bring this interim account of Blair's life to an end.

Notes

1. MORI opinion poll, *News of the World*, 17 September 2000: 82 per cent said the protesters blockading oil refineries were 'right to take direct action in this way'; 15 per cent said they were wrong.
2. The seven polls conducted by the four main companies, ICM, Gallup, MORI and NOP, between 14 and 23 September put the Conservatives ahead by 2 to 8 points, or level with Labour, which until then had held an average lead of 15 points that year.
3. MORI, *News of the World*, 17 September 2000.
4. Gallup, interviewing between 20 and 26 September, put Labour 3 points ahead, *Daily Telegraph*, 2 October 2000.

5. *Good Housekeeping*, October 1999.
6. Lesley Ann Down, *News of the World*, 29 October 1995.
7. *Good Housekeeping*, October 1999.
8. *Sunday Times*, 11 June 2000.
9. *The Times* and *Sun*, 17 July 2000.

37

Definition Deferred

The Future

'I am never quite sure about those "What would you like to be remembered for?" questions.'

—*Tony Blair, 1995*

Blair is an Augustinian preacher-politician, always promising the virtue of clarity, but not yet. As Leader of the Opposition, he said we would see how radical he would be after the election: 'I don't think any project such as this becomes clear to the public until you are in government and you're doing things.'[1] Once elected, however, we had to wait until after the two years of Conservative spending plans – a period later glossed as 'getting the public finances in order' – before the real Blair would stand up and be counted. It was John Burton, his Sedgefield agent, who said in 1998, 'I can't wait for the two years to be up so that we can get on with the real job,' giving away in advance the strategy which soon became more widely known.[2] Blair emerged in the second half of his first term as a mild social democrat. But this was a rather unheroic, retro posture, and he insisted there was more to him than that, only we would have to wait until the second term before the true, and truly historic, shape of his achievement would become evident.

Certainly his rhetoric often strained towards something on a grander scale than free eye and teeth checks for old-age pensioners, worthy though that might be. But he lacked a story to tell, like the ones Churchill, Attlee and Thatcher (and, in the case of Europe, Heath) could tell about their mission as Prime Minister. Neal Lawson, one of several bright modernisers to work as a researcher for Gordon Brown before moving on, observed: 'The lack of narrative means that we repeat the contents page at an ever-increasing rate but never get to hear the story.'[3]

Blair was in thrall to the idea of the strong leader – the one who sensed the mood of the times or who caught the tide of history, or who forced the nation on to a new path by exercise of will. Thatcher was his model, although for technique rather than content. But, despite at times analysing thoughtfully the challenges of his less ideological times, and despite his love of the word, he had no great 'project' for change. Thus he ended up exercising strong leadership over the Labour Party, but when it came to the big themes of the nation's destiny, his instinct was to run a tight ship and by a show of competence nudge the electorate into accepting his commitment to social justice and a more positive engagement with Europe. And, although he was attracted to the idea of himself as a conviction politician in theory, in practice he was proud of his ability to judge what public opinion would accept. To adapt his jibe against John Major, he might lead his party but he followed his country.

He cannot help but compare himself with other great national leaders, however, at home or abroad. He is a reader of political biographies, from the obscure, such as Henry Campbell-Bannerman, the forgotten Liberal Prime Minister at the opening of the previous century, to the obvious, such as Oliver Cromwell and Charles de Gaulle. He liked grand references to 'the broad sweep of history', such as when praising the fallen Mandelson's record in Northern Ireland. And it was in Northern Ireland that he himself had felt the 'hand of history' on his shoulder, securing a settlement which guaranteed him some kind of place in the broad sweep.

Yet, when he was asked by Fiona Millar in 1995 what he would like to be remembered for, he was reluctant to answer, saying: 'I am certainly not thinking of leaving politics yet. My aim is to win the election. But when I do go, I would like to be remembered for serving my country well and helping to create a more just, united society.'[4] That, in stark contrast to Thatcher, was typical of Blair's fill-in-the-gaps politics, into which anyone could read whatever they wanted to read. But, although the scale of it was obscured by the lack of a simple theme – such as Thatcher's drive for liberal market economics – he did achieve a great deal during his first parliament.

Audit of the first term

The Good Friday Agreement, and its implementation, was the most unambiguous triumph, a settlement which had eluded his predecessors since Gladstone. Most of the other business of war and peace was more contested, and Blair's achievements uneven, although it was possible to detect the unsteady advance of the possibility of law-based, and hence ethically-based, international relations. Kosovo was the shining example of this, but lesser claims could be made of policy in Sierra Leone and even the case of Augusto Pinochet.

There was a consistency between attempts supported by Blair to bring war criminals from the former Yugoslavia to justice at The Hague and his (initial) willingness to allow the former Chilean dictator, arrested in London in October 1998 on a charge brought by a Spanish magistrate, to stand trial for crimes against humanity. Blair could have intervened through Jack Straw, the Home Secretary, to throw out the extradition case. But they chose to let the emerging cross-border law of human rights take its course – until Pinochet suffered two strokes while under genteel house arrest in Surrey a year later. Straw then sent him back to Chile on medical grounds, but the precedent had been established and attempts to hold the General to account for his reign of terror continued through Chile's own judicial system.

Relations with Russia and China, however, were characterised by the cynical pursuit of interest-based politics. Blair was so eager to ingratiate himself with Boris Yeltsin's successor, Vladimir Putin, that he breached protocol to visit him while he was still fighting the presidential election campaign. Not only that, but Putin had just fought the second war of suppression in the Russian republic of Chechnya. Blair was again attacked by those who argued that if Britain could not right every injustice in the world it should right none. Military intervention on behalf of the oppressed Chechens was 'neither feasible nor desirable', as Blair said, even if this did illustrate the 'obvious limits' of the doctrine he himself had set out.[5] The arguments against intervention were purely practical, in that Russia was a significant military power with nuclear weapons, but no less persuasive for that.

In the cases of both Russia and China, Blair argued that engagement rather than isolation was the best way to work against internal brutality – but it was an argument that would have been more credible had he engaged with Putin after the presidential elections rather than before.

Since the foundation in 1957 of what would become the European Union, one of the most important judgments of British prime ministers at the court of history has been that of their relations with the rest of Europe. Blair hoped his approach of leadership by stealth at home and energetic diplomacy on the continent would gradually bring the British people round to realising that it was in their economic interest to be fully part of a single European economy. His energy and charm enabled him to break into the Franco-German alliance that was the dominant engine of the EU. He waited for Helmut Kohl to leave the stage, while preparing the ground with the opposition Social Democrats, tying Kohl's successor Gerhard Schröder into the Third Way. He flattered Jacques Chirac, and even co-opted a more reluctant Lionel Jospin. Meanwhile he developed good relations with other member states, which will become more important after enlargement. But public opinion in Britain remained sceptical about membership of the EU and increasingly hostile to the euro. The prospect of winning a referendum on the euro looked as remote at the end of Blair's first parliament as it did at the beginning – while a difference of opinion had opened up semi-publicly between him and his Chancellor on the issue.

If Blair's big legacy could not be the adoption of the euro, he would have to find something else. It could have been the reform of the constitution – he had after all devolved power to Scotland, Wales, Northern Ireland and London; he had got rid of most of the hereditary peers from the House of Lords; and he had passed the Human Rights Act, a legally-enforceable declaration of the fundamental rights of all British citizens. Historians may well look back on all of these as significant, but they were not linked and Blair himself was unenthusiastic about each of them.

A connected 'project' could have been a coalition with the Liberal Democrats, which held a broad-sweep-of-history attraction about which Blair *was* enthusiastic – until it came to the details of a system of proportional representation which would be the condition. Some kind of deal between Labour and the Liberal Democrats may still be possible, but it is unlikely to carry the full weight of 'the Century of the Radicals' proclaimed by Blair in his millenarian mode.

It was not just the squeeze on public spending over the first two years, therefore, which accounted for Blair's tardiness in paying close attention to the problems of delivering better public services. It was that, without the euro, he would need an alternative claim to his place in history. Gordon Brown's programme of redistribution by stealth was important and worthy, as was his own attempt to tackle the multiple causes of 'social exclusion' by trying to get departments to work together. But they lacked the electoral and sweep-of-history appeal of being able to claim after two terms in government to be the Prime Minister who 're-founded the NHS' or who made the British education system 'the envy of the world'. One of the factors which will determine Blair's ultimate place in the rankings of prime ministers is whether such objectives are achievable, and whether public services can be improved so sharply that the electorate will be impressed.

Strengths and weaknesses

If the record of his first four years in government left the core of his political beliefs still surprisingly unclear, it revealed much more about his strengths and weaknesses as a politician. Although he was lucky in his double inheritance – of a sound economy and a dysfunctional Opposition – he managed to avoid squandering either opportunity. It is easy to overlook the importance of avoiding mistakes in politics, and Blair, an unnaturally careful, sharp and risk-averse politician, has made remarkably few of them.

He understood very well, from the beginning, that a political career can be finished in an instant by one false move. His is an unusual character, therefore, in that he combines great self-confidence with great caution. He refused a television debate with William Hague, just as he did with John Major, not because he did not think he was better than them but because he did not think the small risk of his making a damaging mistake was worth it. He also used to be terribly nervous before speeches or interviews, but these were actor's nerves, always about the technical aspects of the performance and never about his right to the centre of the stage.

There is a tension, however, between the lower Blair, who plays percentage politics, always calculating the odds and usually deciding not to take the risk, and the higher Blair, who talks of instinct, conviction and destiny. In fact, that tension is more apparent than real, because the lower Blair almost always has the upper hand. He does have instincts, but they are not so much for what he feels is right, but for what he feels will go down well with the voters.

Thus although he can agonise for hours over how exactly he should respond to a particular question if it is asked, in order to maximise his political advantage, he can also give a spontaneous answer to those unexpected personal questions which often produce the off-key remark which defines a politician forever in the public mind. The best example is his answer to the question asked by *Parents* magazine in 1996: did he smack his children when they were younger? It is the sort of question that a politician is almost bound to get wrong, but he managed to go straight down the middle. Yes, he said, but 'I always regretted it because there are lots of ways of disciplining a child and I don't believe that belting them is the best one'.[6]

That ability to pick up and reflect back the banality of majority was one of his great political strengths. As he climbed the ladder of ambition, his feel for the conventional wisdom of the focus group, his knack of not making enemies and his skill in telling people what they wanted to hear were assets. As Prime Minister, they sometimes became limiting.

There was one outstanding exception to the dominance of the lower Blair, and that was the Kosovo war, in which the high moral imperative of resisting 'ethnic cleansing' took priority and the risks were all on the downside. The lessons of that episode were ambiguous, however. Blair's boldness was vindicated completely – not only were the Kosovo Albanians liberated from Slobodan Milosevic's oppression but Milosevic himself was overthrown democratically by the Serbs themselves eighteen months later. And yet Blair's reward in domestic politics was approximately nil. While he might have gained confidence in his judgment, there was no incentive to take further risks.

In his first term, then, Blair has been a competent Prime Minister with one-off achievements in Ireland and Kosovo to his name, but no great advances which earn him reserves of gratitude and loyalty among his party or the mass of his fellow citizens. But he has demonstrated the confidence and – with the sacking of his friend Peter Mandelson – the brutality to do more.

Notes

1. *New Yorker*, 5 February 1996.
2. Roy Hattersley, *Observer*, 3 May 1998.
3. *Renewal*, Spring 2000.
4. *House Magazine*, 2 October 1995.
5. Mansion House speech, 22 November 1999.
6. *Parents* magazine, 5 June 1996.

Appendix I
Chronology

6 May 1953	Anthony Charles Lynton Blair born, Edinburgh
1955–58	Family lives in Adelaide, Australia, before settling in Durham
1958–61	Attends Western Hill pre–preparatory school, Durham
1961–66	Attends Chorister School, Durham
4 July 1964	Father Leo deprived of the power of speech for three years by a stroke
26 March 1966	Conservative candidate in school mock election
1966–71	Attends Fettes College, Edinburgh: A-levels in English, French and History
1971–72	Year off in London: 'manages' rock bands
1972–75	Reads law at St John's College, Oxford: Upper Second class degree
Spring 1974	Confirmed in the Church of England by College chaplain
1974–75	Lead singer in Ugly Rumours, student rock band
28 June 1975	Mother Hazel dies
Autumn 1975	Moves to Earl's Court, London; joins Chelsea Labour Party
October 1975	Starts one-year Bar course at Lincoln's Inn
Early 1976	Meets fellow law student Cherie Booth
Summer 1976	Works in a bar in Paris

Autumn 1976	Begins pupillage to Derry Irvine, with Cherie Booth
Summer 1977	Secures tenancy in Derry Irvine's chambers
29 March 1980	Marries Cherie Booth, St John's College Chapel, Oxford
27 May 1982	Contests Beaconsfield by-election during Falklands War (loses deposit)
20 May 1983	Selected as candidate for Sedgefield, after election campaign began
9 June 1983	Elected MP for Sedgefield; Cherie comes third in Thanet North
7 November 1984	Appointed junior Treasury spokesman
11 June 1987	General Election
8 July 1987	Second runner-up at first attempt, shadow Cabinet election; promoted to spokesman on the City and consumer affairs, deputy to Bryan Gould, shadow Trade and Industry Secretary
10 November 1988	Elected to shadow Cabinet; appointed shadow Energy Secretary
November 1989	Appointed shadow Employment Secretary
17 December 1989	Announces Labour's support for law against the closed shop
9 April 1992	General Election
18 July 1992	John Smith and Margaret Beckett elected Labour leader, deputy leader
July 1992	Gordon Brown first, Blair second, in shadow Cabinet elections; appointed shadow Chancellor and shadow Home Secretary
October 1992	Elected at first attempt with Brown to Labour National Executive
29 September 1993	One member, one vote carried at Labour conference, Blackpool
12 May 1994	John Smith dies
21 July 1994	Blair elected leader of the Labour Party
29 April 1995	Special Labour conference approved new Clause IV, Westminster
17 March 1997	John Major granted dissolution of parliament
1 May 1997	General Election

Government, 1997

2 May	Tony Blair appointed Prime Minister
6 May	Bank of England made independent
16 May	Blair to Belfast to re-start peace talks
12 June	Lord Irvine's refurbishment, including authentic wallpaper, reported
16 June	Inter-governmental conference at Amsterdam agrees minor amendments to European Union treaties
19 June	Blair's decision to save the Millennium Dome announced; William Hague elected Conservative leader
22–23 June	G7 summit in Denver
30 June	Hong Kong handed back to China
2 July	First Budget: windfall tax on privatised utilities, new tax on pension funds
20 July	IRA restores its ceasefire
22 July	Liberal Democrats join Cabinet committee on constitutional reform
23 July	Student fees plan announced
31 July	Conservatives increase majority in Uxbridge by-election
3 August	Robin Cook, Foreign Secretary, announces he is leaving his wife
30 August	Diana, Princess of Wales, and Dodi Fayed killed in Paris car crash
11 September	'Yes–Yes' vote in referendum on Scottish parliament
18 September	Narrow 'Yes' vote in referendum on Welsh assembly
29 September	Peter Mandelson loses to Ken Livingstone in National Executive election
18 October	'Brown rules out single currency for lifetime of this parliament' headline on *Times* interview with Chancellor
27 October	Brown statement on the euro in the Commons
5 November	Plan to exempt Formula 1 from tobacco advertising ban reported
11 November	Formula One chief Bernie Ecclestone reveals £1m donation to Labour
16 November	Blair apologises in television interview for handling of Ecclestone affair

30 November	Paymaster General Geoffrey Robinson's £12m Guernsey trust reported
1 December	Roy Jenkins appointed to chair electoral reform commission
8 December	Social Exclusion Unit announced
10 December	Forty-seven Labour MPs vote against cut in lone-parent benefit

Government, 1998

1 January	Home Secretary Jack Straw's son named as teenager who sold cannabis
1 January	Start of Britain's six-month presidency of the European Union
9 January	Gordon Brown's resentment revealed in premature release of biography
18 January	Source close to Blair despairs of Brown's 'psychological flaws'
13 March	Private Member's Bill to ban fox-hunting talked out
17 March	Second Budget: Working Families Tax Credit; partial retreat on lone-parent benefit
24 March	Blair's address in French to the National Assembly in Paris
10 April	Good Friday Agreement reached at Stormont, Northern Ireland
2 May	Appointment of Wim Duisenberg as European Central Bank president agreed at London summit
3 May	Press 'hoo-ha' begins over arms to Sierra Leone
7 May	'Yes' vote on low turnout in referendum on London mayor and authority
22 May	'Yes' vote in Irish referendums, north and south
18 June	Minimum wage set for April 1999: £3.60 p.h. and £3 for under-22s
25 June	Elections to Northern Ireland assembly
5 July	Derek Draper's boasts of influence-peddling reported by the *Observer*
14 July	Comprehensive Spending Review: plans for three years from April 1999
27 July	Cabinet reshuffle: Peter Mandelson, Stephen Byers, Margaret Jay in; Harriet Harman, Ivor Richard out; Frank Field resigns

15 August	Omagh bomb kills twenty-eight
2–3 September	UK and Irish parliaments recalled to pass new anti-terrorist laws
21 September	Blair at Third Way seminar in New York with Bill Clinton
27 September	Gerhard Schröder defeats Helmut Kohl in German election
16 October	Augusto Pinochet arrested in London on Spanish extradition warrant
27 October	Ron Davies resigns as Welsh Secretary
29 October	Roy Jenkins's report advocates 'Alternative Vote Plus' electoral system
7 November	Nick Brown, Agriculture Minister, announces he is gay
2 December	Robert Cranborne sacked as Tory leader in the Lords for dealing with Blair over rights of hereditary peers
16 December	American–British Operation Desert Fox launched against Iraq
21 December	The *Guardian* reports Trade and Industry Secretary Peter Mandelson's £373,000 loan from Geoffrey Robinson, Paymaster General
23 December	Peter Mandelson and Geoffrey Robinson resign from government

Government, 1999

1 January	Launch of euro: currencies of eleven EU countries locked together
20 January	Paddy Ashdown announces retirement as Liberal Democrat leader
23 February	Blair statement in Commons on National Changeover Plan to the euro
24 February	Macpherson report on killing of Stephen Lawrence published
9 March	Third Budget: narrow 10p starting rate of income tax replaces broad 20p band; next year's cut in basic rate from 22p to 22p announced
15 March	Entire European Commission resigns after inquiry found nepotism and incompetence
18 March	Pledge at Toynbee Hall to 'end child poverty' in twenty years

24 March	Nato begins bombing Yugoslavia in response to 'ethnic cleansing' in Kosovo
9 April	Stephen Byers, Trade and Industry Secretary, rejects Rupert Murdoch's bid for Manchester United
22 April	Blair's speech on the 'doctrine of international community' in Chicago
6 May	First elections for Scottish parliament and Welsh assembly: Labour fails to win a majority in either
20 May	Sixty-five Labour MPs rebel against cuts in Incapacity Benefit
3 June	Yugoslav President Slobodan Milosevic agrees to Nato terms on Kosovo
10 June	European Parliament elections under new proportional system: Conservatives 36 per cent, Labour 28 per cent, on turnout of 23 per cent
14 July	European Union orders ban on British beef to be lifted (it isn't)
14 July	Ulster Unionist Party executive rejects Blair–Ahern *Way Forward* plan
22 July	Conservatives hold Eddisbury in by-election with barely changed majority
28 July	'Night of the Short Knives': Cabinet escapes in reshuffle of lower ranks
23 September	Strong Scottish National Party challenge in Hamilton South by-election
11 October	Mandelson back in Cabinet as Northern Ireland Secretary in further reshuffle
18 November	George Mitchell publishes review of Northern Ireland peace talks
18 November	Announcement that the Blairs are expecting their fourth child
27 November	Ulster Unionist Party council accepts Mitchell review proposals
29 November	Northern Ireland Assembly elects ministers including Sinn Fein
18 December	Shaun Woodward MP defects from Conservatives to Labour
31 December	Blair holds hands with the Queen at millennium celebration in the Dome

Government, 2000

12 January	Jack Straw announces he is minded to send Pinochet back to Chile; Pinochet goes on 2 March
16 January	Blair pledges on *Breakfast With Frost* to raise health spending by a quarter in real terms to the EU average by 2005
20 January	House of Lords votes against restricting the right to trial by jury
30 January	Peter Kilfoyle resigns as defence minister, criticising New Labour
9 February	Alun Michael resigns as first minister of Wales before confidence vote
11 February	Northern Ireland assembly suspended after ten weeks
20 February	Frank Dobson selected as Labour candidate for London mayor over Ken Livingstone, who announces as an independent candidate on 6 March
21 March	Gordon Brown's fourth Budget confirms spending increases on the NHS
3 April	Forty-one Labour MPs rebel in vote on 75p-a-week rise in state pension
4 May	Ken Livingstone elected London mayor; Lib Dems win Romsey from Conservatives in by-election
6 May	IRA statement offers to put arms dumps verifiably 'beyond use'
7 May	Paratroopers deployed to Sierra Leone
9 May	Forty-six Labour MPs rebel in vote on part-privatisation of National Air Traffic Service
20 May	Blair's fourth child Leo born
27 May	Ulster Unionist Council votes to return to power-sharing, which resumes 30 May
7 June	Blair heckled at Women's Institute conference, Wembley Arena
30 June	Short-lived plan for cashpoint fines for drunken traffic-cone-throwers
6 July	Euan Blair, sixteen, arrested 'drunk and incapable' in Leicester Square
17 July	Leak of 'Touchstone Issues' memo, admitting perception as soft on crime
18 July	Second Comprehensive Spending Review: plans for three years from April 2001

8 September	Blockades of petrol refineries begin, called off 14 September
17 October	High-speed derailment near Hatfield kills four, requiring disruptive speed restrictions throughout the rail network
6–10 December	Nice summit agrees terms for European Union expansion

Government, 2001

2 and 4 January	Donations to Labour of £2m apiece announced from Lord Hamlyn and Christopher Ondaatje, and confirmed from Lord (David) Sainsbury
17 January	House of Commons votes (again) to ban fox-hunting
24 January	Peter Mandelson resigns from the Cabinet for a second time

Appendix II

Family Tree

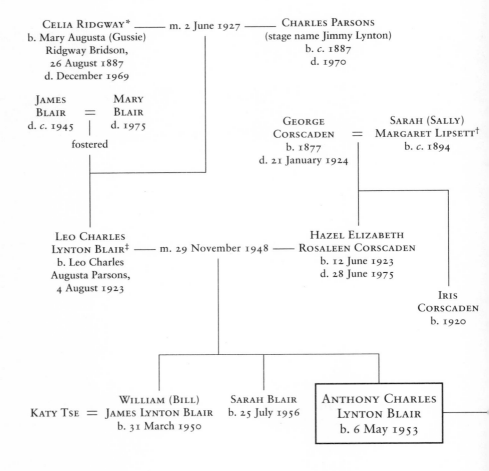

CELIA RIDGWAY* ———— m. 2 June 1927 ———— CHARLES PARSONS
b. Mary Augusta (Gussie) (stage name Jimmy Lynton)
Ridgway Bridson, b. *c.* 1887
26 August 1887 d. 1970
d. December 1969

JAMES MARY
BLAIR = BLAIR GEORGE SARAH (SALLY)
d. *c.* 1945 | d. 1975 CORSCADEN = MARGARET LIPSETT†
 fostered b. 1877 b. *c.* 1894
 d. 21 January 1924

LEO CHARLES HAZEL ELIZABETH
LYNTON BLAIR‡ ——— m. 29 November 1948 ——— ROSALEEN CORSCADEN
b. Leo Charles b. 12 June 1923
Augusta Parsons, d. 28 June 1975
4 August 1923
 IRIS
 CORSCADEN
 b. 1920

 WILLIAM (BILL) SARAH BLAIR ANTHONY CHARLES
KATY TSE = JAMES LYNTON BLAIR b. 25 July 1956 LYNTON BLAIR
 b. 31 March 1950 b. 6 May 1953

* Celia Ridgway's first two marriages had been to a Mr Tordiffe and to Hugh Wilson.
† Sally Lipsett subsequently married William (Willy) McLay, in 1926.
‡ Leo Blair subsequently married Olwen, on 2 August 1980.

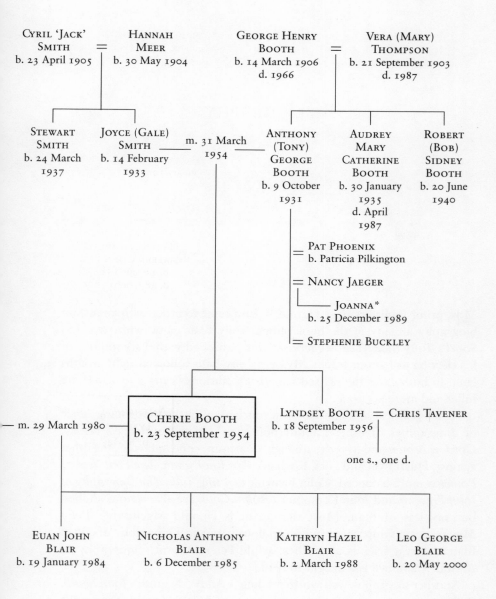

Cyril 'Jack' Smith
b. 23 April 1905
= Hannah Meer
b. 30 May 1904

- Stewart Smith
  b. 24 March 1937
- Joyce (Gale) Smith
  b. 14 February 1933

George Henry Booth
b. 14 March 1906
d. 1966
= Vera (Mary) Thompson
b. 21 September 1903
d. 1987

- Anthony (Tony) George Booth
  b. 9 October 1931
- Audrey Mary Catherine Booth
  b. 30 January 1935
  d. April 1987
- Robert (Bob) Sidney Booth
  b. 20 June 1940

Joyce (Gale) Smith — m. 31 March 1954 — Anthony (Tony) George Booth

Anthony (Tony) George Booth
= Pat Phoenix
b. Patricia Pilkington
= Nancy Jaeger
- Joanna*
  b. 25 December 1989
= Stephenie Buckley

Children of Joyce (Gale) Smith and Anthony (Tony) George Booth:
- Cherie Booth
  b. 23 September 1954
- Lyndsey Booth
  b. 18 September 1956
  = Chris Tavener
  - one s., one d.

— m. 29 March 1980 — Cherie Booth

- Euan John Blair
  b. 19 January 1984
- Nicholas Anthony Blair
  b. 6 December 1985
- Kathryn Hazel Blair
  b. 2 March 1988
- Leo George Blair
  b. 20 May 2000

* Tony Booth's other children (Cherie's half-sisters) are Jenia and Bronwen Booth (by Julie Allan) and Lauren (born Sarah Jane) and Emma Booth (by Suzie Riley-Smith).

Bibliography

Most prime ministers since Harold Wilson came to office with an instant biography already in the book shops. Tony Blair came with two. Jon Sopel's *Tony Blair: The Moderniser* was published within six months of his election as Labour leader. My own *Tony Blair* followed eight months later. In both cases the revised paperback editions (1995 and 1996) are fuller and more accurate.

Blair's political life has also been touched on in the burgeoning range of biographies of other Labour politicians. Paul Routledge's books, *Gordon Brown* and *Mandy*, are highly partisan – one in favour, the other against. Hugh Pym and Nick Kochan's *Gordon Brown: The First Year of Power* is more balanced. Colin Brown's *Fighting Talk: The Biography of John Prescott* and John Kampfner's *Robin Cook* are also serious studies, but say less of Blair. Most significant is Donald Macintyre's *Peter Mandelson*, a sympathetic but scrupulously sceptical biography of one of Blair's closest friends and allies, while Peter Oborne's biography of Alastair Campbell is a delight to read.

Another biography well worth reading is Andy McSmith's *John Smith: A Life, 1938–1994*, and McSmith's *Faces of Labour* (again, choose the revised paperback edition) contains an excellent chapter on Blair.

Not only do biographies come earlier these days, but the memoirs – which used to wait for the twilight years of retirement – started with the Blair government not eighteen months old. Philip Gould, opinion polling adviser to the Labour Party and to Blair personally, published *The*

Unfinished Revolution: How the Modernisers Saved the Labour Party in 1998. As its subtitle makes clear, it is a strongly biased account, and yet provides important insights into Blair's thinking and that of the clique around him.

The political diaries started to be published earlier than before, too, with Ivor Richard providing glimpses of Blair, who sacked him as Labour leader in the House of Lords in July 1998, through the diaries of his wife Janet Jones, *Labour of Love*. The former Liberal Democrat leader's *The Ashdown Diaries* gave a fuller picture of Blair and his ways of working, albeit through the lens of Paddy Ashdown's unrequited desire for coalition.

For Blair's beliefs, *The Personal World: John Macmurray on Self and Society*, edited by Philip Cornford, is the best introduction to the Prime Minister's mentor. Blair's own foreword to *Reclaiming the Ground*, edited by Christopher Bryant, is a short statement of his Christian socialism. A collection of Blair's articles and speeches was published before the election under the title *New Britain*.

Several analyses of Blair's government are worth reading. Peter Hennessy's *The Prime Minister* is an outstanding contemporary history of the office and how Blair has used it; the coda, Chapter 19, measuring Blair up to his post-war predecessors, is a gem of concise assessment. Andrew Rawnsley's *Servants of the People* is a better and more serious analysis of Blair's first term than the sensational reporting of one or two of its colourful third-hand quotations suggested.

The following bibliography lists the books cited. The place of publication is London unless specified.

Leo Abse, *The Man Behind the Smile: Tony Blair and the Politics of Perversion* (Robson Books, 1996)

Paul Anderson and Nyta Mann, *Safety First: The Making of New Labour* (Granta Books, 1997)

Anonymous (Joe Klein), *Primary Colors* (Chatto & Windus, 1996)

Paddy Ashdown, *The Ashdown Diaries, Volume I: 1988–1997* (Allen Lane/The Penguin Press, 2000)

Clement Attlee, *As It Happened* (Heinemann, 1954)

Anthony Barker, *Ruling by Task Force: The Politico's Guide to Labour's New Elite* (Politico's Publishing in association with Democratic Audit, 1999)

Martin Bell, *An Accidental MP* (Viking, 2000)

Tony Blair, *New Britain: My Vision of a Young Country* (collection of speeches, articles and interviews; Fourth Estate, 1996)

David Blunkett, *On a Clear Day* (Michael O'Mara Books, 1995)

Tony Booth, *Stroll On: An Autobiography* (Sidgwick & Jackson, 1989)

Gyles Brandreth, *Breaking the Code: Westminster Diaries* (Weidenfeld & Nicolson, 1999)

Colin Brown, *Fighting Talk: The Biography of John Prescott* (Simon & Schuster, 1997)

Gordon Brown and James Naughtie (eds), *John Smith: Life and Soul of the Party* (Edinburgh: Mainstream, 1994)

Michael Brunson, *A Ringside Seat* (Hodder & Stoughton, 2000)

Christopher Bryant (ed.), *Reclaiming the Ground* (Hodder & Stoughton, 1993)

Trevor Burridge, *Clement Attlee* (Jonathan Cape, 1985)

David Butler and Dennis Kavanagh, *The British General Election of 1983* (Macmillan, 1984)

——, *The British General Election of 1997* (Macmillan, 1997)

James Callaghan, *Time and Chance* (Collins, 1987)

John Campbell, *Margaret Thatcher, Volume I: The Grocer's Daughter* (Jonathan Cape, 2000)

Alan Clark, *Diaries* (Weidenfeld & Nicolson, 1993)

Peter Clarke, *A Question of Leadership: From Gladstone to Blair* (Penguin, *1991*; second edition, 1999)

Ken Coates (ed.), *Clause IV: Common Ownership and the Labour Party* (Nottingham: Spokesman, 1995)

Margaret Cook, *A Slight and Delicate Creature* (Weidenfeld & Nicolson, 1999)

Michael Crick, *Militant* (Faber & Faber, 1984)

Ralf Dahrendorf, *LSE: A History of the London School of Economics and Political Science, 1895–1995* (Oxford: OUP, 1995)

Hunter Davies, *Born 1900: A Human History of the Twentieth Century – For Everyone Who Was There* (Little, Brown & Co., 1998)

Norman Dennis and A. H. Halsey, *English Ethical Socialism: Thomas More to R. H. Tawney* (Oxford: Clarendon Press, 1988)

Derek Draper, *Blair's Hundred Days* (Faber & Faber, 1997)

Roger Eatwell, *The Labour Government, 1945–51* (Batsford Academic, 1979)

Dominic Egan, *Irvine: Politically Correct?* (Edinburgh: Mainstream, 1999)

Geoffrey Evans and Pippa Norris (eds), *British Parties and Voters in Long-Term Perspective* (Sage, 1999)

Frank Field, *How to Pay for the Future: Building a Stakeholders' Welfare* (Institute of Community Studies, 1996)

Michael Foot, *Another Heart and Other Pulses* (Collins, 1984)
Misha Glenny, *The Balkans, 1804–1999: Nationalism, War and the Great Powers* (Granta Books, 1999)
Dean Godson, *David Trimble* (HarperCollins, 2000)
Bryan Gould, *Goodbye to All That* (Macmillan, 1995)
Philip Gould, *The Unfinished Revolution: How the Modernisers Saved the Labour Party* (Little, Brown & Co., 1998)
A. H. Halsey, *No Discouragement: An Autobiography* (Macmillan, 1996)
——, *see also* Norman Dennis
Eric Hammond, *Maverick: The Life of a Union Rebel* (Weidenfeld & Nicolson, 1992)
David Hare, *Asking Around* (Faber & Faber, 1993)
Robert Harris, *The Making of Neil Kinnock* (Faber & Faber, 1984)
Bob Hawke, *The Hawke Memoirs* (Heinemann, 1994)
Anthony Heath, Roger Jowell and John Curtice, *How Britain Votes* (Oxford: Pergamon Press, 1985)
Anthony Heath *et al.*, *Understanding Political Change* (Oxford: Pergamon Press, 1991)
Peter Hennessy, *The Prime Minister: The Office and Its Holders Since 1945* (Allen Lane/The Penguin Press, 2000)
Dave Hill, *Out for the Count: Politicians and the People* (Macmillan, 1992)
Christopher Hitchens, *No One Left to Lie to: The Triangulations of William Jefferson Clinton* (Verso, 1999)
Alistair Horne, *Macmillan, 1957–1986: Volume II of the Official Biography* (Macmillan, 1989)
Colin Hughes and Patrick Wintour, *Labour Rebuilt: The New Model Party* (Fourth Estate, 1990)
Kevin Jefferys (ed.), *Leading Labour: From Keir Hardie to Tony Blair* (I. B. Tauris, 1999)
Janet Jones (wife of Ivor Richard, Labour leader in the House of Lords, 1997–98), *Labour of Love: The 'Partly-Political' Diary of a Cabinet Minister's Wife* (Politico's Publishing, 1999)
Mervyn Jones, *Michael Foot* (Victor Gollancz, 1994)
Nicholas Jones, *Soundbites and Spin Doctors* (Cassell, 1995)
——, *Election '97* (Cassell, 1997)
——, *Sultans of Spin* (Victor Gollancz, 1999)
John Kampfner, *Robin Cook* (Victor Gollancz, 1998)
Dennis Kavanagh and Anthony Seldon, *The Powers Behind the Prime Minister: The Hidden Influence of Number Ten* (HarperCollins, 1999)

Joe Klein, *see* Anonymous

David Kogan and Maurice Kogan, *The Battle for the Labour Party* (Fontana, 1982)

David Kusnet, *Speaking American: How the Democrats Can Win the Nineties* (New York: Thunder's Mouth Press, 1992)

Norman Lamont, *In Office* (Little, Brown & Co., 1999)

Jack Lawson, *Peter Lee* (The Epworth Press, 1949)

Nigel Lawson, *The View from No. 11* (Bantam Press, 1992; Corgi, 1993)

Ken Livingstone, *If Voting Changed Anything, They'd Abolish It* (Collins, 1987)

Donald Macintyre, *Mandelson: The Biography* (HarperCollins, 1999)

David McKittrick, *Through the Minefield* (Belfast: Blackstaff Press, 1999)

John Macmurray, *The Self as Agent* (Faber & Faber, 1957; new edition, 1995)

——, *Persons in Relation* (Faber & Faber, 1961; new edition, 1995)

——, *The Personal World: John Macmurray on Self and Society*, selected and introduced by Philip Cornford (Edinburgh: Floris Books, 1996)

Andy McSmith, *John Smith: A Life, 1938–1994*, revised edition of *Playing the Long Game* (Mandarin, 1994)

——, *Faces of Labour* (Verso, 1997)

John Major, *The Autobiography* (HarperCollins, 1999)

Noel Malcolm, *Kosovo: A Short History* (Macmillan, 1998)

Peter Mandelson and Roger Liddle, *The Blair Revolution: Can New Labour Deliver?* (Faber & Faber, 1996)

Will Marshall and Martin Schram (eds), *Mandate for Change* (New York: Berkley Books, 1993)

Mary Matalin and James Carville, *All's Fair: Love, War and Running for President* (Hutchinson, 1994)

Austin Mitchell, *Beyond the Blue Horizon* (Bellew, 1989)

George Mitchell, *Making Peace: The Inside Story of the Making of the Good Friday Agreement* (William Heinemann, 1999)

Kenneth O. Morgan, *Callaghan: A Life* (Oxford: OUP, 1997)

Andrew Neil, *Full Disclosure* (Macmillan, 1996; Pan, 1997)

Pippa Norris, John Curtice, David Sanders, Margaret Scammell and Holli Semetko, *On Message: Communicating the Campaign* (Sage, 1999)

Michael Oakeshott, *Rationalism in Politics* (Methuen, 1962)

Peter Oborne, *Alastair Campbell: New Labour and the Rise of the Media Class* (Aurum Press, 1999)

Matthew Parris, *Look Behind You!* (Robson Books, 1993)

Robert Philp, *A Keen Wind Blows: The Story of Fettes College* (James & James, 1998)

Pat Phoenix (Patricia Pilkington), *Love, Curiosity, Freckles & Doubt* (Granada, 1983)

Ben Pimlott, *Harold Wilson* (HarperCollins, 1992)

Raymond Postgate, *The Life of George Lansbury* (Longman, 1951)

Hugh Pym and Nick Kochan, *Gordon Brown: The First Year of Power* (Bloomsbury, 1998)

Andrew Rawnsley, *Servants of the People: The Inside Story of New Labour* (Hamish Hamilton, 2000)

John Rentoul, *Tony Blair* (Little, Brown & Co., 1995)

Geoffrey Robinson, *The Unconventional Minister: My Life Inside New Labour* (Michael Joseph, 2000)

Paul Routledge, *Gordon Brown: The Biography* (Simon & Schuster, 1998)

——, *Mandy: The Unauthorised Biography of Peter Mandelson* (Simon & Schuster, 1999)

Michael J. Sandel, *Liberalism and Limits of Justice* (Cambridge: CUP, 1982)

David Selbourne, *The Principle of Duty* (Sinclair-Stevenson, 1994)

Anthony Seldon, *John Major: A Political Life* (Weidenfeld & Nicolson, 1997)

——, *see also* Dennis Kavanagh

Patrick Seyd and Paul Whiteley, *Labour's Grass Roots: The Politics of Party Membership* (Oxford: Clarendon Press, 1992)

Robert Shepherd, *Iain Macleod* (Hutchinson, 1994)

Peter Shore, *Leading the Left* (Weidenfeld & Nicolson, 1993)

Jon Sopel, *Tony Blair: The Moderniser* (Michael Joseph, 1995)

George Stephanopoulos, *All Too Human: A Political Education* (New York: Little, Brown, 1999)

R. H. Tawney, *Equality* (Allen & Unwin, 1931; fourth revised edition, 1952)

Norman Tebbit, *Upwardly Mobile* (Futura, 1989)

Margaret Thatcher, *The Revival of Britain: Speeches on Home and European Affairs, 1975–88* (Aurum Press, 1989)

——, *The Downing Street Years* (HarperCollins, 1993)

——, *The Path to Power* (HarperCollins, 1995)

Alexis de Tocqueville, *Democracy in America* (1835; edited by Phillips Bradley, New York: Vintage, 1945)

Martin Walker, *Clinton: The President They Deserve* (Fourth Estate, 1996)

Alan Wilkinson, *Christian Socialism: Scott Holland to Tony Blair* (SCM Press, 1998)

John Williams and Tom Stoddart, *Victory: With Tony Blair on the Road to a Landslide* (Bookman, 1997)

Philip M. Williams, *Hugh Gaitskell: A Political Biography* (Jonathan Cape, 1979)

Harold Wilson, *The New Britain: Labour's Plan Outlined by Harold Wilson* (selected speeches; Harmondsworth: Penguin Books, 1964)

——, *The Governance of Britain* (Weidenfeld & Nicolson, 1976)

Tony Blair's main government speeches as Prime Minister are on the Internet at:

www.number-10.gov.uk

Many of his more recent Labour Party speeches are at:

www.labour.org.uk

Select committee reports can be found at:

www.parliament.the-stationery-office.co.uk/pa/cm/cmselect

Index

Abacha, General Sani, 425
Abbott, Diane, 262, 307
abortion, 199
Abse, Leo, 7n.
Adams, Gerry, 402, 403, 404, 410, 411, 412, 414–15, 417, 424
Adelaide, 9
Adonis, Andrew, 312, 552
advertising: Tory anti-Labour adverts, 285, 297; tobacco advertising ban, 307, 358, 364–70, 546; Labour leadership election, 359
Advertising Standards Authority, 285
Afghanistan, 410, 424
African National Congress (ANC), 193, 416–17
agriculture, 441
Ahern, Bertie, 405, 406, 408, 409–10, 412, 413, 418
Ahtisaari, Martti, 416, 529
Ailes, Roger, 501n.
Albania, 528, 529; Albanians in Kosovo, 510–11, 513, 514, 518–20, 523, 527
Albright, Madeleine, 524
Alderdice, John, 334, 405, 406
Alexander, Douglas, 386
Allan, Alex, 332, 536
Allan, Tim, 240, 277
Alton, David, 199
Amess, David, 178
Amiel, Barbara, 186–7, 303
Anderson, Eric, 15, 17, 18, 20, 21
Archer, Jeffrey, 563
Argentina, 82
Armstrong, Ernie, 91–2
Armstrong, Hilary, 92, 104
Ashdown, Paddy, 333, 393, 397, 456, 481; and TB as Labour leader, 251; possible coalition, 289–90, 325–6, 389, 488–9, 490–3, 497, 498; and electoral reform, 292, 493–9; retirement, 497; and Balkan conflicts, 509
Asquith, H. H., 7, 328, 449
Atkinson, Rowan, 10
Attlee, Clement, 13, 24, 199, 254, 264, 293, 315, 316, 332, 354n., 383, 505n., 512, 580
Australia, 9, 46, 69, 170, 195, 279–81
Avila da Silva, Reinaldo, 469, 470
Ayling, Bob, 559

Baker, James, 128
Balfour, Arthur, 506
Balkans, 509–12, 513–15, 517–31

Balliol College, Oxford, 20–1
Balls, Ed, 331, 382, 383, 387, 389, 543
Bank of England, 132, 314, 330–1, 437, 475, 476, 540
Banks, Tony, 366
Barak, Daphne, 300
Barbour, Haley, 431, 436
Barker, Anthony, 545
Barker, Godfrey, 82, 86
Barlow Clowes, 138, 147
Barnett, Joel, 104
Baxter, Sarah, 228
BBC, 85, 87, 100, 127, 131, 142, 144, 154, 167, 178, 185, 186, 192–3, 207, 228, 235, 314, 355, 368–9, 387, 397, 414, 443, 484, 494, 511, 547
Beaconsfield by-election (1982), 73–4, 79, 81–8, 530, 562
Beckett, Margaret: 1992 election, 168, 177; deputy leadership election (1992), 181, 184–5, 186; 'one member, one vote' issue, 214, 236–7, 242; opinion polls, 230, 235; deputy leadership campaign (1994), 236–7, 238, 242–3, 247, 359; in Cabinet, 326, 385, 542
Begala, Paul, 194–5, 197–8, 432
Beith, Alan, 492, 493
Bell, Martin, 305, 562
Bell, Ronald, 81
Bell, Stuart, 67
Beloff, Michael, 302–3
Benn, Caroline, 292–3
Benn, Tony, 51, 83, 88, 92–3, 105, 123, 125, 341, 413, 492; Labour leadership contest (1980), 65, 66–7, 71; deputy leadership election (1981), 75, 139, 242; and the Labour Co-ordinating Committee, 76–7; and the Beaconsfield by-election, 84, 85, 93; 1983 election, 113; loses National Executive seat, 213; opposition to Kosovo war, 523
Berger, Sandy, 524–5
Berlusconi, Silvio, 391
Bernstein, Alex, 362
Beswick, Colin, 10
Bevan, Aneurin, 198–9, 253, 293, 341, 547
Bevins, Anthony, 385 and n.
Bickerstaffe, Rodney, 545
Birt, John, 545
Black, Conrad, 230
Blair, Euan (TB's son), 149, 185, 244, 300, 324, 344, 575; birth, 122–3; education, 257–8, 281–2, 283–4; 1997 election, 314; arrested for drunkenness, 484, 544, 576
Blair, Hazel (TB's mother), 29; and Leo's stroke, 3, 4–5, 12; her daughter's illness, 5, 12; early life, 8; in Australia, 9; and TB's childhood, 11–12; relations with TB, 16, 47; death, 47–8
Blair, James, 5, 6
Blair, Kathryn (TB's daughter), 122–3, 168, 300, 324, 504
Blair, Leo (TB's father), 22, 29, 324; suffers stroke, 3–5, 11, 12; political ambitions, 4, 9–10; early life, 5–8; academic career, 8–9; in Australia, 9; legal career, 9; and TB's education, 10, 14; relations with TB, 16; and his wife's death, 47–8; 1983 election, 108; 1997 election, 314
Blair, Leo (TB's son), 544, 574, 575, 576
Blair, Mary, 5, 6, 7
Blair, Nicholas ('Nicky', TB's son), 122, 244, 300, 314, 324, 344
Blair, Olwen (TB's stepmother), 324
Blair, Sarah (TB's sister), 5, 9, 12, 48, 60, 324, 575
Blair, Tony:
  early life and education: and his father's stroke, 3–4, 11, 12; family background, 5–8; birth, 8; in Australia, 9; Durham Chorister School, 10–11, 12; holidays, 11; Conservatism, 12–13; Fettes College, 14–25; left-wing leanings, 23–4; gap year in London, 28–34; lack of interest in politics, 33; at Oxford, 35–47; formation of political views, 35–7, 40–3, 45–6, 47, 49; girlfriends, 40; his mother's death, 47–8; legal career, 48–9, 52, 54–6, 57; journalism, 58–9
  early political career: early political ambition, 3, 4, 56; joins Labour Party, 51, 52; in Hackney South Labour Party, 65, 66, 67–9, 89; 'one member, one vote' issue, 65–6, 99; looks for

parliamentary seat, 67–8, 72–3, 80–1, 91–2; Australian lecture, 69–70, 73, 77–80, 88, 90, 113, 114, 231; as a 'moderniser', 70, 114–16; Solidarity Campaign, 71–2, 74, 77; CND membership, 72–3; Beaconsfield by-election, 73–4, 79, 81–8; position on Europe, 73–4, 83–5, 96, 105, 107; Labour Co-ordinating Committee (LCC), 76–7, 137; battle against Militant, 90–1, 183; adopted as candidate in Sedgefield, 82, 93, 95–107; 1983 election, 95, 107–9, 113; curriculum vitae, 101–3

as an MP: 1983 leadership election, 113–14; relationship with Kinnock, 114; maiden speech, 115–16; relationship with Gordon Brown, 117, 118, 131, 185; joins Tribune Group, 118, 137; and the 1984 Trade Union Act, 119, 120–2; and the miners' strike, 124; media appearances, 127; and the Exchange Rate Mechanism, 129–31

in shadow Cabinet: in shadow Treasury team, 124–31, 133; modernisation of Labour, 126–7, 139–44, 171–3; advisers, 132, 136, 145–6; 1987 election, 133–4; shadow Cabinet elections, 136–7, 147, 153, 187; in shadow Trade and Industry team, 137–9; seniority gap with Brown, 138, 153, 159, 185, 188, 190; journalism, 146; Barlow Clowes affair, 147; shadow Energy Secretary, 148–51, 153; party political broadcasts, 149, 155–6; party conferences, 150–1, 163, 170; shadow Employment Secretary, 153–8, 160–2, 164–7, 213; as potential leader, 158–9, 170–1, 187–90; Mandelson advises, 160; 1992 election, 168–9, 175–8; deputy leadership election (1992), 178–86; as shadow Home Secretary, 187, 188–9, 192–4, 199–205; 1994 leadership election, 188, 359–60; 'one member, one vote' issue, 188, 207–12, 214–16; Clinton's influence, 194–8, 207, 267, 278; social moralism, 198–202, 205, 234–5, 249–50; adopts Conservative language, 200–1, 202; relations with John Smith, 216–17; and Smith's death, 221–4; leadership campaign, 224–41, 244–7; rift with Brown, 229, 232–3; and deputy leadership election, 242–3; relationship with Prescott, 242, 243

as Leader of the Opposition: Support for, 223; and New Labour, 223, 255, 263; and Clause IV, 249, 252–7, 259–63; strategy, 249–52, 263, 264–5; party conferences, 255–6, 269–70, 289; Prime Minister's Questions, 262–3, 272, 309; preparation for power, 267–93; Alan Howarth's defection, 270–1; shadow Cabinet, 271, 284–5; and Mandelson, 272–5; Thatcher's influence, 276–8, 581; use of media, 279–81; image, 284; and Liberal Democrats, 289–93, 325–6, 332; taxation policy, 296–8; 1997 election, 299–317, 575; blind trust, 361–2

as Prime Minister: first hundred days, 323–42, 343; forms Cabinet, 326–7, 332; Prime Minister's Questions, 332–3, 341, 466, 546, 550; Northern Ireland, 334, 400–18; 'Third Way', 172, 335, 422, 431–45; and Europe, 335–6; welfare reforms, 337, 339, 373–81; meets the public, 338–9, 378; 'family values', 340, 355; relations with Brown, 340, 382–9, 470, 542, 543; Ecclestone affair, 341, 358, 363–71, 466; death of Princess Diana, 344–7; salary, 358; Cabinet reshuffles, 385, 413, 541–2, 552; possible successor, 386–8; and media moguls, 391–3; Campbell's role, 393–4, 395–8; media management, 394–9; journalism, 396–7, 431; foreign policy, 420–9; Labour attitudes to, 435–6, 565–7; and equality, 439–41; attacks forces of conservatism, 443–5; House of Lords reform, 447–54; devolution, 454–9; Mandelson's home loan, 461–4, 468–9; accused of cronyism, 467; and the single currency, 472–86;

Blair, Tony – *contd*
as Prime Minister – contd
and Liberal Democrats, 488–99; and electoral reform, 493–8; education policy, 501–7; approval ratings, 504, 574; Kosovo war, 83, 336, 429, 509–12, 513–15, 516–31, 585; air strikes against Iraq, 512–13, 515–16; 'scars in my back' remark, 534, 537; Prime Minister's office, 535–7; special advisers, 535–6; management style, 538–47, 551–2; and the health service, 547–51; Millennium Dome, 555–9; elections for London's mayor, 561–5; loses touch with public opinion, 567–9; fuel crisis, 570–3, 576; leaked memos, 576; plans for 2001 election, 576, 578; Mandelson's second resignation, 577–8, 585; achievements as Prime Minister, 580–5
character and private life: early influences, 7; sporting ability, 10, 17, 36; religious beliefs, 11–12, 19, 28–9, 33, 43–4, 202, 236, 350–7; class background, 13–14, 24; accent, 14, 19; rebelliousness, 16–18, 20, 21–2; relations with parents, 16, 47; acting ability, 18–19, 21, 39–40; interest in rock music, 22, 28–30, 32–3, 37–9, 299–300; appearance, 31, 32, 37–8; and Cherie, 52–3, 55, 60, 63; homes, 65, 123, 168–9, 327–9; children, 122–3, 149, 300, 301, 328, 336, 574–6, 584; lists his own strengths, 236; children's education, 257–8, 283–4, 504, 505; holidays, 288–9, 339, 360, 462, 467, 469; defensiveness, 296; pessimism, 299; Euan's arrest, 484; blend of self-confidence and caution, 584–5
Blair, William (TB's brother), 4, 8, 9, 10, 14, 21, 60, 227, 324, 337, 575
Blishen, Chris, 28–9
block vote issue, 207–12, 213–16, 242, 263
Blunkett, David, 186, 213, 242, 387, 543, 575; social moralism, 202; in shadow Cabinet, 258–9, 271, 281–2, 283; in Cabinet, 341; university tuition fees, 438; education policy, 502–3, 505, 507
Bolton, Tim, 52
Booth, Cherie, 101, 145; education, 21, 52–3, 61–2; on TB, 51, 93; meets TB, 52–3, 55; legal training, 53, 54–5; early political activity, 56, 63; family background and early life, 60–3; marriage, 60, 63; in Hackney South Labour Party, 65, 66, 89; and LCC, 76–7, 93, 123–4; tries to become parliamentary candidate, 80; Beaconsfield by-election (1982), 86; as candidate for Thanet, 88, 91, 92–3; 1983 election, 107, 108; children, 122–3, 574, 575; and the miners' strike, 123–4; character, 161, 303–4; and 1992 deputy leadership election, 182, 185; TB's leadership campaign, 224–5, 241, 244; children's education, 257–8, 283–4, 504; 1997 election, 301–2, 308, 314, 315; appearance, 302; legal career, 302–3; TB becomes Prime Minister, 327–8; death of Princess Diana, 347; Catholicism, 348, 350–1; and Kosovo war, 528; role of, 543, 544; holidays, 544; at the Millennium Dome, 555–6
Booth, Gale, 60–3, 324, 327–8, 575
Booth, Lyndsey, 60, 61, 62, 575
Booth, Tony, 60–2, 63, 68, 75, 86, 92, 107, 124, 241–2, 304, 575
Boothroyd, Betty, 331–2, 333
Bosnia, 403, 509–12, 513, 514, 527, 530
Boycott, Rosie, 385
Boyson, Rhodes, 117
BP, 464–6, 538
Bragg, Melvyn, 359–60
Brampton, Sally, 35
Brandreth, Gyles, 300
Branson, Richard, 363, 483, 545, 562
Breakfast With Frost, 547, 550
Bremner, Rory, 189, 237
'Britain in Europe', 481–2, 483
British Airways, 336, 559
British Rail, 259
British Steel Corporation (BSC), 58–9
British Telecom (BT), 142, 151, 159, 270, 363, 559
British Venture Capital Association, 533
Brittan, Leon, 85
Brookes, Peter, 96–7, 98, 104, 108, 238

Brown, George, 68
Brown, Gordon: political background, 117; relationship with TB, 117, 118, 131, 185, 340, 382–9, 470, 542, 543; and the Tribune Group, 117, 118; on shadow front bench, 125; advisers, 132, 160; 1987 election, 133; rivalry with Bryan Gould, 137; in shadow Cabinet, 137, 138, 144, 147, 153, 187; seniority gap with TB, 138, 153, 159, 185, 188, 190; shadow Trade and Industry Secretary, 151, 159; employment policy, 164, 166, 213; and Exchange Rate Mechanism, 165, 189; 1992 election, 168, 170, 175–7; modernisation of Labour, 171, 173; deputy leadership election (1992), 179–86; feud with Mandelson, 179, 256, 267, 268–9, 271–5, 463; as shadow Chancellor, 187, 188, 189; provides TB with slogan, 193–4; Clinton's influence, 194–8; TB gains ascendancy over, 207–8; 'one member, one vote' issue, 211, 212; as potential successor to John Smith, 217; and Smith's death, 221; TB's leadership campaign, 224–8, 230–5, 246; Routledge's biography of, 224, 225, 232, 378, 382–3, 384, 385; rift with TB, 229, 232–3; Mandelson's letter to, 231; 'New Economics', 232, 242; accused of 'psychological flaws', 233, 383–4; deputy leadership election (1994), 242–3; and Clause IV, 254; preparation for power, 268; taxation policy, 288, 297–9, 364, 583; 1997 election, 306; gives independence to Bank of England, 314, 330–1; in Cabinet, 326; moves into Number Ten, 327; Budgets, 337–8, 408n.; Ecclestone affair, 367; and welfare reform, 373–6, 378, 380; as TB's successor, 386–8; economic policy, 388–9; and equality, 440–1; Laura Spence case, 444; donations from Robinson, 462; and the single currency, 472, 474, 475, 476–9, 483–4; opposition to electoral reform, 496; education spending, 503; and the health service, 548, 550, 551; and the Millennium Dome, 557, 558n.; fuel crisis, 570, 573
Brown, Nick, 100, 163, 331; shadow Cabinet elections, 137; and 1992 deputy leadership election, 181, 182, 184; Gordon Brown withdraws from leadership race, 235; Cabinet reshuffle, 385
Brown, Ron, 68–9, 74, 87
Browne, John, 538
Bruce, Malcolm, 496
Brunson, Michael, 133, 244, 545
Bruton, John, 401
Bryant, Chris, 348
BSkyB, 453, 559
Bulgaria, 528–9
Bulger, James, 200
Bundesbank, 130, 165
Burchill, Julie, 346
Burford, Earl of, 452
Burke, Edmund, 42, 201
Burlison, Tom, 67, 100, 210
Burnett, Nicholas, 16
Burt, Norman, 30
Burton, John, 95–6, 97, 98, 99, 100, 101, 104, 105, 106, 108, 116, 159, 246, 315, 580
Burton, Michael, 55
Bush, George, 282, 423, 524
Butler, David, 108
Butler, Sir Michael, 475–6
Butler, R. A., 506
Butler, Richard, 515, 516
Butler, Sir Robin, 190, 324, 329, 333, 465, 535–6, 538
Byers, Stephen, 286, 385, 559
Byrne, Colin, 182–3

Cabinet meetings, 540–1
Cabinet Office, 536
Caborn, Dick, 493
Callaghan, James, 7, 51, 56, 69, 74, 153, 232, 233, 330, 354n., 492n.; 1979 election, 57–8; resignation, 65–6; as Chancellor, 189; and the Church of England, 350; and devolution, 454; children's education, 505; education policy, 506–7
Campaign Group, 136, 150
Campaign for Labour Victory, 72

Campaign for Nuclear Disarmament (CND), 72–3, 101, 103, 144, 251–2, 422, 429, 509
Campbell, Alastair, 213, 355, 568; on TB's abilities, 131; advises TB, 132; trade union law reform, 156; TB's leadership campaign, 187, 228, 230, 240; role of, 252, 256, 277, 379, 393–4, 395–8, 483, 535, 542, 544, 551, 577N., 578; and Clause IV, 254, 256; rivalry with Mandelson, 256; preparation for power, 268; Alan Howarth's defection, 270–1; and focus groups, 279; and Harriet Harman's son's education, 282; and Claire Short, 284, 285; taxation policy, 296; 1997 election, 299, 306, 308, 309, 312, 313, 315; and first Cabinet meeting, 332; and Cook's affair, 339–40; death of Princess Diana, 344–6, 347; Ecclestone affair, 367, 368; relations with Brown, 383, 384; TB alleged to have lobbied for Murdoch, 391–2; and Northern Ireland, 405, 407, 409, 413; and Iraq, 423, 512; and Sierra Leone, 426; Ron Davies' 'moment of madness', 455; Mandelson's home loan, 461, 463–4; Kosovo war, 520, 522, 524, 528; press office, 537; on TB's reshuffles, 541–2; and Peter Mandelson's resignation, 577
Campbell, Menzies, 493
Cardoso, Fernando Henrique, 433
Carey, George, Archbishop of Canterbury, 555
Carman, George, 55
Carr, John, 76
Carter, Denis, 450, 452
Carville, James, 197
Castle, Barbara, 80, 93, 153
Catto, Chris, 22
Chamberlain, Neville, 485, 540, 552
Change and National Renewal, 244–5
Channel Four, 228, 229, 283, 377
Charles, Prince of Wales, 15, 343–4, 345, 346, 347, 348, 546
Chastelain, General John de, 412, 415
Chater, David, 37, 40
Chequers, 551
Chernomyrdin, Viktor, 529, 530
Chile, 582
China, 337, 427–8, 429, 433, 531, 582
Chinn, Sir Trevor, 362
Chirac, Jacques, 367, 583
Chisholm, Malcolm, 377
Christian Socialist Movement, 202, 348
Church of England, 347–8, 350
Churchill, Winston, 485, 491, 513, 552, 580
civil service, 535–6, 537, 538
Clapham, Mick, 377
Clark, Alan, 121–2, 241
Clark, David, 536
Clark, Wesley, 514, 515, 518, 520, 530
Clarke, Charles, 76, 77, 124, 154, 155, 169, 170, 190, 225, 232–3
Clarke, Kenneth, 138, 143, 202–4, 278, 311, 331, 341, 474, 481, 483
Clarke, Nick, 192–3
Clarke, Peter, 201
Clarke, Tom, 385, 541
Clause IV, 115, 142, 152, 215, 249, 252–7, 259–63
Clinton, Bill, 34, 239n., 242, 312, 410, 420, 445, 573; influence on TB, 194–8, 207, 267, 278; taxation policy, 297, 440; congratulates TB, 315; inauguration, 324–5; visits TB, 335; and Northern Ireland, 402, 407–8, 409, 418; and Iraq, 422–3, 513, 516; Lewinsky affair, 423, 424, 432, 434, 516; and the Third Way, 432–3, 434–5; Kosovo war, 514, 519, 521, 524–6, 527, 529–30
Clinton, Hillary, 335, 432, 435, 528
Coates, Ken, 262
Cockerell, Michael, 397
Coffman, Hilary, 346–7
Collenette, Alan, 28–33
Committee on Standards in Public Life *see* Nolan committee
Commonwealth, 426
Communist Party, 7
communitarianism, 198
Confederation of British Industry (CBI), 250
Connarty, Mike, 123
Conran, Terence, 545
Conservative Party: Leo Blair's political ambitions, 9–10; Thatcher becomes

leader, 51–2; 1979 election, 316; by-elections, 87, 317, 530; 1983 election, 113; 1987 election, 133–4, 140; trade union law reform, 157, 161; and Exchange Rate Mechanism, 163, 209, 477; Thatcher's resignation, 163; under Major, 163–4; 1992 election, 175–6, 178; TB adopts language of, 200–1, 202; and the Prevention of Terrorism Act, 203, 271; membership, 216; TB's strategy against, 231; 1994 by-elections, 237; and TB as Labour leader, 251–2; Alan Howarth's defection, 270–1; anti-Labour advertisements, 285, 297; taxation policy, 297, 298; 1997 election, 305, 309, 310–11, 316–17; 'cash for questions' affair, 305; Hague becomes leader, 341; and the Nolan Committee, 360–1; welfare reform, 375–6; attacks Campbell, 393–4; attitudes to TB, 435; Brown keeps spending plans, 440, 550, 551; and House of Lords reform, 447–53; and the single currency, 474, 476, 485; dominance of twentieth century, 489; education policy, 502; fuel crisis, 572; plans for 2001 election, 576
constitutional reform, 287, 447–59
Convery, Paul, 117–18, 126–7
Cook, Margaret, 339–40
Cook, Robin, 118, 176, 213, 273; in shadow Cabinet, 153, 271; deputy leadership election (1992), 180, 184; and modernisation of Labour, 186; 'one member, one vote' issue, 212; opinion polls, 230, 235; and Clause IV, 256n., 259; draft manifesto, 286; and electoral reform, 289, 291, 292; 1997 election, 307, 311; in Cabinet, 326, 386n.; marriage break-up, 339–40, 355; 'ethical foreign policy', 420–1, 424, 428, 429, 516; and Sierra Leone, 425–6; opposes fox-hunting ban, 442; and devolution, 455; and the single currency, 474, 477, 483–4; Balkan conflicts, 509–10; and Iraq, 512, 513–14; Kosovo war, 517, 519n.; lack of influence, 543
Copyright Bill, 138
Cornwall, Nick, 145, 551
Corscaden, George, 8
Countryside Alliance, 441–3, 571
Court of Appeal, 59
Cox, Barry, 76, 224–5, 238, 240, 359
Cranborne, Viscount, 447–9, 450, 451–2
crime, 192–4, 198, 199–201, 203–4
Crosby, Brian, 10
Crosland, Anthony, 80, 93, 145, 187, 281, 293, 445, 506
Crossman, Richard, 116
Cryer, Bob, 116
Cunningham, Jack, 271; support for nuclear power, 151; 1992 election, 176, 177; deputy leadership election (1992), 182; in Cabinet, 326; Cabinet reshuffles, 385, 509–10, 542; and the Millennium Dome, 557
Cunningham, Sir Knox, 18
Curtice, John, 494

Daily Express, 86, 178, 283–4, 305, 385
Daily Mail, 5, 178, 230, 250, 301, 305, 334, 376, 380, 444, 481, 502, 568
Daily Mirror see *Mirror*
Daily Telegraph, 82, 86, 87–8, 250, 253, 277, 305, 338, 397, 481
Daily Worker, 7
Dalyell, Tam, 118–19
d'Ancona, Matthew, 353
Darling, Alistair, 379, 380–1
Darlington by-election (1983), 92
David, Wayne, 123
Davies, Chris, 269
Davies, Gavyn, 433
Davies, Liz, 270
Davies, Ron, 455–6
Davis, Mike, 67, 81
Davis, Terry, 133
Day, Billy, 171
Day, Sir Robin, 491
Dean, Brenda, 361
Dearing, Sir Ron, 437
Defence and Overseas Policy (DOP) committee, 521
Delors, Jacques, 129
Democratic Party (USA), 276, 286, 362
Denham, John, 123
Denmark, 472
Denning, Lord, 59–60
Department of Health, 365, 366

Department for International Development, 420, 428
Department of Trade and Industry (DTI), 462, 467, 468, 476
devolution, 287–8, 306, 415–17, 454–9, 583
Dewar, Donald, 169, 233, 240, 289, 455
Diana, Princess of Wales, 343, 344–7
Dimbleby, David, 308
Dineen, Molly, 575
Dobson, Frank, 339; and the NHS, 326, 549, 550; tobacco advertising ban, 365, 367; Cabinet reshuffle, 542; elections for London's mayor, 561, 562–3, 564
Dome *see* Millennium Dome
Donaldson, Jeffrey, 406–7
Dow, Graham, 43
Draper, Derek, 467–8, 542
Dromey, Jack, 153, 156, 282, 347
Drucker, Henry, 361, 362
Dubbins, Tony, 156–7
Dubs, Alf, 58
Duisenberg, Wim, 480
Dunwoody, Gwyneth, 85
Durham, 9, 13
Durham Cathedral, 104
Durham Chorister School, 10–11, 12, 14
Durham University, 9
Dyke, Greg, 359, 545

Earl, Robert, 369–70
East Timor, 421, 422
Eatwell, John, 151, 164, 165, 225
Ecclestone, Bernie, 341, 358, 363–71, 466
Economic Club, 526
The Economist, 550–1
Ede, James Chuter, 198, 199
Edinburgh, 14, 24
Edmonds, John, 186, 212, 286
education: Labour policy, 250, 257–9, 501–7; TB's children's education, 257–8, 504, 505; Harriet Harman's son's education, 281–3; 1997 election, 307; university tuition fees, 437–9, 445, 457; spending increases, 441
EETPU, 67, 72
Elder, Murray, 235
electoral reform, 290–2, 325, 489–90, 492–9, 546, 583
electricity privatisation, 148–51
Elizabeth II, Queen, 11, 304, 323, 334, 344, 345, 346–8, 556
Ellen, Mark, 37–9, 40
Elliott, George, 171
Elrick, Michael, 217
Emanual, Rahm, 432
employment policy, 164, 165, 213–14
Europe: The Third Way, 435
European Central Bank, 480
European Commission, 481
European Court, 59, 481
European Economic Community, 51
European Parliament, 481, 492, 530, 565
European Union: TB's position on, 73–4, 83–5, 96, 105, 582–3; single currency, 129, 311–12, 331, 364, 389, 472–86, 582; Social Chapter, 154–5, 156, 158, 330; beef ban, 279; summit meetings, 335–6; tobacco advertising ban, 365–7, 369; and Iraq, 423; British presidency of, 479–80; health spending, 548, 550
Evans, David, 360
Evening Standard, 31, 222, 228, 334, 504
Ewing, Winnie, 454
Exchange Rate Mechanism (ERM), 129–31, 163, 164–5, 189, 209, 477, 544

Fabian Society, 118, 246, 293, 431
Falconer, Charles, 185; meets TB, 57; on TB as a moderniser, 114; on TB's awe of Brown, 118; on TB's family life, 123; on Cherie Booth, 241; Mandelson's home loan, 463–4; relationship with TB, 543–4; and the Millennium Dome, 556; peerage, 566
Falklands War (1982), 78, 82–3, 87, 88, 512, 513, 524, 528, 530
Fatchett, Derek, 284
Fawcett, Colin, 53
Fayed, Dodi, 344
Fayed, Mohamed, 128, 305
Fédération Internationale de l'Automobile (FIA), 363, 365–6
Fenton, James, 13–14
Ferguson, George, 92, 98, 100, 106, 107
Fettes College, Edinburgh, 4, 14–25, 58, 108
Field, Frank, 326, 374–5, 378–80, 386, 477–8

Filkin, Elizabeth, 468, 470
Finance Bill (1987), 138–9
Financial Times, 78, 156, 326, 331, 362, 426, 453, 476
Fisher, Colin, 254
Flight, Howard, 392
Flynn, Padraig, 365
focus groups, 241, 279, 288, 297, 409, 434, 570, 584
Follett, Barbara, 398
Follett, Ken, 397–8, 545
Foot, Michael, 24, 81, 88, 246–7, 382; becomes Labour leader, 66; Falklands War, 82; endorses TB, 85, 97, 101–2, 104; European policy, 85; battle against Militant, 89–90, 105, 116; 1983 election, 95, 107; resignation, 113, 114; and House of Lords reform, 449
Foreign Office, and Sierra Leone, 425–6
Formula 1 racing, 363–70
Foster, Derek, 541
Foster, Michael, 442
Fowler, Norman, 157, 160
fox-hunting, 441, 442–3
France, 54, 195, 252, 435, 473, 474–5, 479, 571
Friend, Adrian, 33
Frost, David, 238, 547, 550, 566
Fryer, John, 167
fuel crisis (2000), 570–3, 576
Fulbrook, Julian, 53
Fursdon, David, 56

G7, 336
Gaitskell, Hugh, 24, 80, 123, 189, 247, 253, 254, 255, 264
Gallop, Geoff, 35, 37, 41, 46, 49, 56, 69
Galloway, George, 382, 516
Gallup polls, 127, 235, 338
Galtieri, General Leopoldo, 87
'Gang of Four', 66, 250
Gapes, Mike, 83, 123
Gardner, David, 35–6, 37, 74, 83–4
Garrett, John, 542
Gascoigne, Michael, 14–15, 24–5
Gavron, Bob, 362
GCHQ, 155, 330
General Elections: March 1966, 12; February 1974, 45, 46; October 1974, 46; May 1979, 316; June 1983, 91, 93, 95, 107–9, 113; June 1987, 125, 132, 133–4, 139, 140; April 1992, 167–9, 170, 175–8, 241–2; May 1997, 223, 299–317, 489, 494
General and Municipal Workers' Union, 67, 100; *see also* GMB
George, Eddie, 331
Germany, 193, 195, 261, 447, 583; Exchange Rate Mechanism, 130, 165; tobacco advertising ban, 365n.; social democrats win election, 435; and the single currency, 472, 473, 480–1; Kosovo war, 514, 515, 520
Gerrard, Neil, 377
Giddens, Anthony, 172, 433
Giffin, Bill, 105, 106
Gilbert, John, 566
Giuliani, Rudolph, 434
Gladstone, William, 201, 351, 401, 431, 506, 528–9, 552, 581
GMB, 67, 179, 181, 182, 186, 210, 211, 212, 214, 286, 456
GMTV, 539
Good Friday Agreement (1998), 401, 404–12, 413, 415–18, 424, 543, 544, 581–2
Gorbachev, Mikhail, 144
Gore, Al, 352, 424
Goudie, James, 71–2
Goudie, Mary, 71, 106
Gould, Bryan, 88; 1983 leadership election, 113–14; on TB, 130–1, 158; 1987 election, 132, 134; in shadow Cabinet, 136, 137–8, 147; rivalry with Brown, 137; supports privatisation, 142; loses Trade and Industry brief, 151; and Exchange Rate Mechanism, 164; 1992 election, 176; deputy leadership election (1992), 179, 180–1, 182, 184, 186; resignation, 189, 209
Gould, Philip, 385; supports TB, 132, 187; 1989 elections, 149; 1992 election, 168; Clinton's influence, 194; and New Labour, 223, 255; and TB's bid for leadership, 228, 231, 235, 236, 240–1; and deputy leadership election, 243; and Clause IV, 254; 'Unfinished Revolution' memo, 268–9, 278–9; draft manifesto,

Gould, Philip – *contd*
286; focus groups, 288, 297, 409, 570; taxation policy, 297; 1997 election, 313, 314; Uxbridge by-election, 339; and the single currency, 484n.; role of, 543, 544; and the fuel crisis, 570; and TB's speech to WI, 576
Government Information Service, 393, 395
Granada TV, 300
Greater London Assembly, 562–3, 564, 567
Greater London Council, 68, 89, 561
Greece, 365, 472, 486, 514, 520
Green Party, 149
Greenberg, Stan, 279, 313, 484n.
Greenspan, Alan, 331
Greer, Ian, 128
Grice, Andrew, 229, 239, 252
Griffiths, Frank, 81
Griffiths, Nigel, 385
Grocott, Bruce, 567
Grove, Canon John, 9, 11, 12, 29, 47
Grylls, Sir Michael, 128
Guardian, 59, 68, 73, 78, 83, 84, 103, 125, 182–3, 259, 262, 268, 273, 310, 379, 382, 463, 464
Gulf War (1991), 422, 513, 519, 524
Gummer, John Selwyn, 121, 336
Guthrie, General Sir Charles, 512, 514, 521–2, 523, 531

Hackney South Labour Party, 65, 66, 67–9, 89
Hague, William, 392, 443, 565, 568, 569, 578; early life, 33; becomes Conservative leader, 341; and Ecclestone affair, 368; attacks Labour spin-doctors, 399; Republican adviser, 436; and House of Lords reform, 447–9, 451; Prime Minister's Questions, 466, 546; abandons 'tax guarantee', 550; and fuel crisis, 571, 572; plans for 2001 election, 576, 584
Hain, Peter, 123, 386n.
Haiti, 525–6
Hall, Julie, 182
Hall, Phil, 313
Halsey, A. H., 353
Hamilton, Neil, 289, 305
Hannay, Sir David, 476
Hansard, 126, 144
Hardie, Keir, 245n., 292, 354
Harding, Pauline, 5, 6
Harman, Harriet, 118, 213, 347; works for National Council for Civil Liberties, 59; on TB as potential leader, 158; and 1992 deputy leadership election, 182; and TB's bid for leadership, 225–6; deputy leadership election (1994), 243; son's education, 282–3, 284; in Cabinet, 326; and welfare reform, 373–4, 375–6, 377, 378, 379; returns to back benches, 379–80, 541
Harries, Richard, 285
Harris, Martyn, 56
Harris, Nigel, 210, 215
Harris, Robert, 44n., 179, 552
Harron, Mary, 40
Harvey, Nick, 493
Haselhurst, Sir Alan, 523
Haskel, Simon, 361
Haslam, Jonathan, 393, 394
Hattersley, Roy, 133, 169, 254; Solidarity Campaign, 71; Beaconsfield by-election, 85; on TB, 95, 155; TB selected as candidate for Sedgefield, 106; 1983 leadership election, 108, 113, 114, 132; TB on shadow front bench, 124–5, 126; shadow Cabinet elections, 137; 1992 election, 170, 176; resignation, 184; advises TB, 188; 'Statement of Aims and Values', 205; and TB's bid for leadership, 226; on Prescott, 242; critical of TB and New Labour, 257, 281, 391, 433, 435, 436
Hawke, Bob, 170, 195
Haworth, Alan, 75–7, 90–1, 217, 347
Healey, Denis, 150, 189, 388; deputy leadership election, 67, 71, 74, 75, 139; Beaconsfield by-election, 85; 1983 election, 107; and TB's bid for leadership, 228
Heath, Edward, 45, 233, 483, 552, 580
Heffer, Eric, 113
Heffer, Simon, 230
Helm, Toby, 208
Henderson, Arthur, 252, 326
Henderson, Doug, 386n.

Hennessy, Peter, 512–13, 535, 540, 552, 558n.
Heseltine, Michael, 46, 162, 221, 251–2, 392, 427, 481, 483, 540, 541, 556–7
Hewitt, Patricia, 169–70
Heywood, Jeremy, 543, 544
Hill, David, 176, 177, 221, 262
Hinduja, Srichand, 559, 577–8
Hislop, Ian, 329
Hoban, Simon, 97
Hodge, Henry, 230
Hodge, Margaret, 123, 230, 270–1
Hoey, Kate, 123, 315
Holbrooke, Richard, 515, 517–18, 519
Hollick, Clive, 385
Hollis, Patricia, 375
Hollis Industries, 466–7
Holmes, John, 405, 512, 536, 544
Home Office, 59
Hong Kong, 337
House of Commons, 199; Falklands War, 82; TB's maiden speech, 115–16; Prime Minister's Questions, 125–6, 332–3, 341; TB develops reputation in, 125–6, 127–8; television coverage, 154; and devolution, 458; air strikes against Iraq, 512–13
House of Lords, 91, 199; reform of, 287, 447–54, 546, 583; and fox-hunting ban, 442
Howard, Anthony, 395
Howard, Michael, 119, 160–1, 166, 204, 426, 538
Howarth, Alan, 270–1
Howe, Geoffrey, 85, 129, 130
Hoyle, Cherie, 61
Huckfield, Les, 92, 97, 99, 100, 104–5, 106, 116
Hudson, Hugh, 168
Hughes, Simon, 493, 499
Human Rights Act, 583
Hume, Cardinal Basil, 352–3
Hume, John, 407, 408, 411, 417, 418
Humphrys, John, 369
Hunter, Anji, 75–6, 221, 222, 272, 277, 543; early life, 22–3; at Oxford, 40; becomes TB's adviser, 145; 1992 election, 177n.; and TB's leadership campaign, 226, 238, 246; TB's rift with Brown, 232; 1997 election, 315; loan from Robinson, 462; role of, 537, 551
Hurd, Douglas, 163, 421
Hurley, John, 82
Hutton, Will, 312, 388
Hyman, Peter, 240, 288

ICM, 310
Independent, 166, 277, 283, 288, 401
Independent on Sunday, 463
Indonesia, 421–2, 427, 429
inflation, 330–1
Ingram, Adam, 225
International Monetary Fund, 57, 150
Internet, 539, 546
Iraq, 394, 422–3, 429, 461, 462, 512–13, 515–16, 575
Ireland, 11, 405, 410, 415, 416, 418, 485; *see also* Northern Ireland
Irish Republican Army (IRA), 78, 334, 400–3, 406–7, 409–12, 414–17, 424, 578
Irvine, Derry, 58, 76, 93, 118, 334; on TB, 47; and TB's legal career, 53–4, 55–6; early political life, 54; battle against Militant, 90, 91, 183; peerage, 154; and trade union law, 154; on TB as Smith's successor, 217; and John Smith's death, 221, 233; and TB's bid for leadership, 229, 246; and Clause IV, 260; role of, 287, 543; and Cherie Booth's legal career, 302–3; 1997 election, 307, 310; refurbishes apartment, 337; Ecclestone affair, 367; and House of Lords reform, 450–1, 452, 492; Scottish devolution, 454, 492; Mandelson's home loan, 463–4
Islam, 351, 529
Italy: Blair family holidays in, 288–9, 339, 360, 462, 467, 469; and Murdoch's bid for Mediaset, 391; Kosovo war, 514, 520
ITN, 244, 521
ITV, 133

Jack, Ian, 313
Jackson, Glenda, 562
Jackson, Michael, 530

Jacques, Martin, 172
Jaded (rock band), 29–30
Jagger, Mick, 21, 32, 39
James, Howell, 261
Japan, 397n., 427, 479
Jay, Douglas, 255
Jay, Margaret, 361, 362, 385, 449n., 451, 505
Jenkin, Patrick, 85
Jenkins, Roy, 59, 187, 189, 306, 388, 473, 489; leaves Labour Party, 66, 69; wins Glasgow Hillhead, 82; as Home Secretary, 198, 199; endorses TB, 250; and electoral reform, 291, 292, 493–9; and the single currency, 482–3, 485; 'lighthouse' principle, 548
Jenkins, Simon, 556n., 557
Jiang Zemin, 428
Johnson, Boris, 293
Johnson, Joy, 272
Johnson, Paul, 230
Joint Consultative Committee, 491–2
Joint Policy Committee, 209
Jones, James, Bishop of Liverpool, 355
Jospin, Lionel, 335, 435 and n., 583
Jowell, Tessa, 366, 367

Kabbah, Ahmad Tejan, 425, 426
Kaufman, Gerald, 95, 133, 168, 233, 392
Kaye, Sir Emmanuel, 362
Keating, Paul, 195, 280–1, 297
Kellaway, Alec, 237
Kellett, Hugh, 20, 22
Kellner, Peter, 44
Kennedy, Charles, 33, 456–7, 483, 495, 497, 499, 570
Kennedy, David, 3, 20, 21
Kennedy, Helena, 453
Kennedy, John F., 264, 323, 339, 524, 575
Kilfoyle, Peter, 225, 238
King, Tom, 119
Kinnock, Glenys, 234
Kinnock, Neil, 70, 75, 76, 213, 222, 230, 247, 251, 327; tries to unify Labour, 77; Beaconsfield by-election, 85–6; 1983 election, 95; leadership election (1983), 113, 114, 116; relationship with TB, 114; and Gordon Brown, 117; and the Tribune Group, 117, 118; and the miners' strike, 124; promotes TB to shadow front bench, 124, 147–8; in Opposition, 125; modernisation of Labour Party, 134, 139–44, 151–2, 171; trade union law reform, 153, 155, 156, 161–2; sees TB as potential leader, 158–9, 190; employment policy, 164, 165; 1992 election, 168, 170, 175–8, 490–1; Smith's threat to leadership, 169–70; loses leadership, 179, 184; deputy leadership election (1992), 180–1, 182, 183; communitarianism, 205; voting reforms, 208; feud with Prescott, 241; and Clause IV, 254; 1997 election, 316; and devolution, 457; and the single currency, 472
Kirkwood, Archy, 289
Kohl, Helmut, 336, 435, 480, 583
Kosovo, 83, 335, 336, 394, 411, 429, 510–12, 513–15, 516–31, 582, 585
Kosovo Liberation Army (KLA), 511, 513, 517–18
Kramer, Susan, 563
Kusnet, David, 276
Kyoto summit (1997), 337

Labour Party: 1966 election, 12; TB joins, 51, 52, 65; Cherie Booth joins, 63; TB looks for parliamentary seat, 65, 67–8, 72–3, 80–1, 91–2; deputy leadership election (1981), 66–7, 71, 74, 75; Solidarity Campaign, 71–2, 74, 76, 77; Labour Co-ordinating Committee, 76–7, 90–1, 93, 117–18, 123–4, 126–7, 137; Beaconsfield by-election (1982), 81–8; European policy, 84–5, 105; battle against Militant, 89–91; TB selected as candidate for Sedgefield, 93, 95–107; 1983 election, 95, 107–9, 113; leadership election (1983), 113–14; modernisation of, 114–16, 123, 126–7, 134, 139–44, 151–2, 171–3, 186; Clause IV, 115, 142, 152, 215, 249, 252–7, 259–63; 1987 election, 125, 132, 133–4, 139, 140; and the Exchange Rate Mechanism, 129–31, 164–5, 189; shadow Cabinet elections, 136–7, 187; and proportional representation, 139–40; 1989 elections, 149; trade union law reform, 153–8, 161–3; TB as potential leader, 158–9, 170–1, 187–90; party conferences, 162–3, 170, 213–14, 255–6, 269–70, 289; in opposition to Major, 163–4; employment policy, 164, 165, 213–14; 'training revolution', 165–6; and the minimum wage, 166–7; 1992 election, 167–9, 170, 175–8; threats to Kinnock's leadership, 169–70; 'Third Way', 172, 335, 422, 431–45; deputy leadership election (1992), 178–86; 'one member, one vote' issue, 65–6, 99, 188, 207–12, 213–16, 242, 565; Clinton's influence, 194–8, 267, 278; social moralism, 198–202, 205; and the Prevention of Terrorism Act, 203, 271; membership, 209–10, 216, 263, 565; New Labour, 212, 223, 255, 263, 269, 278, 316, 323; John Smith's death, 221–4; leadership election (1994), 188, 224–47, 359–60; by-elections, 237, 299, 339, 386, 530; defections to, 237, 255, 270–1; TB's strategy, 249–52, 263, 264–5; education policy, 257–9, 281–3; preparation for power, 267–93; membership balloted, 286; taxation policy, 296–8; 1997 election, 223, 299–317, 538; first hundred days in government, 330–42; fundraising, 358–71, 469; and welfare reform, 373–81; attitudes to TB, 435–6, 565–7; House of Lords reform, 447–54; and the single currency, 472–86; possible coalition with Liberal Democrats, 488–93, 497–8; opposition to Kosovo war, 523–4; and power of Cabinet, 541; women MPs, 566; *see also* National Executive

Labour Weekly, 89

Lafontaine, Oskar, 447, 481

Lamont, Norman, 128, 138–9, 161, 175, 209, 541, 544, 570

Lansman, Jon, 90

Lascelles, James, 29

Lawson, Dominic, 354n., 473

Lawson, Neal, 580

Lawson, Nigel, 126, 127–8, 129, 130, 147, 161, 162, 164, 165, 384, 540

LBC radio, 147

Lee, Jennie, 253

Lee-Potter, Lynda, 301

Legg, Sir Thomas, 426

Leggett, Miles, 67

Leigh, David, 59

Lester-Cribb, Michael, 20

Levy, Michael, 29, 33, 361–2

Lewinsky, Monica, 423, 424, 432, 434, 516

Liberal Democrats, 149; by-elections, 237, 269; and TB as Labour leader, 250–1; co-operation with Labour, 289–93, 325–6, 332, 389; 1997 election, 316; and devolution, 454, 455, 456–7; possible coalition, 488–93, 497–9, 583; and electoral reform, 493–9

Liberal–SDP Alliance, 127; 1983 election, 70, 108; by-elections, 80, 81; and the Exchange Rate Mechanism, 129, 130; 1987 election, 133, 140; merger of two parties, 139

Liddell, Helen, 433

Liddle, Roger, 72, 254–5, 272, 290, 311, 467, 536

Lilley, Peter, 310, 376, 378

Limehouse Declaration, 66, 68

Littlejohns, Sylvia, 144, 145–6

Livingstone, Ken, 76, 569; on Ron Brown, 68; seizes control of GLC, 81; TB's dislike of, 89, 92, 561, 567; election as London's mayor, 457, 556, 561–5

Lloyd, John, 68–9, 74, 99, 133

Lloyd, Tony, 284, 511

Lloyd George, David, 7, 293, 338, 389, 401, 489, 540

London: elections for mayor, 216, 413, 457, 561–5; IRA bomb, 401

London Labour Briefing, 78

London Oratory, 257–8, 282, 502

London Weekend Television (LWT), 76, 132, 359

lone-parent benefits, 375–8, 379, 380, 381, 540

Looking to the Future, 162, 165

Lords Appointments Commission, 453

Lowton, Nicholas, 40

Luff, Peter, 458

Maastricht Treaty (1991), 155, 188, 196, 242, 336, 473, 474–5

MacAskill, Norman, 221–2
McCain, John, 527
McCourt, Warren, 97, 105, 106
McCurry, Mike, 432
McDonagh, Margaret, 288, 562, 564
MacDonald, Oonagh, 133
MacDonald, Ramsay, 5, 326, 328, 354n., 489, 505n.
McElvoy, Anne, 501, 504
McFadden, Pat, 386
McGee, Alan, 545
McGuinness, Martin, 412, 415
McIntosh, Ian, 15, 20, 23, 24
Macintyre, Donald, 180, 182, 226, 231–2, 239, 273, 274, 559
McIntyre, Pat, 105, 106
Mackay, Lord, 449
Mackenzie Stuart, Amanda, 23–4, 30, 57
Mackenzie-Stuart, Lord, 23, 24
McKittrick, David, 401
McLay, Sally, 8, 12
McLay, William, 8
Maclennan, Robert, 289, 492–3
Macleod, Iain, 14, 323, 339
Macmillan, Harold, 328, 333, 516, 524, 552
Macmurray, John, 41–3, 45, 47, 115–16, 198, 201
McNamara, Kevin, 203, 402
McSmith, Andy, 137–8, 159–60, 228
Maginnis, Ken, 404
Maguire, Kevin, 409
Mahon, Alice, 377
Mail on Sunday, 258, 283, 285, 387–8, 558n.
Major, John, 7, 138, 170, 187, 217, 230, 233, 283, 323, 324, 327, 464, 467, 581; and Exchange Rate Mechanism, 163; becomes Prime Minister, 163; 1992 election, 178; and the Prevention of Terrorism Act, 203; 1997 election, 223, 300, 304, 305, 307–11, 315, 316n., 317, 584; and TB as Labour leader, 251; Prime Minister's Questions, 262–3, 272, 333; majority dwindles, 271; re-election as leader, 272, 541; and Mrs Thatcher, 276, 277; taxation policy, 298; at Number Ten, 329, 535; and Northern Ireland, 334, 400–1, 402–3, 405, 408–9, 412, 418; and the Nolan committee, 360, 363, 370, 371; press secretaries, 393; and Sierra Leone, 425; loyalty to ministers, 469, 541; and the single currency, 472–3, 475; children's education, 505n.; education policy, 507; Balkan conflicts, 510; Gulf War, 524; management style, 552
Major, Norma, 301
Malcolm, Noel, 510, 511
Mallon, Seamus, 408
Mandela, Nelson, 531
Mandelson, Peter, 72, 146, 149, 222, 542, 562; background, 131–2; 1987 election, 132, 133; trade union law reform, 156; selected as candidate for Hartlepool, 159–60; as Blair and Brown's adviser, 160; and Kinnock's leadership, 169, 170; 1992 election, 177; deputy leadership election (1992), 179–83, 186; feud with Brown, 179, 231, 256, 267, 268–9, 271–5, 463; supports Blair, 187; and 'Clintonisation', 196; 'one member, one vote' issue, 212; and TB's leadership campaign, 224, 226–32, 234–7, 238–40, 244; and TB's rift with Brown, 229; reputation as schemer, 231, 239n.; and Clause IV, 254–5, 256, 260–1; rivalry with Campbell, 256; wants more prominent role, 269, 272, 275, 314; *The Blair Revolution*, 272–3, 536; influence on TB, 272; on New Labour, 278; complains about Conservative advertisements, 285; and Liberal Democrats, 291–2; taxation policy, 297; 1997 election, 306, 308, 314, 315; and Cook's affair, 340; and monarchy, 347; joins Cabinet, 385, 386, 394, 541; media management, 396; home loan, 289, 385, 461–4, 468–9, 577; first resignation, 233, 461, 464, 469–70, 552; code of conduct for ministers, 465–6; and Northern Ireland, 413–16, 470, 543, 578, 581; and the single currency, 478, 480, 481, 483–4; on TB's attitude to risk, 525; on role of Cabinet Office, 536; and the Millennium Dome, 557–9; resignation over Hinduja passport application, 577–8, 585

Marr, Andrew, 296
Martin, Tony, 568
Marxism, 45, 47, 261
Marxism Today, 102n., 172, 276
Maxwell, Robert, 466
Mayhew, Sir Patrick, 404
Meacher, Michael, 76, 143, 147, 153–4, 161–2, 541
Meale, Alan, 99
Mediaset, 391
Meet the Challenge, Make the Change, 152
Mellor, David, 370, 541, 545
Members' Interests, Select Committee on, 128–9
Merchant, Piers, 305
Meyer, Christopher, 393
Michael, Alun, 147, 339, 455–7, 542
Mikardo, Ian, 121
Milburn, Alan, 433, 543, 549
Miliband, David, 240, 260, 286, 307, 431, 433, 536–7, 543
Militant, 76, 89–91, 93, 105, 116–17, 183
Millar, Fiona, 187, 302, 581
Millbank Tower, London, 268, 272, 306, 323
Millennium Dome, 389, 540, 555–9, 575, 577–8
Mills, Joe, 99–100, 105
Milne, Seumas, 382
Milosevic, Slobodan, 335, 416, 429, 509–12, 513–15, 517–21, 523–4, 527–8, 530, 585
minimum wage, 166–7
Ministry of Defence, 521
Mirror, 131, 204, 273, 278, 283, 298, 313, 338, 384, 385, 409, 463, 530, 546, 573
Mitchell, Austin, 79, 311
Mitchell, George, 401, 404, 405–6, 408, 414, 415, 418
Monks, John, 334
Moon, James, 34, 38, 39, 40
Moore, John, 126
Morgan, Rhodri, 455–7
Morgan, Sally, 537, 564
MORI, 230
Morris, Bill, 545
Morris, Dick, 239n., 434, 525
Morris, John, 326n., 521
Morrison, Herbert, 132, 557
Mosley, Max, 363–4, 365–6, 370
Mountfield, Sir Robin, 397n.
Mowlam, Mo, 387, 397, 398, 562; in shadow Cabinet, 138; and TB's leadership campaign, 225, 238; and deputy leadership election, 242–3; in Cabinet, 326, 542; and Northern Ireland, 402, 404, 413
MSF (Manufacturing, Science and Finance union), 213, 214
Mulgan, Geoff, 44, 431
Mullin, Chris, 150
Murdoch, Rupert, 230, 279–81, 304, 313, 338, 391–3, 396, 480, 559, 568
Murphy, Patricia, 52
Murphy, Paul, 542
Muslims, 351, 529

National Council for Civil Liberties (NCCL), 59
National Executive (Committee of the Labour Party), 83; and the Labour Co-ordinating Committee, 76; battle against Militant, 90; modernisation of Labour Party, 139; and trade union law reform, 157, 162; and 'one member, one vote', 208, 209, 212; Blair and Brown elected to, 209, 213; elections, 213, 215, 284, 562; and Clause IV, 253, 256–7, 259, 260; and air strikes against Iraq, 516
National Front, 46
National Health Service (NHS), 140–1, 177, 288, 324, 441, 547–51, 576, 583
National Insurance, 175–6, 380
National Lottery, 300, 301, 557, 558–9
National Policy Forum, 271, 286, 543
National Union of Journalists, 59
National Union of Mineworkers, 100, 261
National Union of Teachers, 259
nationalisation, 141–2, 148, 151–2, 159, 259, 269–70
Nato, 144; security pact with Russia, 335; Kosovo war, 429, 511, 513, 514, 515, 517–25, 527–31; and Bosnia, 510, 512, 513, 514; Robertson becomes Secretary-General, 542
Naughtie, James, 252
Neil, Andrew, 187, 230, 392
Neill, Lord, 362, 367–8

Nellist, Dave, 116
New Labour, New Life for Britain, 286
New Paths to Victory, 186, 213
New Statesman, 40, 58, 70, 133, 139–40, 141, 269, 285, 288–9, 291, 475
Newham North-East Labour Party, 75
News at Ten, 244, 478
News of the World, 285, 304, 313, 339–40, 391, 397, 409, 570
NewsCorp, 279–80, 392
Newsnight, 85, 100, 115, 147, 156–7, 228, 304–5, 355, 478–9, 496, 499, 504, 534
Nicolson, Adam, 304
Nigeria, 425–6
Nixon, Richard, 335n.
Nolan committee, 360, 362, 367–8, 545
NOP, 279, 310
Norris, Steven, 563
Northern Ireland, 203, 334, 394, 400–18, 470, 578, 581–2, 583
Nuclear Electric, 150–1
nuclear weapons, 72–3, 107, 144, 307, 324
Number Ten Policy Unit, 375, 431, 467, 536–7, 552
NUPE, 139
Nye, Sue, 227

O'Brien, Mike, 577
Observer, 138, 181, 263n., 271, 290, 293, 312–13, 383, 384, 410, 467, 577
Ogilvy, David, 23
Oliver, Margaret, 53
Omagh, IRA bomb, 409–10, 417
On the Record, 186, 207, 210, 235, 368–9, 371, 388n.
'one member, one vote' issue, 188, 207–12, 213–16, 242, 565
O'Neill, Martin, 144
opinion polls, 230, 235, 279, 296, 299, 310, 316, 331, 338, 399, 434, 504, 555, 556, 562, 563, 572–3, 574
Orange Order, 402, 412
Organisation for Security and Co-operation in Europe (OSCE), 515, 517, 518
Orme, Stan, 85
Otunna, Olara, 36–7, 44, 48
Owen, David, 66, 69, 72, 124, 187, 360
Owen, John, 250
Oxford Union, 46
Oxford University, 20–1, 35–47, 60, 131–2, 444, 506

Page, Jennie, 557
Paisley, Ian, 403–4
Palast, Greg, 467
Palley, Marc, 36, 37, 40, 44, 46–7, 49, 51, 56
Panorama, 238, 308, 344, 533
Paramaecium (discussion society), 20
Parker, Sir Peter, 127
Parker Bowles, Camilla, 344, 347
Parkinson, Cecil, 148–9, 150, 160, 512
Parris, Matthew, 161, 203
Parsons, Charles, 5–6
Parsons, Suzanne, 40
Patten, Chris, 427
Paxman, Jeremy, 33, 304–5, 496
Pendry, Tom, 75, 82
Penfold, Peter, 425
'People at Work' group, 143, 154
Performance and Innovation Unit (PIU), 539
petrol prices, 570–3, 576
Phillips, Dr Anthony, 60
Philp, Robert, 18, 19, 20
Phoenix, Pat, 86, 107
Pimlott, Ben, 104, 145
Pinochet, General Augusto, 582
Pischetsrieder, Bernd, 363–4
Plaid Cymru, 456
Poland, 71, 518
Political Animal Lobby, 443n.
Pollack, Anita, 123
Porter, Shirley, 89
Portillo, Michael, 315, 550, 572
Powell, Charles, 240, 276–7, 405, 536
Powell, Chris, 240, 277
Powell, Enoch, 449
Powell, Jonathan, 240, 475, 493; Clinton's influence, 194; preparation for power, 268; role of, 276–7, 287n., 535–6, 542, 543, 544; 1997 election, 313, 314, 315; transition to power, 324–5, 327, 329; Ecclestone affair, 367; and Northern Ireland, 402, 403, 405, 407, 413; sound-bites, 501n.; and Iraq, 512

Prentice, Gordon, 377
Prentice, Reg, 75, 506
Prescott, John, 149, 217, 543; and trade union law reform, 157; employment policy, 164, 213–14; 1992 election, 167, 241–2; deputy leadership election (1992), 181, 182, 185; attacks 'Clintonisation', 196; opinion polls, 230, 235; deputy leadership campaign, 237, 238, 242–3, 247, 359; background, 241–2; relationship with TB, 242, 243; and Clause IV, 255, 256, 263; in shadow Cabinet, 271; and Labour's pledges, 288; 1997 election, 314; in Cabinet, 243, 326, 358; environmental issues, 336–7; opposition to electoral reform, 494, 496; Cabinet reshuffle, 542; and the Millennium Dome, 557–8; and the fuel crisis, 571, 572; transport policy, 573, 574
Preston, Roz, 177n.
Prevention of Terrorism Act, 203, 271
Pringle, Sandy, 52, 65, 72
Private Eye, 44, 148, 157, 187, 190, 308, 328–9, 384 and n., 444n.
privatisation, 141–3, 148–52, 259, 269–70
Privy Council, 535
Prodi, Romano, 391–2, 435
Purnell, James, 177n.
Putin, Vladimir, 582
Puttnam, David, 359–60, 545

quangos, 545
Queensbridge Labour Party *see* Hackney South Labour Party
Question Time, 127, 308, 309, 443, 484
Quin, Joyce, 284
Quirke, Paddy, 29

Race, Reg, 105, 106
Race Relations Act, 60
Radice, Giles, 99
Rae, Maggie, 60, 62, 65, 75, 90, 217
Railtrack, 269
Raison, Timothy, 155
Ramaphosa, Cyril, 416
Rambouillet conference (1999), 517
Randall, John, 339
Rank and File Mobilising Committee, 76
Rawnsley, Andrew, 383
Raynsford, Nick, 493
Reagan, Ronald, 73, 144, 194, 422, 440, 524
Redwood, John, 465
Rees, Merlyn, 59, 85, 361
Regan, Gaynor, 339–40
Register of Members' Interests, 128–9, 360, 363, 467
Reich, Robert, 312
Reid, John, 457
Renwick, Sir Robin, 476
Republican Party (USA), 286, 362
Restrick, Tom, 240
Reynolds, Albert, 401
Reynolds, Fiona, 149, 150
Richard, Ivor, 287, 450–1, 557
Ridgway, Celia, 5–6
Roberts, Bob, 21, 22
Robertson, George, 512, 527, 542
Robinson, Anne, 304
Robinson, Geoffrey: Blair family stays in his Tuscan villa, 288–9, 339, 360, 462, 467, 468–9; Mandelson's home loan, 289, 461–4, 468–9, 577; offshore trust, 383, 466; Cabinet reshuffle, 386; DTI investigation, 466–7, 468; resignation, 233
Robson, Frank, 105, 106
Roche, Barbara, 123
Rodgers, William, 66, 69, 250
Rogers, Richard, 558
Rolling Stones, 32, 39
Roman Catholic Church, 257–8, 348, 351–3, 504
Rothermere, Lord, 230, 334–5
Routledge, Paul, 180, 224, 225, 232, 378, 382–3, 384, 385, 463, 470
Royal Ulster Constabulary, 417
Rugova, Ibrahim, 511, 517
Russia, 335, 513, 515, 529, 530, 531, 582
Ryden, Nick, 17–18, 21–2, 24

Saatchi, Charles, 311
Saatchi, Maurice, 311
Saddam Hussein, 422, 423, 429, 512–13, 515–16
Sainsbury, Sir David, 359–60, 465, 469
St John's College, Oxford, 21, 37, 40, 60

St Olave's, Orpington, 282–3
Sandel, Michael, 42
Sandline, 425
Sawyer, Tom, 139, 268, 367
Scargill, Arthur, 88, 162, 256, 261, 270, 435, 436
Scharping, Rudolf, 193
Scholar, Michael, 465
Schröder, Gerhard, 435, 472, 583
Scotland: devolution, 287–8, 306, 412, 454–5, 457–8, 495, 583; 1997 election, 306
Scotsman, 306
Scott, Derek, 331
Scott, Nicholas, 51
Scott, Sir Walter, 15, 20
Scottish Labour Party, 117, 259–60, 288, 306, 382
Scottish National Party (SNP), 454
Scottish Young Communist League, 7
Sedgefield: seat created, 91–2; TB selected as candidate for, 82, 93, 95–107; 1983 election, 107–9; TB's home in, 123, 329; 1987 election, 133, 134; 1992 election, 178; Labour Party membership, 209–10; TB's leadership campaign, 237
Sedgemore, Brian, 377
Selby Wright, Ronald, 19, 21–2, 30
Self, Will, 249–50
Serbia, 509–12, 513–15, 517–31
Shadow Communications Agency, 149
Sharples, Adam, 38, 83, 139
Sheppard, David, Bishop of Liverpool, 350
Sheppard, Mike, 29–30, 33
Shersby, Sir Michael, 339
Shore, Peter, 71, 85, 87, 95, 113–14, 189
Short, Clare, 267, 270, 288–9, 305, 398; and 'Clintonisation', 196; 'one member, one vote' issue, 215; in shadow Cabinet, 284–5; and International Development, 420, 428; and House of Lords reform, 449n.; and Kosovo war, 521, 523
Short, Ted, 438
Sieff, Adam, 29, 33
Sierra Leone, 424–7, 429, 527, 582
Silkin, John, 74
Silkin, Sam, 59
Silverman, Sidney, 198
Simon, Sir David, 326, 464–6, 475–6, 477–8, 481, 482
Simpson, John, 524
Single European Act (1986), 129, 131
Sinn Fein, 334, 400–4, 406–7, 409–12, 414, 416
Skeet, Mavis, 547
Skinner, Dennis, 116, 307
Sky TV, 167
Slaughter, Andrew, 339
Sloot, Theo, 29
Smerdon, Denis, 62
Smith, Adam, 41–2
Smith, Andrew, 238, 386
Smith, Chris, 226, 273, 326, 364, 370, 379, 386, 557, 558, 577
Smith, Cyril, 87
Smith, Godric, 397
Smith, John, 54, 82, 122, 230, 296, 384, 468; background, 24; early contacts with TB, 58, 72; reforms Labour leadership elections, 66; Beaconsfield by-election, 85; advances TB's career, 118–19, 120; shadow Cabinet, 137, 144, 153; heart condition, 147, 217–18; employment policy, 164, 213–14; and Exchange Rate Mechanism, 165, 189, 209; 1992 election, 166, 168, 170, 175–8; relations with TB, 169, 216–17; and Labour leadership, 44, 169–70, 186–7, 359; deputy leadership election (1992), 178–85; and modernisation of Labour, 186; and 'Clintonisation', 196; social moralism, 201–2; and the Prevention of Terrorism Act, 203; 'one member, one vote' issue, 207, 208–9, 210, 211–12, 213–14; and Clause IV, 254; on Mandelson, 256; and electoral reform, 290, 291; taxation policy, 298, 374, 544; religious beliefs, 354; blind trust, 361; and devolution, 457–8; and the single currency, 472–3; possible coalition with Liberal Democrats, 491; death, 5, 21, 179, 221–4, 225, 227–8; funeral and memorial service, 233, 246, 347
Smith, Maureen, 221
Smith, Paul, 545

Smith, Tim, 87, 128, 305
Snow, Jon, 556
Social Democratic and Labour Party (SDLP), 407
Social Democratic Party (SDP), 68–70, 72, 81, 108, 127, 239, 250–1, 261; *see also* Liberal–SDP Alliance
Social Exclusion Unit, 436
socialism: Clause IV, 115, 142, 152, 215, 249, 252–7, 259–63; and the Third Way, 431–9
Socialist Labour Party, 270
Socialist Organiser Alliance, 78
Socialist Workers' Party, 259
Society of Labour Lawyers, 89
Solana, Javier, 521, 525, 528
Soley, Clive, 386n.
Solidarity Campaign, 71–2, 74, 76, 77, 176
South Africa, 46, 516
Southern, Sir Richard, 47
Spectator, 34, 58
Spellar, John, 72
Spence, Laura, 444
Spennymoor, 103–5, 116
Spicer, Lieutenant-Colonel Tim, 425
spin-doctors, 397–9
Standards and Privileges Committee, 468
Stanley, Martin, 56
Stanley, Nigel, 147
Steel, Sir David, 454, 492n.
Stephanopoulos, George, 239n., 325, 333, 525, 526
Stevenson, Dennis, 453
Stewart, Neil, 155, 157
Stoddart, Tom, 315
Stothard, Peter, 277
Stott, Roger, 92, 105
Strategic Communications Unit, 537, 540
Strathclyde, Lord, 449, 450, 451
Straw, Jack, 344, 387, 538, 539n., 582; social moralism, 202; and the right to silence, 204; and TB's leadership campaign, 225, 238, 242; and Clause IV, 254; in shadow Cabinet, 258, 271; and electoral reform, 291, 492; in Cabinet, 326, 341; and the Third Way, 433; and fox-hunting ban, 442; and Kosovo war, 521; and the Millennium Dome, 557
Sudan, 410, 424
Sugar, Alan, 363
Suharto, President of Indonesia, 421, 429
Sun, 178, 200, 277–8, 299–300, 301, 303, 304–5, 311, 328, 332, 338, 339, 355, 391, 397, 409, 444, 480, 481, 520–1, 528, 530, 549, 568, 575
Sunday Express, 86, 187, 379, 384
Sunday Telegraph, 56, 82, 199, 208, 304, 353–4, 473, 520, 521
Sunday Times, 186–7, 229, 239, 258, 285, 302, 304, 313, 392, 395
Sutcliffe, John, 17–18
Sweden, 429, 439, 472

Talbott, Strobe, 527
targets, business model of government, 546
task forces, 545
Tatchell, Peter, 85
Tawney, R. H., 115, 281, 506–7
taxation, 195, 271; Smith's 'shadow budget', 175; National Insurance contributions, 175–6; Scottish devolution, 288; Labour promises not to raise basic rate of income tax, 288, 296–9, 364, 365; Brown's first Budget, 337–8; Working Families Tax Credit, 380, 436; and the Third Way, 438–9; and equality, 439–40; fuel duty escalator, 570
Taylor, Ann, 250, 326, 385
Taylor, Matthew, 495
Teasdale, Anthony, 311
Tebbit, Norman, 87
'Tebbit Bill' (1982 Employment Act), 70, 88–9, 119
Teesside Thornaby, 80–1
Terrans, George 'Mick', 98, 106
terrorism, 203, 271, 400–3, 409–10, 417, 511
Thanet, 88, 91, 92–3, 108
Thatcher, Margaret, 7n., 45, 85, 148, 230, 312, 337, 498, 538, 571, 580; becomes Conservative leader, 51–2; becomes Prime Minister, 58, 63, 316, 323, 327; Falklands War, 82, 83, 87, 512, 513, 524, 528, 530; 1983 election, 91, 93, 108; Prime Minister's Questions, 125–6, 333; and the Exchange Rate Mechanism,

Thatcher, Margaret – *contd*
129, 130, 163; 1987 election, 133–4, 140–1; privatisation, 142; condemns Social Charter, 154–5; and trade union law reform, 157; unpopularity, 162; resignation, 163; Brixton riots, 200; influence on TB, 245, 276–8, 581; 1997 election, 315; and Church of England appointments, 350; religious beliefs, 352, 354, 356; on opposition parties, 362; and single parents, 376; relations with Lawson, 384; and Northern Ireland, 400; relations with USA, 422; and Iraq, 423; endorses TB, 435, 531; taxation policy, 440; Balkan conflicts, 510; special advisers, 535; Cabinet meetings, 540, 541; dislike of sacking ministers, 541; NHS review, 549; management style, 552
The Third Way: New Politics for the New Century, 431, 434
This Week Next Week, 144
Thomson, Peter, 24, 35–7, 41, 43, 45, 46, 48, 69, 76, 293
Thornton, Glenys, 76
The Times, 78, 140–1, 143, 146, 197, 199, 222, 234, 252, 256, 273, 274, 277, 302, 304, 311, 368, 476–7, 478
Tisdall, Sarah, 125
tobacco advertising ban, 307, 358, 364–70, 546
Today newspaper, 213, 346
Today radio programme, 243, 251–2, 298, 521
Todd, Ron, 154
Townend, John, 120
Trade Union Act (1984), 119, 120–2
trade unions: law reform, 153–8, 161–3; and modernisation of Labour, 173; 'one member, one vote' issue, 207–12, 213–16, 242; Conservative employment laws, 243; TB appeals to Middle England, 249; and Clause IV, 257, 262; Labour fundraising, 361
Trades Union Congress (TUC), 166, 213, 268, 334
Transport and General Workers' Union (TGWU), 99–100, 105, 154, 156, 179, 181, 214, 243, 263, 572
Treasury: TB on shadow front bench, 124–31, 133; and welfare reform, 375; and Performance and Innovation Unit, 539
Tribune, 81, 117, 150, 242, 257
Tribune Group, 117, 118, 136–7
Trimble, David, 402, 403–4, 406–8, 410, 412, 413, 414–18
Trimdon, 95–7, 98, 100, 107, 108, 123, 314–15
Trippett, Paul, 96, 97–8, 101, 104, 109, 317, 345
Trotskyism, 90
Tse, Katy, 337
Turner, Adair, 250
Twigg, Stephen, 315
Tyler, Paul, 87

Udwin, Emma, 147
Ugly Rumours (rock band), 33, 34, 37–9, 83, 238
Ulster Democratic Party, 404
Ulster Unionist Council, 415–16, 417
Ulster Unionist Party, 334, 401–7, 410–15
Ulster Volunteer Force, 404
unemployment, 164, 165, 378, 441
Union Links Review Group, 208, 209, 210, 211–12, 215, 242
Unison, 262
Unitary Tax Campaign, 128
United Nations, 336, 429, 434; and Iraq, 422, 423, 512, 513, 515; and Sierra Leone, 425, 426; and China, 427; Kosovo war, 514, 516–17, 521, 527, 531; environmental summit, 575
United Nations Development Programme, 428
United States of America, 420, 473; TB visits, 128–9; Clinton's influence on TB, 194–8, 207, 267, 278; taxation, 297; and Northern Ireland, 402, 423–4; and Iraq, 422–3, 513; 'special relationship' with Britain, 422–4; and the Third Way, 432–3, 434–5; Balkan conflicts, 510; Kosovo war, 514–15, 517–18, 519, 521, 522, 524–6, 527, 529–30
university tuition fees, 437–9, 445, 457

Vangen, Doug, 82

Velani, Anwal, 37
Vineyard Congregationalist church, Richmond, 30, 32

Wachner, Linda, 470
Wakeham, John, 453
Walden, Brian, 249
Wales, 211, 216, 287, 288, 454, 455–8, 583
Wales Labour Party, 234, 455–7
Wall, Sir Stephen, 472
Wallace, Jim, 455
Walters, Alan, 130
Walters, Simon, 384
Ward, David, 181, 183–4, 212, 217–18, 254, 363, 366, 367, 370
Ward, Reg, 92, 106
Ward, Terry, 95, 96, 97
Watkins, David, 92, 104
The Way Forward, 412–13, 415
Webb, Beatrice, 268
Webb, Sidney, 252, 268
Webster, Philip, 274
A Week in Politics, 229
Wegg-Prosser, Benjamin, 463
Weighell, Sid, 104
welfare reform, 337, 339, 373–81, 540
Wells, John, 120–1, 122
Welsh Assembly, 412, 495
Whelan, Charlie, 232, 268–9, 383; and Brown's bid for leadership, 229, 235–6; and Brown's feud with Mandelson, 273; and Routledge's biography of Brown, 382; loses job, 233, 397, 470; and Mandelson home loan, 463, 464; Brown's interview on the single currency, 477
White, Sharon, 375
White, Vivian, 142
Who's Who, 125, 303
William, Prince, 344
Williams, John, 313, 384
Williams, Marcia, 145, 329, 537
Williams, Shirley, 66, 69, 80, 81, 93, 187, 250
Wills, Michael, 254, 275, 463
Wilson, Brian, 284
Wilson, Harold, 5, 13, 45, 51, 57, 69, 189, 232, 245, 247, 354n., 453; 1966 election, 12; and Marcia Williams, 145; denounces Prescott, 241; and Clause IV, 253; on the Labour Party, 263; TB compared to, 264; first hundred days, 323, 339; plots against his leadership, 383; and leaks to media, 394–5; and House of Lords reform, 449, 450; EEC referendum, 474; his children's education, 505n.; Prime Minister's office, 534–5, 537; Cabinet meetings, 540; Cabinet reshuffles, 542
Wilson, Mary, 301
Wilson, Phil, 97, 101, 104, 109, 146, 246, 329–30, 345
Wilson, Sir Richard, 394, 462, 522, 538, 543, 544
Winston, Robert, 547
Wintour, Patrick, 312–13
Woman's Hour, 379
Women's Institute (WI), 576
The World at One, 379
The World This Weekend, 192–3, 194
Wrigglesworth, Ian, 80–1, 128
Wright, Billy, 404

Yelland, David, 480
Young, David, 138
Young, Hugo, 473
Young, Jimmy, 387
Young Socialists, 63
Yugoslavia, 411, 509–12, 513–15, 517–31